ANCIENT ROMAN CIVILIZATION

ANCIENT ROMAN CIVILIZATION

HISTORY AND SOURCES
753 BCE TO 640 CE

Ralph W. Mathisen

NEW YORK, OXFORD
OXFORD UNIVERSITY PRESS

Oxford University Press is a department of the University of Oxford. It furthers the University's objective of excellence in research, scholarship, and education by publishing worldwide. Oxford is a registered trade mark of Oxford University Press in the UK and certain other countries.

Published in the United States of America by Oxford University Press
198 Madison Avenue, New York, NY 10016, United States of America.

© 2019 by Oxford University Press

Library of Congress Cataloging-in-Publication Data

Names: Mathisen, Ralph W., 1947- author. | Mathisen, Ralph W., 1947- Ancient Mediterranean civilizations. | Mathisen, Ralph W., 1947- Sources for Ancient Mediterranean civilizations.
Title: Ancient Roman Civilization : History and Sources, 753 BCE to 640 CE / Ralph W. Mathisen.
Description: New York : Oxford University Press, 2018. | Includes material from author's earlier works: Ancient Mediterranean Civilizations and Sources for Ancient Mediterranean Civilizations. | Includes bibliographical references and index.
Identifiers: LCCN 2018011374 (print) | LCCN 2018025145 (ebook) | ISBN 9780190849610 (E-Book) | ISBN 9780190849603 (print book)
Subjects: LCSH: Rome—Civilization—Textbooks. | Rome—Civilization—Sources.
Classification: LCC DG77 (ebook) | LCC DG77 .M375 2018 (print) | DDC 937—dc23 LC record available at https://lccn.loc.gov/2018011374

BRIEF CONTENTS

CONTENTS

LIST OF MAPS

SPECIAL FEATURES

Cultural Encounters

PREFACE

One well might ask what the rationale would be for publishing another Roman history textbook, when there already are so many of them available, all covering pretty much the same material (with the exception of the ones that do not yet extend into Late Antiquity). The goal here is to produce not another generic textbook, but a textbook that responds more effectively, indeed uniquely, to current trends in both the classroom and the scholarly world. There has been a growing interest in introducing students to original documents, to allow them to piece together the history for themselves, in the words of the original actors, rather than getting the history either from the textbook or the instructor. Dealing with original source documents has many pedagogical advantages:

1. It gives student a ready-made opportunity to write short research papers based on their understanding of the documents. This is consistent with another classroom trend, especially in General Education classes: the writing component.
2. It provides discussion material for instructors who adopt the "flipped classroom" approach. Students are responsible for reading the textbook for themselves, and then have the opportunity to put that knowledge to use in a classroom discussion of an original source document;
3. Using original documents also can take some of the weight off the shoulders of non-specialists who have been thrust into a Roman history classroom. If the students can read the documents themselves, then the instructor might not be in the awkward position of trying to explicate unfamiliar material.

But as things currently stand, it can be very difficult and time-consuming to find documents. Some textbooks include boxed features that include document extracts, but these are hardly enough to build a class around. Nor are there available up-to-date and comprehensive readers dealing with Roman civilization.

Ancient Roman Civilization: History and Sources offers a solution to the problem of balancing the study of primary sources with the need for a narrative baseline. It integrates in a single volume both a historical narrative and translated primary sources. Covering the periods from the founding of Rome in 753 BCE to the end of the ancient world circa 640 CE, this combination of narrative and primary sources will have several pedagogical advantages:

1. The historical narrative and documentary sources are designed to go together. Thus, much of the narrative can be enhanced by looking at the parallel primary source documents.
2. The documents are designed to be interrelated, on repetitious themes, so students can use them to follow the same trends throughout the course of the narrative.
3. The majority of the documents are not bits and snippets, but are of sufficient size that students could easily craft an extended discussion of how the documents relate either to the historical narrative or to each other or could use them as source documents for research papers.
4. And last but not least, this textbook is very friendly to the student pocketbook, given that students would need to purchase only one text, as opposed to two, or even more.

Approach and Coverage

The central chapters of *Ancient Roman Civilization* provide the traditional coverage of Roman history, ranging from the founding of Rome circa 753 to the end of the Western Roman Empire. The beginning and the end of the volume are a bit more nontraditional. On the one hand, given that one of the book's unifying themes is the concept of "Cultural Confrontation"—that is, how the Romans interacted or engaged with a multitude of other Mediterranean, Asiatic, and African cultures—rather than jumping right into Roman history *in medias res*, this text commences with an introductory chapter that places the Romans in their wider geographical and cultural context, with discussions of the peoples of western Europe (Iberians and Celts), North Africa (Carthaginians and Garamantians), the eastern Mediterranean (the Greeks of "Great Greece" in southern Italy and Sicily, Hellenistic Greece, Nabataean Arabs, and the Jews), and central Asia (Scythians and Parthians). Thus, when these peoples then appear on the Roman stage during the course of the historical narrative, students already will be familiar with them. Likewise, the second chapter commences with discussions of the peoples whom the Romans engaged with in Italy, the Etruscans, western Greeks, and Italic peoples.

As for the end of the volume, its termination date reflects current thinking on when the ancient world ended. In recent years, texts dealing with ancient and Roman history have been inching their coverage later and later, toward what is now considered to be the canonical end of antiquity in the mid seventh century CE. This book thus continues "all the way" into the seventh century, with

Heraclius and the rise of Islam, where Late Antiquity finally meets the Middle Ages. This text therefore is consistent with the current thought that Late Antiquity marks the true boundary between classical antiquity and the Middle Ages.

Learning Aids

Ancient Roman Civilization offers a number of features intended to catch the attention of students. Collectively, the features are designed to show students how they can interpret historical evidence, both written and material, to form a reasoned analysis of what happened in the past and what it meant. Special features—all of which can stand on their own and thus be useful either for classroom discussions or out-of-class assignments—include (1) **"A Picture Is Worth a Thousand Words,"** in which a material artifact, such as a building, fresco, pot, statue, and so on, is discussed in detail, in the context of the chapter themes, to show how nonliterary material can shed light on an ancient cultures; (2) **"Historical Controversy,"** dealing with divergent modern models or interpretations of an ancient phenomenon; (3) **"Mysteries of History,"** dealing with an unknown aspect of the past; (4) **"History Laboratory,"** which shows how scientific methods, theoretical models, and quantification can be used to understand ancient history on the one hand and debunk pseudoscience and modern popularizers on the other; (5) **"Digging Antiquity,"** an archaeologically based feature that discusses specific sites, many of which still can be visited; and (6) **"Cultural Encounters,"** which builds on the theme of giving special attention to the peoples with whom the Romans interacted.

Interspersed throughout the chapters are smaller boxed features that provide additional learning opportunities. These "sticky notes" draw attention to modern analogies to or survivals of ancient phenomena, present alternative histories, or pose questions that ask students to consider issues of causality, race, ethnicity, gender, and culture.

Throughout the text, important terms, events, and concepts are highlighted in bold to draw students' attention. These words are defined in the Glossary. Each chapter concludes with a "Looking Back/Looking Ahead" section that summarizes the key takeaways of the chapter and outlines the main points that will be examined in the next chapter. The "Further Readings" section points the interested reader toward scholarly works where in-depth investigation of a theme or topic can be pursued.

The book's companion website offers chapter quizzes for students and a test-item file and Power Point slides for instructors. Please visit https://oup-arc-com/access/mathisen-roman

ACKNOWLEDGMENTS

The genesis of this project began with an idea that Charles Cavaliere, executive editor at Oxford University Press, pitched to me in 2016. Charles saw the need for a new Roman history text that combined narrative and sources, and he was perceptive in seeing how the Roman material from my other two books I have published with him—*Ancient Mediterranean Civilizations* (second edition 2015) and *Sources in Ancient Mediterranean Civilizations* (2017)—could form the basis for this new project. Charles's assistant Katie Tunkavige deftly assembled the final manuscript. Project editor Patricia Berube kept me on task and on schedule. I very much appreciate and acknowledge the dedication, engagement, professionalism, and friendliness of everyone at OUP.

I would also like to thank the many colleagues (including several who wished to remain anonymous) who read the initial prospectus and drafts of the manuscript:

Timothy Doran, California State University, Los Angeles
Brian Duvick, University of Colorado, Colorado Springs
Colin Elliot, Indiana University
Thomas Govero, John Cabot University, Rome
Matt Klemm, Ithaca College
Christine Arnold-Lourie, College of Southern Maryland

Their careful readings and trenchant comments have made this a much better volume. All errors, of course, remain my own.

NOTE ON SPELLING AND PRONUNCIATION

Because ancient names and words were written in languages other than English, they can be converted into English using many different methods. The spellings used here are the most widely used spellings, but readers should be aware that other publications sometimes will use spellings that are different from the ones used here.

In addition, a few general guidelines can make it easier to approximate the pronunciation of many foreign words:

1. In diaeresis, the second of two adjoining vowels is printed with an umlaut and is pronounced separately. For example:

Tanaïs =	Tah nah ees'
Arsinoë =	Ar sin' oh ee
Aëtius =	Ah ee' shus

    also

limetanei =	lee meh tah' neh ee
basileus =	bah see leh' oos

2. Foreign words and names do not have silent e's at the end. For example:

Cyrene =	Sigh ree' nee	not	Sigh reen'

3. Some letters of modern languages are printed with diacritical marks. For example:
    Ć and š = 'ch" and "sh" (e.g., Ćašmak)

4. Pronunciation of vowels in Greek words (printed in italics in the text):

a =	"ah" as in "shah"
ē =	"a" as in "cake"
ō =	"o" as in "vote"
y =	"oo" as in "room"

5.   Pronunciation of Latin words:

(1)   Every vowel or diphthong represents a separate syllable, e.g.,

proles =   pro' lace   not   proles

(2a)   In words that have not been anglicized, there are no silent vowels, and words are divided into syllables following a vowel and/or preceding a consonant, e.g.,

familia =   fa mee' lee ah   not   fa mil' ee ah
Trasimene =   Tra si mee' nee   not   Tras ih mene'

(2b)   But some Latin words have been made into English words and thus are pronounced in English; for example, "Caesar" is pronounced "See' zer" in English not "Ky' sar" (as it would be in Latin).

TIMELINE

2000–1200 BCE	Italian Bronze Age
1200–700 BCE	Villanovan Culture, central and northern Italy
ca. 800–700 BCE	Intensive Greek colonization of Sicily and southern Italy
814 BCE	Founding of Carthage; Greek civilization emerges from Dark Ages
753 BCE	Legendary founding of Rome
ca. 600 BCE	Etruscans occupy Rome, construction of Roman Forum; Iberian Culture flourishes in western Mediterranean
587 BCE	Judah falls to the New Babylonians, beginning of Jewish diaspora
509 BCE	Expulsion of last King of Rome; beginning of Roman Republic
ca. 500 BCE	Earliest Greek references to the Celts
ca. 500 BCE–287 BCE	Conflict of the Orders
490–479 BCE	Persian invasions of Greece
451–450 BCE	Twelve Tables of Roman law
ca. 400 BCE	Carthage controls most of coastal North Africa and western Mediterranean
390 BCE	Gauls sack Rome
343–268 BCE	Romans gain control of all of Italy south of the Po River
343–290	Samnite Wars
338 BCE	Philip of Macedon defeats coalition of Greek city-states, Great Latin Revolt
280–275	Pyrrhic Wars
323 BCE	Death of Alexander the Great, beginning of Hellenistic Age

264–241 BCE	First Punic War
247 BCE–224 CE	Parthian Empire
229–219 BCE	Illyrian and Celtic Wars
218–201 BCE	Second Punic War
216 BCE	Hannibal decisively defeats Romans at the Battle of Cannae
201 BCE	Scipio defeats Hannibal at the Battle of Zama
200–146 BCE	Romans engaged in near-constant warfare in eastern Mediterranean
200–168 BCE	Macedonian Wars
181–133 BCE	Celtiberian Wars in Spain
135–132 BCE	Slave revolt in Sicily
133 BCE	Tiberius Gracchus murdered
121 BCE	Gaius Gracchus murdered
107 BCE	Gaius Marius creates the volunteer army
104–100 BCE	Slave revolt in Sicily
90–88 BCE	Revolt of the Italian Allies
88 BCE	Sulla uses his army to overthrow the government
82 BCE	Sulla appointed Dictator
73–71 BCE	Revolt of Spartacus
63 BCE	Pompey deposes the last Seleucid king; Julius Caesar elected Pontifex Maximus
60 BCE	First Triumvirate of Pompey, Crassus, and Caesar
58–51 BCE	Campaigns of Caesar in Gaul
53 BCE	Battle of Carrhae, Crassus defeated and killed by the Parthians
52 BCE	Caesar defeats Vercingetorix at Alesia
49 BCE	Caesar crosses the Rubicon
48 BCE	Caesar defeats Pompey at Battle of Pharsalus
46 BCE	Julian calendar introduced
44 BCE	Caesar appointed "Perpetual Dictator"; Caesar stabbed to death on the Ides of March; Octavian returns to Rome to claim Caesar's legacy
43 BCE	Second Triumvirate of Antony, Lepidus, and Octavian
31 BCE	Antony and Cleopatra defeated by Octavian at the Battle of Actium
30 BCE	Antony and Cleopatra commit suicide; Egypt becomes a Roman province
27 BCE	Establishment of the Principate; Octavian is named "Augustus"
27 BCE–14 CE	Augustan Golden Age of Roman Literature
27 BCE–68 CE	Julio-Claudian Dynasty
13 BCE	Augustus becomes Pontifex Maximus

9 BCE	Germans slaughter Romans at Battle of Teutoburg Forest; Rhine and Danube rivers become northern frontier of the Empire
14 CE	Death of Augustus
14–192 CE	Silver Age of Roman Literature
28 CE	Pontius Pilate executes Jesus of Nazareth
43 CE	Conquest of Britain begins
60 CE	Boudicca leads failed revolt against Roman rule in Britain
64 CE	Fire burns much of Rome; Nero persecutes Christians as scapegoats
66–70 CE	First Jewish Revolt
69 CE	Year of the Four Emperors
69–96 CE	Flavian Dynasty
70 CE	Titus suppresses Jewish revolt, destroys the Second Temple in Jerusalem; construction of Colosseum in Rome begins
79 CE	Volcanic eruption of Mt. Vesuvius destroys Pompeii
96–192 CE	Antonine Dynasty and Roman Peace
117 CE	Death of Trajan; Roman Empire at its greatest extent
132–135 CE	Bar Kochba Revolt of the Jews in Palestine
161–180	Reign of Marcus Aurelius, author of *The Meditations*
192 CE	Commodus assassinated
193–235 CE	Severan Dynasty
212 CE	Caracalla issues the Antonine Constitution
224 CE	Fall of the Parthian Empire; creation of the New Persian Empire
235–284 CE	Imperial Crisis
249–251	Trajan Decius requires loyalty oath and then is killed fighting the Goths
260 CE	Valerian captured by Persian king Shapur
267–274 CE	Queen Zenobia rules the Palmyrene Empire
284–305 CE	Reign of Diocletian; beginning of Late Roman Empire
293 CE	Tetrarchy formed
303 CE	Great Persecution of Christians begins
306–363 CE	Constantinian Dynasty
312 CE	Constantine defeats Maxentius at the Battle of the Milvian Bridge
313 CE	Edict of Milan makes Christianity a fully legal religion
325 CE	Council of Nicaea

330 CE	Founding of Constantinople
361–363 CE	Reign of Julian, last pagan emperor of the entire empire
364–457 CE	Dynasty of Valentinian and Theodosius
376 CE	Visigoths allowed to cross the Danube
378 CE	Roman army annihilated by Visigoths at Battle of Adrianople
395 CE	De facto split of empire into eastern and western halves
410 CE	Visigoths sack Rome; Britain is abandoned
429 CE	Vandals invade North Africa
430 CE	Death of St. Augustine of Hippo
437 CE	Theodosius II issues the Theodosian Code
451 CE	Attila and the Huns defeated by Aëtius at Battle of Catalaunian Fields
455 CE	Vandals sack Rome
476 CE	Romulus Augustulus, last emperor in Rome, is deposed by Odovacar
480 CE	Death of Julius Nepos; end of empire in the west
496 CE	Frankish king Clovis converts to Christianity
527–565 CE	Reign of Justinian
529–534 CE	Code of Justinian compiled
532–555 CE	Construction of Hagia Sophia, Constantinople
ca. 570 CE	Birth of Muhammad
620 CE	Greek becomes official language of the Byzantine Empire
628 CE	Heraclius defeats New Persians
632 CE	Death of Muhammad
634–644 CE	Muslims advance out of Arabia and conquer Syria, Palestine, Egypt, Iraq, and Persia
689 CE	Muslim forces conquer Byzantine North Africa
711 CE	Spain falls to Muslim armies
768–811 CE	Reign of Charlemagne

ABOUT THE AUTHOR

Ralph W. Mathisen has appointments in history, classics, and medieval studies at the University of Illinois at Urbana-Champaign. His research interests include ecclesiastical history, barbarian studies, late Latin literature, prosopography, and the society, culture, and religion of late antiquity. He has authored, coauthored, or edited fourteen books, including *The Battle of Vouillé, 507 CE: Where France Began* (De Gruyter, 2012) (with D.R. Shanzer); *Making Europe: People, Politics, and Culture* (coauthor) (Houghton Mifflin 2009, 2014); *People, Personal Expression, and Social Relations in Late Antiquity*, 2 vols. (University of Michigan 2003); *Law, Society, and Authority in Late Antiquity* (Oxford University Press 2001); and *Ruricius of Limoges and Friends: A Collection of Letters from Visigothic Aquitania* (Liverpool University Press 1999). He currently is working on books on the end of the western Roman Empire; on the late Roman comedy "The Querolus"; and on the life and letters of Desiderius of Cahors. He has published more than 100 scholarly articles. He is director of the Biographical Database for Late Antiquity Project and a fellow of the American Numismatic Society. He has degrees in astronomy and physics (B.S., University of Wisconsin, 1969), mechanical engineering (M.S., Rensselaer Polytechnic Institute, 1972), classical languages (M.A., University of Wisconsin, 1973), and ancient history (Ph.D., University of Wisconsin, 1979). He enjoys photography, running, traveling, and ballroom dancing.

ANCIENT ROMAN CIVILIZATION

THE ORIGINS OF ROME

CHAPTER 1

THE WIDER WORLD OF EARLY ROME: CULTURAL ENCOUNTERS

For the first 500 years after its foundation in 753 BCE—that is, until the 260s BCE—the history of Rome was confined primarily to Italy. Outside Italy lay a much wider world of regions, peoples, and cultures that eventually would influence the Romans in multifarious manners. Indeed, Roman history in many ways is a history of the Romans' engagement with, borrowing from, and integration of the initially foreign peoples with whom they came into contact. In antiquity, both the Romans and Greeks were fascinated by the curious if not bizarre customs of foreign peoples. But whereas the Greeks, who considered all foreign peoples, including the Romans, to be "barbarians," disseminated many negative and even pejorative stereotypes about foreign peoples, the Romans were generally more tolerant. The Roman historian Tacitus, for example, painted a very sympathetic picture of Germanic culture. One might even suggest that the single greatest contributing factor to the Romans' success as a people and as a government was the way they generally respected foreign cultures, admitted foreign peoples to full Roman citizenship, and created a true international culture. It is important for us to acknowledge the significance of cultures other than those of Greece and Rome, some of them far from the Mediterranean world, not only because of their own impact on the Greek and Roman world but also because we always must remind ourselves that the Greeks and Romans were not the only civilizations of antiquity, and other cultures had significance in their own right, not merely as a consequence of the Greeks or Romans.

Given the significance of the Romans' cultural encounters with other peoples throughout the course of their history, this introductory chapter will place Archaic and Republican Rome in its world context, outside of Italy. Along with the Greeks, it also will scrutinize other peoples who existed on the periphery of the Greek and Roman worlds, including Iberians, Celts, and Germans in Europe; Garamantes, Berbers, and Carthaginians in North Africa; Greeks in the eastern

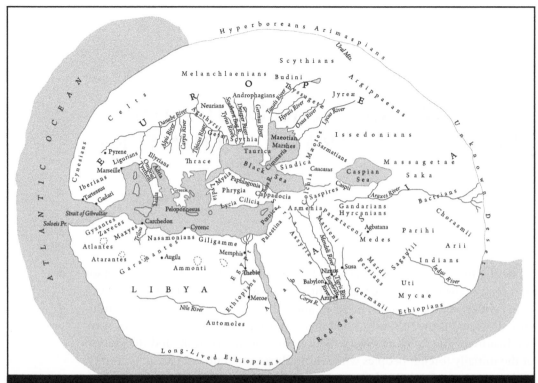

A reconstruction of the world described by the Greek historian Herodotus about 440 BCE. Herodotus rejected the prevalent ideas that Libya (Africa), Europe, and Asia were all the same size and that a single ocean encircled the whole world.

Mediterranean; and Jews, Nabataean Arabs, Scythians, and Parthians in western and central Asia. The characteristics and significance of these peoples all too often have been unappreciated, both then and now. In the modern day, these peoples can be submerged or marginalized as a consequence of the natural focus on the two civilizations that had such a tremendous impact on the future development of western history and culture. And in Greek and Roman antiquity, views of the peoples who lived beyond the known world became more and more fanciful the farther away one got. Indeed, in the mid-fifth century BCE, the Greek historian Herodotus expressed the view that "the extreme regions of the earth, which surround and shut up within themselves all other countries, produce the things that are the rarest."

Greek concepts of world geography went back at least as early as the Ionian philosopher Anaximander of Miletus in the first half of the sixth century BCE. Anaximander crafted a map that ranged from the Strait of Gibraltar in the west to Ethiopia in the south to Europe in the north and the Caspian Sea in the east. Circa 440 BCE Herodotus—who made fun of Greeks who attempted to make maps of the world—himself described a world that extended even farther, to the **Hyperboreans** in the far north and India in the east. This image was expanded by Greek geographers of the third century BCE such as Eratosthenes, who extended the eastern frontiers of the known world to Ceylon and the Ganges River, and the north to include Bretannia (Britain), and even "Thule," which modern cartography has placed anywhere from the Orkney Islands to Norway. In the fully developed Greek view of ancient geography, the world was divided into three continents—Europe, Libya (Africa), and Asia—and was encircled by a single ocean.

The name Thule *now is borne by the United States' northernmost military base, 750 miles (1200 kilometers) north of the Arctic Circle in Greenland.*

THE PEOPLES OF WESTERN EUROPE

In the western Mediterranean, outside Italy, a number of cultures in Spain and inland Europe came to have crucially significant interactions with the Romans.

The Iberian Culture of Spain

In southern Spain, the city of Tartessus, on the southern Iberian coast at the mouth of the Baetis (Guadalquivir) River, developed a mercantile economy in the early first millennium BCE that eventually exploited trade routes leading through the Strait of Gibraltar into the Atlantic Ocean. The city is first mentioned by Herodotus, who reported that in the late seventh century BCE Greek merchants from Samos who had been blown off course eventually fetched up at Tartessus. He commented, "This trading-place was at that time untouched by any, so that when these returned back home they made profit from their cargo greater than any other Hellenes." The Iberian people known as the Cynesians, likewise mentioned by Herodotus and whose main city of Conistorgis was located just west of Tartessus as of the seventh century BCE, shared in the Tartessian Culture. But suggested identifications of Tartessus as the "Tarshish" or "Tarsisi" mentioned in the Old Testament and Assyrian records (which more reasonably refer to the Hittite city of Tarsus in southern Anatolia) are problematic. Hypothesized connections with Plato's Atlantis are even more untenable.

Characteristic Tartessian geometric, internally burnished pottery dates from the tenth century BCE. The Tartessians developed a writing system, attested in ninety-seven preserved documents mostly from the seventh century BCE, that was used to write an as yet undeciphered non–Indo-European language perhaps related to Basque. Eventually, Tartessian Culture extended into Andalusia in Spain and southern Portugal. The primary Tartessian trading route extended north up the Atlantic coast to Gaul, where merchants obtained amber and iron, and thence to Britain, the primary ancient source of tin. Tartessus had excellent local sources of silver, gold, lead, and copper in the Sierra Morena, mountains along the Rio Tinto ("Red River") where mining operations are attested as early as 3000 BCE.

As of the eighth century BCE at least, Tartessus maintained close trading ties first with the Phoenicians and their trading colony at Gades, and then with the Carthaginians in North Africa, who did their best to exclude the Greeks from this lucrative market. Tartessus vanished from history toward the end of the sixth century BCE, a result of either flooding or Carthaginian expansion, if not both. Many Tartessian sites were abandoned soon afterward. The actual site of the city has not been discovered; it may be buried under the wetlands of the Guadalquivir delta, perhaps in the area of the modern city of Huelva.

Tartessian culture was inherited by the Iberian people known as the **Turdetani**, about whom the first-century CE geographer Strabo commented, "The Turdetanians are ranked as the wisest of the Iberians; and they make use of an alphabet, and possess records of their ancient history, poems, and laws written in verse that are six thousand years old, as they assert."

The Turdetani were one of the several disunited peoples of Spain, who also included the Ceretani, Ilergetes, Oretani, and Sordones, who represent the Iberian Culture (ca. 500 BCE–100 CE). These peoples originally had arrived in eastern Spain from farther east in the Mediterranean during the Neolithic Period as early as the fifth millennium BCE. The Iberians traded extensively with Mediterranean peoples such as the Phoenicians and Greeks, and their pottery was distributed throughout the western Mediterranean world. By the fourth century BCE, they had developed their own writing system, based on the Tartessian Script, for their non–Indo-European language. Iberian communities were marked by agriculture and metalworking, fortified towns, and a fully developed aristocratic social hierarchy. A noteworthy characteristic was the production of elaborate funerary busts for high-ranking women.

The Celts

The European Iron Age, with the use of iron for weapons in particular, began in Europe with the **Hallstatt Culture** (ca. 800–450 BCE), named after a site near the upper Danube River. It appeared first in the lower Danube River area, and spread through Europe by commerce and migration into Britain, Ireland, and Scandinavia by 600 BCE and into Spain in the sixth century BCE. It manifested an interconnected cultural network with shared farming technology, tools, and housing types that covered nearly all of Europe except for Greece and Italy.

The Hallstatt Culture was characterized by fortified hilltop settlements and by fine metalwork in iron, bronze, gold, and silver. The economy was primarily agricultural and people were mostly farmers, raising crops and herding animals. A complex trading network with the Mediterranean world was facilitated by the Etruscans of northwestern Italy and the Greek city of Marseille. High-status individuals had mostly inhumation burials, sometimes wearing full armor and accompanied by a chariot.

The widespread use of iron for tools occurred with the succeeding **La Tène Culture** (ca. 500–15 BCE), named after a pile-dwelling site in Switzerland. It evolved seamlessly out of the Hallstatt Culture, to some degree under the

A PICTURE IS WORTH A THOUSAND WORDS

DAMA DE ELCHE

In 1897 a stone bust some twenty-two inches (fifty-six centimeters) high was discovered near Elche, near the coast of southeastern Spain. Known as the Dama de Elche ("the Lady of Elche"), it depicts an aristocratic woman and is dated to the fourth century BCE. A hollow space in the rear suggests that it, and other similar sculptures, might have served as funerary urns. Although influenced by Phoenician (Carthaginian) and Greek artistic styles, it is a product of a native Iberian artistic tradition that can be traced back to the Bronze Age. The Carthaginian association is seen in interpretations that associate the woman with the goddess Tanit, who was very popular in Punic-Iberian Spain. The woman wears a very extravagant headdress marked by elaborate coils on both sides of the head, something that is markedly different from standard Greek and Roman art and identifies the sculpture as the product of a completely independent artistic tradition. Only tiny traces of the original painted surface remain. Immediately after its discovery the sculpture was purchased by a French collector and placed in the Louvre Museum in Paris. But in 1941 the Franco government in Spain obtained its return from the French Vichy government, and since then the bust has been in the National Archaeological Museum in Madrid. Suggestions that the sculpture is a modern forgery are belied by the confirmation of many of its features on subsequently discovered examples of Iberian sculpture.

influence of Greek and Etruscan cultures, without any clear break. It spread to Spain and northern Italy by 400 BCE, and to Britain, the Netherlands, Belgium, Germany, Austria, Hungary, and Slovakia by 200 BCE.

By 500 BCE, the peoples of the Hallstatt and La Tène cultures were known to the Greeks as the Keltoi, or **Celts**, a name at least some of these people apparently used for themselves. Herodotus, who did not have extensive knowledge of western European peoples, correctly located the center of the La Tène Culture, reporting, "The Danube crosses all of Europe, rising among the Celts, who are the most westerly dwellers in Europe, except for the Cynesians, who are the westernmost of all the peoples inhabiting Europe." In this mid-fifth-century BCE

Celts is pronounced "Kelts." If pronounced with an "s" ("Selts"), it's a basketball team.

view, the Celts already inhabited the territory from the Danube to southern Spain. Subsequently the Celts of Gaul and elsewhere also were known as the Galli, or **Gauls**. Attempts to trace the origin of the Celts back to the Urnfield Culture, (ca. 1300–750 BCE) or even to the earlier Bell-Beaker Culture (2800–1800 BCE), have not found wide support, nor has a recent suggestion that the Celts arose not from the Hallstatt Culture but from the contemporaneous Atlantic Bronze Age Culture (ca. 1300–700 BCE).

Rather than being united into a single country or nation, the Celts were composed of many different groups. In Gaul, Celtic peoples included the Aedui and Arverni in central Gaul, the Santones and Pictones in the west, the Veneti in Brittany, the Belgae in the north, and the Sequani and Helvetii in the east. In the Po River valley in northern Italy were the Insubres, Boii, and Senones. The Celts of Iberia, who came to be known generically as Celtiberians because of interactions with the local Iberian culture, included the Vettones in the west central region, the Lusitani in the west, the Gallaeci in the northwest, and those actually called Celtiberi in the east central area. And in Britain, Celtic peoples included the Iceni, Trinovantes, and Catuvellauni in the east; the Silures, Ordovices, and Cornovii in the west; and the Brigantes and Novantae in the north.

The various Celtic peoples shared many of the same cultural attributes. In particular, the Celts spoke the Indo-European Celtic language. As with the Greeks, in many ways it was shared language that made a person "Celtic." Although writing was not widespread among the Celts, it was not completely unknown. Celts of the Golasecca Culture of northern Italy wrote documents in the Lepontic language as early as the seventh century BCE using a derivative of the Etruscan alphabet. And Celtiberian inscriptions of the second and first centuries BCE were written using the preexisting Iberian script. It also has been suggested that the Celtic Ogham alphabet, not actually attested until the fourth century CE, might have originated as early as the sixth century BCE.

Celtic settlements often consisted of a large town dominated by a hill fort known as an *oppidum*. Although the primary occupation remained agriculture, the Celts also maintained extensive trading networks in all directions throughout Europe and into Asia. The Celts mined copper, tin, iron, silver, and gold, and Celtic metalwork was especially prized. Characteristic manufactured items included torques (neck rings), *fibulae* (brooches), weapons, and jewelry. In general, Celtic art manifested stylized, abstract forms that allowed artists to express their individuality. Favored motifs included spirals, wavy animal and plant forms, complex curvilinear patterns, and decapitated heads. Celtic imports ranged from Athenian pottery to Baltic amber to African ivory.

Celtic polytheistic religion was administered by a class of priests known as **Druids**, who carried out rituals such as divination and sacrifice to the gods. Little is known about specific Druidic practices, although the derivation of the name suggests a connection with oak trees, which is consistent with the location of

Celtic shrines in isolated places such as groves of trees and sacred pools. Greeks and Romans, who often wanted to make the Celts seem as barbaric as possible, claimed that the Druids engaged in human sacrifice. Julius Caesar, for example, provocatively reported,

> The Gauls are extremely devoted to superstitious rites. When they are about to engage in battles and dangers they sacrifice men as victims and employ the Druids as the performers of those sacrifices because they think that unless the life of a man is offered the mind of the immortal gods cannot be made favorable. They have figures of vast size made of wicker that they fill with living men, which are set on fire and the men perish enveloped in the flames.

A modern reenactment of Celtic human sacrifice is recreated in the film "The Wicker Man."

Other accounts suggest a belief in reincarnation, a large amount of poetry that had to be memorized, and a role in judicial processes. The political significance of the Druids is suggested by the later, successful, Roman effort to suppress them.

Celtic women were known not only for their freedom to engage in sexual liaisons, but also for their participation in warfare and in government. Celtic men, on the other hand, were reputed to prefer male to female lovers, which might reflect male bonding rituals similar to those used by the Greeks.

Celtic culture and language still survive in Ireland, Cornwall, Wales, Scotland, the Isle of Man, and Brittany.

The Celtic peoples functioned as independent nations, making treaties with foreign powers and issuing their own coinage. In some ways, they were like the Greeks. Each people was governed either by a *rix* ("king") or by a council of warrior aristocrats or oligarchs. If the regular presence of weapons among grave goods is any indicator, the Celts of the La Tène period were even more militaristic than their progenitors of the Hallstatt period. Also like the Greeks, the Celts often engaged in conflict. But Celtic warfare was undisciplined and very unlike Greek warfare. Celtic warriors had metal torques, often of gold or silver and very ornate, forged around their necks. The only way to remove a torque was by decapitating a slain warrior, a practice for which the Celts were famous. The primary Celtic weapon remained the long slashing sword that went back to the Urnfield Culture. Celtic fighters made themselves look more terrifying before a battle by smearing wet lime into their hair to make it stand straight back when it dried. Some Celtic warriors fought in the nude, believing that the magical powers of their torques would protect them. A battle began with Celtic soldiers jumping about and shouting insults at their enemy. After they had worked themselves up into the famous "Celtic fury," they charged. In their initial encounters with the Celts, no Mediterranean people could resist the terrifying assault of hordes of naked six-foot Celts wildly swinging their yard-long swords.

A bronze Celtic belt buckle dating to between the eighth and fifth centuries BCE depicts an aristocratic horseman followed by a shield- and spear-bearing infantryman.

Northern Europe

At the same time that some Greek sailors were exploring and seeking new markets in the east, others went out of the Mediterranean and north into the Atlantic. For example, Pytheas, a Greek sailor from Marseille, reported on a low-budget voyage made about 300 BCE from the Phoenician colony of Gades (Cadiz) in Spain. He sailed up the Atlantic coast to Albion, as he called Britain, and to the Cassiterides, or "Tin Islands" (probably modern Cornwall). Along the way, he took careful measurements, and he was the first Greek known to have connected the tides with the motion of the moon. He reported that six days north of Britain was an island called Thule, identified as the Shetland Islands or the Orkneys, where navigation was rendered nearly impossible by a weather condition with no distinction among the air, sea, and earth, probably a reference to thick fog. He also reported that on the summer solstice, June 21, the day was twenty-four hours long, suggesting that he may even have reached the Arctic Circle. Pytheas made the geographically impossible claim to have surveyed the northern coast of Europe to the east as far as the Tanaïs (Don) River in Russia, in the course of which he found a source of amber. But this would have been based on the standard misconception of the time that the known world was surrounded by a single great ocean. What he thought was the Don probably was the Elbe or another river that flowed into the North Sea or the Baltic Sea.

The Iron Age in northern Europe—the Netherlands and northern Germany—began around 600 BCE when iron, used for both tools and weapons, began to be smelted from ore found in peat bogs. Burials continued to be cremations placed in urns as in the earlier Urnfield Culture. As of the first century BCE these peoples were referred to by the Romans generically as "Germans," a term that could refer to people ranging from less cultured Celts to people who spoke non-Celtic languages to people who lived north of the Rhine River. Like the Celts, the Germans lived in hierarchical societies based on agricultural villages.

A noteworthy practice of these northern European peoples was the use of peat bogs for the deposit of votive offerings, such as torques, bracelets, and ankle rings. Also deposited in bogs were human corpses, both male and female, now commonly known as the "bog people." Some of these remain in

One of the most spectacular finds of the Northern European Iron Age is the Gundestrup cauldron, a large silver vessel, twenty-seven inches (sixty-nine centimeters) in diameter, found in a peat bog in Denmark. It probably dates to the first century BCE and is elaborately decorated with portrayals of animals and deities, such as an antlered man often identified as the Celtic god Cernunnos seated cross-legged and holding a torque in one hand and a long snake in the other.

a nearly perfect state of preservation as a result of the acidic, low-temperature, and anaerobic bog conditions. Nearly two thousand such burials, many of them naked and victims of violent deaths, have been found. It is unclear whether they represent human sacrifices or criminal punishments. The Roman historian Tacitus, in his book *On the Germans*, believed it was the latter, saying, "Penalties are distinguished according to the offence. Traitors and deserters are hanged on trees; the coward, the unwarlike, the man stained with abominable vices, is plunged into the mire of the morass with a hurdle put over him."

THE PEOPLES OF NORTH AFRICA

In the ancient concept of geography, the continent of Africa lay south of the Mediterranean Sea. Peoples and cultures with whom the Romans interacted developed not only in coastal regions, but even in the heart of the Sahara Desert.

The Saharan World

The first-century CE geographer Strabo described the interior of Libya—the Greek word for Africa—as "like a leopard's skin, spotted with inhabited places, which the Egyptians call oases, that are surrounded by waterless desert." He also noted, "Most of the peoples of Libya are unknown to us; not much of it is visited by men from outside and very few of the natives from far inland ever visit us." Strabo was quite correct. The peoples of the Sahara Desert are much less well documented than those of the Nile valley and Mediterranean coast, and no connected history of them can be written. According to Herodotus, the Libyans inhabited the Sahara from the frontiers of Egypt to "the great Lake Tritonis" in southern Tunisia, which survives now only as Chott el Djerid, a salt lake that is nearly dry in the summer. They were composed of several peoples, including, from east to west, the Adyrmachidae, Giligammae, Asbystae, **Nasamonians**, **Garamantes**, Macea, Gindanes, Lotophagi ("Lotus Eaters"), Machlyans, and Auseans. As was his custom, Herodotus provided one or two supposed characteristic customs of each people. For example, the Nasamonians were nomadic herders who harvested wild dates and locusts; the Macea sported Mohawk hairstyles; and the women of the Gindanes wore on their legs a leather anklet for each lover they had had. Otherwise, most of these peoples are just names, and are known from hardly any other source.

The best-known people of the deeper Sahara Desert, attested in antiquity between 500 BCE and 700 CE, are the Garamantes, whose kingdom was centered in the Fezzan area of central and southern Libya. Knowledge about them comes both from occasional mentions in Greek and Roman sources and from recent archaeological investigations. The Garamantes had several towns, of which the most important was Garama (modern Germa), along with a large number of smaller fortified settlements, with preserved walls over ten feet high, many of which have been revealed recently by satellite imagery.

The Garamantes were primarily peaceful farmers, as suggested by Herodotus' description of them as people "who avoid all society with their fellow-men, have no weapon of war, and do not know how to defend themselves." They pursued agriculture in the oases of desert regions with negligible rainfall by utilizing wells, cistern water storage, and elaborate irrigation systems. Beginning about 200 BCE, hundreds of miles of underground *foggara*, artificial channels about two by five feet (0.6 by 1.5 meters) large and up to 130 feet (forty meters) deep, were constructed to access **fossil water** sources. The Garamantes primarily raised wheat, along with some figs, dates, olives, and grapes. Their interactions with the more settled areas nearer the Mediterranean coast included occasional raiding, which accounts for the majority of mentions in the Greek and Roman sources, and trading. They imported wine, olive oil, and fine pottery in exchange for wheat, salt, and slaves. They also quarried amazonite, a green gemstone, in the Tibesti Mountains. Peaceful contacts with the Garamantes are attested in a memo made in the third century CE at a Roman frontier outpost reading, "In November the Garamantes entered leading four mules and two Egyptians who were bearing letters to you, along with an escaped slave, Lieutenant Gtasazeiheme. The officer's name suggests that he was a native who had made his way up in the ranks.

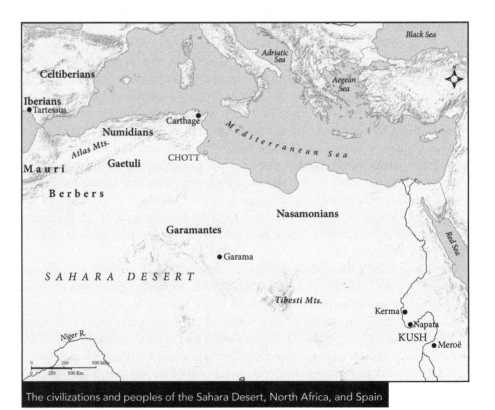

The civilizations and peoples of the Sahara Desert, North Africa, and Spain

Farther to the west, between the Atlantic and Tunisia, the people known generically as the **Berbers** (a derivative of "barbarians") lived on the fringes of the Sahara south of the densely populated coastal regions. To the east, the **Numidians**, famous for their cavalry, occupied the area closer to the Mediterranean coast, and the **Gaetuli**, known for horses and purple dye, inhabited the region between the Atlas Mountains and the Saharan oases. To the west of them, in Mauretania, in the shadow of the Atlas Mountains, lived the **Mauri** (Moors or Mauretanians), whose name also could be applied more loosely to all the Berber peoples. Those Berbers living more to the north practiced settled agriculture, whereas those in the south led oasis-based nomadic lives, keeping herds of cattle, sheep, and goats. Camels were not introduced until around the second century CE. Like the other peoples of North Africa to the east, all of these peoples spoke Afroasiatic languages, a North African linguistic group that also included the Semitic languages of the Levant, Arabia, and Mesopotamia.

In the modern day, most Berber-speaking people live in Algeria and Morocco.

The Berbers had various forms of interaction with the settled peoples on the North African coast. Nomads could move their flocks north to the area of Chott el Djerid in the fall and find work as day laborers in the fields during harvest time. Milk products and valuables such as gold and ivory that trickled across the Sahara could be traded for cereals, olive oil, and wine. Berbers also were regularly recruited into first the Carthaginian and later the Roman army.

The Mediterranean world also had contact with Sub-Saharan Africa. Herodotus, for example, told a tale of five young Nasamonians who had gone exploring in the fifth century BCE and encountered Pygmies:

> After they passed through the desert and having passed through a great tract of sand in many days, they saw at last trees . . . [when] they were beginning to pluck the fruit there came upon them small men, who seized them and carried them away; and neither could the Nasamonians understand anything of their speech nor could those who were carrying them off understand anything of the speech of the Nasamonians. And they led them through very great swamps, and they came to a city in which all the men were of the same size and in color of skin black; and by the city ran a great river, which ran from the west, and in it were seen crocodiles.

If Herodotus' geography is at all correct, the river may be the Niger River, in Mali, the only major African river that has a section flowing from the west. This would put the Pygmy city near the future trading city of Timbuktu and in the area of grasslands extending the width of Africa known as the Sahel.

Recent study suggests that the kingdom of the Garamantes was the primary beneficiary of trans-Saharan trade. The Garamantes were both transporters and consumers of trade goods, and enjoyed a long period of economic prosperity based on the exploitation of both commerce and agriculture. In addition, there was not only a trade in slaves, but slaves also might have been the main component of trans-Saharan trade, especially in the Roman period.

THE HISTORY LABORATORY

ANCIENT CIVILIZATIONS FROM ABOVE

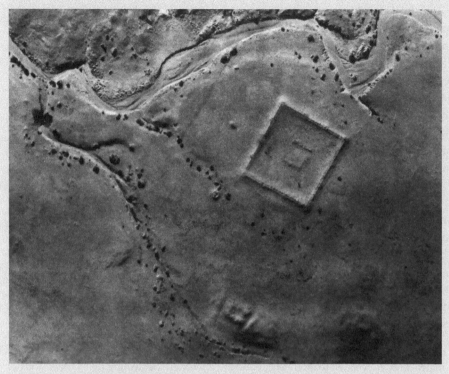

An aerial photograph reveals one of the way stations along the Roman frontier.

Ever since the Second World War, when tens of thousands of aerial reconnaissance photographs were made, aerial imaging has been one of the primary means by which the impact of ancient civilizations on the Sahara Desert area has been assessed. Beginning in 1949, for example, the work of Col. Jean Baradez began the rediscovery and mapping of the Roman fortification system on the fringes of the Sahara, similar to Hadrian's Wall, known as the "Fossatum Africae" ("The African Trench") or the "Limes Africae" ("The African Frontier"). The *fossatum* consists of a ditch surrounded by earth ramparts, accompanied by watchtowers and small forts. Previously, both local legend and historical interpretation wrongly had believed the *fossatum* was part of an irrigation system. Current historical research suggests that the system was intended to control traffic and collect customs tolls.

Carthage

The most significant non-Greek, non-Roman state of ancient North Africa developed on the northern coast of Tunisia. In the late ninth century BCE, the Phoenician city of Tyre established **Carthage** as a trading post on a well-protected harbor

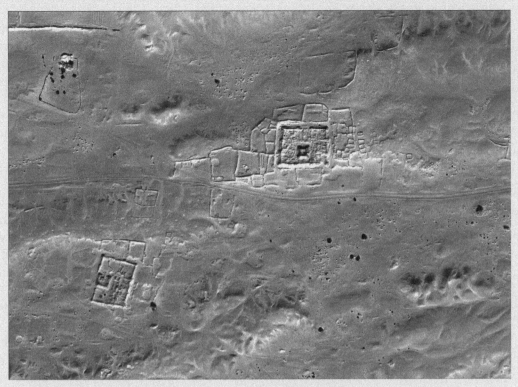

A Garamantian Saharan farming complex as revealed by satellite imaging.

More recently, satellite observations from space have revealed much about the nature of ancient life in the Sahara Desert. For example, the existence of vast lake and river structures that did not finally peter out until as recently as circa 2000 BCE has been revealed. In some places, water from these ancient aquifers lies just tens of feet under the surface and seeps out to form oases.

High-resolution satellite images, some of which were made in the search for oil, also have brought to light the remains of the Garamantian civilization of Libya. More than a hundred sites dating from between 200 BCE and 500 CE and ranging from fortified farms to small settlements have been brought to light. The high settlement density indicates that very efficient methods of irrigation and agriculture must have been in use.

In the case of the aerial observations of both the *fossatum* and the Garamantes, follow-up archaeological excavations on the ground have confirmed and fleshed out the views presented from above.

on the coast of modern Tunisia. According to tradition, the city was founded by **Dido**, a refugee queen from Tyre. A famous story related that when she asked for land from the local Berber king, she was dismissively told that she could have only as much land as could be covered by a single oxhide. So Dido ingeniously cut the oxhide into very thin strips that encircled the **Byrsa**, a high point that became the acropolis of Carthage. For some time Carthage paid tribute to local Berber peoples to ensure the peace.

By about 600 BCE, Carthage had established its independence from Tyre and become a rich and powerful trading city in its own right. In the sixth century BCE, when Tyre was attacked first by the New Babylonians and then by the Persians, many of its inhabitants fled to Carthage. This not only increased the city's population but also made it even more into a center for the preservation of Phoenician traditions. The Carthaginian version of the Phoenician language, known as Punic, became a common language of the western Mediterranean world and has been referred to as "Mediterranean Phoenician."

Carthage established its own commercial empire and became the most prosperous city in the world. Carthaginian craftspeople used raw materials such as gold, silver, bronze, iron, lead, wood, glass, ivory, alabaster, and precious stones to create a wide range of manufactured goods, such as weapons, finely crafted dyed textiles, embroidered silk, inlaid furniture, fine and everyday pottery, glassware, wine, salted fish, garum (fish sauce), perfumes, incense, mirrors, and jewelry. Other trade goods included the famous North African horses, similar to modern Arabian horses, that even appeared on Carthaginian coinage. These products could either be traded for cash in the Mediterranean world or used to acquire additional raw materials elsewhere.

Carthaginian merchants traded all over the ancient world, including by land and sea with Sub-Saharan Africa to the south, whence they obtained gold, peacocks, apes, ebony, and ivory; and from across the Sahara to the east, for spices from Arabia and India. Trade with the city of **Tartessus** and the **Celtiberians** in Spain brought in massive amounts of silver. Carthage also became the primary supplier of tin, imported from Britain, for the Mediterranean and Near Eastern worlds. From Scandinavia and the Celts came furs and highly sought amber. Slaves were imported from just about everywhere. Closer to home, the Carthaginians created their own source of purple dye, worth twenty times its weight in gold, from transplanted Phoenician murex marine snails.

The Carthaginian economy also benefited from increasingly extensive exploitation of the surrounding rich agricultural lands, utilizing sophisticated agricultural techniques including iron ploughs, crop rotation, and advanced irrigation methods. A treatise on agriculture written in Punic by the Carthaginian **Mago** later was translated into Latin and became a standard work on the topic.

When the Greeks began to establish colonies in Sicily in the mid-seventh century BCE, conflict over commerce inevitably resulted. By 600 BCE the

This Carthaginian gold shekel of ca. 300 BCE, depicting the goddess Tanit on one side and a North African horse on the other, attests to Carthage's economic power.

Carthaginians were restricted to the western part of Sicily, and warfare had broken out. In order to resist continued Greek inroads, the Carthaginians made common cause with the Etruscans of northwestern Italy. Around 535 BCE, at the Battle of Alalia off the eastern coast of Corsica, a joint Carthaginian–Etruscan fleet inflicted such damage on Greek colonists from Phocaea that the Greeks were forced to withdraw, leaving the Carthaginians in control of Sardinia and sharing Corsica with the Etruscans.

HISTORICAL CAUSALITY

What kinds of circumstances led to Carthage developing such a successful mercantile economy?

Carthage then avoided entanglement in the expansion of the Persian Empire when the Phoenicians declined to provide ships for a proposed Persian attack in 525. Subsequently, Carthage was able to defeat a Spartan attempt to found a colony on African soil and to prevent further Greek expansion in Sicily.

As a consequence of Greek control of the eastern and central Mediterranean, the Carthaginians focused their commercial efforts to the west, in Spain and out into the Atlantic Ocean, north to the British Isles and south down the west African coast. Indeed, somewhat after 500 BCE, it seems, the Carthaginian **Hanno**, who also served as king of Carthage, wrote a *periplus* (voyage account) describing a journey down the west coast of Africa at least as far the Congo River on which hippopotamuses and hairy creatures called "gorillas" were sighted. At about the same time another Carthaginian noble, **Himilco**, followed the trade routes of the Tartessians and explored the Atlantic coast all the way to northwestern France in the search for tin and other trade goods. In an attempt to scare away Greek competitors, Himilco reported encountering whirlpools, thick fog, impenetrable masses of seaweed, and sea monsters.

On the North African mainland, during the fifth century BCE the Carthaginians asserted their hegemony over the coastal Phoenician colonies. Some, such as the great North African city of Utica, remained independent allies of Carthage. Others paid tribute but retained their local autonomy. Still others had magistrates directly appointed from Carthage, resulting in resentment against Carthage. All were expected to follow Carthaginian foreign policy.

At the same time, Carthage expanded its control inland at the expense of the native Berber peoples and ceased paying them tribute. Berbers living near Carthage were required to pay half of their produce in taxes and had few legal rights. But other native peoples, such as the Numidians and Mauri to the west, the Gaetuli to the south, and the Saharan Garamantes remained independent. By 400 BCE, Carthage controlled not only the North African coast from Cyrenaica and the borders of Egypt in the east to Gibraltar in the west but also Sardinia, Malta, the Balearic Islands, the western third of Sicily, and parts of Corsica and the southern coast of Spain.

The fifth and fourth centuries BCE saw an interminable series of conflicts between Carthage and the Greek cities of Sicily, primarily Syracuse, for control of the island. Carthaginian interests suffered a major setback in 480 BCE when the plans of King Hamilcar to expand in Sicily were disastrously defeated by an alliance of Greek cities at the Battle of Himera. The next 150 years saw constant give and take. The only result, however, was that each side just wore the other down, with no significant changes in the Greek and Carthaginian positions. In the late 320s, Carthage had a scare when Alexander the Great began making preparations to attack Carthage, Italy, and Spain. His early death forestalled this effort.

The disastrous campaigns in Sicily had consequences for Carthaginian government. Carthage initially was ruled by kings who were elected as war leaders for a fixed time period by a *Gerousia* (Senate) whose members were chosen from the wealthiest and most influential families. But as a result of the Battle of Himera, the monarchy was completely discredited, and Carthage began conversion to a republic. Powers came to be apportioned among several units of government. Two **Suffets** ("judges"), still often, and confusingly, referred to as "Kings," were chosen each year from the most influential families to head the government. The *Gerousia* took charge of expenditures and foreign relations, including the appointment of generals. And a newly created "**Council of 104**," whose members were appointed for life and compared by Aristotle to the Spartan Ephors, had oversight of the government and, in particular, the generals, who could be crucified for failure. A popular assembly had the right to make the final decision in cases where the Suffets and *Gerousia* did not unanimously agree.

By the beginning of the fourth century, Carthage had become an oligarchy, and the Carthaginian constitution was included by Aristotle in his collection of constitutions, something quite unusual given that the Greeks otherwise considered the Carthaginians to be "barbarians." Carthaginian citizenship was a prized possession and not readily extended to outsiders. Citizens worked mostly in commerce and were exempt from taxes and, eventually, military service.

Because of the need to protect its seaborne commerce, the Carthaginians possessed a powerful navy of over three hundred warships, kept ready to go to sea in a specially constructed circular war harbor. The navy, which was responsible for protecting the Carthaginian homeland, was recruited primarily from native Carthaginians, and, as at Athens, provided a livelihood for the poor. The Carthaginian army, on the other hand, was used mostly for foreign wars and, given the need for Carthaginian citizens to work in commerce, relied heavily on North African and Spanish mercenaries, such as the famous Numidian cavalry. It also included several hundred African war elephants. The peoples incorporated into the Carthaginian Empire thus could expect to receive protection from the Carthaginian army and navy from attacks on themselves and their trade.

Carthaginian religion was very similar to that of the Phoenicians. The Carthaginians brought with them Melqart, the chief god of Tyre, whose temples also

The Tophet as preserved in modern Carthage, with a large number of grave stelae, is used as evidence for Carthaginian infant sacrifice.

are attested in Spain at the Phoenician colony of Gades (Cadiz) and the Carthaginian colony of Carthago Nova ("New Carthage," modern Cartagena). The name of Melqart is embodied, for example, in the Carthaginian name Hamilcar, and Melqart's most famous devotee was the later general Hannibal. Carthage occasionally made large offerings to the Temple of Melqart back in Tyre.

At the head of the Carthaginian pantheon was a divine couple composed of the fertility goddess **Tanit** (who in Ugarit was an eater of flesh and blood) and the creator god Ba'al Hammon (the Carthaginian version of the Phoenician El). Later Roman sources reported that in times of stress, Carthaginian parents sacrificed infant children to these two deities. Modern archaeological excavations have in fact discovered the burned remains of some twenty thousand infants in urns dating to the fourth and third centuries BCE in the sacred area near the Temple of Tanit and Ba'al Hammon now called the "Tophet" (from a Phoenician word meaning "roasting place"). It is unclear, however, whether they represent actual infant sacrifice or simply the normal cremation of infants who died of natural causes and perhaps then were offered to the gods.

As of the early third century BCE, Carthage was unquestionably the strongest power in the western Mediterranean, and few would have supposed that it would soon be brought down by a newly arisen power in central Italy.

CARTHAGE

A reconstructed plan in the Bardo Museum in Tunis depicts the city of Carthage in antiquity. The outer merchant harbor and inner war harbor are in the foreground and the Byrsa is at the back.

Until the nineteenth century, the ancient site of Carthage served as a stone quarry and a source of souvenir antiquities sold by local residents. Carthaginian marble made its way to Vienna and Constantinople. Modern archaeological excavations began in the late 1850s with the work of an Anglican missionary, Nathan Davis, whose personal friendship with Muhammad IV, the Bey of Tunis, got him the necessary permits. The work was funded by the British Foreign Office and has been described as simple "plundering." Entire mosaic floors were lifted out of context and shipped to England, where Davis' finds now grace the British Museum. In 1874, more than two thousand scavenged Punic inscriptions were lost in a shipwreck. The Catholic Church even encouraged excavations in hopes of achieving a Christian revival in Muslim North Africa. About 1880, scientific excavations were undertaken by the French priest

Alfred Louis Delattre. The finds of Delattre and others were housed in the Bardo Museum in Tunis, which had been established in 1888 in a thirteenth-century palace. Most of this and later French work on the site focused on the Roman remains. In the 1920s, Francis W. Kelsey of the University of Michigan excavated Punic sites in Carthage.

Efforts to preserve the archaeological heritage of Carthage from urban development received a major boost in 1972 with UNESCO's "Save Carthage" campaign, overseen by the Tunisian Institut National d'Archéologie et d'Art with assistance from Canada, Bulgaria, Denmark, France, Germany, the Netherlands, Italy, Poland, Sweden, Tunisia, the United Kingdom, and the United States. As a result, many excavations were carried out between 1974 and 1984, and the archaeological excavation of Carthage continues into the modern day.

THE GREEKS

In the eastern Mediterranean, the primary people that the Romans encountered were the Greeks. After the extinction of the Bronze Age Mycenaean civilization circa 1100 BCE, not that long after the end of the legendary Trojan War, ancient Greece entered the so-called "Dark Ages," when most attributes of civilization, such as urbanism, stone architecture, large-scale manufacturing, long-distance trade, and even writing were lost. Only three hundred years later, in the early eighth century BCE, at just about the same time of the foundation of Rome, did Greece emerge into the "Archaic Age," with the revival of long-distance trade and the recovery of traditions of trade, manufacturing, and literacy. The Greeks then created a culture and civilization that in many ways defines ancient civilization. By this time, Greece was governed by a multitude of city-states, all of which were independent nations. The two most powerful city-states were Sparta and Athens, which united to resist two Persian invasions of Greece (490–479 BCE). But this happy condition was not to last. The Greeks were their own worst enemies, and rounds of warfare between the cities of Athens and Sparta in the fifth century BCE left them so weakened that they were ripe for invasion from outside. Thus, in 338 a coalition of Greek city-states was defeated by Philip II (359–336), king of Macedonia, a Greek kingdom of northwestern Greece. Between 334 and 323 BCE, Philip's son Alexander III, better known as Alexander the Great, defeated the Persians and created the largest empire the world yet had known. It extended from Greece in the west all the way to the Indus River valley in India. After Alexander's death, his generals carved up his empire. Ultimately, the families of Ptolemy, Antigonus, and Seleucid established Hellenistic kingdoms that survived until the coming of the Romans beginning in the second century BCE. This period is known as the **Hellenistic Age** (323–31 BCE).

The Wars of the Successors

One thing Alexander had neglected to do was to provide an heir to his throne. When he was asked, as he was dying, who should succeed him, some thought that he answered, "The strongest man." His wife, Roxana, did not bear his only son, Alexander IV (323–309 BCE), until after his death, and this infant and Alexander's half-brother Philip III (323–317 BCE), mentally incapacitated as a result of a botched poisoning attempt, were named joint kings, although neither was in any position actually to govern. Alexander's generals, known as the *Diadochi*, or "successors," began to squabble among themselves in attempts to carve out chunks of the empire for themselves.

Soon after Alexander's death, in the "Partition of Babylon," Perdiccas was named regent for the two kings and Alexander's generals were named satraps (governors) in the territories throughout the empire. Antipater, for example, received Macedonia and Greece; Lysimachus was granted Thrace; **Antigonus I Monopthalmos** ("the One-Eyed") gained most of Anatolia; **Ptolemy I** obtained Egypt; **Seleucus** was assigned Babylonia; and so on. Two years later, in 321 BCE, Perdiccas was killed by his own troops while he was attacking Ptolemy, and a new arrangement, mostly affecting the more minor players, was established at the "Partition of Triparadisus" (a place in Lebanon): Antipater was named regent, but the holdings of the other main contenders remained essentially the same.

A series of "Wars of the *Diadochi*" then ensued, in which Alexander's generals attempted to expand their holdings and even to restore the empire. This was an age of great generals and elaborate campaigns. A few major players soon consolidated their holdings at the expense of lesser figures. Because armies now included mostly mercenaries, warfare took on a different perspective. Rather than fights to the death, as often had happened among the Greeks, Hellenistic commanders and soldiers alike were much more attuned to reaching accommodations and preserving their forces. It was customary for battles to be rather genteel affairs. Soldiers were expensive to train and difficult to recruit. They certainly were not to be wasted. As soon as one side had the upper hand, fighting would cease. The commanders would reach an agreement in which the winner got something, the loser lost something, and almost everybody lived to fight another day. It was not uncommon for a losing army simply to go into the service of the winner. As a result of this more enlightened approach to battle, with the exception of Egypt, the wealthiest and most easily defended satrapy, which remained firmly in the hands of Ptolemy, territories repeatedly changed hands.

In Macedonia, in 317 BCE Antipater was replaced by his son Cassander, who governed in the name of Philip III but was opposed by Alexander's still-ambitious mother Olympias, who supported the infant Alexander IV. In the course of the conflict, Olympias had Philip executed, but Cassander soon turned the tables, executing first Olympias and then, in 309 BCE, Roxana and the child Alexander IV. In 305, Cassander had himself declared king of Macedon. Farther east, Antigonus the One-Eyed, aided by his able and ambitious son Demetrius, had managed to gain control of the entire empire from Anatolia to Persia by 316. But this caused Cassander, Ptolemy, and Seleucus (whom Antigonus had expelled from Babylonia) to ally against him, and the tide of battle flowed back and forth. Ptolemy defeated Demetrius in 312, and Seleucus reoccupied Babylonia. But in 306, Ptolemy, attempting to attack Anatolia, was defeated in a naval battle by Demetrius, who occupied Cyprus. Antigonus then declared himself *basileus* (king), a move that removed any fiction that there still was a united empire, and was copied by Cassander, Lysimachus, Seleucus, and Ptolemy.

The fighting continued. In 305 BCE, Demetrius mounted a great siege of the island city of **Rhodes**, located off the southwestern coast of Anatolia, the primary stopping point for commercial traffic traveling along the Anatolian coast. Demetrius constructed siege engines of such great size that he gained the nickname Poliorcetes, or "Besieger of Cities." But the siege failed, and the Rhodians melted down the metal from the siege engines to create a 110-foot-tall statue of the sun god Helios known as the Colossus of Rhodes, which stood at the entrance to their harbor and became one of the Seven Wonders of the World. The city then became rich on harbor tolls, and, in order to protect its trade, it developed a powerful navy for the suppression of piracy.

In 301 BCE, Antigonus was attacked by the combined armies of Lysimachus and Seleucus and at the Battle of Ipsus in Phrygia was defeated and killed at eighty-one years of age. His kingdom was divided by the victors. But Demetrius still had his own ambitions. In 297 Cassander died, and Demetrius saw his opportunity. In 294, he seized Athens, murdered the son of Cassander, and established himself as the king of Macedon, only to be expelled in 288 while in the process of making plans of his own to recover Alexander's empire. Lysimachus then occupied Macedonia. The last of the *Diadochi* to strive to reclaim Alexander's empire was eighty-year-old Seleucus, who in 281 defeated and killed Lysimachus, also eighty years old, at the Battle of Corupedium in Lydia. Seleucus thus added Macedonia and Thrace to his dominions in Asia and had recombined nearly all of Alexander's empire except for Egypt. But this was a short-lived triumph, for later in the same year Seleucus, the last living comrade of Alexander, was assassinated by Ptolemy Keraunos ("The Thunderbolt"), an adventurer son of Ptolemy I. The age of the *Diadochi* was over.

The Hellenistic Greek Kingdoms

As of 280 BCE, Egypt (where Ptolemy II [309–246 BCE] had succeeded his father Ptolemy I, who died at eighty-four in 283), Palestine, and Cyprus now were controlled by the **Ptolemaic Dynasty** (323–31 BCE), also known as the "Lagids," after Ptolemy I's father Lagus. The Ptolemies had to rule over both Greek and Egyptian populations. To Greeks, they were Macedonian successors to Alexander. But to Egyptians, they were a Ptolemaic dynasty of pharaohs, and, up to a point, they behaved like pharaohs. They built new temples to the ancient Egyptian gods, married their sisters, and were worshipped as if they were gods. Priests of the ancient Egyptian gods recognized the Macedonian kings as pharaohs, and portrayed them using the same iconography as had been used to represent pharaohs in the past. Ptolemaic queens named Arsinoë, Berenice, and Cleopatra continued the tradition of strong Egyptian female rulers; some ruled in their own names, and others exerted a strong influence over their husbands, brothers, or sons.

Although the Ptolemies outwardly adopted aspects of Egyptian culture that suited their political agendas, culturally they remained completely Greek; indeed, only the last Ptolemaic ruler, another female pharaoh, Cleopatra VII (51–30 BCE), was even said to have learned Egyptian. As their capital the Ptolemies chose the great port city of Alexandria, located on the Mediterranean coast twenty miles (thirty-seven kilometers) west of the mouths of the Nile. The double harbor was

The "pharos," or lighthouse, of Alexandria, here depicted in a sixth-century CE Byzantine mosaic from Libya, was one of the Seven Wonders of the World. It stood at the entry to the harbor of Alexandria and was about 450 feet high; a large fire reflected by a great mirror was visible from up to thirty miles (forty-eight kilometers) out to sea.

A tetradrachm of Gonatas displays on the obverse the horned head of the god Pan, who inspired the Gauls with panic terror at the Battle of Lysimacheia, surrounded by Macedonian shields; the reverse depicts a fighting Athena with the legend "of king Antigonus," for by now all of the Hellenistic monarchs had adopted the royal title.

protected by a long causeway extending out to the island of Pharos, where a famous lighthouse was located.

As of circa 200 BCE, the Ptolemies were confronted by several Egyptian revolts, to some degree facilitated by the admission of native Egyptians into the army. Ptolemaic military strength thus rapidly declined. Much of the next 160 years of Ptolemaic Egypt was beset by dynastic quarreling that sapped the kingdom's ability to restore its political position. In addition, as of the 140s BCE, Ptolemaic Egypt came increasingly under the influence of Rome, and the top priority of Ptolemaic rulers became keeping the Romans happy.

Anatolia and all the rest of the Asian satrapies, from Anatolia to the frontiers of India, were ruled by Antiochus I, the son of Seleucus, and the **Seleucid Dynasty** (312–63 BCE). It was easily the most heterogeneous of the successor states and the most difficult to hold together. It contained a huge non-Greek population, and it was difficult to attract additional Greek settlers. Realizing that their Greek population was far too small to scatter about the countryside as had been done in Egypt, the Seleucids continued Alexander's policy of colonization and established hundreds of colonies not only as focal points of Seleucid rule but also as a means of creating increased commercial activity, and thus raising income. In Syria, which became the core of the empire, Seleucus founded a new capital, the great city of Antioch, named after his father Antiochus, on the Orontes River. The city eventually had a population approaching a half million. A second capital was created in Mesopotamia at Seleucia on the Tigris River north of Babylon, which became the center of Greek culture and administration in the eastern part of the empire. Seleucus also was said to have founded sixteen other Antiochs.

Back in Macedonia, in 279, a huge army of Celts, also called Gauls, from the Danube region invaded Macedonia, defeated and killed Ptolemy Keraunos, and looted Macedonia and northern Greece. Two years later, a large contingent of Gauls was ambushed and destroyed by **Antigonus Gonatas**, the son of Demetrius Poliorcetes, at the Battle of Lysimacheia. Gonatas then laid claim to the throne of Macedonia as Antigonus II (277–239 BCE) and established the **Antigonid Dynasty** for good.

It was the Ptolemaic, Seleucid, and Antigonid dynasties that would confront the Romans when they eventually expanded into the eastern Mediterranean beginning in 200 BCE.

THE PEOPLES OF WESTERN ASIA

In the east, Roman interests eventually extended from Anatolia and the Levant all the way to Mesopotamia and Armenia. Several peoples from this region attracted particular attention from the Romans.

The Jews

The homeland of a people who would have inordinate influence on Roman history lay in Palestine, near the southern coast of the Levant. The kingdom of the Jews initially was established under King Saul, circa 1050 BCE. Around 930 BCE, the kingdom fragmented into two parts, Israel in the north and Judah in the south. The kingdom of Israel was destroyed by the Assyrians in 721 BCE, and Judah fell to the New Babylonians in 587 BCE. Many Jews then were exiled to Babylonia in what became known as the "Babylonian Captivity," which marked the beginning of the Jewish diaspora, the spread of Jewish populations outside of Judaea. The territory of Judah then was incorporated into the Persian Empire, the empire of Alexander the Great, and the Seleucid Empire. Under Alexander, the Jews continued to enjoy the same freedom of worship as under the Persians, but later, unlike the Ptolemies and other Greco-Macedonian rulers, the Seleucids sometimes tried to force Hellenism on their subjects as a means of unifying their kingdom. Many Jews, mostly well-to-do and engaged in public life, embraced Hellenistic culture. They learned Greek, studied Greek literature, and adopted Greek religious and philosophical beliefs. This may have led King Antiochus IV Epiphanes (175–164 BCE), whose epithet meant "God Made Manifest," to believe that other Jews also could be Hellenized. But his efforts to impose Greek culture aroused great opposition, especially among less privileged Jews led by the Hasidim ("the pious ones"), who feared that any adoption of Greek culture could lead to their destruction. Antiochus responded by actively attempting to undermine Jewish practices. He not only prohibited circumcision, studying the **Torah** (the first five books of the Hebrew Bible, containing the most significant parts of Jewish religious law), and observing the Sabbath, but he even instituted ritual prostitution in the Temple in Jerusalem, where he also placed a statue and altar to Zeus on which pigs, which the Jews believed were unclean, were sacrificed, something the Jews called the "abomination of desolation."

Rebellion broke out led by Judah, nicknamed Maccabee ("The Hammer"); the rebels' goal was not just religious freedom but also political independence.

The reconsecration of the Jewish temple still is commemorated each year in the Jewish festival of Hanukkah ("the Dedication").

Against all odds, Judah defeated Antiochus in 165 BCE and liberated Jerusalem, marking one of the very few times in antiquity that a popular revolt succeeded in gaining a people's independence. The following year, the temple was cleansed and reopened. In 140 BCE, Simon, the brother of Judah, was named both high priest and king of the Jews, thus reestablishing a Jewish kingdom. This marked the beginning of the Hasmonean Dynasty (140–37 BCE), which would last for another hundred years and would be the last independent Jewish nation until 1949 CE.

Jewish independence did not, however, mean an end to disagreements among the Jews. Hellenism still attracted many Jews, such as members of the Sadducees, who oversaw the temple in Jerusalem. The Sadducees interpreted Jewish law narrowly, relying solely on written scriptures. The Pharisees, on the other hand, the successors of the Hasidim, supported a rigorous enforcement of Jewish religious law, including orally transmitted law, and oversaw the study of scripture in the synagogues.

At the same time, the Jewish diaspora continued the spread of Jews throughout the Mediterranean world, especially in Mesopotamia and in Alexandria, where a large population of Jews made up of exiles, merchants, and mercenaries eventually outnumbered the Jews of Palestine. These foreign Jews were remarkably successful at being able to preserve much of their culture in the midst of foreign customs. But with respect to language, the Jews of Alexandria eventually functioned in Greek rather than in Hebrew. To make scripture available to them, beginning in the third century BCE a Greek version of the Hebrew Bible was created, known as the Septuagint, from the Latin word meaning "seventy," because it supposedly had been made by seventy translators.

The Nabataean Arabs

A people who benefited from commerce between east and west was the **Nabataeans**, oasis-based Arabs who inhabited the arid territory between Syria and Arabia, from the Euphrates River to the Red Sea. The Nabataeans first appeared in the period after the Babylonian Captivity of the Jews in the sixth century BCE. Their familiarity with desert life enabled them to retain their independence. In the late fourth century BCE, for example, they defeated a Seleucid attack. Soon thereafter they expanded to occupy the port city of Aqaba on the Red Sea and gained a reputation as pirates.

Imaginative irrigation techniques that maximized the effect of the minimal rainfall allowed for the cultivation of date palms and balsam poplar. The Nabataeans also raised horses, and engaged in trade with southern Arabia in frankincense, myrrh, and spices, and in bitumen with Egypt. As a result of the decline of the Seleucid Kingdom in the early first century BCE, the Nabataeans extended their control all the way to Syria and Damascus. At the same time, the Nabataeans expanded the construction of their capital city of **Petra** (Raqmu in the Nabataean language), which was graced by an extensive system of water collection that preserved water from flash floods in cisterns for use during dry periods. The city was approached through a narrow gorge that opened in front of the "Treasury," the city's most impressive monument. With a population of some twenty thousand, Petra was the center of a camel trading network that extended across the desert to the Persian Gulf, north to Damascus, and south to the Red Sea.

It was perhaps in the context of their commerce that the Nabataeans developed a written language using the Aramaic alphabet, which had developed out of the Phoenician alphabet in the eighth century BCE. A cursive form of the Nabataean script later evolved into the Arabic alphabet. The Aramaic alphabet featured added characters that indicated the presence of vowels. No Nabataean literature or official documents, however, survive, and all the attested examples of the written language are found in graffiti, which suggests that the Nabataeans must have had a rather high rate of literacy, no doubt a consequence of its usefulness for commercial transactions. With regard to religion, Nabataean gods were represented as simple blocks of stone, some of which were hewn out of cliffs or mountain tops.

Steppe Nomads: Scythians and Sarmatians

The southern Eurasian steppe lands that extended from the Ukraine, north of the Black Sea, all the way to Mongolia were the homeland of Indo-European peoples who also interacted with Rome. The Indo-Europeans are identified by similarities in their languages, although in other ways their cultures were very different. Over the course of the millennia, beginning around 2000 BCE, groups of Indo-Europeans migrated to India, Iran, Anatolia, and western Europe. The Greeks referred to the Indo-Europeans who remained in central Asia generically as "Scythians," although they also went under many other names. Collectively, the Scythians had a long history of interaction and conflict with their neighbors to the south and west. At some point around 700 BCE, they occupied the steppe territory of the Cimmerians, who responded by invading Anatolia. Subsequently, "Cimmerian" became an alternate term for "Scythian." Around 640 BCE, invading Scythians known to the Assyrians as the "Ashkuza"—a term thought to prefigure the Jewish Ashkenazi—and to the Persians as the "**Saka**" were expelled from Media by Cyaxares, the first king of the Medes. A few decades later, Scythians were first allies and then enemies of the Assyrians, participating in the destruction of Nineveh in 612 BCE. In the next century, the first Persian king, Cyrus, was killed in battle against the Massagetae, an offshoot of the Scythians, in 531 BCE, and in 513 BCE Darius I undertook a massively unsuccessful invasion of the Scythian homeland. In 339 BCE, the Scythian king Ataias was killed in a battle in the Dobrudja with Philip II of Macedon, and ten years later Alexander the Great defeated a Scythian army west of the Caspian Sea, his farthest advance north.

Life among the Scythians served as a backdrop for the "Scythian Suite," composed by the Russian Sergei Prokofiev in 1915.

A typical Scythian horseman carrying the traditional drinking goblet on his belt as depicted on a tapestry of ca. 300 BCE, now in the State Hermitage Museum in St. Petersburg.

The Scythian sweat lodge ritual has a superficial similarity to ceremonies practiced by Native Americans in the modern day.

In general, both the Greeks and the Romans were fascinated by the strange characteristics of the nomadic Scythians and their world. The Greeks often portrayed the Scythians as violent and bloodthirsty. Herodotus, for example, reported that Scythian warriors drank the blood of the first man they killed and brought the heads of others to the king in order to lay claim to a share of the loot after a campaign. The scalps were softened and used as napkins, and the skulls were covered with leather or even gold and used as drinking cups that were shared with distinguished guests. Kings, Herodotus went on to say, were buried under vast mounds, and were accompanied in death by a slaughtered concubine, cook, groom, servant, and cup-bearer, as well as by several horses and golden treasures. Fifty slaughtered youths and horses then were mounted around the tomb. But, as always among the Greeks, opinions varied. A century later, the historian Ephorus wrote that the Scythians "excel all men in justice." And the Scythian philosopher **Anacharsis** was counted as one of the Seven Wise Men of the Greek world and believed to have invented the bellows and the potter's wheel. Upon returning home, however, Anacharsis was immediately executed for participating in Greek culture.

Peoples associated with the Scythians also were given various distinguishing characteristics. The Massagetae, Herodotus said, dwelt near the Caspian Sea, worshipped the sun, lived mostly on milk, and cannibalized their dead. The Sarmatians, who inhabited the area from the Ukrainian steppes just north of the Black Sea eastward to the Caspian Sea and appeared regularly in Roman sources, were believed to have sprung from a union of Scythians and Amazon women. As a consequence, they were described as "women-ruled" and, it was said, "Their women ride, shoot and throw the javelin while mounted, frequently hunt on horseback, in war take the field, and wear the very same dress as the men. . . . No girl can marry until she has killed a man in battle."

In order to assess the reliability of ancient reports about peoples who lived so far beyond the Greek and Roman worlds, one can turn to their material culture. In outline at least, many of the Scythian customs reported by Herodotus and others are confirmed by archaeology. For example, many of the details about Scythian royal burials—such as the large pit covered by a mound, spears planted in the ground, the accompanying concubine and servants, the horse burials, the gold grave goods, and even the slaughtered horses and riders—have been confirmed by excavations. One mound is over sixty-five feet (twenty meters) high, and another was found with four hundred horses accompanying its deceased inhabitant. In addition, the common presence in tombs of armed women easily could have led to legends about Amazons.

Moreover, mummies with western Eurasian genetic markers dating to the Scythian period found in the **Tarim Basin** in northwestern China have been found accompanied by bags of cannabis, thus confirming Herodotus' reports of Scythian marijuana smoking. And recent excavations also have unearthed in the Ukraine the remains of a large settlement dated to the fifth and fourth centuries BCE that has been identified as the wooden city of Gelonus, the only Scythian town mentioned by Herodotus.

The Scythian love of gold likewise is confirmed by archaeological finds of many kinds of golden artifacts used for personal ornamentation, including not only earrings, armbands, and brooches, but also decorations attached to belts, scabbards, and helmets. These attest to Scythian accumulation of wealth from gold mining in rivers and streams, raids on the more settled world to the south, and trade, especially in grain, apparently grown by more settled subject peoples. They also manifest Scythian appreciation of certain kinds of artistic motifs, such as animals—lions, leopards, bears, eagles, stags, and even griffins—engaged in combat. Opinions continue to differ as to whether these finely wrought ornaments were created by Greek or native Scythian craftspeople. The characteristic Scythian animal art style spread east, west, and south to other parts of the ancient world. It also is attested in Scythian tattoos, as seen on a frozen Scythian mummy tattooed with a stag, a ram, a fish, and two griffins. Up until now, however, no examples of skull drinking cups have been unearthed.

In this detail from a piece of golden Scythian animal artwork dated to the fourth century BCE and now in Kiev, griffins attack a horse.

The Parthians

Another Indo-European steppe people said to have been related to the Scythians was the Parthians, who ultimately would become Rome's primary competitor in the east. According to legend, the Parthians originated with the Scythian Arsaces, the leader of a people known as the Parni who lived on the lower Oxus (Amu Darya) River on the southern Eurasian steppe. In 238 BCE they invaded and occupied the Seleucid satrapy of Parthia in northeastern Iran, from which they took their name. Arsaces founded the **Arsacid Dynasty** of Parthian kings, and the Parthians established their first capital city at Hecatompylos ("City of a Hundred Gates") in Khorasan in northeastern Persia.

Parthian society was structured into four classes: (1) the royal family, (2) nobles and priests, (3) merchants, and (4) farmers and herders. The nobility controlled large estates and were responsible for raising the Parthian army and for selecting the king, who often had difficulty keeping the independently minded nobles under control. In fact, in order to maintain their own authority, the nobles sometimes would purposely select a weak king.

The Parthians, and in particular the privileged elements of society, became heavily Hellenized. Much of their writing and recordkeeping was done in Greek, and Parthian coins were modeled on Greek coins and had legends in Greek.

But aspects of native Parthian culture also survived and even prospered. A few documents written in the Parthian Indo-European language remain, nearly all of them relating to commercial transactions. A noteworthy characteristic of Parthian culture was the *gōsān*, or musician-poet, a wandering male or female entertainer who composed poems about ancient kings and heroes for all levels of society.

In spite of dynastic succession issues, the Parthian Empire grew, in the west at the expense of the Seleucid Empire. The defeat and death of the Seleucid king Antiochus VII in 129 BCE consolidated Parthian expansion to the Euphrates River and the frontier of Syria. Once this had happened, the Parthians constructed a new capital city at **Ctesiphon**, just across the Tigris River from the great Greek city of Seleucia. On their northeastern frontier, however, the Parthians continued to be threatened by steppe nomads, and engaged in repeated conflicts with the Saka and Tocharians. Two Parthian kings, Phraates II (132–126 BCE) and Artabanus II (ca. 122–121 BCE), were killed in battle. It took until 100 BCE for King Mithridates II (121–91 BCE) definitively to drive them off. By then, the Parthian Empire had expanded to its maximum extent, extending eastward to the borders of India, and had become the closest thing yet to a native successor to the Persian Empire.

Like the Persians, the Parthians had no standing army except for the relatively small bodyguard of the king. Military contingents were raised by Parthian nobles, so it was important for the king to be on good terms with them. The most effective part of the Parthian army was its cavalry. Heavy cataphracts, which the Parthians introduced to the western world, carried long lances and were, along with their horses, protected by scale armor. The cataphracts were recruited from the Parthian nobility and served as the primary attack force. Well-to-do Parthian farmers and merchants could serve as horse archers, who harassed attackers by using composite bows to shoot arrows as they rode toward an enemy and then, using the famous "Parthian shot," to shoot backward as they rode away. Lightly armed infantry, recruited from poorer Parthians, was used primarily to mop up an enemy army that already had been defeated.

Although the Parthian economy was primarily rural, the Parthians also benefited from their control of a newly opened lucrative trade route to the east. In 125 BCE, the Chinese diplomat Zhang Qian, who had been sent westward by the Han emperor Wu Di (141–87 BCE) to find allies against the Hsiung-Nu, returned to China after fifteen years of exploration. According to the Chinese historical source known as the *Shiji*, written around 100 BCE, "The emperor learned of the Dayuan [Ionians; that is,

A spiral-haired Parthian of the first century CE depicted in a belted decorated tunic with a dagger at his side and perhaps engaged in worship. Perhaps from the ancient province of Khorasan in western Iran.

Greek colonists settled at Alexandria Eschata in Sogdiana], Daxia [Bactria], Anxi [Arsacids, the Parthians], and the others, all great states rich in unusual products whose people cultivated the land and made their living in much the same way as the Chinese. All these states, he was told, prized Han goods and wealth." After embassies were sent by Wu Di to Mithridates II of Parthia, a four-thousand-mile trade route known as the "**Silk Road**" was opened in 114 BCE that linked China with Parthia, and thence to Syria.

The creation of this route was greatly aided by the expansion of Greek trading networks into central Asia, which now could be linked via the Tarim Basin directly to China. Oasis cities such as Khotan, reputedly established by a son of Asoka, and Loulan prospered greatly. But it was the cagey Parthians, who controlled the route, who served as the primary middlemen. They even went so far as to reweave Chinese silks into more complex patterns and then sell them back to the Chinese. The Parthians also had an interest in the southern sea route that led from northeastern Africa to the Persian Gulf, India, and even China, although, regarding the last of these, one source noted, "few men come from there, and seldom."

⇦ LOOKING BACK

A look at the cultures and civilizations that arose outside the vicinity of Rome can provide a more nuanced understanding of cultural and political developments in the Mediterranean world once the Romans began to expand out of Italy. In addition, a consideration of the peoples and societies that developed beyond the world of Rome reminds us that Rome did not exist in a hermetically sealed world and was not isolated from outside influence. Quite the contrary. There was a great deal of interchange between the Romans and the rest of the Mediterranean and Asian worlds, and cultural influences migrated in both directions. Only by understanding the neighbors of the Romans can we even to begin to understand the true significance of the evolution of Roman culture.

LOOKING AHEAD ⇨

Discussion now can turn to Italy, where a new power was developing. Over the course of five hundred years, Rome grew from a small village in central Italy to become the most powerful state in the Mediterranean world. It took the eastern powers a while, however, to understand that balance of power was changing, and in the second century BCE, Antigonid Macedonia and Seleucid Syria would have a rude awakening when Roman armies appeared on their doorsteps. By 146 BCE, it will be seen, Rome had become the undisputed master of the entire Mediterranean world.

FURTHER READING

Baradez, J. *Fossatum Africae. Recherches aériennes sur l'organisation des confins Sahariens à l'époque Romaine.* Paris: Arts et Métiers Graphiques, 1949.

Brett, Michael, and Elizabeth Fentress. *The Berbers.* Oxford & Malden, MA: Wiley-Blackwell, 1997.

Cunliffe, Barry. *The Ancient Celts.* Oxford: Oxford Univ. Press, 1997.

Curtis, Vesta Sarkhosh, and Sarah Stewart. *The Age of the Parthians.* London & New York: I. B. Tauris, 2007.

Errington, R. M. *A History of the Hellenistic World.* Oxford: Blackwell, 2008.

Gimbutas, Marija. *Bronze Age Cultures in Central and Eastern Europe.* Berlin: De Gruyter, 1965.

Gojda, Martin. "Military Activities on Rome's Frontier: The Evidence of Aerial Archaeology." In *Mitteleuropa zur Zeit Marbods*, edited by Vladimír Salač and Jan Bemmann, 1–20. Prague & Bonn, 2009.

Ivantchik, Askold. "The Funeral of Scythian Kings: The Historical Reality and the Description of Herodotus (IV, 71–72)." In *The Barbarians of Ancient Europe: Realities and Interactions*, edited by Larissa Bonfante, 71–106. Cambridge, UK: Cambridge Univ. Press, 2011.

James, Simon. *The Atlantic Celts: Ancient People or Modern Invention?* Madison: University of Wisconsin Press, 1999.

Lancel, Serge. *Carthage: A History.* Oxford: Blackwell, 1997.

Mattingly, David, ed. *Archaeology of Fazzan.* Vol. 1, Synthesis. London: Society for Libyan Studies, 2003.

Miles, Richard. *Carthage Must Be Destroyed: The Rise and Fall of an Ancient Civilization.* London: Allen Lane, 2010.

Pydyn, A. *Exchange and Cultural Interactions: A Study of Long-Distance Trade and Cross-Cultural Contacts in the Late Bronze Age and Early Iron Age in Central and Eastern Europe.* Oxford: Archaeopress, 1999.

SOURCES

THE EXPANSION OF THE CELTS INTO GREECE AND ANATOLIA (279–277 BCE)

JUSTIN, *PHILIPPIC HISTORIES*, BOOKS 24–28

A golden torque, or neck ring, worn by Celtic warriors as a magical amulet that supposedly protected them in battle. The torque was forged as a single piece around the neck and was most easily removed by decapitation, which Celtic warriors practiced after they had killed an enemy in battle. The use of decapitation also was adopted by the Roman army.

As of the sixth century BCE, Celts, also known to the Greeks and Romans as Gauls, occupied the inland regions of western Europe—that is, Spain, Gaul, northern Italy, Britain, and the areas along the Danube River. Although they were politically disunified, they shared the same complex culture and civilization. In the early third century BCE, not long after the dismemberment of the empire of Alexander, groups of Celts began to move south into Greece. Some reached as far as Anatolia. The story of the Celtic attack on Greece in 279 was related in the *Philippic Histories* of the Augustan writer Pompeius Trogus. His work does not survive, but an epitome made circa the second or third century CE by Marcus Junianus Justinus, or simply Justin, does.

Source: John Selby Watson, *Marcus Junius Justinus, Epitome of the Philippic History of Pompeius Trogus* (London: Bohn, 1853).

The Gauls, when the land that had produced them was unable, because of their excessive increase of population, to contain them, sent out three hundred thousand men as a sacred spring,[1] to seek new settlements. Of these adventurers part settled in Italy,[2] and took and burnt the city of Rome, and part penetrated into the remotest parts of Illyricum under the direction of a flight of birds, for the Gauls are skilled in augury beyond other nations. Making their way amid great slaughter of

---

[1] When some ancient groups of people became too large, they would declare a "Sacred Spring," in which all of the children born in a certain year would be sent away to find new homes after they had reached the age of about twenty.

[2] During the fifth century BCE, groups of Gallic Celts seized the Po River valley in northern Italy from the Etruscans.

the barbarous phylē's,[3] they fixed their abode in Pannonia.[4] They were a savage, bold, and warlike nation, and were the first after Hercules, to whom that undertaking procured great admiration for his valor, and a belief in his immortality, to pass the unconquered heights of the Alps, and places uninhabitable from excess of cold. After having subdued the Pannonians, they carried on various wars with their neighbors for many years. Success encouraging them, they betook themselves, in separate bands, some to Greece, and some to Macedonia,[5] laying waste all before them with the sword. Such indeed was the terror of the Gallic name, that even kings, before they were attacked, purchased peace from them with large sums of money.

Ptolemy alone, the King of Macedonia,[6] heard of the approach of the Gauls without alarm, and, hurried on by the madness that distracted him for his unnatural crimes, went out to meet them with a few undisciplined troops, as if wars could be dispatched with as little difficulty as murders.[7] An embassy from the Dardanians,[8] offering him twenty thousand armed men for his assistance, he spurned, adding insulting language, and saying that "the Macedonians would be in a sad condition if, after having subdued the whole east without assistance, they now required aid from the Dardanians to defend their country; and that he had for soldiers the sons of those who had served under Alexander the Great, and had been victorious throughout the world." This answer being repeated to the Dardanian prince, he observed that the famous kingdom of Macedonia would soon fall as a sacrifice to the rashness of a raw youth.

The Gauls, under the command of Belgius,[9] sent deputies to Ptolemy to sound out the disposition of the Macedonians, offering him peace if he wanted to purchase it, but Ptolemy bragged to his courtiers that the Gauls sued for peace from fear of war. Nor was his manner less boastful before the ambassadors than before his own adherents, saying that he would grant peace only on condition that they would give their chiefs as hostages and deliver up their arms; for he would put no trust in them until they were disarmed. When the deputies brought back this answer, the Gauls laughed and exclaimed throughout their camp that Ptolemy would soon see whether they had offered peace from regard for themselves or for him. Some days after a battle was fought, and the Macedonians were defeated and cut to pieces. Ptolemy, after receiving several wounds, was captured and his head, cut off and stuck on a lance, was carried round the whole army to strike terror into the enemy.[10] Flight saved a few of the Macedonians; the rest were either taken or slain.

When the news of this event was spread through all Macedonia, the gates of the cities were shut and all places were filled with mourning. Sometimes the Macedonians lamented their bereavement, from the loss of their children; sometimes they were seized with dread, lest their cities should be destroyed; and at other times they called on the names of their kings, Alexander and Philip,[11] as deities, to protect them; saying that under them they were not only secure, but conquerors of the world, and begging that they would guard their country, whose fame they had raised to heaven by the glory of their exploits, and give assistance to the afflicted, whom the insanity and rashness of Ptolemy had ruined. While all were thus in despair, Sosthenes,[12] one of the Macedonian chiefs, thinking that nothing would be effected by prayers, assembled such as were of age for war, repulsed the Gauls in the midst of their exultation at their victory, and saved Macedonia from devastation. For these great services, he, although of humble extraction, was chosen before many nobles that aspired to the throne of Macedonia. Although he was saluted as king by the

---

[3] Peoples.

[4] Modern Hungary.

[5] In 279 BCE.

[6] Ptolemy Keraunos ("The Thunderbolt"), the eldest son of Ptolemy I of Egypt, who briefly seized control of Macedonia in 281.

[7] Among others, Ptolemy had murdered Seleucus I in 281 BCE.

[8] Dardania was a region northeast of Macedonia.

[9] A Gallic leader sometimes thought to be connected to the Belgae ("Belgians"), a Celtic people of northern Gaul.

---

[10] The Celts had a reputation as head hunters.

[11] Alexander the Great and his father, Philip II.

[12] Macedonian general who ruled as a king from 279 to 278 BCE.

army, he made the soldiers take an oath to him, not as king, but as general.

In the meantime Brennus,[13] under whose command a part of the Gauls had made an attack into Greece,[14] having heard of the success of their countrymen, who, under the leadership of Belgius, had defeated the Macedonians, and being indignant that so rich a booty, consisting of the spoils of the east, had been so lightly abandoned, assembled an army of a hundred and fifty thousand foot and fifteen thousand horse,[15] and suddenly invaded Macedonia. As he was laying waste the fields and villages, Sosthenes met him with his army of Macedonians in full array, but being few in number, and in some consternation, they were easily overcome by the more numerous and powerful Gauls. The defeated Macedonians retired within the walls of their cities and the victorious Brennus, meeting with no opposition, ravaged the lands throughout the whole of Macedonia. Soon after, as if the spoils of mortals were too mean for him, he turned his thoughts to the temples of the immortal gods, saying, with a profane jest, that the gods, being rich, ought to be liberal to men. He suddenly, therefore, directed his march toward Delphi,[16] regarding plunder more than religion and caring for gold more than for the wrath of the deities, "Who," he said, "stood in no need of riches, as being accustomed rather to bestow them on mortals."

The Temple of Apollo at Delphi is situated on Mount Parnassus, on a rock steep on all sides. A concourse of people, who, collecting from the parts around on account of veneration for the majesty of the god had settled on the rock, formed a city there. Thus, not walls, but precipices, not defenses formed by the hand, but by nature, protect the temple and the city, so that it is utterly uncertain whether the strength of the place, or the influence of the deity

residing in it, attracts more admiration. The central part of the rock falls back in the shape of an amphitheater, and, in consequence, if ever shouts are raised or if the noise of trumpets is mingled with them the sound, from the rocks echoing and re-echoing to one another, is heard many times repeated, and louder than it was made at first. The effect on those who are ignorant of its cause and are struck with wonder at it produces a greater awe of the power of the god. In the winding of the rock, about half way up the hill, there is a small plain and in it a deep fissure in the ground that is open for giving oracles, for a cold exhalation, driven upward by some force, as it were by a wind, produces in the minds of the priestesses a certain madness and compels them, filled with the influence of the god, to give answers to such as consult them.[17] Hence many rich presents of kings and nations are to be seen there, which, by their magnificence, testify to the grateful feelings of those that have paid their vows, and their belief in the oracles given by the deity.

Brennus, when he came within sight of the temple, deliberated for some time as to whether he should at once make an attempt upon it or should allow his soldiers, wearied with their march, a night to refresh themselves. The captains of the Aeniani and Thessalori,[18] who had joined him for a share in the booty, advised that no delay should be made, while the enemy were unprovided for defense and the alarm at their coming still fresh, that in the interval of a night, the courage of the enemy would perhaps revive and assistance come to them, and that the approaches, which now were open, might be blocked up. But the common soldiers, when, after a long endurance of scarcity, they found a country abounding with wine and other provisions, had dispersed themselves over the fields, rejoicing as much at the plenty as if they

---

[13] A Gallic leader with the same name as the Brennus who sacked Rome in 390 BCE.

[14] In 279 BCE.

[15] A gross exaggeration.

[16] On the northern coast of the Gulf of Corinth, the site of a richly endowed oracle and shrine of Apollo.

[17] The priestesses of Apollo served as oracles and responded to questions posed to them, as by Romulus when he founded Rome, and by the Romans during the Second Punic War.

[18] Peoples of central Greece who had joined up with the Gauls.

had gained a victory, and leaving their standards deserted wandered about to seize on everything like conquerors. This conduct gave some respite to the Delphians.

At the first report that the Gauls were approaching, the country people are said to have been prohibited by the Oracle from carrying away their grain and wine from their houses. The salutariness of this prohibition was not understood, until, because this abundance of wine and other provisions had been thrown in the way of the Gauls as a stop to their progress, reinforcements from their neighbors had time to collect. The Delphians, accordingly, supported by the strength of their allies, secured their city before the Gauls, who clung to the wine-skins on which they had seized, could be recalled to their standards. Brennus had sixty-five thousand infantry, selected from his whole army; of the Delphians there were not more than four thousand, in utter contempt of whom Brennus, to rouse the courage of his men, pointed to the vast quantity of spoil before them, declaring that the statues and four-horse chariots, of which a great number were visible at a distance, were made of solid gold, and would provide greater prices when they came to be weighed than they were in appearance.

The Gauls, animated by these assertions, and disordered at the same time on account of the wine that they had drunk the day before, rushed to battle without any fear of danger. The Delphians, on the other hand, placing more confidence in the god than in their own strength, resisted the enemy with contempt, and, from the top of the hill, repelled the Gauls as they climbed up, partly with pieces of rock and partly with their weapons. Amid this contest between the two, the priests of all the temples as well as the priestesses themselves, with their hair loose and with their decorations and fillets, rushed, trembling and frantic, into the front ranks of the combatants, exclaiming that the god had come, that they had seen him leap down into his temple through the opening roof, that, while they were all humbly imploring aid of the deity, a youth of extraordinary beauty, far above that of mortals, and two armed virgins, coming from the neighboring temples of Diana and Minerva,[19] met them; that they had not only perceived them with their eyes but also had heard also the sound of a bow and the rattling of arms, and they therefore conjured them with the strongest entreaties not to delay, when the gods were leading them on, to spread slaughter among the enemy, and to share the victory with the powers of heaven. Incited by these exhortations, they all rushed eagerly to the field of battle, where they themselves also soon perceived the presence of the divinity, for a part of the mountain, broken off by an earthquake, overwhelmed a host of the Gauls and some of the densest bodies of the enemy were scattered abroad, not without wounds, and fell to the earth. A tempest then followed, which destroyed, with hail and cold, those that were suffering from bodily injuries.

General Brennus himself, unable to endure the pain of his wounds, ended his life with his dagger. The other general, after punishing the advisers of the war, made off from Greece with all haste, accompanied with ten thousand wounded men. But neither was fortune more favorable to those who fled, for in their terror they passed no night under shelter and no day without hardship and danger. Continual rains, snow congealed by the frost, famine, fatigue, and, what was the greatest evil, the constant want of sleep, consumed the wretched remains of the unfortunate army. The nations and people too, through whom they marched, pursued their stragglers in order to despoil them. Hence it happened that, of so great an army that, little before, presuming on its strength contended even against the gods, not a man was left to be a memorial of its destruction.

After peace was made between the two kings, Antigonus[20] and Antiochus,[21] a new enemy suddenly started up against Antigonus as he was returning to Macedonia. The Gauls who had been left behind to

---

[19] Greek Artemis and Athena.

[20] Antigonus Gonatas (277–239 BCE), son of Demetrius Poliorcetes, the son of Antigonus I "the One-Eyed"; he still lacked a kingdom.

[21] Antiochus I (281–261 BCE), son of Seleucus I and ruler of the Seleucid Empire.

defend the borders of their country by their general Brennus when he marched into Greece, armed fifteen thousand foot and three thousand horse and having routed the forces of the Getae and Triballi,[22] and preparing to invade Macedonia, sent ambassadors to Antigonus to offer him peace if he would pay for it, and to play the part of spies, at the same time, in his camp. Antigonus, with royal munificence, invited them to a banquet, and entertained them with a sumptuous display of luxuries. The Gauls were so struck with the vast quantity of gold and silver set before them, and so tempted with the richness of such a spoil, that they returned more inclined to war than they had come. The king also ordered his elephants to be shown them, as monsters unknown to those barbarians, and his ships laden with stores to be displayed, little thinking that he was thus exciting the desire to seize his treasures among those whom he sought to strike with terror by the ostentation of his strength.[23] The ambassadors, returning to their countrymen, and exaggerating everything excessively, set forth at once the wealth and unsuspiciousness of the king; saying that his camp was filled with gold and silver, but secured neither by rampart nor trench, and that the Macedonians, as if they had sufficient protection in their wealth, neglected all military duties, apparently thinking that, as they had plenty of gold, they had no use for steel.

By this statement, the desires of a covetous people were sufficiently stimulated to take possession of such spoil. The example of Belgius, too, had its influence with them, who, a little before, had cut to pieces the army of the Macedonians and their king. Being all of one mind, therefore, they attacked the king's camp by night, but he, foreseeing the storm that threatened him, had given notice to his soldiers to remove all their baggage and to conceal themselves noiselessly in a neighboring wood, and the camp was only saved because

it was deserted. The Gauls, when they found the camp destitute not only of defenders but also of sentinels, suspecting that there was not a flight but some stratagem on the part of the enemy, were for some time afraid to enter the gates.[24] At last, leaving the defenses entire and untouched, and more like men come to explore than to plunder, they took possession of the camp, and then, carrying off what they found, they directed their course toward the coast. Here, as they were incautiously plundering the vessels and fearing no attack, they were cut down by the sailors and a part of the army that had fled thither with their wives and children.[25] Such was the slaughter among them that the report of this victory procured Antigonus peace, not only from the Gauls, but from his other barbarous neighbors.[26]

The nation of the Gaul was at that time so prolific that they filled all Asia as with one swarm. The kings of the east carried on no wars without a mercenary army of Gauls, nor, if they were driven from their thrones, did they seek protection with any other people than the Gauls. Such indeed was the terror of the Gallic name, and the unvaried good fortune of their arms, that princes thought they could neither maintain their power in security, nor recover it if lost, without the assistance of Gallic valor. Hence, being called by the king of Bithynia[27] to his aid, and having gained him the victory over his enemies, they shared his kingdom with him and called their part of it Gallograecia.[28]

---

[22] Peoples of Thrace, north of Greece and Macedonia.

[23] The rest of the story suggests that Antigonus, an experienced general, was in fact trying to lure the Gauls into an ambush.

[24] See Chapter 3 for a similar situation during the sack of Rome by the Gauls in 390 BCE.

[25] The Gauls in fact were destroyed by Antigonus and his army in a successful ambush.

[26] The Battle of Lysimacheia in 277 BCE. Antigonus' victory gained for him the throne of Macedonia.

[27] A kingdom on the southern coast of the Black Sea.

[28] That is, "Gallic Greece." In 278 BCE Nicomedes, King of Bithynia, invited several bands of Gauls into Anatolia as mercenaries. They remained and established their own kingdoms in central Anatolia in what came to be called Galatia.

1.2 THE CONSTITUTION OF CARTHAGE (ca. 340 BCE)

ARISTOTLE, *POLITICS*, BOOK 2, CHAPTER 11

Even though the Carthaginians would have been considered "barbarians" by Greek standards, in his book the *Politics*, the late-fourth-century philosopher Aristotle nevertheless thought them civilized enough to include their constitution in his catalogue of model forms of government, illustrating well the ambivalence that even the most chauvinistic of ancient peoples felt toward other peoples.

Source: Benjamin Jowett, trans., *The Politics of Aristotle* (London: Colonial Press, 1900), 49–51.

The Carthaginians also are considered to have an excellent form of government, which differs from that of any other state in several respects, although it is in some ways very like the Spartan. Indeed, all three states, the Spartan, the Cretan, and the Carthaginian, nearly resemble one another, and are very different from any others. Many of the Carthaginian institutions are excellent. The superiority of their constitution is proved by the fact that the common people remain loyal to the constitution. The Carthaginians never have had any rebellion worth speaking of, and never have been under the rule of a tyrant. Among the points in which the Carthaginian constitution resembles the Spartan are the following: the common tables of the clubs answer to the Spartan *pheiditia*,[29] and their magistracy of the Hundred-Four[30] to the Ephors; but, whereas the Ephors are any chance persons, the magistrates of the Carthaginians are elected according to merit: this is an improvement. They have also their kings and their *Gerousia*, or council of elders, who correspond to the kings and elders of Sparta. Their kings,[31] unlike the Spartan, are not always of the same family, nor that an ordinary one, but if there is some distinguished family they are selected[32] out of it and not appointed by seniority: this is far better. Such officers have great power, and therefore, if they are persons of little worth, they do a great deal of harm, and they already have done harm at Sparta.

Most of the defects or deviations from the perfect state, for which the Carthaginian constitution would be censured, apply equally to all the forms of government that we have mentioned. But of the deflections from aristocracy and constitutional government, some incline more to democracy and some to oligarchy. The kings and elders, if unanimous, may determine whether they will or will not bring a matter before the people, but when they are not unanimous, the people decide on such matters as well.[33] And whatever the kings and elders bring before the people is not only heard but also determined by them, and anyone who likes may oppose it; now this is not permitted in Sparta and Crete. That the magistrates of five who have under them many important matters should be co-opted,[34] that they should choose the supreme council of One Hundred and Four and should hold office longer than other magistrates (for they are virtually rulers both before and after they hold office), these are oligarchical features, their being without salary and not elected by lot, and any similar points, such as the practice of having all suits tried by the magistrates, and not some by one class of judges or jurors and some by another, as at Sparta, are characteristic of aristocracy.

The Carthaginian constitution deviates from aristocracy and inclines to oligarchy, chiefly on

---

[29] An obligatory daily military meal.

[30] The Council of 104 oversaw the Carthaginian government.

[31] In the fifth century, single kings were replaced by two Suffets, who also were called kings.

[32] By the *Gerousia*.

---

[33] In a popular assembly.

[34] From among the wealthy, not elected.

a point where popular opinion is on their side. For men in general think that magistrates should be chosen not only for their merit, but for their wealth: a man, they say, who is poor cannot rule well, for he has not the leisure. If, then, election of magistrates for their wealth be characteristic of oligarchy, and election for merit of aristocracy, there will be a third form under which the constitution of Carthage is comprehended, for the Carthaginians choose their magistrates, and particularly the highest of them, their kings and generals, with an eye both to merit and to wealth. But we must acknowledge that, in thus deviating from aristocracy, the legislator has committed an error. Nothing is more absolutely necessary than to provide that the highest class, not only when in office but also when out of office, should have leisure and not disgrace themselves in any way, and to this their attention should be first directed. Even if you must have regard to wealth, in order to secure leisure, yet it is surely a bad thing that the greatest offices, such as those of kings and generals, should be bought. The law that allows this abuse makes wealth of more account than virtue, and the whole state becomes avaricious.

For, whenever the chiefs of the state deem anything honorable, the other citizens are sure to follow their example, and, where virtue has not the first place, their aristocracy cannot be firmly established. Those who have been at the expense of purchasing their places will be in the habit of re-paying themselves, and it is absurd to suppose that a poor and honest man will be wanting to make gains, and that a lower stamp of man who has incurred a great expense will not. Wherefore they should rule who are able to rule best. And even if the legislator does not care to protect the good from poverty, he should at any rate secure leisure for them when in office. It would seem also to be a bad principle that the same person should hold many offices, which is a favorite practice among the Carthaginians, for one business is better done by one man.

The government of the Carthaginians is oligarchical, but they successfully escape the evils of oligarchy by enriching one portion of the people after another by sending them to their colonies. This is their panacea and the means by which they give stability to the state. Accident favors them, but the legislator should be able to provide against revolution without trusting to accidents. As things are, if any misfortune occurred, and the bulk of the subjects revolted, there would be no way of restoring peace by legal methods.

JUSTIN, *PHILIPPIC HISTORIES*, BOOK 13

A silver tetradrachm (four-drachm coin) issued ca. 311–305 BCE by Alexander's general Seleucus, who became satrap of Babylonia in the division of Alexander's empire after his death. Seleucus showed his respect for local culture not only by not divorcing his Persian wife but also by portraying on the obverse of this coin an image of the eastern god Ba'al of Tarsus seated and holding a scepter and on the reverse a lion walking left with an anchor, a Seleucid symbol, above.

After the death of Alexander the Great in 323 BCE, some generals, especially Perdiccas, Eumenes, and Polyperchon, wished to hold the empire together in the name of Alexander's infant son. But most other generals looked to their own advantage. The generals therefore parceled out sections of the empire among themselves. These included Perdiccas, Craterus, and Antipater, the guardians of Alexander's infant son Alexander IV; and Polyperchon, governor of Greece and Macedonia; as well as Eumenes; Antigonus the One-Eyed; Lysimachus; Ptolemy; and Seleucus, who in the initial division, respectively, received Cappadocia and Paphlagonia, "Greater Phrygia," Thrace, Egypt, and "The Command of the Camp." Conflicts immediately ensued as these generals attempted to expand their holdings, and there was a rapid shakeout as many soon fell by the wayside. Alliances changed quickly as the generals ganged up on anyone who appeared to be getting too powerful. Soon only a handful were left. Just when it looked like Antigonus the One-Eyed and his son Demetrius "The Besieger of Cities" were on the verge of reconstituting Alexander's empire, they were defeated at the Battle of Ipsus in 301 by a coalition including Ptolemy, Lysimachus, and Seleucus. It was not until 281 BCE, when the eighty-year-old Seleucus defeated Lysimachus at the Battle of Couropedium, that the Wars of the Successors finally came to an end. The story of these conflicts was related in the *Philippic Histories* of the Augustan writer Pompeius Trogus, epitomized circa the second or third century CE by Marcus Junianus Justinus, or simply Justin.

Source: John Selby Watson, trans., *Marcus Junius Justinus, Epitome of the Philippic History of Pompeius Trogus* (London: Bohn, 1853).

When this allotment,[35] like a gift from the Fates,[36] was made to each, it was to many of them a great occasion for improving their fortunes, for not long after, as if they had divided kingdoms, not governments, among themselves, they became princes instead of prefects,[37] and not only secured great power to themselves but also bequeathed it to their descendents. Afterward a war arose between Antigonus[38] and Perdiccas.[39] Craterus and Antipater,[40] who, having made peace with the Athenians, had appointed Polyperchon to govern Greece and Macedonia, lent their aid to Antigonus. Perdiccas, as the aspect of affairs was unfavorable, called Arridaeus[41] and Alexander the Great's son,[42] then in Cappadocia,[43] the charge of both of whom had been committed to him, to a consultation concerning the management of the war. It seemed more to the purpose to begin with Egypt, lest, while they were gone into Macedonia, Asia should be seized by Ptolemy.[44] Ptolemy, by his wise exertions in Egypt, was acquiring great power. He had secured the favor of the Egyptians by his extraordinary

prudence. He had attached the neighboring princes by acts of kindness and courtesy. He had extended the boundaries of his kingdom by getting possession of the city Cyrene,[45] and was grown so great that he did not fear his enemies so much as he was feared by them.

Ptolemy, having increased his strength from the forces of this city, made preparations for war against the coming of Perdiccas. But the hatred that Perdiccas had incurred by his arrogance did him more injury than the power of the enemy. For his allies, detesting his overbearingness, went over in troops to Antipater. Neoptolemus,[46] too, who had been left to support Eumenes,[47] intended not only to desert to Antipater but also to betray the force of his party. Eumenes, understanding his design, thought it a matter of necessity to engage the traitor in the field. Neoptolemus, being worsted, fled to Antipater and Polyperchon, and persuaded them to surprise Eumenes, by marching without intermission, while he was full of joy for his victory, and freed from apprehension by Neoptolemus' flight. But this project did not escape Eumenes. The plot was in consequence turned upon the contrivers of it, and they who expected to attack him unguarded were attacked themselves when they were on their march and wearied with watching through the previous night. In this battle, Polyperchon was killed. Neoptolemus, too, engaging hand to hand with Eumenes, and maintaining a long struggle with him, in which both were wounded more than once, was at last overpowered and fell.

Eumenes, therefore, being victorious in two successive battles, supported in some degree the spirits of his party, which had been cast down by the desertion of their allies. At last, however, Perdiccas having been killed,[48] Eumenes was declared an enemy by the army, and the conduct of the war against him was committed to Antigonus. When

---

[35] The division of Alexander's empire made in Babylon after his death in 323 BCE.

[36] Goddesses depicted as elderly women who control human destiny: Clotho spun the thread of life, Lachesis measured how long it would be, and Atropos cut it off at the end.

[37] That is, governors.

[38] Nicknamed "Monopthalmos," "The One-Eyed." He received "Greater Phrygia" in central Anatolia in the original division of territories but went on to reconquer nearly the entire empire.

[39] After Alexander's death he was appointed guardian of Alexander's young son Alexander IV and, as "Regent of the Empire," for a brief time was the effective ruler of the empire.

[40] Craterus and Antipater also were guardians of Alexander IV and wanted to maintain the integrity of the empire.

[41] Philip III (323–317), Alexander's incapable brother who succeeded him as King of Macedon.

[42] Alexander IV only would have been a few years old at the time.

[43] A mountainous region of northern Anatolia that remained under the control of a Persian dynasty until it was incorporated into the Roman Empire in 17 CE.

[44] One of the main instigators of the division of Alexander's empire; he received the rich satrapy of Egypt.

[45] On the coast of Libya.

[46] A Macedonian general who had been assigned the satrapy of Armenia.

[47] A supporter of Perdiccas, he received the territories of Paphlagonia and Cappadocia, which had not yet been conquered.

[48] Assassinated in 321 BCE.

Eumenes found that Perdiccas was slain, that he himself was declared an enemy by the Macedonians, and that the conduct of the war against him was committed to Antigonus, he at once made known the state of affairs to his troops, lest report should either exaggerate matters, or alarm the minds of the men with the unexpected nature of the events. When he returned to his camp, letters were found scattered through it in which great rewards were offered to any that should bring the head of Eumenes to Antigonus.

In the meantime Antigonus came up with his army, and having pitched his camp, offered battle on the following day. Nor did Eumenes delay to engage with him, but, being defeated, he fled to a fortress, where, when he saw that he must submit to the hazard of a siege, he dismissed the greater part of his army, lest he should either be delivered to the enemy by consent of the multitude, or the sufferings of the siege should be aggravated by too great a number. He then sent a deputation to Antipater, who was the only general that seemed a match for the power of Antigonus, to entreat his aid; and Antigonus, hearing that succor was dispatched by Antipater to Eumenes, gave up the siege. Eumenes was thus for a time, indeed, relieved from fear of death, but, as so great a portion of his army had been sent away, he had no great hope of ultimate safety. After taking everything into consideration, therefore, he thought it best to apply to the Argyraspides[49] of Alexander the Great, a body of men that had never yet been conquered.

At length, when it was announced that Antigonus was approaching with his army, he obliged the Argyraspides to march into the field, where, slighting the orders of their general, they were defeated by the bravery of the enemy. In this battle they lost, with their wives and children, not only their glory from so many wars but also the booty obtained in their long service. Immediately after, without the knowledge of their leaders, they sent deputies to Antigonus, requesting that "he would order what was theirs to be restored to them." Antigonus promised that he would restore what they asked if they would deliver up Eumenes to him, saying that his

single victory was so far more glorious to Antigonus than so many other victories had been to Alexander, and that whereas Alexander subdued the east, Antigonus had defeated those by whom the east had been subdued.

Perdiccas and his brother, with Eumenes and Polyperchon, and other leaders of the opposite party, having been killed,[50] the contention among the successors of Alexander seemed to be at an end, when, on a sudden, a dispute arose among the conquerors themselves, for Ptolemy, Cassander,[51] and Lysimachus,[52] demanding that the money taken among the spoil, and the provinces, should be divided. Antigonus said that he would admit no partners in the advantages of a war of which he alone had undergone the perils. And that he might seem to engage in an honorable contest with his confederates, he gave out that his object was to avenge the death of Olympias,[53] who had been murdered by Cassander, and to release the son of Alexander, his king, with his mother,[54] from their confinement at Amphipolis.[55] On hearing this news, Ptolemy and Cassander, forming an alliance with Lysimachus and Seleucus,[56] made vigorous preparations for war by land and sea. Ptolemy had possession of Egypt, with the greater part of Africa, Cyprus, and Phoenicia. Macedonia and Greece were subject to Cassander. Antigonus had taken possession of Asia and the eastern countries. Demetrius, the son of Antigonus, was defeated in the first engagement by Ptolemy, at Gamala.[57]

Ptolemy meanwhile engaged a second time with Demetrius at sea,[58] and, having lost his fleet, and left the victory to the enemy, fled back to Egypt.

---

[49] The "Silver Shields," an elite body of Alexander's troops.

[50] Eumenes was executed by Antigonus in 316 BCE, but Polyperchon survived until 304 BCE or later.

[51] The son of Antipater; in 317 BCE he became King of Macedon.

[52] The satrap of Thrace, northeast of Greece in the Balkans.

[53] The mother of Alexander the Great.

[54] Roxanne, Alexander's first wife.

[55] One of the capital cities of Macedonia, on the northern coast of the Aegean Sea.

[56] The satrap of Babylonia, who had been accumulating additional territory in the eastern regions of the empire.

[57] The Battle of Gaza, in 312 BCE.

[58] The Battle of Myus, a city in Caria in southern Anatolia.

Antigonus, being elated with this victory, gave orders that he himself, as well as his son Demetrius, should be styled "basileus" ("king") by the people.[59] Ptolemy also, so that he might not appear of less authority among his subjects, was called "king" by his army. Cassander and Lysimachus, too, when they heard of these proceedings, assumed regal dignity themselves. They all abstained, however, from taking the insignia of royalty,[60] as long as any sons of their king[61] survived. Such forbearance was there in them, that, although they had the power, they yet contentedly remained without the distinction of kings as long as Alexander had a proper heir. But Ptolemy and Cassander, and the other leaders of the opposite faction, perceiving that they were individually weakened by Antigonus,[62] whereas each regarded the war, not as the common concern of all, but as merely affecting himself, and all were unwilling to give assistance to one another, as if victory would be only for one, and not for all of them, appointed, after encouraging each other by letters, a time and place for a conference, and prepared for the contest with united strength. Cassander, being unable to join in it, because of a war near home, dispatched Lysimachus to the support of his allies with a large force.

Before the war with Antigonus was commenced by Ptolemy and his allies, Seleucus, on a sudden, leaving Greater Asia, came forward as a fresh enemy to Antigonus. The merit of Seleucus was well known, and his birth had been attended with extraordinary circumstances. His mother Laodice, being married to Antiochus, a man of eminence among Philip's generals, seemed to herself, in a dream, to have conceived from a union with Apollo and, after becoming pregnant, to have received from him, as a reward for her compliance, a ring, on the stone of which was engraved an anchor and which she was advised to give to the child that she should bring forth. A ring similarly engraved was found the next day in the bed, and the figure of an anchor, which was visible on the thigh of Seleucus when he was born, made this dream extremely remarkable.[63] After the division of the Macedonian empire among the followers of Alexander, he carried on several wars in the east. He first took Babylon,[64] and then, his strength being increased by this success, subdued the Bactrians. After settling his affairs in the east, Seleucus proceeded to join in the war against Antigonus. As soon as the forces of all the confederates were united, a battle was fought, in which Antigonus was slain, and his son Demetrius put to flight.[65] But the allied generals, after thus terminating the war with the enemy, turned their arms again upon each other, and, as they could not agree about the spoil, they were divided into two parties. Seleucus joined Demetrius, and Ptolemy joined Lysimachus. Thus new wars arose.

---

[59] The first time that any of the successors referred to themselves as "king." Others soon followed.
[60] Such as wearing the royal diadem.
[61] The child Alexander IV.
[62] In 301 BCE.

[63] The anchor then became a Seleucid insignia and often appeared on their coins.
[64] In the Babylonian War, 312–311 BCE, Seleucus drove Antigonus out of Babylonia, thus ending the possibility of a reunification of Alexander's empire.
[65] The Battle of Ipsus in 301 BCE.

THE BOOK OF MACCABEES

A silver tetradrachm (four-drachm coin) of the Seleucid king Antiochus IV Epiphanes depicts the head of Antiochus on the obverse wearing a diadem (a piece of cloth tied around the head) signifying royal status. The reverse portrays Zeus seated and holding a scepter in his left hand and the goddess Nikē (Victory) in his right. The legend reads, "King Antiochus Epiphanes ['God Made Manifest'], Bearer of Victory."

After the Seleucid king Antiochus IV Epiphanes (175–164 BCE), the son of Antiochus III (222–187 BCE), came to power in the Seleucid Empire, he attempted to unify the empire by enforcing the adoption of Greek customs on the Jews of Palestine. This offended many of the Jews in the kingdom. In 167 BCE, one of them, Mattathias, resisted and raised a rebellion. Mattathias was succeeded as leader of the rebellion by his son Judas Maccabaeus, who gave it its name. A full account of the Maccabean revolt is preserved in the biblical Book of Maccabees.

Source: "First Book of Maccabees," *New Revised Standard Version.*

After Alexander[66] son of Philip, the Macedonian, who came from the land of Kittim,[67] had defeated King Darius of the Persians and the Medes, he succeeded him as king. He fought many battles, conquered strongholds, and put to death the kings of the earth. He advanced to the ends of the earth and plundered many nations. When the earth became quiet before him, he was exalted, and his heart was lifted up. He gathered a very strong army and ruled over countries, nations, and princes, and they became tributary to him. After this he fell sick and perceived that he was dying. So he summoned his most honored officers, who had been brought up with him from youth, and divided his kingdom among them while he was still alive.[68] And after

---

[66] That is, Alexander the Great, King of Macedon.

[67] Specifically Cyprus, but, in this case, used to refer generically to "the west."

[68] An error. Alexander failed to indicate the disposition of his empire, which led to a long period of conflicts among his generals.

Alexander had reigned twelve years,[69] he died. Then his officers began to rule, each in his own place. They all put on crowns after his death, and so did their descendents after them for many years, and they caused many evils on the earth. From them came forth a sinful root, Antiochus Epiphanes, son of King Antiochus.[70] He had been a hostage in Rome. He began to reign in the one hundred thirty-seventh year of the kingdom of the Greeks.[71]

In those days certain renegades came out from Israel and misled many, saying, "Let us go and make a covenant with the Gentiles[72] around us, for since we separated from them many disasters have come upon us." This proposal pleased them, and some of the people eagerly went to the king, who authorized them to observe the ordinances of the Gentiles. So they built a gymnasium[73] in Jerusalem, according to Gentile custom, removed the marks of circumcision,[74] and abandoned the holy covenant. They joined with the Gentiles and sold themselves to do evil.

When Antiochus saw that his kingdom was established, he determined to become king of the land of Egypt, in order that he might reign over both kingdoms. So he invaded Egypt with a strong force, with chariots and elephants and cavalry and a large fleet.[75] He engaged King Ptolemy[76] of Egypt in battle, and Ptolemy turned and fled before him, and many were wounded and fell. He captured the fortified cities in the land of Egypt, and he plundered the land of Egypt. After subduing Egypt,[77] Antiochus returned in the one hundred forty-third year.[78] He went up against Israel and came to Jerusalem with a strong force. He arrogantly entered the sanctuary[79] and took the golden altar, the lampstand for the light, and all its utensils. He took also the table for the Bread of the Presence,[80] the cups for drink offerings, the bowls, the golden censers, the curtain, the crowns, and the gold decoration on the front of the temple; he stripped it all off. He took the silver and the gold, and the costly vessels; he took also the hidden treasures that he found. Taking them all, he went into his own land.[81]

Then the king wrote to his whole kingdom that all should be one people, and that all should give up their particular customs. All the Gentiles accepted the command of the king. Many even from Israel gladly adopted his religion; they sacrificed to idols and profaned the sabbath. And the king sent letters by messengers to Jerusalem and the towns of Judah; he directed them to follow customs strange to the land, to forbid burnt offerings and sacrifices and drink offerings in the sanctuary, to profane sabbaths[82] and festivals, to defile the sanctuary and the priests, to build altars and sacred precincts and shrines for idols, to sacrifice swine and other unclean animals, and to leave their sons uncircumcised. They were to make themselves abominable by everything unclean and profane, so that they would forget the law and change all the ordinances. He added, "And whoever does not obey the command of the king shall die."

In those days Mattathias son of John son of Simeon, a priest of the family of Joarib, moved from Jerusalem and settled in Modein.[83] He had five sons,

---

[69] Alexander actually reigned from 336 until 323 BCE.

[70] The Seleucid king Antiochus I (281–261 BCE).

[71] That is, the Seleucid Empire, begun by Seleucus I in 311 BCE.

[72] Non-Jews.

[73] A Greek exercise ground, where participants exercised in the nude.

[74] Permanent restoration of the foreskin was accomplished by epispasm, or decircumcision, which involved slicing the skin of the penis circumferentially to loosen it, extending it over the glans, and then tying it off until it had reattached itself. A temporary process, infibulation, involved pulling the skin of the penis over the glans and then tying it off or pinning it with a fibula.

[75] In 168 BCE.

[76] In 170 BCE Antiochus invaded Egypt and defeated King Ptolemy VI (180–145 BCE); in 168 he invaded Egypt again and defeated both Ptolemy VI and his younger brother, Ptolemy VIII (169–116).

[77] Not exactly. Antiochus was forced by the Romans to evacuate Egypt.

[78] Of the Seleucid Empire, 168 BCE.

[79] Of the Jewish temple in Jerusalem.

[80] Loaves of bread always kept as an offering to God on a special table in the Jewish temple in Jerusalem.

[81] Antiochus needed the money to pay off the war indemnity imposed by the Romans on his father by the Treaty of Apamea in 188 BCE.

[82] Saturday, the Jewish day of worship.

[83] A town in Judaea near Jerusalem.

John surnamed Gaddi, Simon called Thassi, Judas called Maccabeus,[84] Eleazar called Avaran, and Jonathan called Apphus. He saw the blasphemies being committed in Judah and Jerusalem. Then Mattathias and his sons tore their clothes, put on sackcloth, and mourned greatly. The king's officers who were enforcing the apostasy[85] came to the town of Modein to make them offer sacrifice. Many from Israel came to them, and Mattathias and his sons were assembled. Then the king's officers spoke to Mattathias as follows: "You are a leader, honored and great in this town, and supported by sons and brothers. Now be the first to come and do what the king commands, as all the Gentiles and the people of Judah and those that are left in Jerusalem have done. Then you and your sons will be numbered among the friends of the king, and you and your sons will be honored with silver and gold and many gifts."

But Mattathias answered and said in a loud voice, "Even if all the nations that live under the rule of the king obey him, and have chosen to obey his commandments, every one of them abandoning the religion of their ancestors, I and my sons and my brothers will continue to live by the covenant of our ancestors. Far be it from us to desert the law and the ordinances. We will not obey the king's words by turning aside from our religion to the right hand or to the left." When he had finished speaking these words, a Jew came forward in the sight of all to offer sacrifice on the altar in Modein, according to the king's command. When Mattathias saw it, he burned with zeal and his heart was stirred. He gave vent to righteous anger; he ran and killed him on the altar. At the same time he killed the king's officer who was forcing them to sacrifice, and he tore down the altar. Then Mattathias cried out in the town with a loud voice, saying: "Let everyone who is zealous for the law and supports the covenant come out with me!" Then he and his sons fled to the hills and left all that they had in the town.

At that time many who were seeking righteousness and justice went down to the wilderness to live there, they, their sons, their wives, and their livestock, because troubles pressed heavily upon them. And it was reported to the king's officers, and to the troops in Jerusalem the city of David, that those who had rejected the king's command had gone down to the hiding places in the wilderness. Many pursued them, and overtook them; they encamped opposite them and prepared for battle against them on the sabbath day. The troops said to them, "Enough of this! Come out and do what the king commands, and you will live." But the Jews replied, "We will not come out, nor will we do what the king commands and so profane the sabbath day." Then the enemy quickly attacked them. But they did not answer them or hurl a stone at them or block up their hiding places, for they said, "Let us all die in our innocence; heaven and earth testify for us that you are killing us unjustly." So they attacked them on the sabbath, and they died, with their wives and children and livestock, to the number of a thousand persons.

When Mattathias and his friends learned of it, they mourned for them deeply. And all said to their neighbors: "If we all do as our kindred have done and refuse to fight with the Gentiles for our lives and for our ordinances, they will quickly destroy us from the earth." So they made this decision that day: "Let us fight against anyone who comes to attack us on the sabbath day; let us not all die as our kindred died in their hiding places." Then there united with them a company of Hasideans,[86] mighty warriors of Israel, all who offered themselves willingly for the law. And all who became fugitives to escape their troubles joined them and reinforced them. They organized an army, and struck down sinners in their anger and renegades in their wrath; the survivors fled to the Gentiles for safety. And Mattathias and his friends went around and tore down the altars. They forcibly circumcised all the uncircumcised boys that they found within the borders of Israel. They hunted down the arrogant, and the work prospered in their hands. They rescued the law out of the hands of the Gentiles and kings, and they never let the sinner gain the upper hand.

---

[84] A word meaning "the hammer."

[85] To abandon one religion and adopt another one.

[86] A Jewish religious sect.

HERODOTUS, *THE HISTORIES*, BOOK 4

An Attic red-figured plate dated to ca. 510 BCE and now in the British Museum depicts a Scythian archer running left and pulling an arrow out of a quiver.

In the course of his discussion of the attack on the Scythians in 513 BCE by the Persian king Darius, the Greek historian Herodotus, writing about 440 BCE, added a lengthy digression about Scythian customs, reflecting a contemporary Greek fascination with the curious practices of peoples they referred to as "barbarians."

Source: George Rawlinson, Henry Rawlinson, and John Gardner Wilkinson, trans., *The History of Herodotus: A New English Version* (London: Murray, 1862).

The Scythians are provided with the most important necessaries. Their manners and customs come now to be described. They worship only the following gods, namely, Hestia,[87] whom they reverence beyond all the rest, Zeus, and Earth, whom they consider to be the wife of Zeus; and after these Apollo, Heavenly Aphrodite, Hercules, and Ares. These gods are worshipped by the whole nation; the Royal Scythians[88] offer sacrifice likewise to Poseidon. In the Scythian tongue Hestia is called Tabiti, Zeus (very properly, in my judgment) Papaeus, Earth Apia, Apollo Goetosyrus, Celestial Venus Argimpasa, and Neptune Thagimasadas. They use no images, altars, or temples, except in the worship of Ares, but in his worship they do use them.

The manner of their sacrifices is everywhere and in every case the same. The victim[89] stands with its two fore-feet bound together by a cord, and the person who is about to offer, taking his station behind the victim, gives the rope a pull, and thereby throws the animal down. As it falls he invokes the god to whom he is offering, after which he puts a noose round the animal's neck, and, inserting a small stick, twists it round, and so strangles him. No fire is lighted, there is no consecration, and no pouring out of drink-offerings, but as soon as the beast is strangled the sacrificer skins it and then sets to work to boil the flesh.

---

[87] The goddess of the hearth, Roman Vesta.
[88] The Scythian royal family.

[89] A four-footed animal such as a cow, bull, or horse.

As Scythia, moreover, is utterly barren of fire-wood, a plan has had to be contrived for boiling the flesh, which is the following. After flaying the beasts, they take out all the bones, and, if they possess such gear, put the flesh into boilers made in the country, which are very like the cauldrons of the Lesbians, except that they are of a much larger size. Then placing the bones of the animals beneath the cauldron, they set them alight, and so boil the meat. If they do not happen to possess a cauldron, they make the animal's paunch hold the flesh, and pouring in at the same time a little water, lay the bones under and light them. The bones burn beautifully, and the paunch easily contains all the flesh when it is stript from the bones, so that by this plan an ox is made to boil itself, and other victims also to do the like. When the meat is all cooked, the sacrificer makes an offering of a portion of the flesh and of the entrails by casting them on the ground before him. They sacrifice all sorts of cattle, but most commonly horses.

Such are the victims offered to the other gods, and such is the mode in which they are sacrificed, but the rites paid to Ares are different. In every district, at the seat of government, there stands a temple of this god, whereof the following is a description. It is a vast pile of brushwood, in length and breadth three furlongs[90]; in height somewhat less. It has a square platform upon the top, three sides of which are precipitous, whereas the fourth slopes so that people may walk up it. Each year a hundred and fifty wagon-loads of brushwood are added to the pile, which sinks continually by reason of the rains. An antique iron sword is planted on the top of every such mound, and serves as the image of Ares. Yearly sacrifices of cattle and of horses are made to it, and more victims are offered thus than to all the rest of their gods. When prisoners are taken in war, out of every hundred men they sacrifice one, not however with the same rites as the cattle, but with different ones. Libations of wine are first poured upon their heads after which they are slaughtered over a vessel. The vessel then is carried up to the top of the pile, and the blood poured upon the scimitar. While this takes place at the top of the mound,

below, by the side of the temple, the right hands and arms of the slaughtered prisoners are cut off and tossed on high into the air. Then the other victims are slain and those who have offered the sacrifice depart, leaving the hands and arms where they may chance to have fallen, and the bodies also, separate. Such are the observances of the Scythians with respect to sacrifice. They never use swine for the purpose, nor indeed is it their custom to breed them in any part of their country.

In what concerns war, their customs are the following. The Scythian soldier drinks the blood of the first man he overthrows in battle. Whatever number he slays, he cuts off all their heads, and carries them to the king because he is thus entitled to a share of the booty, wherefore he forfeits all claim if he does not produce a head. In order to strip the skull of its covering, he makes a cut round the head above the ears, and, laying hold of the scalp, shakes the skull out; then with the rib of an ox he scrapes the scalp clean of flesh, and softening it by rubbing between the hands, uses it thenceforth as a napkin. The Scythian is proud of these scalps, and hangs them from his bridle-rein; the greater the number of such napkins that a man can show, the more highly is he esteemed among them. Many make themselves cloaks, like the capotes[91] of our peasants, by sewing a quantity of these scalps together. Others flay the right arms of their dead enemies, and make of the skin, which stripped off with the nails hanging to it, a covering for their quivers. Now the skin of a man is thick and glossy, and would in whiteness surpass almost all other hides. Some even flay the entire body of their enemy, and stretching it upon a frame carry it about with them wherever they ride. Such are the Scythian customs with respect to scalps and skins.

The skulls of their enemies, not indeed of all, but of those whom they most detest, they treat as follows. Having sawn off the portion below the eyebrows, and cleaned out the inside, they cover the outside with leather. When a man is poor, this is all that he does, but if he is rich, he also lines the inside with gold. In either case the skull is used as a drinking-cup. They do the same with the skulls

---

[90] A furlong equals 660 feet.

[91] A long hooded coat.

of their own kith and kin if they have been at feud with them and have vanquished them in the presence of the king. When strangers whom they deem of any account come to visit them, these skulls are handed round and the host tells how that these were his relations who made war upon him, and how that he got the better of them; all this being looked upon as proof of bravery.

Once a year the governor of each district, at a set place in his own province, mingles a bowl of wine from which all Scythians who have slain foes have a right to drink, whereas those who have slain no enemy are not allowed to taste of the bowl but sit aloof in disgrace. No greater shame than this can happen to them. Such as have slain a very large number of foes, have two cups instead of one and drink from both.

Scythia has an abundance of soothsayers, who foretell the future by means of a number of willow wands. A large bundle of these wands is brought and laid on the ground. The soothsayer unties the bundle, and places each wand by itself, at the same time uttering his prophecy. Then, while he still is speaking, he gathers the rods together again, and makes them up once more into a bundle. This mode of divination is of home growth in Scythia. The Enarees, or woman-like men, have another method, which they say Aphrodite taught them. It is done with the inner bark of the linden-tree. They take a piece of this bark, and, splitting it into three strips, keep twining the strips about their fingers, and untwining them, while they prophesy.

Whenever the Scythian king falls sick he sends for the three soothsayers of most renown at the time, who come and make trial of their art in the mode above described. Generally, they say that the king is ill because such and such a person, mentioning his name, has sworn falsely by the royal hearth. This is the usual oath among the Scythians, when they wish to swear with very great solemnity. Then the man accused of having foresworn himself is arrested and brought before the king. The soothsayers tell him that by their art it is clear he has sworn a false oath by the royal hearth, and so caused the illness of the king. He denies the charge, protests that he has sworn no false oath, and loudly complains of the wrong done to him. Upon this the king sends for six new soothsayers, who try the matter by soothsaying. If they too find the man guilty of the offense, straightway he is beheaded by those who first accused him and his goods are divided among them: if, on the contrary, they acquit him, other soothsayers, and again others, are sent for, to try the case. Should the greater number decide in favor of the man's innocence, then they who first accused him forfeit their lives.

The mode of their execution of soothsayers is the following: a wagon is loaded with brushwood and oxen are harnessed to it. The soothsayers, with their feet tied together, their hands bound behind their backs, and their mouths gagged, are thrust into the midst of the brushwood. Finally the wood is set alight, and the oxen, being startled, are made to rush off with the wagon. It often happens that the oxen and the soothsayers are both consumed together, but sometimes the pole of the wagon is burnt through, and the oxen escape with a scorching. Lying diviners are burnt in the way described for other causes besides the one here spoken of. When the king puts one of them to death, he takes care not to let any of his sons survive: all the male offspring are slain with the father, only the females being allowed to live.

Oaths among the Scythians are accompanied with the following ceremonies: a large earthen bowl is filled with wine, and the parties to the oath, wounding themselves slightly with a knife or an awl, drop some of their blood into the wine; then they plunge into the mixture a scimitar, some arrows, a battle-axe, and a javelin, all the while repeating prayers. Lastly the two contracting parties drink each a draught from the bowl, as do also the chief men among their followers.

JUSTIN, *PHILIPPIC HISTORIES*, BOOK 41

The Parthians were a steppe people said to have been related to the Scythians. According to legend, the Parthians originated with the Scythian Arsaces, the leader of a people known as the Parni who lived on the lower Oxus (Amu Darya) River on the southern Eurasian steppe. In 238 BCE they invaded and occupied the Seleucid satrapy of Parthia in northeastern Iran, from which they took their name. Arsaces founded the Arsacid Dynasty of Parthian kings. The Parthians, being located intermediate between the western Mediterranean world and the world of the Far East, served as important conduits for commerce and culture between west and east. In the west they interacted first with the Seleucid Empire and then with the Romans before being overthrown by the Sasanid Persians in the 220s CE. This account of Parthian history comes from the *Philippic Histories* of the Augustan writer Pompeius Trogus, which were summarized circa the second or third century CE by Marcus Junianus Justinus, or simply Justin.

Source: John Selby Watson, *Marcus Junius Justinus, Epitome of the Philippic History of Pompeius Trogus* (London: Bohn, 1853).

The Parthians originally were exiles from Scythia. This is apparent from their very name, for in the Scythian language exiles are called Parthi. During the time of the Assyrians and Medes, they were the most obscure of all the people of the east. Subsequently, too, when the empire of the east was transferred from the Medes to the Persians, they were but as a herd without a name, and fell under the power of the stronger.[92] At last they became subject to the Macedonians,[93] when they conquered the east; so that it must seem wonderful to everyone, that they should have reached such a height of good fortune as to rule over those nations under whose sway they had been merely slaves. Being assailed by the Romans, also, in three wars,[94] under the conduct of the greatest generals, and at the most flourishing period of the Republic, they alone, of all nations, were not only a match for them, but came off victorious. It may, however, have been a greater glory to them, indeed, to have been able to rise amid the Assyrian, Median, and Persian empires, so celebrated of old, and the most powerful dominion of Bactria, peopled with a thousand cities, than to have been victorious in war against a people that came from a distance, especially when they were continually harassed by severe wars with the Scythians and other neighboring nations, and pressed with various other formidable contests.

The Parthians, being forced to quit Scythia by discord at home, gradually settled in the deserts between Hyrcania,[95] the Dahae, the Arci, the Sparni, and the Marsiani.[96] They then advanced their borders, although their neighbors, who at first made no opposition, at length endeavored to prevent them, to such an extent, that they not only got possession of the vast level plains, but also of steep hills, and heights of the mountains; and hence it is that an excess of heat or cold prevails in most parts of the Parthian territories, because the snow is troublesome on the higher grounds and the heat in the plains.

The government of the nation, after their revolt from the Macedonian power,[97] was in the hands of kings. Next to the royal authority is the order of the people, from which they take generals in war and

[92] "Parthia" was one of the satrapies of the Persian Empire.
[93] During the campaigns of Alexander the Great.
[94] Perhaps campaigns undertaken by Crassus (54–53 BCE), Ventidius (40 BCE), and Mark Antony (37 BCE); see Chapters 6-7.

[95] On the southern coast of the Caspian Sea.
[96] For some of these peoples, see the map at the beginning of this chapter.
[97] The Seleucid Empire.

magistrates in peace. Their language is something between those of the Scythians and Medes, being a compound of both. Their dress was formerly of a fashion peculiar to themselves; afterward, when their power had increased, it was like that of the Medes, light and full flowing. The fashion of their arms is that of their own country and of Scythia. They have an army, not like other nations, of free men, but chiefly consisting of slaves, the numbers of whom daily increase, the power of manumission being allowed to none, and all their offspring, in consequence, being born slaves. These bondmen they bring up as carefully as their own children, and teach them, with great pains, the arts of riding and shooting with the bow. As anyone is eminent in wealth, so he furnishes the king with a proportionate number of horsemen for war. Indeed when fifty thousand cavalry encountered Antony,[98] as he was making war upon Parthia, only four hundred of them were free men.

Of engaging with the enemy in close fighting and of taking cities by siege, they know nothing. They fight on horseback, either galloping forward or turning their backs. Often, too, they counterfeit flight so that they may throw their pursuers off their guard against being wounded by their arrows. The signal for battle among them is given, not by trumpet but by drum. Nor are they able to fight long, but they would be irresistible if their vigor and perseverance were equal to the fury of their onset. In general, they retire before the enemy in the very heat of the engagement, and, soon after their retreat, return to the battle afresh, so that, when you feel most certain that you have conquered them, you have still to meet the greatest danger from them. Their armor, and that of their horses, is formed of plates, lapping over one another like the feathers of a bird, and covers both man and horse entirely. Of gold and silver, except for adorning their arms, they make no use.

Each man has several wives. They punish no crime more severely than adultery, and accordingly they not only exclude their women from entertainments but also forbid them the very sight

of men. They eat no flesh but that which they take in hunting. They ride on horseback on all occasions; on horses they go to war, and to feasts; on horses they discharge public and private duties; on horses they go abroad, meet together, traffic, and converse. Indeed the difference between slaves and freemen is, that slaves go on foot, but freemen only on horseback. Their general mode of burial is dilaniation[99] by birds or dogs; the bare bones they at last bury in the ground. In their superstitions and worship of the gods the principal veneration is paid to rivers. The disposition of the people is proud, quarrelsome, faithless, and insolent, for they think that a certain roughness of behavior is becoming to men and gentleness only to women. They are always restless and ready for any commotion, at home or abroad. They are taciturn by nature, more ready to act than speak, and consequently they shroud both their successes and miscarriages in silence. They obey their princes, not from humility, but from fear. They are libidinous, but frugal in diet. To their word or promise they have no regard, except as far as suits their interest.

After the death of Alexander the Great, when the kingdoms of the east were divided among his successors, the government of Parthia was committed to Stasanor, a foreign ally, because none of the Macedonians would deign to accept it.[100] Subsequently, when the Macedonians were divided into parties by civil discord, the Parthians, with the other people of Upper Asia, followed Eumenes, and, when he was defeated, went over to Antigonus. After his death they were under the rule of Seleucus Nicator,[101] and then under Antiochus[102] and his successors, from whose great-grandson Seleucus[103] they first revolted, at the time of the First

---

[98] The Roman Triumvir Mark Antony, who invaded Parthia in 37 BCE.

[99] Tearing into pieces.

[100] According to Justin himself, at the "Partition of Babylon" in 323 BCE, Stasanor was granted the administration of the Dranci and Arci, and Nicanor was granted the Parthians.

[101] Seleucus I (311–281 BCE), who founded the Seleucid Empire.

[102] Antiochus I "The Great" (281–261 BCE), son of Seleucus I.

[103] Seleucus II (246–225 BCE).

Punic war, when Lucius Manlius Vulso and Marcus Attilius Regulus were Consuls.[104] For their revolt, the dispute between the two brothers, Seleucus and Antiochus,[105] procured them impunity, for while they sought to wrest the throne from one another they neglected to pursue the revolters.

At the same period, Theodotus, governor of the thousand cities of Bactria, revolted,[106] and assumed the title of king; and all the other people of the east, influenced by his example, fell away from the Macedonians. One Arsaces, a man of uncertain origin, but of undisputed bravery, happened to arise at this time; and he, who was accustomed to live by plunder and depredations, hearing a report that Seleucus was overcome by the Gauls in Asia, and being consequently freed from dread of that prince, invaded Parthia with a band of marauders, overthrew Andragorus, Seleucus' lieutenant,[107] and, after putting him to death,[108] took upon himself the government of the country. Not long after, too, he made himself master of Hyrcania,[109] and thus, invested with authority over two nations, raised a large army, through fear of Seleucus and Theodotus, King of the Bactrians. But being soon relieved of his fears by the death of Theodotus, he made peace and an alliance with his son, who was also named Theodotus, and not long after, engaging with King Seleucus, who came to take vengeance on the revolters, he obtained a victory,[110] and the Parthians observe the day on which it was gained with great solemnity, as the date of the commencement of their liberty.

Seleucus being then recalled into Asia by new disturbances, and respite being thus given to Arsaces, he settled the Parthian government, levied soldiers, built fortresses, and strengthened his towns. He founded a city also, called Dara, in Mount Zapaortenon, of which the situation is such, that no place can be more secure or more pleasant, for it is so encircled with steep rocks that the strength of its position needs no defenders, and such is the fertility of the adjacent soil, that it is stored with its own produce. Such too is the plenty of springs and wood, that it is amply supplied with streams of water and abounds with all the pleasures of hunting. Thus Arsaces, having at once acquired and established a kingdom, and having become no less memorable among the Parthians than Cyrus among the Persians, Alexander among the Macedonians, or Romulus among the Romans, died at a mature old age, and the Parthians paid this honor to his memory, that they called all their kings thenceforward by the name of Arsaces.[111] His son and successor on the throne, whose name also was Arsaces,[112] fought with the greatest bravery against Antiochus, the son of Seleucus, who was at the head of a hundred thousand foot and twenty thousand horse, and was at last taken into alliance with him.

The third king of the Parthians was Priapatius,[113] but he was also called Arsaces, for, as has just been observed, they distinguished all their kings by that name, as the Romans use the titles of Caesar and Augustus. He, after reigning fifteen years, died, leaving two sons, Mithridates and Phraates. The elder, Phraates,[114] being, according to the custom of the nation, heir to the crown, subdued the Mardi, a strong people, by force of arms, and died not long after, leaving several sons, whom he set aside, and left the throne, in preference, to his brother Mithridates,[115] a man of extraordinary ability, thinking that more was due to the name of king than to that of father, and that he ought to consult the interests of his country rather than those of his children.

Almost at the same time that Mithridates ascended the throne among the Parthians, Eucratides[116]

---

[104] 256 BCE; rather earlier than the reign of Seleucus II.

[105] Antiochus Hierax (246–226 BCE), a brother and rival of Seleucus II.

[106] In 250 BCE.

[107] A satrap of Seleucus II who had revolted in the mid-240s.

[108] In 238 BCE.

[109] On the southern coast of the Caspian Sea.

[110] Ca. 235 BCE.

---

[111] The royal family of the Parthians was called the Arsacids.

[112] Arsaces II, King of Parthia from 211 to 185 BCE.

[113] King of Parthia from 185 to 170 BCE.

[114] Phraates I, King of Parthia from 168 to 165 BCE.

[115] Mithridates I, King of Parthia from 165 to 132 BCE.

[116] King of Bactria ca. 170–145 BCE.

began to reign among the Bactrians, both of them being great men. But the fortune of the Parthians, being the more successful, raised them, under this prince, to the highest degree of power, whereas the Bactrians, harassed with various wars, lost not only their dominions, but their liberty, for having suffered from contentions with the Sogdianians, the Drangians, and the Indians, they were at last overcome, as if exhausted, by the weaker Parthians. Eucratides, however, carried on several wars with great spirit, and although much reduced by his losses in them, yet, when he was besieged by Demetrius,[117] king of the Indians, with a garrison of only three hundred soldiers he repulsed, by continual sallies, a force of sixty thousand enemies. Having accordingly escaped, after a five months' siege, he reduced India under his power. But as he was returning from the country, he was killed on his march by his son, with whom he had shared his throne, and who was so far

from concealing the murder, that, as if he had killed an enemy, and not his father, he drove his chariot through his blood, and ordered his body to be cast out unburied.

During the course of these proceedings among the Bactrians, a war arose between the Parthians and Medes, and after fortune on each side had been some time fluctuating, victory at length fell to the Parthians when Mithridates, enforced with this addition to his power, appointed Bacasis over Media, while he himself marched into Hyrcania. On his return from thence, he went to war with the king of the Elymaeans,[118] and having conquered him, added this nation also to his dominions, and extended the Parthian empire, by reducing many other peoples under his yoke, from Mount Caucasus to the river Euphrates. Being then taken ill, he died in an honorable old age, and not inferior in merit to his great-grandfather Arsaces.

---

[117] Several Greek kings of this name are attested; this one may be Demetrius II, who may have reigned ca. 175–150 BCE.

[118] Elymais was in southern Persia on the northwestern shore of the Persian Gulf.

CHAPTER 2

ARCHAIC ROME
(753–509 BCE)

When it was established as a small farming village on the Tiber River in the mid-eighth century BCE, Rome was no different from many thousands of other little farming villages scattered about the ancient world. No one could have guessed that Rome would develop into the strongest power that the world had yet known. Over the centuries, Rome assimilated both population and culture from its neighbors, creating a truly multicultural society.

CULTURAL ENCOUNTERS OF THE EARLY ROMANS

One of the most noteworthy characteristics of the ancient Romans was their ability to assimilate aspects of the cultures of other peoples while at the same time maintaining their own unique identity. One of the reasons for this, no doubt, is that from the very beginning of their history, the Romans were in close contact with neighboring peoples with very different cultural traits. Rather than fearing foreign contacts, the Romans readily borrowed from the cultures of their Italian neighbors.

The Peoples of Italy

The Bronze Age in Italy was represented by several different cultures. In Sardinia, the Nuragic Civilization (ca. 1800–200 BCE) was typified by the construction of cone-shaped towers of uncertain purpose known as *nuraghe* and by the extensive working of bronze. Trade in bronze items such as daggers, swords, bracelets, and axes was carried out with Mycenaean Greece, Crete, and Cyprus. On the Italian mainland, the Italian Bronze Age, also known as the Apennine Culture, lasted from roughly 2000 to 1200 BCE in central and southern Italy and was characterized by inhumation burials. In northern Italy, the middle and late Bronze Age was represented by the Terramare, or "Black Earth," Culture (ca. 1700–1150 BCE),

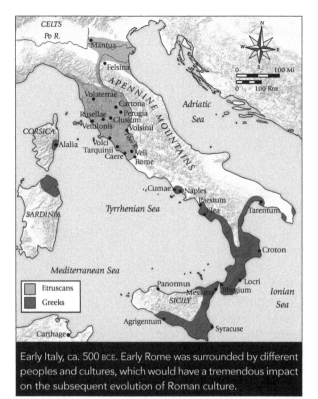

Early Italy, ca. 500 BCE. Early Rome was surrounded by different peoples and cultures, which would have a tremendous impact on the subsequent evolution of Roman culture.

The P and Q speaker distinction survives in Irish (Q) and Breton and Welsh (P) speakers.

marked by villages, protected by earthworks and moats, with rectilinear streets and houses sometimes erected on pilings.

The Iron Age appeared rather suddenly in central and northern Italy with the Villanovan Culture (ca. 1200–700 BCE), an offshoot of the central European Urnfield Culture. One characteristic of the Villanovan Culture was the use of pottery urns, sometimes in the shape of huts, that contained cremated remains. Toward the end of the Villanovan period, there is increased evidence for foreign contacts as manifested by amber necklaces from the area of the Baltic Sea and bronze armor from the Greek world. At the same time, there was a reintroduction of inhumation burials in chamber tombs used by aristocratic elites.

These cultural developments sometimes have been connected to the arrival of groups of Indo-European speakers in the years after circa 2000 BCE, at the same time that Indo-Europeans were moving off the southern Russian steppes into Iran, Anatolia, and the Balkans. According to one model, there were at least two movements into Italy by peoples who spoke related Indo-European languages. The first was by the "Q speakers," for whom, for example, the number "five" was "quinque." Subsequently, the "P speakers," for whom "five" was "pompa," arrived and pushed back the Q speakers. By circa 1000 BCE, the Q speakers inhabited only the rich agricultural plain of Latium, south of the lower Tiber River, and included primarily the people later known as the **Latins,** whose language was Latin. The P speakers, whose dialects included Oscan and Sabellian, developed into the **Italic peoples,** or Sabellians. These included the **Samnites,** Campanians, and Lucanians, who inhabited the mountainous areas of central and southern Italy. Other models, however, discount the "two invasion" hypothesis and attribute the linguistic differences to other causes. Attempts also have been made, with little success, to associate these linguistic patterns with different burial practices—cremation and inhumation—used by different groups of immigrants.

During the eighth century BCE, the Villanovan Culture was superseded in northern Italy by the Etruscan civilization. The proximity of Etruscan cities to Rome, just the other side of the Tiber River, meant that the Etruscans would have a very great influence on the development of early Roman culture. The Italic peoples who inhabited the uplands bordering Latium also would be intimately involved in the development of Rome right from its earliest history. And the Celts who migrated from Gaul to settle in the Po River valley in the fifth century BCE likewise would have a special effect on the course of early Roman history.

The Etruscans

As of the eighth century BCE, the native early Iron Age Villanovan Culture of Italy was replaced in northwestern Italy by the civilization of the **Etruscans**. It remains a matter of great debate whether the Etruscans were an intrusive population, perhaps from the coast of Anatolia, or a local development. The Etruscans did not form a unified nation but consisted of a dodecapolis of twelve independent cities such as Tarquinii, Caere, Clusium, Populonia, and Veii. Each city was ruled initially by a *lucumo* (king), who was supported and advised by a warrior aristocracy. In the sixth century BCE, some of the Etruscan cities developed into aristocracies or oligarchies, much as happened in Greece. The highly developed Etruscan economy was based on trade and manufacturing; the Etruscans were particularly admired for their metalwork. Much Etruscan trade was with the Greeks, and some of the best-preserved Greek pottery comes not from Greece but from Etruria. They used an alphabet developed from that of the Greeks to write a non–Indo-European language that still is undeciphered. For example, the Etruscan name for themselves, the Rasna, cannot be derived from any known language.

The name of the Etruscans survives in the modern Italian region of Tuscany.

Etruscan religion was established on the belief that the natural world was controlled by divinities who could be influenced to a particular course of action. To ascertain the will of the gods, the Etruscans used divination, which was based on the interpretation of signs received from the gods. For example, Etruscan priests took the *auspices* (inspecting flights of birds) and performed *haruspicy* (examining sheep livers) for indications of the outcome of future events.

The Etruscans had a vision of an afterlife that was superficially similar to that of the Egyptians: they believed that "you could take it with you" and that life after death was a perpetuation of all the best aspects of life on earth. Etruscan aristocrats constructed elaborate cities of the dead marked by groves of cypress trees and comprising hundreds of multiroomed stone-cut underground tombs. The walls had carved into them implements that were used in everyday life, and marble coffins, or sarcophagi, contained the remains of married couples who remained united in death just as they had been united in life. Etruscan funerals were marked by athletic contests, such as wrestling matches, in honor not only of the dead but also of the gods of the underworld.

The Etruscans expanded south across the Tiber River in the late seventh century BCE, and as a result came into conflict with the Greeks of southern Italy. They also joined with the Carthaginians to resist Greek intrusions into their markets, and as a result of the Battle of Alalia circa 535 BCE they gained a foothold in Corsica. At about the same time, the Etruscans expanded into the Po River valley of northern Italy and began to exploit the rich soil there.

THE ORIGIN OF THE ETRUSCANS

For at least two reasons, the ancient Etruscans often are referred to as a "mysterious" people. For one thing, their language, although written in a form of the Greek alphabet, is undeciphered, meaning that their history has to be reconstructed from archaeology and the accounts of their enemies, the Greeks and Romans. Second, an enduring controversy has arisen regarding the Etruscans' origin because different historians give different versions. Around 10 BCE, Dionysius of Halicarnassus believed that the Etruscans were native Italians who developed their own idiosyncratic civilization. Nowadays, this version tends to be preferred by Italian historians, who suppose that Italian ancestors of the Etruscans assimilated foreign cultural attributes, much as the Greeks had done during their Archaic Age (776–500 BCE). But other ancient writers thought differently. At about the same time, the Roman historian Livy had the Etruscans originally coming from the Danube region. On the other hand, in the fifth century BCE the Greek historian Herodotus wrote that the Etruscans had migrated to Italy from Lydia around 800 BCE, and Thucydides connected the Etruscans with pirates from Lemnos, an island off the coast of Lydia. This view is consistent with inscriptions found on Lemnos dating to the sixth century BCE and written in an alphabet almost identical to the Etruscan alphabet. DNA study also supports an eastern as opposed to a European origin for the Etruscans, and an eastern origin also could help to explain the many eastern motifs in Etruscan art.

The Lemnos inscription, thought to preserve a form of the Etruscan language.

In the late sixth century BCE, however, the fortunes of the Etruscans began to deteriorate. They suffered several defeats at the hands of the Greeks, and they lost their holdings south of the Tiber River. By 400 BCE, Celts from across the Alps in Gaul had forced them out of the Po Valley, which became known as Cisalpine Gaul, or "Gaul on this side of the Alps." This decline in their political affairs was reflected in their funeral practices, which assumed a more sinister tone. The Etruscans feared that the uncertainty in their earthly lives might follow them after death, and they therefore developed rituals intended to placate the demons of the underworld. The earlier lighthearted funeral games evolved into ritual combats to the death, and even were accompanied by human sacrifice.

The Western Greeks

Between 750 and 550 BCE, the cities of mainland and Ionian Greece established several colonies on the southern Italian coast, the most prominent being Capua, Naples, and Tarentum. Other colonies were founded on the coasts of Sicily (such as Syracuse) and southern France (Marseille). These colonies were carbon copies of the cities back in Greece, and some, Syracuse in Sicily in particular, grew to be as powerful and influential as any city back in the Greek homeland. In the course of their extensive trade, these colonies served as a conduit both for the spread of Greek culture into the European hinterland and for the reception of native culture into the Mediterranean area. During the fifth century BCE, native peoples of the Italian uplands began to move toward the coast, occupying some of the Greek colonies and creating an amalgamation of Greek and Italian culture. It was via these Greek colonies that the early Romans were exposed to and assimilated many aspects of Greek culture.

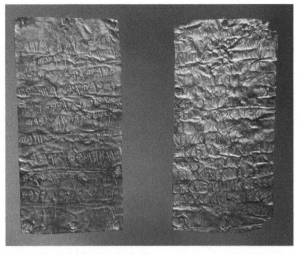

The "Pyrgi Tablets," inscribed on gold plates and dating to around 500 BCE, record in both the Punic and Etruscan languages a dedication made by the Etruscan king of Caere to the Carthaginian goddess Astarte. They attest to the close relations between the Carthaginians and Etruscans.

ROME OF THE KINGS (753–509 BCE)

This multicultural Italian environment saw the rise of Rome, a city that was to establish the most successful Mediterranean empire of all time. In its early days, however, Rome was but one of thousands of small, undistinguished agricultural villages scattered about the Mediterranean, and no contemporary records of its foundation and early history survive. As a result, one must rely on archaeological evidence, legends, and later traditions for evidence about this period. According to Roman tradition, Rome was founded in 753 BCE and first was ruled by kings. For reasons that are not yet clear, the Roman monarchy ended in 509 BCE and was replaced by an initially aristocratic form of government known as the Roman Republic.

Cities such as Naples, Syracuse, and Marseille still are major commercial centers.

The Founding of Rome

Several legends told of the foundation of Rome. A Greek version had Rome being founded by Trojans, led by the hero Aeneas, the son of the goddess Aphrodite (Roman Venus) and the Trojan Anchises, who had fled circa 1184 BCE from the burning city of Troy. This version had Aeneas, like Odysseus, sailing about the Mediterranean for ten years. His travels took him to Carthage, where he had a love affair with Queen Dido, but then abandoned her in his continuing quest for a new home. Eventually he and his people settled near the Tiber River in Italy and founded Rome.

But a more popular local Roman legend had the city established on 21 April 753 BCE. To deal with this chronological inconsistency, later Roman historians had Aeneas founding a city at Alba Longa, not far from the later site of Rome, and Rome actually being founded by his distant descendents. Thirteenth in descent from Aeneas were the brothers Numitor, the legitimate king of Alba Longa, and Amulius. The ambitious Amulius drove out his brother and usurped the throne. To prevent Numitor's daughter Rhea Silvia from having any sons who might challenge him, Amulius compelled her to become a Vestal Virgin, one of the priestesses responsible for keeping the sacred fire burning. Rhea nevertheless became pregnant and blamed the god Mars. In time she gave birth to twins, Romulus and Remus, whom Amulius ordered to be killed so they could not lay claim to the throne. But their executioner did not have the heart to kill them, so he sent them down the Tiber River in a basket. Downstream, the shepherd Faustulus found them under a fig tree being suckled by a wolf (*lupa*, the Latin word for "wolf," also was the word for "prostitute," which could suggest that the twins' birth was not as august as the legend claimed), and they were raised as shepherds.

The story of Romulus and Remus being set adrift reflects a common folktale motif, as seen in similar stories about Sargon of Akkad and Moses.

As young men, the two discovered their true heritage and killed their uncle. But because they had incurred blood guilt for murdering a relative, they were compelled to leave town, and they therefore decided to found a new city on a site with seven hills on the southern bank of the lower Tiber River. After an argument over which twin would have the right to found the city, Romulus killed Remus, and hence the new city was named Rome, after him. In a different version, on the other hand, Rome got its name from a Greek word Romē, meaning "strength."

Romulus then became the first of seven kings of Rome. He and his successors established **Rome of the Kings**, also known as the "Archaic Period," and were believed to have introduced many of the most time-honored customs of Rome. Very little evidence survives from the regal period, and many later legends grew up about the kings, whose existence we can accept even if we doubt many of their supposed activities. For example, it seems clear that later views about the kings were largely based on folk etymologies of their names, such as that Numa (derived from *numen*, or "divine power") had organized Roman religion; that Tullus Hostilius (from *hostilis*, "hostile") had been a successful warrior; and that Servius Tullus (from *servus*, "slave") originally had been a slave. But even though the belief that King Tarquinius Priscus—"Tarquin the Old"—came from the Etruscan city of Tarquinii might be pressing the evidence too far, his name is, in fact, Etruscan. In general, it is simply impossible to say with any certainty what any particular king did or did not do.

Based on what can be projected back from later times, however, we know that the kings had the powers of *imperium*, which gave them authority to lead armies, and *auspicium*, the right to assess the will of the gods. According to legend, the city initially was populated by a variety of bandits, Latins, and Italic peoples; stories such as this gave rise to traditions of Roman willingness to incorporate newcomers. For example, it was believed that, in order to find wives, the early Romans kidnaped women from a neighboring Italic people, the Sabines (an event later known as the "kidnaping of the Sabine women"), whose king, Titus Tatius, later joined forces with the Romans.

Rome Becomes a City

Regardless of how much one credits the patriotic legends, archaeological excavations show that the first settlements on the hills of Rome do in fact date to around 750 BCE. At this time, moreover, Rome was a very modest place, consisting of straw huts perched on the tops of hills. For some 150 years, the inhabitants of Rome were subsistence farmers, grubbing a scanty sustenance from the soil. They were not yet even unified into a single community, although they did share some religious festivals.

According to Roman historical traditions, this situation changed drastically just before 600 BCE, when Rome was occupied by the Etruscans, who provided the last three kings of Rome and who are credited with making Rome into a city. These accounts are generally consistent with archaeological evidence indicating that Rome did become urbanized at this time. The swampy land between the hills was drained (the legends spoke of the construction of the *Cloaca maxima*, or "big sewer"), and the first pebble pavements, the first stone buildings, including the Temple of Jupiter atop the Palatine Hill, and the **forum**, or central meeting place, were built.

At the same time, many aspects of Etruscan culture, such as divination and the Etruscan version of the Greek alphabet, were imported into Rome, and new occupations, including trading (according to legend, King Tarquin the Old originally had been an Etruscan trader) and pottery manufacturing, were adopted. Other Roman concepts that had an Etruscan origin included the *fasces* (bundled rods with axes) that symbolized a high magistrate's power; and Luceres, the name of an ancient Roman tribe, was derived from *lucumo*, Etruscan for "king." Even the Latin word *populus*, "the Roman people," was the name of

TABLE 2.1　THE KINGS OF ROME AND THEIR LEGENDARY DATES AND DEEDS (ALL DATES BCE)

Native Kings		
Romulus	753–716	Established Senate and secular institutions
Numa Pompilius	716–672	Established religious institutions
Tullus Hostilius	672–640	Engaged in warfare
Ancus Martius	640–616	Engaged in warfare and built bridges
Etruscan Kings		
Tarquin the Old	616–578	First Etruscan king, built the Cloaca Maxima
Servius Tullius	578–533	Built the first wall, took the first census
Tarquin the Proud	533–509	Last king, built the Capitoline temple

an Etruscan god. Thus, even though some would argue that the Romans simply adopted aspects of Etruscan culture on their own, the extent of the assimilation suggests that it was the Etruscans who brought urbanization and civilization to Rome; indeed, the very name *Roma* may have been Etruscan.

The legends that recount in great detail the history of regal and early Republican Rome not only include many elaborations but also must be read through the lens of the times in which they came to be written down, not until circa 200 BCE, where they reflect contemporary views of what early Rome must have been like. Early Rome is presented as much more structured, much more like the Rome of 200 BCE, than it actually was. For example, Roman military campaigns are presented as being carried out under the auspices of the Roman government and Roman magistrates. Current scholarship suggests, however, that Roman government and society were very fragmented in the Archaic Period, and that many military campaigns were private affairs initiated by private commanders, sometimes called "warlords." Only on occasion was the government brought in. Some of these campaigns, at least, seem to have been organized by extended families, or *gentes*. Thus, in the early fifth century BCE, the Fabii alone undertook to carry out the campaign against the Etruscan city of Veii, and at the Battle of Cremera in 477 BCE the family was completely exterminated except for one young man who was too young to serve.

Early Roman Society

This period saw the development of several characteristic Roman values and institutions. The Roman character was fundamentally conservative and was based on the concept of **mos maiorum**, "the ways of our ancestors." In general, the Romans felt that the older something was, the better it was. Thus Roman legends tended to retroject into the past some of Rome's most hallowed traditions, in much the same way that the Spartans had done, so as to endow them with greater antiquity and authority. The Romans valued moral qualities such as stability, discipline, industry, frugality, temperance, and fortitude. They had a down-to-earth character that rejected the idealized portraiture of the Greeks, often preferring a realistic style that depicted themselves as they were, warts, wrinkles, and all. Intellect, innovation, and imagination were generally not high on the Roman list of virtues.

The words patrician *and* plebeian *still refer to "upper-class" and "lower-class" people, respectively.*

As a result of economic differentiation, a process by which a few families gained control of most of the wealth, the citizen body evolved into two social orders, or classes: the **patricians** and the **plebeians** (or plebs). The patricians were the Roman equivalent of the Greek aristocrats. They controlled the best land, and about one hundred of them belonged to the **Senate** (from the word for "old men"), which advised the king. The plebeians were mostly peasant farmers who worked either their own small plots or land that belonged to the patricians. Some, however, followed the Etruscan example and became well-to-do in trade and crafts. But no matter how rich they became, there was no way for plebeians to enter the hereditary patrician order, for the distinction between patricians and plebeians involved not wealth but social status and family background.

RECONSTRUCTING EARLY ROME

One of the things that makes it difficult to recover the earliest history of Rome is that no written records survive from that period. The Romans did have legends about early Rome, but they did not begin to write them down until around 200 BCE, and by that time the legends had become greatly embellished and largely if not completely fictional. The best opportunity to try to reconstruct early Rome comes from archaeology. Excavations on the Palatine Hill have recovered artifacts from the very earliest history of Rome. For example,

post holes show where the poles that supported the sides and roofs of huts were set into the ground. This discovery allows historians to establish the floor size of early Roman homes. In addition, excavations of early Roman cemeteries have recovered pottery urns that held the bones and ashes of the cremated dead. These urns were sometimes made in the shape of the huts in which the people they contained had lived. By combining the shape of the cremation urns with the dimensions provided by the post holes, archaeologists can reconstruct with a great degree of accuracy what the simple houses of the early Romans looked like, demonstrating that, at that time, there was nothing to mark Rome for future greatness.

An early Roman funerary urn made in the shape of the huts in which early Romans lived.

A reconstruction of early Rome based on archaeological evidence.

The Romans' concern over status also went far beyond the distinction between patricians and plebeians. Everyone knew his or her place in Roman society. Family life was structured and authoritarian. Within each family the *paterfamilias*, or "father of the family," had life-and-death authority over the household. Fathers undertook the responsibility for educating their sons by taking them along as they fulfilled their own responsibilities in the daily round of public and private life. Most sons lived at home under their fathers' legal authority, even after they were married, until their fathers died, and they then

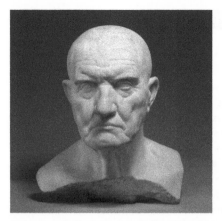

For a typical Roman paterfamilias, life was serious business, as suggested by the expression on this portrait from the later Republic.

became "fathers of the family" in their own right. But there was a way to gain legal freedom in advance: if the father fictitiously sold his son and set him free three times in a row in a process called *emancipatio* (emancipation), the son then was *sui juris*—that is, under his own legal authority.

All women were under the *manus* (legal authority) of some man except for the six **Vestal Virgins**, whose duty was to keep the sacred hearth fire of the goddess Vesta burning. Daughters generally were expected to marry and assume control over a household. Having a marriage recognized under Roman law was very important because it allowed one's children to inherit property and Roman citizenship. Early Rome had three different kinds of marriage, two of which were *in manum*—that is, they transferred *manus* over the wife from the father to the husband. *Confarreatio* ("with spelt") was the most restrictive form and occurred only between patricians. The wedding consisted of the couple sharing a cake made of spelt (a type of wheat) in the presence of ten witnesses, and the woman then passed into the *manus* of her husband. It was required that those wishing to become certain kinds of priests, such as Flamen Dialis (high priest of Jupiter), or Vestal Virgins have parents who were married by *confarreatio*, and divorce was almost impossible. *Coemptio*, or "purchase," was a much more common form of marriage, usually involving a dowry, in which a father fictitiously sold his daughter as a means of transferring *manus* over her to the husband. The third form of marriage, *usus* ("usage"), involved simple cohabitation, equivalent to a modern "common law" marriage. If the woman remained in the husband's home for a year without interruption, she passed into his *manus*, but if she stayed out of his house for three nights during the year, she remained under the more distant *manus* of her father (or another male member of her father's family). Many women preferred the *usus* form of marriage as a means of maintaining some semblance of independence in the marital home.

Roman social relations involved the concept of reciprocal duty and responsibility with respect to the gods, the state, family, friends, and benefactors. If anyone did a Roman a favor, the Roman was beholden to that person until the favor had been repaid. **Senators** felt that it was their duty to participate in public life, and they expected to be rewarded by recognition and office. One of the most important Roman social institutions was the system of *clientela*, in which a patron and a client rendered mutual services to each other and were bound to each other in a quasi-religious union. At this time, the patrons were usually patricians, who would have many plebeian clients. A patrician patron provided physical protection, legal services (only the patricians knew the laws), and economic support, including foodstuffs and seed grain when times were tough and even land to rent if a pleb lost his own. What the patron received in return was an entourage to accompany him when he went to war—for the patricians did most

A PICTURE IS WORTH A THOUSAND WORDS

THE *LAPIS NIGER*

Not even the Romans were sure whether the name *lapis niger* (black stone) referred to a black stone inscription buried in the Roman forum or to the black pavement (five by eleven feet large) that covered it. The inscription, from the mid-sixth century BCE, is the oldest surviving Roman document and the only one dating to the period of Rome of the Kings. It was buried in a shrine in front of the Senate house and managed to escape destruction in the sack by the Gauls in 390 BCE. The Romans eventually forgot what the shrine was for; some later thought that it was the site of Romulus' grave, or the place where Romulus was murdered by the Senate, or where Faustulus the shepherd was killed in battle. It more likely marked the place where the Roman kings addressed the people. Excavations of the site around 1900 turned up small dedicatory statues and the remains of animal sacrifices, attesting to the religious nature of the shrine. The inscription is written in a very early form of Latin using a southern Etruscan alphabet (itself based on the Greek alphabet) used at Veii that became commonly used in Latium. It was this alphabet that eventually evolved into the modern alphabet. Like other very early Latin inscriptions, the text is written in "boustrophedon" (named after the back-and-forth motion of a plowing ox) style, alternating top-down and then bottom-up. Its fragmentary condition makes the inscription difficult to translate, although it seems that it curses anyone who disturbs the shrine. The inclusion of the word, in archaic lettering, "PECEI"—that is, in standard Latin, *regi*, "for the king"—provides concrete proof that Rome was in fact administered by some kind of king in the sixth century BCE (see Source 2.2 for a translation of the inscription).

of the actual fighting—or even when he went into Rome, for one of the measures of the status of a patrician lay in the number of clients who accompanied him. Clients also provided a little help in raising a ransom or dowry. This system of reciprocal responsibility bound Roman society together in a way that Greek society never was, with the result that Romans were inhibited from resorting to violence when disputes arose. But it also was designed to maintain the status quo and to preserve the privileges of the patricians.

The same values were manifested in religion, in which it was believed that various inchoate *numina*, or forces of nature, controlled the environment. Contractual rituals were developed to ensure that each **numen** performed its function. In the sphere of personal religion, for example, every year farmers would sacrifice a red dog at a crossroads to ensure that the red rust, which was controlled by the *numen* Robigus, did not strike their crops. Religious practices to ensure the well-being of Rome were overseen by a chief priest known as the **Pontifex Maximus**, who supervised the Vestal Virgins and other state priests. The chief state gods consisted of the Capitoline Triad of Jupiter Optimus Maximus (Jupiter the Best and Greatest), Juno, and Minerva (Greek Zeus, Hera, and Athena). From their temple atop the Capitoline Hill, they oversaw the welfare of Rome as a whole.

Roman religion was seamlessly integrated into Roman political and everyday life. Annual festivals celebrated many of the gods. The Lupercalia, for example, held on February 15 in honor of Juno, was a purification ceremony intended to stimulate human pregnancy. State religion adopted several Etruscan divination practices, such as the performance of the *haruspices* and the taking of the *auspices*, to determine whether public undertakings could be performed. Other forms of divination, such as interpreting thunderclaps in a clear sky, also were part of the political process. The Roman calendar, which according to legend was reorganized by King Numa with the addition of the months of January and February, established which days of the year were "fas" ("lawful"), when public business could be carried out, or "nefas" ("unlawful"), when public meetings could not be held.

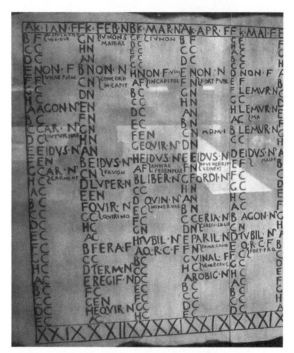

A calendar from Antium in Italy, dating to ca. 85–54 BCE, is the earliest surviving Roman calendar. It lists the Kalends (the first), Nones (the fifth or seventh), and Ides (the thirteenth or fifteenth) of each month and specifies the days when public business could or could not be carried out (indicated by the letters "F," for "fas," or "N," for "nefas"). It also includes Roman festivals, such as the "Lupercalia" in February; the "Robigalia" on April 25, when sacrifices were made to Robigus to safeguard the crops; and the "Lemuria" on May 9, 11, and 13, when exorcism rituals were performed to placate malicious spirits of the dead. Reproduction from the Museum of the Roman Theater of Caesaraugusta in Zaragoza, Spain.

The Fall of the Monarchy

Patriotic legends reported that in 509 BCE Sextus Tarquin, the dissolute son of the autocratic Etruscan king Tarquin the Proud, assaulted the virtuous and aristocratic Roman matron Lucretia, who then committed suicide for dishonoring her family. The native Roman aristocrats then rose in revolt and expelled the kings. Although this legend tells us more about Roman attitudes toward women than about historical events—the most fitting place for a woman was at home spinning wool to make clothing for her family—it correctly reports, at the right point in time, the transition from a monarchical to an aristocratic form of government. This model is analogous to political evolution in Greece, where monarchies had been replaced by aristocracies around the ninth century BCE. Another model suggests that the last few kings of Rome—whose legendary backgrounds included being a slave and a merchant—were not Etruscans at all but were, in fact, native Romans who, akin to Greek tyrants, came to power by appealing to the underprivileged and that their overthrow resulted from an aristocratic revolution. A problem with this interpretation, however, is that other examples of this kind of political devolution are difficult to find—in Greece, for example, tyrannies always followed on aristocracies, not monarchies, and were always replaced by oligarchies and never regressed to aristocracies. However that may be, it is clear that the monarchy did disappear, to be replaced by the *res publica* ("public thing"), or **Republic**, a form of government designed to prevent the Romans from ever again having a *rex* ("king") and in which sovereign authority lay with the people.

⇦ LOOKING BACK

Rome had its beginnings in the middle of the eighth century BCE as an unpretentious farming village located on hills along the Tiber River. During the period of "Rome of Kings" (753–509 BCE), Rome was occupied by the Etruscans, who were responsible for making Rome into a city and from whom the Romans assimilated many significant elements of their culture.

LOOKING AHEAD ⇨

After the expulsion of the Etruscan kings in 509 BCE, the Romans were confronted with the need to establish a government that ensured there would be no more kings, and to deal with social issues that arose between the aristocrats, known as patricians, and the rest of the citizen body.

FURTHER READING

Barchiesi, Alessandro, and Walter Scheidel, eds. *The Oxford Handbook of Roman Studies*. Oxford: Oxford Univ. Press, 2010.

Barker, G., and T. Rasmussen. *The Etruscans*. London: Blackwell, 1998.

Bremmer, Jan. "The Suodales of Poplios Valesios." *Zeitschrift für Papyrologie und Epigraphik* 47 (1982), 133–147.

Cary, M., and H. H. Scullard. *A History of Rome down to the Reign of Constantine*. 3rd ed. New York: St. Martin's Press, 1975.

Cornell, Tim. *The Beginnings of Rome: Italy and Rome from the Bronze Age to the Punic Wars (c. 1000–264 BC)*. New York: Routledge, 1995.

Forsythe, Gary. *A Critical History of Early Rome: From Prehistory to the First Punic War* Berkeley: Univ. of California Press, 2006.

Holloway, Ross. *The Archaeology of Early Rome and Latium*. Exeter, UK: Univ. of Exeter Press, 1994.

Ñaco del Hoyo, Toni, and Fernando López Sánchez, eds. *War, Warlords, and Interstate Relations in the Ancient Mediterranean*. Leiden: Brill, 2017.

SOURCES

2.1 THE FOUNDING OF ROME (753 BCE)

PLUTARCH, LIFE OF ROMULUS

A small copper coin issued ca. 330–335 CE under the emperor Constantine I (306–337) depicts on the obverse a helmeted bust of the goddess Roma with the legend "The City of Rome" and on the reverse a scene from the legends surrounding the foundation of Rome, the infants Romulus and Remus being suckled by a wolf.

By the time that Roman history began to be written down circa 200 BCE, stories of Rome's past existed in many different versions. The most popular version of the founding of Rome involved the twins Romulus and Remus, descended in legend from the hero Aeneas of Troy, who himself was the son of the goddess Venus. The story included several curious elements that had to be incorporated because they were integral parts of the legend. It is up to modern historians to attempt to disentangle the historical kernels of truth from the legendary accretions. The foundation of Rome by Romulus inaugurated the period of "Rome of the Kings" (753–509 BCE). This account comes from the "Parallel Lives" authored by the Greek biographer Plutarch in the mid-second century CE. Plutarch's account makes it clear that there were different versions of the details of the story in circulation.

Source: John Dryden, *The Lives of the Noble Greeks and Romans*, revised by A. H. Clough, Vol. 1 (Boston: Little, Brown, 1910).

The story that has the widest credence and the greatest number of vouchers was first published among the Greeks, in its principal details, by Diocles of Peparethus,[1] and Fabius Pictor[2] follows him in most points. Here again there are variations in the story, but its general outline is as follows. The descendents of Aeneas[3] reigned as kings in Alba, and the succession devolved at length upon two brothers, Numitor and Amulius. Amulius divided

[1] A Greek author of ca. 400 BCE, the earliest known historian to write about the foundation of Rome.
[2] The first Roman writer of history, who wrote in Greek ca. 200 BCE.

[3] A Trojan hero who escaped Troy during its sack by the Greeks and traveled around the Mediterranean, eventually settling at Alba Longa not far from the future site of Rome.

the whole inheritance into two parts, setting the treasures and gold that had been brought from Troy over against the kingdom, and Numitor chose the kingdom. Amulius, then, in possession of the treasure and made more powerful by it than Numitor, easily took the kingdom away from his brother. Fearing lest that brother's daughter should have children, he made her a priestess of Vesta, bound to live unwedded and a virgin all her days. Her name is variously given as Ilia, or Rhea, or Silvia.

Not long after this, she was discovered to be with child, contrary to the established law for the Vestals. She did not, however, suffer the capital punishment that was her due,[4] because the king's daughter, Antho, interceded successfully in her behalf, but she was kept in solitary confinement, that she might not be delivered without the knowledge of Amulius. Delivered she was of two boys, and their size and beauty were more than human. Wherefore Amulius was all the more afraid, and ordered a servant to take the boys and cast them away. This servant's name was Faustulus, according to some, but others give this name to the man who took the boys up. Obeying the king's orders, the servant put the babes into a basket and went down toward the river, intending to cast them in, but when he saw that the stream was much swollen and violent, he was afraid to go close up to it, and setting his burden now near the bank, went his way. Then the overflow of the swollen river took and bore up the basket, floating it gently along, and carried it down to a fairly smooth spot.

Now there was a wild fig-tree hard by, which they called Ruminalis, either from Romulus, as is generally thought, or because cud-chewing, or ruminating, animals spent the noon-tide there for the sake of the shade, or best of all, from the suckling of the babes there, for the ancient Romans called the breast "ruma." Here, then, the babes lay, and the she-wolf of story here gave them suck, and a woodpecker came to help in feeding them and to watch over them. Now these creatures are considered sacred to Mars and this was the chief reason why Rhea Silvia was believed when she declared

that Mars was the father of her babes. And yet it is said that she was deceived into doing this, and really lost her virginity to Amulius himself, who came to her in armor.[5] But some say that the name of the children's nurse, by its ambiguity, deflected the story into the fabulous. For the Latins not only called she-wolves "lupae," but also prostitutes.

As for the babes, they were taken up and reared by Faustulus, a swineherd of Amulius, and no man knew of it, or, as some say with a closer approach to probability, Numitor did know of it, and secretly aided the foster-parents in their task. They applied themselves to generous occasions and pursuits, not esteeming sloth and idleness generous, but rather bodily exercise, hunting, running, driving off robbers, capturing thieves, and rescuing the oppressed from violence. For these things, indeed, they were famous far and near.

When a quarrel arose between the herdsmen of Numitor and Amulius, and some of the latter's cattle were driven off, the brothers would not suffer it, but fell upon the robbers, put them to flight, and intercepted most of the booty. To the displeasure of Numitor they gave little heed, but collected and took into their company many needy men and many slaves, exhibiting thus the beginnings of seditious boldness and temper.

But once when Romulus was busily engaged in some sacrifice, being fond of sacrifices and of divination, the herdsmen of Numitor fell in with Remus as he was walking with a few companions, and a battle ensued. After blows and wounds given and received on both sides, the herdsmen of Numitor prevailed and took Remus prisoner. When Numitor came home,[6] after getting Remus into his hands, he was amazed at the young man's complete superiority in stature and strength of body. Perceiving by his countenance that the boldness and vigor of his soul were unsubdued and unharmed by his present circumstances, and hearing that his acts and deeds corresponded with his looks, but chiefly, as it would seem, because a divinity was aiding and assisting in the inauguration of great events, he

---

[4] Vestal Virgins who violated their vows of chastity normally were buried alive.

[5] That is, dressed like Mars.

[6] In Alba Longa, where he still lived despite having been deposed as king.

grasped the truth by a happy conjecture. He asked him who he was and what were the circumstances of his birth, while his gentle voice and kindly look inspired the youth with confidence and hope.

Then Remus boldly said: "Indeed, I will hide nothing from you; for you seem to be more like a king than Amulius; you hear and weigh before punishing, but he surrenders men without a trial. Formerly, my twin brother and I believed ourselves children of Faustulus and Larentia, servants of the king, but since being accused and slandered before you and brought in peril of our lives, we hear great things concerning ourselves. Whether they are true or not, our present danger is likely to decide. Our birth is said to have been secret, and our nursing and nurture as infants stranger still. We were cast out to birds of prey and wild beasts, only to be nourished by them, by the breasts of a she-wolf and the morsels of a woodpecker, as we lay in a little basket by the side of the great river. The basket still exists and is kept safe, and its bronze girdles are engraved with letters now almost effaced, which may perhaps hereafter prove unavailing tokens of recognition for our parents, when we are dead and gone."

Then Numitor, hearing these words and conjecturing the time that had elapsed from the young man's looks, welcomed the hope that flattered him, and thought how he might talk with his daughter concerning these matters in a secret interview, for she still was kept in the closest custody.[7] Meanwhile, Faustulus, on hearing that Remus had been seized and delivered up to Numitor, called upon Romulus to go to his aid, and then told him clearly the particulars of their birth. Faustulus took the basket and went to see Numitor. Naturally enough, the guards at the king's gate were suspicious of him, and when he was scrutinized by them and made confused replies to their questions, he was found to be concealing the basket in his cloak. Now by chance there was among the guards one of those who had taken the boys to cast them into the river and were concerned in their exposure. This man, now seeing the basket, and recognizing it by its make and inscription, conceived a suspicion of the truth, and without any delay told the matter to

the king and brought Faustulus before him to be examined. In these dire and pressing straits, Faustulus admitted that the boys were alive and well.

Romulus was now close at hand, and many of the citizens who hated and feared Amulius were running forth to join him. He also was leading a large force with him, divided into companies of a hundred men, each company headed by a man who bore aloft a handful of hay and shrubs tied round a pole (the Latin word for handful is "manipulus," and hence in their armies they still call the men in such companies "maniples"). And when Remus incited the citizens within the city to revolt, and at the same time Romulus attacked from without, the tyrant,[8] without taking a single step or making any plan for his own safety, from sheer perplexity and confusion, was seized and put to death.

Amulius now being dead and matters settled in the city, the brothers were neither willing to live in Alba, unless as its rulers, nor to be its rulers while their grandfather[9] was still alive. Having therefore restored the government to him and paid fitting honors to their mother, they resolved to dwell by themselves, and to found a city in the region where, at the first, they were nourished and sustained. But perhaps it was necessary, now that many slaves and fugitives were gathered about them, either to disperse these and have no following at all, or else to dwell apart with them. For that the residents of Alba would not consent to give the fugitives the privilege of intermarriage with them, nor even receive them as fellow-citizens, is clear, in the first place, from the kidnaping of the Sabine women, which was not a deed of wanton daring but one of necessity, owing to the lack of marriages by consent, for they certainly honored the women, after they had carried them off, beyond measure.[10] And in the second place, when their city was first founded, they made a sanctuary of refuge for all fugitives, which they

---

[7] By Numitor's brother, King Amulius.

[8] Amulius is called a "tyrant" because he was an illegal ruler.

[9] Numitor.

[10] To have a legal marriage, a couple needed to have the right of intermarriage in the society where they were getting married; because the early Romans did not have this with their neighbors, they had to kidnap their brides.

called the sanctuary of the God of Asylum. There they received all who came, delivering none up, neither slave to masters, nor debtor to creditors, nor murderer to magistrates, but declaring it to be in obedience to an oracle from Delphi that they made the asylum secure for all men. Therefore the city soon was full of people, for they say that the first houses numbered no more than a thousand. This, however, was later.

When they set out to establish their city, a dispute at once arose concerning the site. Romulus, accordingly, built Roma Quadrata[11] (which means "square"), and wished to have a city on that site, but Remus laid out a strong precinct on the Aventine Hill,[12] which was named from him Remonium, but now is called Rignarium. Agreeing to settle their quarrel by the flight of birds of omen,[13] and taking their seats on the ground apart from one another, six vultures, they say, were seen by Remus, and twice that number by Romulus. Some, however, say that whereas Remus truly saw his six, Romulus lied about his twelve, but that when Remus came to him, then he did see the twelve. Hence it is that at the present time also the Romans chiefly regard vultures when they take auguries from the flight of birds.

When Remus learned of the deceit he was enraged, and as Romulus was digging a trench where his city's wall was to run he ridiculed some parts of the work and obstructed others. At last, when he leaped across it, he was smitten by Romulus himself and fell dead there. Faustulus also fell in the battle. Romulus buried Remus and then set himself to building his city. A circular trench was dug around what is now the Comitium[14] and in this were deposited the first-fruits of all things the use of which was sanctioned by custom as good and by nature as necessary. Finally, every man brought a small portion of the soil of his native land and these were cast in among the first-fruits and mingled with them. Then, taking this as a center, they marked out the city in a circle around it. And the founder, having shod a plough with a bronze ploughshare and having yoked to it a bull and a cow, himself drove a deep furrow round the boundary lines while those who followed after him had to turn the clods, which the plough threw up, inward toward the city, and suffer no clod to lie turned outward. With this line they marked out the course of the wall, and it is called, by contraction, "pomerium."[15] And where they intended to put in a gate, there they took the share out of the ground, lifted the plough over, and left a vacant space. And this is the reason why they regard all the wall as sacred except the gates, for if they held the gates sacred it would not be possible, without religious scruples, to bring into and send out of the city things that are necessary and yet unclean.[16]

Now it is agreed that the city was founded on the twenty-first of April, and this day the Romans celebrate with a festival, calling it the birthday of their country. And at first, as it is said, they sacrificed no living creature at that festival, but thought they ought to keep it pure and without stain of blood, because it commemorated the birth of their country.

---

[11] "Square Rome."

[12] Later a center of the plebeian opposition to the patricians.

[13] A rite of divination known as "taking the auspices."

---

[14] The meeting place in the Forum of the Roman popular assemblies.

[15] That is, from *"post murum,"* "beyond the wall."

[16] Such as corpses, which were buried outside the pomerium.

THE *LAPIS NIGER*

Only a single document survives from the period of Rome of the Kings, the so-called Black Stone, a fragmentary inscription carved onto tufa, a volcanic stone common in the area, whose very archaic form of lettering uses the Etruscan alphabet, which, in turn, was based on the alphabet used by the Greeks of southern Italy. The inscription is written in what is called "boustrophedon" ("ox-turning") style, which alternates between left to right and right to left. Both the archaic form of Latin and the fact that half or more of each line is missing make the inscription very difficult to understand, although it appears to concern religious prohibitions about bringing draft animals into a certain area of the Roman Forum. The following translation of necessity is rather fanciful (see "A Picture is Worth a Thousand Words" on page 65 for a a visual analysis of the *Lapis Niger*).

Source: Paul MacKendrick, *The Mute Stones Speak* (New York: St. Martin's Press, 1960), 94.

Whosoever defiles this spot, let him be forfeit to the shades of the underworld, and whosoever contaminates this spot with refuse, it is right for the king after due process of law, to confiscate his property. Whatsoever persons the king shall discover passing on this road, let him order the summoner to seize their draft animals by the reins, that they may turn out of the road forthwith and take the proper detour. Whosoever persists in traveling this road, and fails to take the proper detour, by due process of law let him be sold to the highest bidder.

THE VIOLATION OF LUCRETIA AND THE FOUNDING OF THE ROMAN REPUBLIC (509 BCE)

LIVY, *FROM THE FOUNDING OF THE CITY*, BOOK 1, CHAPTERS 57–60

The overthrow of Tarquinius Superbus ("Tarquin the Proud"), the last Etruscan king of Rome, and the establishment of the Roman Republic in 509 BCE was one of the most important events in Roman history. It therefore is no surprise that the Romans had a detailed account of how they believed this momentous change had occurred. The cast of characters in the version presented by the Roman historian Livy (ca. 60 BCE–17 CE) in his work *From the Founding of the City* included patriotic Romans, despicable Etruscans, and a virtuous Roman matron. A close reading of the story suggests that the expulsion of the kings resulted not from a popular revolt but from a conspiracy involving the highest officials of the Roman government of the time.

Source: B. O. Foster, trans. *Livy, Books I and II* (Cambridge, MA: Harvard Univ. Press, 1919).

Ardea[17] belonged to the Rutuli,[18] who were a nation of commanding wealth for that place and period. This very fact was the cause of the war, because the Roman king[19] was eager not only to enrich himself, impoverished as he was by the splendor of his public works,[20] but also to appease with booty the feeling of the common people, who, besides the enmity they bore the monarch for other acts of pride, were especially resentful that the king should have kept them employed so long as artisans and doing the work of slaves.

An attempt was made to capture Ardea by assault. Having failed in this, the Romans invested the place with entrenchments, and began to besiege the enemy. Here in their permanent camp, as is usual with a war not sharp but long drawn out, furlough was rather freely granted, although more freely to the leaders than to the soldiers.

The young princes[21] for their part passed their idle hours together at dinners and drinking bouts. It chanced, as they were drinking in the quarters of Sextus Tarquinius, where Tarquinius Collatinus,[22] son of Egerius, also was a guest, that the subject of wives came up. Every man fell to praising his own wife with enthusiasm, and, as their rivalry grew hot, Collatinus asserted that there was no need to talk about it, for it was in their power to know, in a few hours' time, how far the rest were excelled by his own Lucretia: "Come! If the vigor of youth is in us let us mount our horses and see for ourselves the disposition of our wives. Let every man regard as the surest test what meets his eyes when the woman's husband enters unexpected." They were heated with wine. "Agreed!," they all cried, and clapping spurs to their horses were off for Rome.

Arriving there at early dusk, they thence proceeded to Collatia,[23] where Lucretia was discovered behaving very differently from the daughters-in-law of the king. These they had seen at a luxurious banquet, whiling away the time with their young friends, whereas Lucretia, although it was late at

---

[17] A city, like Rome, founded in the eighth century BCE, about twenty-two miles (thirty-five kilometers) southeast of Rome.

[18] An ancient Italic people.

[19] The Etruscan king Tarquinius Superbus ("Tarquin the Proud") (535–509 BCE).

[20] At this time the Etruscan kings were in fact engaged in building projects, such as the Temple of Jupiter on the Capitoline Hill and the construction of the "Great Sewer" for the draining of the forum area.

[21] Tarquin had three sons, Titus, Arruns, and Sextus.

[22] A great-nephew of the first Etruscan king of Rome, Tarquinius Priscus ("Tarquin the Old").

[23] A town where Collatinus' father was stationed and which gave Collatinus his name.

night, was busily engaged upon her wool,[24] while her maidens toiled about her in the lamplight as she sat in the hall of her house. The prize of this contest in womanly virtues fell to Lucretia. When Collatinus and the Tarquinii approached they were graciously received, and the victorious husband courteously invited the young princes to his table.

It was there that Sextus Tarquinius was seized with a wicked desire to debauch Lucretia; not only her beauty but also her proved chastity provoked him. For the present, however, they ended the boyish prank of the night and returned to the camp. When a few days had gone by, Sextus Tarquinius, without letting Collatinus know, took a single attendant and went to Collatia. Being kindly welcomed, for no one suspected his purpose, he was brought after dinner to a guest-chamber. Burning with passion, he waited until it seemed to him that all about him was secure and everybody fast asleep. Then, drawing his sword, he came to the sleeping Lucretia. Holding the woman down he said, "Be still, Lucretia! I am Sextus Tarquinius. My sword is in my hand. Utter a sound, and you die!"

In fear the woman started out of her sleep. No help was in sight, but only imminent death. Then Tarquinius began to declare his love, to plead, to mingle threats with prayers, to bring every resource to bear upon her woman's heart. When he found her obdurate and not to be moved even by fear of death, he went farther and threatened her with disgrace, saying that when she was dead he would kill his slave and lay him naked by her side, that she might be said to have been put to death in adultery with a man of base condition. At this dreadful prospect her resolute modesty was overcome by his victorious lust, and Tarquinius departed, exulting in his conquest of a woman's honor.

Lucretia, grieving at her great disaster, dispatched the same message to her father in Rome and to her husband at Ardea; she asked that they should each take a trusty friend and come, that they must do this and do it quickly, for a frightful thing had

happened. Spurius Lucretius[25] came with Publius Valerius,[26] Volesus' son. Collatinus brought Lucius Junius Brutus,[27] with whom he chanced to be returning to Rome when he was met by the messenger from his wife. They found Lucretia sitting sadly in her chamber. The entrance of her friends brought the tears to her eyes, and to her husband's question, "Is all well?" She replied, "Far from it; for what can be well with a woman when she has lost her honor? The print of a strange man, Collatinus, is in your bed. Yet my body only has been violated. My heart is guiltless, as death shall be my witness. But pledge your right hands and your words that the adulterer shall not go unpunished. Sextus Tarquinius is he that last night returned hostility for hospitality, and brought ruin on me, and on himself no less, if you are men, when he worked his pleasure upon me."

They give their pledges, every man in turn. They seek to comfort her, sick at heart as she is, by diverting the blame from her to the doer of the wrong. They tell her it is the mind that sins, not the body, and that where purpose has been wanting there is no guilt. "It is for you to determine," she answers, "what is due to him. For my own part, although I acquit myself of the sin, I do not absolve myself from punishment, nor in time to come shall ever unchaste woman live through the example of Lucretia."

Taking a knife that she had concealed beneath her dress she plunged it into her heart, and

---

[24] To spin wool for making the family clothing was the most virtuous act that a Roman matron could perform.

[25] Spurius Lucretius Tricipitinus, Lucretia's father.

[26] A leading Roman aristocrat who later held four consulates and established many of the fundamental guiding principles of the Roman Republic; he gained the epithet "Publicola," or "Friend of the People." It is intriguing to consider whether a certain Poplios Valesios, cited in very archaic Latin in an inscription of ca. 500 BCE, is to be identified with Publicola.

[27] The nephew of Tarquin the Proud; although the king had executed his brother, Brutus remained second-in-command to the king and gave the impression of being harmless by pretending to be dull-witted. Brutus had visited the Oracle of Apollo at Delphi with Tarquin's sons to ask who would be the next king of Rome. The Oracle replied that it would be the first one to kiss his mother. On their return, Brutus pretended to trip and surreptitiously kissed the earth. The Brutus who helped to assassinate Julius Caesar in 44 BCE claimed descent from this Brutus.

sinking forward upon the wound, died as she fell. The wail for the dead was raised by her husband and her father. Brutus, while the others were absorbed in grief, drew out the knife from Lucretia's wound, and holding it up, dripping with gore, exclaimed, "By this blood, most chaste until a prince wronged it, I swear, and I take you, gods, to witness, that I will pursue Lucius Tarquinius Superbus and his wicked wife and all his children, with sword, with fire, aye with whatsoever violence I may, and that I will suffer neither them nor any other to be king in Rome!"

The knife he then passed to Collatinus, and from him to Lucretius and Valerius. They were dumbfounded at this miracle. Whence came this new spirit in the breast of Brutus? As he bade them, so they swore. Grief was swallowed up in anger; and when Brutus summoned them to make war from that very moment on the power of the kings, they followed his lead. They carried out Lucretia's corpse from the house and bore it to the market-place, where men crowded about them, attracted, as they were bound to be, by the amazing character of the strange event and its heinousness. Every man had his own complaint to make of the prince's crime and his violence. They were moved, not only by the father's sorrow, but by the fact that it was Brutus who chided their tears and idle lamentations and urged them to take up the sword, as befitted men and Romans, against those who had dared to treat them as enemies.

The boldest of the young men seized their weapons and offered themselves for service, and the others followed their example. Then, leaving Lucretia's father to guard Collatia, and posting sentinels so that no one might announce the rising to the royal family, the rest, equipped for battle and with Brutus in command, set out for Rome. Once there, wherever their armed band advanced it brought terror and confusion; but again, when people saw that in the van were the chief men of the state, they concluded that whatever it was it could be no meaningless disturbance. And in fact there was no less resentment at Rome when this dreadful story was known than there had been at Collatia. So from every quarter of the city men came running to the Forum.

No sooner were they there than a crier summoned the people before the Tribune of the Celeres,[28] which office Brutus happened to be holding. There he made a speech by no means like what might have been expected of the mind and the spirit that he had feigned up to that day. He spoke of the violence and lust of Sextus Tarquinius, of the shameful defilement of Lucretia, and her deplorable death, of the bereavement of Tricipitinus,[29] in whose eyes the death of his daughter was not so outrageous and deplorable as was the cause of her death. He reminded them, besides, of the pride of the king himself and the wretched state of the commons, who were plunged into ditches and sewers and made to clear them out. The men of Rome, he said, the conquerors of all the nations round about, had been transformed from warriors into artisans and stone-cutters. He spoke of the shameful murder of King Tullius, and how his daughter had driven her accursed chariot over her father's body,[30] and he invoked the gods who punish crimes against parents.

With these and, I fancy, even fiercer reproaches, such as occur to a man in the very presence of an outrage, but are far from easy for an historian to reproduce, he inflamed the people, and brought them to abrogate the king's authority and to exile Lucius Tarquinius, together with his wife and children.[31] Brutus himself then enrolled the juniors,[32] who voluntarily gave in their names, and arming them set out for the camp at Ardea to arouse the troops against the king. The command at Rome he left with Lucretius, who had been appointed Prefect of the City[33] by the king

---

[28] The commander of the king's bodyguard.

[29] Lucretia's father.

[30] Servius Tullius (575–535 BCE), the predecessor of Tarquin the Proud, was murdered by his daughter Tullia and her husband Tarquin, who went on to become king.

[31] The Tribune of the Celeres had the power to summon the popular assembly, so in the official Roman version of the story Tarquin had been legally deposed.

[32] The "juniors" of the Roman army were young men who fought in the field, whereas the "seniors" were older men who defended the city.

[33] An official who acted in place of the king when the king was not in Rome.

some time before. During this confusion Tullia[34] fled from her house, cursed wherever she went by men and women, who called down upon her the furies that avenge the wrongs of kindred.

When the news of these events reached the camp, the king, in alarm at the unexpected danger, set out for Rome to put down the revolt. Brutus, who had perceived the king's approach, made a circuit to avoid meeting him, and at almost the same moment, although by different roads, Brutus reached Ardea and Tarquinius Rome. Against Tarquinius the gates were closed and exile was pronounced. The liberator of the city was received with rejoicings in the camp and the sons of the king were driven out of it. Two of them followed their father, and went into exile at Caere, in Etruria. Sextus Tarquinius departed for Gabii,[35] as though it had been his own kingdom, and there the revengers of old quarrels, which he had brought upon himself by murder and rapine, slew him.

Lucius Tarquinius Superbus ruled for five and twenty years. The rule of the kings at Rome, from its foundation to its liberation, lasted two hundred and forty-four years. Two Consuls were then chosen in the Centuriate Assembly,[36] under the presidency of the Prefect of the City, in accordance with the reforms of Servius Tullius.[37] These were Lucius Junius Brutus and Lucius Tarquinius Collatinus.[38]

---

[34] The wife of King Tarquin.

---

[35] A Latin town eleven miles (eighteen kilometers) east of Rome that Sextus had brought under Roman control.
[36] The assembled Roman army, which had the authority to choose its own commanders, in this case the Consuls.
[37] In Roman legend it was believed that the establishment of the Centuriate Assembly, and other reforms, such as the building of the "Servian Wall," had been accomplished under King Servius Tullius; it now appears that these reforms actually occurred during the early Roman Republic.
[38] Collatinus, however, soon was forced to resign and go into exile because of his family relationship to the Etruscan kings.

THE ROMAN REPUBLIC

CHAPTER 3

THE EARLY ROMAN REPUBLIC (509–350 BCE)

The government of the Roman Republic began as an aristocracy in which only the aristocratic patricians could participate. Political and social development was marked by a drawn-out struggle by non-aristocrats, the plebeians, to gain more rights and privileges, and in particular the right to hold political office. By 366 BCE, the most influential of the non-aristocrats had joined with the aristocrats, the patricians, to form a much more stable oligarchy.

THE CREATION OF THE ROMAN REPUBLIC (509–246 BCE)

After the expulsion of the last Etruscan king in 509 BCE, the Roman elite were confronted with creating a form of government designed to prevent a return to monarchy. The result was the creation of the Roman Republic, a form of government that would last for nearly five hundred years.

Roman Republican Government

The administration of the Republic was based on the concept of **collegiality**: no office was overseen by a single person. The king was replaced by two **Consuls** who were elected each year. Like the king, they had the powers of *imperium* and *auspicium* and were accompanied by twelve **Lictors** carrying the fasces who symbolized the Consul's power. They also had the right to oversee the administration of justice and to name new senators and citizens. Other yearly magistrates were the Quaestors, who originally assisted the Consuls in enforcing the laws and later oversaw financial matters. Only in times of dire emergency—if, for example, the state was on the verge of being defeated by

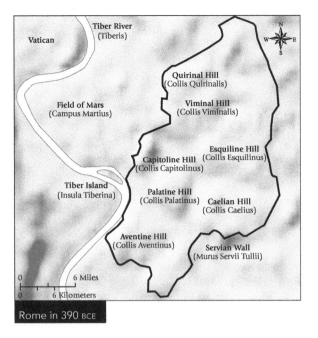

Rome in 390 BCE

a foreign enemy—did the Romans permit a very limited form of one-man rule in which the Consuls appointed a **Dictator**. But there were severe limitations on the Dictator's authority: he could serve only until the emergency was over, and never longer than six months.

Citizenship and Social Organization

Most of the population consisted of citizens, for at this time the slave population was quite small because Rome was not yet very prosperous. Citizens enjoyed private rights, which allowed them to carry on business and to marry under Roman law, and public rights, which permitted them to vote and to run for public office. A significant difference from other ancient societies was that freed slaves became endowed with full Roman citizen rights. The entire citizen body, or *populus*, was organized into three ancient **tribes** (from Latin *tribus,* a third)—the Ramnes (from Romulus), Tities (from Titus Tatius), and Luceres (from Etruscan *lucumo*)—supposedly descended from the Romans, Italians, and Etruscans, respectively, and representing the multiethnic nature of the Roman people. Each tribe consisted of ten *curiae* (singular *curia*), or clans, and the *curiae* were composed of *gentes* (singular *gens*), extended families. Each *gens* was made up of individual *familiae* (singular *familia*), or families, each under the authority of a *paterfamilias.* Roman men bore a first name, such as Gaius, a *gens* (gentilic) name, such as Julius, and a family name, such as Caesar. Family names often were based on an attribute of a distant ancestor (Caesar, for example, meant "hairy"). Women, on the other hand, had a gentilic name, such as Julia, and an iteration number, such as Secunda ("the second").

The thirty *curiae* were organized into a popular (from *populus*) assembly called the **Curiate Assembly** (or assembly organized by *curiae*), which was the sovereign political body of the Roman state. Each *curia* had one vote. Like all later popular assemblies as well, the Curiate Assembly did not have initiative authority. It only considered motions that previously had been approved by the Senate, which grew to about three hundred members (who served for life) and became the primary governing body of Rome. This left the patricians effectively in control of the government. Not only were all the members of the Senate patricians, but patrons also could instruct their clients how to vote when a measure was being considered in a popular assembly. Likewise, the patricians could control who was elected to the

THE ORIGINS OF ROMAN SOCIAL RELATIONS

Controversy continues to swirl about the origin of Roman social and cultural institutions. For example, there has been much recent debate about the role of the Etruscans in early Rome. The conventional interpretation that four Latin kings were followed by three Etruscan kings, and that the Etruscans introduced civilization to Rome, has been challenged on several grounds. It has been suggested, for example, that the last two kings of Rome, Servius Tullius and Tarquin the Proud, were not legitimate kings at all, but rather tyrants, like those who arose in Archaic Age Greece. The prevailing belief that civilization was introduced into Rome by the Etruscans also has been questioned. It has been suggested that both the Romans and the Etruscans participated equally in a kind of common central Italian culture. In this model, the Romans developed a sophisticated culture of their own essentially independently of direct Etruscan influence. This hypothesis, however, has been challenged by even more recent research that focuses on Roman adoption of Etruscan terminology. It has been noted, for example, that the Latin word *sacer* ("sacred") is not Indo-European, and derives from the Etruscan *sacni* ("sanctuary").

In addition, in spite of centuries of research, it remains completely unclear how and when the hereditary patrician class developed. Some see the patriciate as existing under the kings, others as a development of the very early Republic, given that L. Junius Brutus, one of the first two Consuls, may have been a plebeian. The ancient Roman view that the patricians originated with the first one hundred senators appointed by the first king Romulus cannot be supported. Past views relating to racial or ethnic distinctions, or service in the cavalry, likewise have long been dismissed. More recent hypotheses see a connection to control over religious rites, such as the taking of the auspices, and to the holding of priesthoods, both of which also conveyed political authority. Evidence for early status differentiation within the patricians themselves comes from their division into the "major families" and "minor families," although, again, there is no evidence for how this distinction arose. Also to be explained is why some families had patrician and plebeian branches. And any model for the origin of the patricians also would have to explain how they came to control the majority of the landed wealth in early Rome.

New models also dissociate the struggles of poor plebeians to escape oppression by rich landowners from the struggles of well-to-do plebeians to gain political authority. The former, it is suggested, occurred in the fifth century BCE, whereas the latter, what is commonly called the Conflict of the Orders, did not really occur until the fourth century BCE, around the time of the Licinian-Sextian law, which themselves largely created the firm distinctions between patricians and plebeians.

In many ways, therefore, the origins of what ultimately became the greatest empire the world has ever known remain shrouded in mystery and have yet to reveal their secrets to determined and dedicated researchers.

magistracies: even though there was no rule against plebeians running for office, they could not hope to muster sufficient votes to be elected. And, given that the Senate was composed of persons appointed by the Consuls, there was little chance that a plebeian could become a member. At the beginning of the Republic, therefore, the patricians held virtually all the social, political, and economic privileges.

DENARIUS OF MARCUS JUNIUS BRUTUS

The Romans valued their ancient Republican traditions, one of the most significant of which was the replacement of the Etruscan kings by two annually elected Consuls in 509 BCE. One of the first two Consuls was Lucius Tarquinius Collatinus, who had led the Roman rebellion against the Etruscans after his wife Lucretia had been assaulted by the son of King Tarquin the Proud and committed suicide. But because Collatinus was himself related to the Etruscan royal family, he was soon forced to go into exile. The other Consul, Lucius Junius Brutus, also was closely connected to the Etruscan kings, being the grandson of King Tarquin the Old and the nephew of Tarquin the Proud. After the expulsion of the kings, Brutus had the Roman people swear an oath that there would be no more kings. Then, when Brutus' two sons became involved in a conspiracy to restore the Etruscan kings, he dutifully oversaw their execution. Brutus then was killed in battle against the Etruscans before he too could be purged for his Etruscan connections. This silver *denarius* issued in the first century BCE by Marcus Junius Brutus, one of the assassins of Julius Caesar, shows on the reverse his distant ancestor Brutus walking between two Lictors carrying the fasces, a bundle of rods containing an ax, and preceded by an *Accensus*, who summoned people to court. The obverse of the coin depicts the personification "Libertas" (that is, "liberty"). The coin was intended to remind people of Brutus' connection to one of the founders of the Republic and to ancient Roman concepts of freedom. The fasces, which symbolize the power to rule with force and gave their name to Fascism, appear in the iconography of the United States on the Mercury dime, issued from 1916 until 1946, and behind the podium in the U.S. House of Representatives.

THE CONFLICT OF THE ORDERS (500–287 BCE)

The early Roman Republic was beset by a long period of nonviolent domestic unrest known as the **Conflict of the Orders** (500–287 BCE), during which plebeians attempted to obtain expanded rights and opportunities. The plebeians had several complaints against the patricians. They had no officials to look out for their interests. To a large degree they did not know what the laws were, and they also did not know how to prosecute court cases. Well-to-do plebeians had no realistic chance of being elected to office or becoming members of the Senate. Poorer plebeians could be sold into slavery if they defaulted on loans, which usually were made by patricians. The patricians, however, were determined to maintain the status quo and resisted calls for change.

Strength in Numbers

Given the close ties that bound Roman society together, violence and revolution were not viable options when it came to the plebeians gaining greater rights. So the plebeians did exactly what the patricians had done to hold on to power: they got organized and used their class solidarity. Two factors in particular helped the plebeians to pursue their goals. For one thing, it soon became apparent to the patricians that they could not hope to defend Rome without plebeian assistance. According to Roman tradition, for example, 306 members of the patrician Fabian family had been killed in 479 BCE in a battle with the city of Veii. Therefore, soon after 500 BCE, the **Servian Reforms**—later attributed to King Servius Tullius in order to endow them with even greater antiquity—were implemented. They allowed the wealthiest plebeians to serve in the army, for only those Romans who could afford to purchase their own weaponry were allowed to be soldiers. The citizen body was divided into 193 units, called "centuries," that were distributed among different classes based on wealth. Thus the highest-ranking class, the *equites* ("**Equestrians**," or "Knights"), was assigned eighteen centuries and consisted of those who nominally were rich enough to afford not only a full panoply of arms and armor but also a horse. Class I, eighty centuries, contained men who could afford a complete panoply; the men of Class II, twenty centuries, could manage not quite an entire panoply; and so it went, down to Class V, thirty centuries, men who could afford just a single weapon. The largest group, the **proletariate**, was those who had no property and could provide only their offspring (*proles*) to support the state; they were assigned five centuries and did not fight.

The citizenry under arms then became another popular assembly, the **Centuriate Assembly** (assembly organized by centuries), also known as the Army Assembly, which assumed several of the duties of the old Curiate Assembly, such as declaring war and electing the Consuls. Each century had one vote even though the poorer centuries contained many more people than the rich ones. Thus, the patricians were able to control the votes, because, as long as the equestrians and Class I, which contained all the patricians, voted together—as they initially always did—their ninety-eight votes outnumbered the ninety-five votes of everybody else. But at the same time, wealthy and influential plebeians in the Equestrians and Class I served in the army side by side with patricians and had the opportunity, based on their military ability, to serve as Military Tribunes in command

TABLE 3.1   **THE CENTURIATE ASSEMBLY**

Class	Number of Centuries/Votes
Equestrians	18
Class I	80
Class II	20
Class III	20
Class IIII	20
Class V	30
Proletariate	5
Total Centuries/Votes	*193*

of army units. Army service meant that the patricians now needed the collective cooperation of the plebs to a far greater extent than they had before.

The plebeians also found strength in numbers and organization in another way. They formed their own assembly, known as the **Council of the Plebs**. Its organization was based on twenty geographical tribes into which the people were divided based on where they lived; each tribe had one vote. It issued pronouncements, or **plebiscites**, that were binding only on the plebeians, although they could become Roman law if ratified by the Senate and one of the other popular assemblies. Each year the plebeians also elected ten **Tribunes of the Plebs**, whose responsibility was to defend the interests of the plebeians against patrician oppression and to preside over the meetings of the Council of the Plebs. The plebs swore to avenge themselves on any patrician who ever harmed a Tribune. The Tribunes appropriated the authority to say **"veto"** ("I forbid") if the patricians ever did anything against plebeian interests. On such occasions, the plebs went on strike until the Tribune could be induced to remove his veto. In extreme cases the plebs could threaten to secede from the state and to withdraw to the Aventine Hill and establish their own nation. The plebs sometimes did so when Rome was under military threat as a means of coercing the patricians into making political concessions.

In the United States, only chief executive officers, such as the president and governors, have veto power.

Social and Political Reforms

One of the plebeians' earliest demands was to know the laws. The patricians, too, might have seen benefits in this. As a result, in 451 BCE the patricians appointed a board of ten men, the **Decemvirs**, who were charged with writing down the laws. After being reappointed for a second term in 450 BCE, the Decemvirs issued the famous **Twelve Tables** of Roman law, which, with few exceptions, did not create new law but merely recorded existing law. They stated the fundamental concepts of Roman law, such as *mancipatio* (transferring ownership over property), *stipulatio* (making a contract between two parties), *emancipatio* (freeing someone from slavery), and *nexum* (reducing someone to slavery). The code also covered criminal law, with crimes such as arson, casting spells, and stealing crops being punishable by death, but because there were no state police or prosecutors, criminal prosecutions had to be instituted by the wronged parties themselves.

The laws offered little redress for plebeian complaints. For example, they still permitted those who fell into debt to be sold as slaves; the law even specified that a defaulted debtor had to be bound with at least fifteen pounds of chains. And to add insult to injury, one of the new laws added in 450 BCE prohibited marriages between patricians and plebeians and thus blocked the only means by which members of a plebeian family could enter the aristocracy, for if a plebeian woman married a patrician man, their children would be patricians. The plebeians were sufficiently incensed that they seceded. In 449, the patricians responded with the Valerio-Horatian Laws (named after the Consuls Valerius and Horatius, who had introduced them), which acknowledged

TABLE 3.2 COMPOSITION OF ROMAN POPULAR ASSEMBLIES

Name	Members	Unit	No. of Units	Membership Basis
Curiate Assembly	All citizens	*Curia*	30	Family
Centuriate Assembly	All citizens	Century	198	Property
Council of the Plebs	Plebeians	Tribe	20/35*	Residence
Council of the People	All citizens	Tribe	20/35*	Residence

*The number of geographical tribes grew from 20 to 35 (4 urban and 31 rural) as Rome expanded.

the validity of plebiscites, subject to ratification by the Senate; guaranteed the *sacrosanctitas* (sacrosanctity, or personal security) of the Tribunes of the Plebs; and allowed the Council of the Plebs to appoint two Aediles, who oversaw the markets, streets, and public buildings. At the same time, it seems, a new popular assembly, the **Council of the People by Tribes**, was introduced, modeled on the Council of the Plebs but also including the patricians. It was more inclusive than the Curiate Assembly because it automatically included new citizens who did not belong to one of the family-based *curiae*.

Continued agitation by the most influential plebeians brought the Canuleian Law, named after a Tribune of the Plebs, Canuleius, which in 445 BCE repealed the ban on intermarriage. But the patricians balked when the plebeians insisted on being given a realistic opportunity to be Consuls. Being unable to contemplate the idea of having a plebeian Consul, the patricians responded in 444 by abolishing the consulate altogether and replacing it with the office of Military Tribune with Consular Powers. At least two, and as many as six, were appointed each year. The new office absorbed the military functions of the Consuls and could be held by plebeians, who, after their terms of service, then entered the Senate. Meanwhile, other consular duties were transferred to another new official, the **Censor**, two of whom were appointed every five years by the Centuriate Assembly. They served for eighteen months and ranked above the Consuls. It was their responsibility to take the census of citizen property, to appoint new members to the Senate, to let out contracts for public works construction, and to oversee public morality. Only patricians were chosen for this office. Thus, even though the patricians were willing to make concessions to plebeian demands for increased opportunity when circumstances demanded, they did so only grudgingly and in small doses.

The Censors' moral duties survive in modern "censoring."

Consolidation of Senate Authority

Nevertheless, as the years went by, many influential plebeians became members of the Senate and were able to participate in truly substantive decision making. Eventually, this factor, combined with intermarriage, led the patricians and these powerful plebeians to make common cause. In 367, the **Licinio-Sextian Law** restored the consulate: henceforward one of the Consuls would be a plebeian. But here, too, the patricians fought a rear-guard action to retain something of their past privileges. They introduced at the same time two new Aediles to oversee public works and the Urban **Praetor**, an official with *imperium* who had jurisdiction over legal cases involving Roman citizens. Initially, the new offices were open only to patricians as a means of limiting plebeian authority. But such ploys were short-lived. In 356 BCE, the first plebeian Dictator was appointed; in 351 BCE, the office of Censor was opened to plebs; and in 337 the praetorship was as well. The plebeians achieved final victory in 287, when the **Hortensian Law** gave the plebiscites issued by the Council of the Plebs' independent authority binding on the whole state without the need to get Senate approval. By then, the Conflict of the Orders was unquestionably at an end.

The end result of these developments was an evolution from an aristocracy, in which Rome was governed essentially just by the patricians, to an oligarchy, in which patricians and influential plebeians served together in the Senate and shared the rule. Eventually, all ex-office holders became members. Within the Senate, senators jockeyed for status. Those whose ancestors had ever been Consuls became an inside group called the **Nobles**, who jealously guarded access to the consulate. Only the most able and ambitious non-nobles were able to become Consuls, and this was so unusual that one who did so was designated a *novus homo*, or **New Man**. Every five years, the Censors drew up a list of the Senate in rank order. Every senator's ambition was to be named the *Princeps senatus*, or First Man of the Senate, for all of the other senators then would have to yield precedence to him. The key to the successful functioning of the government lay in the willingness of the senators to share the rule among themselves.

TABLE 3.3   OFFICIALS OF THE ROMAN REPUBLIC (AS OF 197 BCE)

Title	No.	Duties	Term of Office
Annually Elected Officials (in rank order)			
Consul	2	Lead Roman army, preside at assemblies	1 year
Praetor	6	Oversee law courts, govern some provinces	1 year
Aedile	4	Oversee public works and markets in Rome	1 year
Quaestor	6	Oversee treasury and financial matters	1 year
Tribune	10	Preside over Council of the Plebs	1 year
Nonannual Officials			
Dictator	1	Outranks Consuls in grave emergencies	6 months maximum
Censor	2	Property assessments, appoint senators	18 months
Proconsul	varies	Has the authority but not title of a Consul outside of Rome	varies

Roman Law

From the very beginning of Rome, the Romans believed in the concept of "**rule of law**" to which everyone in Roman society, from the highest-ranking senator to the least distinguished plebeian, was subject. Their inherent belief in the role of law made the Romans into the greatest lawmakers of the ancient world. This sense of subordination to the law continued throughout Roman history and was one of the great contributions that Romans made not only to western civilization but also to world civilization.

In "rule of law," law is an overarching guiding principle; in "rule by law," law is simply a tool used by the government to enforce its authority.

In the Republic, only the popular assemblies had the constitutional authority to issue laws binding on the entire Roman state, but the powers of the assemblies were very limited. They could not initiate legislation, which was presented to them by their presiding magistrates, either a Consul or Tribune; nor could they discuss or emend measures presented to them. All they could do was vote "yes" or "no." Real lawmaking went on behind the scenes, and real legislative power lay in the hands of the Senate. Although the Senate had no constitutional authority to issue legislation—that right belonged only to the popular assemblies—it had a very powerful advisory position. A Consul or Tribune who wanted to introduce a law was expected to receive Senate approval before presenting it to an assembly. The Senate thus issued *senatus consulta*, Resolutions of the Senate, which were advice to magistrates or interpretations of existing Roman law. In practice, the advice was almost always followed, and these Resolutions of the Senate gained the de facto force of law. The Senate also performed important executive functions, including overseeing state expenditures and managing foreign policy. As a consequence, the Senate was the real governing body of the Republic.

Technically, Roman jus civile (civil law, or "the law of citizens") applied to what we in the modern day would consider to be both civil and criminal law.

Roman private law was administered by the Urban Praetor, who heard cases involving citizens, and the Peregrine Praetor, an office introduced in 246 BCE to hear cases involving foreigners. The Urban Praetors put into practice the concepts embodied in the private law of the Twelve Tables and developed standard *formulae* (legal forms) for different kinds of legal actions involving, for example, purchases, sales, contracts, property disputes, personal injuries, and so on. If a *formula* did not already exist for a particular kind of case, the Praetor created one. All of the *formulae* were collected into a constantly expanding Praetor's Edict. Lawsuits took place in two phases: in the *actio* (action) phase, the Praetor himself drew up the *formula*, which included the plaintiff's claim and the penalty that the accused stood to suffer. For the *judicium* (judgment) phase, the Praetor then appointed a *judex* (judge), who could be anyone, to try the case based only on what was in the *formula*. At the trial, litigants and lawyers called witnesses, presented evidence, cited legal precedents, and made their arguments. The final decision lay solely in the hands of the judge, and there was no appeal.

STRUGGLING TO SURVIVE (509–350 BCE)

The early years of the Republic were a struggle for survival as the Romans not only fought off Etruscan attempts to retake the city but also competed with neighboring Latins and Italic peoples for control of **Latium**. The situation was exacerbated in 390 BCE when Rome was attacked by a raiding party of Gauls from Northern Italy.

Early Conflicts

According to an alternate version of the legend, Lars Porsenna actually did recapture Rome, and the Etruscans then were expelled a second time.

During the fifth century BCE, the combined army of patricians and plebeians defended Rome against attacks from Etruscans, Latins, and Italian peoples such as the Aequi, Volsci, and Hernici. Many heroic legends arose. For example, it was believed that in 508 BCE the Etruscan king Lars Porsenna of Clusium besieged Rome in an attempt to recapture the city. A young Roman patrician named Gaius Mucius was sent by the Senate to assassinate Porsenna, but he failed and was captured. Mucius told the king that three hundred Roman young men had sworn an oath to kill him, and even if he had failed one of them surely would succeed. Then, to demonstrate Roman commitment, Mucius put his right hand into a fire on an altar and did not flinch while it was burned to a crisp. Impressed with the young man's resolve, Porsenna released him and made peace with the Romans. Young Mucius, meanwhile, then gained the nickname "Scaevola," or "Lefty."

Soon thereafter, in or about 498, the Romans were said to have engaged in the Battle of Lake Regillus with the Latin League, a confederation of Latin cities, for control of Latium. According to legend, the Romans were on the verge of defeat when the heroes Castor and Pollux came to their rescue. In the resultant Cassian Treaty, the first treaty made by the Romans, the Romans and Latins agreed to be equal partners in any future wars, to share any war booty, and to share legal rights. The Romans also built at this time a temple to Castor and Pollux, part of which still survives. There also was the tale of the ex-Consul Cincinnatus, who was plowing his fields in 458 BCE when word came that a Roman army was trapped by the Aequi and that he had been appointed Dictator. Cincinnatus raised a force of old men and boys, rescued the army, and then went back to plowing his fields after only sixteen days as Dictator, the very model of Roman virtue. Whether these patriotic tales actually occurred is beside the point; Romans believed that they had happened and used them to establish a value system revolving around the importance of doing one's duty for the Roman state.

All that survives of the original fifth-century BCE Temple of Castor and Pollux in the Roman Forum is the foundation; the rest is the result of several subsequent reconstructions, the most recent dating to the emperor Tiberius (14–37 CE).

It was not until 396 BCE, with the defeat of the Etruscan city of Veii, that the Romans were able markedly to increase their territory. The newly won land was distributed to landless plebeians in order to make them eligible for military service and remove a potential source of unrest from Rome. Immediately after this victory, however, Roman fortunes took a decided turn for the worse.

The Gallic Sack of Rome

In 390 BCE a raiding party of Celts from the Po River valley, called "Gauls" by the Romans, attacked Rome. The Roman army, packed together in the traditional phalanx formation, was completely flabbergasted by the horrifying, undisciplined charge of the howling Celtic warriors. The Romans turned tail and ran, leaving the Gauls to occupy, sack, and burn the city of Rome, destroying in the process any records, such as the original copy of the Twelve Tables, that existed. Only by paying a hefty ransom were the Romans able to induce the Gauls to depart. According to one account, after the Romans complained that the ransom paid to the Gauls was too great, the Gallic chieftain Brennus threw his sword onto the scales and said, "Vae victis"—that is, "Woe to the conquered."

The Roman equivalent of the English saying "We've got our backs to the wall" was "We're back to the triarii."

The sack of Rome in 390 BCE by the Gauls subsequently was commemorated yearly as a *dies ater*, or "dark day." The Romans swore that such a humiliation would never happen again. To this end, they protected the city by building the massive Servian Wall, later attributed to King Servius Tullius, and restructured the army, abandoning the old phalanx in favor of a more flexible tactical structure based on 120-man units known as **maniples**, which could act independently and accommodate themselves to the landscape. In addition, the need to pull together after the sack no doubt was another one of the factors that contributed to the final settlement between the patricians and plebeians in 367 BCE, with the agreement that henceforth one Consul must be a plebeian.

After the Gallic sack, the Romans were back on the defensive as their neighbors attempted to benefit from the Roman defeat. It took some forty years for the Romans to recover their strength and once again become a significant power in central Italy.

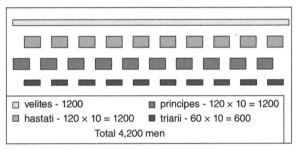

velites - 1200	principes - 120 × 10 = 1200
hastati - 120 × 10 = 1200	triarii - 60 × 10 = 600
Total 4,200 men	

After the Gallic sack of Rome in 390 BCE, the battle formation of Roman *legions* was reconfigured to two lines of 120-man maniples and one line of 60-man maniples. The first line of young *hastati* ("spear men") went into action first. If things got tough they could withdraw through the second line of more experienced men, the *principes* ("leading men"), who then went into action. If they could not win the battle, then the *hastati* and *principes*, armed with the *pilum* (throwing spear) and *gladius* (short sword), would withdraw behind the veteran *triarii* ("third-line men"), armed with the long *hasta*, or thrusting spear, who would simply try to hold the enemy off. A screen of young *velites* ("speedy men") serving as skirmishers started out in front of the formation; they withdrew to the rear as soon as the real fighting started.

THE SERVIAN WALL

One of the consequences of the Gallic sack of Rome was that it made the Romans even more sensitive to the threats that foreign enemies could present and to the need to defend the city. Unable to deal with such a huge undertaking themselves, the Romans hired Greek stonemasons from Campania to build a large stone wall to enclose a city that had greatly expanded since the regal period. The Greek masons used huge polygonal (squared-off) stone blocks of yellowish tuff (a volcanic rock) imported from Veii to construct the wall. The blocks were laid as headers (lengthwise) and stretchers (with the butt end out) to strengthen the wall. The finished wall had sixteen gates and was seven miles (eleven kilometers) long and up to thirty-three feet (ten meters) high and twelve feet (3.6 meters) wide. Parts of the wall had either a ditch in front or an earthen ramp behind to increase its effective height.

Later in their history, the Romans, out of their desire to retroject great events from their history as far into the past as possible, called the wall the Servian Wall, attributing it to King Servius back in the sixth century BCE.

The wall stood the Romans in good stead; in 211 BCE, during the Second Punic War, when the Carthaginian general Hannibal marched his army right up to it but could not break through. It continued to be maintained until the end of the Roman Republic. The next wall built to protect Rome would not be constructed for another 650 years, attesting to the future success the Romans had in protecting themselves from foreign threats.

Only bits and pieces of the wall survive, scattered about the modern city. The biggest chunk stands next to the main train station.

⇦ LOOKING BACK

The Romans' shared values, sense of social responsibility, and belief in the concept of the "rule of law" allowed them to make accommodations between patricians and plebeians that avoided violence and provided opportunities for social advancement. Their form of government co-opted the abilities of powerful and ambitious senators who somehow found a way to work together. At the same time, the Romans also had to contend with threats from their neighbors that culminated in the sack of Rome by the Gauls in 390 BCE.

LOOKING AHEAD ⇨

By 350 BCE, the Rome had recovered its strength. Only then did the Romans begin the long road to becoming the strongest power first in Italy, and then in the entire Mediterranean.

FURTHER READING

Broughton, T. Robert S. *The Magistrates of the Roman Republic.* 3 vols. New York: American Philological Association, 1951.

Byrd, Robert C. *The Senate of the Roman Republic.* Honolulu: Univ. Press of the Pacific, 2001.

Cary, M., and H. H. Scullard. *A History of Rome down to the Reign of Constantine.* 3rd ed. New York: St. Martin's Press, 1975.

Cornell, Tim. *The Beginnings of Rome: Italy and Rome from the Bronze Age to the Punic Wars (c. 1000–264 BC).* New York: Routledge, 1995.

Farney, Gary D., *Ethnic Identity and Aristocratic Competition in Republican Rome.* Cambridge, UK: Cambridge Univ. Press, 2007.

Raaflaub, Kurt, ed. *Social Struggles in Archaic Rome: New Perspectives on the Conflict of the Orders.* Berkeley: University of California Press, 1986; updated Oxford: Blackwell, 2005.

Vecchi, Italo. *Italian Cast Coinage, A Descriptive Catalogue of the Cast Coinage of Rome and Italy.* 2nd ed. London: London Ancient Coins, 2013.

SOURCES

THE "TWELVE TABLES"

The monetary fines in later editions of the "Twelve Tables" were cited in "asses," large copper coins that were not introduced until ca. 280 BCE, attesting to the slowness with which the Romans adopted an actual currency. The "as" weighed one pound of copper. Such a cumbersome coin was not useful for large transactions but would have been suitable for the payment of ritualized amounts such as those found in the Twelve Tables.

Soon after the establishment of the Roman Republic in 509 BCE, the plebeians (the unprivileged citizens) began to agitate against the patricians (the Roman aristocrats) to have greater rights. One of their earliest demands was to know the laws. As a result, in 451 BCE the patricians appointed a board of ten men, the Decemvirs, who were charged with writing down the laws. After being reappointed for a second term in 450 BCE, the Decemvirs issued the famous "Twelve Tables" of Roman law, which, with few exceptions, did not create new law but merely recorded existing law. They stated the fundamental concepts of Roman law, such as *mancipatio* (transferring ownership over property), *stipulatio* (making a contract), *emancipatio* (freeing someone from slavery), and *nexum* (reducing someone to slavery). The code also covered criminal law, with crimes such as arson, casting spells, and stealing crops being punishable by death. Because there were no state police or prosecutors, criminal prosecutions had to be initiated by the wronged parties themselves. The Twelve Tables can be compared with other ancient law codes, such as those of Ur-Nammu and Hammurabi in Mesopotamia and of the Hebrews.

Source: S. P. Scott, trans., *The Civil Law Including the Twelve Tables, the Institutes of Gaius, the Rules of Ulpian, the Opinions of Paulus, the Enactments, Vol. 1* (Cincinnati: Central Trust, 1932).

Table I. *Concerning the summons to court.*

Law I. When anyone summons another before the tribunal of a judge, the latter must, without hesitation, immediately appear.

Law II. If, after having been summoned, he does not appear, or refuses to come before the tribunal of the judge, let the party who summoned him call upon any citizens who are present to bear witness. Then let him seize his reluctant adversary; so that he may be brought into court, as a captive, by apparent force.

Law III. When anyone who has been summoned to court is guilty of evasion, or attempts to flee, let him be arrested by the plaintiff.

Law IIII. If bodily infirmity or advanced age should prevent the party summoned to court from appearing, let him who summoned him furnish him with an animal as a means of transport. If he is unwilling to accept it, the plaintiff cannot legally be compelled to provide the defendant with a vehicle constructed of boards or a covered litter.

Law V. If he who is summoned has either a sponsor or a defender, let him be dismissed, and his representative can take his place in court.

Law VI. The defender, or the surety[1] of a wealthy man, must himself be rich, but anyone who desires to do so can come to the assistance of a person who is poor and occupy his place.

Law VII. When litigants wish to settle their dispute among themselves, even while they are on their way to appear before the Praetor,[2] they shall have the right to make peace. Whatever agreement they enter into shall be considered just and shall be confirmed.

Law VIII. If the plaintiff and defendant do not settle their dispute, as above mentioned, let them state their cases either in the Comitium[3] or the Forum, by making a brief statement in the presence of the judge,[4] between the rising of the sun and noon, and, both of them being present, let them speak so that each party may hear.

Law IX. In the afternoon, let the judge grant the right to bring the action,[5] and render his decision in the presence of the plaintiff and the defendant.

Law X. The setting of the sun shall be the extreme limit of time within which a judge must render his decision.

Table II. *Concerning judgments and thefts.*

Law I. When issue has been joined in the presence of the judge, sureties and their substitutes for appearance at the trial must be furnished on both sides. The parties shall appear in person, unless prevented by disease of a serious character, or where vows that they have taken must be discharged to the gods, or where the proceedings are interrupted through their absence on business for the State, or where a day has been appointed by them to meet an alien.[6]

Law II. If any of the above-mentioned occurrences takes place, that is, if one of the parties is seriously ill, or a vow has to be performed, or one of them is absent on business for the State, or a day has been appointed for an interview with an alien, so that the judge, the arbiter, or the defendant is prevented from being present, and the furnishing of security is postponed on this account, the hearing of the case shall be deferred.

Law III. Where anyone is deprived of the evidence of a witness let him call him with a loud voice in front of his house, on three market-days.[7]

Law IIII. Where anyone commits a theft by night, and having been caught in the act is killed, he is legally killed.

Law V. If anyone commits a theft during the day, and is caught in the act, he shall be whipped, and given up as a slave to the person against whom the theft was committed. If he who perpetrated the theft is a slave, he shall be beaten with rods and hurled from the Tarpeian Rock.[8] If he is under the

---

[1] Someone who ensures that a person will appear in court and abide by the settlement.

[2] The Roman magistrate who ranked just below the Consul and oversaw the Roman court system; this office was not created until 367 BCE.

[3] The area of the Forum where popular assemblies met.

[4] The Praetor.

[5] That is, the legal case.

[6] A non-Roman.

[7] In the Roman calendar, market days occurred every eight days.

[8] A rocky prominence eighty feet high on the south side of the Capitoline Hill.

age of puberty, the Praetor shall decide whether he shall be whipped and surrendered by way of reparation for the injury.

Law VI. When any persons commit a theft during the day and in the light, whether they be freemen or slaves, of full age or minors, and attempt to defend themselves with weapons, or with any kind of implements, and the party against whom the violence is committed raises the cry of thief, and calls upon other persons, if any are present, to come to his assistance; and this is done, and the thieves are killed by him in the defense of his person and property, it is legal, and no liability attaches to the homicide.

Law VII. If a theft be detected by means of a dish and a girdle,[9] it is the same as manifest theft,[10] and shall be punished as such.

Law VIII. When anyone accuses and convicts another of theft that is not manifest, and no stolen property is found, judgment shall be rendered to compel the thief to pay double the value of what was stolen.

Law IX. Where anyone secretly cuts down trees belonging to another, he shall pay twenty-five *asses*[11] for each tree cut down.

Law X. Where anyone, in order to favor a thief, makes a compromise for the loss sustained, he cannot afterward prosecute him for theft.

Law XI. Stolen property shall always be his to whom it formerly belonged, nor can the lawful owner ever be deprived of it by long possession, without regard to its duration, nor can it ever be acquired by another, no matter in what way this may take place.

Table III. *Concerning Property that is Lent.*

Law I. When anyone, with fraudulent intent, appropriates property deposited with him for safe keeping, he shall be condemned to pay double its value.

Law II. When anyone collects interest on money loaned at a higher rate per annum than that of the *unciae*,[12] he shall pay quadruple the amount by way of penalty.

Law III. An alien cannot acquire the property of another by usucaption,[13] but a Roman citizen, who is the lawful owner of the property, always shall have the right to demand it from him.

Law IIII. Where anyone, having acknowledged a debt, has a judgment rendered against him requiring payment, thirty days shall be given to him in which to pay the money and satisfy the judgment.

Law V. After the term of thirty days granted by the law to debtors who have had judgment rendered against them has expired, and in the meantime, they have not satisfied the judgment, their creditors shall be permitted to forcibly seize them and bring them again into court.

Law VI. When a defendant, after thirty days have elapsed, is brought into court a second time by the plaintiff, and does not satisfy the judgment, or, in the meantime, another party, or his surety does not pay it out of his own money, the creditor, or the plaintiff, after the debtor has been delivered up to him, can take the latter with him and bind him or place him in fetters, provided his chains are not of more than fifteen pounds weight; he can, however, place him in others that are lighter, if he desires to do so.

Law VII. If, after a debtor has been delivered up to his creditor, or has been placed in chains, he desires to obtain food and has the means, he shall be permitted to support himself out of his own property. But if he has nothing on which to live, his creditor, who holds him in chains, shall give him a pound of grain every day, or he can give him more than a pound, if he wishes to do so.

Law VIII. In the meantime, the party who has been delivered up to his creditor can make terms with him. If he does not, he shall be kept in chains for sixty days, and for three consecutive market-days he shall be brought before the Praetor in the place of assembly in the Forum, and the amount

---

[9] Apparently someone making an accusation of theft could search the premises of the accused dressed only in a girdle, for decency's sake, and carrying a dish into which any stolen property could be put. This would ensure that the accuser was not perpetrating a false accusation by bringing in the supposedly stolen goods himself.

[10] Being caught in the act.

[11] The *as*, a copper coin initially weighing a pound of copper, was not introduced until ca. 280 BCE.

---

[12] The *uncia*, or ounce, was one-twelfth of a pound, or eight and one-third percent.

[13] To gain ownership of something by using it for a specified period of time.

of the judgment against him shall be publicly proclaimed.

Law IX. After he has been kept in chains for sixty days, and the sum for which he is liable has been three times publicly proclaimed in the Forum, he shall be condemned to be reduced to slavery by him to whom he was delivered up; or, if the latter prefers, he can be sold beyond the Tiber.[14]

Law X. Where a party is delivered up to several persons, on account of a debt, after he has been exposed in the Forum on three market days, they shall be permitted to divide their debtor into different parts, if they desire to do so; and if anyone of them should, by the division, obtain more or less than he is entitled to, he shall not be responsible.

Table IV. *Concerning the Rights of a Father, and of Marriage.*

Law I. A father shall have the right of life and death over his son born in lawful marriage, and also shall have the power to render him independent, after he has been sold[15] three times.

Law II. If a father sells his son three times, the latter shall be free from paternal authority.

Law III. A father shall immediately put to death a son recently born who is a monster or has a form different from that of members of the human race.[16]

Law IIII. When a woman brings forth a son within the next ten months after the death of her husband, he shall be born in lawful marriage, and shall be the legal heir of his estate.

Table V. *Concerning Estates and Guardianships.*

Law I. No matter in what way the head of a household may dispose of his estate, and appoint heirs to the same, or guardians; it shall have the force and effect of law.

Law II. Where a father dies intestate, without leaving any proper heir, his nearest agnate,[17] or,

if there is none, the next of kin among his family, shall be his heir.

Law III. When a freedman dies intestate, and does not leave any proper heir, but his patron, or the children of the latter survive him; the inheritance of the estate of the freedman shall be adjudged to the next of kin of the patron.

Law IIII. When a creditor or a debtor dies, his heirs can only sue, or be sued, in proportion to their shares in the estate; and any claims, or remaining property, shall be divided among them in the same proportion.

Law V. Where co-heirs desire to obtain their shares of the property of an estate, which has not yet been divided, it shall be divided. In order that this may be properly done and no loss be sustained by the litigants, the Praetor shall appoint three arbiters, who can give to each one that to which he is entitled in accordance with law and equity.

Law VI. When the head of a family dies intestate, and leaves a proper heir who has not reached the age of puberty, his nearest agnate shall obtain the guardianship.

Law VII. When no guardian has been appointed for an insane person, or a spendthrift, his nearest agnates, or if there are none, his other relatives, must take charge of his property.

Table VI. *Concerning Ownership and Possession.*

Law I. When anyone contracts a legal obligation with reference to his property, or sells it, by making a verbal statement or agreement concerning the same, this shall have the force and effect of law. If the party should afterward deny his statements, and legal proceedings are instituted, he shall, by way of penalty, pay double the value of the property in question.

Law II. Where a slave is ordered to be free by a will, upon his compliance with a certain condition, and he complies with the condition; or if, after having paid his price to the purchaser, he claims his liberty, he shall be free.

Law III. Where property has been sold, even though it may have been delivered, it shall by no means be acquired by the purchaser until the price

---

[14] So as not to become an object of pity and create social unrest.

[15] And then set free.

[16] This practice can be compared to the inspection of newborn infants at Sparta.

[17] "Agnates" were male relatives from the same *gens*, or extended family.

has been paid, or a surety or a pledge has been given, and the vendor satisfied in this manner.

Law IIII. Immovable property shall be acquired by usucaption after the lapse of two years; other property after the lapse of one year.

Law V. Where a woman, who has not been united to a man in marriage, lives with him for an entire year without the usucaption of her being interrupted for three nights, she shall pass into his power as his legal wife.[18]

Law VI. Where parties have a dispute with reference to property before the tribunal of the Praetor, both of them shall be permitted to state their claims in the presence of witnesses.

Law VII. Where anyone demands freedom for another against the claim of servitude, the Praetor shall render judgment in favor of liberty.

Law VIII. No material forming part of either a building or a vineyard shall be removed therefrom. Anyone who, without the knowledge or consent of the owner, attaches a beam or anything else to his house or vineyard shall be condemned to pay double its value.

Law IX. Timbers that have been dressed and prepared for building purposes, but which have not yet been attached to a building or a vineyard can legally be recovered by the owner, if they are stolen from him.

Law X. If a husband desires to divorce his wife, and dissolve his marriage, he must give a reason for doing so.

Table VII. *Concerning Crimes.*

Law I. If a quadruped causes injury to anyone, let the owner tender him the estimated amount of the damage, and if he is unwilling to accept it, the owner shall, by way of reparation, surrender the animal that caused the injury.

Law II. If you cause any unlawful damage accidentally and unintentionally, you must make good the loss, either by tendering what has caused it or by payment.

Law III. Anyone who, by means of incantations and magic arts, prevents grain or crops of any kind belonging to another from growing shall be sacrificed to Ceres.[19]

Law IIII. If anyone who has arrived at puberty, secretly, and by night, destroys or cuts and appropriates to his own use the crop of another, which the owner of the land has obtained laboriously by plowing and the cultivation of the soil, he shall be sacrificed to Ceres, and hung.

If he is under the age of puberty, and not yet old enough to be accountable, he shall be whipped, in the discretion of the Praetor, and shall make good the loss by paying double its amount.

Law V. Anyone who turns cattle on the land of another, for the purpose of pasture, shall surrender the cattle by way of reparation.

Law VI. Anyone who, knowingly and maliciously, burns a building, or a heap of grain left near a building, after having been placed in chains and whipped shall be put to death by fire. If, however, he caused the damage by accident and without malice, he shall make it good, or, if he has not the means to do so, he shall receive a lighter punishment.

Law VII. When a person, in any way, causes an injury to another that is not serious he shall be punished with a fine of twenty *asses*.

Law VIII. When anyone publicly abuses another in a loud voice or writes a poem for the purpose of insulting him or rendering him infamous,[20] he shall be beaten with a rod until he dies.

Law IX. When anyone breaks a member of another, and is unwilling to come to make a settlement with him, he shall be punished by the law of retaliation.[21]

Law X. When anyone knocks a tooth out of the gum of a freeman, he shall be fined three hundred *asses*; if he knocks one out of the gum of a slave, he shall be fined a hundred and fifty *asses*.

---

[18] That is, that he will gain legal authority over her; otherwise, she remained under the legal authority of her father or, if her father were deceased, of her father's male relatives.

[19] The goddess of grain, Demeter to the Greeks.

[20] Personal honor was very important and disrespect of one's personal honor was a grave offence.

[21] That is, by the imposition of the same injury, the "eye for an eye" law, as in the Old Testament of the Bible.

Law XI. If anyone, after having been asked, appears either as a witness or a balance-holder at a sale or the execution of a will and refuses to testify when this is required to prove the genuineness of the transaction, he shall become infamous[22] and cannot afterward give evidence.

Law XII. Anyone who gives false testimony shall be hurled from the Tarpeian Rock.

Law XIII. If anyone knowingly and maliciously kills a freeman, he shall be guilty of a capital crime. If he kills him by accident, without malice and unintentionally, let him substitute a ram to be sacrificed publicly by way of expiation for the homicide of the deceased and for the purpose of appeasing the children of the latter.

Law XIV. Anyone who annoys another by means of magic incantations or diabolical arts, and renders him inactive, or ill, or who prepares or administers poison to him, is guilty of a capital crime, and shall be punished with death.

Law XV. Anyone who kills an ascendant[23] shall have his head wrapped in a cloth, and, after having been sewed up in a sack, shall be thrown into the water.

Law XVI. Where anyone is guilty of fraud in the administration of a guardianship, he shall be considered infamous; and, even after the guardianship has been terminated, if any theft is proved to have been committed, he shall, by the payment of double damages, be compelled to make good the loss that he caused.

Law XVII. When a patron defrauds his client, he shall be dedicated to the infernal gods.[24]

Table VIII. *Concerning the Laws of Real Property.*

Law I. A space of two feet and a half must be left between neighboring buildings.

Law II. Societies and associations that have the right to assemble can make, promulgate, and confirm for themselves such contracts and rules as they may desire, provided nothing is done by them contrary to public enactments or which does not violate the common law.[25]

Law III. The space of five feet shall be left between adjoining fields, by means of which the owners can visit their property, or drive and plow around it. No one shall ever have the right to acquire this space by usucaption.

Law IIII. If any persons are in possession of adjoining fields and a dispute arises with reference to the boundaries of the same, the Praetor shall appoint three arbiters, who shall take cognizance of the case. After the boundaries have been established, he shall assign to each party that to which he is entitled.

Law V. When a tree overhangs the land of a neighbor so as to cause injury by its branches and its shade, it shall be cut off fifteen feet from the ground.

Law VI. When the fruit of a tree falls upon the premises of a neighbor, the owner of the tree shall have a right to gather and remove it.

Law VII. When rain falls upon the land of one person in such a quantity as to cause water to rise and injure the property of another, the Praetor shall appoint three arbiters for the purpose of confining the water and providing against damage to the other party.

Law VIII. Where a road runs in a straight line, it shall be eight feet, and where it curves, it shall be sixteen feet in width.

Law IX. When a man's land lies adjacent to the highway he can enclose it in any way that he chooses; but if he neglects to do so, any other person can drive an animal over the land wherever he pleases.

Table IX. *Concerning Public Law.*

Law I. No privileges or statutes shall be enacted in favor of private persons, to the injury of others contrary to the law common to all citizens, and which individuals, no matter of what rank, have a right to make use of.

Law II. The same rights shall be conferred upon, and the same laws have been enacted for good and steadfast Roman citizens, shall be considered to

---

[22] The punishment of *infamia* brought a diminution of one's citizenship rights.

[23] An older male relative.

[24] That is, sacrificed to the gods of the underworld.

---

[25] The right to form private associations was severely restricted in the future.

have been enacted for all the people residing in and beyond Latium.[26]

Law III. When a judge, or an arbiter appointed to hear a case, accepts money, or other gifts, for the purpose of influencing his decision, he shall suffer the penalty of death.

Law IIII. No decision with reference to the life or liberty of a Roman citizen shall be rendered except by the vote of the Greater Comitia.[27]

Law V. Public accusers in capital cases shall be appointed by the people.

Law VI. If anyone should cause nocturnal assemblies in the city, he shall be put to death.

Law VII. If anyone should stir up war against his country, or delivers a Roman citizen into the hands of the enemy, he shall be punished with death.

Table X. *Concerning Religious Law.*

Law I. An oath shall have the greatest force and effect for the purpose of compelling good faith.

Law II. Where a family adopts private religious rites every member of it can, afterward, always make use of them.

Law III. No burial or cremation of a corpse shall take place in a city.

Law IIII. No greater expenses or mourning than is proper shall be permitted in funeral ceremonies.

Law V. No one shall, hereafter, exceed the limit established by these laws for the celebration of funeral rites.

Law VI. Wood employed for the purpose of constructing a funeral pyre shall not be finished, but shall be rough and unpolished.

Law VII. When a corpse is prepared for burial at home, not more than three women with their heads covered with mourning veils shall be permitted to perform this service. The body may be enveloped in purple robes, and when borne outside, ten flute players, at the most, may accompany the funeral procession.

Law VIII. Women shall not during a funeral lacerate their faces, or tear their cheeks with their nails, nor shall they utter loud cries bewailing the dead.

Law IX. No bones shall be taken from the body of a person who is dead, or from his ashes after cremation, in order that funeral ceremonies may again be held elsewhere. When, however, anyone dies in a foreign country, or is killed in war, a part of his remains may be transferred to the burial place of his ancestors.

Law X. The body of no dead slave shall be anointed, nor shall any drinking take place at his funeral, nor shall a banquet of any kind be instituted in his honor.

Law XI. No wine flavored with myrrh, or any other precious beverage, shall be poured upon a corpse while it is burning, nor shall the funeral pyre be sprinkled with wine.

Law XII. Large wreaths shall not be borne at a funeral; nor shall perfumes be burned on the altars.

Law XIII. Anyone who has rendered himself deserving of a wreath as the reward of bravery in war or through his having been the victor in public contests or games, whether he has obtained it through his own exertions or by means of others in his own name, and by his own money, through his horses, or his slaves, shall have a right to have the said wreath placed upon his dead body, or upon that of any of his ascendants, as long as the corpse is at his home, as well as when it is borne away, so that, during his funeral rites he may enjoy the honor that in his lifetime he acquired by his bravery or his good fortune.

Law XIV. Only one funeral of an individual can take place, and it shall not be permitted to prepare several biers.

Law XV. Gold, no matter in what form it may be present, shall, by all means, be removed from the corpse at the time of the funeral, but if anyone's teeth should be fastened with gold, it shall be lawful either to burn or bury it with the body.[28]

---

[26] That is, Roman citizens who reside outside of Roman territory.

[27] The Centuriate, or Army, Assembly.

[28] The Romans had two forms of interment, inhumation (the burial of the body intact) and cremation (the burning of the body, followed by the gathering of the bones for burial).

Law XVI. No one, without the knowledge or consent of the owner, shall erect a funeral pyre or a tomb nearer than sixty feet to the building of another.

Law XVII. No one can acquire by usucaption either the vestibule or approach to a tomb or the tomb itself.

Law XVIII. No assembly of the people shall take place during the obsequies of any man distinguished in the State.

Table XI. *Supplement to the Five Preceding Tables.*

Law I. Affairs of great importance shall not be transacted without the vote of the people, with whom rests the power to appoint magistrates, to condemn citizens, and to enact laws. Laws subsequently passed always take preference over former ones.

Law II. Those who belong to the Senatorial Order and are styled Fathers shall not contract marriage with plebeians.[29]

Table XII. *Supplement to the Five Preceding Laws.*

Law I. No one shall render sacred[30] any property with reference to which there is a controversy in court, where issue has already been joined; and if anyone does render such property sacred, he shall pay double its value as a penalty.

Law II. If the claim of anyone in whose favor judgment was rendered after the property had been illegally seized, or after possession of the same had been delivered, is found to be false, the Praetor shall appoint three arbiters by whose award double the amount of the profits shall be restored by him in whose favor the judgment was rendered.

Law III. If a slave, with the knowledge of his master, should commit a theft, or cause damage to anyone, his master shall be given up to the other party by way of reparation for the theft, injury, or damage committed by the slave.

---

[29] A very contentious ruling added to the law code in 450 BCE.

[30] Dedicate to the gods.

LIVY, *FROM THE FOUNDING OF THE CITY*, BOOK 5, CHAPTERS 32–42

It was not until 396 BCE, with the defeat of the Etruscan city of Veii, that the Romans were able markedly to increase their territory. Immediately after this victory, however, Roman fortunes took a decided turn for the worse. In 390 BCE, as graphically recounted by the Roman historian Livy (ca. 60 BCE–17 CE) in his work *From the Founding of the City*, a raiding party of Gauls from the Po River valley attacked Rome. The Roman army, packed together in the traditional phalanx formation, was completely flabbergasted by the horrifying, undisciplined charge of the howling Celtic warriors. The Romans turned tail and ran, leaving the Gauls to occupy, sack, and burn the city of Rome, destroying in the process any written records, such as the original copy of the Twelve Tables, that existed. After the sack, it was only by paying a hefty ransom that the Romans were able to induce the Gauls to depart. According to one account, after the Romans complained that the ransom paid to the Gauls was too great, the Gallic chieftain Brennus threw his sword onto the scales and said, "Vae victis"—that is, "Woe to the conquered." The Romans also patriotically claimed that under the Dictator Camillus they eventually regrouped and defeated the Gauls before they could depart with their treasure. The Romans vowed that such a disaster would never happen again.

Source: Canon Roberts, trans., *Titus Livius. The History of Rome, Vol. 1* (London: Dent, 1905).

In this year[31] Marcus Caedicius, a member of the plebs, reported to the Tribunes that while he was in the Via Nova[32] he heard in the silence of the night a voice more powerful than any human voice bidding the magistrates be told that the Gauls were approaching. No notice was taken of this, partly owing to the humble rank of the informant, and partly because the Gauls were a distant and therefore an unknown nation. Ambassadors came from Clusium[33] begging for assistance against the Gauls. The tradition is that this nation, attracted by the report of the delicious fruits and especially of the wine, a novel pleasure to them, crossed the Alps and occupied the lands formerly cultivated by the Etruscans. As a matter of fact, Gauls crossed into Italy two centuries before they attacked Clusium and took Rome. Nor were the Clusines the first Etruscans with whom the Gallic armies came into conflict; long before that they had fought many battles with the Etruscans who dwelt between the Apennines and the Alps.[34]

The people of Clusium were appalled by this strange war, when they saw the numbers, the extraordinary appearance of the men, and the kind of weapons they used, and heard that the armies of Etruria had been often routed by them on both sides of the Po. Although they had no claim on Rome, either on the ground of alliance or friendly relations, unless it was that they had not defended their kinsmen at Veii[35] against the Romans, they nevertheless sent ambassadors to ask the Senate for assistance. Active assistance they did not obtain. The three sons of M. Fabius Ambustus[36] were sent

---

[31] 390 BCE.

[32] The "New Way," the second road built in Rome; it branched off from the first, the Via Sacra ("Sacred Way"), and ran along the base of the Palatine Hill.

[33] An Etruscan city.

[34] These Gauls had expanded there at the expense of the Etruscans.

[35] An Etruscan city that had been conquered very recently, in 396 BCE, by the Romans.

[36] The *Pontifex Maximus* (Chief priest) of Rome. The Fabii were one of the most distinguished aristocratic families of Rome.

as ambassadors to negotiate with the Gauls and warn them not to attack those from whom they had suffered no injury, who were allies and friends of Rome, and who, if circumstances compelled them, must be defended by the armed force of Rome. They preferred that actual war should be avoided, and that they should make acquaintance with the Gauls, who were strangers to them, in peace rather than in arms.

A peaceable enough mission, had it not contained envoys of a violent temper, more like Gauls than Romans.[37] After they had delivered their instructions in the council of the Gauls, the following reply was given: "Although we are hearing the name of Romans for the first time, we believe nevertheless that you are brave men, because the Clusines are imploring your assistance in their time of danger. Because you prefer to protect your allies against us by negotiation rather than by armed force, we on our side do not reject the peace you offer, on condition that the Clusines cede to us Gauls, who are in need of land, a portion of that territory that they possess to a greater extent than they can cultivate. On any other conditions peace cannot be granted. We wish to receive their reply in your presence, and if territory is refused us we shall fight, while you are still here, so that you may report to those at home how far the Gauls surpass all other men in courage."

The Romans asked them what right they had to demand, under threat of war, territory from those who were its owners, and what business the Gauls had in Etruria. The haughty answer was returned that they carried their right in their weapons, and that everything belonged to the brave. Passions were kindled on both sides; they flew to arms and joined battle. Thereupon, contrary to the Law of Nations,[38] the envoys seized their weapons,

for the Fates[39] already were urging Rome to its ruin. The fact of three of the noblest and bravest Romans fighting in the front line of the Etruscan army could not be concealed, so conspicuous was the valor of the strangers. And what was more, Q. Fabius rode forward at a Gallic chieftain, who was impetuously charging right at the Etruscan standards, ran his spear through his side and slew him. While he was in the act of despoiling the body the Gauls recognized him, and the word was passed through the whole army that it was a Roman ambassador. Forgetting their rage against the Clusines, and breathing threats against the Romans, they sounded the retreat.

Some Gauls were for an instant advance on Rome. The older men thought that ambassadors should first be sent to Rome to make a formal complaint and demand the surrender of the Fabii as satisfaction for this violation of the Law of Nations. After the ambassadors had stated their case, the Senate, while disapproving of the conduct of the Fabii and recognizing the justice of the demand that the barbarians made, were prevented by political interests from placing their convictions on record in the form of a recommendation in the case of men of such high rank. In order, therefore, that the blame for any defeat that might be incurred in a war with the Gauls might not rest on them alone, they referred the consideration of the Gauls' demands to the people. Here personal popularity and influence had so much more weight that the very men whose punishment was under discussion were elected Consular Tribunes[40] for the next year.

The Gauls regarded this procedure as it deserved to be regarded, namely, as an act of

---

[37] A stereotype of Gauls was that they were quick-tempered and violent.

[38] The "Ius gentium" ("Law of Nations") were established customs that applied to all peoples. Ambassadors were supposed to be inviolate and were not supposed to engage in military conflicts while they were on their missions.

---

[39] Goddesses depicted as elderly women who control human destiny: Clotho spun the thread of life, Lachesis measured how long it would be, and Atropos cut it off at the end.

[40] In 444 BCE, when the plebs demanded the right to hold the office of Consul, the patricians abolished the consulate and replaced it with the office of Military Tribune with Consular Powers, which plebeians could hold.

hostility, and after openly threatening war, returned to their people. Burning with rage, for as a nation they cannot control their passions, they seized their standards and hurriedly set out on their march. At the sound of their tumult as they swept by, the affrighted cities flew to arms and the country folk took to flight. Horses and men, spread far and wide, covered an immense tract of country; wherever they went they made it understood by loud shouts that they were going to Rome. But although they were preceded by rumors and by messages from Clusium, and then from one town after another, it was the swiftness of their approach that created most alarm in Rome. An army hastily raised by a levy en masse marched out to meet them. The two forces met hardly eleven miles (eighteen kilometers) from Rome, at a spot where the Allia River, flowing in a very deep channel from the Crustuminian Mountains, joins the river Tiber a little below the road to Crustumerium.[41] The whole country in front and around was now swarming with the enemy, who, being as a nation given to wild outbreaks, had by their hideous howls and discordant clamor filled everything with dreadful noise.

The Consular Tribunes had secured no position for their camp, had constructed no entrenchments behind which to retire, and had shown as much disregard of the gods as of the enemy, for they formed their order of battle without having obtained favorable auspices.[42] They extended their line on either wing to prevent their being outflanked, but even so they could not make their front equal to the enemy's, while by thus thinning their line they weakened the center so that it could hardly keep in touch. On their right was a small eminence that they decided to hold with reserves, and this disposition, although it was the beginning of the panic and flight, proved to be the only means of safety to the fugitives. For Brennus, the Gallic chieftain, fearing some ruse in the scanty numbers of the enemy, and thinking that the rising ground was occupied in order

that the reserves might attack the flank and rear of the Gauls while their front was engaged with the legions, directed his attack upon the reserves, feeling quite certain that if he drove them from their position, his overwhelming numbers would give him an easy victory on the level ground. So not only Fortune but tactics also were on the side of the barbarians.

In the other army there was nothing to remind one of Romans either among the generals or the private soldiers. They were terrified and all they thought about was flight, and so utterly had they lost their heads that a far greater number fled to Veii, although the Tiber lay in their way, rather than by the direct road to Rome, to their wives and children. For a short time the reserves were protected by their position. In the rest of the army, no sooner was the battle-shout heard on their flank by those nearest to the reserves, and then by those at the other end of the line heard in their rear, than they fled, whole and unhurt, almost before they had seen their untried foe, without any attempt to fight or even to give back the battle-shout. None were slain while actually fighting; they were cut down from behind while hindering one another's flight in a confused, struggling mass. Along the bank of the Tiber, whither the whole of the left wing had fled, after throwing away their arms, there was great slaughter. Many who were unable to swim or were hampered by the weight of their cuirasses and other armor were sucked down by the current. The greater number, however, reached Veii in safety, yet not only were no troops sent from there to defend Rome but not even was a messenger dispatched to report the defeat to Rome. All the men on the right wing, which had been stationed some distance from the river and nearer to the foot of the hill, made for Rome and took refuge in the Citadel without even closing the city gates.

The Gauls for their part were almost dumb with astonishment at so sudden and extraordinary a victory. At first they did not dare to move from the spot, as though puzzled by what had happened, then they began to fear a surprise, at last they began to despoil the dead, and, as their custom is, to pile up the arms in heaps. Finally, as no hostile

---

[41] A Latin town conquered by the Romans around 500 BCE.
[42] Religious rites intended to secure the good will of the gods before important undertakings.

movement was anywhere visible, they commenced their march and reached Rome shortly before sunset. The cavalry, who had ridden on in front, reported that the gates were not shut, there were no pickets on guard in front of them, no troops on the walls. This second surprise, as extraordinary as the previous one, held them back, and fearing a nocturnal conflict in the streets of an unknown city, they halted and bivouacked between Rome and the Anio.[43] Reconnoitering parties were sent out to examine the circuit of the walls and the other gates, and to ascertain what plans their enemies were forming in their desperate plight.

As for the Romans, because the greater number had fled from the field in the direction of Veii instead of Rome, it was universally believed that the only survivors were those who had found refuge in Rome, and the mourning for all who were lost, whether living or dead, filled the whole city with the cries of lamentation. But the sounds of private grief were stifled by the general terror when it was announced that the enemy were at hand. Presently the yells and wild war-whoops of the squadrons were heard as they rode round the walls. All the time until the next day's dawn the citizens were in such a state of suspense that they expected from moment to moment an attack on the city. They expected it first when the enemy approached the walls, for they would have remained at the Allia had not this been their object; then just before sunset they thought the enemy would attack because there was not much daylight left; and then when night was fallen they imagined that the attack was delayed until then to create all the greater terror. Finally, the approach of the next day deprived them of their senses; the entrance of the enemy's standards within the gates was the dreadful climax to fears that had known no respite.

But all through that night and the following day the citizens afforded an utter contrast to those who had fled in such terror at the Allia. Realising the hopelessness of attempting any defense of the city with the small numbers that were left, they decided that the men of military age and the able-bodied among the senators should, with their wives and children, withdraw into the Citadel[44] and the Capitol,[45] and after getting in stores of arms and provisions, should from that fortified position defend their gods, themselves, and the great name of Rome. The Flamen[46] and priestesses of Vesta[47] were to carry the sacred things of the State far away from the bloodshed and the fire, and their sacred cult should not be abandoned as long as a single person survived to observe it. If only the Citadel and the Capitol, the abode of gods; if only the Senate, the guiding mind of the national policy; if only the men of military age survived the impending ruin of the city, then the loss of the crowd of old men left behind in the city could be easily borne; in any case, they themselves were certain to perish. To reconcile the aged plebeians[48] to their fate, the men who had been Consuls and enjoyed triumphs gave out that they would meet their fate side by side with them, and not burden the scanty force of fighting men with bodies too weak to carry arms or defend their country.

Thus they sought to comfort one another, these aged men doomed to death. Then they turned with words of encouragement to the younger men on their way to the Citadel and Capitol, and solemnly commended to their strength and courage all that was left of the fortunes of a city that for 360 years[49] had been victorious in all its wars. As those who were carrying with them all hope and succor finally separated from those who had resolved not to survive the fall of the city the misery of the scene was heightened by the distress of the women. Their tears, their distracted running about as they followed first their husbands then their sons, their imploring appeals to them not to leave them[50] to

---

[43] The modern Aniene River; it joins the Tiber River just north of Rome.

[44] A high point on the north end of the Capitoline Hill.

[45] The Temple of "Jupiter the Best and Greatest" atop the Capitoline Hill.

[46] The Flamen dialis, the high priest of Jupiter.

[47] The six Vestal Virgins.

[48] Who at this point time still were not eligible to be Consuls.

[49] Rounded; actually 363 years from the founding of Rome in 753 BCE.

[50] The elderly men.

their fate, made up a picture in which no element of human misery was wanting.

After all the arrangements that circumstances permitted had been made for the defense of the Capitol, the old men returned to their respective homes and, fully prepared to die, awaited the coming of the enemy. Those who had filled curule offices[51] resolved to meet their fate wearing the insignia of their former rank and honor and distinctions. They put on the splendid dress that they wore when conducting the chariots of the gods or riding in triumph through the city, and thus arrayed, they seated themselves in their ivory chairs in front of their houses. Some writers record that, led by Marcus Fabius, the *Pontifex Maximus*, they recited the solemn formula in which they devoted themselves to death for their country.[52]

As the Gauls were refreshed by a night's rest after a battle that had at no point been seriously contested, and as they were not now taking the city by assault or storm, their entrance the next day was not marked by any signs of excitement or anger. Passing the Colline Gate,[53] which was standing open, they came to the Forum and gazed round at the temples and at the Citadel, which alone wore any appearance of war. They left there a small body to guard against any attack from the Citadel or Capitol while they were scattered, and then they dispersed in quest of plunder through streets in which they did not meet a soul. Some poured in a body into all the houses near, others made for the most distant ones, expecting to find them untouched and full of spoils.

Appalled by the very desolation of the place and dreading lest some stratagem should surprise the stragglers, they returned to the neighborhood of the Forum in close order. The houses of the plebeians were barricaded, the halls of the patricians stood open, but they felt greater hesitation about entering the open houses than those that were closed. They gazed with feelings of real veneration upon the men who were seated in the porticoes of their mansions, not only because of the superhuman magnificence of their apparel and their whole bearing and demeanor, but also because of the majestic expression of their countenances, wearing the very aspect of gods. So they stood, gazing at them as if they were statues, until, as it is asserted, one of the patricians, M. Papirius, roused the passion of a Gaul, who began to stroke his beard, which in those days was universally worn long, by smiting him on the head with his ivory staff. He was the first to be killed, the others were butchered in their chairs. After this slaughter of the magnates, no living being was thenceforth spared; the houses were rifled, and then set on fire.[54]

Now, whether it was that the Gauls were not all animated by a passion for the destruction of the city, or whether their chiefs had decided on the one hand to present the spectacle of a few fires as a means of intimidating the besieged into surrender from a desire to save their homes, and on the other, by abstaining from a universal conflagration, hold what remained of the city as a pledge by which to weaken their enemies' determination, it is certain that the fires were far from being so indiscriminate or so extensive as might be expected on the first day of a captured city. As the Romans beheld from the Citadel the city filled with the enemy who were running about in all the streets while some new disaster was constantly occurring, first in one quarter then in another, they could no longer control their eyes and ears, let alone their thoughts and feelings. In whatever direction their attention was drawn by the shouts of the enemy, the shrieks of the women and boys, the roar of the flames, and the crash of houses falling in, thither they turned their eyes and minds as though set by Fortune to be spectators of their country's fall, powerless to protect anything left of all they possessed beyond their lives.

---

[51] Offices whose holders had the power of *imperium* (the power to command armies) and were permitted to use the curule chair; at this time, this included Consular Tribunes, Consuls, and Dictators.

[52] The ceremony of *devotio* ("devotion"), in which a contract was made with the gods; in exchange for sacrificing themselves, distinguished Romans expected that the gods would give their support to Rome.

[53] The site of a crucial battle in 82 BCE between the rebel general Sulla and supporters of the Senate.

---

[54] This would have destroyed many records of earlier Roman history.

CHAPTER 4

THE EXPANSION OF THE ROMAN REPUBLIC (350–120 BCE)

During the course of the Middle Republic (ca. 350–146 BCE), the Romans engaged in wars that took them farther and farther from Rome. Even though these wars were not fought for purely imperialistic purposes, as a consequence of them the Romans gradually acquired more and more overseas territories that they were responsible for governing. Thus, paradoxically, what we call the Roman Empire largely developed during the Roman Republic. Between 350 and 268 BCE the Romans gained control of all of Italy south of the Po River. Soon afterward they expanded into the Mediterranean and by 146 they had defeated all the primary Mediterranean powers, in most cases several times.

WARS IN ITALY (350–268 BCE)

It took the Romans about fifty years to recover from the Gallic sack, during which time they learned how to deal with the wild Gallic charge: if they could withstand the initial assault, the Gauls would get tired out and flee. They then became engaged in a protracted series of Italian military conflicts lasting from 343 to 268 BCE that eventually gave them control of all of Italy south of the Po River valley.

The Nature of Roman Warfare in the Middle Republic

The Gallic sack engendered in the Romans a virtually paranoid fear of strong neighbors. This led to a policy of **defensive aggression**, as a result of which the Romans would sometimes preemptively attack neighbors whom they felt were becoming potential threats. Other factors that could encourage the Romans to go to war included a desire by Consuls to gain military glory, wishes to obtain land for land-hungry plebeians, dutiful responses to pleas for assistance from their neighbors, and genuine threats. In their earlier wars the

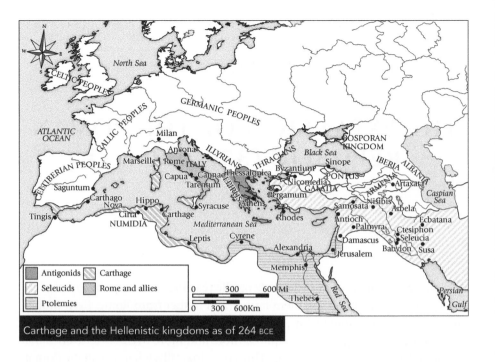

Carthage and the Hellenistic kingdoms as of 264 BCE

Romans lost more battles than they won, a consequence of having untrained armies and generals with little experience. The Romans prevailed more by persistence and a willingness to take greater losses than by military skill. There is little indication, moreover, that before around 150 BCE the Romans engaged in calculated imperialism out of a desire for large-scale political, financial, or territorial gain.

The First Samnite War (343–341 BCE)

In 343 BCE, the city of Capua in Campania requested Roman assistance against attacks by the Samnites, an Italic mountain people who were expanding west toward the Bay of Naples. Although in 354 the Romans had concluded a mutual defense treaty with the Samnites, they now were fearful of growing Samnite strength. When the Capuans unilaterally surrendered to the Romans, the Senate accepted the invitation. This First Samnite War (343–341 BCE) ended in a draw in 341 BCE when the Romans had to withdraw because of a mutiny in the Roman army by soldiers unhappy at being away from home for so long. As often was the case with the Romans, this initial involvement set a crucial precedent, and the Romans now found themselves committed to maintaining a presence in Campania. They may even have annexed Capua and made its citizens *cives sine suffragio*—that is, "citizens without the vote," a form of partial citizenship that included only the private rights of a Roman citizen.

A PICTURE IS WORTH A THOUSAND WORDS

DENARIUS OF MARCUS SERGIUS SILUS

A *denarius* issued by the Quaestor Marcus Sergius Silus in 115 BCE commemorated the heroic deeds of his ancestor Sergius, who had fought in the Second Punic War (218–201 BCE). According to the *Natural History* of Pliny the Elder, written toward the end of the first century CE, the elder Silus lost his right hand in his second campaign but continued to fight with an iron hand attached to his right wrist. He served in the cavalry and fought one-handed in four battles, having two horses killed underneath him. When he was serving as Praetor, his enemies attempted to exclude him from religious ceremonies because of his deformity, for priests were expected to be free of any blemish. Silus successfully defended himself in a speech that Pliny consulted for his information. This coin depicts on the obverse the head of the goddess Roma in a winged helmet with the legend "ROMA" and "Ex S.C.," or "By decree of the Senate," for at this time coinage was issued under the authority of the Senate. The character $\bar{X}$ to the left of Roma's neck represents the Roman numeral XVI, or sixteen, indicating that the value of the *denarius* has been increased from 10 *asses* to 16 *asses*, a significant increase in value. The reverse of the coin shows what must be an event, unmentioned by Pliny, from Silus' military career, a horseman galloping to the left and holding in his left hand both a sword and a severed head and bearing a shield on his right arm, all attesting to the loss of his right hand. The reference probably is to an encounter with the Gauls serving in Hannibal's army, for the Gauls practiced head-hunting, and this tactic was adopted by the Romans when fighting barbarian enemies.

The Great Latin Revolt (340–338 BCE)

In the short term, however, the Romans were confronted in 340 BCE by the Great Latin Revolt (340–338 BCE) after the Latins felt that they were being drawn into Rome's wars and that the terms of the Cassian Treaty were not being observed. After the defeat of the Latins in 338, the Romans dissolved the Latin League and simply annexed the Latin towns. Those living closer to Rome were made full Roman citizens, and those farther away were granted the *jus Latinum,* or "Latin

Right," a form of partial Roman citizenship that gave the Latins all the private rights of a Roman citizen plus the right to vote if they happened to be in Rome, but denied them the right to hold office. By these means, the Romans began the process whereby they shared their citizenship rights with increasing numbers of other peoples, something that was unheard of among the Greeks.

The Second Samnite War (326–304 BCE)

In 326 BCE the Romans entered the Second Samnite War (326–304 BCE) after the Samnites had occupied the Greek city of Naples. The war was marked by repeated Roman defeats. In 321, a Roman army was trapped and captured at the Battle of the Caudine Forks and then forced to suffer the humiliation of "passing under the yoke," where defeated soldiers were compelled to bow as they went underneath a gateway made of their own captured spears that represented the yoke connecting a pair of oxen, as if the soldiers had become beasts of burden. In 315, the Romans again were routed at the Battle of Lautulae. The Romans did, however, get some good news with the defeat of the Etruscans, who had allied themselves with the Samnites, at the Battle of Lake Vadimon in 310. And at the same time that the Romans were losing battles against the Samnites, they were establishing their strategic superiority. They began the construction of military colonies on the borders of Samnium: destitute Roman citizens gave up their citizenship in exchange for the opportunity to receive land grants and a new start. And in 312 BCE the Censor Appius Claudius Caecus began the construction of the Appian Way, an all-weather military road from Rome to Capua, which allowed for the speedy concentration of troops and supplies in the south. At the same time, the Romans recaptured territory gained by the Samnites outside of Samnium. By 304, the Samnites were hemmed in and exhausted and sued for peace, which was made based on a return to the status quo before the war and a renewal of the treaty of 354.

The Third Samnite War (298–290 BCE)

The Third Samnite War (298–290 BCE) commenced in 298 BCE after the Samnites formed a great Italian coalition against the Romans. The decisive encounter occurred at the Battle of Sentinum in 295, where a combined force of Samnites, Etruscans, and Gauls was on the verge of defeating the Romans when Decius Mus, one of the Roman Consuls, performed the ancient ritual of *devotio*. He dedicated himself to the gods, charged into the enemy ranks, and was killed. Instead of causing demoralization, his brave act gave courage to the soldiers, who, confident that the gods now would do their part and grant the Romans victory, rallied to defeat the enemy. In 290, the Samnites submitted to Rome and, although allowed to remain independent, were made into dependent Roman *socii*, or allies.

As an epilogue to the Samnite wars, in the 280s the Romans conducted reprisals against the Gauls of northeastern Italy, defeating them, again at Lake Vadimon, in 283 BCE and laying waste to an area called the *ager Gallicus* ("Gallic field") that remained a desert for the next fifty years.

The Pyrrhic War (280–275 BCE)

In 282 BCE, Rome came into conflict with the Greeks of southern Italy after the city of Tarentum sank a small Roman scouting fleet and, what was worse from the Roman perspective, spattered mud on the togas of some Roman ambassadors, an act that grievously offended the Roman sense of *dignitas* (dignity). Knowing they could not stand up to Roman retaliation by themselves, the Tarentines appealed for help to the most able Greek general of the day, King Pyrrhus of Epirus. Pyrrhus, who had notions of his own about expanding his influence into Great Greece in southern Italy and Sicily, accepted the challenge, and in 280 BCE he sailed to Italy with his army, which included war elephants. During the Pyrrhic War (280–275 BCE), the Romans fought three arduous battles with Pyrrhus, at Heraclea in 280, Asculum in 279, and Beneventum in 275. Even though Pyrrhus won the first two and the third was indecisive, his losses were very heavy; after one battle, he commented, "Another victory like this and I shall be totally ruined." The losses of the Romans were even greater, but unlike typical Hellenistic states, they simply refused to negotiate. One of Pyrrhus' ambassadors returned from Rome complaining that the Senate acted like an "assembly of kings." By 275 BCE Pyrrhus had had enough and returned to Greece, supposedly with the words, "What a battlefield I am leaving for Rome and Carthage." This left the Greeks of southern Italy unable to resist, and by 268 BCE all had surrendered to Rome.

The term Pyrrhic victory *still refers to a victory with enough losses to qualify as a defeat.*

In these campaigns, the Romans often prevailed primarily because of their persistence, their willingness to suffer great losses, and their ability to create long-term strategies for defeating enemies by constructing roads and military colonies. In their wars during this period, they usually lost more battles than they won, often because their generals, who were in office for just a single year, were amateurs and had a tendency to take risks in a rush for personal military glory. Senatorial generals strove to gain the greatest honor that a senator could be granted, a **triumph** after a military victory. In a triumph, the victorious general, painted red like the god Jupiter, led a procession of cheering soldiers, disconsolate captives, and wagons piled with loot along the Sacred Way through the forum in Rome and up to the Capitoline temple.

By 268 BCE, Rome had become the dominant power in Italy south of the Po River valley. Curiously, however, aside from confiscating tracts of land called *ager publicus* ("public land") in strategic areas, the Romans showed little interest in actually taking over the territory of their defeated neighbors. Part of the public land was used to establish military colonies at strategic points, such as river fords and mountain

An Etruscan dish depicts a western war elephant. Never having seen elephants before, the Romans called Pyrrhus' war elephants "Lucanian cows," after the region of Italy in which they were fighting.

THE NATURE OF ROMAN IMPERIALISM

The policies and practices that resulted in Rome's acquisition of overseas territories known as "provinces" continue to be much discussed. Embedded in these debates is the question of whether Roman expansion during the Republic should be described as "imperialism." Some historians simply assume that Roman expansion must have been "imperialistic," supposing that any acquisition of foreign territory by a government is by its very nature "imperialistic." But this very straightforward interpretation begs the more nuanced question of whether the Romans were being intentionally imperialistic. Some historians presume that the Romans did they have a conscious policy of acquiring foreign territories in the same manner as other empires, such as the Assyrian, Persian, Macedonian, and British Empires did. Thus, one historian recently referred to "Rome's extraordinary long-term commitment to expansion." But for a good 250 years the Romans in fact were very chary about expansion. In Italy, they did not annex defeated enemies but turned them into allies. When the Romans initially expanded into the Mediterranean, they went to extraordinary lengths to avoid annexing defeated enemies, a policy that resulted in repeated wars with the same rival; thus, two wars with the Illyrians, three with the

Carthaginians, three with the Celtiberians, and four with the Macedonians. Overseas provinces (Sicily, Sardinia, and Spain) were annexed only to keep an enemy, Carthage, from having them. In 146 BCE, Carthage and Macedonia finally were annexed, but only as a last resort. This kind of imperialism often is called "defensive imperialism"—that is, engaging in foreign wars, and even acquiring overseas territories, as a proactive means of protection against possible future attacks. The Roman policy toward acquiring overseas provinces did not obviously change until 133 BCE, with the self-serving decision to annex the Kingdom of Pergamum, which then became a new province of "Asia." Subsequently, in what certainly qualifies as "imperialism," ambitious generals such as Pompey and Caesar expanded their personal authority by annexing new provinces, Syria and Gaul respectively. Ultimately, a tradition of imperialism became so embedded that during the Roman Empire an emperor was expected to be a *propagator imperii* ("expander of the empire") even though, after the first emperor Augustus, there was in fact hardly any further expansion. When speaking of Roman imperialism, therefore, it is important to specify which period one is discussing, and in particular, before or after 133 BCE.

passes. The colonies also allowed the Romans to make land grants to landless plebeians and thus make them eligible for military service.

The Romans' primary concern was to weaken potential adversaries in Italy to a point at which they no longer posed a threat to Rome. Their usual policy was to impose a bilateral treaty on a defeated enemy, with Rome as the patron and the enemy as the client. The former enemy became a Roman *socius*, or ally. It relinquished its independent foreign policy and was required to have "the same friends and enemies" as Rome. Whenever Rome went to war, its allies were expected to contribute manpower for the Roman armies. The result of this **Italian Alliance** was that, even though Roman territory did not expand greatly after these victories, Rome gained access to a manpower reserve of over half a million soldiers. Roman society now consisted of two groups of people: senators and plebeians, who had Roman citizenship, and Italian allies and slaves, who did not.

WARS IN THE WESTERN MEDITERRANEAN (264–201 BCE)

It was only a short time before Rome became entangled in additional wars on an even greater scale, especially between 264 and 201 BCE with the North African city of Carthage, which at this time controlled an empire that included the coastal regions of North Africa, the western third of Sicily, the islands of Sardinia and Corsica, and part of southern Spain, and was the most powerful state in the western Mediterranean. Earlier in its history, Rome had entered into several treaties with Carthage in which each recognized the sphere of influence of the other: Rome in Italy, and Carthage in the Mediterranean.

Carthage was especially interested in expanding its authority over the Greek cities in eastern Sicily, and it was this ambition that brought it into conflict with Rome.

The First Punic War (264–241 BCE)

In the 280s BCE a band of Campanian mercenaries called the Mamertines, or "Sons of Mars," seized the Sicilian Greek city of Messana, located on the Strait of Messina just nine miles (fifteen kilometers) from Italy. In 265 they were attacked by the powerful city of Syracuse. Fearful of being defeated and executed, the Mamertines accepted aid from the Carthaginians, who were delighted to gain a foothold in eastern Sicily. The Carthaginians then refused to leave, and the Mamertines responded by offering to become allies of Rome.

Even though the Romans had no obligation at all to these disreputable mercenaries, the matter was debated in the Senate. The Senate, however, could not decide what to do and, in an unprecedented move, passed the motion to the Centuriate Assembly without any recommendation. The Consul-elect Appius Claudius Pulcher, eager to win personal glory in a war, played on fears of strong neighbors and argued that the Romans "could fight the Carthaginians either in Sicily or before the gates of Rome." War was declared, and Rome became committed to its first overseas conflict, the First Punic War (264–241 BCE), from *Poenus*, the Latin word for Phoenician.

Sicily was an island, so the Romans, who had little seafaring experience, were compelled to construct a navy from scratch. It was said that they reverse-engineered a wrecked Carthaginian warship that had washed up on shore and practiced rowing on benches set up on the beach. The Carthaginians, of course, were much better sailors than the Romans, so the Roman tactic was to turn a sea battle into a land battle. They outfitted each warship with a *corvus*, or "beak," a long plank with a spike at the end. At the Battle of Mylae in 260 BCE, the Roman captains maneuvered their ships close to the overconfident Carthaginians and dropped the gangplanks. Roman troops swarmed over the surprised Carthaginians. The result was an overwhelming Roman victory. Although the Carthaginians were not fooled again, this unexpectedly easy triumph only strengthened the Romans' commitment to fight on until they had won.

Meanwhile, in Sicily, the war bogged down into largely unproductive siege warfare, the only result being the devastation of much of the Sicilian countryside.

An attempted Roman invasion of Africa under Marcus Regulus in 256 BCE was defeated by the Spartan mercenary commander Xanthippus, and the Carthaginian commander in Sicily, Hamilcar Barca, consistently outwitted the Romans. Finally, in 241, after their supply fleet had been destroyed at the Battle of the Aegates Islands and they were faced with a renewed Roman offensive, the Carthaginians decided to cut their losses and sue for peace. Carthage evacuated Sicily and agreed to pay a war **indemnity** of 3,200 talents of silver (a talent being about fifty-six pounds), for the Romans expected defeated foreign enemies to pay the costs associated with the war.

In the very next year, the Carthaginians faced a new threat when their mercenaries, who formed the backbone of their army, mutinied because they had not been paid. Unable to deal with them, the Carthaginians appealed to their new Roman patrons for help, and the Romans assisted in the suppression of the revolt. In 238 BCE, however, this friendly Roman attitude changed after Hamilcar Barca, Rome's nemesis in Sicily, commenced restoring Carthaginian military strength. When the Carthaginian mercenaries in Sardinia offered to turn the island over to Rome, the Romans accepted. The Carthaginian protest was met by a Roman declaration of war. The weakened Carthaginians had no choice but to accept a revised treaty that added an extra 1,700 talents to the indemnity and required them to evacuate Sardinia and Corsica as well. This callous Roman opportunism infuriated many Carthaginians.

The question remained of what to do with the territories Carthage had abandoned. Fearful of having the rich island of Sicily fall into the wrong hands, the Romans annexed it and in 227 BCE made it their first **province**, or foreign territory over which Rome assumed direct control. In the same year, Sardinia and Corsica became a second province. Having no method of governing these new territories, the Romans created two new Praetors to serve as governors. But otherwise, the Roman policy toward the provinces might be best described as benign neglect.

The Illyrian and Celtic Wars (229–219 BCE)

Hitherto, the Romans had confined their attentions almost exclusively to the western Mediterranean and had shown little interest in the Greek world. This changed in 229 BCE, when pirates from Illyria, roughly modern Albania, killed a Roman ambassador on the Adriatic Sea. That was all it took for the Romans to declare war on the Illyrian queen Teuta, initiating the First Illyrian War (229 BCE). The Illyrians could not hope to resist. Teuta promised not to do it again, and the Romans' two-hundred-warship fleet departed, but not before acknowledging as *amici* ("friends") some of the Greek peoples near the Adriatic coast. In 219 BCE, after another spate of piracy, the Romans had to return to Illyria in the Second Illyrian War (219 BCE). These rather inglorious episodes had the effect of giving the Romans a precedent for future involvements on the Greek mainland.

This decade also saw the last Gallic invasion of Italy when in 225 BCE a coalition of some seventy thousand Gauls from the Po River valley, augmented by Gallic mercenaries from Transalpine Gaul ("Gaul across the Alps"), advanced south. They were met at the Battle of Telamon, on the coast of Etruria, by two

Roman armies who caught them from both sides. After a savage battle, the Gauls were defeated, and thousands were sold into slavery. Subsequently, the Romans decided to deal with the problem of the north Italian Celts once and for all and invaded the Po valley. By 220, nearly all the Italian Gauls had been defeated, and the Romans established military colonies to keep a further eye on them.

The Second Punic War (218–201 BCE)

In the interim, the Carthaginians had been recovering their strength in Spain, where whey found silver and Celtiberian mercenaries under the leadership of Hannibal, the son of Hamilcar Barca. It was later thought by the Romans that in his youth Hannibal had sworn to his father that he would destroy Rome. In the Ebro Treaty of 226, Rome prohibited the Carthaginians from going north of the Ebro River in Spain but acknowledged Carthaginian authority south of the Ebro. Nevertheless, in 219 BCE, when the city of Saguntum, well south of the Ebro, appealed to Rome for help against a besieging Carthaginian army, the Romans ordered Hannibal to withdraw. Hannibal refused and captured Saguntum, along with a vast amount of booty. The Romans thus sent the ambassador Quintus Fabius Maximus to the Carthaginian Senate with a demand that Hannibal be handed over to Rome, but when the Carthaginians blamed the Romans for the violation of the Ebro Treaty, Fabius reached into a fold in his toga and said, "Here I bring you war and peace. Which do you choose?" When the Carthaginians told him to pick whichever he wanted himself, Fabius replied, "Then war it must be." And Hannibal, too, having observed many examples of unwarranted Roman interference in Carthaginian affairs, saw no alternative to war and determined to attack the Romans on their home territory and to try to break up Rome's Italian Alliance, which he saw as the real source of Rome's strength.

A Carthaginian silver double shekel, now in the British Museum in London, issued by the general Hamilcar Barca, the father of Hannibal, in Spain ca. 230 BCE. The obverse depicts the god Melqart in the form of Hercules, with a club over his shoulder, and the reverse portrays a Carthaginian war elephant. Most of Hannibal's elephants died crossing the Alps; the survivors only participated in one battle, at the Trebia River in 218, and only one, nicknamed "The Syrian," survived the war.

Therefore, in 218 BCE Hannibal led his mercenary army of Celtiberian infantry and Numidian cavalry, accompanied by seventeen war elephants, out of Spain, through the Alps, and into Cisalpine Gaul, where he expected that the Cisalpine Gauls would flock to join him. Thus began the Second Punic War (218–201 BCE). But the Gauls, who recently had been defeated by the Romans, were reluctant to take up arms. In 218, 217, and 216, making effective use of his cavalry and his experienced mercenary army, Hannibal inflicted three devastating defeats on the Romans at the Battle of the Trebia River in Cisalpine Gaul, the Battle of Lake Trasimene in Etruria, and the Battle of Cannae in southeastern Italy. For the last of these, the Romans had raised a double consular army of over fifty thousand men, but Roman operations were paralyzed by bickering between the Consuls Varro, a New Man, and his patrician colleague Paullus. In the ensuing battle, the Roman army was virtually annihilated after being surrounded by Hannibal's smaller (thirty-thousand-man) army. Paullus died with his men; eighty other senators were killed. This was the worst disaster Rome had ever suffered. When Varro, who survived and saved as much of the army as possible, returned to Rome, he was met by the Senate, who publicly thanked him for not despairing of Rome. And as for Hannibal, he was rebuked for not immediately attacking Rome by Maharbal, one of his cavalry commanders, with the famous words, "You know how to win a victory, Hannibal, but not how to use it." But at that point, Hannibal's army was too exhausted to go anywhere. And these spectacular victories now did induce some Gauls to join Hannibal.

The Carthaginian victory at Cannae created complete consternation in Rome. The historian Livy later reported, "Never before, while the city itself was still safe, had there been such panic within its walls." The ancient Sibylline Books were consulted. These were a collection of oracles believed to have been purchased from a mysterious elderly woman by King Tarquin the Proud and intended to be used only in grave emergencies. Obeying the oracle, the Romans resorted to human sacrifice, burying alive pairs of Greeks and Gauls, a man and woman each, in the "Cattle Forum" in Rome.

"Fabian strategy" still refers to a tactical avoidance of battle, which George Washington employed at Valley Forge.

The Senate responded by appointing a Dictator, Quintus Fabius Maximus, who refused to fight Hannibal in the field but shadowed him so closely that Hannibal could control only the patch of ground on which his army was camped. At one point, Hannibal actually did march his army up to the gates of Rome, but, safe behind the Servian Wall, the Romans refused to fight him; in fact, the chauvinistic Romans later said that the Roman who owned the land on which Hannibal camped sold the property that day and made money on the deal. Rather than giving in, the Romans showed their commitment to persevere by raising additional armies and expanding to a four-front war. They sent armies to Sicily, where Syracuse had revolted. They dispatched troops to Spain, the primary source of Carthage's financial and manpower reserves. And they even invaded Greece, where King Philip V of Macedon (220–179 BCE) had allied himself with Hannibal, resulting in the First Macedonian War (214–205), the sole intent of which was to prevent Philip from crossing to Italy.

Gradually, the Romans disentangled themselves from the other theaters of the war. Syracuse was betrayed and sacked in 211 BCE. In 210 the command in Spain was given to Publius Cornelius Scipio, who as a young Military Tribune had survived the Battle of Cannae and whose father and uncle had been killed in Spain the previous year. Even though Scipio was only a twenty-five-year-old ex-Aedile, there was so much popular sympathy for him that he was very irregularly granted a proconsular *imperium*—that is, the *imperium* of a Proconsul (an ex-Consul). Mimicking the tactics of Hannibal, he was able to achieve total victory in Spain by 206. And in 205, after they realized that Philip had no intention of invading Italy, the Romans extricated themselves from Greece by negotiating the Peace of Phoenice with the Macedonians. They abandoned their Greek friends, making this the only Republican war settled by a treaty that the Romans lost. But Hannibal still was unopposed in Italy.

At this point, Scipio, as Consul for the year 205, with only reluctant support from the Senate took an army consisting primarily of the survivors from Cannae to Africa to attack the Carthaginian homeland. Scipio found a local ally in Masinissa, an ambitious Numidian chieftain who supplied the Roman army with much-needed cavalry. In 203 the Carthaginians were defeated at the Battle of the Great Plains. At the same time that Scipio offered them a very favorable peace treaty they recalled Hannibal from Italy. Hannibal arrived before the treaty could be signed, and the war again was on. The final showdown came the next year at the Battle of Zama Regia, in which the Roman and Numidian cavalry was able to slip behind and surround the Carthaginian army. Hannibal finally was defeated, and Scipio gained the victory title Africanus, or "conqueror of Africa." The Carthaginians had no choice but to make peace. They were compelled to relinquish all claims to Spain, to reduce their navy to ten warships, and to pay an indemnity of twenty thousand talents in fifty annual installments. They also were prohibited from making war or even defending themselves without the consent of Rome. Carthage never again would be a strong military power.

The Second Punic War involved the entire western Mediterranean, just as the Peloponnesian War had involved nearly the entire Greek world. It demonstrated the strength of Rome's Italian Alliance, for nearly all of Rome's Italian allies had held firm. The Romans later looked back to their defeat of the terrifying Hannibal as their defining moment, and they never forgot it. For hundreds of years, Roman mothers would frighten their children into obedience by saying, "Hannibal's at the gates!" Its victory left Rome as the only power in the western Mediterranean, and one of its unanticipated consequences was that the Romans felt compelled to lay claim to Spain, if for no other reason than to keep the Carthaginians away from it. In 197 BCE two new provinces were created there, Nearer and Further Spain, governed by two additional Praetors, although at this time Rome controlled only the coastal areas.

WARFARE SPREADS TO THE EAST (200–146 BCE)

The end of the Second Punic War found Rome absolutely drained. Tens of thousands of soldiers had been killed, and the property losses in Italy were staggering. One would have thought that the Romans would have wanted nothing more than to rest and recover their strength. But this was not to be. In addition to continuing wars in the west, between 200 and 146 BCE Rome also was drawn into involvements with the Hellenistic states that had succeeded to the empire of Alexander the Great. These included not only Antigonid Macedonia, Seleucid Syria, and Ptolemaic Egypt but also a number of smaller states, such as Pergamum in western Anatolia, the island of Rhodes, and the Achaean and Aetolian Leagues of Greece.

The Second Macedonian War (200–197 BCE)

The first of these wars involved unfinished business. The Romans had not forgotten the unsatisfactory conclusion of the First Macedonian War. In addition, the Roman fears about strong neighbors were revived in 203 BCE when Rhodes and Pergamum reported that Philip V, ruler of Macedon, and King Antiochus III, ruler of the Seleucid Empire, had concluded a "Secret Treaty" whereby they planned to carve up the possessions of the Ptolemaic kingdom of Egypt. With the full support of the Consuls, who would have the opportunity to gain military glory, the Senate therefore recommended that war be declared on Macedonia. But then something completely unprecedented happened: the Centuriate Assembly, tired of war, rejected the motion. Only after a revised motion exempted military veterans from service was war declared. Even though the Macedonians could not hope to resist the full might of the Roman army, it was not until 197 BCE that the Romans found a capable general, Titus Quinctius Flamininus, who ended the Second Macedonian War (200–197 BCE) by defeating the wily Philip at the Battle of Cynoscephalae (Dogs' Heads). But rather than occupying any Greek territory, the Romans were content to weaken Macedonia by requiring Philip to pay a war indemnity, give up his navy, and evacuate his holdings in Greece. They declared the Greek cities "free," and then returned home.

The Syrian War (192–188 BCE)

At this point, King Antiochus III (223–187 BCE), ruler of the vast Seleucid Empire of Syria and the east, saw an opportunity to gain control of much of the empire of Alexander. In 192 he invaded Greece, and the Romans were compelled to send another army to the east to deal with what they perceived as a grave threat. The Syrian War (192–188 BCE) began with a Roman victory at the Battle of Thermopylae in 191 BCE, which forced Antiochus out of Greece. The Romans then pursued Antiochus into Asia, and at the Battle of Magnesia in Lydia in 190 BCE, the well-trained thirty-thousand-man Roman army, commanded by the Consul Lucius Cornelius

Scipio, who was advised by his brother Scipio Africanus, demolished the motley seventy-thousand-man Seleucid army, which still employed war elephants and even scythe chariots. In the Treaty of Apamea in 188 BCE, the Romans once again occupied no new territory, but they did compel the Seleucids to pay a war indemnity of fifteen thousand talents over the course of twelve years and to evacuate most of their holdings in Anatolia, which the Romans granted to Pergamum.

The Third Macedonian War (170–168 BCE)

During the succeeding years, Macedonia regained its strength. A new king, Perseus (179–168 BCE), began to expand his influence to the north. A rumor reached Rome that he planned to hire the Bastarnae, a Celtic people living near the Danube, to attack Rome. Fears of a new Macedonian threat led the Romans again to declare war in 171 BCE. The Third Macedonian War (171–168 BCE) played out much like the second. Not until 168 BCE did a competent general emerge, Lucius Aemilius Paulus, who defeated Perseus at the Battle of Pydna, a set battle that definitively demonstrated the superiority of the Roman legions over the Macedonian phalanx. This time the Romans took more serious measures to prevent future problems. They did not take over any territory, but they divided Macedonia up into four independent republics, which were forbidden contact with each other. They then departed, confident that the Macedonian threat had been eliminated.

After the Third Macedonian War, the Romans began to act like the bullies of the Mediterranean, as they became increasingly aware that no one could resist them. On the way home from Macedonia in 168 BCE, the Roman army pillaged Epirus, enslaving 150,000 inhabitants in belated retaliation for the Pyrrhic War. In the same year, the Seleucid king Antiochus IV (215–164 BCE) conquered Ptolemaic Egypt. On being notified that a Roman ambassador, Popillius Laenas, had arrived in Alexandria, Antiochus honored him by greeting him on the beach. But the ambassador, an old friend of Antiochus, formally notified him, "The Senate and the Roman people want you to get out of Egypt." When Antiochus asked for more time to think it over, the ambassador replied he could have as long as he wanted so long as he did not leave a circle the ambassador drew around him in the sand. Antiochus, offended by Roman arrogance but very aware of Rome's power, had no choice but to comply. In 162 BCE, the Romans again demonstrated their lack of respect for the Seleucids by sending an embassy to Syria that arrogantly destroyed the Seleucid navy and pitilessly hamstrung the Seleucid war elephants. Public opinion against this atrocity was so great that the Roman emissary, an ex-Consul, was assassinated.

TABLE 4.1 ROMAN WARS, 390–146 BCE (ALL DATES BCE)

390	Gallic sack of Rome
343–341	First Samnite War
340–338	Great Latin Revolt
326–304	Second Samnite War
298–290	Third Samnite War
280–275	Pyrrhic War
264–241	First Punic War
229–227	First Illyrian War
219–218	Second Illyrian War
218–201	Second Punic War
215–204	First Macedonian War
200–197	Second Macedonian War
192–188	Syrian War
181–179	First Celtiberian War
171–168	Third Macedonian War
154–133	Second Celtiberian War
149–146	Third Punic War
149–148	Fourth Macedonian War
146	Achaean Revolt

The Third Punic War (149–146 BCE)

Carthage, too, which had rebuilt itself as an economic, although not as a military, powerhouse, experienced Roman high-handedness. The hawkish senator Marcus Porcius Cato the Elder, a New Man, was jealous of Carthage's wealth and ended his speeches in the Senate with the words, "And in other regards, I think that Carthage must be destroyed." In 150 BCE, the Carthaginians paid off the last of the installments of the indemnity of 201. The next year, the Romans declared war after the Carthaginians violated the treaty of 201 by defending themselves against attacks by the Numidians. This began the Third Punic War (149–146 BCE), which dragged on until the Romans found a skilled general in Scipio Aemilianus, the adoptive grandson of Scipio Africanus. In 146 BCE the city was captured in desperate house-to-house fighting, during which many Carthaginians threw themselves into the burning Temple of Tanit rather than be taken captive.

The popular story that the Romans sowed the site of Carthage with salt is an urban legend dating to the eighteenth century.

The Fourth Macedonian War and Achaean Revolt (149–146 BCE)

In 149 Rome also faced a Fourth Macedonian War (149–148 BCE) in Greece, where a pretender to the Macedonian throne had reconstituted the kingdom. He was defeated in 148, but in 146 BCE the Achaean League, manifesting increasing Greek discontent with Roman high-handedness, also revolted. The Roman general Mummius swiftly suppressed the Achaean revolt. In the same year the Romans decided that a lesson had to be provided to those who contemplated resisting the will of Rome in the future. Thus, in 146 BCE the Romans destroyed two of the most famous cities of the Mediterranean world, Corinth in Greece and Carthage in North Africa. In addition, Macedonia and Achaea were annexed as the new province of Macedonia, and the territory of Carthage became the province of Africa. The Roman lesson finally was learned, and there was no further serious resistance against the Romans in the Mediterranean.

These acquisitions brought to an end the Roman reluctance to acquire foreign territory, and the Romans soon began to occupy additional overseas provinces. Thus, when King Attalus III of Pergamum died in 133 BCE and, lacking an heir, willed his kingdom to Rome, the Roman government accepted the offer. After a short-lived popular revolt led by a certain Aristonicus, who claimed to be Attalus' long-lost brother, had been easily suppressed, Pergamum was incorporated as a new province grandiosely named **Asia**. And in 121 BCE, to facilitate land communications to Spain, the province of Narbonese Gaul was annexed in southern Gaul.

Narbonese Gaul came to be known simply as provincia ("the province"), leading to the modern designation Provence.

The Wars in Spain (181–133 BCE)

Meanwhile, endemic warfare in Spain continued to drain Roman resources and manpower as the Romans gradually extended their control over the peninsula. Two Celtiberian Wars (181–179, 154–133 BCE) were interspersed with incessant guerilla warfare, and any general who wanted military glory always could look for it in Spain if there were no wars going on anywhere else. The losses suffered have led to Spain being referred to as "the Graveyard of the Roman Republic." The conflict came to head in the 140s with joint rebellions in north-central Spain, centered on the *oppidum* (hill fort) of Numantia, also known as the Numantine War, and in Lusitania (modern Portugal) in the west, led by the charismatic chieftain Viriathus. After winning several victories, Viriathus was betrayed and killed in 139. Meanwhile, the Numantines were besieged on and off beginning in 143 BCE. After several inglorious episodes in which defeated Roman generals were forced to grant the Numantines a treaty only to have it repudiated by the Senate, Scipio Aemilianus, the victor at Carthage in 146, was given the command. The following year, after Scipio had constructed a five-and-a-half-mile-long ring of fortifications around the city, the inhabitants, realizing their cause was hopeless, burned the city and largely committed suicide. Only a few hundred survived. This was the last organized local resistance against Rome, and the pacification of Spain then proceeded more smoothly.

⇦ LOOKING BACK

Following the disastrous sack of Rome by the Gauls, the Romans developed an army that could be used not only for defense, but also to attack peoples who were seen as threats. Their lenient treatment of defeated peoples in Italy gave the Romans access to a huge military recruiting pool. By 120 BCE Rome had defeated all the other powers of the Mediterranean world and created a network of overseas provinces that extended across the Mediterranean.

LOOKING AHEAD ⇨

The Roman expansion into the Mediterranean had serious and unanticipated consequences for the Roman way of life. Every element of Roman culture was affected, ranging from administrative affairs to the economy to religious practices. As a consequence of Roman contacts with other peoples, the Roman ability to assimilate aspects of other cultures now was put to the test.

FURTHER READING

Burton, Paul J. *Friendship and Empire. Roman Diplomacy and Imperialism in the Middle Republic (353–146 BC)*. Cambridge: Cambridge Univ. Press, 2011.

Byrd, Robert C. *The Senate of the Roman Republic.* Honolulu: Univ. Press of the Pacific, 2001.

Champion, Craige B., ed. *Roman Imperialism: Readings and Sources.* Oxford: Blackwell, 2004.

Cornell, Tim. *The Beginnings of Rome: Italy and Rome from the Bronze Age to the Punic Wars (c. 1000–264 BC).* New York: Routledge, 1995.

Eckstein, Arthur M. *Mediterranean Anarchy, Interstate War, and the Rise of Rome.* Berkeley: Univ. of California Press, 2006.

Errington, R. M. *The Dawn of Empire: Rome's Rise to World Power*. Ithaca, NY: Cornell Univ. Press, 1972.

Gabba, Emilio. *Republican Rome, the Army, and the Allies*. Berkeley: Univ. of California Press, 1976.

Gruen, Erich S. *The Hellenistic World and the Coming of Rome*. 2 vols. Berkeley: University of California Press, 1984.

Harris, William V. *War and Imperialism in Republican Rome 327–70 B.C.* Oxford: Oxford Univ. Press, 1979.

Hin, Saskia. *The Demography of Roman Italy. Population Dynamics in an Ancient Conquest Society 201 BCE–CE 14*. Cambridge, UK: Cambridge Univ. Press, 2013.

Hoyos, Dexter. *Roman Imperialism: A Concise History of the Rise and Expansion of Ancient Rome*. London: I. B. Tauris, 2017.

Rosenstein, Nathan S. *Imperatores victi: Military Defeat and Aristocratic Competition in the Middle and Late Republic*. Berkeley: Univ. of California Press, 1990.

SOURCES

4.1 THE DEVOTION OF DECIUS MUS (295 BCE)

LIVY, *FROM THE FOUNDING OF THE CITY*, BOOK 10, CHAPTERS 27–29

In 295 BCE, during the Third Samnite War (298–290 BCE), a Roman army led by the Consuls Publius Decius Mus and Quintus Fabius Maximus Rullianus encountered a huge army of Samnites, Gauls, Umbrians, and Etruscans at Sentinum. With the Roman army on the verge of defeat, Mus made use of the ancient ritual of *devotio*, or "devotion," a form of contract. Mus dedicated himself to the gods of the underworld on the understanding that once he had sacrificed himself, the gods then would support the Roman cause.

Source: D. Spillan and Cyrus Edmonds, trans., *The History of Rome by Titus Livius: Books Nine to Twenty-Six* (London: Bohn, 1868).

The Consuls,[1] having crossed the Apennines, came up with the enemy[2] in the territory of Sentinum,[3] their camp was pitched there at the distance of about four miles (six and a half kilometers). Several councils were then held by the enemy, and their plan of operations was thus settled: that they should not encamp together, nor go out together to battle; the Gauls were united to the Samnites, the Umbrians to the Etruscans. The day of battle was fixed. The part of maintaining the fight was committed to the Samnites and Gauls; and the Etruscans and Umbrians were ordered to attack the Roman camp during the heat of the engagement. This plan was frustrated by

---

[1] Quintus Fabius Maximus Rullianus and Publius Decius Mus.

[2] A combined army of Samnites, Etruscans, Umbrians (an Italian people of central Italy), and Gauls.

[3] In east-central Italy.

three Clusian[4] deserters, who came over by night to Fabius, and after disclosing the above designs, were sent back with presents, in order that they might discover, and bring intelligence of, any new scheme which should be determined on. The Consuls then wrote to Flavius and Postumius[5] to move their armies, the one from the Faliscian, the other from the Vatican[6] region, toward Clusium; and to ruin the enemy's territory by every means in their power. The news of these depredations drew the Etrurians from Sentinum to protect their own region.

The Consuls, in their absence, practised every means to bring on an engagement. For two days they endeavored, by several attacks, to provoke the enemy to fight; in which time, however, nothing worth mention was performed. A few fell on each side, but still the minds of the Romans were irritated to wish for a general engagement; yet nothing decisive was hazarded. On the third day, both parties marched out their whole force to the field: here, while the armies stood in order of battle, a deer chased by a wolf from the mountains, ran through the plain between the two lines: there the animals taking different directions, the deer bent its course toward the Gauls, the wolf toward the Romans: way was made between the ranks for the wolf, the Gauls slew the deer with their javelins; on which one of the Roman soldiers in the van said, "To that side, where you see an animal, sacred to Diana, lying prostrate, flight and slaughter are directed; on this side the victorious wolf of Mars, safe and untouched, reminds us of our founder, and of our descent from that deity."

The Gauls were posted on the right wing, the Samnites on the left: against the latter, Fabius drew up, as his right wing, the first and third legions: against the Gauls, Decius formed the left wing of the fifth and sixth. The second and fourth were employed in the war in Samnium, under the Proconsul[7] Lucius Volumnius. In the first encounter the action was supported with strength so equal on both sides that had the Etruscans and Umbrians been present, either in the field or at the camp, in whichever place they might have employed their force, the Romans must have been defeated.

Although the victory was still undecided, fortune not having declared in favor of either party, yet the course of the fight was by no means similar on both right and left wings. The Romans under Fabius rather repelled than offered assault, and the contest was protracted until very late in the day, for their general knew very well that both Samnites and Gauls were furious in the first onset, so that, to withstand them would be sufficient. It was known, too, that in a protracted contest the spirits of the Samnites gradually flagged, and even the bodies of the Gauls, remarkably ill able to bear labor and heat, became quite relaxed, and although, in their first efforts, they were more than men, yet in their last they were less than women. He, therefore, reserved the strength of his men as unimpaired as possible, until the time when the enemy were the more likely to be worsted.

Decius, more impetuous, as being in the prime of life and full flow of spirits, exerted whatever force he had to the utmost in the first encounter, and, thinking the infantry not sufficiently energetic, brought up the cavalry to the fight. Putting himself at the head of a troop of young horsemen of distinguished bravery, he besought those youths, the flower of the army, to charge the enemy with him, telling them that they would reap a double share of glory, if through their means the victory should commence on the left wing. Twice they compelled the Gallic cavalry to give way. At the second charge, when they advanced farther and were briskly

---

[4] Etruscans from Clusium, the home of king Lars Porsenna, who had besieged Rome in 508 BCE.

[5] Roman generals who were ordered to attack Etruscan territory to try to lure the Etruscan part of the army away.

[6] An area just across the Tiber River from Rome.

[7] A former Consul who had his command extended.

engaged in the midst of the enemy's squadrons by a method of fighting new to them, they were thrown into dismay. A number of the enemy, mounted on chariots, made toward them with such a prodigious clatter from the trampling of the cattle and rolling of wheels that it frightened the horses of the Romans, unaccustomed to such tumultuous operation. By this means the victorious cavalry were dispersed in panic, and men and horses, in their headlong flight, were tumbled promiscuously on the ground. Hence also the battalions of the legions were thrown into disorder, through the impetuosity of the horses, and of the carriages which they dragged through the ranks, many of the soldiers in the van were trodden or bruised to death, while the Gallic line, as soon as they saw their enemy in confusion, pursued the advantage, nor allowed them time to take breath or recover themselves.

Decius, calling aloud, "Where are they fleeing, or what hope could they have in running away?", strove to stop them as they turned their backs, but finding that he could not, by any efforts, prevail on them to keep their posts, so thoroughly were they dismayed, he called on his father, Publius Decius, by name, saying, "Why do I any longer defer the fate laid on my family? It is destined to our race, that we should serve as expiatory victims to avert the public danger. I will now offer the legions of the enemy, together with myself, to be immolated to the Earth and the infernal gods." Having thus said, he commanded Marcus Livius, a pontiff,[8] whom, at his coming out to the field, he had charged not to stir from him, to dictate the form of words in which he was to devote himself, and the legions of the enemy, for the army of the Roman people, the Quirites.[9] He was accordingly devoted with the same imprecations, and in the same habit, in which his father, Publius Decius, had ordered himself to be devoted at the Veseris in the Latin war.[10] Then, immediately after the solemn

imprecation, he added that he drove before him dismay and flight, slaughter and blood, and the wrath of the gods celestial and infernal, and that, with the contagious influence of the furies, the ministers of death, he would infect the standards, the weapons, and the armor of the enemy, and that the same spot should be that of his perdition, and that of the Gauls and Samnites. After uttering these execrations on himself and the foe, he spurred forward his horse, where he saw the line of the Gauls thickest, and, rushing upon the enemy's weapons, met his death.

Thenceforward the battle seemed to be fought with a degree of force scarcely human. The Romans, on the loss of their general, a circumstance which, on other occasions, is wont to inspire terror, stopped their flight, and were anxious to begin the combat afresh.[11] The Gauls, and especially the multitude which encircled the Consul's body, as if deprived of reason, cast their javelins at random without execution, some became so stupefied as not to think of either fighting or flying, whereas on the other side, Livius, the pontiff, to whom Decius had transferred his Lictors, with orders to act as Propraetor,[12] cried out aloud, that the Romans were victorious, being saved by the death of their Consul. That the Gauls and Samnites were now the victims of mother Earth and the infernal gods, that Decius was summoning and dragging to himself the army devoted along with him, and that, among the enemy, all was full of dismay, and the vengeance of all the furies. While the soldiers were busy in restoring the fight, Lucius Cornelius Scipio and Caius Marcius, with some reserved troops from the rear, who had been sent by Quintus Fabius, the Consul, to the support of his colleague, came up. There the fate of Decius was ascertained, a powerful stimulus to brave every danger in the cause of the public good.

---

[8] A *pontifex*, or Roman priest.

[9] Roman religious rites had to be performed using the exactly correct formulas; if the wrong words were used, the ritual was invalid.

[10] In 340 BCE, during the Great Latin War, Decius Mus' father likewise had devoted himself to the gods, on the Veseris River in Campania, in order to obtain victory.

---

[11] The soldiers perked up in the belief that because Mus had fulfilled his part of the contract by sacrificing himself, the gods now would fulfill their part and bring ruin on the enemy.

[12] An official with the authority but not the office of a Praetor.

Therefore, when the Gauls stood in close order, with their shields formed into a fence before them, and had but little prospect of success from a close fight, the javelins, which lay scattered between the two lines, were, therefore, by order of the lieutenants-general, gathered up from the ground, and thrown against the enemy's shields, and as most of them pierced the fence, the long pointed ones even into their bodies, their compact band was overthrown in such a manner that a great many, who were unhurt, yet fell as if thunderstruck. Such were the changes of fortune on the left wing of the Romans. On the right, Fabius had at first protracted the time, as we mentioned above, in slow operations, then, as soon as he perceived that neither the shout, nor the efforts of the enemy, nor the weapons which they threw, retained their former force, having ordered the commanders of the cavalry to lead round their squadrons to the flank of the Samnites, he commanded them to charge them in flank with all possible violence and his infantry to advance leisurely, and drive the enemy from their ground. When he saw that the enemy were unable to make resistance, and that their exhaustion was certain, drawing together all his reserves, whom he had kept fresh for that occasion, he made a brisk push with the legions, and gave the cavalry the signal to charge. The Samnites could not support the shock, but fled precipitately to their camp, passing by the line of the Gauls, and leaving their allies to fight by themselves. These stood in close order under cover of their shields.

Fabius, therefore, having heard of the death of his colleague, ordered the squadron of Campanian cavalry, in number about five hundred, to fall back from the ranks, and riding round, to attack the rear of the Gallic line, then the chief strength of the third legion to follow, with directions that wherever they should see the enemy's troops disordered by the charge, to follow the blow, and cut them to pieces, when in a state of consternation. After vowing a temple and the spoils of the enemy to Jupiter the Victorious,[13] he proceeded to the camp of the Samnites, where all their forces were hurrying in confusion. The gates not affording entrance to such very great numbers, those who were necessarily excluded, attempted resistance just at the foot of the rampart, and here fell Gellius Egnatius, the Samnite general. These, however, were soon driven within the rampart. The camp was taken after a slight resistance, and at the same time the Gauls were attacked on the rear, and overpowered. There were slain of the enemy on that day twenty-five thousand: eight thousand were taken prisoners. Nor was the victory an unbloody one; for, of the army of Publius Decius, the killed amounted to seven thousand; of the army of Fabius, to one thousand two hundred. Fabius, after sending persons to search for the body of his colleague, had the spoils of the enemy collected into a heap, and burned them as an offering to Jupiter the Victorious. The Consul's body could not be found that day, being hid under a heap of slaughtered Gauls: on the following day, it was discovered and brought to the camp, amidst an abundance of tears shed by the soldiers. Fabius, discarding all concern about any other business, solemnized the funeral of his colleague in the most honorable manner, passing on him the high encomiums that he had justly merited.

---

[13] The Temple of Jupiter Victor survived into the Roman imperial period.

LIVY, *FROM THE FOUNDING OF THE CITY*, BOOK 22, CHAPTERS 34–57

The Battle of Cannae in 216 BCE was Rome's defining moment. After the Romans had lost fifty thousand soldiers in the first two years of the war, at Cannae Hannibal's smaller army surrounded the much larger Roman one and totally destroyed it. The Romans lost another fifty thousand men; only ten thousand escaped to tell the tale. It appeared that the Romans were about to lose the war. But not only did they continue the fight; they even expanded the theaters of operation. Livy's account of the battle begins with the contentiousness that arose over the Consular elections for 216 BCE, where two bitterly opposed Consuls were elected, Gaius Terentius Varro, an inexperienced rabble-rousing plebeian whose emotional appeals to the plebs opposed the delaying tactics of the Dictator Quintus Fabius Maximus and rashly promised a quick end to the war with Hannibal, and Lucius Aemilius Paullus, a distinguished, experienced, and cautious patrician implacably opposed to Varro and the plebeians. The two were at odds throughout the campaign, with disastrous results. The Roman historian Livy (ca. 60 BCE–17 CE), in his work *From the Founding of the City*, described the events leading up to the battle and the battle itself in great detail.

Source: Canon Roberts, trans., *Titus Livius. The History of Rome*, Vol. 3 (London: Dent, 1905).

The elections[14] were held amid a bitter struggle between the patricians and the plebs. C. Terentius Varro,[15] a member of their own order, had ingratiated himself with the plebs by his attacks upon the leading men in the state and by all the tricks known to the demagogue. His success in shaking the influence of Fabius[16] and weakening the authority of the Dictator had invested him with a certain glory in the eyes of the mob, and they did their utmost to raise him to the consulship. The patricians opposed him with their utmost strength, dreading lest it should become a common practice for men to attack them as a means of rising to an equality with them. Q. Baebius Herennius, a relation of Varro, strengthened the feeling in favor of his own candidate. "It was by the nobility," he declared, "who had for many years been trying to get up a war, that Hannibal was brought into Italy, and when the war might have been brought to a close, it was they who were unscrupulously protracting it. We shall never see the end of the war until we have elected as our Consul a man who is really a plebeian, that is, one from the ranks. The plebeian nobility[17] have all been initiated into the same mysteries; when they are no longer looked down upon by the patricians they at once begin to look down upon the plebs. One consulship at all events belongs to the Roman plebs; the people will freely dispose of it and give it to the man who prefers an early victory to prolonged command."

Harangues like these kindled intense excitement among the plebs. There also were three patrician candidates in the field, P. Cornelius Merenda, L. Manlius Vulso, and M. Aemilius Lepidus, and two

---

[14] For the year 216 BCE.

[15] Varro was a complete outsider, a "New Man"—that is, a person none of whose ancestors had held the office of Consul.

[16] Quintus Fabius Maximus, who had been appointed Dictator after the disastrous Roman defeat at the Battle of Lake Trasimene in 217 BCE. By implementing his "Fabian Strategy" of restricting military operations to raids and guerilla warfare but not engaging Hannibal's main army, Fabius got the nickname Cunctator, "The Delayer."

[17] Plebeians who, unlike Varro, did have a Consul in their family background. The consulate had been open to plebeians since 367 BCE.

plebeians who now were ennobled, C. Atilius Serranus and Q. Aelius Paetus. But the only one elected was C. Terentius Varro, so that the elections for appointing his colleague were in his hands. The nobility compelled L. Aemilius Paullus to come forward. On the next election day, after all Varro's opponents had retired, Paullus was given to him not so much to be his colleague as to oppose him on equal terms.

The armies were increased, but as to what additions were made to the infantry and cavalry, the authorities vary so much, both as to the numbers and nature of the forces, that I should hardly venture to assert anything as positively certain. Some say that 10,000 recruits were called out to make up the losses; others, that four new legions were enrolled so that they might carry on the war with eight legions. Some authorities record that both horse and foot in the legions were made stronger by the addition of 1000 infantry and 100 cavalry to each, so that they contained 5000 infantry and 300 cavalry, whereas the allies[18] furnished double the number of cavalry and an equal number of infantry. Thus, according to these writers, there were 87,200 men in the Roman camp when the Battle of Cannae[19] was fought. One thing is quite certain; the struggle was resumed with greater vigor and energy than in former years, because the Dictator had given them reason to hope that the enemy might be conquered.[20] But before the newly raised legions left the city the Decemvirs[21] were ordered to consult the Sibylline Books[22] owing to the general alarm that had been created by fresh portents. It was reported that showers of stones had fallen simultaneously on

the Aventine in Rome and at Aricia; that the statues of the gods among the Sabines had sweated blood, and cold water had flowed from the hot springs. This latter portent created more terror, because it had happened several times. In the colonnade near the Campus Martius[23] several men had been killed by lightning. The proper expiation of these portents was ascertained from the Sibylline Books.

After completing the enrolment the Consuls waited a few days for the contingents furnished by the Latins and the allies to come in. Then a new departure was made; the soldiers were sworn in by the Military Tribunes.[24] Up to that day there had only been the military oath binding the men to assemble at the bidding of the Consuls and not to disband until they received orders to do so. It had also been the custom among the soldiers, when the infantry were formed into companies of 100, and the cavalry into troops of 10, for all the men in each company or troop to take a voluntary oath to each other that they would not leave their comrades for fear or for flight, and that they would not quit the ranks save to fetch or pick up a weapon, to strike an enemy, or to save a comrade. This voluntary covenant was now changed into a formal oath taken before the Tribunes.

Before they marched out of the city, Varro delivered several violent harangues, in which he declared that the war had been brought into Italy by the nobles, and would continue to feed on the vitals of the Republic if there were more generals like Fabius; he, Varro, would finish off the war the very day he caught sight of the enemy. His colleague, Paullus, made only one speech, in which there was much more truth than the people cared to hear. He passed no strictures on Varro, but he did express surprise that any general, while still in the city before he had taken up his command, or become acquainted with either his own army or that of the enemy, or gained any information as to the lie of the country and the nature of the ground, should know in what way he should conduct the

---

[18] The "socii," or Italian allies, defeated peoples and cities of Italy not governed by Rome but expected to contribute troops for Rome's wars.

[19] In Apulia in far southeastern Italy, the site of one of Rome's most disastrous military defeats.

[20] By his policy of harassing but not directly confronting Hannibal.

[21] The "Ten Men in Charge of Carrying out Sacrificial Duties," five patricians and five plebeians. They were in charge of consulting the Sibylline Books.

[22] Books believed to have been purchased from a Sibyl (a prophetess) by King Tarquin the Proud. They were consulted in times of emergencies to find the proper expiatory rites needed to regain the favor of the gods.

---

[23] The "Field of Mars," where, in earlier Roman history, the army was accustomed to assemble.

[24] Each legion had six Military Tribunes, chosen by the Senate and by vote of the people.

campaign and be able to foretell the day on which he would fight a decisive battle with the enemy.

As for himself, Paullus said that he would not anticipate events by disclosing his measures, for, after all, circumstances determined measures for men much more than men made circumstances subservient to measures. He hoped and prayed that such measures as were taken with due caution and foresight might turn out successful; so far rashness, besides being foolish, had proved disastrous. He made it quite clear that he would prefer safe to hasty counsels, and in order to strengthen him in this resolve Fabius is said to have addressed him on his departure in the following terms:

"You are mistaken, Lucius Paullus, if you imagine that you will have less difficulty with Gaius Terentius than with Hannibal. I rather think the former will prove a more dangerous enemy than the latter. With the one you will only have to contend in the field, the opposition of the other you will have to meet everywhere and always. Against Hannibal and his legions you will have your cavalry and infantry, when Varro is in command he will use your own men against you. If he carries out his threat and brings on an action at once, some place or other will be rendered more notorious by our defeat than even Trasimene.[25] The only rational method of carrying on war against Hannibal is the one that I have followed. We are carrying on war in Italy, in our own country on our own soil, everywhere round us are citizens and allies, and time and circumstance are making us more efficient, more circumspect, more self-reliant. Hannibal, on the other hand, is in a foreign and hostile land, far from his home and country, confronted everywhere by opposition and danger; nowhere by land or sea can he find peace; nowhere does he see anything that he can call his own, he has to live on each day's pillage. He has hardly a third of the army with which he crossed the Ebro.[26] He has lost

more by famine than by the sword, and even the few he has cannot get enough to support life. Do you doubt then, that if we sit still we shall get the better of a man who is growing weaker day by day, who has neither supplies nor reinforcements nor money? Varro, although he is a Roman Consul, will desire just what Hannibal the Carthaginian commander desires. Hannibal will only feel contempt for a man who runs all risks; he will be afraid of one who never takes a rash step."

The Consul's reply was far from being a cheerful one, for he admitted that the advice given was true, but not easy to put into practice. What power or authority would a Consul have against a violent and headstrong colleague? With these words Paullus, it is said, set forward, escorted by the foremost men among the patricians; the plebeian Consul was attended by his plebeian friends, more conspicuous for their numbers than for the quality of the men who composed the crowd. When they came into camp the recruits and the old soldiers were formed into one army, and two separate camps were formed, the new camp, which was the smaller one, being nearer to Hannibal, while in the old camp the larger part of the army and the best troops were stationed.

An incident occurred that still further encouraged Varro's impetuous and headstrong temperament. Parties were sent to drive off the foragers; a confused fight ensued owing to the soldiers rushing forward without any preconcerted plan or orders from their commanders, and the contest went heavily against the Carthaginians. As many as 1700 of them were killed, the loss of the Romans and the allies did not amount to more than 100. The Consuls commanded on alternate days, and that day happened to be Paullus' turn. He checked the victors who were pursuing the enemy in great disorder, for he feared an ambuscade. Varro was furious, and loudly exclaimed that the enemy had been allowed to slip out of their hands, and if the pursuit had not been stopped the war could have been brought to a close. Hannibal did not very much regret his losses. On the contrary, he believed that they would serve as a bait to the impetuosity of the Consul and his newly-raised troops, and that he would be more headstrong than ever. What was going on in the enemy's camp was quite as well

---

[25] The Roman defeat at the Battle of Lake Trasimene the year before, where incompetent Roman generals had allowed the Roman army to be trapped between a mountain and a lake.
[26] The Spanish river that marked the northern boundary of Carthaginian territory. It was Rome's violation of the Ebro Treaty of 226 that had led to the Second Punic War.

known to him as what was going on in his own; he was fully aware that there were differences and quarrels between the commanders, and that two-thirds of the army consisted of new recruits.

Owing to the want of grain, Hannibal decided to move into the warmer parts of Apulia, where the harvest was earlier and where, owing to the greater distance from the enemy, desertion would be rendered more difficult for the fickle-minded part of his force. He ordered campfires to be lighted, and a few tents left where they could be easily seen, in order that the Romans, remembering a similar stratagem,[27] might be afraid to move. Statilius, however, was sent to reconnoiter with his Lucanians.[28] He reported that he had caught a distant view of the enemy in line of march, and the question of pursuit was discussed. As usual, the views of the two Consuls were opposed, but almost all present supported Varro, not a single voice was given in favor of Paullus, except that of Servilius, Consul in the preceding year. The opinion of the majority of the council prevailed, and so, driven by destiny, they went forward to render Cannae famous in the annals of Roman defeats. It was in the neighborhood of this village that Hannibal had fixed his camp with his back to the sirocco that blows from Mount Vulture[29] and fills the arid plains with clouds of dust. This arrangement was a very convenient one for his camp, and it proved to be extremely advantageous afterward, when he was forming his order of battle, for his own men, with the wind behind them, blowing only on their backs, would fight with an enemy who was blinded by volumes of dust.

The Consuls followed the Carthaginians, and when they reached Cannae and had the enemy in view they formed two entrenched camps. Hannibal now saw his hopes fulfilled, that the Consuls would give him an opportunity of fighting on ground naturally adapted for the movements of cavalry, the arm in which he had so far been invincible, and accordingly he placed his army in order of battle,

and tried to provoke his foe to action by repeated charges of his Numidians.[30] The Roman camp was again disturbed by a mutinous soldiery and Consuls at variance, Paullus bringing up against Varro the fatal rashness of Sempronius and Flaminius,[31] Varro retorting by pointing to Fabius as the favorite model of cowardly and inert commanders, and calling gods and men to witness that it was through no fault of his that Hannibal had acquired, so to speak, a prescriptive right to Italy; he had had his hands tied by his colleague; his soldiers, furious and eager for fight, had had their swords and arms taken away from them. Paullus, on the other hand, declared that if anything happened to the legions flung recklessly and betrayed into an ill-considered and imprudent action, he was free from all responsibility for it, although he would have to share in all the consequences. "See to it," he said to Varro, "that those who are so free and ready with their tongues are equally so with their hands in the day of battle." While time was thus being wasted in disputes instead of deliberation, Hannibal withdrew the bulk of his army, who had been standing most of the day in order of battle, into camp. He sent his Numidians, however, across the river[32] to attack the parties who were getting water for the smaller camp. They had hardly gained the opposite bank when with their shouting and uproar they sent the crowd flying in wild disorder, and galloping on as far as the outpost in front of the rampart, they nearly reached the gates of the camp. It was looked upon as such an insult for a Roman camp to be actually terrorized by irregular auxiliaries that one thing, and one thing alone, held back the Romans from instantly crossing the river and forming their battle line—the supreme command that day rested with Paullus. The following day Varro, whose turn it now was, without any consultation with his colleague, exhibited the signal for battle and led his forces drawn up for action across the river. Paullus

---

[27] A stratagem previously used by the Dictator Fabius Maximus to escape from Hannibal.

[28] An Italic people of southern Italy.

[29] An extinct volcano in Lucania in southern Italy.

[30] A native North African people known for its excellent cavalry.

[31] Sempronius had lost the Battle of the Trebia River in 218 BCE and Flaminius had lost the Battle of Lake Trasimene in 217.

[32] The Aufidus River, just south of the battle site.

followed, for although he disapproved of the measure, he was bound to support it. After crossing, they strengthened their line with the force in the smaller camp and completed their formation. On the right, which was nearest to the river, the Roman cavalry were posted, then came the infantry; on the extreme left were the cavalry of the allies, their infantry were between them and the Roman legions. The javelin men with the rest of the light-armed auxiliaries formed the front line. The Consuls took their stations on the wings, Terentius Varro on the left, Aemilius Paullus on the right.

As soon as it grew light Hannibal sent forward the Balearics[33] and the other light infantry. He then crossed the river in person and as each division was brought across he assigned it its place in the line. The Gallic and Spanish horse he posted near the bank on the left wing in front of the Roman cavalry; the right wing was assigned to the Numidian troopers. The center consisted of a strong force of infantry, the Gauls and Spaniards in the middle, the Africans at either end of them. You might fancy that the Africans were for the most part a body of Romans from the way they were armed, they were so completely equipped with the arms, some of which they had taken at the Trebia, but the most part at Trasimene. The Gauls and Spaniards had shields almost of the same shape but their swords were totally different, those of the Gauls being very long and without a point, the Spaniard, accustomed to thrust more than to cut, had a short handy sword, pointed like a dagger. These nations, more than any other, inspired terror by the vastness of their stature and their frightful appearance: the Gauls were naked above the waist, the Spaniards had taken up their position wearing white tunics embroidered with purple, of dazzling brilliancy. The total number of infantry in the field was 40,000, and there were 10,000 cavalry. Hasdrubal was in command of the left wing, Maharbal of the right; Hannibal himself with his brother Mago commanded the center. It was a great convenience to both armies that the sun shone obliquely on them, whether it was that they had purposely

so placed themselves, or whether it happened by accident, because the Romans faced the north, the Carthaginians the south. The wind, called by the inhabitants the Vulturnus,[34] was against the Romans, and blew great clouds of dust into their faces, making it impossible for them to see in front of them.

When the battle shout was raised the auxiliaries ran forward, and the battle began with the light infantry. Then the Gauls and Spaniards on the left engaged the Roman cavalry on the right; the battle was not at all like a cavalry fight, for there was no room for maneuvering, the river on the one side and the infantry on the other hemming them in, compelled them to fight face to face. Each side tried to force their way straight forward, until at last the horses were standing in a closely pressed mass, and the riders seized their opponents and tried to drag them from their horses. It had become mainly a struggle of infantry, fierce but short, and the Roman cavalry was repulsed and fled. Just as this battle of the cavalry was finished, the infantry became engaged, and as long as the Gauls and Spaniards kept their ranks unbroken, both sides were equally matched in strength and courage. At length after long and repeated efforts the Romans closed up their ranks, echeloned their front,[35] and by the sheer weight of their deep column bore down the division of the enemy that was stationed in front of Hannibal's line and was too thin and weak to resist the pressure. Without a moment's pause they followed up their broken and hastily retreating foe until they took to headlong flight. Cutting their way through the mass of fugitives, who offered no resistance, they penetrated as far as the Africans who were stationed on both wings, somewhat further back than the Gauls and Spaniards who had formed the advanced center. As the latter fell back the whole front became level, and as they continued to give ground it became concave and crescent-shaped, the Africans at either end forming the horns. As the Romans rushed on

---

[33] From the Balearic Islands in the Mediterranean Sea east of Spain; known for their skill as slingers.

[34] The Roman god of the east wind.

[35] By advancing in misaligned columns, a tactic made famous by the Theban general Epaminondas in the 370s and 360s BCE.

incautiously between them, they were enfiladed[36] by the two wings, which extended and closed round them in the rear. On this, the Romans, who had fought one battle to no purpose, left the Gauls and Spaniards, whose rear they had been slaughtering, and commenced a fresh struggle with the Africans. The contest was a very one-sided one, for not only were they hemmed in on all sides, but wearied with the previous fighting they were meeting fresh and vigorous opponents.

By this time the Roman left wing, where the allied cavalry were fronting the Numidians, had become engaged, but the fighting was slack at first owing to a Carthaginian stratagem. About 500 Numidians, carrying, besides their usual arms and missiles, swords concealed under their coats of mail, rode out from their own line with their shields slung behind their backs as though they were deserters, and suddenly leaped from their horses and flung their shields and javelins at the feet of their enemy. They were received into their ranks, conducted to the rear, and ordered to remain quiet. While the battle was spreading to the various parts of the field they remained quiet, but when the eyes and minds of all were wholly taken up with the fighting they seized the large Roman shields that were lying everywhere among the heaps of slain and commenced a furious attack upon the rear of the Roman line. Slashing away at backs and hips, they made a great slaughter and a still greater panic and confusion. Amid the rout and panic in one part of the field and the obstinate but hopeless struggle in the other, Hasdrubal, who was in command of that arm, withdrew some Numidians from the center of the right wing, where the fighting was feebly kept up, and sent them in pursuit of the fugitives, and at the same time sent the Spanish and Gallic horse to the aid of the Africans, who were by this time more wearied by slaughter than by fighting.

Paullus was on the other side of the field. In spite of his having been seriously wounded at the commencement of the action by a bullet from a sling, he frequently encountered Hannibal with a compact body of troops, and in several places restored the battle. The Roman cavalry formed a bodyguard

round him, but at last, as he became too weak to manage his horse, they all dismounted. It is stated that when someone reported to Hannibal that the Consul had ordered his men to fight on foot, he remarked, "I would rather he handed them over to me bound hand and foot." Now that the victory of the enemy was no longer doubtful this struggle of the dismounted cavalry was such as might be expected when men preferred to die where they stood rather than flee, and the victors, furious at them for delaying the victory, butchered without mercy those whom they could not dislodge. They did, however, repulse a few survivors exhausted with their exertions and their wounds.

All were at last scattered, and those who could regained their horses for flight. Cn. Lentulus, a Military Tribune, saw, as he rode by, the Consul covered with blood sitting on a boulder. "Lucius Aemilius," he said, "the one man whom the gods must hold guiltless of this day's disaster, take this horse while you have still some strength left." The Consul replied: "Cornelius, do not waste in useless pity the few moments left in which to escape from the hands of the enemy. Go, announce publicly to the Senate that they must fortify Rome before the victorious enemy approaches, and tell Q. Fabius privately that I have ever remembered his precepts in life and in death. Suffer me to breathe my last among my slaughtered soldiers." Lentulus escaped on horseback in the rush. The other Consul escaped with about fifty cavalry to Venusia. 45,500 infantry, 2700 cavalry, almost an equal proportion of Romans and allies, are said to have been killed.

Such was the battle of Cannae, a battle as famous as the disastrous one at the Allia River[37]; not so serious in its results, owing to the inaction of the enemy, but more serious and more horrible in view of the slaughter of the army. For the flight at the Allia saved the army although it lost the city, whereas at Cannae hardly fifty men shared the Consul's flight, nearly the whole army met their death in company with the other Consul.

Hannibal's officers all surrounded him and congratulated him on his victory, and urged that after

---

[36] Surrounded.

[37] Where the Romans were defeated by the Gauls in 390 BCE.

such a magnificent success he should allow himself and his exhausted men to rest. Maharbal, however, the commandant of the cavalry, thought that they ought not to lose a moment. "That you may know," he said to Hannibal, "what has been gained by this battle I prophesy that in five days you will be feasting as victor in the Capitol. Follow me; I will go in advance with the cavalry; they will know that you are come before they know that you are coming." Hannibal told Maharbal that he commended his zeal, but he needed time to think out his plans. Maharbal replied, "You know how to win victory, Hannibal, but you do not how to use it."[38] That delay is believed to have saved the city and the nation.

The reports that reached Rome left no room for hope that even these remnants of citizens and allies were still surviving; it was asserted that the army with its two Consuls had been annihilated and the whole of the forces wiped out. Never before, while the city itself was still safe, had there been such excitement and panic within its walls. Over and above these serious disasters, considerable alarm was created by portents that occurred. Two Vestal virgins, Opimia and Floronia, were found guilty of unchastity. One was buried alive, as is the custom, at the Colline Gate,[39] the other committed suicide. L. Cantilius, one of the pontifical secretaries, now called "Minor Pontiffs," who had been guilty with Floronia, was whipped in the Comitium by the *Pontifex Maximus* so severely that he died under it. This act of wickedness, coming as it did among so many calamities, was regarded as a portent, and the Decemvirs were ordered to consult the Sibylline Books. Q. Fabius Pictor[40] was sent to consult the Oracle of Delphi as to what forms of prayer and supplication they were to use to propitiate the gods, and what was to be the end of all these terrible disasters. Meanwhile, in obedience to the Sibylline Books, some strange and unusual sacrifices were made, human sacrifices among them. A Gallic man and a Gallic woman and a Greek man and a Greek woman were buried alive under the Forum Boarium.[41] They were lowered into a stone vault, which had on a previous occasion also been polluted by human victims, a practice most repulsive to Roman feelings.

Yet, in spite of all their disasters, no one anywhere in Rome mentioned the word "Peace," either before the Consul's return or after his arrival. Such a lofty spirit did the citizens exhibit in those days that although the Consul[42] was coming back from a terrible defeat for which they knew he was mainly responsible, he was met by a vast concourse drawn from every class of society, and thanks were formally voted to him because he "had not despaired of the Republic." Had he been commander-in-chief of the Carthaginians there was no torture to which he would not have been subjected.[43]

---

[38] One of the most famous quotations of antiquity.
[39] One of the gates of Rome.

[40] The first Roman writer of history, who wrote in Greek ca. 200 BCE.
[41] The "Cattle Forum" in Rome.
[42] Varro.
[43] The Carthaginians executed defeated generals.

CHAPTER 5

THE IMPACT OF EXPANSION ON ROME IN THE SECOND CENTURY BCE

By 133 BCE, Rome controlled territory extending from Spain to Anatolia, giving rise to what has been known as the **Republican Empire.** This expansion had far-reaching economic, social, and cultural effects as the Romans came into close contact with a multitude of other peoples. The days of Rome as a simple central Italian city-state now were long gone, and, like it or not, the Romans had to face the consequences. The most significant impact of warfare was not simply the acquisition of foreign territory, but the consequences of encounters with foreign peoples on Roman society, religion, economy, culture, and politics.

ECONOMIC DEVELOPMENTS

Roman expansion had significant effects on the Roman economy. For centuries, the Romans had primarily an agricultural economy, and trade, manufacturing, and commerce did not play a tremendous role. But Roman expansion brought a need for not only liquid capital but also financial managers.

Roman Coinage

Warfare created the need for an effective monetary system to pay for it. The earliest Roman money had consisted of large copper bricks known as *aes signatum* ("stamped copper") with symbols, such as a cow, pig, or elephant, imprinted on them. Indeed, the Latin word for money, *pecunia*, was derived from *pecus*, or herd of cows, suggesting that the Roman economy initially was on the cow standard. Copper coins, first issued in 289 BCE, were cumbersome and crude: the *as*, a coin valued at a pound of copper, actually weighed a pound. Soon afterward, a silver coinage, based on Greek models, was created. The standard Roman silver coin, the *denarius*, was introduced around 212 BCE, when tremendous amounts of coinage were needed to pay the expenses of the Second Punic War. A gold *aureus* was issued

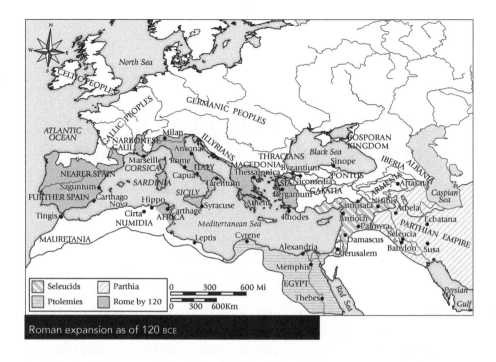

Roman expansion as of 120 BCE

only in times of great emergency, such as when the Romans consolidated their resources in the fight against Hannibal. By then, moreover, the Romans also had become more financially sophisticated, and they realized that by linking the value of the copper and silver coinages—one silver *denarius* was initially valued at ten copper *asses*—they could float a loan on the population by using smaller, cheaply produced copper coins in place of silver ones. Once the Romans had gained political control of the Mediterranean world, their economic influence became so great that the silver *denarius* became the standard currency of the Mediterranean world.

The word "penny" comes from denarius.

TABLE 5.1   COIN DENOMINATIONS OF THE ROMAN REPUBLIC

Metal	Denomination	Value
Gold	Aureus (aurei)	First 18, then 20 denarii
Silver	Denarius (denarii)	First 10, then 16 asses
Silver	Quinarius	½ denarius: 5, then 8 asses
Silver	Sestertius (sesterces)	¼ denarius: 2½, then 4 asses
Copper	As (asses)	12 unciae
Copper	Semis	6 unciae, ½ as
Copper	Triens	4 unciae, ⅓ as
Copper	Quadrans	3 unciae, ¼ as
Copper	Sextans	2 unciae, ⅙ as
Copper	Uncia	1 uncia (ounce)

Public Expenses

A consequence of having increased economic resources was the expansion of building projects and public entertainments. Aqueducts, beginning with the Aqua Appia built in conjunction with the Appian Way in the late fourth century BCE, brought fresh water into Rome. Old-fashioned buildings, such as the temple of Jupiter on the Capitoline Hill, were remodeled, and new public buildings, such as basilicas, where the Praetors could hear legal cases, were constructed. Imaginative forms of architectural construction used bricks and concrete, as well as stone, to build the arch, the vault, and the dome and replaced the rather predictable Greek marble-block, rectangular-temple format. People also came to expect elaborate entertainments, such as chariot racing and gladiatorial combats, to commemorate festivals and special events. Regular chariot races, borrowed from the Etruscans and Greeks and held on racecourses known as circuses, were held as of 211 BCE in a festival honoring Apollo. And gladiatorial contests, likewise borrowed from the Etruscans, were presented at the funerals of important persons commencing toward the end of the third century. Eventually, however, they were put on purely for entertainment.

The Rise of the Equestrians

A social consequence of Rome's economic expansion was the rise of a new social class, the equestrians (or knights), who adopted the name (but not the function) of the old top class of the Centuriate Assembly and ranked between the senators and the plebeians. These opportunistic individuals made their fortunes in trade, manufacturing, money lending, and tax collecting, activities that were considered unsuitable for conservative senators, who believed that land was the only respectable kind of investment. Indeed, a law of 218 BCE even prohibited senators from owning merchant ships. Roman political control over the Mediterranean world gave the equestrians business advantages over non-Romans, such as access to large financial resources and legal preference in Roman courts.

WHAT TO DO WITH THE PROVINCES

The establishment, between 227 and 133 BCE, of provinces that extended from Spain in the west to Asia in the east created critical pressure for the Roman administration, which had been instituted to govern a small city-state, not a Mediterranean-wide empire. The strain became so serious that in several ways Rome was simply unable to cope with the consequences and responsibilities that came with these new territories. Never having really wanted most of them in the first place, and often having acquired them simply to keep them out of the hands of potential enemies, the Romans saw little reason to alter their city-state form of government in order to accommodate them.

Provincial Administration

As a result, direct Roman administration was very minimal. Provinces were governed by **Proconsuls** (who in the past, usually the year before, had been Consuls) and by Praetors. Proconsuls had the same *imperium* as Consuls, and thus could issue laws and lead armies, which generally were stationed in the provinces only on an as-needed basis because of the expense involved. Provincial governors generally served for one year and had only a very small staff, consisting of a Quaestor to handle the finances and a few Legates to whom authority (and *imperium*) could be delegated.

A governor's main responsibilities were to oversee the administration of justice, provide military defense, and collect the taxes. Their small staffs meant that nearly all the aspects of day-to-day local administration were left in the hands of locals. This was done by dividing up the province into smaller territorial units, each administered by the city council of a *civitas* (city). If a province did not already have cities, as was the case in western European regions such as Spain, the Romans created them and, for purposes of local administration, divided up the province's territory among them. In many cases, the territory of a *civitas* capital roughly matched the territory of Celtic peoples, although the actual city was established not at one of the old hill fort sites but at a more accessible place. Governors made a regular circuit of the cities in their provinces to remind the **provincials**, the inhabitants of the provinces who did not have Roman citizenship, of the Roman presence and to adjudicate legal disputes that could not be settled locally.

Many cities created in western Europe by the Romans continue to be important cities in the modern day.

Problems in the Provinces

Even though the Romans did not intend to exploit or misgovern the provinces, there were potential problems with Roman policies and administrative methods. For example, the provincials had no established means of interaction with the Roman government. There was no centralized office of provincial administration either in Rome or in the individual provinces, the provincials had no rights in Rome, and the governor was the last court of appeal. In addition, there was no regular means by which provincials could become Roman citizens, although governors, by virtue of their power of *imperium*, did have the power to create citizens in an ad hoc way.

The greatest complaint with provincial administration, in some provinces at least, involved the taxes. Not that Roman taxes were excessive; indeed, sometimes they were lower than before the Roman conquest. The problem had to do with how the taxes were collected. Taxes were assessed by two different processes, depending on the system that had been in place at the time the Romans created a province. In economically sophisticated provinces where there already was extensive exploitation of agriculture, such as Sicily and Asia, the taxation system known as the **tithe** was in effect. In the tithe system, farmers paid one-tenth of their annual crop in taxes. This meant that in a good farming year taxes would be high, and in a bad year they would be low. This could have been a fair system, but in practice, because of the lack of Roman administrative oversight, there were many opportunities for abuse, as when the locally hired tax collectors, known as *publicani* ("publicans"), seized large quantities of crops and called it "a tenth." As a result, *publicani* developed a very unsavory reputation. In provinces that were less economically developed, a form of tax known as *tributum*, or tribute, was assessed. This was a fixed amount that was paid each year irrespective of how economically productive a province had been during the year. The tribute system was less liable to corruption because there was no uncertainty about exactly how much each taxpayer owed.

TABLE 5.2 ROMAN PROVINCES, 227–121 BCE

Province	Date Annexed	Governor
Sicily	227 BCE	Praetor
Sardinia and Corsica	227 BCE	Praetor
Nearer Spain	197 BCE	Praetor
Further Spain	197 BCE	Praetor
Africa	146 BCE	Proconsul
Macedonia	146 BCE	Proconsul
Asia	129 BCE	Proconsul
Narbonese Gaul	121 BCE	Proconsul

Because the government did not have staffing to arrange to collect the taxes itself, the right to do so in various regions was auctioned off to "tax-farming" companies. These paid the Roman government a lump sum and then extorted as much as they could from the provincials. Even if a governor protested against or tried to limit abuses, he often had little ability to prevent it. And to make it even more difficult to restrain unscrupulous tax collectors, the tax-farming companies were increasingly operated not by wealthy provincials but by even wealthier Roman equestrians, who often were the only ones with financial resources sufficient to raise the huge amounts of money needed to bid. The equestrians' connections in Rome made it even more difficult for provincial governors to repress corruption in the provinces, given that the equestrians were behind the corruption, and once a governor's term of service was up he could expect resentment and resistance from ambitious equestrians and their senatorial allies back in Rome.

The Extortion Court

In most regards, the Roman government paid little attention to the provinces. It did not intend to exploit the provinces, and it rarely made money. Any corruption that arose through the sale of justice or problems in tax collection benefited individual profiteers or governors, not the Roman government. The government just had no procedures for policing the provinces. A senatorial *Quaestio de repetundis*, or **Extortion Court**, established in 149 BCE, was meant to try governors for corruption but often ended up being used to trump up charges against a senator's political enemies, and as a consequence good governors sometimes ended up being the ones charged with "corruption." One of the main failures of the Republic was that it never found a way to integrate the provinces and the provincials into Roman government, administration, and society.

SOCIAL AND CULTURAL CONSEQUENCES OF EXPANSION

Roman expansion also exposed the Romans to many foreign cultural influences, especially from Greece. Indeed, the poet Horace later wrote that "captured Greece overcame her savage conqueror and introduced the arts into rustic Latium." The adoption of aspects of foreign culture had both its supporters and detractors.

Intellectual and Literary Development

Greek theories of rhetoric found a receptive audience among the Romans, for whom public speaking was a necessity of political life. Greek philosophical beliefs, which gave people the opportunity to define their own personal place and role in the world, also made their way into Rome. For example, Zeno, a native of Citium on Cyprus who settled in Athens about 300 BCE, developed a teaching called **Stoicism** because he taught in the *Stoa Poikilē*, or "Painted Portico." His teachings were centered on a materialistic universe that was highly structured into a pattern established by a rational governing force called the *logos*. But all the *logos* did was to set the universe in motion; otherwise the Stoic universe had no gods. It rather was like a very predictable finely tuned machine that repeated itself about every twenty-six thousand years. Every individual person represented one tiny part of the machine, and it was everyone's duty to perform the role that they had been assigned by god. The Stoic creed was "Lead me, O Zeus, wherever you will, and I will follow willingly, and if I do not, you will drag me." The only choice a Stoic had was either to accept the inevitable, which already had been determined by the *logos*, or to fight against it and inevitably be destroyed. The importance given to the performance of duty made Stoicism well suited for individuals committed to duty and public service, and it found many Roman adherents.

The philosopher Epicurus of Samos, who founded a school called the Garden in Athens circa 300 BCE, likewise took a materialistic approach, but one that was completely unstructured, to understanding one's personal place in the world. His teachings, which came to be known as **Epicureanism**, proposed that there were no gods or good or bad luck and that the universe consisted simply of atoms randomly falling through space without any guiding principle. Sometimes the atoms swerved, clumped together, and created the material world, including people. The swerve also gave people the free will to pursue the Epicurean goal of gaining *ataraxia*, peace of mind, by pursuing hedonism, or pleasure. But for

Epicurus, pleasure meant preventing one's atoms from getting jangled, and this meant avoiding pain. Thus pleasures that caused pain, such as overeating or drunkenness, were to be avoided. To attain *ataraxia*, one needed to avoid being affected by circumstances. Epicurus thus recommended avoiding public service and pursuing a life of seclusion spent with like-minded friends. Epicurus' school was unusual in that it admitted women. At the same time, however, with its focus on self-indulgence Epicureanism was so offensive to some influential Romans that in the second century BCE Epicurean teachers were expelled from Rome.

At the same time, Roman playwrights such as Plautus and Terence wrote Latin comedies modeled on Greek originals. And in the years after 200 BCE, the first histories of Rome were written in Greek by both Romans and Greeks, most notably Polybius, a Greek hostage who accompanied Scipio Aemilianus at the fall of Carthage and wrote by far the best surviving account of Rome's third-century BCE wars. The adaptation of Greek literary styles and genres to Roman purposes was supported by influential senators such as Scipio Aemilianus, whose Scipionic Circle included not only writers such as Terence, Polybius, the satirist Lucilius, and the Stoic philosopher Panaetius of Rhodes but also senatorial patrons of the arts, such as C. Laelius Sapiens.

Satire continues to be popular, as still seen in political cartoons.

But other Romans were chary of the adoption of too much Greek culture. The conservative senator Cato the Elder, fearing that Rome would be overwhelmed by Hellenism, insisted on writing his own history of Rome in Latin, and later writers followed in his footsteps. At the same time, the Romans developed their own national literary genre, satire, introduced by the writer Lucilius, which took a critical but humorous look at society, morality, and personal behavior. It was written in both poetry and prose and was full of parody, obscenity, and invective. By the end of the second century BCE, Latin had become an established literary language in its own right. And Greece, having lost its political significance, became a place where young Romans went to continue their studies in subjects such as rhetoric and philosophy, especially in Athens.

LEARNING FROM HISTORY

Many Romans would have liked to maintain their old established customs at the same time that they were extending their authority throughout the Mediterranean. Do you think that a world power can keep its culture isolated from politics as it expands to absorb other peoples?

Religious Assimilation

The Romans not only enthusiastically adopted Greek myths and legends, but also assimilated eastern religious practices, such as **mystery cults** (from Greek *mysterion*, or "secret"), which promised a happy afterlife. All of the mystery cults involved the worship of a god or goddess who suffered, died, and was resurrected, and participants went through an **initiation** rite in which they learned the secrets that would grant them, too, eternal life. During the ceremony, the human participant in some way shared the identity of the god and as a consequence shared in the god's immortality. If the god could be resurrected, then so could you. Different cults created this mystical union with the god in different ways. Initiates were sworn to secrecy, but enough of the ritual slipped out for us to be able to form a general picture of what happened. The ceremony usually began with a purification ritual that enabled the initiate to come into contact with the deity. It then entailed sitting through, or actually participating in, an elaborate performance explaining the cycle of life and death.

In order to be initiated into most mystery cults, all people had to do was show up, although some cults made greater demands than others. Whereas some initiations, such as into the Eleusinian mysteries in Athens, occurred only in single location, others could occur anywhere. For example, the ancient Egyptian **cult of Isis**, in which Osiris was brought back from the dead after being dismembered and thrown into the Nile, was refurbished to make it more attractive to a mass audience. The account given by the third-century CE writer Apuleius provides the most accurate account of the initiation process. First of all, those desiring initiation were expected to live in the temple for a while with the priests and to attend temple rites. Eventually, participants received during the night a sign from the goddess that they were ready to proceed. The next morning the initiates were instructed from an ancient book written in strange characters, probably a reference to hieroglyphs. Then, asking pardon from the gods for their sins, they were baptized with water identified as sacred water from the Nile and were reborn just as Osiris had been reborn from the Nile. Following their baptism, the initiates remained pure for ten days by refraining from drinking wine, eating meat, and having sex. The final initiation rite began at sunset on the tenth day, when the candidates were taken to the innermost part of the temple and metaphorically became Osiris, undergoing a ritual death, traveling to the underworld, and seeing the gods; in one account, Isis herself said to an initiate, "When you descend to the underworld, there you will see me shining and you will worship me as the one who has favored you." The initiates then were reborn with the rising sun the next morning.

In the initiation into the cult of the wine-god **Dionysus**, a son of Zeus known as the "twice born" because Zeus had recreated him after he was eaten by the Titans, participants first drank wine, which represented the god's blood. The next sacrament was the "feast of the raw flesh" in which they tore apart and ate raw a wild animal, such as a fawn, which represented Dionysus himself. By sharing Dionysus' flesh and blood, initiates partook of his divinity and immortality. On some occasions, Dionysian rites known as the Bacchanalia (after Bacchus, another name for Dionysus) turned into sexual orgies brought on by the wine and religious ecstacy.

The most demanding mystery cult was that of **Cybele**, an Anatolian mother goddess. In myth, Cybele fell in love with her son Attis, a vegetation god, but when the young man preferred a local princess, the goddess drove him mad, and he castrated himself with a sharp stone and died under a pine tree. But Cybele brought him back to life in the spring, and, like vegetation, he was ready to die again. The annual festival of Cybele, celebrated in March, recreated the death and rebirth of Attis. A pine tree representing the dead Attis was brought to the

Temple of Cybele, and devotees then mourned his death by abstaining for a day from drinking wine and from eating fruits and vegetables. The climax came on March 24, "the Day of Blood." Participants worked themselves into a frenzy by madly dancing to the sound of clashing cymbals, blaring horns, and beating drums. They also slashed themselves with knives, sprinkling fertilizing blood on the pine tree in order to restore Attis to life. The Greek satirist Lucian described what then could happen: "Frenzy comes upon many who have come simply to watch. The initiate throws off his clothes, takes up a sword, and castrates himself. Then he runs through the city holding the parts he has cut off. He takes female clothing and adornment from whatever house he throws the parts into." By this means, the initiate not only became Attis, the consort of Cybele, but also, in a sense, became Cybele herself, and thus was able to gain immortality. Having taken this irrevocable step, the initiate, if he survived, also became one of the wandering priests of Cybele known as the Galli.

There was nothing complicated about mystery cults. People gained salvation simply by having a brief devotion to a mystery deity and by engaging in the appropriate rituals. There was no need for any long-term commitment or any continued ritual. Nor were the cults exclusive, and people could be initiated into any number of mystery cults. These were the first religions of redemption open to all, and they were extraordinarily popular. Thus there was a widespread belief that it was possible to gain a life after death by following the model of a god who had done the same thing and by participating in a ceremony that mimicked the experiences of the god.

Sometimes the importation of eastern mystery cults into Rome was done officially, as when during the closing days of the Second Punic War, the Romans again consulted the Sibylline Books and were told to bring the "Great Mother" from Anatolia. As a result, a meteoric stone representing Cybele was brought to Rome in 204, and after the quickly ensuing defeat of Hannibal in 201, a Temple of Cybele was dedicated in 191 BCE and an annual festival known as the "Megalensia" (from the Greek word for "great") was inaugurated.

On other occasions, however, the introduction of eastern religions created official anxiety. In 186 BCE, the Consul Spurius Postumius received a report from Hispala, an ex-slave, that worshippers of the wine god Bacchus were holding secret orgies. According to the later historian Livy, "There was nothing wicked that was not practiced among them. There was more frequent pollution of men with each other than with women. If any were unwilling to commit vice, they were sacrificed as victims." The Senate not only feared a threat to conventional morality but also was concerned that the clandestine gatherings might lead to conspiracies against the government. Many of those convicted of engaging in these Bacchanalian rites were condemned to death, with women turned over to their families "so they could inflict the punishment in private." As a reward for coming forward, Hispala was granted the unusual privilege of being permitted to marry a man of higher social status.

The Changing Status of Women

The example of Hispala demonstrates that by the second century BCE, women were becoming more outspoken and assertive. Women gained additional influence in other ways, too, with a liberalization of some of the more restrictive aspects of Roman treatment of women. Some women became so dissatisfied that they took matters into their own hands. In a celebrated case of 331 BCE, 170 women were convicted of trying to poison their husbands. On another occasion, in 195 BCE, women protested against the Oppian Law, which had been issued in the trying times after the Battle of Cannae and ordered that no woman should own more than a half-ounce of gold, or wear multicolored clothing, or ride in Rome in a carriage. The women blockaded the forum and confronted the senators. This kind of political activism by women was absolutely unprecedented. Even though the conservative Consul Cato the Elder complained, "Our freedom is conquered by female fury; we even now let them meddle in the Forum and our assemblies," the offensive law was repealed.

Other demands by women no doubt were pursued behind the scenes, and over the course of time women gained additional rights. The "usage" type of marriage began to be replaced by a marriage *sine manu*, "without authority," in which a woman technically remained under the authority of her father and her property was kept separate from that of her husband. When her father died she then became *sui juris*, "under her own authority," with independent ownership of her own property. Women also obtained the right to initiate various kinds of legal proceedings, such as divorces, buying and selling property, or making wills, although they still needed a cooperative male "guardian" to conduct the legal formalities.

THE AGRICULTURAL-MILITARY CRISIS

During the second half of the second century BCE, a number of problems that had been developing over the course of the previous century, such as the failure of Roman methods for administering the provinces, became so serious that they threatened the very existence of the Republic. The most dramatic problem with the gravest consequences had to do with military recruitment.

Tiberius Gracchus and the Distribution of Public Land

Roman expansion and the annexation of provinces also created problems in other ways. The very act of acquiring them necessarily involved another Roman institution: the army. Ever since the Samnite Wars (343–290 BCE), Roman armies had been fighting farther from home for longer periods. This created problems for the agricultural economy. The ancient military recruiting policies specified by the Servian Reforms required soldiers to be property owners. This meant that rather than tilling the soil, thousands of small farmers were far from home fighting Rome's wars. Many of them did not return, and those who did often had little desire to return to tedious farm life and were happy to sell their plots to senators, who always were looking to acquire additional land. As a consequence, the recruiting base for the army became ever smaller, leaving Rome facing an **agricultural-military crisis**.

It might seem that there would have been two possible solutions to this dilemma: either to abandon the property requirement altogether or to distribute state-owned *ager publicus*, or "public land," to landless plebeians and thus make them eligible for military service. In typical fashion, however, the conservative Senate opposed any attempt at reform: in 140 BCE, the Consul Laelius was dissuaded from introducing a land distribution law and as a result gained the nickname Sapiens ("The Wise"). The problem thus continued to fester.

In 133 BCE a Tribune of the Plebs, **Tiberius Gracchus**, attempted to deal with the recruitment crisis after observing that most of the land in Etruria was being worked not by Roman peasant farmers eligible for military service but, as reported by Plutarch, by "barbarian slaves working as cultivators and shepherds." Now, Tiberius came from the most blue-blooded of Roman senatorial families. His mother, Cornelia, was the daughter of Scipio Africanus, and his sister, Sempronia, was married to Scipio Aemilianus. After the death of her husband, Cornelia turned down an offer of marriage from Ptolemy VII, king of Egypt, and raised and educated Tiberius, Sempronia, and their brother Gaius by herself. She became a classic model of Roman female virtue. According to one story, when she was questioned by fancily adorned Roman matrons about why she, too, was not showing off her jewelry, she called in her sons and stated, "These are my jewels." Tiberius embarked on the standard senatorial career. As a Military Tribune, he was the first over the wall in the final Roman assault on Carthage in 146 BCE, and as Quaestor in Spain in 137, he rescued a defeated Roman army by negotiating a treaty with the Celtiberians. Tiberius thus could have looked forward to an outstanding traditional political career including, no doubt, the consulate. But he instead chose to become a reformer by introducing legislation in the Council of the Plebs to distribute plots of thirty *jugera* (a *jugerum* was about two-thirds of an acre) each of public land to the poor, thus increasing the number of Romans eligible to serve in the army.

Even though Tiberius was supported by some of the most influential senators, the sticking point in his bill was that much of the public land already was being rented by powerful, land-hungry senators who had come to look on it as their own, and this in spite of a law dating back to 367 specifying that no one could lease more than 500 *jugera* of public land. In an attempt to defuse senatorial objections, Tiberius' law granted 500 *jugera* to each senator and 250 to each son of a senator free and clear. But even that was not enough to gain Senate support. When hostile senators induced another Tribune to veto Tiberius' law, Tiberius simply had him deposed and then took the extraordinarily divisive step of failing to gain prior Senate approval and taking his law directly to the Council of the Plebs, where it was duly passed. The opportunity to do this had been enhanced just six years earlier with the passage of a law replacing the old method of verbal voting with secret ballot voting, which weakened the patronage hold of senators on plebeian voters.

A PICTURE IS WORTH A THOUSAND WORDS

DENARIUS OF PUBLIUS LICINIUS NERVA

The reforms of Tiberius Gracchus were facilitated by the introduction of a secret ballot in the popular assemblies in 139 BCE, only six years earlier. The law was intended to reduce bribery and intimidation, but a more significant result was that voters no longer could be observed directly by their patrons and thus were able to vote more freely. A *denarius* issued in 113 BCE by the moneyer Nerva commemorates the introduction of the secret ballot with a voting scene on the reverse depicting one plebeian receiving a ballot from an attendant and another voter placing a ballot in an urn on the right. In the background is a dividing line with a sign bearing the letter "P," which identifies the section of the Comitium, the area of the forum where the assemblies met, marked off for the voting of the thirty-five geographical tribes (tribes whose names began with the letter "P" included Palatina, an urban tribe, and Papira, Polla, Popillia, and Pupinia, rural tribes). The obverse of the coin depicts the goddess Roma in full armor, with a winged helmet, a spear, and a shield depicting a cavalryman. Behind the bust is the legend "ROMA," and the symbol X (shorthand for XVI) to her left reflects the revaluing of the denarius from 10 to 16 asses. The office of moneyer was held by young men, usually from senatorial families, just beginning their political careers. Licinius Nerva went on to serve as Praetor in Sicily in 104 BCE; he was relieved of duty when he was unable to restrain a major slave revolt, which was not finally put down until 101 BCE.

When the Senate then refused to allocate any funding to put the **land law** into effect, Tiberius threatened to introduce a law assigning it the wealth of the newly acquired kingdom of Pergamum, and the Senate was forced to yield, only exacerbating the hard feelings of many senators toward Tiberius. The law then took effect, and public land began to be allocated to landless plebs. But when Tiberius announced a provocative intention to run for reelection as Tribune to ensure the success of the land law, conservative senators had had enough; Tiberius had violated too many time-tested traditions. On election day, rioting broke out. In the Senate, the senator Scipio Nasica, an ex-Consul and the cousin of Tiberius, declared, "All who want to save the state, follow me." A number of senators, using pieces of broken furniture, then clubbed Tiberius and three hundred of his supporters to death. The willingness of the senators to violate the principle of *sacrosanctitas*, which made the persons of Tribunes inviolate, demonstrates the degree to which they were prepared to violate past traditions in pursuit of their agendas. Subsequently, senatorial kangaroo courts executed or exiled many of Tiberius' supporters.

The murder of Tiberius and his supporters marked the first appearance of serious violence in Republican politics. And the tactics used by both Tiberius and the Senate marked the beginning of the breakdown of the carefully nurtured cooperation among senators that had made the Republic work. Senators now increasingly looked out for their own self-interest. They adopted different strategies for doing so. Some, known as the *optimates* ("the best people"), preferred to work within the Senate, often in an obstructionist manner, in an attempt to prevent any reform of the Roman political, economic, and social system. Others, the *populares* ("men of the people"), sought support for political programs directly from the people and were characterized by programs intended to gain popular support, such as land distribution or subsidized foodstuffs. *Populares* also made common cause with the equestrians, and even with Italians, in an attempt to find support outside the Senate. But the distinction between *optimates* and *populares* refers strictly to the kinds of political methods they used and should not be confused with political parties, for those who used these different tactics did not have any common political agendas. All would have claimed that they supported the rights of the Senate and were working for the greater glory of Rome as each politician pursued his own immediate personal ambitions, not the long-term goals of any group.

What to Do with the Italian Allies?

Military recruitment policies related to Roman expansion also created another kind of problem. Over time, Rome's Italian allies had provided an ever-greater percentage of Rome's armies, rising from half in the third century BCE to two-thirds by the early first century. The Italians felt that they were bearing more and more of the burden for Rome's wars but were sharing less and less in the benefits. Not only that, but the Roman government was behaving increasingly high-handedly toward them. On one occasion, the wife of a Roman magistrate wanted to use the men's baths at an Italian town. The town's chief magistrate was publicly flogged when he was slow in clearing out the baths. And after the passage of Tiberius Gracchus' land law, the Romans attempted to confiscate Italian land for distribution, giving rise to howls of protest.

Italian concerns coalesced into demands to be granted Roman citizenship. Only in this way could the Italians share in the benefits of expansion in business and commerce, be protected under Roman law, and be immune from oppression by Roman officials. But these demands were resisted both by senators, who feared that the addition of hundreds of thousands of new citizens would weaken their ability to use their ties of patronage to control the voting in the popular assemblies, and by plebeians, who feared that the dilution of the citizen ranks would lessen the privileges that they gained from citizenship. In 125 BCE the Consul Fulvius Flaccus, an ally of the Gracchi, introduced a bill to make Italians citizens, but he was induced by the Senate to withdraw the measure by the offer of an attractive military command in Gaul. When Flaccus' bill came to nought, the Latin town of Fregellae attempted to withdraw from its alliance with Rome. The Roman response was quick and deadly: Fregellae was razed to the ground by the Praetor Opimius.

Gaius Gracchus and the Expansion of Popular Tactics

These events set the stage for the rise to prominence of Tiberius' younger brother **Gaius Gracchus**, who was elected Tribune of the Plebs for the year 123 BCE. Gaius made no attempt to hide his antipathy toward the Senate, which he viewed as being directly responsible for his brother's death. As one of the most preeminent orators of Rome, Gaius was able to influence the Council of the Plebs to approve many reform measures. He reaffirmed and expanded the program of land distribution, increasing the size of the plots and founding colonies for those who wanted to settle together. He even attempted to found an overseas colony in Africa, near, but not on, the site of Carthage. Back in Rome, in order to maintain his support among the urban mob, Gaius passed legislation providing subsidized foodstuffs to needy plebeians. Having secured his electoral base, Gaius then took his revenge on the Senate, transferring control of the Extortion Court from the Senate to the equestrians, the very people who were the cause of most of the extortion. This meant that a governor who actually suppressed extortion in a province could be put on trial and convicted for extortion back in Rome, as happened in 92 BCE when the ex-Consul Rufus, a New Man, was convicted of extortion in Asia after he had gallantly suppressed the abuses of the equestrians. He spent his exile in Asia, where he was welcomed with open arms. Gaius was said to have called this law "a dagger in the side of the Senate." This act also acknowledged the equestrians as an important political entity and marked another step in the weakening of the Senate's authority. Gaius also favored the equestrians with a law stipulating that the right to collect the taxes for the entire province of Asia was to be auctioned off in Rome, something that only opportunistic equestrians could afford.

Gaius was reelected as Tribune for 122 BCE and was joined by Fulvius Flaccus, who took the unprecedented step of running for Tribune after already having been Consul. The two revived the plan to grant Roman citizenship to the Italians, but they were opposed by another Tribune, Drusus, an ally of the Senate. Drusus' strategy was to out-Gaius Gaius by making even more popular proposals, such as a plan to found twelve colonies for the poorest Roman citizens, that he and his senatorial allies never intended to implement. Drusus then vetoed Gaius' franchise bill, and Gaius felt too weakened to do anything about it. When Gaius ran for a third tribunate in 121 BCE, he was soundly defeated. He and Flaccus then occupied the Aventine Hill, the traditional place of plebeian resistance, with armed bands, at which the Senate passed the *Senatus consultum ultimum*, the **"Last Recommendation of the Senate,"** which commanded the Consuls to take whatever measures they thought were necessary to see to it that the state came to no harm. At this, the Consul Opimius—who as Praetor had destroyed Fregellae—raised an armed band of citizens. Flaccus was killed in the general mêlée, Gaius ordered a trusted slave to stab him to death, and in the aftermath three thousand of Gaius' followers were executed.

The end of Gaius and his supporters made it even more clear that the old Roman Republican "gentlemen's agreement" among senators—to work together to avoid dissension and to keep power in the hands of the Senate and preserve old traditions while at the same time favoring the ambitions of a few prese-lected nobles—just was not working anymore. Cagy politicians had learned that they could achieve their goals by looking for support further down the social scale, from equestrians, plebeians, and even Italian allies. No matter how much senatorial *optimates* attempted to close ranks, resist change, and hold on to authority, the united front on which they had prided themselves so much in the past was broken.

⇦ LOOKING BACK

As the Romans expanded out of Latium into Italy, and then out of Italy into the wider Mediterranean world, they assimilated elements of the cultures of the peoples with whom they came into contact. As a consequence, the Romans eventually had to cope with significant changes to their economy, society, culture, and religious practices. The rise of Rome as a world power thus brought many disruptive influences into Rome: tremendous wealth, the opportunity for great military power, and the realization that there were additional sources of wealth, culture, authority, and prestige outside of Rome. In particular, expansion brought political changes and the breakdown of the carefully maintained senatorial united front.

LOOKING AHEAD ⇨

By the middle of the second century BCE, the big question was whether the Romans would be able to preserve the way of life that had made Roman government work ever since 509 BCE. Until this time, senators had been able to distribute power and authority among themselves in a way that kept powerful, status-conscious senators sufficiently happy that they were willing to continue to bring all their many resources to bear in support of the government. As the stakes became higher and the rewards became greater, would powerful senators be willing, or able, to continue to put Rome first?

FURTHER READING

Brunt, P. A. *Italian Manpower 225 B.C.–A.D. 14.* Oxford: Clarendon Press, 1971.

Byrd, Robert C. *The Senate of the Roman Republic.* Honolulu: Univ. Press of the Pacific, 2001.

Crawford, Michael H. *Coinage and Money under the Roman Republic.* London: Methuen, 1985.

de Ligt, L., and S. J. Northwood, eds. *People, Land, and Politics. Demographic Developments and the Transformation of Roman Italy, 300 BC–AD 14.* Leiden: Brill, 2008.

Errington, R. M. *The Dawn of Empire: Rome's Rise to World Power.* Ithaca, NY: Cornell Univ. Press, 1972.

Gabba, Emilio. *Republican Rome, the Army, and the Allies.* Berkeley: Univ. of California Press, 1976.

Gardner, J. F. *Women in Roman Law and Society.* Bloomington: Indiana Univ. Press, 1986.

Harris, William V. *War and Imperialism in Republican Rome 327–70 B.C.* Oxford: Oxford Univ. Press, 1979.

Lintott, A. *Violence in Republican Rome.* Oxford: Clarendon Press, 1968.

Millar, Fergus. *Rome, the Greek World, and the East: Volume 1: The Roman Republic and the Augustan Revolution.* Chapel Hill: Univ. of North Carolina Press, 2002.

Mouritsen, H. *Plebs and Politics in Late Republican Rome.* Cambridge, UK: Cambridge Univ. Press, 2001.

Scullard, H. H. *From the Gracchi to Nero: A History of Rome from 133 BC to AD 68.* 5th ed. Oxford: Routledge, 1982.

Stockton, D. L. *The Gracchi.* Oxford: Clarendon Press, 1979.

Yakobson, A. *Elections and Electioneering in Rome: A Study in the Political System of the Late Republic.* Stuttgart: Steiner, 1999.

SOURCES

THE BACCHANALIAN SCANDAL AND A CRIMINAL INVESTIGATION OF THE IMPACT OF FOREIGN CULTURES ON ROME (186 BCE)

LIVY, *FROM THE FOUNDING OF THE CITY*, BOOK 39, CHAPTERS 5–19, AND "THE RECOMMENDATION OF THE SENATE ON THE BACCHANALIANS"

An original copy of the "Recommendation of the Senate on the Bacchanalians," engraved on a bronze plate, still survives, preserved in the Kunsthistorisches Museum in Vienna.

One of the very few records of an actual criminal investigation to survive from the Roman Republic is contained in a "Recommendation of the Senate Concerning the Worshippers of Bacchus" that was issued to the Consuls in 186 BCE. It demonstrates that even though the Senate was just an advisory body, it often acted as if it had direct authority to issue regulations and to instruct magistrates to take specific actions. It included the actual minutes of a meeting of the Senate that recorded investigations into the activities of worshippers of the wine god Bacchus, another name for Dionysus, in the year 186 BCE. During the course of the inquiry, Roman concerns arose regarding threats to their way of life posed by exposure to foreign customs. Roman discomfort about illegal organizations, and especially those that met at night (see the "Twelve Tables" above, Chapter 3), also surfaced. It is our good fortune that two detailed sources on this controversy survive, in the Roman historian Livy's *From the Founding of the City* and in an original copy of the Recommendation[1] of the Senate issued to the two Consuls, inscribed on bronze and set up for all to see. It is preserved in the Kunsthistorisches Museum in Vienna.

---

[1] Traditionally, the Latin term *senatus consultum* has been translated as "Decree of the Senate." But the Senate was not a constitutional body and did not issue legislation. The most it could do was give advice and make recommendations. The advice usually was followed, and had the de facto force of law, but de iure, all the Senate did was issue *Consultationes* ("Recommendations").

(a) Livy, *From the Founding of the City*, Book 39, Chapters 5–19

Oliver J. Thatcher, ed., *The Library of Original Sources: Vol. III: The Roman World*, (Milwaukee: Univ. Research Extension Co., 1907), 65–77.

The following year diverted Spurius Postumius Albinus and Quintus Marcius Philippus[2] from the care of armies, and wars, and provinces, to the punishing of an intestine conspiracy. Both Consuls were advised to make an inquisition concerning clandestine meetings. A Greek of mean condition came into Etruria, a low operator in sacrifices, and a soothsayer, and a priest of secret and nocturnal rites. These mysterious rites were, at first, imparted to a few, but afterward communicated to great numbers, both men and women. To their religious performances were added the pleasures of wine and feasting, to allure a greater number of proselytes. When wine, lascivious discourse, night, and the mingling of the sexes had extinguished every sentiment of modesty, then debaucheries of every kind began to be practiced, as every person found at hand that sort of enjoyment to which he was disposed by the passion predominant in his nature.

Nor were they confined to one species of vice, the promiscuous mingling of free-born men and women, but from this store-house of villainy proceeded false witnesses, counterfeit seals, false evidences, and pretended discoveries. From the same place, too, proceeded poison and secret murders, so that in some cases, not even the bodies could be found for burial. Many of their audacious deeds were brought about by treachery, but most of them by force. It served to conceal the violence, that, on account of the loud shouting, and the noise of drums and cymbals, none of the cries uttered by the persons suffering violence or murder could be heard abroad.

The infection of this mischief, like that from the contagion of disease, spread from Etruria to Rome, where the size of the city affording greater room for such evils and more means of concealment, cloaked it at first, but information of it was at length brought to the Consul, Postumius, principally in the following manner. Publius Aebutius, whose father had held equestrian rank in the army,[3] was left an orphan, and his guardians having died, he was educated under the eye of his mother Duronia, and his stepfather Titus Sempronius Rutilus. Duronia was entirely devoted to her husband; and Sempronius, having managed the guardianship in such a manner that he could not give an account of the property, wished that his ward should be either made away with, or bound to compliance with his will by some strong tie. The Bacchanalian rites were the only way to effect the ruin of the youth. His mother told him that, "during his sickness, she had made a vow for him, that if he should recover, she would initiate him among the Bacchanalians."

There was a freedwoman called Hispala Fecenia, a noted courtesan, but deserving of a better lot than the mode of life to which she had been accustomed when very young and a slave, and by which she had maintained herself since her manumission. As they lived in the same neighborhood, an intimacy subsisted between her and Aebutius, which was far from being injurious to the young man's character or property, for he had been loved and wooed by her unsolicited, and as his friends supplied his wants ungenerously, he was supported by the generosity of this woman. To such a length did she go under the influence of her affection, that, on the death of her patron, because she was under the protection of no one, having petitioned the Tribunes and Praetors for a guardian[4] when she was making her will, she constituted Aebutius her sole heir.

As neither kept anything secret from the other, the young man, jokingly, bid her not be surprised if he separated himself from her for a few nights, as, on account of a religious duty, to discharge a vow made for his health, he intended to be initiated among the Bacchanalians. On hearing this,

---

[2] Consuls for the year 186 BCE.

[3] That is, that he had been granted a "public horse," a great honor.

[4] A temporary guardian, just for the purpose of filing the will. Women were not allowed to submit documents with their own hand, so courts had stand-in men to perform this service.

the woman, greatly alarmed, cried out, "May the gods will more favorably!", affirming that it would be better, both for him and her, to lose their lives than that he should do such a thing. She then imprecated curses, vengeance, and destruction on the head of those who advised him to such a step. The young man, surprised both at her expressions and at the violence of her alarm, bid her refrain from curses, for it was his mother who ordered him to do so, with the approbation of his stepfather. "Then," said she, "your stepfather is in haste to destroy, by that act, your chastity, your character, your hopes, and your life."

To him, now surprised by such language, and inquiring what was the matter, she said that when she was a slave, she had gone into that place of worship as an attendant on her mistress, but that, since she had obtained her liberty, she had never once gone near it: that she knew it to be the receptacle of all kinds of debaucheries; that it was well known that, for two years past, no one older than twenty had been initiated there. When any person was introduced he was delivered as a victim to the priests, who led him away to a place resounding with shouts, the sound of music, and the beating of cymbals and drums, lest his cries, while suffering violation, should be heard abroad. She then entreated and besought him to put an end to that matter in some way or other and not to plunge himself into a situation where he must first suffer, and afterward commit, everything that was abominable. Nor did she quit him until the young man gave her his promise to keep himself clear of those rites.

When he came home, he told his mother that he did not intend to be initiated. His stepfather was present at this discourse. His mother on one side and his stepfather on the other, loading him with reproaches, drove him out of the house, assisted by four slaves. The youth repaired to his aunt Aebutia, told her the reason of his being turned out by his mother, and the next day, by her advice, gave information of the affair to the Consul Postumius, without any witnesses of the interview.

The Consul dismissed him, with an order to come again on the third day following. In the meantime, he inquired of his mother-in-law Sulpicia, a woman of respectable character, whether she knew an old matron called Aebutia, who lived on the Aventine Hill. When she answered that she knew her well, and that Aebutia was a woman of virtue, and of the ancient purity of morals, he said that he required a conference with her, and that a messenger should be sent for her to come. Aebutia, on receiving the message, came to Sulpicia's house, and the Consul, soon after, coming in, as if by accident, introduced a conversation about Aebutius, her brother's son. The tears of the woman burst forth, and she began to lament the unhappy lot of the youth, who, after being robbed of his property by persons whom it least of all became, was then residing with her, being driven out of doors by his mother, because, being a good youth, he refused to be initiated in ceremonies devoted to lewdness, as report goes.

The Consul, thinking that he had made sufficient inquiries concerning Aebutius, and that his testimony was unquestionable, having dismissed Aebutia, requested his mother-in-law to send again to the Aventine, and bring from that quarter Hispala, a freedwoman, not unknown in that neighborhood, for there were some queries that he wished to make of her. Hispala being alarmed because she was sent for by a woman of such high rank and respectable character, and being ignorant of the cause, after that she saw the Lictors[5] in the porch, the multitude attending on the Consul and the Consul himself, was very near fainting. The Consul led her into a retired part of the house, and, in the presence of his mother-in-law, told her that she need not be uneasy, if she could resolve to speak the truth she might receive a promise of protection either from Sulpicia, a matron of such dignified character, or from himself. And that she ought to tell him what was accustomed to be done at the Bacchanalia, in the nocturnal orgies in the grove of Stimula.

---

[5] Twelve attendants of the Consul who carried the fasces, bundles of wooden rods with an ax-head projecting from them, symbolizing the power of life and death. In the city proper, the ax-head was removed.

When the woman heard this, such terror and trembling of all her limbs seized her, that for a long time she was unable to speak. But recovering, at length she then gave a full account of the origin of the mysteries. "At first," she said, "those rites were performed by women. No man used to be admitted. They had three stated days in the year on which persons were initiated among the Bacchanalians, in the daytime. The matrons used to be appointed priestesses, in rotation. Paculla Minia, a Campanian, when priestess, made an alteration in every particular, as if by the direction of the gods. For she first introduced men; changed the time of celebration, from day to night; and, instead of three days in the year, appointed five days of initiation in each month.

From the time that the rites were thus made common, and men were intermixed with women, and the licentious freedom of the night was added, there was nothing wicked, nothing flagitious, that had not been practiced among them. There was more frequent pollution of men with each other than with women. If any were less patient in submitting to dishonor, or more averse to the commission of vice, they were sacrificed as victims. To think nothing unlawful was the grand maxim of their religion.

The men, as if bereft of reason, uttered predictions, with frantic contortions of their bodies; the women, in the habit of *Bacchantes,* with their hair disheveled, and carrying blazing torches, ran down to the Tiber, where, dipping their torches in the water, they drew them up again with the flame unextinguished, being composed of native sulphur and charcoal. Their number was exceedingly great now, almost a second state in themselves, and among them were many men and women of noble families."

When she had completed her information, she entreated the Consul that he might send her out of the country. The Consul requested his mother-in-law to clear some part of the house, into which Hispala might remove. Accordingly, an apartment was assigned her in the upper part of it. Aebutius, also, was ordered to remove to the house of one of the Consul's clients. When both the informers were by these means in his power, Postumius represented the affair to the Senate. Great consternation seized on the senators, not only on the public account, lest such conspiracies and nightly meetings might be productive of secret treachery and mischief, but, likewise, on account of their own particular families, lest some of their relations might be involved in this infamous affair.

The Senate voted, moreover, that thanks should be given to the Consul because he had investigated the matter with singular diligence and without exciting any alarm. The senators then committed to the Consuls the holding of an inquiry, out of the common course, concerning the Bacchanals and their nocturnal orgies. They ordered them to take care that the informers, Aebutius and Fecenia, might suffer no injury on that account, and to invite other informers in the matter, by offering rewards. They ordered that the officials in those rites, whether men or women, should be sought for, and be delivered over to the power of the Consuls; and also that proclamation should be made that no persons initiated in the Bacchanalian rites should presume to come together or assemble on account of those rites, or to perform any such kind of worship; and above all, that search should be made for those who had assembled or conspired for personal abuse, or for any other flagitious practices.

The Senate resolved these things. The Consuls directed the Curule Aediles[6] to make strict inquiry after all the priests of those mysteries, and to keep such as they could apprehend in custody until their trial; they at the same time charged the Plebeian Aediles[7] to take care that no religious ceremonies should be performed in private. To the Capitol Triumvirs[8] the task was assigned to post watches in proper places of the city and to use vigilance in preventing any meetings by night.

---

[6] Two junior magistrates elected from the patrician class to oversee the city infrastructure; they had *imperium* and were allowed two Lictors each.

[7] Two junior magistrates chosen from among the plebeians to care for the city.

[8] Junior magistrates in charge of holding prisoners and executions; they oversaw the closest thing there was to a police force at this time.

After dispatching these officers to their several employments, the Consuls mounted the rostrum; and, having summoned a *contio*[9] of the people. One of the Consuls, when he had finished the solemn form of prayer that the magistrates are accustomed to pronounce before they address the people, proceeded thus:

Romans, to no former *contio* was this solemn supplication to the gods more suitable or even more necessary, as it serves to remind you, that these are the deities whom your forefathers pointed out as the objects of your worship, veneration, and prayers, and not those that infatuated men's minds with corrupt and foreign modes of religion, and drove them, as if goaded by the furies, to every lust and every vice. That the Bacchanalian rites have subsisted for some time past in every country in Italy, and are at present performed in many parts of this city also, I am sure you must have been informed, not only by report but also by the nightly noises and horrid yells that resound through the whole city, but still you are ignorant of the nature of that business. As regards the number, they are many thousands. A great part of them are women, and this was the source of the evil. The rest are males, but nearly resembling women, debauchers and the debauched, night revelers, driven frantic by wine, noises of instruments, and clamors. The conspiracy, as yet, has no strength, but it has abundant means of acquiring strength, for they are becoming more numerous every day.

The impious assembly at present confines itself to outrages on private citizens because it has not yet acquired force sufficient to crush the Republic, but the evil increases and spreads daily. It already is too great for the private ranks of life to contain it, and aims its views at the body of the state. Unless you take timely precautions, Romans, their nightly assembly may become as large as this, held in open day, and legally summoned by a Consul. Now they one by one dread you collected together in the *contio*; presently, when you shall have separated and retired to your several dwellings, in town and country, they will again come together, and will hold a consultation on the means of their own safety, and, at the same time, of your destruction. Thus united, they will cause terror to every one of you.

How often in the ages of our fathers was it given in charge to the magistrates to prohibit the performance of any foreign religious rites; to banish strolling sacrificers and soothsayers from the Forum, the circus, and the city; to search for, and burn, books of divination; and to abolish every mode of sacrificing that was not conformable to the Roman practice? We shall do all these things with the favor and approbation of the gods, who, because they were indignant that their divinity was dishonored by those people's lusts and crimes, have drawn forth their proceedings from hidden darkness into the open light and have directed them to be exposed, not that they may escape with impunity but in order that they may be punished and suppressed.

The Senate has committed to me and my colleague an extraordinary inquisition[10] concerning this affair. The charge of posting watches through the city during the night we have committed to the inferior magistrates, and, for your part, it is incumbent on you to execute vigorously whatever duties are assigned you, and in the several places where each will be placed, to perform whatever orders you shall receive, and to use your best endeavors that no danger or tumult may arise from the treachery of the party involved in the guilt.

---

[9] A general meeting of the entire population for informational purposes, as opposed to a meeting of a popular assembly.

[10] Because the Roman government had no permanent officials, offices, or bodies to investigate crimes against the state, all such investigations were ad hoc in nature.

They then ordered the Recommendation of the Senate to be read and published a reward for any discoverer who should bring any of the guilty before them, or give information against any of the absent. They then issued an edict,[11] that no person whatever should presume to buy or sell anything for the purpose of leaving the country; or to receive or conceal, or by any means aid the fugitives. On the *contio* being dismissed, great terror spread throughout the city; nor was it confined merely within the walls, or to the Roman territory, for everywhere throughout the whole of Italy alarm began to be felt when the letters from guest-friends[12] were received, concerning the Recommendation of the Senate, and what passed in the *contio*, and the edict of the Consuls.

During the night, great numbers, attempting to flee, were seized, and brought back by the Triumvirs, who had posted guards at all gates, and accusations were lodged against many, some of whom, both men and women, put themselves to death. Those who, as it appeared, had been only initiated, and had made after the priest, and in the most solemn form, the prescribed imprecations, in which the conspiracy for the perpetration of every crime and lust was contained, but who had not themselves committed, or compelled others to commit, any of those acts to which they were bound by the oath, all such they left in prison.[13] But those who had forcibly committed personal defilements or murders, or were stained with the guilt of false evidence, counterfeit seals, forged wills, or other frauds, all these they punished with death.

A greater number were executed than thrown into prison; indeed, the multitude of men and women who suffered in both ways was very considerable. The Consuls delivered the women who were condemned to their relations, or to those under whose guardianship they were, so that they might

inflict the punishment in private. If there did not appear any proper person of the kind to execute the sentence, the punishment was inflicted in public.

With regard to the future, the Senate passed a recommendation that no Bacchanalian rites should be celebrated in Rome or in Italy, and ordering that, in case any person should believe some such kind of worship incumbent upon him, and necessary; and that he could not, without offense to religion, and incurring guilt, omit it, he should represent this to the Urban Praetor, and the Praetor should lay the business before the Senate. If permission were granted by the Senate, when not less than one hundred members were present, then he might perform those rites, provided that no more than five persons should be present at the sacrifice, and that they should have no common stock of money, nor any president of the ceremonies, nor priest.

Spurius Postumius some time after came to Rome, and on his proposing the question, concerning the reward to be given to Publius Aebutius and Hispala Fecenia, because the Bacchanalian ceremonies were discovered by their exertions, the Senate passed a vote, that the City Quaestors should give to each of them, out of the public treasury, one hundred thousand *asses*; and that the Consuls should desire the Tribunes of the Plebs to propose to the plebs,[14] that Publius Aebutius should not become a soldier against his wishes.

They voted also, that Hispala Fecenia should enjoy the privileges of alienating her property by gift or deed; of marrying out of her rank, and of choosing a guardian, as if a husband had conferred these privileges by will; that she should be at liberty to wed a man of honorable birth[15]; and that there should be no disgrace or ignominy to him who should marry her, and that the Consuls and Praetors then in office, and their successors, should take care that no injury should be offered to that woman, and that she might live in safety. All these particulars were proposed to the Council of the Plebs, and executed, in accordance with

---

[11] Like Praetors, who could issue certain forms of law in the law courts, Consuls had the power, usually exercised only outside Rome, to issue edicts based on their power of *imperium*.

[12] Romans who had ties of friendship to Italians passed along reports of what had transpired at the meeting.

[13] Not as punishment, but to await trial.

---

[14] That is, to the Council of the Plebs.

[15] There usually were severe restrictions against marriages between full Roman citizens and persons with a servile background.

the Recommendation of the Senate, and full permission was given to the Consuls to determine respecting the impunity and rewards of the other informers.[16]

(b) *Senatus Consultum de Bacchanalibus* ("Recommendation of the Senate on the Bacchanalians")

Nina Weston, trans., in Oliver Joseph Thatcher, ed., *The Ideas That Have Influenced Civilization, in the Original Documents: Vol. III, The Roman World* (Manchester, UK: Roberts-Manchester, 1901), 76–77.

Quintus Marcius, the son of Lucius, and Spurius Postumius consulted the Senate on the Nones of October[17] at the Temple of Bellona.[18] Marcus Claudius, son of Marcus, Lucius Valerius, son of Publius, and Quintus Minucius, son of Gaius, were the committee for drawing up the report. Regarding the Bacchanalia, it was resolved to give the following directions to those who are in alliance with us. No one of them is to possess a place where the festivals of Bacchus are celebrated; if there are any who claim that it is necessary for them to have such a place, they are to come to Rome to the Urban Praetor, and the Senate is to decide on those matters after their claims have been heard, provided that not less than one hundred senators are present when the affair is discussed. No man is to be a Bacchantian, neither a Roman citizen, nor one of the Latin name, nor any of our allies unless they come to the Urban Praetor, and he in accordance with the opinion of the Senate expressed when not less than one hundred senators are present at the discussion, shall have given leave. Carried.

No man is to be a priest; no one, either man or woman, is to be an officer to manage the temporal affairs of the organization; nor is anyone of them to have charge of a common treasury; no one shall appoint either man or woman to be master or to act as master; henceforth they shall not form conspiracies among themselves, stir up any disorder, make mutual promises or agreements, or interchange pledges; no one shall observe the sacred rites either in public or private or outside the city, unless he comes to the Urban Praetor, and he, in accordance with the opinion of the Senate, expressed when no less than one hundred senators are present at the discussion, shall have given leave. Carried.

No one in a company of more than five persons altogether, men and women, shall observe the sacred rites, nor in that company shall there be present more than two men or three women, unless in accordance with the opinion of the Urban Praetor and the Senate as written above. See that you declare it in the assembly for not less than three market days, so that you may know the opinion of the Senate that this was their judgment. If there are any who have acted contrary to what was written above, they have decided that a proceeding for a capital offense should be instituted against them. The Senate has justly recommended that you should inscribe this on a bronze tablet, and that you should order it to be placed where it can be easiest to read. See to it that the revelries of Bacchus, if there be any, except in case there be concerned in the matter something sacred, as was written above, be disbanded within ten days after this letter shall be delivered to you.

In the Teuranian field.[19]

---

[16] All grants of special privileges had to be approved by the Council of the Plebs.

[17] 7 October.

[18] Meetings of the Senate regarding warfare were held on the Capitoline Hill in the Temple of Bellona, an ancient war goddess sometimes said to be married to Mars.

---

[19] A comment appended to the document attesting to the place where it was posted in Bruttium in southern Italy, where the tablet was found.

A ROMAN "NEW MAN" CONFRONTS GREEK CULTURE (234–149 BCE)

PLUTARCH, *LIFE OF CATO THE ELDER*

A severely depicted portrait bust from the Museum of the Villa Torlonia in Rome known as the "Patrizio Torlonia" ("The Torlonian Patrician") is a second-century CE copy of an original dating to 80–70 BCE and is thought to represent Marcus Porcius Cato the Elder.

During the second century BCE, the Romans experienced intense cultural pressures as a result of Roman expansion, which brought exposure to different cultures and the assimilation of foreign populations. Some Romans, such as Scipio Aemilianus, the grandson of Scipio Africanus, who had defeated Hannibal, embraced Greek culture and welcomed Greek writers and scholars to Rome. But more conservative Romans were chary of excessive foreign contacts, fearing that old Roman values and virtues were threatened by what they viewed as Greek self-indulgence, immorality, frivolity, and general lack of respect for Roman values. No one was more conservative than Marcus Porcius Cato the Elder, a "New Man" from a very undistinguished family who rose to the august offices of Consul in 195 BCE and Censor in 184 BCE. As a newcomer to the Roman nobility, Cato established a reputation for being more senatorial than the established senators by espousing the most extreme practice of what he considered old Roman virtues.

Source: John Dryden, *The Lives of the Noble Greeks and Romans, Vol. 1*, revised by A. H. Clough (Boston: Little, Brown, 1910).

The family of Marcus Cato, it is said, was of Tusculan[20] origin. His ancestors commonly passed for men of no note whatever, but Cato himself extols his father, Marcus, as a brave man and good soldier. He also says that his grandfather, Cato, often won prizes for soldierly valor, and received from the state treasury, because of his bravery, the price of five horses which had been killed under him in battle. The Romans used to call men who had no family distinction, but were coming into public notice through their own achievements, "New Men," and such they called Cato.[21] But he himself used to say that as far as office and distinction went, he was indeed new, but having regard to ancestral deeds of valor, he was oldest of the old. Near his fields was the cottage which had once belonged to Manius Curius, a hero of three triumphs. To this he would often go, and the sight of the small farm and the mean dwelling led him to think of their former owner, who, although he had become the greatest of the Romans, had subdued the most warlike nations, and driven Pyrrhus out of Italy,[22] nevertheless tilled this little patch of ground with his own hands and occupied this cottage, after three triumphs.[23] He did not learn Greek until late in life, and was quite well on in years when he took to reading Greek books. He never paid more than fifteen hundred *denarii* for a slave because he did not want them to be delicately beautiful, but sturdy workers, such as grooms and herdsmen, and these he thought it his duty to sell when they got oldish, instead of feeding them when they were useless.[24]

There was at Rome a certain man of the highest birth and greatest influence, who had the power to discern excellence in the bud, and the grace to cultivate it and bring it into general esteem. This man was Valerius Flaccus.[25] He had a farm next to that of Cato, and learned from Cato's servants of their master's laborious and frugal way of living. He was amazed to hear them tell how Cato, early in the morning, went on foot to the market-place and pleaded the cases of all who wished his aid[26]; then came back to his farm, where he worked with his servants and then sat down with them to eat of the same bread and drink of the same wine. They told Valerius many other instances of Cato's fairness and moderation, until at last Valerius gave command that Cato be invited to dine with him. After this, discovering by converse with him that his nature was gentle and polite, and needed, like a growing tree, only cultivation and room to expand, Valerius urged and at last persuaded him to engage in public life at Rome. Accordingly, taking up his abode in the city, his own efforts as an advocate at once won him admiring friends, and the favor of Valerius brought him great honor and influence, so that he was made Military Tribune first, and then Quaestor.[27] After this, being now launched on an eminent and brilliant career, he shared the highest honors with Valerius, becoming Consul with him, and afterward Censor.

Ten years after his consulship, Cato stood for the censorship. This office towered, as it were, above every other civic honor, and was, in a way, the culmination of a political career. Therefore, when Cato stood for it, nearly all the best known and most influential men of the senatorial party united to oppose him. The men of noble parentage among them were moved by jealousy, thinking that

---

[20] From Tusculum, a city of Latium, fifteen miles southeast of Rome.

[21] More specifically, "New Men" were individuals who gained the office of Consul after never having had a consular ancestor.

[22] The Roman war with Pyrrhus of Epirus lasted between 280 and 275 BCE. Even though he defeated the Romans several times in battle, he eventually returned to Greece because his extensive losses of manpower had nearly ruined him.

[23] It was believed that the greatest virtue that a Roman senator could manifest was to plow his own fields.

[24] This kind of callous behavior toward agricultural slaves was one of the reasons for the slave revolts of 135, 104, and especially that led by Spartacus in 70 BCE.

---

[25] For a person from an undistinguished family to have political success, it was necessary to have powerful patrons. In Cato's case, it was the patrician Lucius Valerius Flaccus, whose father had been Consul in 227 BCE and with whom Cato shared the consulate in 195 BCE and the office of Censor in 183 BCE.

[26] Many newcomers to politics, such as Cicero, initially made names for themselves as lawyers.

[27] The typical beginning of a senatorial career.

nobility of birth would be trampled in the mire if men of ignoble origin forced their way up to the summits of honor and power, whereas those who were conscious of base practices and of a departure from ancestral customs feared the severity of the man, which was sure to be harsh and inexorable in the exercise of power. Therefore, after due consultation and preparation, they put up in opposition to Cato seven candidates for the office, who sought the favor of the multitude with promises of mild conduct in office, supposing that it wanted to be ruled with a lax and indulgent hand. Cato, on the contrary, threatened wrong-doers in his speeches, and loudly cried that the city had need of a great purification. He adjured the people, if they were wise, not to choose the most agreeable physician, but the one who was most in earnest. He himself, he said, was such a physician, and so was Valerius Flaccus, of the patricians. With him as colleague, he thought he could cut and sear the luxury and effeminacy of the time. So truly great was the Roman people, and so worthy of great leaders, that they elected Flaccus to the office along with Cato. As Censor, Cato made Lucius Valerius Flaccus, his colleague and friend, chief senator.[28] He also expelled many members of the Senate,[29] including a senator who was thought to have good prospects for the consulship, namely, Manilius, because he embraced his wife in open day before the eyes of his daughter. For his own part, he said, he never embraced his wife unless it thundered loudly and it was a pleasantry of his to remark that he was a happy man when it thundered.

Cato was not only his son's reading teacher, but also his tutor in law and his athletic trainer, and he taught his son not merely to hurl the javelin and fight in armor and ride the horse, but also to box, to

endure heat and cold, and to swim lustily through the eddies and billows of the Tiber. His *History of Rome*, as he tells us himself, he wrote out with his own hand[30] and in large characters, that his son might have in his own home an aid to acquaintance with his country's ancient traditions. He declares that his son's presence, as much as that of the so-called Vestal Virgins,[31] put him on his guard against indecencies of speech, and that he never bathed with him. This, indeed, would seem to have been a general custom with the Romans, for even fathers-in-law avoided bathing with their sons-in-law, because they were ashamed to uncover their nakedness. Afterward, however, when the Romans had learned from the Greeks their freedom in going naked, they in their turn infected the Greeks with the practice even when women were present.

When Cato was now well on in years, there came as ambassadors from Athens to Rome, Carneades the Academic,[32] and Diogenes, the Stoic philosopher,[33] to beg the reversal of a certain decision against the Athenian people, which imposed upon them a fine of five hundred talents. Upon the arrival of these philosophers, the most studious of the city's youth hastened to wait upon them, and became their devoted and admiring listeners. The charm of Carneades especially, which had boundless power, and a fame not inferior to its power, won large and sympathetic audiences, and filled the city, like a rushing mighty wind, with the noise of his praises. Report spread far and wide that a Greek of amazing talent, who disarmed all opposition by the magic of his eloquence, had infused a tremendous passion into the youth of the city,

---

[28] That is, Cato repaid Flaccus for his support by granting him the title of "Princeps Senatus" ("First Man of the Senate"), the greatest honor a Roman senator could receive.

[29] Censors had the right both to admit new worthy members to the Senate and to expel those whom they thought were guilty of misbehavior. Cato used this power to revenge himself on some of his enemies, and in so doing he created for himself even more enemies.

[30] Cato wrote his history, which does not survive, in Latin, contrary to the existing custom of writing in Greek. Subsequently, Latin became a literary language in its own right.

[31] The six most distinguished women in Rome, in whose presence one always was on one's best behavior.

[32] Carneades was the head of the "Academy," the philosophical school founded by the Athenian philosopher Plato. He espoused "Skepticism," the belief that it was impossible to know anything about anything exactly.

[33] A Greek from Seleucia in Babylonia and the head of the Stoic school in Athens. A third Greek philosopher on the embassy was Critolaus, who represented the "Peripatetic" school based on the teachings of Aristotle.

in consequence of which they forsook their other pleasures and pursuits and were "possessed" about philosophy. The other Romans were pleased at this, and glad to see their young men lay hold of Greek culture and consort with such admirable men.

Cato, however, at the very outset, when this zeal for discussion came pouring into the city, was distressed, fearing lest the young men, by giving this direction to their ambition, should come to love a reputation based on mere words more than one achieved by martial deeds. And when the fame of the visiting philosophers rose yet higher in the city, and their first speeches before the Senate were interpreted, at his own instance and request by so conspicuous a man as Gaius Acilius,[34] Cato determined, on some decent pretext or other, to rid and purge the city of them all. So he rose in the Senate and censured the magistrates for keeping in such long suspense an embassy composed of men who could easily secure anything they wished, so persuasive were they. "We ought," he said, "to make up our minds one way or another, and vote on what the embassy proposes, in order that these men may return to their schools and lecture to the sons of Greece, while the youth of Rome give ear to their laws and magistrates, as heretofore."

This he did, not, as some think, out of personal hostility to Carneades, but because he was wholly averse to philosophy, and made mock of all Greek culture and training, out of patriotic zeal. He said, for instance, that Socrates[35] was a mighty prattler, who attempted, as best he could, to be his country's tyrant, by abolishing its customs, and by enticing his fellow citizens into opinions contrary to the laws. He made fun of the school of Isocrates,[36] declaring that his pupils kept on studying with him until they were old men, as if they were to practice their arts and plead their cases before Minos in

Hades.[37] And seeking to prejudice his son against Greek culture, he indulged in an utterance all too rash for his years, declaring, in the tone of a prophet or a seer, that Rome would lose her empire when she had become infected with Greek letters. But time has certainly shown the emptiness of this ill-boding speech of his, for while the city was at the zenith of its empire, she made every form of Greek learning and culture her own.[38]

It was not only Greek philosophers that he hated, but he also was suspicious of Greeks who practiced medicine at Rome. He had heard, it would seem, of Hippocrates'[39] reply when the Great King of Persia consulted him, with the promise of a fee of many talents, namely, that he would never put his skill at the service of barbarians who were enemies of Greece. He said all Greek physicians had taken a similar oath, and urged his son to beware of them all. He himself, he said, had written a book of recipes, which he followed in the treatment and regimen of any who were sick in his family. He never required his patients to fast, but fed them on greens, and on bits of duck, pigeon, or hare. Such a diet, he said, was light and good for sick people, except that it often causes dreams. By following such treatment and regimen he said he had good health himself, and kept his family in good health.

He composed speeches, then, on all sorts of subjects, and histories, and as for farming, he followed it in earnest when he was young and poor, indeed, he says he then had only two ways of getting money, farming and frugality, but in later life he was only a theoretical and fancy farmer. He also composed a book on farming,[40] in which he actually gave recipes for making cakes and preserving fruit, so ambitious was he to be superior and peculiar in everything.

---

[34] A Roman senator who interpreted the speeches of the Greek philosophers and wrote, in Greek, a history of Rome.

[35] An Athenian philosopher whose teachings were recorded by Plato.

[36] A famous Athenian teacher of oratory in the first half of the fourth century BCE.

---

[37] Minos, the legendary king of Crete, became the judge of deceased spirits in Hades, the underworld.

[38] Plutarch, a Greek himself, naturally spoke here on behalf of Greek culture.

[39] The most famous Greek physician, from the Aegean island of Cos; he practiced just before and after 400 BCE.

[40] Cato's *On Agriculture* still survives.

The last of his public services is supposed to have been the destruction of Carthage. It was Scipio the Younger[41] who actually brought the task to completion, but it was largely in consequence of the advice and counsel of Cato that the Romans undertook the war. It was in this manner. Cato was sent on an embassy to the Carthaginians and to Masinissa the Numidian,[42] who were at war with one another, to inquire into the grounds of their quarrel. Masinissa had been a friend of the Roman people from the first, and the Carthaginians had entered into treaty relations with Rome after their defeat by the elder Scipio.[43] The treaty deprived them of their empire and imposed a grievous money tribute upon them. Cato, however, found the city by no means in a poor and lowly state, as the Romans supposed, but rather teeming with vigorous fighting men, overflowing with enormous wealth, filled with arms of every sort and with military supplies, and not a little puffed up by all this. He therefore thought it no time for the Romans to be ordering and arranging the affairs of Masinissa and the Numidians, but that unless they should repress a city that had always been their malignant foe, now that its power was so incredibly grown, they would be involved again in dangers as great as before.[44] Accordingly, he returned with speed to Rome, and advised the Senate that the former calamitous defeats of the Carthaginians had diminished not so much their power as their foolhardiness, and were likely to render them in the end not weaker, but more expert in war. Their present contest with Numidia was but a prelude to a contest with Rome, whereas peace and treaty were mere names wherewith to cover their postponement of war until a fit occasion offered.

In addition to this, it is said that Cato contrived to drop a Libyan fig in the Senate, as he shook out the folds of his toga, and then, as the senators admired its size and beauty, said that the country where it grew was only three days' sail from Rome. And in one thing he was even more savage, namely, in adding to his vote on any question whatsoever these words: "In my opinion, Carthage must be destroyed." In this way Cato is said to have brought to pass the third and last war against Carthage,[45] but it had no sooner begun than he died.

---

[41] Scipio Aemilianus, adopted by Scipio the son of Scipio Africanus, who had defeated Hannibal. He was a great supporter of Greek culture.

[42] The peace treaty between Rome and Carthage in 201 BCE had prohibited the Carthaginians from going to war without permission of the Romans. As a result, the native Numidians, led by King Masinissa, had been nibbling away at Carthaginian territory, but the Romans had refused to allow the Carthaginians to defend themselves.

[43] At the Battle of Zama in 202 BCE, where Scipio defeated Hannibal.

---

[44] A manifestation of the typical Roman paranoia about strong neighbors who might repeat the Sack of Rome by the Gauls in 390 BCE.

[45] From 149 to 146 BCE, when Carthage finally was captured and destroyed by Scipio Aemilianus.

THE LAND LAW OF TIBERIUS GRACCHUS (133 BCE)

PLUTARCH, *LIFE OF TIBERIUS GRACCHUS*

In 133 BCE, Tiberius Gracchus was a decorated war hero with impeccable family credentials: he was the maternal grandson of Scipio Africanus, who had defeated Hannibal in 202 BCE, and his sister was married to Scipio Aemilianus, who had destroyed Carthage in 146 BCE. If he had worked within the system, he could have expected to have a stellar political career, but instead he chose to become a reformer. Realizing that it was becoming more and more difficult to find recruits for the Roman army who met the requirement for property ownership, as Tribune of the Plebs he proposed legislation to distribute public land (land owned by the government) to landless plebeians and thus make them eligible for military service. The introduction of this law brought a resurgence of the same class conflicts as had been manifested between the Consuls Paullus and Varro before the Battle of Cannae in 216 CE. The law was opposed vigorously by senators who had been renting the land and looked on it as their own. Tiberius therefore ignored tradition and took his law directly to the Council of the Plebs without consulting the Senate. The law passed. Soon thereafter, Tiberius again violated tradition for running for Tribune of the Plebs a second time in a row. This was too much for the senators, who instigated a riot and clubbed Tiberius to death. This was the first use of violence in Roman politics; it would not be the last. These reforms of Tiberius and the subsequent reforms of his brother Gaius Gracchus (123–121 BCE) marked the beginning of the end of the Roman Republic. Senators on both sides of issues were no longer able to reach behind-the-scenes compromises as they had in the past and were increasingly willing to put their own personal ideas about what was good for Rome ahead of the best interests of the state as a whole. As a result, the hard-won unity within the Senate that had allowed the Senate to govern effectively began to break down, and other groups, such as the equestrians, the Italian allies, and the plebs, assumed greater roles in politics. The pursuit of senatorial self-interest would culminate with generals who were willing to use their armies to seize control of the government. Tiberius' career is fulsomely discussed by the second-century CE Greek biographer Plutarch.

Source: John Dryden, *The Lives of the Noble Greeks and Romans, Vol. 2*, revised by A. H. Clough (Boston: Little, Brown, 1910).

Tiberius and Gaius were sons of Tiberius Gracchus, who, although he had been Censor[46] at Rome, twice Consul, and had celebrated two triumphs, derived his more illustrious dignity from his virtue. Therefore, after the death of the Scipio who conquered Hannibal, he was judged worthy to take Scipio's daughter Cornelia in marriage. A short time afterward he died, leaving Cornelia with twelve children by him. Cornelia took charge of the children and of the estate, and showed herself so discreet, so good a mother, and so magnanimous, that Tiberius was thought to have made no bad decision when he elected to die. For when Ptolemy the king offered to share his crown with her and sought her hand in marriage, she refused him, and remained a widow. In this state she lost most of her children, but three survived; one daughter, who married Scipio the Younger,[47] and two sons, Tiberius and Gaius, whose lives I now relate. These sons Cornelia reared with such scrupulous care that although confessedly no other Romans were so well endowed by nature, they were thought to owe their virtues more to education than to nature. The younger Tiberius, accordingly, serving in

---

[46] Two Censors were appointed every five years to take the census (a survey of property ownership), oversee the membership list of the Senate, and let out contracts for construction work.

[47] Cornelia's daughter Sempronia married her cousin, Scipio Aemilianus, grandson of Scipio Africanus.

Africa under the younger Scipio, who had married his sister, and sharing his commander's tent, soon learned to understand that commander's nature and led all the young men in discipline and bravery; yes, he was first to scale the enemy wall.[48]

While he remained with the army Tiberius was the object of much good will, and on leaving it he was greatly missed. Tiberius then began to agitate his agrarian laws. The occasion of this was as follows. Of the territory that the Romans won in war from their neighbors, a part they sold, and part they made public land, and assigned it for occupation to the poor and indigent among the citizens on payment of a small rent into the public treasury. And when the rich began to offer larger rents and drove out the poor, a law was enacted forbidding the holding by one person of more than five hundred acres of land. For a short time this enactment gave a check to the rapacity of the rich, and was of assistance to the poor, who remained in their places on the land that they had rented and occupied the allotment that each had held from the outset. But later on the neighboring rich men, by means of fictitious personages, transferred these rentals to themselves and finally held most of the land openly in their own names. Then the poor, who had been ejected from their land, no longer showed themselves eager for military service and neglected the bringing up of children. Soon all Italy was conscious of a dearth of freemen and was filled with gangs of foreign slaves, by whose aid the rich cultivated their estates, from which they had driven away the free citizens. An attempt was therefore made to rectify this evil by Gaius Laelius the comrade of Scipio,[49] but the men of influence opposed his measures, and he, fearing the disturbance that might ensue, desisted, and received the surname of "The Wise" (for the Latin word "sapiens" has that meaning). Tiberius, however, on being elected Tribune of the Plebs, took the matter directly in hand. His brother Gaius, in a certain pamphlet, wrote

that as Tiberius was passing through Tuscany[50] on his way to Numantia,[51] and observed the dearth of inhabitants in the country and that those who tilled its soil or tended its flocks there were barbarian slaves, he then first conceived the public policy that was the cause of countless ills to the two brothers. The energy and ambition of Tiberius, however, were most of all kindled by the people themselves, who posted writings on porticoes, house-walls, and monuments calling upon him to recover for the poor the public land.

He did not, however, draw up his law by himself, but took counsel with the citizens who were foremost in virtue and reputation, among whom were Crassus the *Pontifex Maximus*, Mucius Scaevola the jurist,[52] who then was Consul, and Appius Claudius,[53] his father-in-law. And it is thought that a law dealing with such great injustice and rapacity never was drawn up in milder and gentler terms. For men who ought to have been punished for their disobedience and to have surrendered with payment of a fine the land that they were illegally enjoying, these men it merely ordered to abandon their unjust acquisitions upon being paid the value and to admit into ownership of them such citizens as needed assistance. But although the rectification of the wrong was so considerate, the people were satisfied to let bygones be bygones if they could be secure from such wrong in the future. The men of wealth and substance, however, were led by their greed to hate the law, and by their wrath and contentiousness to hate the law-giver, and tried to dissuade the people by alleging that Tiberius was introducing a re-distribution of land for the confusion of the body politic and was stirring up a general revolution.

But they accomplished nothing, for Tiberius, striving to support a measure that was honorable and just with an eloquence that would have adorned even a meaner cause, was formidable and invincible whenever, with the people crowding around

---

[48] The first soldier to scale the wall of an enemy city received the "corona muralis," or "mural crown," one of the highest Roman military decorations.

[49] That is, Scipio Africanus.

[50] In northwestern Italy, homeland of the Etruscans.

[51] The final stronghold of rebels in Spain.

[52] A legal expert.

[53] Appius Claudius Pulcher, Consul in 143 BCE and later a Censor.

the rostra,[54] he took his stand there and pleaded for the poor. "The wild beasts that roam over Italy," he would say, "have every one of them a cave or lair to lurk in, but the men who fight and die for Italy enjoy the common air and light, indeed, but nothing else. Houseless and homeless they wander about with their wives and children. And it is with lying lips that their Imperators[55] exhort the soldiers in their battles to defend tombs and shrines from the enemy, for not a man of them has a hereditary altar, not one of all these many Romans an ancestral tomb, but they fight and die to support others in wealth and luxury, and although they are styled masters of the world they have not a single clod of earth that is their own."

Such words as these, the product of a lofty spirit and genuine feeling, and falling upon the ears of a people profoundly moved and fully aroused to the speaker's support, no adversary of Tiberius could successfully withstand. Abandoning therefore all counter-pleading, they addressed themselves to Marcus Octavius,[56] another one of the Tribunes of the Plebs, a young man of sober character, discreet, and an intimate companion of Tiberius. On this account Octavius at first tried to hold himself aloof, out of regard for Tiberius, but he was forced from his position, as it were, by the prayers and supplications of many influential men, so he set himself in opposition to Tiberius and staved off the passage of the law. Now, the decisive power is in the hands of any Tribune who interposes his veto, for the wishes of the majority avail not if one Tribune is in opposition. Incensed at this procedure, Tiberius withdrew his considerate law, and introduced this time one that was more agreeable to the multitude and more severe against the wrongdoers, because it simply ordered them to vacate without compensation the land that they had acquired in violation of the earlier laws.

When the appointed day was come and Tiberius was summoning the people to the vote, the voting urns were stolen away by the party of the rich, and great confusion arose. The supporters of Tiberius, however, were numerous enough to force the issue, and were banding together for this purpose, when

Manlius and Fulvius, men of consular dignity, fell down before Tiberius, clasped his hands, and with tears besought him to desist. Tiberius, conscious that the future was now all but desperate, and moved by respect for the men, asked them what they would have him do. They replied that they were not competent to advise in so grave a crisis, and urged him with entreaties to submit the case to the Senate. To this Tiberius consented.

But the Senate in its session accomplished nothing, owing to the prevailing influence of the wealthy class in it, and therefore Tiberius resorted to a measure that was illegal and unseemly, the ejection of Octavius from his office, for he was unable in any other way to bring his law to the vote. In the first place, however, he begged Octavius in public, addressing him with kindly words and clasping his hands, to give in and gratify the people, who demanded only their just rights, and would receive only a trifling return for great toils and perils. But Octavius rejected the petition, and therefore Tiberius, after premising that, because they were colleagues in office with equal powers and differed on weighty measures, it was impossible for them to complete their term of office without open war, said he saw only one remedy for this, and that was for one or the other of them to give up his office. Indeed, he urged Octavius to put to the people a vote on his own case first, promising to retire at once to private life if this should be the will of the citizens. But Octavius was unwilling, and therefore Tiberius declared that he would put the case of Octavius unless Octavius should change his mind upon reflection.

With this understanding, he dissolved the assembly for that day, but on the following day, after the people had come together, he mounted the rostra and once more attempted to persuade Octavius. When, however, Octavius was not to be persuaded, Tiberius introduced a law depriving him of his tribuneship, and summoned the citizens to cast their votes upon it at once. Now, there were five and thirty tribes,[57] and when seventeen of them

---

[54] The speaker's platform in the Roman Forum.

[55] Victorious army generals.

[56] An ancestor of Augustus, the first Roman emperor.

[57] Originally, Roman citizens were distributed among three tribes (from Latin *tribus*, "one third") based on family descent; subsequently thirty-five geographic tribes, based on place of residence, were used for political voting purposes.

had cast their votes, and the addition of one more would make it necessary for Octavius to become a private citizen, Tiberius called a halt in the voting, and again entreated Octavius, embracing him and kissing him in the sight of the people and fervently begging him not to allow himself to be dishonored, and not to attach to a friend responsibility for a measure so grievous and severe.

On hearing these entreaties, we are told, Octavius was not altogether untouched or unmoved; his eyes filled with tears and he stood silent for a long time. But when he turned his gaze toward the men of wealth and substance who were standing in a body together, his awe of them, as it would seem, and his fear of ill repute among them, led him to take every risk with boldness and bid Tiberius do what he pleased. And so the law was passed, and Tiberius ordered one of his freedmen to drag Octavius from the rostra, for Tiberius used his freedmen as officers, and this made the sight of Octavius insultingly dragged along a more pitiful one. Moreover, people made a rush at him, and although the men of wealth ran in a body to his assistance and spread out their hands against the crowd, it was with difficulty that Octavius was snatched away and safely rescued from the crowd; and a trusty servant of his who stood in front of his master and protected him, had his eyes torn out, against the protest of Tiberius, who, when he perceived what had been going on, ran down with great haste to appease the tumult.

After this the agrarian law was passed, and three men were chosen for the survey and distribution of the public land, Tiberius himself, Appius Claudius his father-in-law, and Gaius Gracchus his brother, who was not at Rome, but was serving under Scipio[58] in the expedition against Numantia. These measures were carried out by Tiberius quietly and without opposition. The aristocrats,[59] however, who were vexed at these proceedings and feared the growing power of Tiberius, heaped insult upon him in the Senate. When he asked for the customary tent at public expense for his use when dividing

up the public land, they would not give it, although other men often had obtained one for less important purposes, and they fixed his daily allowance for expenses at nine obols.[60] These things were done on motion of Publius Nasica,[61] who surrendered completely to his hatred of Tiberius. For he was a very large holder of public land, and bitterly resented his being forced to give it up.

And now Attalus Philometor[62] died, and Eudemus of Pergamum brought to Rome the king's last will and testament, by which the Roman people was made his heir. At once Tiberius courted popular favor by bringing in a bill that provided that the money of King Attalus, when brought to Rome, should be given to the citizens who received a parcel of the public land, to aid them in stocking and tilling their farms. And as regarded the cities that were included in the kingdom of Attalus, he said it did not belong to the Senate to deliberate about them, but he himself would submit a pertinent resolution to the people. By this proceeding he gave more offense than ever to the Senate, and Pompeius,[63] rising to speak there, said that he was a neighbor of Tiberius, and therefore knew that Eudemus of Pergamum had presented Tiberius with a royal diadem and purple robe, believing that he was going to be king in Rome.[64]

And now Tiberius' friends, observing the threats and the hostile combination against him, thought that he ought to be made Tribune again for the following year. Once more, therefore, Tiberius sought to win the favor of the multitude by fresh laws, reducing the time of military service, granting appeal to the people from the verdicts of the judges, adding to the judges, who at that time were composed of senators only, an equal number from the

---

[58] Scipio Aemilianus, who had been appointed when the Roman offensive against the Spaniards bogged down.

[59] The senators who opposed Tiberius.

[60] A small Greek silver coin; this was an insultingly small sum.

[61] Publius Scipio Nasica, a cousin of Scipio Aemilianus and Consul in 138 BCE.

[62] Attalus III (138–133 be), king of Pergamum in western Anatolia.

[63] Elected Tribune of the Plebs in the next year, 132 BCE, he continued to oppose the Gracchi brothers.

[64] Claiming that a politician wanted to become "king" was the worst accusation that could be made.

equestrian order, and in every way at length trying to maim the power of the Senate from motives of anger and contentiousness rather than from calculations of justice and the public good. And when, as the voting was going on, the friends of Tiberius perceived that their opponents were getting the better of the contest, because all the people were not present, and in the first place resorted to abuse of his fellow Tribunes, and so protracted the time. Next, they dismissed the assembly, and ordered that it should convene on the following day. Then Tiberius, going down into the Forum, at first supplicated the citizens in a humble manner and with tears in his eyes. Next, he declared he was afraid that his enemies would break into his house by night and kill him, and thereby so wrought upon his hearers that great numbers of them took up their station about his house and spent the night there on guard.

At break of day there came to the house the man who brought the birds with which auspices are taken, and he threw food before them. But the birds would not come out of the cage, with the exception of one, although the keeper shook the cage right hard and even the one that came out would not touch the food, but raised its left wing, stretched out its leg, and then ran back into the cage.[65] At the same time also many of his friends on the Capitol came running to Tiberius with urgent appeals to hasten thither, because matters there were going well. And in fact things turned out splendidly for Tiberius at first, as soon as he came into view the crowd raised a friendly shout, and as he came up the hill they gave him a cordial welcome and ranged themselves about him, that no stranger might approach.

But after Mucius[66] began once more to summon the tribes to the vote, none of the customary forms could be observed because of the disturbance that arose on the outskirt of the throng, where there was crowding back and forth between the friends of Tiberius and their opponents, who were striving to force their way in and mingle with the rest. Moreover, at this juncture Fulvius Flaccus, a senator, posted himself in a conspicuous place and because it was impossible to make his voice heard so far, indicated with his hand that he wished to tell Tiberius something meant for his ear alone. Tiberius ordered the crowd to part for Flavius, who made his way up to him with difficulty, and told him that at a session of the Senate the party of the rich, because they could not prevail upon the Consul to do so, were purposing to kill Tiberius themselves, and for this purpose had under arms a multitude of their friends and slaves.

Tiberius, accordingly, reported this to those who stood about him, and they at once girded up their togas, and breaking in pieces the spear-shafts with which the officers keep back the crowd, distributed the fragments among themselves, that they might defend themselves against their assailants. Those who were farther off, however, wondered at what was going on and asked what it meant. Whereupon Tiberius put his hand to his head, making this visible sign that his life was in danger, because the questioners could not hear his voice. But his opponents, on seeing this, ran to the Senate and told that body that Tiberius was asking for a crown; and that his putting his hand to his head was a sign having that meaning. All the senators, of course, were greatly disturbed, and Nasica demanded that the Consul should come to the rescue of the state and put down the tyrant. The Consul replied with mildness that he would resort to no violence and would put no citizen to death without a trial; if, however, the people, under persuasion or compulsion from Tiberius, should vote anything that was unlawful, he would not regard this vote as binding. Thereupon Nasica sprang to his feet and said: "Because, then, the chief magistrate[67] betrays the state, all you who wish to preserve the laws, follow me!" With these words he covered his head with the skirt of his toga and set out for the Capitol. All the senators who followed him wrapped their togas about their left arms[68] and pushed aside those who stood

---

[65] This was a very bad omen.

[66] Publius Mucius Scaevola, one of the two Consuls and a legal expert.

[67] The Consul Mucius.

[68] To give themselves more room to maneuver because the toga was a very confining garment.

in their path, no man opposing them, in view of their dignity, but all taking to flight and trampling upon one another.

Now, the attendants of the senators carried clubs and staves that they had brought from home, and the senators themselves seized the fragments and legs of the benches that were shattered by the crowd in its flight, and went up against Tiberius, at the same time smiting those who were drawn up to protect him. Of these there was a rout and a slaughter, and as Tiberius himself turned to flee, someone laid hold of his garments. So he let his toga go and fled in his tunic. But he stumbled and fell to the ground among some bodies that lay in front of him. As he strove to rise to his feet, he received his first blow, as everybody admits, from Publius Satyreius, one of his colleagues,[69] who smote him on the head with the leg of a bench. And of the rest more than three hundred were slain by blows from sticks and stones, but not one by the sword.

This is said to have been the first sedition at Rome, since the abolition of royal power, to end in bloodshed and the death of citizens; the rest although neither trifling nor raised for trifling objects, were settled by mutual concessions, the nobles yielding from fear of the multitude, and the people out of respect for the Senate. And it was thought that even on this occasion Tiberius would have given way without difficulty had persuasion been brought to bear upon him, and would have yielded still more easily if his assailants had not resorted to wounds and bloodshed, for his adherents numbered not more than three thousand. But the combination against him would seem to have arisen from the hatred and anger of the rich rather than from the pretexts that they alleged, and there is strong proof of this in their lawless and savage treatment of his dead body. For they would not listen to his brother's request that he might take up the body and bury it by night, but threw it into the river along with the other dead. Nor was this all; they banished some of his friends without a trial and others they arrested and put to death.

But the Senate, trying to conciliate the people now that matters had gone too far, no longer opposed the distribution of the public land, and proposed that the people should elect a commissioner in place of Tiberius. So they took a ballot and elected Publius Crassus, who was a relative of Gracchus. Moreover, because the people felt bitterly over the death of Tiberius and were clearly awaiting an opportunity for revenge, and because Nasica was already threatened with prosecutions, the Senate, fearing for his safety, voted to send him to Asia. For when people met Nasica they did not try to hide their hatred of him, but grew savage and cried out upon him wherever he chanced to be, calling him an accursed man and a tyrant, who had defiled with the murder of an inviolable and sacred person the holiest and most awe-inspiring of the city's sanctuaries. And so Nasica stealthily left Italy. He roamed and wandered about in foreign lands ignominiously, and after a short time ended his life at Pergamum.

---

[69] Another one of the Tribunes of the Plebs.

CHAPTER 6

THE DECLINE OF THE ROMAN REPUBLIC (120–44 BCE)

During the second century BCE, Rome became the most powerful state in the Mediterranean world, and, even though we still call it the Republic, by 120 BCE it had amassed an empire of provinces extending from Spain to Anatolia. The creation of this "Republican Empire" placed tremendous stress on administration and politics. Rome's city-state form of government was not equipped to handle the administration of overseas provinces. The need to raise large professional armies was inconsistent with the Roman tradition of armies recruited from peasant farmers. And powerful ambitious senators, in command of these large armies, increasingly tended to put their own personal ambitions ahead of the best interests of the Roman state. A consequence was the acquisition of additional overseas provinces, and the end result was civil wars to determine which senatorial general would prevail. Combined, these factors eventually led to the fall of the Republic as it initially had been established.

FROM ONE CRISIS TO THE NEXT (113–88 BCE)

After the murder of Gaius Gracchus in 121 BCE, the Roman political scene had the appearance of returning to business as usual. But not for long. Beginning in the last decade of the second century BCE, the problems caused by expansion resurfaced with a vengeance to create even more disruption in Roman politics.

Marius and the Volunteer Army

In spite of Tiberius' murder, his land law went into effect, and a land commission began distributing public land to landless plebeians. It soon became apparent that the new land distribution policy was not sufficient to stem the reduction in the recruiting pool. The Romans limped along using the old system, which continued to be marginally functional as long as there were no large recruiting demands. But it broke down completely in the years after 113 BCE, when the

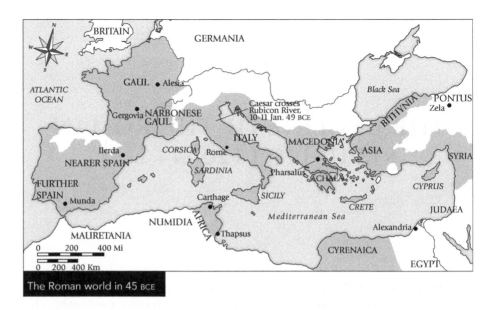

The Roman world in 45 BCE

Romans were compelled to fight no less than three crucial campaigns during the same period. The first crisis began when two large groups of Celts from northern Europe, the **Cimbri**, under King Boiorix, and the **Teutones**, under King Teutobod, left their homes, perhaps because of seacoast flooding in Jutland, and arrived in southern Gaul looking for new homes. Peoples friendly to Rome called on Roman assistance, and the Romans sent several armies north.

By now, the Celts were even more formidable fighters than before. Rather than fighting naked with just a longsword, as they often had done in Italy, they now wore metal helmets and armor and were organized into phalanxes. In 113 BCE the Cimbri and Teutones defeated the Consul Carbo at the Battle of Noreia in the territory of Noricum near the Danube River. In 109 they requested land to settle on in exchange for military service, and when that offer was refused, they destroyed the army of the Consul Silanus at an unidentified place in Narbonese Gaul. Other peoples, such as the Tigurini, also joined in the attacks. In 107 BCE, at the Battle of Agen, near Bordeaux, the Consul Longinus was killed and the Roman survivors were disgraced by being forced to pass under the yoke. But the biggest disaster occurred in 105 BCE, when at the Battle of Arausio (Orange) the aristocratic Proconsul Caepio refused to cooperate with the Consul Maximus, a New Man. The Romans suffered their worst defeat since Cannae; the two generals and a few hundred men escaped, but the Romans lost eighty thousand men that they could ill afford to lose. It was only their own lack of direction that kept the Cimbri and Teutones from invading Italy.

At the same time, in 111 BCE, Rome also declared war on Jugurtha, a Numidian king whose army had massacred some Italians in North Africa. Roman armies had little success in the guerilla war that Jugurtha pursued. And the military situation was made even worse in 104 BCE by a second slave revolt in Sicily (a revolt in 135 BCE led by a certain Eunus had taken three years to suppress), led by a slave named Salvius, who took the name Tryphon, the name of an earlier Seleucid rebel general, and raised an army of more than twenty thousand men. He then was joined by another army of rebellious slaves led by the Cilician Athenion. The Roman recruiting base simply could not bear the load.

A solution to the problem came from another ambitious New Man, Gaius **Marius**, an equestrian from southern Latium who, after distinguished military service in Spain in the 130s, embarked on a political career and was elected Consul for 107 BCE. He was assigned the war in Africa, and to raise an army he resorted, on his own authority, to enlisting men who had no property at all. This created the **volunteer army**, in which soldiers were not fighting for the greater glory of Rome, as the Senate liked to think, but to gain personal profit. Nor did the Senate then assume responsibility either for funding this new army or for rewarding the soldiers with land after the war was over. This was left to the general, which raised a disturbing possibility that such armies, as clients, would have more loyalty toward their generals than toward the state.

Marius also reorganized the army tactically, abandoning the old maniples in favor of more stable six-hundred-man **cohorts**, each consisting of six one-hundred-man centuries. Ten cohorts made up a legion of six thousand men. Each soldier was equipped with a *pilum* (javelin), a *gladius* (a short Spanish sword useful for both hacking and thrusting), and two six-foot wooden stakes used for constructing palisades around camps while the army was on the march. The soldiers, now laden with fifty pounds of equipment, referred to themselves as "Marius' mules." With his new army, Marius was able to hem Jugurtha in, but not to defeat him—that was accomplished in 106 BCE only by treachery, when Marius' lieutenant Lucius Cornelius **Sulla**, a member of an old patrician family fallen on hard times, induced the Mauretanian chieftain Bocchus to hand Jugurtha over. Marius then spent three years training his army for the expected next attack by the Cimbri, Teutones, and Tigurini. This came in 102 BCE, when the Celts finally had a plan, a three-pronged attack on Italy. Later in the year, Marius fell upon the Cimbri as they approached through southern France. At the Battle of Aquae Sextiae (Aix), they were completely defeated, and thousands were enslaved. The following year, when the Teutones invaded northern Italy, Marius met and defeated them at the Battle of Vercelli. Although some of the women killed themselves and their children to escape slavery, thousands more were enslaved. In the same year Sulla drove off the Tigurini, and the barbarian threat was ended. Finally, in 100 BCE, the Sicilian slave revolt was suppressed by Manius Aquillius, a protégé of Marius.

Gaius Marius, creator of the volunteer army.

CLIMATE AND HISTORY, THE CIMBRIAN FLOOD

Writing in the early second century CE, the Roman historian Florus emphatically stated that the Cimbri and other peoples had had been set into motion circa 113 BCE by coastal flooding in far northern Europe, saying, "The Cimbri, Teutones, and Tigurini were refugees from the furthest parts of Gaul, for after the ocean had inundated their lands they sought new homes throughout the world."

The geographer Strabo, however, writing around the turn of the first century BCE, doubted that the story was true, relating,

> As for the Cimbri, some things that are told about them are extremely improbable. For instance, one could not accept as a reason for their having become a wandering folk that while they were dwelling on a peninsula they were driven out of their habitations by a great flood-tide. . . . It is ridiculous to suppose that they departed from their homes on account of a phenomenon that is natural and eternal, occurring twice every day. And the assertion that an excessive flood-tide once occurred looks like a fabrication, for when the ocean is affected in this way it is subject to increases and diminutions, but these are regulated and periodical.

Strabo clearly believed that the flood story simply was related to the tides, but modern scientific investigations suggest that something quite different might have been involved. Some studies propose that the homeland of the Cimbri was the area of the Zuider Zee in the Netherlands, a shallow bay on the North Sea known for flooding well back into the Middle Ages.

But the preponderance of the evidence suggests somewhere further east. Strabo, for example, stated that the Cimbri lived on a peninsula. At about the same time, the emperor Augustus, in his *Res gestae*, noted, "My fleet sailed from the mouth of the Rhine eastward as far as the lands of the Cimbri." And the geographer Ptolemy reported that the ancient name of Jutland was the "Cimbric Peninsula" and that the Cimbri lived on the northern end of it. It thus would appear that Jutland (modern Denmark), which divides the North Sea from the Baltic Sea, probably was where the Cimbri began their trek.

Now, scientific study indicates that coastal dunes on the western coast of Jutland formed in the years after 5000 BCE and that sand movements sporadically occurred until the end of the nineteenth century, often associated with increased storminess. For example, by circa 600 BCE, the sea level had risen over twenty-three feet (seven meters) above its normal level. On occasion, storms can break through sand barriers and cause massive flooding in the areas behind, as happened as recently as 1825, when the northernmost part of Jutland—the very region once inhabited by the Cimbri—was separated from the mainland by a great flood and became the North Jutlandic Island.

It therefore would seem quite possible that the uncertainties of coastal dwelling during one of the periods of seacoast variability might have induced some—but by no means all—of the Cimbri to begin a journey to attempt to locate new homes, and it probably would be imprudent to dismiss the flood account out of hand.

Thus the recruitment needs of the Roman army had been met, and the agricultural-military crisis had been solved. But Rome now was left with an even more perilous problem: armies whose loyalty to the Roman government was dependent on the good will of the senatorial generals who commanded them. Indeed, when the Senate resisted granting land to Marius' veterans, Marius was compelled to ally himself with two rabble-rousing Tribunes, Saturninus and Glaucia, and to call in his troops to ensure that the law was passed. But when these two began to use open violence to secure their political goals, the Senate issued the Last Recommendation of the Senate and ordered Marius to deal with the crisis. Marius obeyed, and both Tribunes were killed in the subsequent rioting. As a consequence, Marius—a much better general than politician—lost credibility as a popular leader, and his political career was ruined. He also provided a lesson to later politicians about the need to hold on to their political power base.

The Revolt of the Italian Allies

Meanwhile, Italian discontent about being forced to serve in Rome's wars without the opportunity to become Roman citizens finally boiled over in the 90s BCE. In 95 BCE, Italians living in Rome were expelled, and in 91 BCE another reforming Tribune of the Plebs, Drusus, the son of Gaius Gracchus' opponent, once again proposed to enfranchise the Italians. He was assassinated, and Roman supporters of the Italians were put on trial. This was the last straw, In 90 BCE a massive coordinated revolt of the Italian Allies, also known as the **Social War**, from the Latin word *socii*, or "allies," broke out. The Italians established their own country, called **Italia**, with its own Senate, modeled on that of Rome, and a capital city at Corfinium, and raised 100,000 soldiers.

The Romans mobilized armies in northern and southern Italy but could not hope to win such a war quickly, if at all, so, in typical fashion, when they were forced to introduce change, they were quite willing to do so. In the first year of the revolt, the Consul L. Julius Caesar issued the Julian Law, which granted Roman citizenship to all Italian cities that were not yet in revolt. And in the next year the Tribunes M. Plautius and C. Papirius sponsored the Plautian-Papirian Law granting citizenship to all rebels who laid down their arms and reported to a Roman Praetor within sixty days. The vast majority of the Italians now had what they wanted, and by 88 BCE the revolt had collapsed; only the Samnites continued to hold out. The result was another alteration in the structure of Roman society. The status of "Italian ally" disappeared, and all the free population of Italy became Roman citizens. The composition of the army necessarily also changed. Italians now enrolled in the legions, and there were no more units of allied Italians. This compelled Roman generals to look further afield, out into the provinces, when it came to recruiting bands of auxiliary soldiers.

A *denarius* issued by the Italians during the Italian Revolt. The obverse bears the head of the personification of Italy and the legend "Italia"; the reverse depicts eight Italian soldiers sacrificing a pig and swearing an oath not to surrender to the Romans.

AN AGE OF GENERALS (88–60 BCE)

At the end of the Italian Revolt, the Roman government was confronted by three overwhelming problems: the ineffective administration of the provinces, the need to control a volunteer army that was loyal to its generals, and the increasing disinclination of ambitious senators to get along with each other. The ineffectiveness of the Senate in dealing with these problems ultimately would lead to the demise of the Republic itself as a viable form of government.

The *Regnum Sullanum*

Dissatisfaction with provincial administration continued to fester and was particularly rampant in economically developed provinces such as Asia and Sicily, which offered greater opportunity for corruption. In 88 BCE resentment boiled over into open revolt in Asia. This provided an opening for **Mithridates VI** (119–63 BCE), the ambitious king of Pontus, located on the southeastern coast of the Black Sea, and a supposed descendent of the Persian King-of-Kings Darius I, to expand his territory. After first occupying the neighboring kingdom of Bithynia, he then invaded the Roman province of Asia. In the so-called Asiatic Vespers, it was said that eighty thousand Romans were murdered on a single day. The Roman Legate Manius Aquillius, the victor over the Sicilian slaves in 100 BCE, was executed by having molten gold poured down his throat, accompanied by the words, "And now let the Roman thirst for gold be satisfied."

In Rome, the command of the war against Mithridates was given to the Consul Lucius Cornelius Sulla, an experienced general who had served in North Africa and defeated the Tigurini. In 88 BCE, Sulla recruited his own volunteer army and was on the point of departure when he learned that Marius had induced the Senate to transfer the command to himself. Rather than passively acquiescing to this setback, Sulla appealed to his soldiers. With their support, he marched on Rome. In a virtual coup d'état, he put Marius to flight, seized the city, and forced the government to give the command back to him. He then sailed off to do battle in the east.

Meanwhile, back in Rome Marius returned, raised an army, and instituted a reign of terror against Sulla's supporters, with the heads of executed enemies displayed in the Forum. Even though he himself soon died, his adherents, such as the Consuls Cornelius Cinna and Papirius Carbo, continued to oppose Sulla and even planned to send an army against him to Greece; but Cinna was murdered by his own soldiers because they did not want to engage in a profitless civil war. In 83 BCE, after duly defeating Mithridates and gathering all the loot that he could, Sulla returned to Italy . Over the course of the following year, he defeated all of his enemies, including the Samnites, who in 82 BCE made a last-ditch stand and died to a man at the Battle of the Colline Gate outside Rome. Sulla's first order of business was to raise resources to reward his troops, and in doing so he also was able to revenge

Mithridates VI of Pontus portrayed as Hercules wearing a lion skin, attesting to his claims to divine status.

himself on his enemies. He published lists of enemies known as **Proscriptions**: both the lives and the property of those on it were forfeit, and several thousand wealthy persons throughout Italy perished. By these means, which amounted to little more than state-sanctioned murder, Sulla found land for 120,000 of his army veterans.

In spite of his unconstitutional actions, Sulla, as a Roman who believed implicitly in the concept of rule of law, desired to find some quasi-constitutional method for holding absolute authority. He therefore had himself appointed Dictator for Restoring the Republic, but without the customary six-month limitation, a decidedly unconstitutional situation. Sulla then governed so high-handedly that his regime was known as the *Regnum Sullanum*, or "Kingdom of Sulla." He attempted to ensure that no one else would do what he had just done by imposing reforms that attempted to weaken the power of popular politicians and strengthen the authority of the Senate. He restored the Senate's right to preapprove measures submitted to popular assemblies, and he

Ambitious Republican politicians often sponsored the construction of public works in order to gain popular support and demonstrate their public spirit. One of the few such buildings to survive is the *tabularium*, or government archives, built by the Consul Catulus in 78 BCE. It was built from travertine, tufa, and concrete and preserved records formerly stored in the Temple of Saturn. In the modern period, an upper storey was removed by Michelangelo, and what remains now is part of the City Hall of Rome.

transferred jurisdiction over criminal cases from the assemblies to the Senate. To make the office of Tribune less attractive, the tribunician veto was outlawed, and Tribunes were not permitted to run for higher office. He increased the number of Quaestors and Praetors in order to expand the membership of the Senate and thus make it more representative of the optimates. In 78 BCE Sulla retired, and, racked by illness, he died the following year.

Although Sulla tried to undo what he had done and restore power to the Senate, his most important legacy was his example of using his army to take control of the state and to subvert constitutional government. Others were quick to follow his precedent. Marcus Aemilius **Lepidus**, one of the Consuls for 78 BCE, for example, attempted to gain power by adopting a popular program, such as offering to restore land confiscated by Sulla. Assigned the province of Narbonese Gaul, Lepidus raised an army. When the Senate ordered him to return to Rome, he brought his army with him, intending to do what Sulla had done and seize control of the government. But Catulus, the other Consul, defeated him on the outskirts of Rome. Lepidus fled and soon died of disease.

It now had reached the point at which it was almost a necessity for senators who wanted to have influential positions in the state to control large armies, for one's soldiers could be used not only to win glory away from home but also to manipulate votes in the Senate and popular assemblies. The only way to gain control of an army was to be assigned a province where there was a war going on.

Therefore, ambitious senators became even more eager for military commands than they had been before. The question now was no longer which faction in the Senate would have political predominance, but which individual would. In the post-Sullan period, three senatorial generals in particular were to engage in a tumultuous struggle for power: Crassus, Pompey, and Caesar.

Crassus and the Revolt of Spartacus

Yet another result of Rome's expansion and many wars was a large increase in the slave population of Italy and Sicily, where war captives labored on large senatorial estates called *latifundia*, a word meaning "wide fields." These agricultural slaves were not always well treated. Because they cost so little, the senator Cato the Elder recommended working them to death and then buying new ones. Sicilian slave revolts in 135 and 103 attested to the discontent that could arise among the slave population as a result of such attitudes.

An even more serious slave problem arose in 73 BCE, when **Spartacus**, a Thracian slave being trained as a gladiator at Capua, led an insurrection among the slave population of Italy. The slave army, which numbered more than seventy thousand and included many former soldiers, defeated several Roman armies sent against them. Spartacus' plan was to lead the slaves north out of Italy, whence they could disperse to their homes, but the slaves chose to continue looting in Italy. Ultimately, Marcus Licinius **Crassus** Dives ("The Rich") was given the military command. Most of Crassus' noble family had been killed during the Marian purge, but Crassus' support of Sulla had allowed him not only to recover the family wealth but also to become the richest man in Rome. After restoring discipline in the Roman army, in part by using the old Roman military punishment of **decimation**, wherein every tenth man in a disgraced army unit was chosen by lot for execution by his own comrades, Crassus hemmed in the slaves in southern Italy. The slave army was defeated in 71 BCE, and the rebels were mercilessly punished: six thousand were crucified at one-hundred-yard intervals on the Appian Way outside Rome. There were no further large slave rebellions after this. On the other hand, however, the treatment of slaves also improved, in part because the Romans had learned their lesson about what could happen if slaves were treated too badly. His suppression of the slave revolt made Crassus into one of the most powerful senators in Rome, but it also left the Senate reluctant to grant him another command that would allow him to acquire even greater glory and power.

The Rise of Pompey

Another ambitious senator was Gnaeus **Pompey**, the son of the Consul Pompey Strabo, a New Man who had distinguished himself in the Italian Revolt. After his father, a supporter of Sulla, died of the plague in 87 BCE, nineteen-year-old Pompey kept his father's army together. In 83 BCE he offered his own support to Sulla, who sent him to Sicily; there, Pompey's enthusiastic execution of one of

Sulla's enemies gained him the nickname *Adulescens carnifex*, or "the Teenage Butcher." Pompey realized very early in his career the importance of controlling an army in order to gain political advancement, and he did everything he could to obtain military commands. During the 70s BCE, he put down the revolt of Sertorius, a supporter of Cinna who had established a separatist state among the native peoples of Spain, and he returned just in time to claim the credit for mopping up the last of the defeated slaves in 71 BCE. A major quarrel with Crassus over this was averted when both were named Consuls for 70 BCE.

In 67 BCE, the Gabinian Law gave Pompey an extraordinary command, on the sea and fifty miles (eighty kilometers) inland, against the pirates who then infested the Mediterranean. In a well-organized campaign he swept from Gibraltar to the Levant, rounding up the pirates as he went and eventually settling them, as his clients, in Pompeiopolis, a city in southern Anatolia named after himself. Meanwhile, another war against Mithridates was going on, the Third Mithridatic War (73–63 BCE), in which Mithridates had been joined by King Tigranes of Armenia. The Roman commander Lucullus had been militarily successful, but his lack of troops prevented him from concluding the war.

Thus, in 66 BCE, the Manilian Law put Pompey in charge of the war against Mithridates, and Pompey's campaigns resulted in many additional engagements with the peoples of western Asia. Pompey made an alliance with Phraates III, king of Parthia, and the two then engaged in joint operations. After campaigning in Armenia and the Caucasus Mountains, Pompey turned south. Mithridates, meanwhile, had fled to the Kingdom of the Bosporus in the Crimea. When his son Pharnaces II (63–47 BCE) revolted, Mithridates attempted to commit an honorable suicide by taking arsenic, a move that failed because Mithridates, afraid of being poisoned, had been regularly taking small doses and had built up an immunity. So he was reduced to falling on his sword.

Pompey then took the opportunity to settle the affairs of the entire eastern Mediterranean. In 64 BCE he deposed the last Seleucid king, Philip II Philoromaeus ("Roman-Lover") (65-63 BCE), abolished the Seleucid Empire, and in the next year made Syria, the most Hellenized part of the old Seleucid kingdom, into a Roman province. This left Ptolemaic Egypt, a slavish adherent to the Roman line, as the last independent Hellenistic kingdom. Pompey also was called upon to intervene in Jewish dynastic quarreling, which resulted in a cultural encounter that initially did not go well. After a three-month siege of the temple mount in Jerusalem, the fortifications were stormed and twelve thousand Jews were massacred. Pompey then offended the Jews even further by entering the temple sanctuary, something reserved only for the priests; out of his respect for religion, however, he did leave the temple treasures untouched. Part of the Jewish kingdom was annexed to the new province of Syria, but the inland section was left to be ruled by a loyal client, Hyrcanus II, who was made Jewish High Priest and given the title of "Ethnarch." In addition, Arethas III (87–62 BCE), king of the Nabataean Arabs, who had created a kingdom that extended from northern Arabia to

While serving as Quaestor in 64 BCE, Marcus Aemilius Scaurus was made a Military Tribune by Pompey, his brother-in-law. In 62 BCE, Pompey left Scaurus in charge of prosecuting a war against the Nabataean Arab king Arethras III, which resulted in Arethas becoming a Roman client king. As Aedile in 58 BCE, Scaurus issued a *denarius* glorifying his eastern military experience. Arethas is depicted next to a camel on his knees as a suppliant, with the legend "King Aretas." Above is the legend, "Marcus Scaurus, Curule Aedile."

Damascus in southern Syria, likewise became a Roman client. When he returned to Rome in 62 BCE, Pompey had the potential to become the most politically powerful senator in Rome, but he turned out to be as naïve a politician as he was a shrewd general. Pompey found the Senate jealous of his great successes and unwilling to approve his eastern settlement or to pass a law granting land to the veterans of his army.

Marcus Tullius Cicero and the Conspiracy of Catiline

Another influential politician of this period, Marcus Tullius **Cicero**, was something of a throwback and an anomaly. He made his reputation not by his military prowess but by his legal and oratorical talents. Cicero came from a family of equestrians from Arpinum, a town south of Rome. After a token attempt to pursue a military career under Pompey Strabo and Sulla during the Revolt of the Italian Allies, he studied rhetoric and philosophy in Greece and followed a legal career. Following a string of successful defenses and prosecutions of influential senators, as a result of which many powerful senators became indebted to him, Cicero ran for Consul for 63 BCE. He gained election when the senatorial optimates, with whom he wished to associate himself but who never really accepted him, were forced to back him against Crassus' candidate Lucius Sergius Catilina, or **Catiline**, who was proposing an extensive reform program. The disappointed Catiline then raised an army, and in a series of famous Catilinarian speeches Cicero warned that Catiline planned to overthrow the state. The Senate issued the Last Recommendation of the Senate, and Cicero had Catiline's supporters arrested and executed without a trial, an act that later would come back to haunt Cicero. Shortly thereafter, Catiline's ragtag army was defeated, with Catiline himself dying in the front ranks.

JULIUS CAESAR AND THE FIRST TRIUMVIRATE (60–44 BCE)

The increasing role played by powerful generals in the last years of the Roman Republic was seen in the creation of two triumvirates, groups of three ultrapowerful senators who banded together in pursuit of their own interests. With authority based on their possession of large armies, these senators effectively removed whatever vestiges of independent authority the Senate possessed.

The Rise of Julius Caesar

The third powerful general of this period was a late bloomer. Gaius Julius **Caesar**, a member of a patrician family supposedly descended from Venus, had been named in Sulla's proscription lists—his aunt Julia was married to Marius, and he himself was married to the daughter of Cinna—and had barely escaped with his life. His political career, therefore, got off to a slow start. As Aedile in 65 BCE, he laid claim to popular support by restoring the trophies of his uncle Marius to the Capitoline temple and sponsoring the most elaborate public entertainment yet, with no less than 320 pairs of gladiators fighting in silver-gilt armor. In 63 BCE Caesar parlayed this popularity into election as *Pontifex Maximus*, chief priest of Rome. His first military command did not come until 62 BCE, when he served as a Praetor in Spain, but in 60 BCE he was forced by the Senate to give up his claims on a triumph in order to run for, and win, the consulate. Like any ambitious senator, Caesar then wished to receive a province, where, as Proconsul, he could recruit a large army and acquire glory and power. The Senate, however, was reluctant to permit him to pursue his ambitions and insultingly allocated to him "the foot paths and cattle trails of Italy."

Portrait bust of Julius Caesar.

The First Triumvirate

Crassus, Pompey, and Caesar then made common cause. The desires of all three in one way or another had been thwarted by the Senate. They therefore formed an unofficial alliance called the **First Triumvirate** (a "group of three men") in which each agreed to look out for the interests of the others. Pompey needed to have his legislation passed, and Caesar, as Consul in 59 BCE, saw to it that this was done. Caesar wanted a suitable province, and he now was assigned both Cisalpine and Narbonese Gaul, the latter of which gave him the opportunity to make military interventions to the north, where a number of appeals for Roman assistance had been received. And Crassus, fearful of being the odd man out, desired to restore his own military standing. He eventually was granted a command against the Parthians, who had succeeded to all but the westernmost parts of the old Seleucid Empire. In addition, Cicero was exiled for having illegally executed Catiline's supporters.

In 58 BCE Caesar, having raised ten legions, went to Gaul, where he remained for nine years. He reported the progress of his campaigns in a series of dispatches that collectively became known as the *Gallic War*, one of the most famous historical accounts to survive from antiquity. By making effective use of the Roman maxim "Divide and conquer," he played off one Celtic people against another. In 58 BCE, Caesar inflicted substantial defeats on the Helvetii, a people of modern Switzerland who had planned to migrate into Gaul, and on the Suebi, a Germanic people led by King Ariovistus who had established settlements in northern Gaul. A year later, the Belgae of northwestern Gaul, including in particular the powerful Nervii, likewise were defeated. The next year, 56 BCE, was spent in mopping-up operations against western Gallic peoples.

Caesar was so successful at extending Roman authority into Gaul that in 55 BCE he was able to undertake a punitive raid across the Rhine River against the Suebi and peoples referred to as "Germans." It is unclear, however, just what Caesar meant by "Germans." At the beginning of the *Gallic War*, he described them simply as "those who live across the Rhine," without any indication of ethnic attributes, such as language. So it is not at all clear that Caesar's "Germans" are the same Germans who appear later in Roman history. Some Roman writers even thought that the later Germans originally had come from the Belgic area of Gaul, and the possibility exists that Caesar's Germans were actually Celts, and that actual Germanic speakers lived nearer to the Elbe River. By building a full-scale bridge in only ten days, Caesar was able not only to impress the peoples of Germany with Roman engineering expertise but also to craft a descriptive passage so riddled with technical vocabulary that it still troubles modern Latin students. After burning a few villages and making a show of force to impress his audience back in Rome, Caesar returned to Gaul after only eighteen days.

Still in 55 BCE Caesar also made a reconnaissance of Britain, followed by a full-scale invasion in 54 BCE. Even though Caesar failed to occupy any British territory permanently—and it is unclear whether he had intended to do so—he did install client kings and set a precedent for further Roman intervention there. As of 54 BCE it therefore looked as if Caesar was satisfied that Gaul had been well and truly subdued and was just marking time until he could return in triumph to Rome.

But any sense of final victory was illusory. As had happened in Spain, a charismatic leader arose, **Vercingetorix**, a chief of the Arverni, and united the Gauls in a great revolt against Rome in 52 BCE. Caesar's attempt to suppress the revolt began badly with a defeat at the hill fort of Gergovia, near modern Clermont-Ferrand. It looked like the whole conquest of Gaul was on the verge of collapse. Only after a tremendous battle before the hill fort of Alesia were the Gauls definitively defeated. As a result of his Gallic campaigns, Caesar built up not only a massive amount of wealth but also an effective and battle-hardened army and many Gallic clients.

Meanwhile, in 54 BCE Crassus went off to fight the Parthians. The campaign was a disaster from the start. Before the crossing of the Euphrates, it was said, one of the eagles (the military standard of a legion) became so stuck in the ground that it could only with difficulty be pulled out. This was a very bad omen that suggested to the superstitious soldiers that the standard did not want to attack the Parthians (or more reasonably that the soldiers did not want to). Crassus' soldiers became bogged down in the sands of Mesopotamia. Unable to bring the Parthian horse-archers to battle, all they could do was hunker down behind their shields while their water ran out. Eventually, Crassus attempted to parley with the Parthians but was butchered and beheaded instead. Most of his soldiers were captured and enslaved, and his head was used as a stage prop in a production of *The Bacchae*, a Greek tragedy by Euripides, in Ctesiphon, the Parthian capital. The triumvirate thus became a less stable duovirate.

THE SIEGE OF ALESIA

To give himself time to assemble all his forces in the Gallic revolt against Caesar in 52 BCE, Vercingetorix withdrew to the hill fort of Alesia with 80,000 troops to await the arrival of 100,000 reinforcements. Caesar knew that he could not permit the two forces to unite, so he besieged Vercingetorix in Alesia with his army of 60,000 Romans. Caesar was vastly outnumbered, so he did what the Romans did best: he built fortifications, which Caesar himself described in great detail in his *Gallic War*. First, over a period of three weeks a line of circumvallation eleven miles (twenty-nine kilometers) long and thirteen feet (four meters) high, fronted by a ditch fifteen feet (four and a half meters) wide and deep and with towers at intervals, was built around Alesia to prevent the besieged Gauls from escaping and to starve them out. Caesar took great pains to discuss all of the work that his men put into building booby traps to keep the Gauls from even reaching the walls. Sharpened stakes placed in pits were jokingly called *lilia* ("lilies") by the men, groups of brambles were called *cippi* ("gravestones"), and *stimuli* ("spurs") were wooden blocks with iron hooks in them extending just above ground level. Then an even longer, similarly designed, fourteen-mile wall of contravallation was constructed to keep the relief force from attacking Caesar's rear.

The final showdown came in September of 52 BCE. After a furious battle in which one area of the Roman fortifications was almost completely overrun and in which Caesar himself led the Roman cavalry reserves in a desperate attempt to save the day, the Gauls were finally forced to retreat. That decided the issue, for Alesia could no longer hold out, and Vercingetorix surrendered the next day.

In later French history, the heroic resistance of Vercingetorix served as an example of French resistance to invaders, and ever since the nineteenth century attempts have been made to identify the site of the battle. In the 1860s, when France was threatened by an attack from Germany, the French emperor Napoleon III (1852–1870) sponsored excavations at Alise-Sainte Reine near Dijon that claimed to have found remains of the battle, and a great monument was erected. The only problem was that the site did not match Caesar's description very well. Many other possible sites also have been proposed, as at Alaise in the Franche-Comté, or near either Chaux-des-Crotenay or Salins-les-Bains in the Jura Mountains in eastern France, or atop Mont-Auxois, where an artifact with the words "In Alisiia" ("In Alesia") was found.

Although the dispute over the location of the battle no doubt will continue, Caesar's careful descriptions allow his fortifications to be reconstructed with a fair degree of accuracy, and many models, large and small, have been made. One can only imagine the degree of apprehension the Gauls must have felt when attempting to attack such formidable defenses.

The Civil War

Back in Rome, senators such as Cicero had been playing on Pompey's vanity and naïveté in an effort to detach him from his ally Caesar. After the death of Pompey's beloved wife Julia, Caesar's daughter, in 54 BCE, they were successful. In 50 BCE, Caesar was refused the right to run for Consul in absentia and ordered to return to Rome as a private citizen. He realized that doing so would be political suicide, for it would leave him open to trumped-up charges by his rivals. He therefore felt that he had no recourse but to return—not without his army, but with it. In 49 BCE, saying, "The die is cast," he crossed the shallow **Rubicon River**, the boundary between Cisalpine Gaul and Italy. Doing so automatically put him into rebellion against the Roman state.

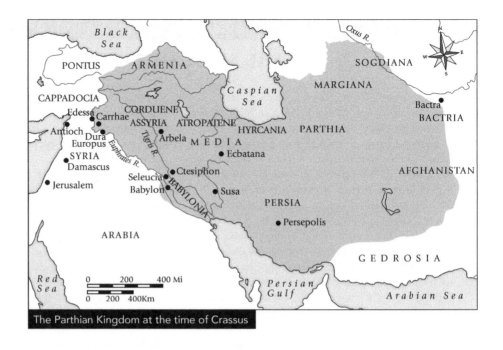

The Parthian Kingdom at the time of Crassus

Pompey was caught largely unprepared. He fled to Greece with his senatorial supporters in order to gather his resources and strengthen his army. After being duly legitimized by what was left of the Senate in Rome, Caesar too crossed to Greece. At the Battle of Pharsalus in 48 BCE the army of Pompey was defeated, and Pompey fled to the opulent kingdom of Ptolemaic Egypt in a last effort to rebuild his forces. He was met by King Ptolemy XII (51–47 BCE), who, thinking to do Caesar a favor, beheaded him. Caesar, who arrived soon thereafter, was not amused by the idea of an Egyptian king decapitating a distinguished Roman general who also was his son-in-law, and he deposed Ptolemy in favor of his twenty-year-old sister and co-regent, **Cleopatra VII** (51–30 BCE).

Caesar was forced to remain in Egypt for the winter, and nine months later Cleopatra bore his son, Caesarion. In the spring of 47 BCE, Caesar returned to Rome after making a detour to Anatolia, where Pharnaces II, the son of Mithridates, was attempting to expand his territory. After a five-day war and a quick victory at the Battle of Zela, Caesar sent his famous words to the Senate, "veni, vidi, vici" ("I came, I saw, I conquered"). He spent the next two years defeating his remaining rivals at the Battles of Thapsus in Africa and Munda in Spain.

In his attempts to act within the constraints of Roman legal tradition, Caesar sought to remain in power by using—and misusing—existing offices and powers. He attempted to preserve his position as head of state not only by repeatedly serving as Consul but also by holding the quite irregular position of *Dictator perpetuus,* or Dictator for Life. In order to maintain popular support for his abnormal position, he made many benefactions to the Roman people. Using spoils from the Gallic war (unlike Sulla, Caesar did not confiscate wealth from his personal enemies), Caesar undertook a large-scale renovation of the forum. He constructed a new law court, the *Basilica Julia* ("Julian basilica"); reconstructed the rostra, or speaker's platform; and began a reconstruction of the *curia*, or Senate house, in a new form, the *Curia Julia* ("Julian *curia*"). He also built a new forum to take some of the pressure off the old Republican forum, which no longer had sufficient capacity to meet the needs of the growing population of Rome. The highlight of the Forum of Caesar was a temple of Venus Genetrix, "Venus the Ancestress," an allusion to Caesar's putative descent direct from the goddess Venus; the temple also contained a statue of Cleopatra.

Caesar's position of supreme authority also gave him the power to attempt to deal with some of the problems facing the Republic. For example, his extension of Roman citizenship to some cities outside Italy assisted in the integration of the provinces into the Roman world, as did his creation of overseas colonies at Seville in Spain, Arles in Gaul, Carthage in Africa, and Corinth in Greece to provide land for 100,000 army veterans. He attempted to reduce extortion by replacing the Asian and Sicilian tithe with tribute. He made the Senate more representative by expanding it to nine hundred members and including some non-Italians. And, because the Roman calendar had gotten out of synch, with December occurring in the summer, he made the year 45 BCE to be 445 days long and he introduced the **Julian calendar** of 365 days, with a leap year every fourth year; the month Sextilis also was renamed "July" in his honor. Caesar's short period of rule and repeated military distractions meant that he did not have the opportunity to introduce any systematic or comprehensive reforms, but he did demonstrate that a single ruler could deal with problems much more effectively and efficiently than the Senate had.

One of Caesar's policies had been to show *clementia* (clemency) and to pardon defeated enemies in an attempt to restore normalcy to the state. These magnanimous gestures came back to haunt him when, on the **Ides of March** (March 15) in 44 BCE, just before his departure for a war against the Parthians, he was stabbed to death at a meeting of the Senate by a group of conspirators who objected to his unconstitutional holding of power. Ironically, he died in a theater built by Pompey at the feet of Pompey's statue. His assassins included a number of pardoned enemies, such as Marcus Brutus and Gaius Cassius.

ALTERNATIVE HISTORY

Are there any other ways that Caesar could have modeled his position in the state that might have worked more effectively? How would Roman history have played out if Caesar had not gone to the Senate meeting on the Ides of March?

LATE REPUBLICAN LITERATURE

The late Republic also saw the flowering of Latin literary culture. The Romans had gotten off to a rather late start when it came to the development of literary traditions, but by the Late Republic Latin had become a fully fledged literary language in its own right.

Late Republican Poets

As before, some writers, particularly poets, made their reputations primarily on the basis of their literary efforts. Catullus, writing in the 60s and 50s BCE, was known primarily for his love poetry, addressed to a fictitious lover named Lesbia. But he also wrote other kinds of elegiac poetry, ranging from a tender "farewell" to his deceased brother to various kinds of invective, as when he lampooned a Romanized Celt for supposedly engaging in the Spanish practice of brushing his teeth with urine. Catullus was one of the first Latin writers to apply Greek lyric verse meters to Latin. And in the 50s BCE, the Epicurean philosopher Lucretius authored a poem, *On the Nature of Things*, that presented an atheistic model intended to free one from fear of death. The concept of a universe composed of atoms falling through a void influenced later concepts of "atomism," and Lucretius also is considered to have originated the system that divides the human past into the Stone, Bronze, and Iron Ages.

The poem of Lucretius influenced the materialistic thought of Karl Marx.

Politicians at Leisure

At the same time, the senatorial ideal now included the expectations that a senator not only would participate in public life but also would engage in leisure activities that included both reading and writing various kinds of literary works. Indeed, the most famous late Republican prose writers, Caesar, Cicero, Sallust, and Varro, all were very active in politics. Caesar, of course, wrote the *Gallic War* and the *Civil War*, both intended to portray his own political actions in the most positive light. And Cicero published not only his speeches and letters, likewise intended to enhance his personal reputation, but also works on oratory and philosophy. In later years, Cicero set the standard of Latin prose writing against which all other authors were measured.

In addition, Sallust, a supporter of Caesar during the civil war who used ill-gotten gains in the provinces to create famous gardens on the Quirinal Hill in Rome, wrote surviving historical accounts of the *War against Jugurtha* and the *Conspiracy of Catiline*; his *Histories* of the post-Sullan period, however, have been lost. Rather than merely narrating events, Sallust attempted to explain the human motivations and weaknesses and the historical processes lying behind them, and thus he set the stage for a more nuanced writing of Roman history. And Varro, a supporter of Pompey pardoned by Caesar, was believed to have written no less than 620 books, most of which do not survive, on various topics. In the field of history, he developed the standard historical chronological framework for Roman history based on lists of Consuls beginning in 509 BCE and on the foundation of Rome in 753 BCE; in this scheme, dates were expressed in years "AUC," or *Ab urbe condita* ("from the foundation of the city"). Two of his works, practical in nature, survive: *On the Latin Language*, a grammatical treatise, and *On Agricultural Matters*, a handbook on farming. Influential Roman senators in public life thus also saw themselves as the representatives of Roman culture and values.

⇦ LOOKING BACK

The last century of the Roman Republic was marked by the Senate's increasing inability to deal with problems that had accumulated during Rome's period of rapid expansion. These included the failure to take responsibility for governing provinces effectively, the inability to bring the volunteer army under its control, and, in particular, the pursuit of personal ambitions by powerful senatorial generals who put their own interests ahead of the interests of the state as a whole. One crisis led to another. The institutionalized violence that had been introduced during the age of the Gracchi escalated into civil wars in which Sulla and Caesar used their armies to seize control of the Roman world. Neither, however, was able to deal with the accumulated problems, and after the assassination of Caesar in 44 BCE there still were no solutions in sight. The military campaigns of generals such as Pompey and Caesar also resulted in closer cultural interactions with peoples on the fringes of the Roman world such as Armenians, Parthians, Jews, Arabs, Gauls, and Germans.

LOOKING AHEAD ⇨

The assassins of Caesar had naïvely assumed that once Caesar was gone there would be a return to the old Republic. But those days were gone, and the only result would be yet another round of civil wars.

FURTHER READING

Badian, Ernst. *Roman Imperialism in the Late Republic.* Ithaca, NY: Cornell Univ. Press, 1971.

Badian, Ernst. *Sulla, the Deadly Reformer.* Sydney: Sydney Univ. Press, 1970.

Bradley, K. R. *Slavery and Rebellion in the Roman World 140 B.C.–70 B.C.* Bloomington: Indiana Univ. Press, 1989.

Brunt, P. A. *The Fall of the Roman Republic.* Oxford: Clarendon Press, 1988.

Canfora, Luciano. *Julius Caesar: The People's Dictator.* Edinburgh: Edinburgh Univ. Press, 2006.

Evans, Richard J. *Gaius Marius: A Political Biography.* Pretoria: Univ. of South Africa, 1994.

Gruen, Erich S. *The Last Generation of the Roman Republic.* Berkeley: Univ. of California Press, 1995.

Keaveney, A. *Sulla: The Last Republican.* 2nd ed. Oxford & New York: Routledge, 2005.

Lintott, A. *Violence in Republican Rome.* Oxford: Clarendon Press, 1968.

McCullough, Colleen. *First Man in Rome.* New York: Avon Books, 1991 [A historical novel about the days of Sulla and Marius].

Mouritsen, H. *Plebs and Politics in Late Republican Rome.* Cambridge, UK: Cambridge Univ. Press, 2001.

Osgood, Josiah. *Caesar's Legacy: Civil War and the Emergence of the Roman Empire.* New York: Cambridge Univ. Press, 2006.

Rawson, E. *Intellectual Life in the Late Roman Republic.* Baltimore: Johns Hopkins Univ. Press, 1985.

Scullard, H. H. *From the Gracchi to Nero: A History of Rome from 133 BC to AD 68.* 5th ed. Oxford: Routledge, 1982.

Syme, Ronald. *The Roman Revolution.* Oxford: Oxford Univ. Press, 1939.

Taylor, Lilly Ross. *Party Politics in the Age of Caesar.* Berkeley: Univ. of California Press, 1961.

Yakobson, A. *Elections and Electioneering in Rome: A Study in the Political System of the Late Republic.* Stuttgart: Steiner, 1999.

SOURCES

PLUTARCH, *LIFE OF SULLA*

In 88 BCE the Consul Sulla assembled an army in Campania for the war against King Mithridates of Pontus. But before he could depart, politics intervened when Marius attempted to take over Sulla's command. The result was great disruption and a near civil war, as related by the biographer Plutarch.

Source: John Dryden, *The Lives of the Noble Greeks and Romans, Vol. 1*, revised by A. H. Clough (Boston: Little, Brown, 1910).

At the time of which I speak, Sulla's thoughts soared to the Mithridatic war. But here he found a rival in Marius, who was possessed by ambition and a mad desire for fame. And when Sulla had set out for his camp, Marius contrived that most fatal sedition, which wrought Rome more harm than all her wars together had done, as indeed the heavenly powers foreshowed to them. Marius now made alliance with Sulpicius who was a Tribune of the Plebs, a man second to none in prime villainies, so that the question was not whom else he surpassed in wickedness, but in what he surpassed his own wickedness. For the combination of cruelty, effrontery, and rapacity in him was regardless of shame and of all evil, since he sold the Roman citizenship to freedmen and aliens at public sale, and counted out the price on a money-table which stood in the forum. Moreover, he maintained three thousand swordsmen, and had about him a body of young men of the equestrian order who were ready for everything, and whom he called his anti-senate. This man was now let loose upon the people by Marius, and after confounding all things by force and the sword, he proposed certain vicious laws, and particularly one offering to Marius the command in the Mithridatic war. To prevent voting on these, the Consuls[1] decreed suspension of public business, as they were holding an assembly near the Temple of

Castor and Pollux,[2] and, among many others, slew also the young son of Pompeius the Consul in the forum; but Pompeius made his escape unnoticed. Sulla, however, after having been pursued into the house of Marius, was forced to come forth and rescind the decree for suspension of public business, and it was because he did this that Sulpicius, although he deposed Pompeius, did not take the consulship away from Sulla, but merely transferred the expedition against Mithridates to the command of Marius. He also sent Military Tribunes[3] at once to Nola,[4] who were to take over the army there and conduct it to Marius.

But Sulla succeeded in making his escape and reached the camp first, and his soldiers, when they learned what had happened, stoned the Tribunes to death. In return for this, Marius and his partisans in the city went to slaying the friends of Sulla and plundering their property. Then there were removals and flights, some passing continually from camp to city, and others from city to camp. The senate was not its own master, but was governed by the dictates of Marius and Sulpicius, and when it learned that Sulla was marching against the city, it sent two of the Praetors, Brutus and Servilius, to forbid his advance. These men addressed Sulla with too much boldness, whereupon his soldiers

---

[1] That is, Pompeius and Sulla.

[2] An ancient temple in the Roman forum where the Senate often met.
[3] Military officers, not Tribunes of the Plebs.
[4] An Italian city just west of Naples.

would have gladly torn them to pieces, but contented themselves with breaking their fasces, stripping them of their senatorial togas, insulting them in many ways, and then sending them back to the city. Here a terrible dejection was produced by the mere sight of them, stripped of their praetorial insignia, and by their announcement that the sedition could no longer be checked, but must run its course.

Marius and his partisans, then, busied themselves with preparations, while Sulla, at the head of six full legions, moved with his colleague from Nola, his army, as he saw, being eager to march at once against the city, although he himself wavered in his own mind, and feared the danger. But after he had offered a sacrifice, Postumius the soothsayer learned what the omens were, and stretching out both hands to Sulla, begged that he might be bound and kept a prisoner until the battle, assuring him that he was willing to undergo the extremest penalty if all things did not speedily come to a good issue for him.[5] It is said, also, that to Sulla himself there appeared in his dreams a goddess whom the Romans learned to worship from the Cappadocians,[6] whether she is Luna, or Minerva, or Bellona.[7] This goddess, as Sulla fancied, stood by his side and put into his hand a thunder-bolt, and naming his enemies one by one, bade him smite them with it; and they were all smitten, and fell, and vanished away. Encouraged by the vision, he told it to his colleague, and at break of day led on toward Rome.

When he had reached Pictae,[8] he was met by a deputation from the city, which begged him not to advance to an immediate attack, because the Senate had voted that he should have all his rights. He therefore agreed to encamp there, and ordered his officers to measure out the ground, as was usual, for the camp, so that the deputation

returned to the city believing that he would do so. But no sooner were they gone than he sent forward Lucius Basillus and Gaius Mummius, who seized for him the city-gate and the walls on the Esquiline hill; then he himself followed hard after them with all speed.

Basillus and his men burst into the city and were forcing their way along, when the unarmed multitude pelted them with stones and tiles from the roofs of the houses, stopped their further progress, and crowded them back to the wall. But by this time Sulla was at hand, and seeing what was going on, shouted orders to set fire to the houses, and seizing a blazing torch, led the way himself, and ordered his archers to use their fire-bolts and shoot them up at the roofs. This he did not from any calm calculation, but in a passion, and having surrendered to his anger the command over his actions, because he thought only of his enemies, and without any regard or even pity for friends and kindred and relations, made his entry by the aid of fire, which made no distinction between the guilty and the innocent. Meanwhile Marius, who had been driven back to the Temple of Tellus, made a proclamation calling the slaves to his support under promise of freedom; but the enemy coming on, he was overpowered and fled from the city.

Sulla now called together the Senate, and had a sentence of death passed on Marius himself and a few others, among whom was Sulpicius the Tribune of Plebs. But Sulpicius was killed, after he had been betrayed by a slave, to whom Sulla first gave his freedom and then had him thrown down the Tarpeian Rock.[9] Moreover, he set a price on the head of Marius, an act both ungrateful and impolitic, because it was in his house that he had found refuge and surrendered himself a little before this, and had been let off safe.[10]

---

[5] That is, the omens were good and the gods supposedly favored Sulla's undertakings.

[6] A people of eastern Anatolia.

[7] Goddesses of the moon, wisdom, and warfare respectively.

[8] A few miles southwest of Rome.

---

[9] A site on top of the Capitoline Hill. The worst offenders against the Roman state were hurled from there to their death. The slave was executed because he had betrayed his owner and patron.

[10] So in this case, it was Sulla who was betraying his own patron.

PLUTARCH, *LIFE OF CRASSUS*

Roman mistreatment of large numbers of agricultural slaves purchased at low costs led to several massive slave revolts, as in Sicily between 135 and 132 BCE and then again from 104 to 100 BCE. The greatest slave revolt began in 73 BCE right at home, in Italy, when Spartacus, a Thracian slave being trained as a gladiator, organized a massive revolt that eventually included more than 100,000 slaves. After defeating several Roman military units, the slaves finally were defeated in 71 BCE by the Roman general Crassus. Even though the revolt had failed, the Romans did learn their lesson, and the treatment of slaves generally improved. This was the last of the Roman slave revolts.

Source: John Dryden, *The Lives of the Noble Greeks and Romans, Vol. 1*, revised by A. H. Clough (Boston: Little, Brown, 1910).

The insurrection of the gladiators and the devastation of Italy, commonly called the War of Spartacus, began upon this occasion. One Lentulus Batiates trained up a great many gladiators in Capua,[11] most of them Gauls and Thracians,[12] who, not for any fault by them committed, but simply through the cruelty of their master, were kept in confinement for this object of fighting one with another. Two hundred of these formed a plan to escape, but being discovered, those of them who became aware of it in time to anticipate their master, being seventy-eight, got out of a cook's shop chopping-knives and spits, and made their way through the city, and meeting along the way several wagons carrying gladiators' arms to another city, they seized them and armed themselves. And occupying a defensible place, they chose three captains, of whom Spartacus was chief, a Thracian of one of the nomadic peoples, and a man not only of high spirit and valiant, but in understanding, also, and in gentleness superior to his condition, and more of a Grecian than the people of his country usually are. When he first came to be sold at Rome, they say a snake coiled itself upon his face as he lay asleep, and his wife, who at this latter time also accompanied him in his flight, his countrywoman, a kind of prophetess, and one of those possessed with the bacchanal[13] frenzy, declared that it was a sign portending great and formidable power to him with no happy event.

First, then, routing those that came out of Capua against them, and thus procuring a quantity of proper soldiers' arms, they gladly threw away their own as barbarous and dishonorable. Afterward Claudius,[14] the Praetor, took the command against them with a body of three thousand men from Rome and besieged them within a mountain, accessible only by one narrow and difficult passage, which Claudius kept guarded, encompassed on all other sides with steep and slippery precipices. Upon the top, however, grew a great many wild vines, and cutting down as many of their boughs as they had need of, they twisted them into strong ladders long enough to reach from thence to the bottom, by which, without any danger, they got down all but one, who stayed there to throw them down their arms, and after this succeeded in saving himself. The Romans were ignorant of all this, and, therefore, coming upon them in the rear, they assaulted them unawares and took their camp. Several shepherds and herdsmen that were there, stout and nimble fellows, also revolted over to them, to some of whom they gave complete arms, and

[11] An ancient city inland from the Bay of Naples in Italy.
[12] From a rugged area of the Balkans northeast of Greece and Macedonia.

[13] The Bacchanalians were the female worshippers of Dionysus, known for their enthusiastic worship.
[14] Gaius Claudius Glaber, otherwise unknown.

made use of others as scouts and light-armed soldiers.

Publius Varinius,[15] the Praetor, was now sent against them, whose lieutenant, Furius, with two thousand men, they fought and routed. Then Cossinius[16] was sent with considerable forces to give his assistance and advice, and Spartacus barely missed capturing him in person, as he was bathing at Salinae.[17] With great difficulty he made his escape, while Spartacus possessed himself of his baggage, and following the chase with a great slaughter, stormed his camp and took it, where Cossinius himself was slain. After many successful skirmishes with the Praetor himself, in one of which Spartacus took his Lictors and his own horse, he began to be great and terrible, but wisely considering that he was not to expect to match the force of the Republic, he marched his army toward the Alps, intending, when he had passed them, that every man should go to his own home, some to Thrace, some to Gaul. But the slaves, grown confident in their numbers and puffed up with their success, would give no obedience to him and went about and ravaged Italy.

The Senate now not only was moved at the indignity and baseness, both of the enemy and of the insurrection, but also, looking upon it as a matter of alarm and of dangerous consequence, sent out both the Consuls,[18] as to a great and difficult enterprise. The Consul Gellius, falling suddenly upon a party of Germans, who through contempt and confidence had straggled from Spartacus, cut them all to pieces. But when Lentulus with a large army besieged Spartacus, he sallied out upon him, and, joining battle, defeated his chief officers and captured all his baggage. As he made toward the Alps, Cassius, who was Praetor of that part of Gaul that lies about the Po,[19] met him with ten thousand men, but being overcome in the battle, he

had much ado to escape himself, with the loss of a great many of his men.

When the Senate understood this, it was displeased at the Consuls and, ordering them to meddle no further, it appointed Crassus[20] general of the war, and a great many of the nobility went as volunteers with him, partly out of friendship and partly to get honor. He stayed himself on the borders of Picenum,[21] expecting Spartacus would come that way, and sent his lieutenant, Mummius, with two legions, to wheel about and observe the enemy's motions, but upon no account to engage or skirmish. But Mummius, upon the first opportunity, joined battle, and was routed, having a great many of his men slain and a great many only saving their lives with the loss of their arms. Crassus rebuked Mummius severely, and arming the soldiers again, he made them find sureties[22] for their arms, that they would part with them no more, and five hundred that were the first to flee he divided into fifty tens, and one of each was to die by lot, thus reviving the ancient Roman punishment of decimation,[23] where ignominy is added to the penalty of death, with a variety of appalling and terrible circumstances, presented before the eyes of the whole army, assembled as spectators.

After he thus had reclaimed his men, he led them against the enemy; but Spartacus retreated through Lucania[24] toward the sea, and in the straits meeting with some Cilician[25] pirate ships, he had thoughts of attempting Sicily, where, by landing two thousand men, he hoped to rekindle the war of the slaves, which was but lately extinguished,[26] and seemed to need but little fuel to set it burning

---

[15] Another Roman officer largely unknown aside from his defeat by Spartacus.

[16] Another lieutenant of the Praetor Varinius.

[17] A spa at an unknown location.

[18] The two Consuls were Lucius Gellius Publicola and Gnaeus Cornelius Lentulus Clodianus.

[19] That is, Cisalpine Gaul.

---

[20] Marcus Licinius Crassus Dives ("The Rich"); given that there already were two Consuls, he was given the rank of Praetor.

[21] A region on the northeastern coast of Italy.

[22] Guarantors.

[23] A punishment where every tenth man is selected to be beaten to death by his own comrades.

[24] A region of southern Italy.

[25] Cicilia was a mountainous area on the coast of southern Anatolia where Pompey had settled captured pirates and it still was known for its pirates.

[26] Actually, twenty-nine years earlier, in 100 BCE.

again. But after the pirates had struck a bargain with him, and received his earnest they deceived him and sailed away. He thereupon retired again from the sea and established his army in the peninsula of Rhegium.[27] There Crassus came upon him, and considering the nature of the place he set to work to build a wall across the isthmus, thus keeping his soldiers at once from idleness and his foes from forage. This great and difficult work he perfected in a space of time short beyond all expectation, making a ditch from one sea to the other, over the neck of land, three hundred furlongs[28] long, fifteen feet broad, and as much in depth, and above it built a wonderfully high and strong wall. All of which Spartacus at first slighted and despised, but when provisions began to fail and he found he was walled in and no more food was to be had in the peninsula, taking the opportunity of a snowy, stormy night, he filled up part of the ditch with earth and boughs of trees and so passed the third part of his army over.

Crassus was afraid lest Spartacus should march directly to Rome, but was soon eased of that fear when he saw many of his men break out in a mutiny and quit him and encamp by themselves upon the Lucanian lake. Crassus, falling upon these, beat them from the lake, but he could not pursue the slaughter because of Spartacus suddenly coming up and checking the flight. Now he began to repent that he had previously written to the Senate to call Lucullus out of Thrace[29] and Pompey out of Spain,[30] so that he did all he could to finish the war before they came, knowing that the honor of the action would redound to him that came to his assistance. Resolving, therefore, first to set upon those that had mutinied and encamped apart, whom Gaius Cannicius and Castus commanded, he sent six thousand men before to secure a little

eminence and to do it as secretly as possible. To do so, they covered their helmets, but having been discovered by two women who were sacrificing for the enemy, they would have been in great danger had not Crassus immediately appeared and engaged in a battle that proved a most bloody one. Of twelve thousand three hundred whom he killed, two only were found wounded in their backs, the rest all having died standing in their ranks and fighting bravely.

Spartacus, after this discomfiture, retired to the mountains of Petelia,[31] but Quintius, one of Crassus' officers, and Scrofa, the Quaestor, pursued and overtook him. But when Spartacus rallied and faced them, they were utterly routed and fled, and had much ado to carry off their Quaestor, who was wounded. This success, however, ruined Spartacus, because it encouraged the slaves, who now disdained any longer to avoid fighting or to obey their officers. While they were upon the march they came to their officers with their swords in their hands and compelled them to lead them back again through Lucania, against the Romans, the very thing that Crassus was eager for. For news already had arrived that Pompey was at hand, and people began to talk openly that the honor was reserved to him, who would come and at once oblige the enemy to fight and put an end to the war. Crassus, therefore, eager to fight a decisive battle, encamped very near the enemy, and began to make lines of circumvallation,[32] but the slaves made a sally and attacked the workers. Spartacus, seeing there was no avoiding it, set all his army in array and when his horse was brought him, he drew out his sword and killed him, saying that if he won the day he would have a great many better horses of the enemies and if he lost it he should have no need of a horse. And so making directly toward Crassus himself, through the midst of arms and wounds, he missed him, but slew two Centurions that fell upon him together. At last being deserted by those that were about him, he himself stood his ground, and, surrounded by the enemy, bravely defending himself, he was cut in pieces.

---

[27] On the top of the toe of Italy.

[28] A furlong equals 660 feet.

[29] Marcus Lucullus was Consul in 73 BCE and then in the following year was Proconsul of Macedonia, where he fought the Bessi in Thrace, northeast of Greece, before being recalled to assist in the campaign against Spartacus.

[30] The Roman general Gnaeus Pompey was in Spain suppressing a revolt by the Roman general Sertorius.

---

[31] On the coast of southwestern Italy.

[32] A circular line of siege works.

Although Crassus had good fortune, and not only played the part of a good general but also gallantly exposed his person, yet Pompey received much of the credit of the action. For he met with many of the fugitives and slew them, and wrote to the Senate that Crassus indeed had vanquished the slaves in a pitched battle but that he had put an end to the war. Pompey was honored with a magnificent triumph for his conquest over Sertorius and Spain, whereas Crassus could not so much as desire a triumph in its full form, and it even was thought mean of him to accept of the lesser honor, called the ovation, for a servile war, and perform a procession on foot.[33]

---

[33] A triumph was granted for victories over foreign enemies; in an ovation, a lesser ceremony, the victorious general walked rather than being driven in a chariot.

CICERO, *FIRST SPEECH AGAINST CATILINE*

A fresco by Cesare Maccari (1840–1919) in the Palazzo Madama in Rome, often reproduced in Latin textbooks, depicts Cicero denouncing Catiline, seated alone by himself at the right, before the Senate. In reality, however, Catiline was not actually present when Cicero delivered his famous Catilinarian speeches.

The late Roman Republican politician Marcus Tullius Cicero made his reputation as a good speaker, especially in court cases. By successfully defending influential Roman senators, he made them into his clients. In 64 BCE, he called in his favors and was elected Consul for the following year. In that year, Rome was faced with a crisis when Lucius Sergius Catilina, or Catiline, a failed candidate for Consul, formed a conspiracy to take control of the government. Cicero made several anti-Catiline speeches in the Senate, addressing Catiline as if he were present, when in reality he was in Etruria raising his army. Citing previous examples of when the Senate had caused the deaths of its political opponents, Cicero succeeded in having several of Catiline's co-conspirators executed without a trial. This act was completely contrary to Roman law and eventually led to Cicero's exile.

Source: Charles Duke Yonge, trans., *Select Orations of M. T. Cicero* (New York: Harper, 1877), 1–14..

When, O Catiline, do you mean to cease abusing our patience? How long is that madness of yours still to mock us? When is there to be an end of that unbridled audacity of yours, swaggering about as it does now? Do not the night guards placed on the Palatine Hill,[34] do not the watches posted throughout the city, does not the alarm of the people, and the union of all good men, does not the precaution taken of assembling the Senate in this most defensible place, do not the looks and countenances of this venerable body here present, have any effect upon you?[35] Do you not feel that your plans are detected? Do you not see that your conspiracy is already arrested and rendered powerless by the knowledge that everyone here possesses of it? What is there that you did last night, what the night before, where it is that you were, who was there that you summoned to meet you, what design was there that was adopted by you, with which you think that any one of us is unacquainted?

Shame on the age and on its principles! The Senate is aware of these things; the Consul[36] sees them, and yet this man lives. Lives! Aye, he comes even into the Senate. He takes a part in the public deliberations; he is watching and marking down and checking off for slaughter every individual among us. And we, gallant men that we are, think that we are doing our duty to the Republic if we keep out of the way of his frenzied attacks. You ought, O Catiline, long ago to have been led to execution by command of the Consul. The destruction that you have been long plotting against us ought to have already fallen on your own head.

What? Did not that most illustrious man, Publius Scipio, the *Pontifex Maximus*, in his capacity of a private citizen, put to death Tiberius Gracchus, although but slightly undermining the constitution?[37] And shall we, who are the Consuls,[38] tolerate Catiline, openly desirous to destroy the whole world with fire and slaughter? For I pass over older instances, such as how Gaius Servilius Ahala with his own hand slew Spurius Maelius when he was plotting a revolution in the state.[39] There was, there was once such virtue in this Republic that brave men would repress mischievous citizens with severer chastisement than the most bitter enemy. For we have a Recommendation of the Senate, a formidable and authoritative recommendation against you, O Catiline; the wisdom of the Republic is not at fault, nor the dignity of this senatorial body. We, we alone, I say it openly, we, the Consuls, are wanting in our duty.

The Senate once passed a recommendation that Lucius Opimius, the Consul, should take care that the Republic suffered no injury.[40] Not one night elapsed. There was put to death, on some mere suspicion of disaffection, Gaius Gracchus, a man whose family had borne the most unblemished reputation for many generations. There was slain Marcus Fulvius, a man of consular rank, and all his children. By a like Recommendation of the Senate the safety of the Republic was entrusted to Gaius Marius and Lucius Valerius,[41] the Consuls. Did not the vengeance of the Republic, did not

---

[34] The important hill adjoining the Forum and the site of many posh residences.

[35] Cicero pretends to address Catiline as if he were actually present, but he already had departed to his army in Etruria.

[36] That is, Cicero himself.

---

[37] Scipio Nasica, whom, as a consequence of his implication in Tiberius' murder in 133 BCE, the Senate in fact sent away from Rome to Asia, where he died in the same year. Given the importance that Romans placed on following tradition, Cicero's acknowledgment that Nasica acted unconstitutionally raises a suspicion that Cicero himself was planning to do the same.

[38] Cicero's colleague as Consul was Gaius Antonius Hybrida, the uncle of the Triumvir Mark Antony.

[39] In 439 BCE; Ahala in fact was charged with murder and, like Nasica, escaped conviction only by going into exile.

[40] In 121 BCE during a protest organized by Gaius Gracchus, the brother of Tiberius; the first example of the *Senatus consultum ultimum* ("The Last Recommendation of the Senate"), which asks the Consuls to see to the safety of the Republic. Gaius and three thousand of his supporters were murdered.

[41] Consuls in 100 BCE.

execution overtake Lucius Saturninus,[42] a Tribune of the Plebs, and Gaius Servilius,[43] the Praetor, without the delay of one single day? But we, for these twenty days, have been allowing the edge of the Senate's authority to grow blunt, as it were. For we are in possession of a similar Recommendation of the Senate, but we keep it locked up in its parchment, buried, I may say, in the sheath; and according to this recommendation you ought, O Catiline, to be put to death this instant. You live, and you live not to lay aside but to persist in your audacity.

I wish, O Conscript Fathers,[44] to be merciful; I wish not to appear negligent amid such danger to the state; but I do now accuse myself of remissness and culpable inactivity. A camp is pitched in Italy, at the entrance of Etruria, in hostility to the Republic; the number of the enemy increases every day and yet the general of that camp, the leader of those enemies, we see within the walls, aye, and even in the Senate, planning every day some internal injury to the Republic. If, O Catiline, I should now order you to be arrested, to be put to death, I should, I suppose, have to fear lest all good men should say that I had acted tardily, rather than that anyone should affirm that I acted cruelly. But yet this, which ought to have been done long since, I have good reason for not doing as yet. I will put you to death, then, when there shall be not one person possible to be found so wicked, so abandoned, as like yourself, as not to allow that it has been rightly done. As long as one person exists who can dare to defend you, you shall live; but you shall live as you do now, surrounded by my many and trusty guards, so that you shall not be able to stir one finger against the Republic. Many

eyes and ears shall still observe and watch you, as they have hitherto done, although you shall not perceive them.

For what is there, O Catiline, that you can still expect, if night is not able to veil your nefarious meetings in darkness, and if private houses cannot conceal the voice of your conspiracy within their wall, if everything is seen and displayed? Change your mind. Trust me. Forget the slaughter and conflagration you are meditating. You are hemmed in on all sides; all your plans are clearer than the day to us; let me remind you of them. Do you recollect that on the 21st of October I said in the Senate, that on a certain day, which was to be the 27th of October, C. Manlius, the satellite and servant of your audacity, would be in arms? Was I mistaken, Catiline, not only in so important, so atrocious, so incredible a fact, but, what is much more remarkable, in the very day? I said also in the Senate that you had fixed the massacre of the nobles for the 28th of October, when many chief men of the Senate had left Rome, not so much for the sake of saving themselves as of checking your designs. Can you deny that on that very day you were so hemmed in by my guards and my vigilance that you were unable to stir one finger against the Republic, when you said that you would be content with the flight of the rest and the slaughter of us who remained? What? When you made sure that you would be able to seize Praeneste[45] on the first of November by a nocturnal attack, did you not find that that colony was fortified by my order, by my garrison, by my watchfulness and care? You do nothing, you plan nothing, you think of nothing that I not only do not hear but also that I do not see and know every particular of.

Listen while I speak of the night before. You shall now see that I watch far more actively for the safety than you do for the destruction of the Republic. I say that you came the night before into the Scythedealers' street, to the house of Marcus Lecca; that many of your accomplices in the same insanity and wickedness came there too. Do you dare to deny it? Why

---

[42] A Tribune of the Plebs elected for the third time in 100 BCE.

[43] Gaius Servilius Glaucia; in 100 BCE when his candidacy for the office of Consul was failing, he and Saturninus engineered the murder of his opponent, which led the Senate to issue the "Last Recommendation of the Senate." Both men then were killed.

[44] The members of the Senate.

---

[45] Modern Palestrina, twenty-two miles east of Rome.

are you silent? I will prove it if you do deny it, for I see here in the Senate some men who were there with you. O you immortal gods, where on earth are we? In what city are we living? What constitution is ours? There are here, here in our body, O Conscript Fathers, in this most holy and dignified assembly of the whole world, men who meditate my death, and the death of all of us, and the destruction of this city, and of the whole world. I, the Consul, see them; I ask them their opinion about the Republic, and I do not yet attack, even by words, those who ought to be put to death by the sword. You were, then, O Catiline, at Lecca's that night; you divided Italy into sections; you settled where everyone was to go; you fixed whom you were to leave at Rome, whom you were to take with you; you portioned out the divisions of the city for conflagration; you undertook that you yourself would at once leave the city, and said that there was then only this to delay you, that I was still alive. Two Roman equestrians were found to deliver you from this anxiety, and to promise that very night, before daybreak, to slay me in my bed. All this I knew almost before your meeting had broken up. I strengthened and fortified my house with a stronger guard; I refused admittance, when they came, to those whom you sent in the morning to salute me, and of whom I had foretold to many eminent men that they would come to me at that time.

As, then, this is the case, O Catiline, continue as you have begun. Leave the city at last. The gates are open; depart. That Manlian camp[46] of yours has been waiting too long for you as its general. And lead forth with you all your friends, or at least as many as you can. Purge the city of your presence. You will deliver me from a great fear when there is a wall between me and you. Among us you can dwell no longer, I will not bear it, I will not permit it, I will not tolerate it. Great thanks are due to the immortal gods, and to this very Jupiter

Stator,[47] in whose temple we are, the most ancient protector of this city, that we have already so often escaped so foul, so horrible, and so deadly an enemy to the Republic. But the safety of the Republic must not be too often allowed to be risked on one man. As long as you, O Catiline, plotted against me while I was the Consul Elect,[48] I defended myself not with a public guard, but by my own private diligence. When, in the next Consular Comitia,[49] you wished to slay me when I was actually Consul, and your competitors also, in the Campus Martius,[50] I checked your nefarious attempt by the assistance and resources of my own friends, without exciting any disturbance publicly. In short, as often as you attacked me, I by myself opposed you, and that, too, although I saw that my ruin was connected with great disaster to the Republic. But now you are openly attacking the entire republic.

You are summoning to destruction and devastation the temples of the immortal gods, the houses of the city, the lives of all the citizens; in short, all Italy. Wherefore, because I do not yet venture to do that which is the best thing, and which belongs to my office and to the discipline of our ancestors, I will do that which is more merciful if we regard its rigor, and more expedient for the state. For if I order you to be put to death, the rest of the conspirators will still remain in the Republic; if, as I have long been exhorting you, you depart, your companions, those worthless dregs of the Republic, will be drawn off from the city too. What is the matter, Catiline? Do you hesitate to do that when I order you what you were already doing of your own accord? The Consul orders an enemy to depart from the city. Do you ask me, are you to

---

[46] Catiline's army in Etruria, under the command of Gaius Manlius, an ex-Centurion of Sulla, who had seized control of the government in 88 and 82 BCE.

[47] The Senate was meeting not in the Senate house, but in the Temple of Jupiter Stator ("Jupiter the Stayer from Flight") near the Forum.
[48] In late 64 BCE.
[49] The Centuriate, or Army, Assembly,
[50] A region outside the sacred boundary of the city, near the Tiber River.

go into banishment? I do not order it, but, if you consult me, I advise it.

But now, what is that life of yours that you are leading? For I will speak to you not so as to seem influenced by the hatred I ought to feel, but by pity, nothing of which is due to you. You came a little while ago into the Senate. In so numerous an assembly, who of so many friends and connections of yours saluted you? If this in the memory of man never happened to anyone else, are you waiting for insults by word of mouth, when you are overwhelmed by the most irresistible condemnation of silence? Is it nothing that at your arrival all those seats were vacated? That all the men of consular rank, who had often been marked out by you for slaughter, the very moment you sat down, left that part of the benches bare and vacant? With what feelings do you think you ought to bear this? On my honor, if my slaves feared me as all your fellow-citizens fear you, I should think I must leave my house. Do not you think you should leave the city? If I saw that I was even undeservedly so suspected and hated by my fellow-citizens, I would rather flee from their sight than be gazed at by the hostile eyes of everyone. And do you, who, from the consciousness of your wickedness, know that the hatred of all men is just and has been long due to you, hesitate to avoid the sight and presence of those men whose minds and senses you offend? If your parents feared and hated you, and if you could by no means pacify them, you would, I think, depart somewhere out of their sight. Now, your country, which is the common parent of all of us, hates and fears you, and has no other opinion of you, than that you are meditating parricide in her case; and will you neither feel awe of her authority, nor deference for her judgment, nor fear of her power?

And yet, why am I speaking? So that anything may change your purpose? So that you may ever amend your life? So that you may meditate flight or think of voluntary banishment? I wish the gods may give you such a mind, although I see, if alarmed at my words you bring your mind to go into banishment, what a storm of unpopularity hangs over me, if not at present, while the memory of your wickedness is fresh, at all events hereafter. But it is worthwhile to incur that, as long as that is but a private misfortune of my own, and is unconnected with the dangers of the Republic. But we cannot expect that you should be concerned at your own vices, that you should fear the penalties of the laws, or that you should yield to the necessities of the Republic, for you are not, O Catiline, one whom either shame can recall from infamy, or fear from danger, or reason from madness.

You will go at last where your unbridled and mad desire has been long hurrying you. And this causes you no grief, but an incredible pleasure. Nature has formed you, desire has trained you, fortune has preserved you for this insanity. Not only did you never desire quiet, but you never even desired any war but a criminal one; you have collected a band of profligates and worthless men, abandoned not only by all fortune but even by hope. Then what happiness will you enjoy! With what delight will you exult! In what pleasure will you revel! When in so numerous a body of friends, you neither hear nor see one good man. All the toils you have gone through have always pointed to this sort of life; your lying on the ground not merely to lie in wait to gratify your unclean desires, but even to accomplish crimes; your vigilance, not only when plotting against the sleep of husbands, but also against the goods of your murdered victims, have all been preparations for this. Now you have an opportunity of displaying your splendid endurance of hunger, of cold, of want of everything, by which in a short time you will find yourself worn out. All this I effected when I procured your rejection from the consulship,[51] so that you should be reduced to make attempts on your country as an exile instead of being able to distress it as Consul, and so that which had been wickedly

---

[51] In the consular elections in 64 BCE, conservative senators preferred to support Cicero, a "New Man" who was not a member of the nobility, against Catiline, a member of an ancient and distinguished patrician family who sought popularity among the plebeians by proposing to cancel all debts.

undertaken by you should be called piracy rather than war.

Now that I may remove and avert, O Conscript Fathers, any in the least reasonable complaint from myself, listen, I beseech you, carefully to what I say, and lay it up in your inmost hearts and minds. In truth, if my country, which is far dearer to me than my life, if all Italy, if the whole republic were to address me,

> Marcus Tullius, what are you doing? Will you permit that man to depart whom you have ascertained to be an enemy? Whom you see ready to become the general of the war? Whom you know to be expected in the camp of the enemy as their chief, the author of all this wickedness, the head of the conspiracy, the instigator of the slaves and abandoned citizens, so that he shall seem not driven out of the city by you, but let loose by you against the city? Will you not order him to be thrown into prison, to be hurried off to execution, to be put to death with the most prompt severity? What hinders you? Is it the customs of our ancestors? But even private men often in this Republic have slain mischievous citizens. Is it the laws that have been passed about the punishment of Roman citizens? But in this city those who have rebelled against the Republic have never had the rights of citizens. Do you fear odium with posterity? You are showing fine gratitude to the Roman people that has raised you, a man known only by your own actions, of no ancestral renown, through all the degrees of honor at so early an age to the very highest office, if from fear of unpopularity or of any danger you neglect the safety of your fellow-citizens. But if you have a fear of unpopularity, is that arising from the imputation of vigor and boldness, or that arising from that of inactivity and indecision most to be feared? When Italy is laid waste by war, when cities are attacked

and houses in flames, do you not think that you will be then consumed by a perfect conflagration of hatred?

To this holy address of the Republic, and to the feelings of those men who entertain the same opinion, I will make this short answer: If, O Conscript Fathers, I thought it best that Catiline should be punished with death, I would not have given the space of one hour to this gladiator to live in. If, forsooth, those excellent men and most illustrious cities not only did not pollute themselves, but even glorified themselves by the blood of Saturninus, and the Gracchi, and Flaccus, and many others of old time, surely I had no cause to fear lest for slaying this parricidal murderer of the citizens any unpopularity should accrue to me with posterity. And if it did threaten me to ever so great a degree, yet I have always been of the disposition to think unpopularity earned by virtue and glory, not unpopularity. although there are some men in this body who either do not see what threatens, or dissemble what they do see; who have fed the hope of Catiline by mild sentiments, and have strengthened the rising conspiracy by not believing it; influenced by whose authority many, and they not wicked, but only ignorant, if I punished him would say that I had acted cruelly and tyrannically. But I know that if he arrives at the camp of Manlius to which he is going, there will be no one so stupid as not to see that there has been a conspiracy, no one so hardened as not to confess it. But if this man alone were put to death, I know that this disease of the Republic would be only checked for a while, not eradicated forever. But if he banishes himself, and takes with him all his friends, and collects at one point all the ruined men from every quarter, then not only will this full-grown plague of the Republic be extinguished and eradicated, but also the root and seed of all future evils.

We have now for a long time, O Conscript Fathers, lived among these dangers and machinations of conspiracy; but somehow or other, the ripeness of all wickedness, and of this long-standing madness and audacity, has come to a head at the time of my consulship. But if this man alone is removed from this piratical crew, we may appear, perhaps, for a short time relieved from fear and anxiety, but the danger will settle down and lie hid in the veins and bowels of the Republic. As it often happens that men afflicted with a severe disease, when they are tortured with heat and fever, if they drink cold water, seem at first to be relieved, but afterward suffer more and more severely; so this disease that is in the Republic, if relieved by the punishment of this man, will only get worse and worse, as the rest will be still alive.

Wherefore, O Conscript Fathers, let the worthless be gone, let them separate themselves from the good, let them collect in one place, let them, as I have often said before, be separated from us by a wall. Let them cease to plot against the Consul in his own house, to surround the tribunal of the Urban Praetor, to besiege the Senate house with swords, to prepare brands and torches to burn the city. Let it, in short, be written on the brow of every citizen, what are his sentiments about the Republic. I promise you this, O Conscript Fathers, that there shall be so much diligence in us the Consuls, so much authority in you, so much virtue in the Roman equestrians, so much unanimity in all good men, that you shall see everything made plain and manifest by the departure of Catiline, everything checked and punished.

With these omens, O Catiline, be gone to your impious and nefarious war, to the great safety of the Republic, to your own misfortune and injury, and to the destruction of those who have joined themselves to you in every wickedness and atrocity. Then do you, O Jupiter, who were consecrated by Romulus with the same auspices as this city, whom we rightly call the stay of this city and Republic, repel this man and his companions from your altars and from the other temples, from the houses and walls of the city, from the lives and fortunes of all the citizens; and overwhelm all the enemies of good men, the foes of the Republic, the robbers of Italy, men bound together by a treaty and infamous alliance of crimes, dead and alive, with eternal punishments.

CAESAR, *GALLIC WARS, BOOK 7, CHAPTERS 68–89*

A silver *denarius* issued in 48 BCE, four years after the defeat of Vercingetorix, depicts on the obverse not a Roman deity, but a Gallic warrior with his hair stiffened back with dried lime in typical Gallic fashion. On the reverse is a Gallic chariot with a driver and spear thrower. The chain around the neck suggests that this may be Vercingetorix himself, who at this time was imprisoned in Rome. He was strangled after Caesar's Gallic triumph in 46 BCE.

In 52 BCE, it seemed that Caesar's conquest of Gaul, which already had been formed into a Roman province, was complete. But the Gauls then found an inspirational leader, Vercingetorix, a chief of the Arvernians, a people of central Gaul. A massive revolt left Caesar's ten-legion 60,000-man army besieging Vercingetorix and 80,000 Gauls in the hill fortress of Alesia at the same time that a relief army of 100,000 Gauls was on its way. To prevent being trapped between two forces, Caesar's army put its engineering talents to work and constructed massive siegeworks around Alesia.

Source: W. A. McDevitte and W. S. Bohn, trans., *Gaius Julius Caesar. Commentaries on the Gallic War* (New York: Harper, 1869)..

After his cavalry had been routed, Vercingetorix immediately began to march to Alesia, which is a town of the Mandubii,[52] and ordered the baggage to be speedily brought forth from the camp and to follow him closely. Caesar,[53] having conveyed his baggage to the nearest hill, and having left two legions to guard it, pursued as far as the time of day would permit, and after slaying

---

[52] A group of Gallic peoples living in east central Gaul.

[53] So as to make his report seem more objective, Caesar always speaks of himself in the third person.

about three thousand of the rear of the enemy, encamped at Alesia on the next day. On reconnoitering the situation of the city, finding that the enemy were panic-stricken because the cavalry in which they placed their chief reliance had been beaten, he encouraged his men to endure the toil, and began to draw a line of circumvallation[54] around Alesia.

The town itself was situated on the top of a hill, in a very lofty position, so that it did not appear likely to be taken except by a regular siege. Two rivers, on two different sides, washed the foot of the hill. Before the town lay a plain of about three miles (five kilometers) in length, and on every other side hills at a moderate distance, and of an equal degree of height, surrounded the town. The army of the Gauls had filled all the space under the wall, comprising a part of the hill that looked to the rising sun, and had drawn in front a trench and a stone wall six feet (two meters) high. The circuit of the fortification commenced by the Romans extended eleven miles (eighteen kilometers). The camp was pitched in a strong position, and twenty-three fortified places were raised in it, in which sentinels were placed by day, lest any sally should be made suddenly, and by night the same were occupied by watches and strong guards.

The work having been begun, a cavalry action ensues in that plain. The contest is maintained on both sides with the utmost vigor; Caesar sends the Germans to aid our troops when distressed, and draws up the legions in front of the camp, lest any sally should be suddenly made by the enemy's infantry. The courage of our men is increased by the additional support of the legions. The enemy, being put to flight, hinder one another by their numbers, and as only the narrower gates were left open, are crowded together in them. Then the Germans[55] pursue them with vigor even to the fortifications. A great slaughter ensues; some leave their horses and endeavor to cross the ditch and climb the wall. Caesar orders the legions that he had drawn up in front of the rampart to advance a little. The Gauls, who were within the fortifications, were no

less panic-stricken, thinking that the enemy were coming that moment against them, and unanimously shout "to arms"; some in their alarm rush into the town. Vercingetorix orders the gates to be shut, lest the camp should be left undefended. The Germans retreat, after slaying many and taking several horses.

Vercingetorix adopts the design of sending away all his cavalry by night, before the fortifications should be completed by the Romans. He charges them when departing that each of them should go to his respective state and press for the war all who were old enough to bear arms. He states his own merits, and conjures them to consider his safety, and not surrender him who had deserved so well of the general freedom to the enemy for torture. He points out to them that, if they should be remiss, eighty thousand chosen men would perish with him, and that upon making a calculation, he had barely grain for thirty days, but could hold out a little longer by economy. After giving these instructions he silently dismisses the cavalry in the second watch,[56] at the point where our works were not completed. He orders all the grain to be brought to himself; he ordains capital punishment to such as should not obey; he distributes among them, man by man, the cattle, great quantities of which had been driven there by the Mandubii. He began to measure out the grain sparingly, and by little and little, he receives into the town all the forces that he had posted in front of it. In this manner he prepares to await the reinforcements from Gaul and to carry on the war.

Caesar, on learning of these proceedings from deserters and captives, adopted the following system of fortification: he dug a trench twenty feet deep, with perpendicular sides, in such a manner that the base of this trench should extend so far as the edges were apart at the top. He raised all his other works at a distance of four hundred feet from that ditch. He did that with this intention, lest a large number of the enemy should suddenly, or by night, sally against the fortifications, or lest they should by day cast weapons against our men

---

[54] A circular line of siegeworks.
[55] German allies of the Romans.

[56] From about 9 p.m. until midnight.

while occupied with the works. Having left this interval, he drew two trenches fifteen feet broad, and of the same depth; the innermost of them, being in low and level ground, he filled with water conveyed from the river. Behind these he raised a rampart and wall twelve feet high; to this he added a parapet and battlements, with large stakes cut like stags' horns, projecting from the junction of the parapet and battlements, to prevent the enemy from scaling it, and surrounded the entire work with turrets, which were eighty feet distant from one another.

It was necessary, at one and the same time, to procure timber, to lay in supplies of grain, and to raise also extensive fortifications, and the available troops were in consequence of this reduced in number, because they used to advance to some distance from the camp, and sometimes the Gauls endeavored to attack our works and to make a sally from the town by several gates and in great force. Caesar thought that further additions should be made to these works, in order that the fortifications might be defensible by a small number of soldiers. Having, therefore, cut down the trunks of trees or very thick branches, and having stripped their tops of the bark, and sharpened them into a point, he drew a continued trench everywhere five feet deep. These stakes being sunk into this trench, and fastened firmly at the bottom, to prevent the possibility of their being torn up, had their branches only projecting from the ground. There were five rows in connection with, and intersecting each other; and whoever entered within them were likely to impale themselves on very sharp stakes. The soldiers called these "tombstones." Before these, which were arranged in oblique rows in the form of a quincunx,[57] pits three feet deep were dug, which gradually diminished in depth to the bottom. In these pits tapering stakes, of the thickness of a man's thigh; sharpened at the top and hardened in the fire, were sunk in such a manner as to project from the ground not more than four inches (ten centimeters); at the same time for the purpose of giving them strength and stability, they

were each filled with trampled clay to the height of one foot from the bottom: the rest of the pit was covered over with osiers and twigs, to conceal the deceit. Eight rows of this kind were dug, and were three feet distant from each other. They called this a "lily" from its resemblance to that flower. Stakes a foot long, with iron hooks attached to them, were entirely sunk in the ground before these, and were planted in every place at small intervals; these they called "spurs."

After completing these works and having enclosed an area of fourteen miles (twenty-three kilometers), he constructed, against an external enemy, fortifications of the same kind in every respect,[58] and separate from these, so that the guards of the fortifications could not be surrounded even by immense numbers, if such a circumstance should take place owing to the departure of the enemy's cavalry; and in order that the Roman soldiers might not be compelled to go out of the camp with great risk, he orders all to provide forage and grain for thirty days.

While those things are carried on at Alesia, the Gauls, having convened a council of their chief nobility, determine that all who could bear arms should not be called out, which was the opinion of Vercingetorix, but that a fixed number should be levied from each state lest, if too great a multitude assembled together, they could neither govern nor distinguish their men, nor have the means of supplying them with grain. Yet such was the unanimity of the Gauls in asserting their freedom and recovering their ancient renown in war, that all earnestly directed their energies and resources to that war, and they collected eight thousand cavalry, and about two hundred and forty thousand infantry.[59] All march to Alesia, sanguine and full of confidence, nor was there a single individual who imagined that the Romans could withstand the sight of such an immense host, especially in an action carried on both in front and rear, when the besieged would sally from the town and attack the enemy, and on the outside so great forces of cavalry and infantry would be seen.

---

[57] In the shape of the number five on dice.

[58] A wall of contravallation, facing outward rather than inward.

[59] Probably closer to 100,000 soldiers.

But those who were blockaded at Alesia, the day being past on which they had expected auxiliaries from their countrymen, and all their grain being consumed ignorant of what was going on among the Aedui,[60] convened an assembly and deliberated on the exigency of their situation. After various opinions had been expressed among them, some of which proposed a surrender, others a sally, while their strength would support it. When different opinions were expressed, they determined that those who, owing to age or ill health, were unserviceable for war, should depart from the town. The Mandubii, who had admitted them into the town, are compelled to go forth with their wives and children. When these came to the Roman fortifications, weeping, they begged of the soldiers by every entreaty to receive them as slaves and relieve them with food. But Caesar, placing guards on the rampart, forbade them to be admitted.

In the meantime, Commius[61] and the rest of the leaders, to whom the supreme command had been entrusted, came with all their forces to Alesia, and encamped not more than a mile from our fortifications. The following day, having led forth their cavalry from the camp, they fill all that plain, which, we have related, extended three miles (five kilometers) in length, and drew out their infantry a little from that place, and post them on the higher ground. The town Alesia commanded a view of the whole plain. The besieged run together when these auxiliaries were seen; mutual congratulations ensue, and the minds of all are elated with joy. Accordingly, drawing out their troops, they encamp before the town, and cover the nearest trench with hurdles[62] and fill it up with earth, and make ready for a sally and every casualty.

Caesar, having stationed his army on both sides of the fortifications, in order that, if occasion should arise, each should hold and know his own post, orders the cavalry to issue forth from the camp and commence action. There was a commanding view from the entire camp, which occupied a ridge of hills, and the minds of all the soldiers anxiously awaited the issue of the battle. The Gauls had scattered archers and light-armed infantry here and there among their cavalry to give relief to their retreating troops and sustain the impetuosity of our cavalry. Several of our soldiers were unexpectedly wounded by these, and left the battle. When the Gauls were confident that their countrymen were the conquerors in the action, and beheld our men hard pressed by numbers, both those who were hemmed in by the line of circumvallation and those who had come to aid them, they supported the spirits of their men by shouts and yells from every quarter. As the action was carried on in sight of all, neither a brave nor cowardly act could be concealed; both the desire of praise and the fear of ignominy urged on each party to valor. After fighting from noon almost to sunset, without victory inclining in favor of either, the Germans, on one side, made a charge against the enemy in a compact body, and drove them back, and the archers were surrounded and cut to pieces. In other parts, likewise, our men pursued to the camp the retreating enemy, and did not give them an opportunity of rallying. Those who had come forth from Alesia returned into the town dejected and almost despairing of success.

The relieving Gauls, after the interval of a day and after making, during that time, an immense number of hurdles, scaling-ladders, and iron hooks, silently went forth from the camp at midnight and approached the fortifications in the plain. Raising a shout suddenly, that by this intimation those who were besieged in the town might learn their arrival, they began to cast down hurdles and dislodge our men from the rampart by slings, arrows, and stones, and to execute the other movements that are requisite in storming.

While the Gauls were at a distance from the fortification they were more successful, owing to the immense number of their weapons. But after they came nearer, they either unawares impaled themselves on the spurs or were pierced by the darts from the ramparts and towers, and thus perished. After receiving many wounds on all sides, and having forced no part of the works, when day drew nigh, fearing lest they should be surrounded by a

---

[60] The longest and oldest allies of the Romans in Gaul, who likewise had joined the revolt.

[61] King of the Atrebates, a Belgic people, who hitherto had been a loyal ally of Caesar.

[62] Wooden frames used to cover a ditch.

sally made from the higher camp on the exposed flank, they retreated to their countrymen. But those within, when they bring forward those things that had been prepared by Vercingetorix for a sally, fill up the nearest trenches. Having delayed a long time in executing these movements, they learned the retreat of their countrymen before they drew nigh to the fortifications. Thus they returned to the town without accomplishing their object.

The Gauls, having been twice repulsed with great loss, consult what they should do. They avail themselves of the information of those who were well acquainted with the country. From them they ascertain the position and fortification of the upper camp. There was, on the north side, a hill, which our men could not include in their works, on account of the extent of the circuit, and had necessarily made their camp in ground almost disadvantageous, and quite steep. Gaius Antistius Reginus, and Gaius Caninius Rebilus, two of the lieutenants, with two legions, were in possession of this camp. The leaders of the enemy, having reconnoitered the country by their scouts, select from the entire army sixty thousand men belonging to those states that bear the highest character for courage. They privately arrange among themselves what they wished to be done, and in what manner. They decide that the attack should take place when it should seem to be noon. They appoint over their forces Vergasillaunus, the Arvernian, one of the four generals and a near relative of Vercingetorix. He, having issued from the camp at the first watch and having almost completed his march a little before the dawn, hid himself behind the mountain and ordered his soldiers to refresh themselves after their labor during the night. When noon now seemed to draw nigh, he marched hastily against that camp that we have mentioned before, and, at the same time, the cavalry began to approach the fortifications in the plain and the rest of the forces to make a demonstration in front of the camp.

Vercingetorix, having beheld his countrymen from the citadel of Alesia, issues forth from the town. He brings forth from the camp long hooks, movable mantlets,[63] wall hooks, and other things that he had prepared for the purpose of making an attack. They engage on all sides at once and every expedient is adopted. They flocked to whatever part of the works seemed weakest. The army of the Romans is distributed along their extensive lines, and with difficulty meets the enemy in every quarter. The shouts that were raised by the combatants in their rear had a great tendency to intimidate our men, because they perceived that their own protection from danger depended on the bravery of others, for generally all evils that are distant most powerfully alarm men's minds.

Caesar, having selected a commanding situation, sees distinctly whatever is going on in every quarter, and sends assistance to his troops when hard pressed. The idea uppermost in the minds of both parties is that the present is the time in which they would have the fairest opportunity of making a struggle, the Gauls despairing of all safety unless they should succeed in forcing the lines, and the Romans expecting an end to all their labors if they should gain the day. The principal struggle is at the upper lines, to which as we have said Vergasillaunus was sent. The least elevation of ground, added to a declivity,[64] exercises a momentous influence. Some are casting missiles, others, forming a *testudo*,[65] advance to the attack; fresh men by turns relieve the wearied. The earth, heaped up by all against the fortifications, gives the means of ascent to the Gauls, and covers those works that the Romans had concealed in the ground. Our men have no longer arms or strength. Caesar, on observing these movements, sends Labienus[66] with six cohorts to relieve his distressed soldiers. He orders him that if he should be unable to withstand them to draw off the cohorts and make a sally, but not to do this except through necessity. Caesar himself goes to the rest and exhorts them not to succumb to the toil. He shows them that the fruits of all former engagements depend on that day and hour.

---

[63] Portable shelters that offer protection from arrow and sling stone fire.

[64] Low point in the terrain.

[65] The "tortoise," a formation the soldiers made by interlocking their rectangular shields over their heads.

[66] Caesar's second in command in Gaul, he later became one of Caesar's main opponents in the civil war with Pompey.

The Gauls within, despairing of forcing the fortifications in the plains on account of the greatness of the works, attempt the places precipitous in ascent. Here they bring the engines that they had prepared. By the immense number of their missiles they dislodge the defenders from the turrets. They fill the ditches with clay and hurdles, then clear the way. They tear down the rampart and breast-work with hooks. Caesar sends at first young Brutus[67] with six cohorts, and afterward Gaius Fabius, his lieutenant, with seven others. Finally, as the Gauls fought more obstinately, he leads up fresh men to the assistance of his soldiers. After renewing the action, and repulsing the enemy, he marches in the direction in which he had sent Labienus, drafts four cohorts from the nearest redoubt, and orders part of the cavalry to follow him, and part to make the circuit of the external fortifications and attack the enemy in the rear. Labienus, when neither the ramparts or ditches could check the onset of the enemy, informs Caesar by messengers of what he intended to do. Caesar hastens to share in the action.

When his arrival becomes known from the color of his cloak,[68] and the troops of cavalry and the cohorts that he had ordered to follow him being seen, as these low and sloping grounds were plainly visible from the eminences, the enemy join battle. A shout being raised by both sides, it was succeeded by a general shout along the ramparts and whole line of fortifications. Our troops, laying aside their javelins, carry on the engagement with their swords. The cavalry is suddenly seen in the rear of the Gauls; the other cohorts advance rapidly; the enemy turn their backs; the cavalry intercept them in their flight, and a great slaughter ensues. Sedulius the general and chief of the Lemovices[69] is slain; Vergasillaunus the Arvernian is taken alive in the flight. Seventy-four military standards are brought to Caesar, and few out of so great a number return safe to their camp.

The besieged, beholding from the town the slaughter and flight of their countrymen and despairing of safety, lead back their troops from the fortifications. A flight of the Gauls from their camp immediately ensues on hearing of this disaster, and had not the soldiers been wearied by sending frequent reinforcements and the labor of the entire day, all the enemy's forces could have been destroyed. Immediately after midnight, the cavalry are sent out and overtake the rear, a great number are taken or cut to pieces, the rest by flight escape in different directions to their respective states.

Vercingetorix, having convened a council the following day, declares, that he had undertaken that war not on account of his own exigencies but on account of the general freedom, and because he must yield to fortune, he offered himself to them for either purpose, whether they should wish to atone to the Romans by his death, or surrender him alive. Ambassadors are sent to Caesar on this subject. He orders their arms to be surrendered, and their chieftains delivered up. He seated himself at the head of the lines in front of the camp. The Gallic chieftains are brought before him. They surrender Vercingetorix and lay down their arms. Reserving the Aedui and Arverni, to attempt to win over, through their influence, their respective states, he distributes one of the remaining captives to each soldier throughout the entire army as plunder. A supplication[70] of twenty-days is ordered by the Senate at Rome on learning of these successes from Caesar's dispatches.

---

[67] A favorite cousin of Caesar who in 44 BCE brought Caesar to the meeting of Senate where Caesar was assassinated; it is this Brutus to whom Caesar referred in the Shakespeare play *Julius Caesar* when he uttered his last words, "Et tu, Brute?" ("And you too, Brutus?").
[68] The scarlet *paludamentum*, or general's cloak.

---

[69] A Gallic people who gave their name to the city of Limoges.
[70] A *supplicatio* was a period of public prayer to the gods for salvation from a crisis.

CATULLUS, *POEMS*

A wall fresco from Herculaneum, now in the National Archaeological Museum in Naples, depicts a well-to-do Roman couple enjoying each other's company in the same way that Catullus and his lady love "Lesbia" did. Curiously, the small female figure to the left has no legs; it has been suggested that this is not a person at all, but some kind of mechanical device, such as a clock, set on a pedestal.

The Roman poet Catullus was one of the so-called New Poets who composed avant-garde poetry that focused on small-scale personal matters as opposed to more traditional poetry involving gods, heroes, and the Roman state. His poetry is characterized by much use of literary allusion, different meters, and refined vocabulary. His work greatly influenced Augustan poets such as Horace, Ovid, and Vergil.

Source: Francis Warre Cornish, J. P. Postgate, and J. W. Mackail, trans., *Catullus. Tibullus. Pervigilium Veneris*, revised by G. P. Goold, Loeb Classical Library (Cambridge, MA: Harvard Univ. Press, 1913); Francis Ware Cornish, The Poems of Gaius Valerius Catullus with an English Translation (Cambridge, UK: Cambridge Univ. Press, 1904). .

Poem 2: The Sparrow

Sparrow, my lady's pet, with whom she often plays while she holds you in her lap, or gives you her fingertip to peck and provokes you to bite sharply, whenever she, the bright-shining lady of my love, has a mind for some sweet pretty play, in hope, as I think, that when the sharper smart of love abates, she may find some small relief from her pain. Ah, might I but play with you as she does, and lighten the gloomy cares of my heart!

Poem 5: "Let Us Live"

Let us live and love, my Lesbia,[71] and a penny for all the talk of morose old sages! Suns may set and rise again; but we, when once our brief light has set, must sleep through a perpetual night. Give me a

_____

[71] The poetic name of the object of the poet Catullus' affections; she usually is identified as Clodia, the sister of the politician Clodius who was murdered in 52 BCE. The name probably includes an allusion to the famous Greek woman poet Sappho of Lesbos.

thousand kisses, then a hundred, then still another thousand, then a hundred. Then when we shall have made up many thousands, we shall confuse the reckoning, so that we ourselves may not know their amount, nor any spiteful person have it in his power to envy us when he knows that our kisses were so many.

Poem 39: Lampoon of Egnatius

Egnatius, because he has white teeth, is everlastingly smiling. If people come to the prisoner's bench, when the counsel for the defense is making everyone cry, he smiles. If they are wailing at the funeral of an affectionate son, when the bereaved mother is weeping for her only boy, he smiles. Whatever it is, wherever he is, whatever he is doing, he smiles. It is a malady he has, neither an elegant one as I think nor in good taste. So I must give you a bit of advice, my good Egnatius. If you were a Roman or a Sabine or a Tiburtine or a thrifty Umbrian or a plump Etruscan, or a black and tusky Lanuvian, or a Transpadane, to touch on my own people too,[72] or anybody else who washes his teeth with clean water, still I should not like you to be smiling everlastingly, for there is nothing more silly than a silly laugh. As it is, you are a Celtiberian,[73]

now in the Celtiberian country. The natives rub their teeth and red gums every morning with what they have urinated, so that the cleaner your teeth are, the more urine you are shown to have drunk.

Poem 101: On the Burial of His Brother

Wandering through many countries and over many seas

I come, my brother, to these sorrowful obsequies,

To present you with the last guerdon of death,

And speak, although in vain, to your silent ashes,

Because fortune has taken your own self away from me

Alas, my brother, so cruelly torn from me!

Yet now meanwhile take these offerings, which by the custom of our fathers

Have been handed down—a sorrowful tribute—for a funeral sacrifice;

Take them, wet with many tears of a brother, And forever, O my brother, hail and farewell!

---

[72] These all are references to cities or regions in Italy.
[73] One of the Celts of Spain.

PART

THE PRINCIPATE

AUGUSTUS AND THE CREATION OF THE PRINCIPATE (44 BCE–14 CE)

Julius Caesar was the second senatorial general to use his army to seize control of the state. Neither he nor Sulla had been able to find an effective way to maintain his authority except by making unconstitutional uses of the archaic office of Dictator, the only Republican office that provided for any sort of one-man rule. Both of them had aroused extreme jealousy among other senators, who felt, quite justifiably, that these two generalissimos were monopolizing too much of the influence and authority for themselves in a decidedly un-Republican manner and were not sharing enough of the rule with other senators. Neither Sulla nor Caesar, therefore, was able to solve any of the greatest problems that bedeviled the late Republic, especially the problem of ambitious senators who put their own interests ahead of the interests of the state.

For the Romans, Julius Caesar often was thought to have been the first Roman "emperor," however an emperor was defined. But in the modern day, the consensus of opinion is that it was Caesar's grand-nephew and adopted son Octavian who created the Roman Empire in its initial form, known as the "Principate." In the process of doing so Octavian, who soon gained the title and name Augustus, was forced to confront the serious problems that had led to the fall of the Republic while at the same time managing to stay alive.

THE SECOND TRIUMVIRATE (43–31 BCE)

After the assassination of Caesar, it soon became clear that Caesar's assassins had no idea how to deal with any of these problems. They apparently presumed that after Caesar was gone, the old Republic again would begin to function. They were mistaken: the only result of Caesar's assassination was another round of civil wars among additional powerful and ambitious generals.

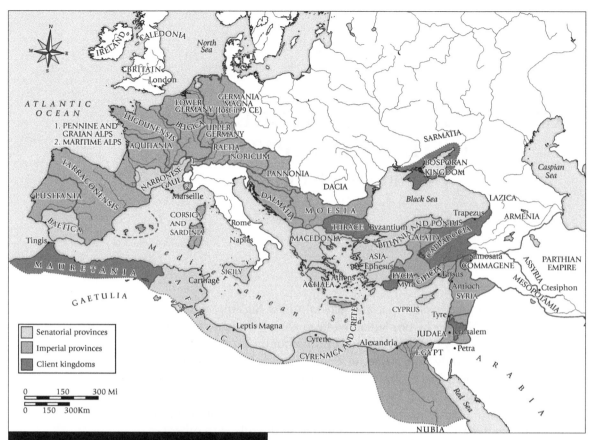

The Roman Empire at the death of Augustus (14 CE)

The Advent of Octavian

Immediately after Caesar's death, two of Caesar's favored generals, Marcus Aemilius **Lepidus** and Marcus Antonius, better known as Mark **Antony**, retained the loyalty of much of Caesar's army. Lepidus, the son of the Lepidus who had led an insurrection in 78 BCE, had managed to restore the family fortunes and risen to the position of Master of Horse, or deputy Dictator, under Caesar in 44 BCE. And Antony, the grandson of a famous orator and a distant cousin of Caesar's, spent a dissolute youth gambling and drinking. After showing military talent in the east, he attached himself to Caesar. As a Tribune in early 49 BCE he tried to veto the Senate's actions against Caesar and was forcibly expelled from Rome. In 47 he, too, was made Caesar's Master of Horse. He was married to Fulvia, the granddaughter of Gaius Gracchus and a politician in her own right; indeed, it was reported that she preferred politically active husbands so she, too, could engage in politics. Her first husband was the demagogue Clodius, who had served as Caesar's man in Rome. After Clodius' murder, she then married Curio, another ally of Caesar, and after his death in Africa she married Antony. At the time of Caesar's assassination in 44 BCE, Antony was sharing the consulate with Caesar.

A newcomer to the scene was Gaius Octavius, Caesar's eighteen-year-old grand-nephew who had been adopted in his will and thus became C. Julius Caesar Octavianus, or **Octavian**. At the time, Octavian was studying in Apollonia in western Greece, but he immediately returned to Italy to lay claim to Caesar's legacy. Initially, the hardened Italian politicians thought little of him, but he soon showed that he possessed a sense of political astuteness well beyond his years. He began by using the name of his adoptive father, C. Julius Caesar, and by making his own play for the loyalty of Caesar's troops, many of whom flocked to his standard.

After some initial bickering, Antony, Lepidus, and Octavian joined forces against Caesar's assassins by forming the **Second Triumvirate** in 43 BCE, and the time had come for them to revenge themselves on their enemies. Cicero, who had delivered a series of speeches called the "Philippics" (an allusion to the Athenian orator Demosthenes' speeches against Philip II of Macedon) against Antony, was murdered, and his head was displayed in the forum with a golden hairpin stuck through its golden tongue by Fulvia. And Caesar was officially **deified**—that is, made into a god. The chief assassins, meanwhile, had fled east, Brutus to Macedonia and Cassius to Syria, where they raised armies of their own. In 42 BCE, the armies met at the Battle of Philippi, in Macedonia, with Octavian facing Brutus and Antony opposing Cassius, Lepidus having been left back in Italy. In the first encounter, Brutus repelled Octavian, but Cassius was defeated and committed suicide. In a second battle three weeks later, Brutus was defeated and likewise killed himself.

Discord among the Triumvirs

There then commenced yet another struggle among senatorial generals to see who would end up on top. The Triumvirs divided up the Roman world, with Lepidus receiving Spain and Africa, Octavian Italy and Gaul, and Antony the east. In 41 BCE, in an effort to further Antony's claims, Fulvia raised eight legions in Italy and seized Rome, but eventually she was forced to surrender and soon died in exile. Fulvia also became the first Roman woman to have her portrait displayed on the coinage. Meanwhile, Sextus Pompey, the son of Pompey the Great, had raised a powerful navy and seized Sicily. Two attacks by Octavian failed, and only in 36 BCE was Sextus defeated by Octavian's loyal and able general Marcus Agrippa. Sextus' illegal execution without a trial the following year brought opprobrium upon Antony. The victory over Sextus left Octavian strong enough to force Lepidus into retirement after the latter attempted to seize Sicily; he was exiled to a small town in Latium where he survived until 13 BCE.

CLEOPATRA, THE LEGEND AND THE REALITY

In the modern day, Queen Cleopatra VII Philopator (69–30 BCE) is legendary for her beauty and sexuality. She has been the *femme fatale* of the cinema for over a hundred years, and the French philosopher Blaise Pascal, alluding to her beauty, even argued, "If Cleopatra's nose had been shorter, the whole face of the world would have been changed." There is no doubt that Cleopatra is one of the most romantic and enigmatic personalities of the Roman past, not to mention one of the most misrepresented. As Egyptian pharaoh (and the only one of the Ptolemies to learn to speak Egyptian), last Macedonian queen of Egypt, and paramour of two of the most powerful Romans of her day, she moved among three different social and cultural worlds. Indeed, her status as a native of North Africa even has given rise to modern beliefs that she was of Sub-Saharan Black African descent.

As the eldest child of Ptolemy XII, Cleopatra was named joint ruler with her father at the age of fourteen, but at his death in 51 BCE his will made her joint ruler with her twelve-year-old brother Ptolemy XIII, whom Cleopatra also married. Cleopatra soon seized sole power and issued coins in her own name. A palace revolt expelled her from power, but she quickly gained reinstatement by gaining the favor of Julius Caesar, who had pursued Pompey to Egypt in 48 BCE. Plutarch reports that "Caesar was first captivated by this proof of Cleopatra's bold wit, and was afterward so overcome by the charm of her society" that he eventually supported her claims and made her queen of Egypt. In 44 BCE, Cleopatra visited Caesar in Rome, creating a scandal when Caesar put a golden statue of her as the goddess Isis in the temple of his own ancestress Venus.

But Cleopatra's true claim to fame lay in her role in Mark Antony's attempts to seize control of the Roman world during his rivalry with Octavian. Ancient writers portrayed Antony as Cleopatra's lackey. According to Plutarch, in 42 BCE, when Cleopatra was summoned to meet Antony at the outset of his Parthian War, "She had faith in her own attractions, which, having formerly recommended her to Caesar, she did not doubt might prove yet more successful with Antony. Caesar's acquaintance was with her when a girl, young and ignorant of the world, but she was to meet Antony in the time of life when women's beauty is most splendid, and their intellects are in full maturity." Antony's

The Roman world then was repartitioned, with Octavian receiving authority in Italy and the west and Antony in Syria and the east. Both knew that it was only a matter of time before a final showdown came, and both raised enormously bloated armies of about forty legions each. Even though Egypt was still an independent state ruled by its queen (or pharaoh) Cleopatra, Antony spent most of his time there exploiting its resources and building up his forces. In the west, Octavian commenced a propaganda war in which Antony was depicted as Cleopatra's lackey. The slanders against Antony seemed to be confirmed when Octavian illegally seized Antony's will from the Vestal Virgins and revealed that, after his death, Antony wished to be buried in Egypt alongside Cleopatra.

In 31 BCE Octavian marched east and Antony west. The two armies met at Actium, on the western coast of Greece. The result of this encounter was something of an anticlimax. Antony's soldiers began to lose heart and to desert to the side of Octavian, who was assisted by the strategy and

LEARNING FROM HISTORY

What does Roman history teach us about the role of self-interest in politics? Even though they claimed to be "supporting the Republic," did these Roman leaders really have the best interests of Rome at heart? Can you think of any politicians in the history of the world who sacrificed their own ambitions for the good of the country?

This tetradrachm of Cleopatra and Mark Antony, probably issued in Antioch around 36 BCE, depicts an elaborately dressed Cleopatra in the position of honor on the obverse, and a bareheaded Antony on the reverse.

preparations to attack Parthia, Plutarch continues, "were all rendered useless to him because of Cleopatra. For, in order to pass the winter with her, the war was pushed on before its due time, as by a man who had no power of control over his faculties, who was under the effect of some drug or magic and whose object was much more to hasten his return than to conquer his enemies."

Soon afterward, Cleopatra and Antony, seated on two golden thrones, divided up the eastern world among their three children: the twins, Cleopatra Selene and Alexander Helius, and Ptolemy Philadelphus. According to Plutarch, "Cleopatra was then, as at other times when she appeared in public, dressed in the habit of the goddess Isis, and gave audience to the people under the name of the New Isis." But these grand plans were not to last. Cleopatra and Antony were defeated at the Battle of Actium in 31 BCE, and a year later both committed suicide. Thus died the last true pharaoh of Egypt, bringing to an end the Ptolemaic Dynasty, and the last of Alexander the Great's successor kingdoms.

But the real Cleopatra might not in fact have been the great beauty of legend, as suggested by the comparison between her and Antony's Roman wife Octavia, the sister of Octavian; Plutarch commented, "The Romans who had seen Cleopatra could report that she in no way had the advantage of Octavia either in youth or in beauty." It may be, then, that to Julius Caesar and Mark Antony she was more attractive for her wealth than for her physical charms. And it was only by an accident of history that her offspring—by either Caesar or Antony—did not end up ruling the Roman Empire.

generalship of Agrippa. Eventually, Antony decided that the most he could hope to do was to flee back to Egypt and live to fight another day. He and Cleopatra attempted to break out by sea, and the result was the **Battle of Actium**. Antony lost most of his fleet, although he and Cleopatra did make good their escape.

Octavian, now in possession of an overwhelmingly large military force, occupied Egypt in the following year. Antony and Cleopatra, not wishing to be humiliated by being led in chains in Octavian's triumph, took the honorable way out and committed suicide, and young Caesarion was put to death. Once again, an ambitious senatorial general had used his army to eliminate his rivals and to gain control of the Roman world. The question now was, what was he going to do with it?

THE ESTABLISHMENT OF THE PRINCIPATE (31–21 BCE)

Fortunately for Rome, Octavian was a much better administrator than he was a general. This was just what Rome needed. Octavian had two primary goals in mind. First of all, he wanted to end the civil wars while at the same time ensuring his own personal security. Second, he wished to deal with the problems that had plagued the Republic and make the Roman state into a more stable, enduring establishment.

From Octavian to Augustus

After gaining control of the Roman world, Octavian confronted the question of what his own future role would be. According to the second-century biographer Suetonius, "He twice thought of restoring the Republic, but reflecting that he himself would not be free from danger if he should retire, and that it would be hazardous to trust the state to the control of more than one person, he continued to keep power in his hands." If he were to control Rome effectively and not arouse undue opposition, Octavian would need to do two things: maintain control of the army and ensure that everything he did was done legally. Most important was the army. To relinquish his military command would only mean a revival of the internecine warfare of the past and would permit another ambitious senator to do to him what he had just done to everyone else. He realized that the solution of Sulla and Caesar, holding the dictatorship, was too unconstitutional and too high-profile and simply would not work. He determined to be more circumspect and at least to give the appearance of working within Republican constitutional traditions.

Octavian therefore worked hard to convey the impression that all he wanted to do was to restore the Republic. He made sure that all of his actions were done legally, by due process. Even though, paradoxically, he knew that any organized opposition was likely to come from the Senate, he went out of his way to consult with it and to respect its ancient perquisites. He understood that without the cooperation of the senators, who embodied all of the civil and military experience, had the greatest social influence, and controlled most of the wealth in the Roman world, he could not hope to govern effectively.

Beginning in 31 BCE, Octavian undertook what is called his "First Settlement," which consisted simply of holding the office of Consul every year. Doing so gave him not only command of the army by virtue of the consular *imperium* but also the right to introduce legislation before the popular assemblies. In 28 BCE, Octavian and his trusty comrade Agrippa were named Censors. Using their authority to expel and add senators, they reconfigured the Senate membership to Octavian's liking and listed Octavian as *Princeps senatus*, the first-ranking senator. Then, in the next year, Octavian went so far as to offer to relinquish all of his powers. The Senate, however, not only declined this magnanimous proposal but also piled new honors on Octavian, including a new title, that of **Augustus**, which was not an office or even a power but only a mark of very great respect and admiration, meaning something like "the one who is revered." Octavian was so proud of his new title that he used it as his name. The title of Augustus continued to be used by the individuals we now identify as Roman emperors, although

A PICTURE IS WORTH A THOUSAND WORDS

CAESARION AND CLEOPATRA

This relief from Dendera in Egypt portrays the continued respect of the Ptolemaic Dynasty for Egyptian customs even in the mid-first century BCE. On the left stands the cow goddess Hathor, a goddess of motherhood, wearing a headdress of a sun disk and cows' horns and holding the ankh, symbol of eternal life, in her right hand, and a long was-scepter, a symbol of power often associated with pharaohs, in her left. On the far right stands Cleopatra, portrayed as Isis, wearing the same cow horns with sun disk, topped by the double plumes of the mother goddess Mut. In front of her, a teenaged pharaoh Caesarion stands in the full regalia of a pharaoh, wearing the double crown of Upper and Lower Egypt. Cleopatra and Caesarion both make offerings to Hathor. The identity of the small figure in front of Hathor wearing the regalia of a pharaoh is uncertain; it may be the deified Ptolemy XIV, Cleopatra's younger brother, who died in 44 BCE. The identity of the even smaller figure between Caesarion and Cleopatra is even more mysterious.

Caesarion, the son of Cleopatra and Caesar, was born in 48 BCE: according to Plutarch, "Caesar left Cleopatra as queen of Egypt, who soon after had a son by him, whom the Alexandrians called Caesarion." Cleopatra made Caesarion co-ruler of Egypt at the age of three after Caesar's assassination and gave him the tongue-twisting title Ptolemy Theos Philopator Philometor Caesar; in modern parlance he is known simply as Ptolemy XV. By doing so, Cleopatra hoped to create a dynasty of rulers who would combine rule of Egypt with rule of the Roman world. But this vision was complicated by Cleopatra's liaison with Mark Antony, with whom she had three more children, who replaced Caesarion in her plans for dominion. After the occupation of Egypt by Octavian in 30 BCE, the eighteen-year-old Caesarion was executed because, in spite of Caesar's will, he could have challenged Octavian's status as the successor to Julius Caesar. The deaths of Cleopatra and Caesarion brought an end to the last of a line of independent pharaohs going back to 3000 BCE.

The Latin word Imperator, *source of the English word* emperor, *in Roman times was simply the title of a victorious army general.*

it must be stressed that Augustus himself claimed neither to have established the Roman Empire nor to have become Roman emperor. These are modern-day concepts, for we know very well that regardless of what Augustus (as he now can be called) said it was, the Roman Republic was dead, and one individual, the Augustus, now controlled the army and otherwise oversaw the affairs of state.

The Principate

We therefore say that the Roman Empire began in 27 BCE. In the form in which it was established by Augustus, it is called the **Principate**. It was based on the assumption that the emperor and the Senate worked in partnership to govern the empire, for the emperor also was the *princeps*, the First Man of the Senate. There was nothing new here; there always had been a *princeps*. This meant that even though the emperor took precedence in the Senate, he still could be perceived as just another senator. It soon became clear, however, that Augustus' monopolization of the consulate, an office that all ambitious and status-conscious senators desired to hold, aroused the same jealousy that Sulla and Caesar had encountered, so much so that several assassination attempts were uncovered. In addition, the official duties became burdensome for the sickly Augustus.

Thus, in 21 BCE, after surviving a nearly mortal illness, Augustus adopted a new, more low-key "Second Settlement" that likewise gave him both command of the army and control of the legislative process. Based on precedents going back to Scipio Africanus, he had the Senate grant him the proconsular *imperium*, or power of a Proconsul, which gave him the *imperium* that allowed him to control certain key provinces and the armies stationed in them. To be on the safe side, he held an *imperium proconsulare maius*, a **greater proconsular imperium**, which allowed him to outrank all generals and officials. In one fell swoop, therefore, Augustus not only kept control the army but also ensured that no other senator could supersede him. In addition, Augustus, who was just as much subject to the rule of law as any Roman, needed to ensure that he always acted legally. He therefore received annually the *tribunicia potestas*, the **tribunician power**. By receiving only the powers and not the actual office, Augustus, a patrician, was able to sidestep

The Prima Porta Augustus depicts the full level of propaganda in the portrayal of the ruler of the Roman world.

the requirement that Tribunes of the Plebs had to be plebeians. The tribunician power permitted Augustus not only to introduce legislation but also to veto the actions of any other magistrate. The mere knowledge that he had this power meant that he never had to use it, for any senator contemplating a legislative initiative made sure to consult Augustus in advance. Another power that Augustus appropriated was the Censor's right to **adlect** (appoint) new members of the Senate, and in so doing to control its composition. In 13 BCE he also assumed the title of *Pontifex Maximus* and thus became the head of the Roman state religion, there being no separation of church and state in the Roman Empire.

The greater proconsular *imperium* and the tribunician power became the two sources of the authority of the Roman emperors during the Principate. They permitted emperors to get things done on the one hand and to keep a low profile on the other. This enabled them to avoid, as much as possible, arousing jealousy, resentment, and opposition in the Senate. Everything the emperor did was done under the rubric of the old Republican constitution, and he was able to claim that no matter what extraordinary authority he had, he was working in partnership with the Senate.

THE AGE OF AUGUSTUS (27 BCE–14 CE)

By finding a way to continue to hold supreme power without looking like a Dictator or autocrat, Augustus was able not only to ensure his personal security but also to deal with the problem of ambitious senators that had contributed so greatly to the fall of the Republic. Once he was fully in control, he was able to turn to the two other problems that the Republic never had been able to solve: dealing with the provinces and keeping the army under control. By addressing these two issues, he would make the Roman Empire into a better governed and more integrated whole that would have the staying power to last over the long term and not just for his own lifetime. The most complex problem that Augustus confronted was dealing with the provinces, which had suffered more than two hundred years of neglect. Augustus' initiatives in the provinces had three components: (1) crafting a coherent imperial policy with respect to expansion and defense, (2) creating an effective system of provincial administration, and (3) finding a way to integrate the millions of provincials into the Roman world.

The Provinces: Expansion and Defense

During the Republic, provinces had been annexed more or less at random, and there had been no consistent concept of systematic expansion or border defense. To correct this, Augustus pursued a policy of consolidating the territories that Rome already controlled and seeking borders that were easy to defend. Regarding consolidation, Augustus did some infill and annexed marginal regions in areas already under Roman control, usually in uplands such as northwestern Spain or the Alps. And as to defensible frontiers, different sections of the empire required different approaches. In the south was the Sahara Desert, which, given the lack of invasion threat, required but a single legion to defend. Egypt, a special case because of its great wealth, became the personal property of the emperor. Farther south, after first being defeated by Kushite archers led by the one-eyed queen Amanirenas, the Romans penetrated as far as the city of Napata, but then withdrew and reached an agreement with the Kingdom of Kush that fostered trade and led to increased prosperity for both sides.

To the east lay the Parthian Empire. After the Republican debacles, which had resulted from personal ambition rather than state policy, Augustus accepted that there was nothing to be gained by campaigning there, so he pursued a policy of peace and negotiated a favorable treaty. Border areas not considered strategically significant enough to annex were left under **client kings**, such as **Herod the Great** in Judaea and Archelaus in Commagene in Anatolia, who were allowed to rule so long as they remained loyal and did not antagonize Rome.

Paradoxically, nearly all of the conquests that created the Roman Empire occurred during the Roman Republic or under Augustus.

The most loyal of all the client kings, **Juba II**, lived in interesting times. His father Juba I, the Berber king of Numidia in western North Africa, had supported the Pompeian side at the Battle of Thapsus in 46 BCE and had died there in a suicide pact with a defeated Pompeian general. Little Juba II, only about five years old, was paraded in Caesar's triumph in Rome and then taken into the households first of Caesar and then of Octavian Augustus. He dedicated himself to the study of Greek and Latin and became a Roman citizen. He also fought with his good friend Octavian at the Battle of Actium in 31 BCE. In the early 20s BCE, Octavian installed Juba as King of Numidia, and soon thereafter he married him to **Cleopatra Selene**, the only daughter of Cleopatra VII, the last pharaoh of Egypt, and Mark Antony. Cleopatra, too, had been led through the streets of Rome in chains, in Augustus' triumph. At about the same time, Augustus also named Juba king of Mauretania.

Juba and Cleopatra then became patrons of the arts, sponsoring elaborate Roman-style building projects in the Mauretanian cities of Caesaria (modern Cherchel) and Volubilis, dramatic productions, and scientific expeditions and research. It was Juba, for example, who named the Canary Islands. Juba wrote books dealing with grammar, history, history, and natural history, and was cited many times by the late-first-century natural historian Pliny the Elder. Juba II was succeeded as client king of Mauretania in 23 CE by his son Ptolemy, whose distinguished pedigree included direct family relationships with the later emperors Caligula, Claudius, and Nero, as well as descent from the pharaohs of Egypt.

Denarius issued by King Juba II of Mauretania and his wife Queen Cleopatra Selene, the daughter of Cleopatra VII of Egypt and Mark Antony. Whereas Juba is depicted in portrait form, Cleopatra is represented by the moon and a star, an allusion to her surname "Selene," the Greek goddess of the moon. Moreover, Juba's name is given in Latin, whereas Cleopatra's is in Greek, the language of her mother, reflecting her desire to perpetuate her mother's memory.

The most serious problem with defense was in the north, where several barbarian peoples threatened the security of the frontier. Augustus proposed to create a defensible border by invading Pannonia and expanding

foreign conquests, the Roman army became a garrison army and often was kept busy on construction projects such as building roads, bridges, and, especially, fortifications.

Because Augustus himself had come to power using his army, it always was possible that someone else would try to do the same. It thus was a top priority of Augustus and later emperors to maintain the army's loyalty. Augustus adopted several means of doing so. First and foremost, there was the question of army command. The only person an emperor could really trust to lead a large army was himself, but even if he had wanted to, which he clearly did not, it was not possible for Augustus to command all his armies in person. It thus was necessary to select reliable and loyal generals. Augustus' method was to use relatives by marriage, Agrippa, Drusus, and Tiberius, as his must trusted generals. But it always was clear that it was the emperor who remained the commander in chief. Any victories won by generals were treated as if they had been won by the emperor, and emperors took "victory titles" after foreign peoples had been defeated. Thus, a victory over the Germans gave an emperor the title "Germanicus," or a victory in Britain made him "Britannicus."

Augustus also professionalized the army by creating a standing army that was not disbanded after each campaign, as had been the case during the Republic. The core of the command structure lay in the **Centurions**, senior noncommissioned officers who commanded units of one hundred men. Army discipline was strictly enforced; the most serious punishment was decimation, the execution of every tenth man in a disgraced unit. A strong sense of esprit de corps developed, and a unit's military standards were accorded a religious reverence.

Soldiers in the legions, who had to be citizens, were paid 225 *denarii* a year, and it also became customary for emperors, upon their succession, to bestow a **donative** of several gold pieces on the Praetorian Guard to solidify their loyalty, a policy that later was extended to the entire army. After seventeen years of service, legionaries retired with a bonus of either three thousand *denarii* or a land allotment, perhaps twenty acres, often in military colonies established around the empire; during his reign, Augustus had to find land for some 150,000 veterans. Whereas the legions were stationed at strong points on the frontier, the auxiliary forces, roughly equal in number to the legions and composed mostly of provincials paid only marginally less than the legions, were spread out in smaller garrisons, often in forward positions. Auxiliary forces also included most of the cavalry, along with specialized units such as slingers and archers. Soldiers' sons often followed in their fathers' footsteps. The rewards bestowed by emperors on the army fostered the natural patron–client relationship between the commander and the troops, meaning that if an army was loyal to the father, it also would be loyal to the family. And yet, in spite of the attractions of army service to both citizens and provincials, emperors always were concerned about finding enough recruits.

Unlike nations in the modern day, the Roman Empire had no police force; small-scale violence was contained by city councils, and serious breaches of the peace had to be dealt with by detached units of the Roman army.

The army also carried Roman culture to the frontiers of the empire and thereby became one of the main purveyors of **Romanization**, or the extension of Roman culture into the provinces. For example, the first thing an auxiliary soldier had to learn was the Latin language, a later consequence of which was the development of the modern Romance languages of Italian, French, Spanish, Portuguese, and Romanian. In addition, during Augustus' reign, eighty colonies were established for army veterans in Spain, North Africa, and Greece, creating centers of Roman administration, society, and culture in the provinces. But at the same time that Greek and Roman culture was spreading into the provinces, provincial culture was making its way into Rome, just as eastern culture had been propagated into Greece during the Hellenistic period. The result of this cultural interchange was the creation of a composite **Mediterranean Culture** that included elements of the cultures of all the peoples incorporated under the Roman umbrella.

Propaganda

Augustus and subsequent emperors used several methods for advertising their achievements, justifying their own existence, and linking the image of the emperor with that of Rome. For mass media, the emperors used the coinage to proclaim their deeds in a manner designed to reach the widest possible audience. Coins could be used to disseminate either specific information, such as a military or diplomatic victory, or general ideologies relating to the emperor's piety or generosity.

Augustus sponsored the construction of a multitude of monuments in Rome to commemorate special events and to demonstrate his generosity. Indeed, according to the second-century biographer Suetonius, Augustus claimed to have changed Rome from a city of brick into one of marble. Augustus' *Ara pacis*, or Altar of Peace, for example, completed in 9 CE, portrayed Augustus as the one who had brought peace to the Roman world; few could contest this claim. A triumphal Arch of Augustus erected in the forum had on one side the official *Fasti consulares*, a list of all the Consuls going back to 509 BCE, and on the other the official *Fasti triumphales*, a list of all the generals who had been granted a triumph. Augustus also built in the forum a temple of *Divus Julius*, "the deified Julius," in honor of Caesar, whose deification had made Augustus into *divi filius*, "the son of the god." Like Caesar, Augustus built a new forum, the Forum of Augustus. This forum contained a temple of Mars Ultor, "Mars the Avenger," which Augustus had vowed to build when he took up arms against the assassins of Caesar. Elsewhere, Augustus built the Theater of Marcellus in honor of his nephew and the great Temple of Apollo on the Palatine Hill; in general, he claimed to have built or restored no less than eighty-two temples. Finally, Augustus constructed a mausoleum, an elaborate tomb designed, like Etruscan tombs, to be covered with a mound of earth planted with cypress trees, to hold the remains of himself and his family.

Augustus and his successors also provided the people with entertainment, most popularly in the form of gladiatorial combats and chariot races. Augustus took control of who sponsored popular entertainments, many of which he underwrote himself, so as to prevent senators from using the sponsorship of games to gain popularity, as had been done during the Republic by his own adoptive father. He sponsored as many as twelve chariot races a day in the Circus Maximus, or "Greatest Circus," which could seat up to 150,000 spectators. Augustus also claimed to have provided *annona* (grain doles) for more than 100,000 persons. And the emperors were the only source of "disaster relief" in the Roman world. For example, after a great earthquake in the province of Asia devastated Sardis and eleven other cities, Augustus' successor Tiberius granted ten million *sestertii* for the relief of the city, and all twelve cities had their taxes remitted for five years.

As *pater patriae* ("Father of the Country"), Augustus felt that it was his duty to restore the moral fiber of a people who had become disheartened after so many years of civil war and lost sight of the values that had made the Romans great. He opposed extravagance in favor of living a simple life. Being something of a prude, he attempted to intrude himself into the most intimate aspects of people's lives. He encouraged marriage and childbearing (which was good for army recruitment): women with three or more children received legal privileges, and men were free of civic obligations, but childless persons were prohibited from receiving inheritances. He also restricted marriages between persons of different social classes, prohibiting slaves and freedwomen from marrying senators. At the same time, he prohibited soldiers from getting married while on active duty. He taxed prostitutes, punished homosexuality, and banished adulterers. Indeed, Augustus' own daughter Julia fell afoul of Augustus' moral agenda when she was convicted of adultery and banished to the tiny island of Pandataria, where she was forbidden to see any men.

In general, the emperor served as both a patron and a unifying element for the entire Roman world, whose population became his clients. The old Roman tradition of *clientela* was therefore brought into service as a model for creating a kind of imperial state that the world had never seen before. The emperor provided offices and honors for the senators, salaries and bonuses for the soldiers, and edibles and entertainment for the urban mob of Rome. As the years went by, more and more power fell into his hands. Bit by bit, the authority of the Senate, which historically had been unwilling to change with the times, dwindled. Sometimes, the only real opportunity the Senate had to express its opinion about an emperor came after the emperor had died, and the Senate could choose to deify him, to do nothing, or, if it really disliked him, to issue a sentence of *damnatio memoriae, Damnation of Memory*, which permitted the mutilation of his images, ordinarily an act of high treason.

The Augustan Golden Age of Roman Literature

In other ways, too, Augustus propagated the idea of a mystique of Rome, with himself as the divinely ordained leader. Poets and writers recruited by Augustus' adviser Maecenas perpetuated the **Golden Age of Roman literature** that had begun in

A PICTURE IS WORTH A THOUSAND WORDS

THE *GEMMA AUGUSTEA*

The *Gemma Augustea* ("Augustan gemstone"), a 7.5- by 9-inch cameo carved from a piece of two-layered white and blue Arabian onyx, now in the Kunsthistorisches Museum in Vienna, probably was made by Dioscorides, Augustus' favorite gem cutter, for display at the imperial court. It is one of the most

the late Republic. Horace became the poet laureate of Augustan Rome and in 17 BCE wrote a hymn in honor of the Secular Games, which took place only every 110 years and marked the beginning of a new age. And the historian Livy authored a massive 142-volume history of Rome, of which about one-quarter survives, that began with the city's foundation and ran up to his own day.

The most famous Augustan poet was Publius Vergilius Maro, or Vergil, who wrote *Georgics* and *Eclogues* on the joys of the rural life, a theme that Augustus wished to promulgate after so many years of war. The *Fourth Eclogue*, later known as the "Messianic" *Eclogue*, told about the birth of a boy who would bring a new Golden Age. Vergil, of course, intended this to be interpreted as Augustus, but in later centuries Christians saw this poem as a foreshadowing of Jesus Christ, and effective pieces of visual political propaganda ever made. The identifications of some of the figures are heavily debated, so one always can feel free to suggest alternate interpretations. According to some interpretations, the upper register depicts Augustus posing as Jupiter, just as on the ubiquitous coins of Alexander the Great, seated partially nude on a throne, holding a *lituus*, a curved stick symbolic of the power of auspicium, in his right hand and a scepter, the symbol of his earthly *imperium*, in his left. The eagle of Jupiter stands underneath and Augustus' astrological sign, Capricorn, is above to his left. Oikumene (the whole world), wearing a turreted crown and veil, stands behind him and crowns him with the *corona civica*, an oak wreath awarded to those who saved Roman lives. In front of her, at the far right, stands Neptune, signifying dominion over the sea, and Italia sits in front of him, accompanied by children representing fertility, the same theme that appeared on Augustus' Altar of Peace. Seated next to Augustus, the goddess Roma, made to look like Augustus' wife Livia, is ready for war, with one hand on a spear and the other on a sword. At the far left, Tiberius, Augustus' stepson and eventual successor, descends from a chariot driven by the goddess Victory, in which he had just triumphed in 12 CE. He already is garbed in the toga after laying down his command, and he is the only other figure holding a scepter, representing the *imperium* already granted him by Augustus. The young military garbed figure on Roma's right seems just to have dismounted from the horse behind and perhaps represents Germanicus, son of Tiberius' brother Drusus and Consul in 12 CE.

The lower register presumably portrays the victory celebration after a battle on the northern frontier and is linked to the upper register by the shields under Augustus' feet. It depicts the power on which Augustus' rule was based and advertises the emperor's role as the one who protected the empire against threatening barbarians. On the left, soldiers raise a trophy of captured weapons above a seated pair of dejected Germanic or Celtic captives, with the man's hands bound and the woman weeping, and to the right additional captives begging for mercy are brought in. According to one interpretation of this scene, the Romans are Roman soldiers, and the different styles of the soldiers' helmets and dress indicate that both Roman legionaries and auxiliary troops are represented. But other scholars interpret the Roman figures as the gods Apollo (at the far left in a Thracian cap), Mars (helmeted), Castor and Pollux (lifting the trophy), Diana (carrying two spears and in hunting clothes), and Mercury (wearing a *petasus*, or sun hat). At the far left, moreover, the shield bears the sign of Scorpio, the sign of Tiberius. The victory has been interpreted as that of Tiberius over the Dalmatians in 9 CE, with the triumph having been delayed as a result of the Varian disaster, or that of Tiberius over the Germans in 12 CE.

as a result Vergil was viewed as a Christian poet, and his works were preserved. Vergil's greatest work, the ***Aeneid***, became the Roman national epic, and sections of it were memorized by every Roman schoolchild. It told the story of the Trojan hero Aeneas, who, with his son Ascanius (also known as Iulus) and father Anchises, had escaped from burning Troy and had wandered for ten years before founding Alba Longa, a city a short way away from the future site of Rome. Aeneas was famous for his *pietas*, or sense of duty, and he foreshadowed later Romans, culminating in Augustus himself, who had dutifully expanded the grandeur of Rome.

Greek writers also participated in the Augustan Golden Age of literature and proclaimed the glories of Augustan Rome. Dionysius of Halicarnassus in Anatolia settled in Rome after the civil wars, studied Latin, and wrote a massive

Greek work called *Roman Antiquities* covering Roman history from Aeneas and Greek mythology until the First Punic War. His work was intended to convince Greeks of the positive aspects of Roman rule and that the Romans were, in fact, an ancient part of the Greek world. Dionysius and Livy provide the only surviving narrative accounts of early Roman history.

There also was a second flowering of Latin love poetry by poets such as Propertius, another client of Maecenas; Sulpicia, a niece of the patron of the arts Messalla and the only female poet whose work survives; Tibullus, a client of Messalla; and Ovid, whose poem *The Metamorphoses* explained Greek mythology in Roman terms and who was banished to distant Tomis on the Black Sea as a result of what he described only as "a poem and a mistake." Their poems, lacking the imperial jingoism of the court authors, provide insights into the personal and private leisure lives of the Roman educated elite.

The Imperial Succession

One final problem that Augustus faced was the choice of a successor. Given that there was no constitutional position of emperor, there likewise was no constitutional means of choosing a new emperor when the current one died. This quandary created the problem of the **Imperial Succession**. Augustus dealt with it in two ways. He granted to the person he wanted to succeed him all the powers that he had. This made the Senate happy, because the transfer was thus done legally. And, because he had no natural sons, he adopted him. This made the army happy, for in Rome loyalties were inherited. But this was only an ad hoc solution and was to result in problems when future emperors did not have the foresight to put their successors in place before they died. Augustus also had decidedly bad luck when it came to selecting successors. One by one, those he chose, including his nephew Marcellus, his friend Agrippa, his grandsons Gaius and Lucius, and his stepson Drusus, all died. Some have attributed this unfortunate chain of events to the machinations of his wife Livia, the first of several imperial women to receive the honorary title of **Augusta** (empress), who supposedly wanted Tiberius, her son by an earlier marriage, to succeed to the throne, although there is no direct evidence for this.

The last thing that Augustus did to ensure the success of his settlement was to live a long time. In spite of his poor health, he died in 14 CE at the age of seventy-six. He immediately was deified by the Senate. It had been more than sixty years since the Republic had operated as such. Few remembered it as anything but ancient history.

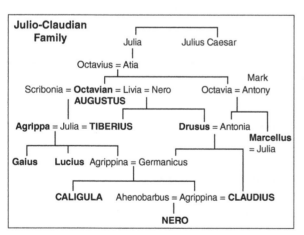

The Julio-Claudian family tree depicts one of the great ironies of Roman imperial history: the last Julio-Claudian emperors were direct descendents of Mark Antony.
Note: Failed successors of Augustus are in bold lowercase and emperors are in bold uppercase.

THE HISTORY LABORATORY

RECONSTRUCTING *THE DEEDS*
OF THE DEIFIED AUGUSTUS

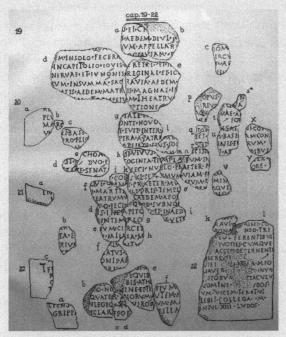

A section of a copy of Augustus' *Res gestae* **found in Ancyra (Ankara) in Turkey.**

Most of the lengthy literary texts that survive from antiquity were preserved as texts written first on papyrus scrolls and then later copied onto parchment manuscripts. But some texts were preserved as inscriptions cut into stone. This form of preservation, of course, was much more costly than writing on a perishable text and was usually done under government auspices—one recalls the decree of the Senate on the worshippers of Bacchus in 186 BCE. During the Roman Empire, the government oversaw the preservation of other documents on stone, including a speech of the emperor Claudius (41–54) and the Edict on Maximum Prices issued by Diocletian in 301. One of the most historically significant texts preserved on stone, and one of the most effective pieces of propaganda ever produced, is the *Res gestae divi Augusti*, or "Deeds of the Deified Augustus," an autobiographical account of his own achievements

that Augustus wrote when he was seventy-six and instructed the Senate to post throughout the empire, in both Latin and Greek, after his death. This was done, but the *Res gestae* do not survive intact anywhere. The original bronze copy from the forum in Rome is lost, and the surviving version had to be pieced together from stone fragments found at Ancyra, where the best copy was found; at Apollonia; and at Antioch.

The reconstructed document is in thirty-five paragraphs preserved on eight tablets. Paragraphs 2–14 record Augustus' political career and are consistent with how Roman senators traditionally were remembered. Paragraphs 15–24 go on to catalogue Augustus' benefactions to the people of Rome, demonstrating that he behaved like a responsible patron. Paragraphs 25–33 detail Augustus' military activities, showing how he had dutifully defended and expanded the empire. And the final two paragraphs summarize Augustus' important role in the state: "In my sixth and seventh consulates [28–27 BCE], after putting out the civil war, having obtained all things by universal consent, I transferred the state from my power to the dominion of the Senate and Roman people. And for this merit of mine, by a Recommendation of the Senate, I was called Augustus."

A brief appendix, added posthumously, summarized Augustus' benefactions to the people, for example, "All the expenditures which he gave either into the treasury or to the Roman plebs or to discharged soldiers: 2,400,000,000 *sestertii*."

By controlling the flow of information about his own reign, Augustus was able to predetermine how he would be perceived by future generations. Both in antiquity and in modern times, the *Res gestae* have been used as a primary source for the reign of Augustus, and much of Augustus' own spin about himself has been accepted into scholarly and popular tradition. By reconstructing original documents of this sort, historians sometimes are able to get much closer to the thoughts and intentions of ancient peoples than they can by studying written traditions that have been recopied, rewritten, and revised over the course of many centuries.

⇦ LOOKING BACK

Octavian was the third powerful and ambitious senator, after Sulla and Caesar, to use his army to seize control of the Roman world. Sulla and Caesar had failed to deal with the accumulated problems that confronted the state. Octavian did a much better job. After receiving the title Augustus from a supine Senate, he created a form of government that he called a restoration of the Roman Republic but that we call the Principate, the first form of the Roman Empire. Although supposedly a partnership with the Senate, the Principate left real legal and military power in the hands of the emperor. By 21 BCE, Augustus had solidified his political control over the Roman government in a way that largely solved the problem of keeping ambitious senators under control. Subsequently, he dealt with accumulated problems in the provinces, including reforming provincial administration, coming up with a defensive strategy, and integrating provincial populations into the Roman world. At the same time, he also developed methods for keeping the army under control.

LOOKING AHEAD ⇨

By and large, Augustus was very successful in bringing peace to the Roman world and creating a stable form of government. Succeeding dynasties built on Augustus' foundation, and more and more power accumulated in the hands of the emperor at the expense of the Senate. One thing that Augustus had not done, however, was to develop a constitutional method of choosing a new emperor in situations where a sitting emperor had not named a successor. His failure to do so would come back to haunt the empire on several occasions.

FURTHER READING

Bowersock, G. W. *Augustus and the Greek World*. Oxford: Oxford Univ. Press, 1965.

Brunt, P. A. *The Fall of the Roman Republic*. Oxford: Clarendon Press, 1988.

Gurval, R. A. *Actium and Augustus*. Ann Arbor: Univ. of Michigan Press, 1995.

Kleiner, Diana E. E. *Cleopatra and Rome*. Cambridge, MA: Harvard Univ. Press, 2005.

Levick, Barbara. *Augustus: Image and Substance*. London: Longman, 2010.

Mellor, Ronald, ed. *From Augustus to Nero: The First Dynasty of Imperial Rome*. East Lansing: Michigan State Univ. Press, 1990.

Osgood, Josiah. *Caesar's Legacy: Civil War and the Emergence of the Roman Empire*. New York: Cambridge Univ. Press (USA), 2006.

Roller, Duane W. *The World of Juba II and Kleopatra Selene*. London: Routledge, 2003.

Scullard, H. H. *From the Gracchi to Nero: A History of Rome from 133 BC to AD 68*. 5th ed. Oxford: Routledge, 1982.

Severy, Beth. *Augustus and the Family at the Birth of the Roman Empire*. Oxford: Routledge, 2003.

Shotter, D. *Augustus Caesar*. London: Routledge, 1991.

Webster, Graham. *The Roman Imperial Army of the First and Second Centuries A.D.* Norman: Univ. of Oklahoma Press, 1998.

Zanker, P. *The Power of Images in the Age of Augustus*. Translated by A. Shapiro. Ann Arbor: University of Michigan Press, 1990.

SOURCES

CLEOPATRA, PHARAOH AND QUEEN OF EGYPT (48–31 BCE)

PLUTARCH, *LIFE OF CAESAR* AND *LIFE OF ANTONY*

A silver *denarius* issued in 32 BCE depicts Cleopatra and Antony. The legend on the obverse reads, "Of Cleopatra, Queen of Kings, whose Sons are Kings," and the reverse reads, "Of Antony, after Armenia had been defeated." The coin thus tactfully remains silent about the defeat of Antony's invasion of Parthia. It also does not give Antony an official title; he no longer was a Triumvir and thus had become, in essence, a dependent general of Cleopatra.

Cleopatra VII was not only the last of the Ptolemaic rulers of Egypt but also the last of a line of Egyptian pharaohs that extended back to circa 3000 BCE. Her career overlaid one of the most portentous periods of Roman history, the period of civil wars that brought the end of the Roman Republic and the creation of the Roman Empire. As a Hellenistic ruler at a time when the domination of Rome extended across the entire Mediterranean, she exhibited ambition, skill, and tact as she attempted to carve out an Egyptian empire of her own. Plutarch's lives of Julius Caesar and Mark Antony, written in the mid-second century CE, have much to say about the relationship between Cleopatra and these two preeminent Roman generals. Cleopatra became, in succession, the lover of both of them, and adroitly used her relationships with them to expand her own authority and power. Antony in particular is portrayed as being completely smitten with Cleopatra and totally under her control. Cleopatra's suicide in 30 BCE, which followed on her and Antony's defeat by Julius Caesar's adopted son Octavian at the Battle of Actium in 31 BCE, brought the independent kingdom of Egypt to an end and helped to make her one of the most admired women of antiquity; a scene of her suicide even appeared in the Christian catacombs of Rome. In Plutarch's *Life of Caesar*, the discussion of Cleopatra picks up after Caesar has followed his defeated rival Pompey to Egypt. Caesar was compelled to spend the winter there and used that opportunity to reorganize the administration of the Ptolemaic kingdom. In the *Life of Antony*, the readings likewise commence after Caesar's victory over Pompey at the Battle of Pharsalus in 48 BCE. In his youth Antony had a reputation in public as an excellent general but in private life as a frivolous, loose-living spendthrift. Both reputations followed him throughout his life.

Source: John Dryden, *Plutarch: The Lives of the Noble Greeks and Romans, Vols. 1 and 2*, revised by A. H. Clough (Boston: Little, Brown, 1910).

Plutarch, *Life of Caesar*

Caesar replied that he did not want Egyptians to be his counselors, and soon after privately sent for Cleopatra from her retirement.[1] She took a small boat and one only of her confidants, Apollodorus the Sicilian, along with her, and in the dusk of the evening landed near the palace. She was at a loss how to get in undiscovered until she thought of putting herself into the coverlet of a bed and lying at length while Apollodorus tied up the bedding and carried it on his back through the gates to Caesar's apartment. Caesar was first captivated by this proof of Cleopatra's bold wit and afterward was so overcome by the charm of her society that he made a reconciliation between her and her brother, on the condition that she should rule as his colleague in the kingdom. There was a plot against Caesar by Achillas, general of the king's forces, who escaped to the army and raised a troublesome and embarrassing war against Caesar. The first difficulty Caesar met with was want of water. Another was, when the enemy endeavored to cut off his communication by sea, he was forced to set fire to his own ships, which, after burning the docks, spread on and

destroyed the great library.[2] A third was when, in an engagement near Pharos, he threw himself into the sea and with much difficulty swam off. At last, the king having gone off to Achillas and his party, Caesar engaged and conquered them. Many fell in that battle, and the king himself was never seen again. Upon this, Caesar left Cleopatra Queen of Egypt, who soon after had a son by him, whom the Alexandrians called Caesarion, and then departed for Syria.[3]

Plutarch, *Life of Antony*

Caesar cured Antony of most of his prodigality and folly by not allowing his errors to pass unnoticed. For Antony put away his reprehensible way of living and turned his thoughts to marriage, taking to wife Fulvia, the widow of Clodius the demagogue.[4] She was a woman who took no thought for spinning or housekeeping, nor would she deign to bear sway over a man of private station, but she wished to rule a ruler and command a commander. Therefore Cleopatra later was indebted to Fulvia for teaching Antony to endure a woman's sway, because she took him over quite tamed and schooled at the outset to obey women.

Such, then, was the nature of Antony, when as a crowning evil his love for Cleopatra supervened,

---

[1] In 51 BCE, eighteen-year-old Cleopatra VII and her younger brother, ten-year-old Ptolemy XIII, had been made joint rulers of Egypt; following Egyptian tradition, the two also married. In 48 BCE Cleopatra was exiled as a result of a palace conspiracy. Caesar, who had pursued his rival Pompey to Egypt only to find him shockingly beheaded by the retinue of young Ptolemy, recalled Cleopatra from exile.

[2] The great library of Alexandria, founded by King Ptolemy I (323–283 BCE), was said to have been destroyed on several occasions: in 48 BCE; also when the city was recaptured by the emperor Aurelian in 272 CE; again when the temple of Serapis was burned by Christians in 391 CE; and finally by the Arab general 'Amr in 641 CE.

[3] In 47 BCE.

[4] A political ally of Julius Caesar killed during rioting in Rome in 52 BCE.

roused, and drove to frenzy many of the passions that were still hidden and quiescent in him, and dissipated and destroyed whatever good and saving qualities still offered resistance. He was taken captive in this manner. As he was getting ready for the Parthian war,[5] he sent to Cleopatra, ordering her to meet him in Cilicia[6] in order to make answer to the charges made against her of giving to Cassius much money for the war.[7] But Dellius, Antony's messenger, when he saw how Cleopatra looked and noticed her subtlety and cleverness in conversation, at once perceived that Antony would not so much as think of doing such a woman any harm but that she would have the greatest influence with him. He therefore resorted to flattery and tried to induce the Egyptian to go to Cilicia "decked out in fine array," as Homer would say. She was persuaded, and judging by the proofs that she had had previously of the effect of her beauty upon Gaius Caesar and Gnaeus the son of Pompey,[8] she had hopes that she would more easily bring Antony to her feet. For Caesar and Gnaeus had known her when she was still a girl and inexperienced in affairs, but she was going to visit Antony at the very time when women have the most brilliant beauty and are at the acme of intellectual power.

Cleopatra therefore provided herself with many gifts, much money, and such ornaments as high position and prosperous kingdom made it natural for her to take, but she went putting her greatest confidence in herself and in the charms and sorceries of her own person. She so despised and laughed the man to scorn as to sail up the Cydnus River[9] in a barge with gilded poop,[10] its sails spread purple, its rowers urging it on with silver oars to the sound of the flute blended with pipes and lutes. She herself reclined beneath a canopy spangled with gold, adorned like Venus in a painting, while boys like Cupids in paintings stood on either side and fanned her. Likewise, the fairest of her serving-maidens, attired like Nereïds and Graces,[11] were stationed, some at the rudder-sweeps and others at the reefing-ropes.[12] Wondrous odors from countless incense-offerings diffused themselves along the river-banks. A rumor spread on every hand that Venus[13] had come to revel with Bacchus[14] for the good of Asia. Antony, therefore, invited her to supper, but she thought it fitting that he should rather come to her. At once, then, Antony obeyed and went. Cleopatra observed in the jests of Antony much of the soldier and the common man and adopted this manner also toward him, boldly and without restraint.

Her beauty was in itself not altogether incomparable nor such as to strike those who saw her, but conversation with her had an irresistible charm, and her presence, combined with the persuasiveness of her discourse and the character that was somehow diffused about her behavior toward others, had something stimulating about it. There was sweetness also in the tones of her voice. Her tongue, like an instrument of many strings, she could readily turn to whatever language she pleased, so that in her interviews with barbarians she very seldom had need of an interpreter, but made her replies to most of them herself and unassisted, whether they were Ethiopians, Troglodytes,[15] Hebrews, Arabians, Syrians, Medes, or Parthians. Nay, it is said that she knew the speech of many other peoples also, although the kings of Egypt before her had not even made an effort to learn the native language, and some actually gave up their Macedonian dialect.[16]

---

[5] In 41 BCE.

[6] At the city of Tarsus, on the coast of southeastern Anatolia.

[7] Cassius was one of the assassins of Julius Caesar in 44 BCE and had been defeated by the Triumvirs Octavian and Antony at the Battle of Philippi in 42 BCE.

[8] This is the only surviving reference to a love affair between Cleopatra and Gnaeus, who in 49 BCE had been sent by his father to obtain aid from Egypt in Pompey's civil war with Julius Caesar. He returned with sixty ships.

[9] The modern Berdan River, next to Tarsus.

[10] The back section of a ship.

---

[11] The Nereïds were sea nymphs who helped sailors during storms. The Graces, known in Greek as the Charites, were minor female goddesses connected to nature and fertility.

[12] The lines used to adjust the sails.

[13] The goddess of love—that is, Cleopatra.

[14] The dissipated god of wine—that is, Antony.

[15] A people from the African coast of the Red Sea.

[16] That is, they only spoke standard Greek.

Accordingly, she made such sport of Antony that, while Fulvia his wife was carrying on war at Rome with Caesar in defense of her husband's interests, and while a Parthian army was hovering about Mesopotamia, he suffered her to hurry him off to Alexandria. There, indulging in the sports and diversions of a young man of leisure, he squandered and spent upon pleasures that which Antiphon[17] calls the most costly outlay, namely, time.[18] They had an association called The Inimitable Livers, and every day they feasted one another, making expenditures of incredible profusion.

Cleopatra, ever contributing some fresh delight and charm to Antony's hours of seriousness or mirth, kept him in constant tutelage, and released him neither night nor day. She played at dice with him, drank with him, hunted with him, and watched him as he exercised himself in arms. When by night he would station himself at the doors or windows of the common folk and scoff at those within, she would go with him on his round of mad follies, wearing the garb of a serving maiden, for Antony also would try to array himself like a servant.

While Antony was indulging in such follies, he was surprised by reports from two quarters: one from Rome, that Lucius his brother and Fulvia his wife had waged war with Octavian Caesar, had lost, and were in flight from Italy, and another, that the Parthians were subduing Asia as far as Lydia and Ionia. He learned that Fulvia had been to blame for the war, being naturally a meddlesome and headstrong woman and hoping to draw Antony away from Cleopatra. It happened, however, that Fulvia fell sick and died at Sicyon.[19] Therefore there was an opportunity for a reconciliation with Caesar.[20] The friends of the two men reconciled them, and divided up the empire assigning the east to Antony, and the west to Caesar. These arrangements needed a stronger security, and this security

Fortune offered. Octavia was a sister of Caesar. Her husband, Caius Marcellus, had died a short time before and she was a widow. Antony, too, was a widower; although he did not deny his relations with Cleopatra, he would not admit that she was his wife, for his reason was still battling with his love for the Egyptian. When both men were agreed, they went up to Rome and celebrated Antony's marriage to Octavia.[21]

Antony, after putting Octavia in Caesar's charge together with his children by her and Fulvia,[22] crossed over into Asia. But the dire evil that had been slumbering for a long time, namely, his passion for Cleopatra, which men thought had been put to rest by sensible considerations, blazed up again with renewed power as he drew near to Syria. Finally, he spurned away all saving and noble counsels and brought Cleopatra to Syria. When she had come, he made her a present of no insignificant addition to her dominions, namely, Phoenicia, Coele Syria, Cyprus, and a large part of Cilicia, and still further, the balsam-producing part of Judaea and all that part of Arabia Nabataea that slopes toward the outer sea.[23] These gifts particularly annoyed the Romans. He also made presents to many private persons of tetrarchies and realms of great peoples,[24] but the shamefulness of the honors conferred upon Cleopatra gave most offense. And he heightened the scandal by acknowledging his two children by her, and called one Alexander and the other Cleopatra, with the surname of "Sun" for the first and of "Moon" for the other.

After sending Cleopatra back to Egypt, Antony proceeded through Arabia and Armenia to the place where his forces were assembled.[25] And yet we are told that all this preparation and power, which terrified even the Indians beyond Bactria and made all Asia quiver, was made of no avail to

---

[17] An Athenian orator of the late fifth century BCE.

[18] Antony spent the winter of the years 41–40 BCE with Cleopatra in Alexandria. At the end of 40 BCE Cleopatra gave birth to twins.

[19] A city in Greece.

[20] That is, Octavian.

[21] In the fall of 40 BCE.

[22] Antony and Octavia's daughter Antonia would become the mother of the emperor Claudius (41–54 CE), the grandmother of the emperor Caligula (37–41 CE), and the great-grandmother of the emperor Nero (54–68 CE).

[23] The ocean, in this case the Indian Ocean.

[24] Apparently a reference to the installation of client rulers.

[25] For the war against Parthia.

Antony by reason of Cleopatra. For so eager was he to spend the winter with her that he began the war before the proper time and managed everything confusedly. He was not master of his own faculties, but, as if he were under the influence of drugs or of magic rites, was ever looking eagerly toward her and thinking more of his speedy return than of conquering the enemy.

[After some initial successes, Antony is forced to retreat until he finally reaches the Euphrates River.]

The front ranks advanced little by little, and the river[26] came in sight. On its bank Antony sent his sick and disabled soldiers across first. When the Parthians saw the river, they unstrung their bows and bade the Romans cross over with good courage, bestowing much praise also upon their valor. Antony held a review of his troops and found that twenty thousand of the infantry and four thousand of the cavalry had perished, not all at the hands of the enemy but more than half by disease. He himself went down to the sea and waited for Cleopatra to come. Because she was slow in arriving he was beside himself with distress, promptly resorting to drinking and intoxication, and in the midst of the drinking would often spring up to look out until she put into port. Afterward, Antony once more invaded Armenia and took Artavasdes[27] in chains down to Alexandria, where he celebrated a triumph. And herein particularly did he give offense to the Romans, because he bestowed the honorable and solemn rites of his native country upon the Egyptians for Cleopatra's sake.[28]

Meanwhile, at Rome Octavia was desirous of sailing to Antony, and Caesar[29] gave her permission to do so, not as a favor to her, but in order that, in case she were neglected and treated with scorn, he might have plausible ground for war. But Cleopatra was afraid that if Octavia added to the dignity of her character and the power of Caesar her assiduous attentions to Antony, she would become invincible and get complete control over her husband. She therefore pretended to be passionately in love with

Antony herself and reduced her body by slender diet. She put on a look of rapture when Antony drew near and one of melancholy when he went away. She contrived often to be seen in tears and then would quickly wipe the tears away and try to hide them, as if she would not have Antony notice them. Her flatterers reviled Antony as hard-hearted and unfeeling, and as the destroyer of a mistress who was devoted only to him. Octavia, they said, had married him as a matter of public policy, but Cleopatra, who was queen of so many people, was called Antony's beloved. At last, Antony became fearful that Cleopatra would throw away her life and went back to Alexandria.

At Rome, Antony was hated for the distribution that he made to his children in Alexandria; it was seen to evince hatred of Rome.[30] For after placing on a tribunal of silver two thrones of gold, one for himself and the other for Cleopatra, and other lower thrones for his sons, in the first place he declared Cleopatra to be Queen of Egypt, Cyprus, Libya, and Coele Syria, and she was to share her throne with Caesarion.[31] Caesarion was believed to be a son of the former Caesar, by whom Cleopatra was left pregnant. In the second place, he proclaimed his own sons by Cleopatra as Kings of Kings. To Alexander he allotted Armenia, Media, and Parthia (when he would have subdued it), and to Ptolemy Phoenicia, Syria, and Cilicia.[32] Cleopatra assumed a robe sacred to Isis and was addressed as the New Isis. By reporting these things to the Senate and by frequent denunciations before the people Caesar tried to inflame the multitude against Antony.

Antony heard of this while he was tarrying in Armenia, and at once he ordered Canidius[33] to take sixteen legions and go down to the sea, but he himself took Cleopatra with him and came to Ephesus.[34] Antony ordered Cleopatra to sail to Egypt

---

[26] The westernmost loop of the Euphrates River.

[27] The King of Armenia.

[28] In 34 BCE.

[29] Octavian.

[30] The so-called Donations of Alexandria, at the same time as Antony's triumph in 34 BCE.

[31] Caesarion thus became Ptolemy XV.

[32] In addition, Cleopatra Selene was allotted Cyrenaica and Libya.

[33] Antony's most important general; he later was executed by Octavian.

[34] A Greek city on the Ionian coast of Anatolia.

and there await the result of the war.[35] Cleopatra, however, fearing that Octavia would again succeed in putting a stop to the war, said that it was neither just to drive away from the war a woman whose contributions to it were so large nor was it for the interest of Antony to dispirit the Egyptians, who formed a large part of his naval force. And besides, it was not easy to see how Cleopatra was inferior in intelligence to anyone of the princes who took part in the expedition, she who for a long time had governed so large a kingdom by herself and by long association with Antony had learned to manage large affairs. These arguments prevailed, and with united forces they sailed to Samos[36] and there made merry.

Meanwhile, Titius and Plancus, friends of Antony and men of consular rank, being abused by Cleopatra, ran away to Caesar and gave him information about Antony's will, which was on deposit with the Vestal Virgins. When Caesar asked for it, they would not give it to him, but if he wanted to, they told him to come and take it. So he assembled the Senate and read it aloud to them. Caesar laid most stress on the clause that directed that Antony's body, even if he should die in Rome, should be borne in state through the Forum and then sent away to Cleopatra in Egypt. And Calvisius, a companion of Caesar, brought forward charges against Antony that he had bestowed upon Cleopatra the libraries from Pergamum, in which there were two hundred thousand volumes[37]; that at a banquet he had stood up and rubbed Cleopatra's feet; that he had consented to have the Ephesians salute Cleopatra as mistress; and that many times, while he was seated on his tribunal and dispensing justice, he received love letters from her and read them.

When Caesar had made sufficient preparations, a vote was passed to wage war against Cleopatra and to take away from Antony the authority that

he had surrendered to a woman. Caesar said in addition that Antony had been drugged and was not even master of himself. When the forces came together for the war,[38] Antony had no fewer than five hundred fighting ships, among which were many vessels of eight and ten banks of oars. He also had one hundred thousand infantry soldiers and twelve thousand horsemen. Caesar had two hundred and fifty ships of war, eighty thousand infantry, and about as many horsemen as his enemies.

To such an extent, now, was Antony an appendage of the woman that although he was far superior on land, he wished the decision to rest with his navy, to please Cleopatra, even though he saw that for lack of crews his trierarchs[39] were recruiting wayfarers, mule-drivers, harvesters, and teenagers, and that even then their ships were not fully manned, but most of them were deficient and sailed wretchedly. Canidius, the commander of the land forces, advised Antony to send Cleopatra away and to decide the issue by a land battle, saying that it would be a strange thing for Antony, who was most experienced in land conflicts, not to avail himself of his numerous legionary soldiers but to distribute his forces among ships and fritter them away. Cleopatra, however, prevailed with her opinion that the war should be decided by the ships.

During that day, then, and the three following days the sea was tossed up by a strong wind and prevented the battle, but on the fifth, the weather becoming fine and the sea calm, they came to an engagement. The sea-fight was undecided and equally favorable to both sides when suddenly the sixty ships of Cleopatra were seen hoisting their sails for flight and making off through the midst of the combatants. The enemy looked on with amazement. Here, Antony made it clear to all the world that he was swayed neither by the sentiments of a commander nor of a brave man, nor even by his own, but he was dragged along by the woman as if he had become incorporate with her and must go where she did. No sooner did he see her ship sailing off than he forgot everything else, betrayed and ran away from those who were fighting and dying in

---

[35] Antony by now had realized that war with Octavian was inevitable.

[36] An island, and city, in the Aegean Sea off the coast of Ionia.

[37] To replace the books that had been burned during Caesar's stay; the library of Pergamum was second only to that of Alexandria.

---

[38] In 31 BCE, at Actium on the coast of western Greece.

[39] Ship captains.

his cause, got into a five-oared galley, and hastened after the woman who had already ruined him and would make his ruin still more complete. Cleopatra recognized him and raised a signal on her ship, so Antony came up and was taken on board, but he neither saw nor was seen by her. Instead, he went forward alone to the prow and sat down by himself in silence, holding his head in both hands. He spent three days by himself at the prow, either because he was angry with Cleopatra or because he was ashamed to see her, and then put in at Taenarum.[40] Here the women in Cleopatra's company persuaded them to eat and sleep together. After Antony had reached the coast of Libya and sent Cleopatra forward into Egypt from Paraetonium,[41] he had the benefit of solitude without end.

Antony tried to kill himself, but was prevented by his friends and brought to Alexandria. Here he found Cleopatra venturing upon a hazardous and great undertaking. The isthmus in Egypt that separates the Red Sea from the Mediterranean Sea and is considered to be the boundary between Asia and Libya, at its narrowest point measures three hundred furlongs. Here Cleopatra undertook to raise her fleet out of water and drag the ships across, and after launching them in the Arabian Gulf with much money and a large force, to settle outside of Egypt, thus escaping war and servitude. But because the Arabians about Petra[42] burned the first ships that were drawn up, and Antony still thought that his land forces at Actium were holding together, she desisted, and guarded the approaches to the country.

Canidius in person brought him word of the loss of his forces at Actium, but none of these things greatly disturbed him, for he gladly laid aside his hopes so that he also might lay aside his anxieties. After he had been received into the palace by Cleopatra, he turned the city to the enjoyment of suppers and drinking-bouts and distributions of gifts. Cleopatra and Antony now dissolved their famous society of Inimitable

Livers and founded another, not at all inferior to that in extravagant outlay, which they called the society of Partners in Death. They passed the time delightfully in a round of suppers. Moreover, Cleopatra was getting together collections of all sorts of deadly poisons. She tested the painless working of each of them by giving them to prisoners under sentence of death. But when she saw that the speedy poisons enhanced the sharpness of death by the pain they caused, whereas the milder poisons were not quick, she made trial of venomous animals. She found that the bite of the asp alone induced a sleepy torpor and sinking, where there was no spasm or groan but rather a gentle perspiration on the face, while the perceptive faculties were easily relaxed and dimmed, and resisted all attempts to rouse and restore them, as is the case with those who are soundly asleep.

When the winter was over, Caesar marched against his enemy through Syria, and his generals through Libya. When Caesar had taken up position near the hippodrome, Antony sallied forth against him and routed his cavalry. Then, exalted by his victory, he went into the palace and kissed Cleopatra, all armed as he was. Antony, conscious that there was no better death for him than that by battle, determined to attack by land and sea at once. He personally posted his infantry on the hills in front of the city and watched his ships as they attacked those of the enemy. But the crews of his ships saluted Caesar's crews with their oars and changed sides. No sooner had Antony seen this than he also was deserted by his cavalry, and after being defeated with his infantry he retired into the city, crying out that he had been betrayed by Cleopatra to those with whom he waged war for her sake. But she, fearing his anger and his madness, fled for refuge into her tomb. Then she sent messengers to tell Antony that she was dead. Antony believed that message, and saying to himself, "Why do you longer delay, Antony? Fortune has taken away your sole remaining excuse for clinging to life," he went into his chamber. Here, as he unfastened his breastplate and laid it aside, he said: "O Cleopatra, I am not grieved to be bereft of you, for I shall straightway join you but I am grieved that

---

[40] A coastal city near Sparta in southern Greece.

[41] Modern Mersa Matruh on the Mediterranean coast of Egypt, now a major tourist destination.

[42] A powerful trading city of northern Arabia.

such an Imperator[43] as I am has been found to be inferior to a woman in courage." And running himself through the belly with his sword he dropped upon the couch. But the wound did not bring a speedy death.

Antony lay writhing and crying out until Diomedes the secretary came from Cleopatra with orders to bring him to her in the tomb. Having learned that Cleopatra was alive, Antony eagerly ordered his servants to raise him up, and he was carried to her tomb. Cleopatra, however, would not open the doors, but showed herself at a window, from which she let down ropes and cords, and she drew him up herself with the aid of the two women whom alone she had admitted with her. Smeared with blood and struggling with death he was drawn up, stretching out his hands to her even as he dangled in the air. For the task was not an easy one, and scarcely could Cleopatra, with clinging hands and strained face, pull up the rope. And when she had thus got him in and laid him down, she rent her garments over him, beat and tore her breasts with her hands, wiped some of his blood upon her face, and called him master, husband, and Imperator; indeed, she almost forgot her own ills in her pity for his. But Antony stopped her lamentations and asked for a drink of wine, either because he was thirsty or in the hope of a speedier release. When he had drunk, he advised her to consult her own safety, if she could do it without disgrace, and among all the companions of Caesar to put most confidence in Proculeius,[44] and not to lament him for his last reverses, but to count him happy for the good things that had been his, because he had become most illustrious of men, had won greatest power, and now had been not ignobly conquered, a Roman by a Roman.

Scarcely was he dead when Caesar sent Proculeius, bidding him, if possible, above all things to get Cleopatra into his power alive, for he was fearful about the treasures in her funeral pyre, and he thought it would add greatly to the glory of his triumph if she were led in the procession. Proculeius

applied a ladder and went in through the window. One of the women imprisoned with Cleopatra cried out, "Wretched Cleopatra, you are taken alive," whereupon the queen turned about, saw Proculeius, and tried to stab herself, for she had at her girdle a dagger such as robbers wear. Proculeius ran swiftly to her, threw both his arms about her, and said: "O Cleopatra, you are wronging both yourself and Caesar by trying to rob him of an opportunity to show great kindness." At the same time he took away her weapon, and shook out her clothing, to see whether she was concealing any poison. And there was also sent from Caesar one of his freedmen, Epaphroditus, with injunctions to keep the queen alive by the strictest vigilance.

After a few days Caesar himself came to talk with her and give her comfort. She was lying on a mean pallet-bed, clad only in her tunic, but she sprang up as he entered and threw herself at his feet. Her hair and face were in terrible disarray, her voice trembled, and her eyes were sunken. There were also visible many marks of the cruel blows upon her bosom; in a word, her body seemed to be no better off than her spirit. Nevertheless, the charm for which she was famous and the boldness of her beauty were not altogether extinguished, but, although she was in such a sorry plight, they shone forth from within and made themselves manifest in the play of her features. Caesar told her that he would give her more splendid treatment than she could possibly expect. Then he went off, supposing that he had deceived her, but he rather had been deceived by her.

Cleopatra begged Caesar that she might be permitted to pour libations for Antony; and when the request was granted, she had herself carried to the tomb, and embracing the urn that held his ashes, she said: "Dear Antony, I buried you but lately with hands still free; now, however, I pour libations for you as a captive, and so carefully guarded that I cannot either with blows or tears disfigure this body of mine, which is a slave's body and closely watched so that it may grace the triumph over you. Do not expect other honors or libations; these are the last from Cleopatra the captive. For although in life nothing could part us from each other, in death we are likely to change places, with you,

---

[43] A general who has won an important victory.

[44] An equestrian and good friend of Octavian, known for his powers of persuasion.

the Roman, lying buried here, while I, the hapless woman, lie in Italy. But if indeed there is any might or power in the gods of that country (for the gods of this country have betrayed us), do not abandon thine own wife while she lives, nor permit a triumph to be celebrated over myself in my person, but hide and bury me here with thyself, because out of all my innumerable ills not one is so great and dreadful as this short time that I have lived apart from you."

After such lamentations, she wreathed and kissed the urn and then ordered a bath to be prepared for herself. After her bath, there came a man from the countryside carrying a basket, and when the guards asked him what he was bringing there, he opened the basket and showed them a dish full of leaves and figs. The guards were amazed at the great size and beauty of the figs, whereupon the man smiled and asked them to take some, so they felt no mistrust and bade him take them in. After her meal, Cleopatra took a tablet that was already written upon and sealed and sent it to Caesar. When Caesar opened the tablet, he found there

supplications of one who begged that he would bury her with Antony and quickly knew what had happened. He ordered messengers to go with all speed and investigate. But the mischief had been swift. When they opened the doors they found Cleopatra lying dead upon a golden couch, arrayed in royal state. Of her two women, the one called Iras was dying at her feet, while Charmion, already tottering and heavy-handed, was trying to arrange the diadem that encircled the queen's brow. Then somebody said in anger: "A fine deed, this, Charmion!" "It is indeed most fine," she said, "and befitting the descendent of so many kings." Not a word more did she speak, but fell there by the side of the couch. It is said that a cobra[45] was brought with those figs and leaves and lay hidden beneath them. When she took away some of the figs and saw it, she said, "There it is, you see," and baring her arm she held it out for the bite. Caesar, although vexed at the death of the woman, admired her lofty spirit; and he gave orders that her body should be buried with that of Antony in splendid and regal fashion.

---

[45] The word used here, "aspis," meaning simply a poisonous snake, does not refer to the European snake called the asp, as it commonly is rendered, but to the Egyptian cobra. Ironically, a rearing cobra known as the "uraeus" was affixed to the forehead of the Pharaoh.

THE "PRAISE OF TURIA"

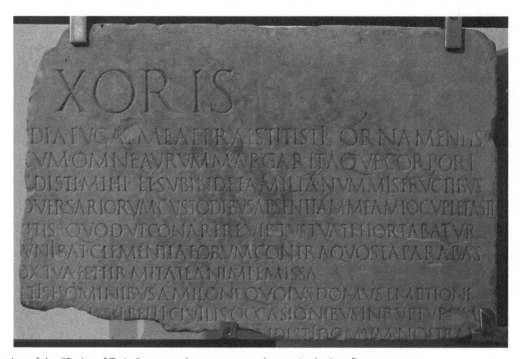

A section of the "Praise of Turia," engraved on a stone tombstone in the late first century BCE.

The "Laudatio Turiae," or "Praise of Turia," is an inscription on a tombstone that preserves a husband's lengthy and very touching eulogy on the virtues of his wife. The woman's name is not preserved on the fragmentary inscription, but she often has been identified with the Turia who was married to Q. Lucretius Vespillo, who was proscribed by the Second Triumvirate in 43 BCE but later rose to become Consul in 19 BCE. His deeds during the proscriptions were described by the authors Valerius Maximus and Appian.

Source: Erik Wistrand, *The So-Called Laudatio Turiae* (Lund, Sweden: Berlingska Boktryckeriet, 1976).

(Heading)

[---] of my wife

(Left-hand column)

(line 1) [---] through the honesty of your character [---] you remained [---]
You became an orphan suddenly before the day of our wedding, when both your parents were murdered together in the solitude of the countryside. It was mainly due to your efforts that the death of your parents was not left unavenged, for I had left for Macedonia, and your sister's husband Cluvius[46] had gone to the province of Africa.

So strenuously did you perform your filial duty by your insistent demands and your pursuit of

---

[46] Otherwise unknown.

justice that we could not have done more if we had been present. These merits you have in common with that most virtuous lady your sister.

While you were engaged in these things, having secured the punishment of the guilty, you immediately left your own house in order to guard your modesty and you came to my mother's house, where you awaited my return. Then pressure was brought to bear on you and your sister to accept the view that your father's will, by which you and I were heirs, had been invalidated by his having contracted a *coemptio*[47] with his wife. If that was the case, then you together with all your father's property would necessarily come under the guardianship of those involved, and your sister would be left without any share at all of that inheritance, because she had been transferred to the *potestas* of Cluvius.[48] How you reacted to this, with what presence of mind you offered resistance, I know full well, although I was absent.

You defended our common cause by asserting the truth, namely, that the will had not in fact been broken, so that we should both keep the property, instead of your getting all of it alone.[49] It was your firm decision that you would defend your father's written word; you would do this anyhow, you declared, by sharing your inheritance with your sister, if you were unable to uphold the validity of the will. And you maintained that you would not come under the state of legal guardianship,[50] because there was no such right against you in law, for there was no proof that your father belonged to any

gens that could by law compel you to do this. For even assuming that your father's will had become void, those who prosecuted had no such right because they did not belong to the same *gens*.[51] They gave way before your firm resolution and did not pursue the matter any further. Thus you on your own brought to a successful conclusion the defense you took up because of your duty to your father, your devotion to your sister, and your faithfulness toward me.

Marriages as long as ours are rare, marriages that are ended by death and not broken by divorce. For we were fortunate enough to see our marriage last without disharmony for fully forty years. I wish that our long union had come to its final end through something that had befallen me instead of you; it would have been more just if I as the older partner had had to yield to fate through such an event.

Why should I mention your domestic virtues: your loyalty, obedience, affability, reasonableness, industry in working wool,[52] religion without superstition, sobriety of attire, modesty of appearance? Why dwell on your love for your relatives, your devotion to your family? You have shown the same attention to my mother as you did to your own parents, and have taken care to secure an equally peaceful life for her as you did for your own people, and you have innumerable other merits in common with all married women who care for their good name. It is your very own virtues that I am asserting, and very few women have encountered comparable circumstances to make them endure such sufferings and perform such deeds. Providentially Fate has made such hard tests rare for women.

We have preserved all the property you inherited from your parents under common custody, for you were not concerned to make your own what you had given to me without any restriction. We divided our duties in such a way that I had the guardianship of your property and you had the care of mine.

---

[47] That is, the property had been put into trust. Guardians would have been appointed, and Turia and her husband would not have had direct access to the property.

[48] That is, she had entered a marriage *cum manu* ("with authority"), in which she came under the legal authority of her husband. Doing so disqualified her from being an heir of her father.

[49] If the will had been disallowed, Turia would have inherited everything as the only surviving child still under the *potestas* (legal authority) of her father, which indicates that her marriage must have been *sine manu* ("without authority"), in which she remained under her own legal authority.

[50] Having the property put under someone else's guardianship was to be avoided because guardians sometimes mismanaged the property put in their care.

---

[51] In Roman law, guardians were to be appointed from among a person's nearest agnates—that is, male relatives from the same *gens* (extended family). Given that the accusers were not agnates, they had no legal right to bring a case, and the will thus stood.

[52] The preeminent virtue of Roman women.

Concerning this side of our relationship I pass over much, in case I should take a share myself in what is properly yours. May it be enough for me to have said this much to indicate how you felt and thought.

Your generosity you have manifested to many friends and particularly to your beloved relatives. On this point someone might mention with praise other women, but the only equal you have had has been your sister. For you brought up your female relations who deserved such kindness in your own houses with us. You also provided dowries for them so that they could obtain marriages worthy of your family. The dowries you had decided upon Cluvius and I by common accord took upon ourselves to pay,[53] and because we approved of your generosity we did not wish that you should let your own patrimony suffer diminution but substituted our own money and gave our own estates as dowries. I have mentioned this not from a wish to commend ourselves but to make clear that it was a point of honor for us to execute with our means what you had conceived in a spirit of generous family affection.

A number of other benefits of yours I have preferred not to mention [---]

(several lines missing)

(Right-hand column)

You provided abundantly for my needs during my flight[54] and gave me the means for a dignified manner of living, when you took all the gold and jewelry from your own body and sent it to me and over and over again enriched me in my absence with servants, money, and provisions, showing great ingenuity in deceiving the guards posted by our adversaries.

You begged for my life when I was abroad—it was your courage that urged you to this step—and because of your entreaties I was shielded by the clemency of those against whom you marshaled your words. Whatever you said was always said with undaunted courage.

Meanwhile when a troop of men collected by Milo,[55] whose house I had acquired through purchase when he was in exile, tried to profit by the opportunities provided by the civil war and break into our house to plunder, you beat them back successfully and were able to defend our home.

(About twelve lines missing)

[---] exist [---] that I was brought back to my country by him[56] for if you had not, by taking care for my safety, provided what he could save, he would have promised his support in vain. Thus I owe my life no less to your devotion than to Caesar.

Why should I now hold up to view our intimate and secret plans and private conversations. How I was saved by your good advice when I was roused by startling reports to meet sudden and imminent dangers; how you did not allow me imprudently to tempt providence by an overbold step but prepared a safe hiding-place for me when I had given up my ambitious designs, choosing as partners in your plans to save me your sister and her husband Cluvius, all of you taking the same risk? There would be no end, if I tried to go into all this. It is enough for me and for you that I was hidden and my life was saved.

But I must say that the bitterest thing that happened to me in my life befell me through what happened to you. When thanks to the kindness and judgment of the absent Caesar Augustus I had been restored to my county as a citizen, Marcus Lepidus,[57] his colleague, who was present, was confronted with your request concerning my recall, and you lay prostrate at his feet, and you were not only not raised up but were dragged away and carried off brutally like a slave. But although your body was full of bruises, your spirit

---

[53] Because Turia's sister was under the legal authority of Cluvius, the latter had control of her inheritance.

[54] A supporter of Pompey during the latter's civil war with Julius Caesar, he again chose the wrong side and was proscribed by the Second Triumvirate in 43 BCE. He later returned to favor and was named Consul for 19 BCE.

[55] A rabble-rousing Tribune of the Plebs who opposed Julius Caesar; he was exiled in 52 BCE after the murder of Clodius.

[56] Octavian Augustus.

[57] Marcus Aemilius Lepidus, one of the members of the Second Triumvirate; during Antony's and Octavian's campaign against Caesar's assassins in 43 BCE, Lepidus was left in charge back in Rome.

was unbroken and you kept reminding him of Caesar's edict with its expression of pleasure at my reinstatement, and although you had to listen to insulting words and suffer cruel wounds, you pronounced the words of the edict in a loud voice, so that it should be known who was the cause of my deadly perils. This matter was soon to prove harmful for him.[58] What could have been more effective than the virtue you displayed? You managed to give Caesar an opportunity to display his clemency and not only to preserve my life but also to brand Lepidus' insolent cruelty by your admirable endurance.

But why go on? Let me cut my speech short. My words should and can be brief, lest by dwelling on your great deeds I treat them unworthily. In gratitude of your great services toward me let me display before the eyes of all men my public acknowledgement that you saved my life. When peace had been restored throughout the world and the lawful political order reestablished, we began to enjoy quiet and happy times. It is true that we did wish to have children, who had for a long time been denied to us by an envious fate. If it had pleased Fortune to continue to be favorable to us as she was wont to be, what would have been lacking for either of us? But Fortune took a different course, and our hopes were sinking. The courses you considered and the steps you attempted to take because of this would perhaps be remarkable and praiseworthy in some other women, but in you they are nothing to wonder at when compared to your other great qualities and I will not go into them.

When you despaired of your ability to bear children and grieved over my childlessness, you became anxious lest by retaining you in marriage I might lose all hope of having children and be distressed for that reason. So you proposed a divorce outright and offered to yield our house free to another woman's fertility. Your intention was in fact that you yourself, relying on our well-known conformity of sentiment, would search out and provide for me a wife who was worthy

and suitable for me, and you declared that you would regard future children as joint and as your own, and that you would not effect a separation of our property that hitherto had been held in common, but that it would still be under my control and, if I wished so, under your administration: nothing would be kept apart by you, nothing separate, and you would thereafter take upon yourself the duties and the loyalty of a sister and a mother-in-law.[59]

I must admit that I flared up so that I almost lost control of myself; so horrified was I by what you tried to do that I found it difficult to retrieve my composure. To think that separation should be considered between us before fate had so ordained, to think that you had been able to conceive in your mind the idea that you might cease to be my wife while I was still alive, although you had been utterly faithful to me when I was exiled and practically dead!

What desire, what need to have children could I have had that was so great that I should have broken faith for that reason and changed certainty for uncertainty? But no more about this! You remained with me as my wife, for I could not have given in to you without disgrace for me and unhappiness for both of us.

But on your part, what could have been more worthy of commemoration and praise than your efforts in devotion to my interests: when I could not have children from yourself, you wanted me to have them through your good offices, and because you despaired of bearing children, to provide me with offspring by my marriage to another woman.

Would that the life-span of each of us had allowed our marriage to continue until I, as the older partner, had been borne to the grave—that would have been more just—and you had performed for me the last rites, and that I had died leaving you still alive and that I had had you as a daughter to myself in place of my childlessness.

Fate decreed that you should precede me. You bequeathed me sorrow through my longing for you and left me a miserable man without children to

---

[58] Lepidus was forced into retirement by Octavian and Antony in 36 BCE.

[59] To the new wife, that is.

comfort me. I on my part will, however, bend my way of thinking and feeling to your judgments and be guided by your admonitions.

But all your opinions and instructions should give precedence to the praise you have won so that this praise will be a consolation for me and I will not feel too much the loss of what I have consecrated to immortality to be remembered forever.

What you have achieved in your life will not be lost to me. The thought of your fame gives me strength of mind and from your actions I draw instruction so that I shall be able to resist Fortune. Fortune did not rob me of everything because it permitted your memory to be glorified by praise. But along with you I have lost the tranquility of my existence. When I recall how you used to foresee and ward off the dangers that threatened me,

I break down under my calamity and cannot hold steadfastly by my promise.

Natural sorrow wrests away my power of self-control and I am overwhelmed by sorrow. I am tormented by two emotions: grief and fear—and I do not stand firm against either. When I go back in time to my previous misfortunes and when I envisage what the future may have in store for me, fixing my eyes on your glory does not give me strength to bear my sorrow with patience. Rather I seem to be destined to long mourning.

The conclusions of my speech will be that you deserved everything but that it did not fall to my lot to give you everything as I ought. Your last wishes I have regarded as law; whatever it will be in my power to do in addition, I shall do.

I pray that your *Di manes*[60] will grant you rest and protection.

---

[60] "The Remaining Gods," deities that embody the spirits of deceased loved ones; Roman tombstones often began their epitaphs with the large letters "DM," "To spirits that remain."

ANCHISES PROPHESIZES THE FUTURE OF ROME (19 BCE)

VERGIL, *AENEID*, BOOK 6

A mosaic from Hadrumetum in North Africa depicts Vergil with two of the muses, Clio, the muse of history, and Melpomene, the muse of poetry. Preserved now in the Bardo Museum in Tunis.

The *Aeneid* of Vergil, which told of the ten years of wandering by Aeneas as he made his way around the Mediterranean world from burning Troy to a settlement not far from the later site of Rome, was the national poem of Rome during the Roman Empire. It was the first work of literature that anyone learning to read and write Latin studied. In the sixth book, Aeneas visits the Cumaean Sibyl, who utters prophesies on behalf of the god Apollo. The Sibyl leads Aeneas through the underworld, where he eventually meets his father, Anchises, who predicts the future greatness of Rome, including the greatness of the emperor Augustus. In Vergil's view, then, the rise of Augustus and the Roman Empire had been preordained by the gods. The story begins here with Aeneas' arrival in Italy.

Source: H. R. Fairclough, trans., *Vergil. Eclogues, Georgics, Aeneid*, Loeb Classical Library, 2 vols. (Cambridge, MA: Harvard Univ. Press, 1916).

Thus Aeneas at last glides up to the shores of Euboean Cumae.[61] Dutiful[62] Aeneas seeks the heights, where Apollo sits enthroned, and a vast cavern hard by, hidden haunt of the dread Sibyl,[63] into whom the Delian seer[64] breathes a mighty mind and soul, revealing the future. The huge side of the Euboean rock is hewn into a cavern, into which lead a hundred wide mouths, a hundred gateways, from which rush as many voices, the answers of the Sibyl. They had come to the threshold, when the maiden cries: "Tis time to ask the oracles; the god, lo! the god!" As thus she spoke before the doors, suddenly not countenance nor color was the same, nor stayed her tresses braided, but her bosom heaves, her heart swells with wild frenzy, and she

[61] The Italian city of Cumae had been founded by the Greek settlers from the island of Euboea.

[62] The Latin word is *pius*, the customary epithet applied to Aeneas; to do one's duty was the greatest virtue that any Roman could display. As of the second century CE, Roman emperors also bore the epithet "Pius."

[63] A woman who makes prophecies under the influence of some god, often Apollo.

[64] Apollo, who was born on the island of Delos in the Aegean Sea.

is taller to behold, nor has her voice a mortal ring, because now she feels the nearer breath of deity. "Are you slow to vow and to pray?" she cries. "Are you slow, Trojan Aeneas? For until then the mighty mouths of the awestruck house will not gape open." So she spoke and was mute. A chill shudder ran through the Teucrians'[65] sturdy frames, and their king[66] pours forth prayers from his inmost heart: "Phoebus,[67] who never failed to pity Troy's sore agony,[68] who guided the Dardanian[69] shaft and hand of Paris against the body of Aeacus' son,[70] under your guidance did I enter so many seas, skirting mighty lands, now at last is Italy's ever receding shore within our grasp. Thus far only may Troy's fortune have followed us! You, too, may now fitly spare the people of Pergamus,[71] you gods and goddesses[72] all, to whom Troy and Dardania's great glory were an offense. And you, most holy prophetess, who foreknow the future, grant that the Teucrians may rest in Latium,[73] with the wandering gods and storm-tossed powers of Troy. Then to Phoebus and Trivia[74] will I set up a temple of solid marble, and festal days in Phoebus' name. You also a stately shrine awaits in our realm, for here I will place your oracles and mystic utterances, told to my people, and ordain chosen men, O gracious one. Only trust not your verses to leaves, lest they fly in disorder, the sport of rushing winds; chant them yourself, I pray." His lips ceased speaking.

But the prophetess, not yet acknowledging the authority of Phoebus, storms wildly in the cavern, as if to shake the mighty god from her breast, but he tires her raving mouth, tames her wild heart, and molds her by constraint. And now the hundred mighty mouths of the house have opened of their own will, and bring through the air the seer's reply: "O you that have at length survived the great perils of the sea—yet by land more grievous woes lie in wait—into the realm of Lavinium[75] the sons of Dardanus shall come, relieve your heart of this care. Yet they shall not also rejoice in their coming. Wars, grim wars I see, and the Tiber foaming with streams of blood. Even now in Latium a new Achilles[76] has been born, himself a goddess' son, nor shall Juno[77] anywhere fail to dog the Trojans, while you, a suppliant in your need, what peoples, what cities of Italy will you not implore! The cause of all this Trojan woe is again an alien bride, again a foreign marriage![78] Yield not to ills, but go forth all the bolder to face them as far as your destiny will allow!"

In these words the Cumaean Sibyl chants from the shrine her dread enigmas and booms from the cavern, wrapping truth in darkness. As soon as the frenzy ceased and the raving lips were hushed, Aeneas the hero begins: "For me, no form of toils arises, O maiden, that is strange or unlooked for. All this have I foreseen and debated in my mind. One thing I pray: because here is the famed gate of the nether king[79] and the gloomy marsh from Acheron's[80] overflow, be it granted me to pass into my dear father's sight and presence; show the way and open the hallowed portals! Amid flames and a thousand pursuing spears, I rescued him on these shoulders, and brought him safe from the

---

[65] The Trojans, named after Teucer, the legendary first king of Troy.

[66] Aeneas.

[67] An epithet of the god Apollo.

[68] The fall of Troy.

[69] Dardanus was the son of the god Zeus and Electra, the daughter of Atlas. He founded the city of Dardanus near Troy.

[70] Achilles, who was killed by an arrow shot by Paris, son of Priam, the king of Troy.

[71] The citadel of the city of Troy.

[72] The gods and goddesses of the Greeks, such as Athena and Juno, who had been bringing ruin on the Trojans.

[73] The fertile plain south of the lower Tiber River, where Rome later would be founded.

[74] Goddess of witchcraft, Hecate in Greek, identified by the Romans with Artemis, sister of Apollo.

---

[75] A new city named by Aeneas in honor of Lavinia, the daughter of Latinus, king of the Latins.

[76] Turnus, king of the Rutili in Italy, who would be the main antagonist of Aeneas in the *Aeneid*.

[77] The sister and wife of Zeus; she opposed the Trojans during the Trojan War because Paris had judged Venus, and not her, to be the most beautiful of all the goddesses.

[78] The first alien marriage had been that of Helen of Sparta to the Trojan Paris; the second would be the marriage of Aeneas to Lavinia, the daughter of the Latin king Latinus.

[79] The god Hades, king of the underworld.

[80] The "River of Woe," along with the Styx, Lethe, Cocytus, and Pyriphlegethon, one of the five rivers of the underworld.

enemy's midst. He it was who prayed and charged me humbly to seek you and draw near to your threshold. Pity both son and sire, I beseech you, gracious one!"

In such words he prayed and clasped the altar, when thus the prophetess began to speak: "Sprung from blood of gods, son of Trojan Anchises, easy is the descent to Avernus.[81] Night and day the door of gloomy Dis[82] stands open. But to recall one's steps and pass out to the upper air, this is the task, this the toil! In all the mid-space lie woods, and Cocytus[83] girds it, gliding with murky folds. But if such love is in your heart, if such a yearning, twice to swim the Stygian[84] lake, twice to see black Tartarus.[85] and if you are pleased to give rein to the mad endeavor, hear what must first be done. There lurks in a shady tree a bough, golden leaf and pliant stem, held consecrate to nether Juno.[86] It is not given to pass beneath earth's hidden places before someone has plucked from the tree the golden-tressed fruitage. Search then with eyes aloft and, when found, duly pluck it with your hand. Only so will you survey the Stygian groves and realms the living may not tread." She spoke, and with closed lips was silent.

With sad countenance Aeneas wends his way, and ponders in his mind the dark issues, gazing on the boundless forest. He prays, "O if now that golden bough would show itself to us on the tree in the deep wood!" Scarce had he said these words when twin doves came flying from the sky and lit on the green grass. Then the great hero knew them for his mother's[87] birds, and prays with joy: "Be my guides and through the air steer a course into the grove, where the rich bough shades the fruitful ground! And you, goddess-mother, fail not my dark hour!" So speaking, he checked his steps, marking where they direct their course. Then, when they came to the jaws of noisome Avernus, they perch side by side on their chosen goal, a tree, through whose branches flashed the contrasting glimmer of gold. Forthwith Aeneas plucks it and greedily breaks off the clinging bough, and carries it beneath the roof of the prophetic Sibyl.

He fulfils with haste the Sibyl's behest. A deep cave there was, yawning wide and vast, of jagged rock, and sheltered by dark lake and woodland gloom, over which no flying creatures could safely wing their way; such a vapor from those black jaws was wafted to the vaulted sky whence the Greeks spoke of Avernus, the Birdless Place.[88] Here first the priestess set in line four dark-backed heifers, and pours wine upon their brows.[89] Then, plucking the topmost bristles from between the horns, she lays them on the sacred fire for first offering, calling aloud on Hecate, supreme both in Heaven and in Hell. Others set knives to the throat and catch the warm blood in bowls. Aeneas himself sacrifices with the sword a black-fleeced lamb, an offering to the mother of the Eumenides[90] and her great sister,[91] and to you, Proserpina, a barren heifer. But just before the rays and dawning of the early sun the ground rumbled underfoot, the wooded ridges began to quiver, and through the gloom dogs seemed to howl as the goddess[92] drew nigh. The seer shrieks, "Rush on the road and unsheathe your sword! Now, Aeneas, is the hour for courage!" So much she said, and plunged madly into the opened cave. He, with fearless steps, keeps pace with his advancing guide.

On they went dimly, beneath the lonely night amid the gloom, through the empty halls of Dis and his phantom realm. Just before the entrance,

---

[81] A volcanic crater near the city of Cumae, believed to be the entrance to the underworld.

[82] Hades, god of the underworld.

[83] The "River of Lamentation," one of the rivers of the underworld.

[84] The Styx was another of the rivers of the underworld.

[85] The deepest section of the underworld, where the most dangerous creatures were imprisoned.

[86] Proserpina, Persephone in Greek, queen of the underworld.

[87] The goddess Venus.

---

[88] From a Greek word meaning "without birds," perhaps because the volcanic fumes killed any birds that flew over the crater.

[89] Before any great undertaking, sacrifices to the gods had to be performed.

[90] The Furies, avenging goddesses who pursued and punished disrespectful people. They were the daughters of the goddess Night.

[91] Earth.

[92] Hecate.

even within the very jaws of Hell, Grief and avenging Cares have set their bed; there pale Diseases dwell, sad Age, and Fear, and Hunger, temptress to sin, and loathly Want, shapes terrible to view, and Death and Distress. Next, Death's own brother Sleep, and the soul's Guilty Joys, and, on the threshold opposite, the death-dealing War, and the Furies' iron cells, and maddening Strife, her snaky locks entwined with bloody ribbons.

A road leads to the waters of Tartarean Acheron. Here, a whirlpool seethes and belches into Cocytus all its sand. A grim ferry man guards these waters and streams. Charon, on whose chin lies a mass of unkempt hoary hair. His eyes are staring orbs of flame; his squalid garb hangs by a knot from his shoulders. Unaided, he poles the boat, tends the sails, and in his murky craft convoys the dead. Hither rushed all the throng, streaming to the banks; mothers and men and bodies of high-souled heroes, their life now done, boys and unwedded girls, and sons placed on the pyre before their fathers' eyes. They stood, pleading to be the first ferried across, and stretched out hands in yearning for the farther shore. But the surly boatman takes now these, now those, while others he thrusts away, back from the brink.

Then aroused and amazed by the disorder, Aeneas cries, "Tell me, maiden, what means the crowding to the river? What seek the spirits? By what rule do these leave the banks, and those sweep the lurid stream with oars?" To him thus briefly spoke the aged priestess, "Anchises' son, true offspring of gods, all this crowd is helpless and graveless; yonder ferryman is Charon; those whom the flood carries are the buried.[93] He may not carry them over the dreadful banks and hoarse-voiced waters until their bones have found a resting place. A hundred years they roam and flit about these shores; then only are they admitted and revisit the longed-for pools."

They pursue the journey, and draw near to the river. But when the boatman saw them he rebukes them: "Whoever you are who come to our river in arms, tell me, even from there, why you come, and check your step. Living bodies I may not carry in the Stygian boat." In answer the soothsayer spoke briefly: "Trojan Aeneas, famous for piety and arms, descends to his father, to the lowest shades of Erebus.[94] If the picture of such piety in no wise moves you, yet know this bough," and she shows the bough, hidden in her robe. At this his swelling breast subsides from its anger. No more is said, but he, marveling at the dread gift, turns his blue barge and nears the shore. Then other souls that sat on the long thwarts he routs out and at once he takes aboard giant Aeneas. The seamy craft groaned under the weight and through its chinks took in marshy flood. At last, across the water, he lands seer and soldier unharmed on the ugly mire.

These realms huge Cerberus[95] makes ring with his triple-throated baying, his monstrous bulk crouching in a cavern opposite. To him, seeing the snakes now bristling on his necks, the seer flung a morsel drowsy with honey and drugged meal. He, opening his triple throat in ravenous hunger, catches it when thrown and, with monstrous frame relaxed, sinks to earth and stretches his bulk over the entire den. The warder buried in sleep, Aeneas wins the entrance, and swiftly leaves the bank of that stream whence none return.

Not far from here, outspread on every side, are shown the Mourning Fields; such is the name they bear. Here those whom stern Love has consumed with cruel wasting are hidden. Among them, with wound still fresh, Phoenician Dido[96] was wandering in the great forest, and soon as the Trojan hero stood near and knew her, he shed tears, and spoke to her in tender love, "Unhappy Dido! Was the

---

[93] Only the dead who have been buried are permitted to pass immediately to the underworld; the unburied must wait a hundred years.

[94] Another name for Tartarus and the underworld.

[95] The three-headed dog who guards the underworld.

[96] The queen of Carthage, a native of Tyre in Phoenicia, who killed herself after Aeneas abandoned her, creating a pretext for the later enmity between the Carthaginians and Romans.

tale true then that came to me, that you were dead and had sought your doom with the sword? Was I, alas! the cause of your death? I swear by whatever is sacred that unwillingly, queen, I parted from your shores. Stay your step and withdraw not from our view." With these words Aeneas strove to soothe the wrath of the fiery, fierce-eyed queen. She, turning away, kept her looks fixed on the ground. At length she flung herself away and, still his foe, fled back to the shady grove where Sychaeus,[97] her lord of former days, responds to her sorrows and gives her love for love. Yet none the less, stricken by her unjust doom, Aeneas pities her as she goes.

At length they came to a land of joy, the pleasant lawns of the Elysian Fields.[98] Here an ampler ether clothes the meadows with roseate light, and they know their own sun, and stars of their own. Some disport their limbs on the grassy wrestling ground, vie in sports, and grapple on the yellow sand; some tread the rhythm of a dance and chant songs. Others he sees, to right and left, feasting on the sward, and chanting in chorus a joyous paean within a fragrant laurel grove, whence the full flood of the Eridanus[99] rolls upward through the forest. From afar Aeneas marvels at their phantom arms and chariots. These, as they streamed round, the Sibyl thus addressed, Musaeus[100] before all: "Say, happy souls, and you, best of bards, what, what place holds Anchises? For his sake are we come." And to her the hero thus made brief reply, "No one has a fixed home. We dwell in shady groves and in meadows fresh with streams. But if you wish, surmount this ridge, and soon I will set you on an easy path." He spoke and stepped on before, and from above points out the shining fields.

Deep in a green vale father Anchises was surveying with earnest thought the imprisoned souls and counting over the full number of his people and beloved children, their fates and fortunes, their works and ways. And as he saw Aeneas coming toward him over the meadow, he eagerly stretched forth both hands while tears streamed from his eyes and a cry fell from his lips, "Have you come at last, and has the duty that your father expected vanquished the toilsome way? Is it given me to see your face, my son, and hear and utter familiar tones? Over what lands, what wide seas have you journeyed to my welcome? What dangers have beset you, my son? How I feared the realm of Libya might work you harm!" And he answered: "Your sad shade, father, meeting me repeatedly, drove me to seek these portals. Grant me to clasp your hand, father, and withdraw not from my embrace!" So he spoke, his face wet with flooding tears. Thrice there he strove to throw his arms about his neck; thrice the form, vainly clasped, fled from his hands.

Meanwhile, in a retired vale, Aeneas sees a sequestered grove and rustling forest thickets, and the river Lethe[101] drifting past those peaceful homes. About it hovered peoples and nations unnumbered. Aeneas is startled by the sudden sight and asks the cause, "What is that river yonder, and who are the men thronging the banks in such a host?" Then said father Anchises, "Spirits they are to whom second bodies are owed by Fate. At the water of Lethe's stream they drink the soothing draught and long forgetfulness." "But, father, must we think that any souls pass aloft from here to the world above and return a second time to bodily fetters?" "I will surely tell you, my son, and keep you not in doubt," Anchises replies, "All these that you see, when they have rolled time's wheel through a thousand years, the god summons in vast throng to Lethe's river, so that, their memories effaced, they may once more revisit the vault above and conceive the desire of return to the body."

Anchises paused, and drew his son and with him the Sibyl into the heart of the assembly and

---

[97] A priest of Tyre and former husband of Dido; he was murdered by Dido's brother Pygmalion, who wanted to steal his treasure.

[98] The resting place of heroes and those who had led virtuous lives.

[99] A river often associated with the Po River in northern Italy; Vergil speaks of it as if it is in the underworld.

[100] A legendary philosopher and poet of Athens.

[101] The River of Forgetfulness.

buzzing throng, then chose a mound whence he might scan face to face the whole of the long procession, saying,[102] "Now then, the glory henceforth to attend the Trojan people, what children of Italian stock are held in store by fate, glorious souls waiting to inherit our name, this shall I reveal in speech and inform you of your destiny. The youth you see leaning on an untipped spear holds the most immediate place. The first to rise into the upper air with Italian blood in his vein will be Silvius[103] of Alban name, last-born of your children, whom late in your old age your wife Lavinia shall rear, a king and father of kings, with whom our people shall hold sway in Alba Longa. He next is Procas, pride of the Trojan nation, then Capys and Numitor, and he who will resurrect you by his name, Aeneas Silvius, no less eminent in goodness and in arms, if ever he come to reign over Alba.[104] What fine young men are these! Further, a son of Mars shall keep his grandsire company, Romulus, whom his mother Ilia shall bear of Assaracus' stock.[105] Lo, under Romulus' auspices, my son, shall that glorious Rome extend her empire to earth's ends, her ambitions to the skies, and shall embrace seven hills with a single city's wall, blessed in a brood of heroes. Turn hither now your two-eyed gaze, and behold this nation, the Romans that are yours. Here is Caesar and all the seed of Iulus[106] destined to pass under heaven's spacious sphere. And this in truth is he whom you so often hear promised you, Augustus Caesar, son of a god,[107] who will again establish a Golden Age in Latium amid fields once ruled by Saturn. He will advance his empire beyond the Garamantes[108] and Indians to a land that lies beyond our stars, where sky-bearing Atlas wheels on his shoulders the blazing star-studded sphere. Against his coming Caspian[109] realms and the Maeotic land[110] even now shudder at the oracles of their gods, and the mouths of sevenfold Nile[111] quiver in alarm."

"But who is he apart, crowned with sprays of live, offering sacrifice? Ah, I recognize the hoary hair and beard of that king of Rome[112] who will make the infant city secure on a basis of laws. Him shall Tullus[113] next succeed, the breaker of his country's peace, who will rouse to war an inactive folk and armies long unused to triumphs. Hard on his heels follows over-boastful Ancus,[114] who even now enjoys too much the breeze by popular favor. Would you also see the Tarquin kings,[115] the proud spirit of Brutus the Avenger,[116] and the fasces regained? He first shall receive a Consul's power and the cruel axes, and when his sons would stir up revolt, the father will hale them to

---

[102] Anchises now prophesies what the future of Aeneas and, descended from him, the Roman people will be.

[103] The son either of Aeneas himself or of Aeneas' son Ascanius; he succeeded Ascanius as king of Alba Longa.

[104] This list of kings is different from the traditional list, which has Aeneas Silvius as the son of Silvius, then Capys four generations, then Procas six generations after him, followed by his son Numitor.

[105] Romulus was the grandson of Numitor and son of Rhea Silvia, also known as Ilia. Assaracus was the brother of Illus, the founder of Troy.

[106] Iulus (Julius) was another name for Ascanius, the son of Aeneas. The Julian family of Julius Caesar and Octavian claimed descent from this Iulus and thus from Aeneas and the goddess Venus.

---

[107] Augustus was the adopted son of Julius Caesar, who was deified after his assassination in 44 BCE.

[108] A people of the western Sahara Desert.

[109] The Caspian Sea, to the east of the Black Sea.

[110] The Maeotian Lake, the modern Sea of Azov, a northern extension of the Black Sea.

[111] So called because the Nile had seven mouths in the Nile delta.

[112] Numa Pompilius (716–672 BCE), the second king of Rome, known for establishing Roman religion.

[113] Tullus Hostilius (672–640 BCE), the third king of Rome, known for wars.

[114] Ancus Martius (640–616 BCE), also known for wars.

[115] Two Etruscan kings, Tarquinius Priscus ("Tarquin the Old") (616–578 BCE) and Tarquinius Superbus ("Tarquin the Proud") (534–509 BCE), the last king of Rome. Omitted from Vergil's list is Servius Tullius (578–534), who reigned between the two Tarquins.

[116] In 509 BCE, Lucius Junius Brutus avenged the violation of Lucretia at the hands of Sextus Tarquin by masterminding the overthrow of the monarchy; he became one of the first two Roman consuls. He had had his sons executed for trying to overthrow the Republic.

execution in fair freedom's name, unhappy man, however later ages will extol that deed; yet shall a patriot's love prevail and unquenched thirst for fame."

"Now behold over there the Decii and the Drusi,[117] Torquatus[118] of the cruel axe and Camillus[119] bringing the standards home! But they whom you see, resplendent in matching arms, souls now in harmony and as long as they are imprisoned in night, alas, if once they attain the light of life, what mutual strife, what battles and bloodshed will they cause, the bride's father swooping from Alpine ramparts and Monoecus' fort, her husband confronting him with forces from the east![120] Steel not your hearts, my sons, to such wicked war nor vent violent valor on the vitals of your land. And you who draw your lineage from heaven, be you the first to show mercy; cast the sword from your hand, child of my blood!"

"He yonder,[121] triumphant over Corinth, shall drive a victor's chariot to the lofty Capitol, famed for Achaeans he has slain. Yon other[122] shall uproot Argos, Agamemnon's Mycenae, and even an heir of Aeacus, seed of mighty Achilles: he will avenge his Trojan sires and Minerva's polluted shrine.[123]

Who, lordly Cato,[124] could leave you unsung, or you, Cossus,[125] who the Gracchan[126] family or the two Scipios,[127] two thunderbolts of war and the ruin of Carthage, or Fabricius,[128] in penury a prince, or you, Serranus,[129] sowing seed in the soil? Where, O Fabii, do you hurry me all breathless? You are he, the mightiest,[130] who could, as no one else, through inaction preserve our state. Others, I doubt not, shall with softer lines beat out the breathing bronze, coax from the marble features to life, plead cases with greater eloquence, and with a pointer trace heaven's motions and predict the risings of the stars: you, Roman, be sure to rule the world, for these are your arts: to crown peace with justice, to spare the vanquished, and to beat down the proud."[131] Thus Father Anchises adds, "Behold how Marcellus[132] advances, graced with the spoils of the chief he slew, and towers triumphant over all! When the Roman state is reeling under a brutal shock, he will steady

---

[117] Two famous Roman families.

[118] Titus Manlius Torquatus, who in 361 defeated a huge Gaul in single combat, decapitated him, and acquired the torque that he wore around his neck, thus gaining the epithet "Torquatus" ("Torque-wearer") for himself and his descendents.

[119] Marcus Furius Camillus who, in a popular legend, was believed to have recaptured the Roman military standards from the Gauls who sacked Rome in 390 BCE.

[120] A reference to the civil war between Julius Caesar, who in 49 BCE invaded Italy via the Alps, and Pompey, who had married Caesar's daughter Julia. The town of Portus Monoeci is modern-day Monaco.

[121] Lucius Mummius, the Roman general who destroyed Corinth in 146 BCE.

[122] Lucius Aemilius Paullus, who defeated Perseus of Macedon at the Battle of Pydna in 168 BCE.

[123] A reference to the enmity between Romans and Greeks that supposedly went back to the Trojan War; the Greek hero Ajax the Lesser polluted the temple of Minerva (Athena) by carrying off Cassandra, daughter of King Priam of Troy, who had taken refuge there.

[124] Marcus Porcius Cato the Elder, Consul in 195 BCE and Censor in 184 BCE, whose constant advice that "Carthage must be destroyed" incited Rome to the Third Punic War (149–146 BCE).

[125] Aulus Cornelius Cossus, who in the mid-fifth century BCE became one of only three Roman generals to win the *spolia opima* for defeating an enemy commander in single combat.

[126] Represented by the brothers Tiberius and Gaius Gracchus, who in the years 133–121 BCE began the changes that led to the fall of the Roman Republic.

[127] Scipio Africanus, who defeated Hannibal in 202 BCE, and his grandson Scipio Aemilianus, who ended the Third Punic War in 146 BCE.

[128] Gaius Fabricius Luscinus, Consul in 282 and 278 and Censor in 275 BCE, known for his austerity and morality.

[129] Gaius Atilius Regulus Serranus, Consul during the First Punic War, in 257 and 250 BCE, who was said to have received the news of his election as Consul while he was sowing.

[130] Quinus Fabius Maximus, named Dictator after the Roman defeat at the Battle of Cannae in 216 BCE by the Carthaginian Hannibal.

[131] A sentiment that defines the Romans' vision of their mission, and arguably the most famous quotation from Roman literature.

[132] Marcus Claudius Marcellus was Consul five times in the last quarter of the third century BCE. During a war with the Gauls, Marcellus killed the opposing general and thus won the *spolia opima*. Marcellus is glorified here because he was an ancestor of the Marcus Claudius Marcellus who was the nephew of the emperor Augustus and an early choice to be Augustus' successor.

it, will ride down Carthaginians and the insurgent Gaul, and offer up to Father Quirinus[133] a third set of spoils." They wander at large over the whole region in the wide airy plain, taking note of all. After Anchises had led his son over every scene, kindling his soul with longing for the glory that was to be, he then tells of the wars that the hero next must wage.

Two gates of Sleep there are. One, they say, is horn and offers a ready exit to true shades, the other shines with the sheen of polished ivory, but delusive dreams issue upward through it from the world below. Thither Anchises, discoursing thus, escorts his son and with him the Sibyl, and sends them forth by the ivory gate. Aeneas speeds his way to the ships and rejoins his comrades, then straight along the shore he sails. The anchor is cast from the prow; the sterns stand ranged on the shore.

---

[133] An early god of the Roman state, being nearly on a par with Jupiter.

HORACE, "THE SECULAR HYMN"

In 86 CE the emperor Domitian celebrated the next Secular Games after those that Augustus had held in 17 BCE, not quite 110 years later. On the reverse of this *sestertius*, Domitian, on a dais, distributes to a man and child combustibles to be used for making ceremonial torches. The legend on the right reads "Ludi saeculares" ("Secular Games"), and the letters "SVEPD" are thought to mean "combustibles being distributed to the people."

In 17 BCE, as part of his attempt to normalize life in the Roman world, solidify his own position, and create a system of government that we know as the Roman Empire, Augustus celebrated a ceremony that was only held every 110 years or so, the Secular Games, a festival of renewal and purification held at a time when no one who was alive during the previous celebration was still alive. The poet Horace was commissioned to compose a hymn to commemorate the event.

Source: Stephen De Vere translation, in William Stearns Davis, *Rome and the West*
(Boston, New York, & Chicago: Allyn & Bacon, 1913), no. 58, 174–176.

Phoebus,[134] and Diana,[135] you whose sway,
Mountains and woods obey!
Twin glories of the skies,[136] forever worshiped,
     hear!
Accept our prayer this sacred year
When, as the Sibyl's[137] voice ordained

For ages yet to come,
Pure maids and youths unstained
Invoke the gods who love the sevenfold hills of
     Rome.
All bounteous Sun![138]
Forever changing, and forever one!
Who in your lustrous car bear'st forth light,
And hid'st it, setting, in the arms of Night,
Look down on worlds outspread, yet nothing
     see
Greater than Rome, and Rome's high sovereignty.

---

[134] Another name of the sun god Apollo.

[135] Goddess of the moon, Artemis to the Greeks.

[136] The sun and moon.

[137] A Sibyl (a prophetess) sold to King Tarquin the Proud a book of prophecies that were consulted in times of emergencies to find the proper expiatory rites needed to regain the favor of the gods.

---

[138] Apollo.

You Ilithyia,[139] too, whatever name,
Goddess, you do approve,
Lucina, Genitalis,[140] still the same
Aid destined mothers with a mother's love;
Prosper the Senate's wise recommendation,
Fertile of marriage faith and countless progeny![141]
 As centuries progressive wing their flight
For you the grateful hymn shall ever sound;
Thrice by day, and thrice by night
For you the choral dance shall beat the ground.
Fates! whose unfailing word
Spoken from Sibylline lips shall abide,
Ordained, preserved, and sanctified
By Destiny's eternal law, accord
To Rome new blessings that shall last
In chain unbroken from the Past.
Mother of fruits and flocks, prolific Earth!
Bind wreaths of spiked grain round Ceres'[142] hair:
And may soft showers and Jove's[143] benignant
    air
Nurture each infant birth!
Lay down your arrows, god of day!
Smile on your youths elect who singing pray.
You, Crescent Queen,[144] bow down your star-
    crowned head
And on your youthful choir a kindly influence
    shed.
If Rome be all your work, if Troy's[145] sad band
Safe sped by you attained the Etruscan strand,
A chosen remnant, vowed
To seek new Lares,[146] and a changed abode.
A remnant for whom through Ilium's[147] blazing
    gate

Aeneas,[148] orphan of a ruined State,
Opened a pathway wide and free
To happier homes and liberty.
Ye gods! If Rome be yours, to placid age
Give timely rest: to docile youth
Grant the rich heritage
Of morals, modesty, and truth.
On Rome herself bestow a teaming race
Wealth, empire, faith, and all befitting grace
Deliver to Venus' and Anchises' heir,[149]
Who offers at your shrine
Due sacrifice of milk-white kine[150],
Justly to rule, to pity and to dare,
To crush insulting hosts, the prostrate foeman
    spare.
The haughty Mede[151] has learned to fear
The Alban[152] axe, the Latian[153] spear,
And Scythians,[154] suppliant now, await
The conqueror's doom, their coming fate.
Honor and peace, and pristine shame,
And virtue's oft dishonored name,
Have dared, long exiled, to return,
And with them Plenty[155] lifts her golden horn.
Augur Apollo! Bearer of the bow!
Warrior and prophet! Loved one of the Nine!
Healer in sickness! Comforter in woe!
If still the templed crags of Palatine[156]
And Latium's fruitful plains to you are dear,
Perpetuate for cycles yet to come,

---

[139] Goddess of childbirth.

[140] Other names for the goddess of childbirth.

[141] Acting through the Senate, Augustus issued legislation favoring those who had children and penalizing those who did not.

[142] The goddess of grain; Demeter to the Greeks.

[143] Another name for Jupiter.

[144] Diana, Greek Artemis, goddess of the moon, was depicted with a lunar crescent in her hair.

[145] The Trojan refugees were ancestors of the Romans.

[146] Household gods.

[147] Another name for Troy.

---

[148] The Trojan hero Aeneas was the ancestor of Augustus.

[149] Aeneas was the son of the goddess Venus and the Trojan hero Anchises.

[150] Cattle.

[151] The Parthians, who ruled a huge empire east of the Roman Empire. Three years earlier Augustus had recovered from the Parthians the military standards lost by the general Crassus in 53 BCE, a huge propaganda coup.

[152] From Alba Longa, the town founded by Aeneas not far from the future site of Rome.

[153] Latium, the fertile plain on which Rome was situated.

[154] Augustus recently had received an embassy from the nomadic "Scythians" of southern Russia.

[155] Ops, the goddess of plenty and fertility.

[156] A hill of Rome that rises above the Forum; it was a posh residential district and the later site of imperial palaces.

Mightier in each advancing year,
The ever growing might and majesty of Rome.
You, too, Diana, from your Aventine,[157]
And Algidus[158] deep woods, look down and hear
The voice of those who guard the books divine,[159]

And to your youthful choir incline a loving ear.
Return we home! We know that Jove
And all the gods our song approve
To Phoebus and Diana given;
The virgin hymn is heard in Heaven.

---

[157] One of the hills of Rome, just southwest of the Palatine Hill.
[158] Part of a dormant volcano twelve miles southeast of
Rome, site of a famous battle between Rome and the Aequi
in 457 BCE.
[159] The Sibylline Books.

RES GESTAE DIVI AUGUSTI

One of the most historically significant texts preserved on stone, and one of the most effective pieces of propaganda ever produced, is the *Res gestae divi Augusti*, or *Deeds of the Deified Augustus*, an autobiographical account of his own achievements that Augustus wrote when he was seventy-six and instructed the Senate to post throughout the empire, in both Latin and Greek, after his death. This was done, but the *Res gestae* do not survive intact anywhere. The original bronze copy from the Forum in Rome is lost, and the surviving version had been pieced together from stone fragments found in Anatolia at Ancyra, where the best copy survives; Apollonia; Sardis; and Antioch in Pisidia.

Source: Frederick W. Shipley, trans., *Velleius Paterculus and Res Gestae Divi Augusti* (Cambridge, MA: Harvard Univ. Press, 1924), 344–405.

Below is a copy of the acts of the Deified Augustus by which he placed the whole world under the sovereignty of the Roman people, and of the amounts that he expended upon the state and the Roman people, as engraved upon two bronze columns[160] that have been set up in Rome.

At the age of nineteen, on my own initiative and at my own expense, I raised an army by means of which I restored liberty to the Republic, which had been oppressed by the tyranny of a faction.[161] For which service the Senate, with complimentary resolutions, enrolled me in its order, in the consulship of Gaius Pansa and Aulus Hirtius,[162] giving me at the same time consular precedence in voting[163]; it also gave me the *imperium*.[164] As Propraetor[165] it ordered me, along with the Consuls, "to see that the Republic suffered no harm."[166] In the same year, moreover, as both Consuls had fallen in war, the people elected me Consul and a Triumvir[167] for settling the constitution. Those who slew my father I drove into exile, punishing their deed by due process of law, and afterward when they waged war upon the Republic I twice defeated them in battle.[168]

Wars, both civil and foreign, I undertook throughout the world, and when victorious I spared all citizens who sued for pardon. The foreign nations that could with safety be pardoned I preferred to save rather than to destroy. The number of Roman citizens who bound themselves to me by military oath was about 500,000. Of these I settled in colonies or sent back into their own towns after their term of service, something more than 300,000, and to all I assigned lands or gave money as a reward for military service.

The dictatorship offered me by the people and the Roman Senate, in my absence and later when present, in the consulship of Marcus Marcellus and

---

[160] These columns no longer survive.

[161] Encompassing all of Augustus' enemies, including the assassins of Julius Caesar and the supporters of Mark Antony.

[162] In 43 BCE.

[163] Voting in the Senate was done in rank order; thus, those with the status of Consuls voted before those with the status of Praetors, and so on.

[164] The power to command armies.

[165] At this point in his career, Octavian never had held any office, but there were precedents for this kind of irregular grant, as when the later Triumvir Pompey was given the power of a Proconsul in 78 BCE in Spain.

[166] The "Last Recommendation of the Senate."

[167] The "Second Triumvirate"; the other two Triumvirs were Mark Antony and Marcus Aemilius Lepidus.

[168] At Philippi in Macedonia in 42 BCE Augustus, with critical assistance from his comrade Agrippa and Mark Antony, defeated the assassins Brutus and Cassius.

Lucius Arruntius[169] I did not accept. I did not decline at a time of the greatest scarcity of grain the charge of the grain-supply, which I so administered that, within a few days, I freed the entire people, at my own expense, from the fear and danger in which they were. The consulship, either yearly or for life, then offered me I did not accept. I refused to accept any power offered me that was contrary to the traditions of our ancestors. Those things that the Senate at that time wished me to administer I carried out by virtue of my tribunician power.[170]

To the day of writing this I have been *Princeps Senatus*[171] for forty years. I have been *Pontifex Maximus*,[172] Augur,[173] a member of the Fifteen Commissioners for Performing Sacred Rites, one of the Seven for Sacred Feasts, an Arval Brother,[174] a *Sodalis Titius*,[175] and a Fetial priest.[176] By Recommendation of the Senate my name was included in the Salian Hymn,[177] and it was enacted by law that my person should be sacred in perpetuity and that so long as I lived I should hold the tribunician power. When I returned from Spain and Gaul, in the consulship of Tiberius Nero and Publius Quinctilius,[178] after successful operations in those provinces, the Senate voted in honor of my return the consecration of an altar[179] to Pax Augusta in the Campus Martius, and on this altar it ordered the magistrates and priests and Vestal virgins to make annual sacrifice.

The Temple of Janus Quirinus, which our ancestors ordered to be closed whenever there was peace, secured by victory, throughout the whole domain of the Roman people on land and sea, and which, before my birth is recorded to have been closed but twice in all since the foundation of the city,[180] the senate voted to be closed three times during my Principate.[181]

I made twelve distributions of food from grain bought at my own expense, and in the twelfth year of my tribunician power I gave for the third time four hundred *sestertii*[182] to each man. To the municipal towns I paid money for the lands that I assigned to soldiers in my own fourth consulship[183] and afterward in the consulship of Marcus Crassus and Gnaeus Lentulus the Augur.[184] The sum that I paid for estates in Italy was about six hundred million *sestertii*, and the amount that I paid for lands in the provinces was about two hundred and sixty million. I was the first and only one to do this of all those who up to my time settled colonies of soldiers in Italy or in the provinces. And later, in the consulship of Tiberius Nero and Gnaeus Piso, likewise in the consulship of Gaius Antistius and Decimus Laelius, and of Gaius Calvisius and Lucius Passienus, and of Lucius Lentulus and Marcus Messalla, and of Lucius Caninius and Quintus Fabricius,[185] I paid cash gratuities to the soldiers whom I settled in their own towns at the expiration of their service, and for this purpose I expended four hundred million *sestertii* as an act of grace. I furnished from my own purse and my own patrimony tickets for grain and money, sometimes to a hundred thousand persons, sometimes to many more.

---

[169] In 22 BCE.

[170] A power that gave Augustus the right to introduce legislation, veto power, and the sacrosanctity of his person. It was renewed every year and later provided a means to date the years of an emperor's reign.

[171] The first person listed on the official list of the Senate, in rank order.

[172] Chief Priest of the Roman people.

[173] The Augurs were Roman priests charged with taking the auspices—that is, seeing the will of the gods in the flights of birds.

[174] The Arval Brothers were an ancient college of twelve priests who made sacrifices to ensure good harvests.

[175] Priests initially appointed by the Sabine king Titus Tatius.

[176] In the Roman Republic, the Fetials were priests were responsible for declaring war.

[177] A song sung in March of every year by the Salian priests.

[178] In 13 BCE. In 9 CE Publius Quinctilius Varus was defeated and killed by the Germans at the disastrous Battle of the Teutoburg Forest.

[179] The Altar of Peace, which still survives.

---

[180] First during the reign of King Servius Tullius, and then in 235 BCE, after the First Punic War.

[181] In 29, 25, and perhaps 7 BCE, highlighting the perception of Augustus as the one who had brought peace to the Roman world.

[182] About three months' wages for an ordinary worker.

[183] In 30 BCE.

[184] In 14 BCE.

[185] Between 7 and 2 BCE.

I built the *Curia*[186] and the Chalcidicum[187] adjoining it, the Temple of Apollo on the Palatine with its porticoes, the Temple of the deified Julius,[188] I restored the channels of the aqueducts that in several places were falling into disrepair through age, and doubled the capacity of the aqueduct called the Marcia by turning a new spring into its channel. I completed the Julian Forum.[189] On my own ground I built the Temple of Mars Ultor and the Augustan Forum[190] from the spoils of war.

Three times in my own name I gave a show of gladiators, and five times in the name of my sons or grandsons; in these shows there fought about ten thousand men. I conducted the Secular Games[191] in the consulship of Gaius Furnius and Marcus Silanus. In my own name, or that of my sons or grandsons, on twenty-six occasions I gave to the people, in the circus, in the Forum, or in the amphitheater, hunts of African wild beasts, in which about three thousand five hundred beasts were slain. I gave the people the spectacle of a naval battle beyond the Tiber, at the place where now stands the grove of the Caesars, the ground having been excavated for a length of eighteen hundred and a breadth of twelve hundred feet. In this spectacle thirty beaked ships, triremes or biremes, and a large number of smaller vessels met in conflict. In these fleets there fought about three thousand men exclusive of the rowers.

I freed the sea from pirates. About thirty thousand slaves, captured in that war, who had run away from their masters and had taken up arms against the Republic, I delivered to their masters for punishment.[192] I extended the boundaries of all the provinces that were bordered by peoples not yet subject to our empire.[193] The provinces of the Gauls, the Spains, and Germany, bounded by the ocean from Gades[194] to the mouth of the Elbe,[195] I reduced to a state of peace.[196] The Alps, from the region that lies nearest to the Adriatic as far as the Etruscan Sea, I brought to a state of peace without waging on any people an unjust war. My fleet sailed from the mouth of the Rhine eastward as far as the lands of the Cimbri[197] to which, up to that time, no Roman had ever penetrated either by land or by sea, and the Cimbri and Charydes and Semnones and other peoples of the Germans of that same region through their envoys sought my friendship and that of the Roman people. On my order and under my auspices two armies were led, at almost the same time, into Ethiopia and into Arabia that is called the "Happy,"[198] and very large forces of the enemy of both peoples were cut to pieces in battle and many towns were captured. Ethiopia was penetrated as far as the town of Napata, which is next to Meroë.[199] In Arabia the

---

[186] Augustus actually merely completed the rebuilding of the *Curia Julia*, or Julian Senate house, in Rome, which had been begun under Julius Caesar.

[187] An annex or addition to a building.

[188] After his assassination, Julius Caesar, the great-uncle and adoptive father of Augustus, was deified—that is, made into a god.

[189] The Forum of Julius Caesar, which adjoined the Republican Forum on one side and the even newer Forum of Augustus on the other side.

[190] The Forum of Augustus, built next to the Forum of Caesar, contained a temple to "Mars the Avenger" that Augustus had vowed to build if he was able to defeat the assassins of Caesar.

[191] A purification festival, held every 110 years or so, at a time when everyone alive at the time of last one was dead. Augustus celebrated it in 19 BCE and the poet Horace composed a celebratory hymn.

[192] The "pirates" and "slaves" are an allusion to Augustus' war with Sextus Pompey, the son of Pompey the Great, who occupied Sicily and competed with Augustus for power between 42 and 36 BCE.

[193] Augustus added more territory to the Roman Empire, especially in Pannonia (modern Hungary), than any earlier Roman. After his conquests, the empire went into a defensive posture and, with only a few exceptions, under the emperors Claudius (41–54) and Trajan (98–117), further wars of conquests virtually ceased.

[194] Modern Cadiz in Spain.

[195] A river running through Germany into the North Sea; Augustus dissembles here: this German territory later was lost, in 9 CE, in the revolt of Arminius..

[196] Augustus' attempt to expand to the Elbe River in Germany in fact failed disastrously in 9 CE when the charismatic German leader Arminius destroyed three legions at the Battle of the Teutoburg Forest.

[197] A voyage of exploration led by Augustus' stepson Tiberius in 5 CE.

[198] "Arabia Felix" ("Happy Arabia"); modern Yemen.

[199] In the Kingdom of Kush, on the Nile River south of Egypt.

army advanced into the territories of the Sabaeans to the town of Mariba.[200]

I settled colonies of soldiers in Africa, Sicily, Macedonia, both Spains, Achaea, Asia, Syria, Narbonese Gaul, and Pisidia.[201] Moreover, Italy has twenty-eight colonies founded under my auspices. The Parthians I compelled to restore to me the spoils and standards of three Roman armies,[202] and to seek as suppliants the friendship of the Roman people. These standards I deposited in the inner shrine that is in the Temple of Mars Ultor. The peoples of the Pannonians,[203] to which no army of the Roman people had ever penetrated before my Principate, having been subdued by Tiberius Nero who was then my stepson and my legate, I brought under the sovereignty of the Roman people, and I pushed forward the frontier of Illyricum as far as the bank of the river Danube. Embassies were often sent to me from the kings of India, a thing never seen before in the camp of any general of the Romans. Our friendship was sought, through ambassadors, by the Bastarnae[204] and Scythians,[205] and by the kings of the Sarmatians who live on either side of the river Tanaïs,[206] and by the Kings of the Albani[207] and of the Iberians[208] and of the Medes.[209]

In my sixth and seventh consulships,[210] when I had extinguished the flames of civil war, after receiving by universal consent the absolute control of affairs, I transferred the Republic from my own control to the will of the Senate and the Roman people. For this service on my part I was given the title of Augustus by Recommendation of the Senate, and the doorposts of my house were covered with laurels by public act, and a civic crown[211] was fixed above my door, and a golden shield was placed in the *Curia Julia*[212] whose inscription testified that the Senate and the Roman people gave me this in recognition of my Valor, my Clemency, my justice, and my Piety.[213] After that time I took precedence of all in rank, but of power I possessed no more than those who were my colleagues in any magistracy.

---

[200] In modern Yemen; the Sabaeans lived in the ancient kingdom of Sheba, whence came the Queen of Sheba who visited the Jewish king Solomon (1030–1000 BCE). Augustus neglects to mention that the invasion of Arabia and siege of Marib in 26–24 BCE were total disasters; most of the Roman army was lost to disease and battle.

[201] In Anatolia.

[202] The standards lost by the Roman Crassus at the Battle of Carrhae (53 BCE), recovered by Augustus in a treaty of 20 BCE, a huge propaganda coup.

[203] In modern Hungary.

[204] An ancient Celtic people dwelling north of the lower Danube River.

[205] Peoples of the southern Russian steppes.

[206] The Don River in southern Russia, flowing south into the Sea of Azov north of the Black Sea.

[207] A nomadic people living near the Caspian Sea.

[208] Inhabitants of Iberia (modern Georgia) in the Caucasus Mountains between the Black and Caspian seas.

[209] That is, the Parthians.

[210] 28–27 BCE.

[211] A crown of oak leaves awarded for saving the life of Roman citizens.

[212] The Senate house in Rome; construction was begun by Caesar and finished by Augustus.

[213] *Pietas*, or "dutifulness," was the greatest virtue that a Roman could demonstrate.

CHAPTER 8

JULIO-CLAUDIANS, FLAVIANS, AND THE CONSOLIDATION OF EMPIRE (14–96 CE)

The Principate—the Roman Empire as established by Augustus—inaugurated a period of more than two hundred years of peace and prosperity for the Roman world. During the first century of the Roman Empire, the period covered by the Julio-Claudian (27 BCE–14 CE) and Flavian (69–96) Dynasties, the policies instituted by Augustus in his creation of the Principate were consolidated and expanded. As fewer and fewer people even remembered what a functioning Republic had been like, the Republic faded into the past, and the Empire became the only show in town.

THE JULIO-CLAUDIAN DYNASTY (27 BCE–96 CE)

Augustus (27 BCE–14 CE) was the first in a long line of emperors of what modern historians call the Roman Empire. As a means of organizing the emperors, emperors who were related in some way to one another are grouped into dynasties. During the first century CE, two imperial dynasties, the **Julio-Claudian Dynasty** and the **Flavian Dynasty,** established the policies and principles that would guide the Roman Empire through its first three centuries. The Julio-Claudian emperors all were related in some manner to Augustus.

Under the Julio-Claudians, the Principate as established by Augustus was consolidated. Emperors obtained their powers in a package consisting of the greater proconsular *imperium* and the tribunician power. Political and social privilege gradually began to move out of Italy into the provinces. And an imperial bureaucracy that actually could manage the administration of the huge empire gradually coalesced. But problems arose with the lack of an established succession system; indeed, one of the curiosities about the Julio-Claudians is that even though the ideal succession pattern, from the point of view of the army, would

The Roman Empire during the reign of Claudius

have been for a son to succeed a father, none of the four Julio-Claudian emperors who followed Augustus was succeeded by a blood son. The Julio-Claudian dynasty also was marked by several ambitious imperial women, often with the title of Augusta, who played important roles in the selection of future emperors.

Tiberius (14–37)

Ultimately, the only choice for a successor left for Augustus was Livia's son and Augustus' stepson, Tiberius Claudius Nero. Augustus adopted him, making him Tiberius Julius Caesar, and granted him the power of a Tribune and the proconsular *imperium*. Tiberius also was made to divorce his wife Vipsania, the daughter of Agrippa, to whom he was happily married, and to marry Augustus' daughter Julia,

TABLE 8.1 DYNASTIES OF THE FIRST CENTURY

Julio-Claudian Dynasty

Augustus (27 BCE–14 CE)
Tiberius (14–37)
Caligula (37–41)
Claudius (41–54)
Nero (54–68)

Flavian Dynasty

Vespasian (69–79)
Titus (79–81)
Domitian (81–96)

who had a reputation for promiscuity and had unsuccessfully propositioned Tiberius while she was still married. After Augustus' death in 14 CE, Tiberius smoothly succeeded as emperor and at once offered to return to the Senate all the powers that Augustus had granted him. The Senate not only declined but granted to Tiberius all of the powers for life in a single package. This became the standard method by which later emperors received their authority. As a consequence, the historian **Tacitus** later claimed that the Senate had "rushed into servitude."

Like Augustus, Tiberius was an effective administrator. He was efficient and capable, and he had a strong sense of duty. He also was an excellent general, having campaigned extensively on the Danube and Rhine. On the other hand, however, he had difficulty getting along with people, and his long experience as the odd man out in the imperial selection process had given him a suspicious nature. Initially, he cooperated with the Senate, expanding its powers at the expense of the increasingly vestigial Republican popular assemblies. He did this, however, for his own convenience, deeming it easier to work with the Senate, to whom he could delegate authority, rather than with the more rambunctious, cumbersome, and unpredictable assemblies. But at the same time Tiberius, who preferred life in a military camp, was not a politician. He also offended the Senate by turning down many of the honors that were offered to him.

The beginning of Tiberius' reign was marked by some striking military success. His nephew Germanicus, son of his brother Drusus, led a raid of reprisal into Germany, buried the Roman dead at the site of the Battle of the Teutoburg Forest, and recovered the lost Roman standards. Tiberius, who did not need to prove his military prowess to anyone, did not, however, add any new territory to the empire.

Tiberius, like Augustus, had problems finding a successor who could outlive him. His popular nephew Germanicus died in 19 amid rumors of poisoning, and his son Drusus died in 23. The elder sons of Germanicus' wife Agrippina, Nero and another Drusus, then were tabbed. Meanwhile, the Praetorian Prefect **Sejanus** began to exercise increasing influence over the emperor. To increase his own power, Sejanus moved the guard into the *Castra praetoria*, the Praetorian Camp, right outside Rome. In 27 BCE, Tiberius visited the island of Capri, and Sejanus convinced him to remain there. Tiberius never returned to Rome. By the year 30, Agrippina and her sons were dead, and Sejanus, even though just an equestrian, plotted to seize the throne himself. Only in 31 did Tiberius learn of Sejanus' schemes when his sister-in-law Antonia, a daughter of Mark Antony, managed to send him a letter. He recruited Macro, another equestrian who served as Prefect of the Night Watch, to arrest and execute Sejanus and then promoted Macro to be Praetorian Prefect.

Tiberius' suspicions then grew by leaps and bounds, and he set an unfortunate precedent of giving a ready ear to **delators**, or informers, who received one-fourth of the estate of anyone convicted of treason whom they had informed on. When Tiberius died in 37, his parsimonious administration left a full treasury, but no successor had been named. Macro submitted the name of Gaius Julius Caesar Germanicus, the twenty-four-year-old youngest son of Agrippina and the great-grandson of Augustus, to the Senate, which had little choice but to concur. The young man had been born in the army camp of his father, Germanicus, and the little boots that the soldiers made for him resulted in the nickname by which he is better known: Caligula.

Caligula (37–41)

Caligula initially showed promise, recalling those who had been exiled by Tiberius. He also doubled the donative to the Praetorian Guard, raising it from the 250 *denarii* of Augustus to 500, or 20 *aurei* (gold pieces), a dangerous precedent that could suggest financial incentives in making new emperors. But Caligula then became seriously ill, and afterward he exhibited some bizarre behavior. For example, believing himself to be the god Jupiter, he decreed divine honors for himself. Caligula ignored the Senate and, it was said, even made his horse, Incitatus, a Consul.

Caligula also made some equally baffling domestic policy decisions. When Ptolemy, the popular king of Mauretania, pretentiously wore an attractive purple cloak while visiting a gladiatorial show in Rome, Caligula became jealous and immediately had him executed. The result was a serious four-year-long revolt in North Africa. Caligula also rashly ordered that a statue of himself be erected in the Jewish Temple in Jerusalem, something that surely would have led to revolt had it happened. The governor of Syria bravely delayed implementing the order until the client king Herod Agrippa, the grandson of Herod the Great and one of the few people Caligula trusted, was able to talk him out of it.

Eventually Caligula made an emperor's most fatal error: he antagonized the army. A commander on the Rhine was executed for treason, and a proposed invasion of Britain, intended to demonstrate Caligula's military talent, failed dismally. In the latter case, court gossip that Caligula sent soldiers gathering seashells so he could claim victory over Neptune probably misrepresent the use of crushed shells in cement for building lighthouses and seaport facilities. Early in 41 even the Praetorian Guard turned against him after he insulted a guard officer, and he was assassinated, marking the first time that the army had rid itself of an unwanted emperor. It would not be the last.

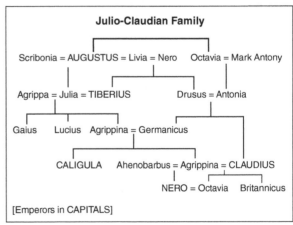

TABLE 8.2 THE JULIO-CLAUDIAN FAMILY

Claudius (41–54)

Once again, the army took matters into its own hands. While the Senate dithered, the Praetorian Guard declared as emperor Caligula's old uncle, Tiberius Claudius Nero, the son of Livia's son Drusus and Antonia, the daughter of Mark Antony. The Senate then had no choice but to confer imperial powers on Claudius. As a youth, Claudius had been afflicted with some type of disability, perhaps infantile paralysis, which left him with a limp and a stammer, and he had been kept very much in the background by the imperial family. As a result, he had taken up the study of ancient history, and had been tutored by the historian Livy. He wrote histories of the Carthaginians and Etruscans, although his proposed history of the civil wars was quashed by the imperial family. After becoming emperor, Claudius, given that he had not been adopted by any of the previous emperors, appropriated the name "Caesar" to advertise a connection to the ruling dynasty. And having been born in Gaul, at Lyon, Claudius became the only emperor of the first century not to have been born in Italy. Given his total reliance on the support of the Praetorian Guard, Claudius raised the donative to whopping 3,750 *denarii*, or 150 gold pieces.

In spite of being lampooned by the Senate for his infirmities, Claudius turned out to be a good administrator, and was popular with the people. He conciliated the Senate by taking his responsibilities seriously, attending meetings, participating in debates, and presiding at trials—even though hostile senatorial writers also accused him of falling asleep during the proceedings and issuing judgments contrary to the laws. He also revived the Senate's right to issue copper coinage. He issued many laws, including several protecting the rights of slaves. For example, in cases where slave owners abandoned sick slaves, the slaves were set free. And owners who killed slaves so they would not have to support them were charged with murder.

In the interest of running the state more efficiently, Claudius put his studies to good use. He extended Roman citizenship to peoples north of Italy and even admitted some Gauls into the Senate. He also relied on ex-slaves to fill important positions in the imperial bureaucracy, reasoning that they would be more loyal to him than powerful senators would be. Claudius gave particular attention to construction projects. He built two new aqueducts in Roma, a road all the way to the German frontier, a canal from the Rhine River to the North Sea, and a port city, "Portus," next to Ostia at the mouth of the Tiber River. This last provided a secure harbor for grain ships from Egypt needed to feed the burgeoning population of Rome. Claudius also established additional Roman colonies in the provinces, and during his reign, the population of Roman citizens increased by one million over what it had been in the reign of Augustus.

In an effort to demonstrate his military prowess, Claudius created a number of new provinces, mostly by annexing the territory of client rulers already dependent on Rome, including Mauretania in North Africa, Noricum on the upper

Danube, Thrace in the northern Balkans, Lycia and Pamphylia in Anatolia, and Judaea. As a consequence of this policy of infill, the empire now consisted of all of the territory up to the imperial frontiers (see map at beginning of chapter). On a much grander scale, Claudius also pursued some of Caligula's unfinished business by commencing in 43 CE the conquest of Britain, which was believed to be a good source of pearls, silver, and lead. The initial invasion force consisted of four legions under the general Plautius. Shortly afterward Claudius visited the front in person, and a temple at Camulodunum (Colchester) was erected in his honor.

Claudius also confronted various kinds of conspiracies, some of which resulted in the execution of senators. He also had domestic difficulties. In 48, his third wife Messalina was implicated in a conspiracy and executed, although their son Britannicus survived. Claudius then married his niece, another Agrippina, who was granted the title of Augusta. She had imperial ambitions for her own son Ahenobarbus, who took the name Nero after being adopted by Claudius and married his daughter Octavia. In 54, Claudius died, after eating poison mushrooms, some said. Agrippina then persuaded the Praetorian Guards with the same 150-gold-piece donative as Claudius to proclaim Nero as the next emperor. After his death, the writer Seneca the Younger made fun of his deification, saying that he had been turned into not a god but a pumpkin.

Nero (54–68)

Nero was only sixteen years old when he became emperor. He had had no administrative experience; indeed, his primary interests included singing accompanied by a lyre, acting, poetry, and chariot racing. In spite of his lack of aptitude for rule, Nero, like Caligula, began his reign auspiciously. Under the guidance of his mother Agrippina, the philosopher Seneca, and experienced administrators, informers were restrained, and the government ran efficiently. Soon, however, the situation worsened, as Nero's true character was revealed. He increasingly gave ear to those who catered to his more prurient interests. In the year 55, Claudius' young son Britannicus, who had a better claim to the throne than he, was poisoned. Then, in 59, desiring to take more direct control of the government, Nero attempted to murder Agrippina by means of a collapsible sailboat. But Agrippina was a good swimmer and made it to shore, where she was simply beaten to death. And in 62, at the instigation of his mistress Poppaea, he murdered his wife Octavia. At that point, Seneca saw the writing on the wall and retired.

Nero, meanwhile, toured the empire entering poetry and athletic competitions, including the Olympic Games. He invariably won the crown of victory, even if, as in the case of the Olympics, he was thrown from his chariot. Such activities, frowned on by the Senate, endeared him to the general populace. In 64, supposedly after Nero had decided to build a new palace in downtown

Rome, a great fire destroyed that very section of Rome. After he was suspected of setting the fire himself, Nero blamed the Christians, some of whom then were burnt alive—the standard punishment for arson—in what came to be known as the first imperial persecution of Christians. Nero then proceeded to build an elaborate two-hundred-acre partially underground palace known as the Golden House.

A number of military problems had to be confronted. In 60 CE, Roman heavy-handedness in Britain had fomented a revolt led by the charismatic queen of the Iceni **Boudicca**, who had united the disparate Celtic peoples. Initially, the Romans were caught off guard. The Celts destroyed the Roman colony of Camulodunum (Colchester). London and Verulamium (St. Albans) received similar treatment; a ten-inch layer of red clay from the burned houses of London still lies beneath London streets. After one cowardly legion refused to march, the Roman commander in Britain, Suetonius Paulinus, could assemble only ten thousand soldiers to face the hundred thousand Celts. At the Battle of Watling Street, Paulinus lined up his troops with his rear and flanks protected by forests. The Celts spent their energy on fruitless assaults on the Roman shield wall, and then the slaughter started. Eighty thousand Celts were killed and Boudicca poisoned herself. Having failed in their revolt, the Celts of Britain, like those of Spain, Pannonia, and Gaul, then accommodated themselves to Roman rule.

A series of wars with Parthia over who was to control the strategic territory of Armenia began in 58. According to the peace settlement of 63, the Armenian king was to be chosen by the Parthians but also was required to travel to Rome to receive his crown from the Roman emperor. The Parthian settlement made Nero particularly popular in the eastern provinces and led to a long period of peaceful relations with Parthia. After this propaganda coup, Nero ceremoniously closed the doors of the Temple of Janus in Rome in 66 CE, ritually signifying that the entire Roman world was at peace. But the temple doors did not stay closed very long at all.

In Judaea, many Jews had been just as resistant to being ruled by Romans as they had been to being ruled by Seleucids. Even though the Romans acknowledged Jewish religious sensibilities by exempting them from the requirement to sacrifice to the Cult of Rome and Augustus, religious conflicts still arose. Thus, in 66 CE, after the Romans plundered the Jewish temple following Jewish tax protests, and, in the same year that Nero closed the doors of the Temple of Janus, simmering tensions in Judaea boiled over. Jewish "Zealots" who advocated for armed resistance spearheaded the "Great Revolt" of the Jews. After a Roman legion was destroyed, Nero appointed the able general Vespasian, who had no connection to the imperial family, as commander of four legions to subdue the revolt. Initially avoiding Jerusalem, Vespasian methodically suppressed resistance in the rest of Judaea, and the revolt dragged on.

Meanwhile, conspiracies and military insurrections threatened Nero more directly. In 65, led by the senator Piso, senators disenchanted with Nero's

CULTURAL ENCOUNTERS

ROME CONFRONTS CHARISMATIC BARBARIAN LEADERS

Roman advances into European regions inhabited by Celts and other peoples followed a predictable pattern. Initially, the Romans would enjoy steady, if sometimes slow, military success. Then the initially disunited people being attacked would find a charismatic leader who would unite them in a great resistance against the Romans. The usual result was a Roman victory after which the territory then would be annexed by the Romans and the people would accommodate themselves to Roman rule. But the Romans were not invincible. On occasion, the people being attacked remained independent, once after a Roman defeat, and once when the Romans withdrew of their own volition.

TABLE 8.3 BARBARIAN LEADERS WHO RESISTED ROME

Leader	People	Date	Place	Battle Result	End Result
Viriathus	Celts	130s BCE	Spain	Roman victory	Roman annexation
Vercingetorix	Celts	52 BCE	Gaul	Roman victory	Roman annexation
Bato (2)	Illyrians	6–9 CE	Pannonia	Roman victory	Roman annexation
Arminius	Germans	9 CE	Germany	Roman defeat	Roman withdrawal
Boudicca	Celts	61 CE	Britain	Roman victory	Roman annexation
Calgacus	Caledonians	84 CE	Caledonia	Roman victory	Roman withdrawal

increasingly autocratic rule and perhaps even wanting to restore the Republic spawned a plan to assassinate the emperor. The plot was betrayed by a freedman, and some twenty senators and equestrians were executed or, like the philosopher Seneca, forced to commit suicide—an option that saved them from the disgrace of execution and preserved their property for their families. Then, in 67–68 CE, Vindex, a Gaul who had been made a senator by Claudius and then appointed a Roman governor, revolted because of Nero's tax policies and encouraged Galba, a governor in Spain, to become emperor. Vindex was quickly defeated and killed by Verginius Rufus, the commander of the legions on the Rhine, whose troops then hailed him as emperor. Verginius declined the offer, but it was a bad sign for Nero.

Back in Rome, the Praetorian Guard declared its support for Galba. Nero, in disguise, fled to the countryside. When the news came that the Senate had declared him a public enemy, Nero proposed to take the honorable way out and commit suicide but did not have the courage. One of his loyal freedmen did the job for him, and Nero's last words supposedly were, "What an artist dies in me." The Senate got the last word by inflicting on Nero a pronouncement of "Damnation of Memory." But in the eastern provinces, Nero was sorely missed, and a belief lasting for hundreds of years arose that Nero would be reborn and that the Golden Age of Nero would return. In the next decade, a number of false Neros even attempted to raise eastern revolts.

The Year of the Four Emperors

The death of Nero brought the Julio-Claudian Dynasty to an end. There were no family members left as obvious candidates for the throne, and the Roman Empire was up for grabs. According to Tacitus, the armies now learned the "secret of Empire": that emperors could be made in other places than Rome. The year 69 became known as the **Year of the Four Emperors**. The first claimant was Galba, but the Rhine legions refused to recognize him and nominated their own commander, Vitellius, instead. Meanwhile, at Rome, Galba's onetime supporter Otho, whose wife Poppaea Nero had taken as his mistress, bribed the Praetorian Guard to lynch him, and Otho immediately was recognized as emperor by the Senate. Soon thereafter, Vitellius' army arrived in northern Italy and defeated Otho, who committed suicide, and Vitellius was duly acknowledged as emperor. But meanwhile the battle-hardened eastern armies had named their own candidate, Vespasian, the commander in Judaea. The powerful Danubian legions followed suit and seized Rome. Vitellius was killed, and Vespasian then was duly granted imperial powers by the Senate.

THE FLAVIAN DYNASTY (69–96 CE)

Vespasian then established the Flavian Dynasty (69–96), which consisted of himself and his two sons, Titus and Domitian. This marked the first father-to-son succession to the throne. Vespasian was a new kind of emperor. He was descended not from an old-line senatorial family, but rather from an Italian equestrian background, and had risen to power in the army. The Flavian Dynasty thus represents an opening up of all of the political and military offices, even the emperorship, to an increasingly broader spectrum of individuals.

Vespasian (69–79)

Vespasian came from an equestrian family: his grandfather Petro, for example, had held only the rank of Centurion in the army of Pompey, and then had become a debt collector. His father Sabinus had been a moneylender and tax collector. Vespasian himself undertook a senatorial career, being elected as Quaestor, Aedile (on his second try), and Praetor. His close relationship with Antonia Caenis, a freedwoman of Antonia, the mother of the emperor Claudius, no doubt helped his political career. His subsequent success as a general gained him the office of Consul in 51 CE. After a period of retirement, Vespasian was called back into service in 66 CE to suppress the revolt of the Jews. Many people thought that a popular eastern prophecy that the ruler of the world would come from Judaea applied to Vespasian, who himself, after hearing of the prophecy from the Jewish historian Josephus, seems to have believed this interpretation. In 69 he was declared emperor by his troops, making him the fourth emperor in the "Year of the Four Emperors."

While he was still fighting Vitellius, Vespasian was confronted by a revolt by the Batavians, a Germanic people living in the Rhine delta who were Roman allies and supplied many recruits for the Roman *auxilia*. Led by the chieftain Civilis, the Batavians took advantage of the Roman civil wars to avenge past insults and mistreatment by the Romans. Other local peoples followed suit. Two Roman legions were first defeated and later destroyed. Refusing an offer of independence from Vespasian, Civilis pressed on with the revolt, which spread to Gaul. A certain Julius Sabinus, who claimed to be a descendent of Caesar, raised a further short-lived revolt. In 70 CE, after securing his own position, Vespasian assembled a huge army of eight legions to deal with the rebels, and the Batavians soon capitulated. In the same year, Jerusalem fell to the besieging Roman armies, now led by Vespasian's son Titus, and the **Jewish temple** was sacked and destroyed.

Vespasian, in an attempt to make a connection with Augustus, portrayed himself as one who had brought peace to the Roman world after a period of civil war. To advertise this, he not only issued large numbers of coins but also built a new forum, the Forum of Peace, at Rome. Vespasian also began construction of what would become the most enduring monument constructed by the Flavians, the Flavian Amphitheater, or Colosseum, which was erected in an attempt to satiate the increasing Roman appetite for blood sports ranging from gladiatorial contests to staged wild beast hunts.

Vespasian was a competent administrator. Confronted with the need to restore the empire's finances after Nero's extravagances and over a year of civil war, he raised taxes in the provinces and confiscated the tax that Jews in the past had paid to the now-destroyed temple in Jerusalem. Vespasian also gained a reputation, no doubt influenced by his and his family's financial experience, for his thriftiness. When he was mocked for having instituted a "urine tax" on public latrines, he reportedly replied, "Money doesn't smell." The government then sold the collected urine to fullers, launderers who, because of its ammonia content, used it for cleaning clothing. In the provinces, Vespasian continued Claudius' policy of expanding Roman rights, granting Latin status to Spain and admitting additional senators from the provinces. Vespasian also fulfilled his duty to expand the empire by having the general Agricola begin an advance into Caledonia (Scotland).

Public urinals are still called vespasiani *in Italy and* vespasiennes *in France.*

Vespasian's reign also saw an expansion of the professional bureaucracy. Secretarial and finance work now tended to be done by equestrians rather than by ex-slaves. The bureaucracy eventually became large and entrenched enough to be able to survive relatively catastrophic changes at the top. At the same time, the status of the Senate continued its inexorable decline. The emperors' consultations came to have more show than substance. The increasing incorporation of non-Italians and proven administrators, who were beholden to the emperors, meant that the Senate had less internal cohesiveness and fewer anti-imperial sentiments. In 79 CE, Vespasian became ill and died: his last words were said to have been, "Oh my, I think that I am becoming a god," a reference to his expected deification after his death. Vespasian, the first emperor who had biological sons, then was smoothly succeeded by his elder son, Titus.

Titus (79–81) and Domitian (81–96)

The emperor Titus (79–81) was popular but short-lived. He had had been left with the task of suppressing the Jewish Revolt after his father had departed for Rome. This he soon accomplished with the capture and sack of Jerusalem in 70 CE, although one group of Jews held out in the fortress of Masada until 74 CE, when the fortress was stormed by the Romans and nearly every Jew committed suicide. During his stay in Judaea, Titus began a well-publicized twelve-year relationship with Berenice, the daughter of the Jewish king Herod Agrippa (41–44 CE) and the sister of the Jewish king Herod Agrippa II (48–73), who supported Vespasian during the Jewish Revolt. Berenice actively participated in government, sharing power with Agrippa II, in much the same manner as the capable women of the Ptolemaic dynasty of Egypt.

Upon his return to Rome, Titus was assigned the politically sensitive position of Praetorian Prefect. Titus then became the first Roman emperor actually to succeed his father. He was a popular emperor. Under Titus, the Colosseum was completed and marked by a hundred straight days of games in which nine thousand wild animals were killed. After the massive eruption of Mt. Vesuvius in 79 CE that buried the cities of **Pompeii** and Herculaneum on the Bay of Naples in Italy, Titus gained additional popularity for his relief efforts. Titus likewise was praised for the support he provided after another great fire in Rome in 80 CE that destroyed, among other buildings, the Pantheon built by Agrippa. And Titus was especially well liked for refusing to listen to delators and for halting the treason trials that had led to the executions of so many senators.

After dying unexpectedly of a fever, Titus was succeeded by his younger brother Domitian (81–96), who previously had been kept in the background, receiving honorary titles such as that of Suffect (replacement) Consul while Titus held positions with actual authority and duties. Domitian thus developed something of an inferiority complex. Nevertheless, when he became emperor, Domitian proved to be a good administrator who was popular with the soldiers—he raised their pay from 225 to 300 *denarii*—and the provincials. His fiscal policies included a revaluation of the *denarius* in which he restored both the weight and silver content, both of which had fallen beginning during the reign of Nero. This revaluation was underwritten by more efficient tax-collection procedures.

Under Domitian, the empire reached its farthest extent in Britain. In 83 CE, the Roman general Agricola defeated the Caledonians led by their charismatic leader Calgacus at the Battle of Mount Graupius. Agricola was on the verge of conquering

A PICTURE IS WORTH A THOUSAND WORDS

THE SACK OF JERUSALEM (70 CE)

One of the most grandiose means by which Roman emperors advertised their greatest military victories was by constructing monumental triumphal arches, usually in Rome, but in other places as well. This was the case after the Jewish Revolt of 66 CE was savagely repressed with the capture and sack of the ancient Jewish capital city of Jerusalem in 70 CE by Titus, the son of the new emperor Vespasian. The Romans also were said to have looted fifty tons of gold and silver from Jerusalem. After becoming emperor in 79 CE, the emperor Titus erected the "Arch of Titus" in Rome to commemorate his victory. This relief from the inside of the arch depicts the sack of the Jewish temple in Jerusalem and shows Roman soldiers carrying off of the great golden seven-branched Menorah, silver trumpets, and the golden Table of Showbread, or offering table, where twelve loaves of bread were constantly displayed and which, according to the Jewish historian Josephus, "weighed many talents." The temple treasures then were put on display in Vespasian's Temple of Peace, where they remained for centuries.

The fate of the temple treasures has intrigued observers ever since antiquity. According to one tradition, they are still in Rome, hidden underneath the Vatican. Other traditions tell different stories. In one, the Table of Showbread ended up with the Visigoths, probably seized during the sack of Rome in 410, from whom it was taken by the Muslim conquerors of Spain in 711 CE. It then was presented to the Muslim Caliph in Damascus. But the most reliable sources indicate that the surviving Jewish temple treasures were looted by the Vandals during their sack of Rome in 455 BCE. The treasures then were repatriated and taken to Constantinople when the emperor Justinian destroyed the Vandal kingdom in 534. After the temple treasures had been displayed in the triumphal procession of general Belisarius, Justinian then sent them to Christian churches in Jerusalem. And meanwhile, the Jewish temple in Jerusalem was never rebuilt, although its western foundations, called the "Wailing Wall," survive as the most sacred site in modern Judaism.

DIGGING ANTIQUITY

POMPEII

A fresco from Pompeii depicts an incident where a contest between the gladiatorial teams of Pompeii and Nuceria led to a riot in which fans (much like modern soccer hooligans) fought one another both inside and outside the arena. Nero punished the participants by shutting down the Pompeii amphitheater for ten years.

During the first century, Pompeii, located on the Bay of Naples in central Italy, was a city just like many cities of the early Principate, home to some twenty thousand people. The city lay at the foot of Mt. Vesuvius, a semi-dormant volcano that had produced recent earthquakes but no eruptions. On 24 August 79 CE, the volcano spectacularly erupted. Superheated gas, ash, mud, and rock known as pyroclastic flow inexorably surged down the mountainside and smashed into the city at a temperature of about 650 degrees Fahrenheit (340 degrees Celsius). Volcanic ash filled the air,

blinding the inhabitants. Some people escaped to the seacoast and were rescued by Roman naval vessels. Indeed, the commander of the Roman naval contingent, Pliny the Elder, stayed too long on the shore conducting scientific observations and was himself killed by the poisonous fumes. Meanwhile, other inhabitants took refuge underground, only to be asphyxiated by the toxic gases. Still others died in collapsing buildings. The entire city soon was covered by a thick layer of ash, rock, and mud. Over half the inhabitants were killed. The buried city was not rediscovered until 1599, and archaeological excavations, which continue until the present, were commenced in 1748.

The city preserves the tiniest details of everyday life. Like most Roman cities, Pompeii had a forum, a theater, an aqueduct, public baths, a senate house, a temple of the imperial cult, and even its own small amphitheater for gladiatorial contests. The poor lived in large apartment buildings, the rich in in-town villas built around a central garden. The streets were laid out on a grid plan, at right angles to each other. Stepping-stones allowed inhabitants to cross the streets without stepping in the animal droppings and other refuse that littered the streets; sewers under the streets carried away the waste when it rained. Street-corner lunch counters served soup, vegetables, and beverages. Vendors sold round loaves of bread. Street musicians entertained passersby. A mosaic at the front entrance to a house depicts a dog and the warning, "Beware the dog." Graffiti carved into the walls preserve the actual words of inhabitants, such as "Restitutus was here with his brother," "Marcus loves Spendusa," and "Money doesn't smell," a saying attributed to the emperor Vespasian. Like no other Roman remains, Pompeii brings the Romans back to life for us.

the last bit of Caledonia (Scotland) when he was recalled ostensibly because of troubles on the Danube, but more likely because the ever-suspicious Domitian, whose father had been declared emperor by a distant army, was concerned about this general becoming too popular with the troops. The northernmost reaches of Britain were abandoned and later served as a staging ground for raids into Roman territory.

On the other hand, however, the area between the Rhine and Danube was occupied and fortified and rendered mostly peaceful for the next 150 years.

In Rome, however, Domitian was not loved by the Senate, who saw him as excessively suspicious and autocratic. He was said to have liked being addressed as "lord and god," and he did not accord the Senate the same respect as had Vespasian and Titus. He underlined the shift of the center of power from the Senate house to the palace by constructing a new imperial palace on the Palatine Hill. Domitian also incurred senatorial hostility by his efficient administration, which curtailed corruption in the provinces. A failed revolt in 88 by Saturninus, a general on the Rhine, resulted in a return of the delators, and in 95 Domitian's two cousins were executed for conspiracy. In 96, his wife Domitia, fearing for her own safety, induced a palace servant to stab Domitian to death while he was engrossed in reading a bogus report of a conspiracy. Domitian then suffered Damnation of Memory at the hands of the Senate. Because he had not named a successor, the Roman Empire once more was in a precarious position, where both the Senate and the army were going to want to have a voice in the choice of the next emperor.

THE ORIGINS OF CHRISTIANITY

It was in the multicultural, multi-religion Roman world, in a world of peace, prosperity, and easy communications for thousands of miles, that a new religion arose in the early years of the Roman Empire: Christianity. The Roman client king Herod the Great (41 BCE–4 CE) ruled the Jews during a period when many Jews were expecting the arrival of a Messiah, or the **Christ** ("the anointed one"), who would restore their independence, lead them to glory, and bring world peace.

Jesus of Nazareth

A number of Jews were seen as possible Messiahs. About 3 CE, for example, a shepherd named Athronges, along with his four brothers, initiated a short-lived Jewish insurrection, directed as much against the Jewish monarchy as against the Romans, that consisted primarily of guerilla attacks. Two other would-be Messiahs are mentioned in the Christian New Testament. Judas the Galilean led an insurrection around 6 CE when the Roman governor imposed new taxes; he was thought to have established the Jewish Zealots, who advocated military resistance against the Romans. A certain Theudas, on the other hand, led a minor insurrection with four hundred followers in the 40s CE. All of these putative Messiahs were associated with armed revolts and all soon were killed.

Another individual identified as the Jewish Messiah—that is, the Christ—who behaved rather differently was Yeshua bar Yosef (Jesus, son of Joseph), better known as **Jesus of Nazareth**, a distant descendent of the Hebrew King David (960–930 BCE). Jesus' teachings that he was the son of God; that the kingdom of God was open to all equally, including the unprivileged; and that the old covenant with Jewish god Yahweh now was to be replaced by a new covenant based on faith in God, brought the enmity of the Sanhedrin, the Jewish governing council, who saw him as a frightening revolutionary. But Jesus never advocated military revolt; indeed, by his famous statement, "Render to Caesar that which is Caesar's," a reference to tax payment, Jesus showed himself to favor compromise with the Romans. Jesus thus was found innocent of the charges against him by the Roman Prefect **Pontius Pilate**, but in order to avoid offending the fractious Jews, Pilate nonetheless consented to Jesus' execution circa 28 CE. After he rose from the dead, it was said, Jesus' followers, who came to be known as Christians—that is, the followers of Christ—continued to proselytize on his behalf.

Christians and Jews

HISTORICAL CAUSALITY

To what extent do you think that the spread of Christianity was affected by the nature of the Roman Empire at the time it arose?

The early Christians retained much in common with their Jewish forebears. They prospered in urban environments: soon, many large cities had Christian communities led by a **bishop**. They had an ethical and moral code for guiding one's life. They preserved their beliefs in written scriptures, now known as the **New Testament**. And Christianity provided a social support system for the underprivileged and a community that held regular communal worship services. Unlike Jews, however, Christians competed with non-Christian mystery cults with their promise of a happy life after death. Their concept of forgiveness for sins also was very popular. And, under the leadership of the apostle Paul, Christians opened up conversion to gentiles, or non-Jews. Doing so gave Christianity the potential to become an empire-wide religion embracing all of the manifold peoples of the empire.

Initially, Romans thought that Christians were just another kind of Jew, had a hard time distinguishing Christians from Jews, and took little notice of them. In the Roman sources, the earliest possible surviving reference to Christians comes from Suetonius, who reported that during the reign of Claudius, "The Jews made disturbances at the instigation of Chrestus" and were expelled from Rome. Their next appearance comes in Tacitus' account of how Nero accused them of setting the "great fire" in Rome in 64 and severely punished them. The general Roman population also had many misconceptions about Christian worship, believing, for example, that they were cannibals because they ate the flesh and drank the blood of their god and that they practiced incest because they called each other "brother" and "sister." As time went on, however, Christians became more and more a part of the mainstream of Roman life.

This graffito, dating to the third century CE and discovered on the Palatine Hill in Rome in 1857, depicts a human figure with a donkey head attached to a cross. Another figure stands to the left, and an inscription in Greek reads, "Alexamenos worships his god." Next to it, in another hand, Alexamenos himself replied, this time in Latin, "Alexamenos is faithful." These kinds of exchanges between pagans and Christians would have been more and more commonplace as Christianity became increasingly widespread.

⇐ LOOKING BACK

During the first century of the Roman Empire, the period covered by the Julio-Claudian (27 BCE–14 CE) and Flavian (69–96) Dynasties, the policies instituted by Augustus in his creation of the Principate were consolidated and expanded. A functioning Republic became a thing of the past, of primarily antiquarian interest, that no one had any personal experience with. Two important processes now were under way: first, the increasing accumulation of authority in the hands of the emperor at the expense of the Senate, and second, a gradual shift in the balance of power between Italy and the provinces, assisted in particular by massive grants of Roman citizenship to provincial populations, in which authority and status increasingly filtered into the provinces at the expense of Italy.

LOOKING AHEAD ⇒

For the Romans, the best was yet to come. The second century CE would bring the Roman Empire to its height with a series of exceptionally well-qualified emperors.

FURTHER READING

Balsdon, J. P. V. D. *Roman Women: Their History and Habits.* Westport, CT: Greenwood Press, 1962.

Barrett, A. A. *Caligula: The Corruption of Power.* New Haven, CT: Yale Univ. Press, 1989.

Bauman, R. *Women and Politics in Ancient Rome.* New York: Routledge, 1992.

Brunt, P. A. "Lex de Imperio Vespasiani." *Journal of Roman Studies* 67 (1977), 95–116.

Champlin, Edward. *Nero.* Cambridge, MA: Harvard Univ. Press, 2005.

Ferrill, A. *Caligula, Emperor of Rome.* London: Thames & Hudson, 1991.

Gradel, Ittai. *Emperor Worship and Roman Religion.* Oxford: Oxford Univ. Press, 2002.

Griffin, Miriam T. *Nero: The End of a Dynasty.* New Haven, CT: Yale Univ. Press, 1985

Keay, S., and N. Terrenato, eds. *Italy and the West: Comparative Issues in Romanization.* Oxford: Oxbow, 2001.

Lenowitz, Harris. *The Jewish Messiahs: From the Galilee to Crown Heights.* New York: Oxford Univ. Press, 1998.

Levick, Barbara. *Claudius.* New Haven, CT: Yale Univ. Press, 1990.

Levick, Barbara. *Tiberius the Politician.* London: Thames & Hudson, 1976.

Levick, Barbara. *Vespasian.* London: Routledge, 2005.

Mellor, Ronald, ed. *From Augustus to Nero: The First Dynasty of Imperial Rome.* Ann Arbor: Michigan State Univ. Press, 1990.

Millar, Fergus. *The Emperor in the Roman World.* London: Duckworth, 2003.

Momigliano, A. *Claudius: The Emperor and his Achievement.* 2nd ed. Oxford: Oxford Univ. Press, 1961.

Morgan, G. *69 A.D. The Year of the Four Emperors.* London: Oxford Univ. Press, 2006.

Price, J. J. *Jerusalem under Siege: The Collapse of the Jewish State.* Leiden, Netherlands: Brill, 1992.

Rhodes, Kevin W. *A Consequence of Legitimacy: Domitian's Conflict with the Senate, and the Imperial Cult's Conflict with Christianity.* Cleburne, TX: Hopkins Publishing, 2014.

Southern, Pat. *Domitian: Tragic Tyrant.* London: Routledge, 2009.

SOURCES

SUETONIUS, *LIFE OF CALIGULA*

A *sestertius* of the emperor Caligula depicts his three sisters, Agrippina, Drusilla, and Julia, on the reverse. Caligula undeniably was very fond of them and subsequently was accused of incest with all of them.

In 37 CE, at the age of twenty-four, Gaius Julius Caesar Augustus Germanicus succeeded Tiberius as emperor. He was the first, but by no means the last, emperor to have had no formal training for the position and whose only qualification was to be a member of the right family. He was known either as Gaius, his *praenomen*, or as Caligula, a nickname given him as a toddler by soldiers who had made little boots for him modeled on the *caligae* (boots) of the soldiers. In the course of his brief four-year reign he became known for bizarre behavior, especially after he suffered and recovered from a mysterious illness, which was gleefully reported by Suetonius, an imperial biographer and court gossip who wrote in the 130s CE.

Source: J. C. Rolfe, trans., *Suetonius. Volume I: The Lives of the Caesars* (Cambridge, MA: Harvard Univ. Press, 1914).

H e began from that time [1] on to lay claim to divine majesty, for after giving orders that such statues of the gods as were especially famous for their sanctity or their artistic merit, including that of Jupiter of Olympia, should be brought from Greece in order to remove their heads and put his own in their place, he built out a part of the palace as far as the Forum, and making the Temple of Castor and Pollux its vestibule he often took his place between the divine brethren, and exhibited himself there to be worshipped by those who presented themselves; some hailed him as Jupiter Latiaris. At night he used constantly to invite the full and radiant moon to his embraces and his bed, whereas in the daytime he would talk confidentially with Jupiter Capitolinus, now whispering

---

[1] After recovering from some kind of mystery illness.

and then in turn putting his ear to the mouth of the god, now in louder and even angry language, for he was heard to make the threat, "Lift me up, or I'll lift you." Finally won by entreaties, as he reported, and even invited to live with the god, he built a bridge over the Temple of the Deified Augustus, and thus joined his palace to the Capitol.[2] When his grandmother Antonia[3] asked for a private interview, he refused it except in the presence of the Prefect Macro,[4] and by such indignities and annoyances he caused her death, although some think that he also gave her poison. After she was dead, he paid her no honor, but viewed her burning pyre from his dining-room. He had his brother Tiberius put to death without warning, suddenly sending a Tribune of the Soldiers to do the deed; besides driving his father-in-law Silanus to end his life by cutting his throat with a razor. As for his uncle Claudius,[5] he spared him merely as a laughingstock.

He lived in habitual incest with all his sisters, and at a large banquet he placed each of them in turn below him whereas his wife reclined above.[6] Of these he is believed to have violated Drusilla when he was still a minor, and even to have been caught lying with her by his grandmother Antonia, at whose house they were brought up in company. Afterward, when she was the wife of Lucius Cassius Longinus, an ex-Consul, he took her from him and openly treated her as his lawful wife. When ill, he made her heir to his property and the throne. The rest of his sisters he did not love with so great affection, nor honor so highly, but often prostituted them to his favorites, so that he was the readier at the trial of Aemilius Lepidus[7] to condemn them as adulteresses and privy to the conspiracies against him.

It would be trivial and pointless to add to this an account of his treatment of his relatives and friends, Ptolemy, son of king Juba, his cousin, for he was the grandson of Marcus Antonius by Antonius' daughter Selene,[8] and in particular Macro himself and even Ennia, who helped him to the throne[9]; all these were rewarded for their kinship and their faithful services by a bloody death. He was no whit more respectful or mild toward the Senate, compelling some who had held the highest offices to run in their togas for several miles beside his chariot and to wait on him at table, standing napkin in hand either at the head of his couch, or at his feet. Others he secretly put to death, yet continued to send for them as if they were alive, and after a few days falsely asserting that they had committed suicide.

The following are special instances of his innate brutality. When cattle to feed the wild beasts that he had provided for a gladiatorial show were rather costly, he selected criminals to be devoured. Many men of honorable rank were first disfigured with the marks of branding-irons and then condemned to the mines, to work at building roads, or to be thrown to the wild beasts, or else he shut them up in cages on all fours, like animals, or had them sawn into pieces. Not all these punishments were for serious offenses, but merely for criticizing one of his shows, or for never having sworn by his Genius.[10]

He seldom had anyone put to death except by numerous slight wounds, his constant order, which soon became well-known, being, "Strike so that he may feel that he is dying." When a different man than he had intended had been killed, through a mistake in the names, he said that the victim too had deserved the same fate. He often uttered the familiar line of the tragic poet, "Let them hate me,

---

[2] The Temple of Jupiter atop the Capitoline Hill.

[3] The daughter of Mark Antony and Octavia, sister of Augustus.

[4] The Praetorian Prefect, commander of the ten thousand elite troops stationed just outside Rome.

[5] Roman emperor 41–54 CE, the successor of Caligula

[6] At a Roman dinner party, three couches were arranged in a "∩" shape; here, Caligula occupied the "low" couch on the left, where the host reclined, whereas his wife was on the "high" couch on the right.

[7] Initially a confidant of Caligula and even named as his heir, he fell out of favor and was executed for conspiracy in 39 CE.

[8] Grandson of Cleopatra and Mark Antony, he was the last king of Mauretania (modern Morocco) at the time of his assassination by Caligula in 40 CE.

[9] The Praetorian Prefect Macro initially had sponsored Caligula as emperor in 37 BCE; Caligula soon felt threatened by him and coerced him and his wife Ennia, who had been Caligula's mistress, into committing suicide.

[10] The emperor's guardian spirit.

so long as they fear me."[11] Angered at the rabble for applauding a faction[12] that he opposed, he cried, "I wish the Roman people had but a single neck." At one of his more sumptuous banquets he suddenly burst into a fit of laughter, and when the Consuls, who were reclining next him, politely inquired at what he was laughing, he replied, "What do you suppose, except that at a single nod of mine both of you could have your throats cut on the spot?" After inviting Ptolemy, whom I have mentioned before, to come from his kingdom, and receiving him with honor, he suddenly had him executed for no other reason than that when giving a gladiatorial show he noticed that Ptolemy on entering the theater attracted general attention by the splendor of his purple cloak.

He respected neither his own chastity nor that of anyone else. He is said to have had unnatural relations with Marcus Lepidus, the pantomimic actor Mnester, and certain hostages. Valerius Catullus, a young man of a consular family, publicly proclaimed that he had violated the emperor and worn himself out in commerce with him. To say nothing of his incest with his sisters and his notorious passion for the concubine Pyrallis, there was scarcely any woman of rank whom he did not approach. These as a rule he invited to dinner with their husbands, and as they passed by the foot of his couch, he would inspect them critically and deliberately, as if buying slaves, even putting out his hand and lifting up the face of anyone who looked down in modesty. Then, as often as the fancy took him he would leave the room, sending for the one who pleased him best, and returning soon afterward with evident signs of what had occurred, he would openly commend or criticize his partner, recounting her charms or defects and commenting on her conduct. To some he personally sent a bill of divorce in the name of their absent husbands and had it entered in the public records.

Having thus impoverished himself, from very need he turned his attention to pillage through a complicated and cunningly devised system of false accusations, auction sales, and imposts. He levied new and unheard of taxes, at first through the publicans[13] and then, because their profit was so great, through the Centurions and Tribunes of the Praetorian Guard. There was no class of commodities or men on which he did not impose some form of tariff. On all eatables sold in any part of the city he levied a fixed and definite charge; on lawsuits and legal processes begun anywhere, a fortieth part of the sum involved, adding a penalty in case anyone was found guilty of compromising or abandoning a suit; on the daily wages of porters, an eighth; on the earnings of prostitutes, as much as each received for one embrace; and a clause was added to this chapter of the law, providing that those who ever had been prostitutes or pimps should be liable to this public tax, and that even matrimony should not be exempt.

He had but one experience with military affairs or war, and then on a sudden impulse. Having gone to Mevania to visit the river Clitumnus[14] and its grove, he was reminded of the necessity of recruiting his body-guard of Batavians[15] and was seized with the idea of an expedition to Germania. So without delay he assembled legions and auxiliaries from all quarters, holding levies everywhere with the utmost strictness and collecting provisions of every kind on an unheard of scale. On reaching his camp, to show his vigilance and strictness as a commander, he dismissed in disgrace the generals who were late in bringing in the auxiliaries from various places, and in reviewing his troops he deprived many of the chief Centurions who were well on in years of their rank, in some cases only a few days before they would have served their time, giving as a reason their age and infirmity; then railing at the rest for their avarice, he reduced the rewards given on completion of full military service to six thousand *sestertii*.[16]

---

[11] A quotation from the play "Atreus" of the mid-second century BCE Latin tragedian Accius.

[12] A chariot-racing team.

[13] Tax collectors.

[14] A small river in Umbria that flowed to the town of Mevania; the site of sacred shrines.

[15] A people of the lower Rhine River often recruited for service in the imperial bodyguard.

[16] Reducing the rewards given to the soldiers always was a potentially dangerous undertaking.

All that he accomplished was to receive the surrender of Adminius, son of Cunobellinus,[17] King of the Britons, who had been banished by his father and had deserted to the Romans with a small force. Presently, finding no one to fight with, he had a few Germans of his bodyguard taken across the river[18] and concealed there, and word brought him after luncheon with great bustle and confusion that the enemy were close at hand. Upon this he rushed out with his friends and a part of the praetorian cavalry to the woods close by, and after cutting the branches from some trees and adorning them like trophies, he returned by torchlight, taunting those who had not followed him as timorous and cowardly, and presenting his companions and the partners in his victory with crowns.

Finally, as if he intended to bring the war to an end, he drew up a line of battle on the shore of the ocean,[19] arranging his ballistas[20] and other artillery, and when no one knew or could imagine what he was going to do, he suddenly bade them gather shells and fill their helmets and the folds of their gowns, calling them spoils from the ocean, due to the Capitol and Palatine.[21]

Then turning his attention to his triumph,[22] in addition to a few captives and deserters from the barbarians he chose all the tallest of the Gauls, and as he expressed it, those who were "worthy of a triumph," as well as some of the chiefs. These he reserved for his parade, compelling them not only to dye their hair red and to let it grow long, but also to learn the language of the Germans and assume barbarian names.

He was very tall and extremely pale, with an unshapely body and very thin neck and legs. His eyes and temples were hollow, his forehead broad and grim, his hair thin and entirely gone on the top of his head, although his body was hairy. Because of this to look upon him from a higher place as he passed by, or for any reason whatever to mention a goat, was treated as a capital offense. He was sound neither of body nor mind. As a boy he was troubled with the falling sickness.[23] While in his youth he had some endurance, yet at times because of sudden faintness he was hardly able to walk, to stand up, to collect his thoughts, or to hold up his head. He himself realized his mental infirmity, and thought at times of going into retirement and clearing his brain. It is thought that his wife Caesonia[24] gave him a drug intended for a love potion, which, however, had the effect of driving him mad. He was especially tormented with sleeplessness; for he never rested more than three hours at night, and even for that length of time he did not sleep quietly but was terrified by strange apparitions.

In his clothing, his shoes, and the rest of his attire he did not follow the usage of his country and his fellow-citizens, not always even that of his sex, or in fact, that of an ordinary mortal. He often appeared in public in embroidered cloaks covered with precious stones, with a long-sleeved tunic and bracelets; sometimes in silk and in a woman's robe, now in slippers or buskins, again in boots, such as the emperor's body-guard wear, and at times in the low shoes that are used by females.

He was so passionately devoted to the green faction[25] that he constantly dined and spent the night in their stables, and in one of his revels with them he gave the driver Eutychus two million *sestertii* in gifts. In order to prevent the horse Incitatus from being disturbed he used to send his soldiers on the day before the games and order silence in the neighborhood. Along with a stall of marble, a manger of ivory, purple blankets and a collar of

---

[17] King of several peoples of Britain. Caligula used the appeal of Cunobellinus' exiled son Adminius as a pretext to lay claim to Britain. Cunobellinus was the title character in Shakespeare's play, "Cymbeline, King of Britain."

[18] The Rhine River.

[19] The Atlantic Ocean.

[20] Torsion weapons, like giant bows, used for shooting spears or stones.

[21] A good example of how Caligula's actions were misrepresented; the shells would have been crushed and used to make waterproof cement for constructing harbor facilities.

[22] Ostensibly for a victory over the Germans.

---

[23] Epilepsy.

[24] Milonia Caesonia, Caligula's fourth and last wife, to whom he was quite devoted. She was murdered shortly after Caligula's assassination in 41 CE.

[25] The fan club of the "Greens," a chariot-racing team.

precious stones, he even gave this horse a house, a troop of slaves, and furniture for the more elegant entertainment of the guests invited in his name. It is also said that he planned to make him Consul.

During this frantic and riotous career several thought of attempting his life. But when one or two conspiracies had been detected and the rest were waiting for a favorable opportunity, two men made common cause and succeeded, with the connivance of his most influential freedmen and the officers of the Praetorian Guard, for although the charge that these last were privy to one of the former conspiracies was false, they realized that Caligula hated and feared them. In fact, he exposed them to great odium by once taking them aside and declaring, drawn sword in hand, that he would kill himself if they too thought he deserved death, and from that time on he never ceased accusing them one to the other and setting them all at odds. When they had decided to attempt his life at the exhibition of the Palatine games, as he went out at noon, Cassius Chaerea, Tribune of a cohort of the Praetorian Guard, claimed for himself the principal part, for Gaius used to taunt him, a man already well on in years, with voluptuousness and effeminacy by every form of insult. When he asked for the watchword Gaius would give him "Priapus" or "Venus," and when Chaerea had occasion to thank him for anything, he would hold out his hand to kiss, forming and moving it in an obscene fashion.

On the ninth day before the Kalends of February[26] at about the seventh hour he hesitated whether or not to get up for luncheon because his stomach was still disordered from excess of food on the day before, but at length he came out at the persuasion of his friends.[27] In the covered passage through which he had to pass, some boys of good birth, who had been summoned from Asia to appear on the stage, were rehearsing their parts, and he stopped to watch and encourage them. Had not the leader of the troop complained that he had a chill, he would have returned and had the performance given at once. From this point there are two versions of the story. Some say that as he was talking with the boys, Chaerea came up behind and gave him a deep cut in the neck, having first cried, "Take that," and that then the Tribune Cornelius Sabinus, who was the other conspirator and faced Gaius, stabbed him in the breast. Others say that Sabinus, after getting rid of the crowd by means of Centurions who were in the plot, asked for the watchword, as soldiers do, and that when Gaius gave him "Jupiter," he cried "So be it," and as Gaius looked around, he split his jawbone with a blow of his sword. As he lay upon the ground and with writhing limbs called out that he still lived, the others dispatched him with thirty wounds, for the general signal was "Strike again." Some even thrust their swords through his privates. At the beginning of the disturbance his bearers ran to his aid with their litter poles and presently the Germans of his body-guard, and they slew several of his assassins along with some inoffensive senators. Gaius lived twenty-nine years and ruled three years, ten months, and eight days.

---

[26] 24 January 41 CE.

[27] A similar story was told about Julius Caesar, who had to be persuaded to attend the Senate meeting where he was assassinated in 44 BCE.

THE "CLAUDIAN RECOMMENDATION OF THE SENATE REGARDING THE RIGHT OF HONORS FOR THE GAULS"; AND TACITUS, *ANNALS*, BOOK 11, CHAPTERS 23–25

The bottom half of a bronze tablet preserves approximately the first half of the speech of Claudius expanding Senate membership to Gauls in 48 CE. It was discovered in 1528 and is displayed in the Musée des Beaux Arts in Lyon.

This speech of the emperor Claudius (41–54 CE) to the Senate in Rome in 48 CE, engraved on a bronze tablet erected in Lyon in Gaul, is one of the very few surviving copies of the original words of an imperial speech. In it, Claudius admitted some Roman citizens from Gaul into the Senate and thus began the process by which the Senate came to represent all the populations of the Empire. The speech was an official transcript and even preserved the words of interruptions from the audience, one of the typical means by which the public could make its views known directly to an emperor. Claudius had a reputation as a historian before becoming emperor, and the examples used in the speech support this impression. The speech also is reported in the *Annals* of Tacitus, allowing one to compare the original text with the slant given to it by a historian.

(a) Claudius, Speech to the Senate

Sources:

Column 1: E. Mary Smallwood, *Documents Illustrating the Principates of Gaius Claudius and Nero* (Cambridge, UK: Cambridge Univ. Press, 1967), 369. Column 2: William Stearns Davis, ed., *Readings in Ancient History: Illustrative Extracts from the Vol. II: Rome and the West* (Boston: Allyn & Bacon, 1912–13), 186–188.

[Column I]

"I should say at the outset that I reject the first thought that will, I am sure, be the very first thing to stand in my way: namely that you will recoil from my suggestion as though I were introducing some revolutionary innovation. Think, instead, of how many changes have taken place over the years in this state and how many forms and constitutions our state has had, from the time of its very foundation.

At one time this city was held by kings,[28] although they did not pass it along to successors from their own families. People from other families came to the throne and even some foreigners. Numa, for example, succeeded Romulus, and was a Sabine; that made him a neighbor, certainly, but at the time he also was a foreigner. Another example is Tarquinius Priscus, who succeeded Ancus Martius: his father was the Corinthian Demaratus and his mother was from Tarquinii, so Tarquinius Priscus supposedly had a Greek father and an Etruscan mother. And although well-born she was very poor, which is why she was forced to marry such a husband. Tarquinius was kept from positions of honor in his own land and thus emigrated to Rome, where he became king. Between Tarquinius and either his son or his grandson (for our authorities disagree on this point) there came Servius Tullius. According to the Roman sources Servius Tullius had as a mother a prisoner-of-war, Ocresia; according to the Etruscans he had been the faithful companion of Caelius Vibenna[29] and took part in his adventures, and later, when he was driven out by a change of

fortune, he left Etruria with all the surviving troops of Caelius and seized the Caelian hill, which thus takes its name from his leader Caelius, and after changing his name, for his Etruscan name was Mastarna, he was given the name I have already mentioned, and became king, to the very great advantage of the state. Then, after the behavior of Tarquinius Superbus[30] came to be hated by our city, and not only his behavior but that of his sons, the people obviously became tired of monarchy, and the administration of state was transferred to the Consuls, who were annual magistrates.

Why need I mention the dictatorship, more powerful even than the consulship, which was what our ancestors came up with when wars were particularly hard or there was serious civil disturbance? Or why need I mention the creation of Tribunes of the Plebs, to provide assistance for the plebs? Why mention transfer of *imperium* from Consuls to the Decemvirs, and at the end of the reign of the Decemvirs the return of *imperium* back to the Consuls?[31] Why mention the distribution of the consular power to multiple recipients, called Military Tribunes with Consular Power,[32] who were first six and then eight in number? Why should I mention the fact that offices that once were patrician ones eventually were shared with the plebeians, religious ones as well as military?

If I were to tell of the wars that our ancestors started with and that have continued down to the present day, I fear that I would appear too boastful and look as though I wanted to boast about my glory in extending the empire beyond the Ocean.[33] But let me instead return to my original point. Citizenship can [---]."[34]

[Column II]

[Claudius]: "It surely is an innovation of the divine Augustus,[35] my great-uncle, and of Tiberius

---

[28] Claudius indulges his interest in ancient history with these historical excurses on the kings of Rome.

[29] An Etruscan chieftain who aided Romulus in his wars against the Sabines.

[30] Tarquin the Proud, the last king of Rome.

[31] In the years 451 and 450 BCE, when the Twelve Tables of Roman law were crafted.

[32] Lasting from 444 until 367 BCE.

[33] The Atlantic Ocean; in 43 CE Claudius had begun the Roman occupation of Britain.

[34] Some text is lost here.

[35] The first emperor, Augustus (27 BCE–14 CE).

Caesar,[36] my uncle, to desire that particularly the flower of the colonies and of the municipal towns,[37] that is to say, all those that contain men of breeding and wealth, should be admitted to this assembly."

[Interruption, seemingly by a senator]: "How now? Is not an Italian senator to be preferred to a provincial senator?"

[Claudius]: "I will soon explain this point to you, when I submit that part of my acts that I performed as Censor,[38] but I do not conceive it needful to repel even the provincials who can do honor to the Senate House. Here is this splendid and powerful colony of Vienna[39] is it so long since it sent senators to us? From that colony comes Lucius Vestinus,[40] one of the glories of the equestrian order, my personal friend, whom I keep close to myself for the management of my private affairs. Let his sons be suffered, I pray you, to become priests of the lowest rank, while waiting until, with the lapse of years, they can follow the advancement of their dignity. As for that robber[41] from Vienna, I will pass over his hateful name. For I detest this hero of the gymnasium, who brought the consulship into his family before even his colony had obtained the full rights of Roman citizenship. I could say as much of his brother, stamped as unworthy by this unlucky relationship, and incapable henceforth of being a useful member of your body."

[Interrupting shout]: "Here now, Tiberius Caesar Germanicus! It is time to let the Conscript Fathers[42] understand what your talk is driving at! Already

you've reached the very limits of Narbonnese Gaul!"[43]

[Claudius]: "All these young men of rank, on whom I cast my glance, you surely do not regret to see among the number of the senators, any more than Persicus, that most high-born gentleman and my friend, is ashamed when he meets upon the images of his ancestors the name Allobrogius.[44] And if such is your thought, what would you desire more? Do I have to point it out to you? Even the territory that is located beyond the province of Narbonese Gaul, has it not already sent you senators? For surely we have no regrets in going clear up to Lugdunum[45] for the members of our order. Assuredly, Conscript Fathers, it is not without some hesitation that I cross the limits of the provinces that are well known and familiar to you, but the moment is come when I must plead openly the cause of Further Gaul.[46] It will be objected that Gaul sustained a war against the divine Julius for ten years.[47] But let there be opposed to this the memory of a hundred years of steadfast fidelity, and a loyalty put to the proof in many trying circumstances. My father, Drusus,[48] was able to force Germany to submit because behind him reigned a profound peace assured by the tranquillity of the Gauls. And note well, that at the moment he was summoned to that war, he was busy instituting the census[49] in Gaul, a new institution among them, and contrary to their customs. And how difficult and perilous to us is

---

[36] Tiberius (14–37 CE), second Roman emperor and adopted son of Augustus.

[37] Colonies and municipalities were cities of Roman citizens that had formal Roman organizational charters.

[38] The ancient Republican magistrate with the authority to adlect (admit) new members to the Senate.

[39] Modern Vienne, on the Rhône River in central France.

[40] Otherwise unknown but probably an ancestor of the Lucius Vestinus who was Consul in 112 CE.

[41] Valerius Asiaticus, whose family had received Roman citizenship ca. 80 BCE. A famous athlete, friendly with the Julio-Claudian emperors, he was the first Gaul to enter the Senate and became Consul in 46 CE. In 47 CE he was accused of adultery and forced by Claudius to commit suicide.

[42] A term for senators.

[43] The original Roman province in southern Gaul, as of ca. 120 BCE; the remainder of Gaul was not annexed by Julius Caesar until 54 BCE

[44] A joke. The Allobroges were a famous Gallic people; Persicus' ancestor got the name not because he was one of them, but because he defeated them.

[45] Modern Lyon, just north of Vienne on the Rhône River in central France.

[46] The part of Gaul on the far side of the Alps, contrasted to Cisalpine Gaul, "Gaul on the Near Side of the Alps."

[47] Not quite; from 58 to 50 BCE at the latest.

[48] Nero Claudius Drusus Germanicus, stepson of the emperor Augustus and brother of the emperor Tiberius. After successful campaigns against the Germans, he died in 9 BCE after a fall from his horse.

[49] The cataloguing of property ownership for the purposes of tax assessment.

this business of the census, although all we require is that our public resources should be known, we have learned by all too much experience."

(b) Tacitus, *Annals*, Book 11, Chapters 23–25

Source: Alfred John Church and William Jackson Brodribb, trans., *Annals of Tacitus* (London: Macmillan, 1876).

In the consulship of Aulus Vitellius and Lucius Vipstanus[50] the question of filling up the Senate was discussed, and the chief men of Gallia Comata,[51] as it was called, who had long possessed the rights of allies and of Roman citizens, sought the privilege of obtaining public offices at Rome. There was much talk of every kind on the subject, and it was argued before the emperor with vehement opposition. "Italy," it was asserted, "is not so feeble as to be unable to furnish its own capital with a Senate. Once our native-born citizens sufficed for peoples of our own kin, and we are by no means dissatisfied with the Rome of the past. To this day we cite examples, which under our old customs the Roman character exhibited as to valor and renown. Is it a small thing that Veneti and Insubres[52] already have burst into the Senate house, unless that now a mob of foreigners, a troop of captives, so to say, is forced upon us? What distinctions will be left for the remnants of our noble houses, or for any impoverished senators from Latium? Every place will be crowded with these millionaires, whose ancestors of the second and third generations at the head of hostile peoples destroyed our armies with fire and sword, and actually besieged the divine Julius at Alesia.[53] These are recent memories. What if there were to rise up the remembrance of those who fell in Rome's citadel and at her altar by the hands of these same barbarians![54] Let them enjoy indeed the title of citizens, but let them not vulgarize the distinctions of the Senate and the honors of office."

These and like arguments failed to impress the emperor. He at once addressed himself to answer them, and thus harangued the assembled Senate.

My ancestors, the most ancient of whom was made at once a citizen and a noble of Rome, encourage me to govern by the same policy of transferring to this city all conspicuous merit, wherever found. And indeed I know, as facts, that the Julii came from Alba,[55] the Coruncanii from Camerium,[56] the Porcii from Tusculum,[57] and not to inquire too minutely into the past, that new members have been brought into the Senate from Etruria and Lucania and the whole of Italy, that Italy itself was at last extended to the Alps, to the end that not only single persons but entire countries and peoples might be united under our name.[58] We had unshaken peace at home; we prospered in all our foreign relations, in the days when Italy beyond the Po was admitted to share our citizenship,[59] and when, enrolling in our ranks the most vigorous of the provincials, under color of settling our legions throughout the world, we recruited our exhausted empire. Are we sorry that the Balbi came to us from Spain, and other men not less illustrious from Narbonese Gaul? Their descendents are still among us, and do not yield to us in patriotism.

What was the ruin of Sparta and Athens,[60] but this, that mighty as they were in war they spurned from them as aliens those whom they had conquered? Our founder Romulus, on the other hand, was so wise that he fought as enemies and then hailed as fellow-citizens several nations on the

---

[50] Consuls in 48 CE.

[51] "Long Haired Gaul," the name given to the areas of Gaul annexed by Julius Caesar in 54 BCE, the same as the "Further Gaul" cited by Claudius in the previous passage.

[52] Peoples of far northern Italy; the Insubres were Celts, the Veneti native peoples.

[53] Actually it was Julius Caesar who besieged the Gauls at Alesia.

---

[54] During the sack of Rome by the Gauls in 390 BCE.

[55] Claudius' own ancestors, the descendents of Iulus, or Ascanius, the son of the Trojan hero Aeneas, who had founded the city of Alba Longa.

[56] An ancient colony of Alba Longa near Rome.

[57] An ancient Latin town.

[58] Claudius again indulges his interests in ancient history.

[59] Cisalpine Gaul received citizenship from Julius Caesar in 49 BCE.

[60] For the disastrous consequences of the warfare between Sparta and Athens.

very same day. Strangers have reigned over us. That freedmen's sons should be entrusted with public offices is not, as many wrongly think, a sudden innovation, but was a common practice in the old Republic. But, it will be said, we have fought with the Senones.[61] I suppose then that the Volsci and Aequi[62] never stood in array against us. Our city was taken by the Gauls. Well, we also gave hostages to the Etruscans, and passed under the yoke of the Samnites.[63] On the whole, if you review all our wars, never has one been finished in a shorter time than that with the Gauls. Thenceforth they have preserved an unbroken and loyal peace. United as they now are with us by manners, education, and intermarriage, let them bring us their gold and their wealth rather than enjoy it in isolation. Everything, senators, that we now hold to be of the highest antiquity once was new. Plebeian magistrates came after patrician; Latin magistrates after plebeian; magistrates of other Italian peoples after Latin. This practice too will establish itself, and what we are this day justifying by precedents, will be itself "a precedent."

The emperor's speech was followed by a Recommendation of the Senate, and the Aedui[64] were the first to obtain the right of becoming senators at Rome. This compliment was paid to their ancient alliance, and to the fact that they alone of the Gauls cling to the name of brothers of the Roman people.

---

[61] Gauls of northern Italy.

[62] Italic peoples who fought the Romans during the early Roman Republic.

[63] After a Roman army was trapped at the Caudine Forks in 321 BCE.

---

[64] An important people of central Gaul.

TACITUS, *ANNALS*, BOOK 14, CHAPTERS 31–37

A silver coin of the Iceni, a Celtic people of Britain, dated to the middle of the first century CE. This coin type often is attributed to Queen Boudicca. In typical Celtic abstract style, it displays a head on the obverse that some claim is Boudicca herself and a horse on the reverse with a wheel above.

In 43 CE the emperor Claudius (41–54 CE) began the conquest of Britain, which proceeded smoothly until 60 CE, when Roman heavy-handedness provoked a revolt led by Boudicca, the charismatic queen of the Iceni, who had united the hitherto disunified Celtic peoples. Initially, the Romans were caught off guard. In particular, the able Roman commander in Britain, Suetonius Paulinus, was occupied in the far west subduing the island of Mona (Anglesey), which had become a refuge for rebels and Celtic priests known as Druids. Boudicca's Celts destroyed the Roman colony of Camulodunum (Colchester). London received similar treatment; a ten-inch layer of red clay from the burned city still lies beneath London streets. After one cowardly legion refused to march, Suetonius could assemble only ten thousand soldiers to face the hundred thousand Celts. At the Battle of Watling Street, Paulinus lined up his troops with his rear and flanks protected by forests. The Celts spent their energy on fruitless assaults on the Roman shield wall, and then the slaughter started. Eighty thousand Celts were killed and Boudicca poisoned herself. Having failed in their revolt, the Celts of Britain, like those of Spain, Pannonia, and Gaul, then accommodated themselves to Roman rule.

Source: Arthur Murphy, *The Works of Tacitus* (Dublin: White, 1794).

During the consulship of Lucius Caesennius Paetus and Publius Petronius Turpilianus,[65] a dreadful calamity befell the army in Britain.

Paulinus Suetonius succeeded to the command; an officer of distinguished merit. His military talents gave him pretensions, and the voice of the people, who never leave exalted merit without a rival, raised him to the highest eminence.

---

[65] 60–61 CE.

By subduing the mutinous spirit of the Britons he hoped to equal the brilliant success of Corbulo in Armenia.[66] With this view, he resolved to subdue the island of Mona[67]; a place inhabited by a warlike people, and a common refuge for all the discontented Britons. In order to facilitate his approach to a difficult and deceitful shore, he ordered a number of flat-bottomed boats to be constructed. In these he transported over the infantry, while the cavalry, partly by fording over the shallows and partly by swimming their horses, advanced to gain a footing on the island.

On the opposite shore stood the Britons, close embodied, and prepared for action. Women were seen running through the ranks in wild disorder, their hair loose to the wind, in their hands flaming torches, and their whole appearance resembling the frantic rage of the Furies. The Druids were ranged in order, with hands uplifted, invoking the gods, and pouring forth horrible imprecations. The novelty of the fight struck the Romans with awe and terror. The exhortations of the general diffused new vigor through the ranks, and the men, by mutual reproaches, inflamed each other to deeds of valor. They felt the disgrace of yielding to a troop of women and a band of fanatic priests. They advanced their standards, and rushed on to the attack with impetuous fury.

The Britons perished in the flames that they themselves had kindled. The island fell, and a garrison was established to retain it in subjection. The religious groves,[68] dedicated to superstition and barbarous rites, were levelled to the ground. In those recesses, the natives stained their altars with the blood of their prisoners, and in the entrails of men explored the will of the gods.[69] While Suetonius was employed in making his

arrangements to secure the island, he received intelligence that Britain had revolted and that the whole province was up in arms.

Prasutagus, the late King of the Iceni,[70] in the course of a long reign had amassed considerable wealth. By his will he left the whole to his two daughters and the emperor in equal shares, conceiving, by that stroke of policy, that he should provide at once for the tranquility of his kingdom and his family. The event was otherwise. His dominions were ravaged by the Centurions, the slaves pillaged his house, and his effects were seized as lawful plunder. His wife, Boudicca, was disgraced with a cruel whipping, her daughters were ravished, and the most illustrious of the Iceni were, by force, deprived of the positions that had been transmitted to them by their ancestors. The whole country was considered as a legacy bequeathed to the plunderers. The relations of the deceased king were reduced to slavery.

Exasperated by their acts of violence, and dreading worse calamities, the Iceni had recourse to arms. The Trinobantes[71] joined in the revolt. The neighboring states, not as yet taught to crouch in bondage, pledged themselves, in secret councils, to stand forth in the cause of liberty. What chiefly fired their indignation was the conduct of the veterans, lately planted as a colony at Camulodunum.[72] These men treated the Britons with cruelty and oppression. They drove the natives from their habitations, and calling them by the shameful names of slaves and captives, added insult to their tyranny. In these acts of oppression, the veterans were supported by the common soldiers, a class of men, by their habits of life, trained to licentiousness, and, in their turn, expecting to reap the same advantages. The temple built in honor of Claudius was another cause of discontent. In the eye of the Britons it seemed the citadel of eternal slavery. The priests appointed to officiate at the altars, with a pretended zeal for religion, devoured the whole substance of the country. To overrun a colony,

---

[66] Corbulo occupied Armenia in 58 CE and it became a Roman client state. In 67 CE he was ordered by the emperor Nero (54–68) to commit suicide.

[67] Anglesey, off the northwestern coast of Wales.

[68] The Druids were believed to worship in groves of oak trees.

[69] In the same way that the Romans practiced the *haruspices*, the inspection of the livers of sacrificial animals, to ascertain the will of the gods.

---

[70] A Celtic people of eastern Britain.

[71] A Celtic people dwelling south of the Iceni.

[72] Modern Colchester.

which lay quite naked and exposed without a single fortification to defend it, did not appear to the incensed and angry Britons an enterprise that threatened either danger or difficulty. The fact was that the Roman generals attended to improvements to taste and elegance but neglected the useful. They embellished the province and took no care to defend it.

While the Britons were preparing to throw off the yoke, the statue of victory, erected at Camulodunum, fell from its base without any apparent cause and lay extended on the ground with its face averted, as if the goddess yielded to the enemies of Rome. Women in restless ecstasy rushed among the people and with frantic screams denounced impending ruin. By these portents the Romans were sunk in despair whereas the Britons anticipated a glorious victory. Suetonius, in the meantime, was detained on the isle of Mona. In this alarming crisis, the veterans at the colony sent to Catus Decianus, the Procurator of the province,[73] for a reinforcement. Two hundred men, and those not completely armed, were all that officer could spare. The colony had but a handful of soldiers. Their temple was strongly fortified and there they hoped to make a stand. But even for the defense of that place no ditch was made and no palisade thrown up, nor were the women and those disabled by age or infirmity sent out of the garrison. Unguarded and unprepared, they were taken by surprise, and, in the moment of profound peace, overpowered by the barbarians in one general assault. The colony was laid waste with fire and sword.

The temple held out, but, after a siege of two days, was taken by storm. Petilius Cerialis, who commanded the Ninth Legion, marched to the relief of the place. The Britons, flushed with success, advanced to give him battle. The legion was routed and the infantry cut to pieces. Cerialis escaped with the cavalry to entrenchments of his camp. Catus Decianus, alarmed at the scene of carnage that he beheld on every side, and further dreading the indignation of a people whom by

rapine and oppression he had driven to despair, betook himself to flight and crossed over into Gaul.

Suetonius, undismayed by this disaster, marched through the heart of the country as far as London, a place not dignified with the name of a colony but the chief residence of merchants and a great center of trade and commerce. At that place he meant to fix the feat of war, but reflecting on the scanty numbers of his little army and the fatal rashness of Cerialis, he resolved to quit the station, and, by giving up one post, secure the rest of the province. Neither supplications nor the tears of the inhabitants could induce him to change his plan. The signal for the march was given. All who chose to follow his banners were taken under his protection. Of all who, on account of their advanced age, the weakness of their sex, of the attractions of the situation, thought proper to remain behind, not one escaped the rage of the barbarians. The inhabitants of Verulamium,[74] a municipal town,[75] in like manner were put to the sword. The genius[76] of a savage people leads them always in quest of plunder, and, accordingly, the Britons left behind them all places of strength. Wherever they expected feeble resistance and considerable booty, there they were sure to attack with the fiercest rage. Military skill was not the talent of barbarians. The number massacred in the places that have been mentioned amounted to no less than seventy thousand, all citizens or allies of Rome. To make prisoners and reserve them for slavery or exchange them was not in the character of a people who despised all the laws of war. They hastened to inflict death, whipping, burning, and crucifixion as if aware they were going to receive retribution but in the meantime were taking their revenge.

The Fourteenth Legion, with the veterans of the Twentieth Legion,[77] and the auxiliaries from the adjacent stations, having joined Suetonius, his army amounted to little less than ten thousand men. Thus reinforced, he resolved, without loss of time, to bring on a decisive action. For this

---

[73] An imperial official in charge of tax collection.

[74] Modern St. Albans.

[75] That is, a city of Roman citizens with a municipal charter.

[76] Guiding spirit.

[77] Another of the four legions stationed in Britain.

purpose he chose a spot encircled with woods, narrow at the entrance, and sheltered in the rear by a thick forest. In that situation he had no fear of an ambush. The enemy, he knew, had no approach but in front. An open plain lay before him. He drew up his men in the following order: the legions in close array formed the center; the light-armed troops were stationed at hand to serve as occasion might require; the cavalry took post in the wings.[78] The Britons brought into the field an incredible multitude. They formed no regular line of battle. Detached parties and loose battalions displayed their numbers, in frantic transport bounding with exultation, and so sure of victory, that they placed their wives in wagons at the extremity of the plain where they might survey the scene of action, and behold the wonders of British valor.

Boudicca, in a chariot, with her two daughters before her, drove through the ranks. She harangued the different nations in their turn: "This," she said, "is not the first time that the Britons have been led to battle by a woman. But now she did not come to boast the pride of a long line of ancestry, nor even to recover her kingdom and the plundered wealth of her family. She took the field, like the meanest among them, to assert the cause of public liberty, and to seek revenge for her body seamed with ignominious stripes, and her two daughters infamously ravished. From the pride and arrogance of the Romans nothing is sacred. All persons are subject to violation; the old endure the whip and the virgins are violated. But the vindictive gods now are at hand. A Roman legion dared to face the warlike Britons. With their lives they paid for their rashness. Those who survived the carnage of that day lie poorly hid behind their entrenchments, meditating nothing but how to save themselves by an ignominious flight.[79] From the din of preparation and the shouts of the British army the Romans, even now, shrink back with terror. What will be their case when the assault begins? Look round, and view your numbers. Behold the proud display of warlike spirits, and consider the motives for which we draw the avenging sword. On this spot we must either conquer, or die with glory. There is no alternative. Although a woman, my resolution is fixed. The men, if they please, may survive with infamy, and live in bondage."

Suetonius, in a moment of such importance, did not remain silent.[80] He expected everything from the valor of his men and yet urged every topic that could inspire and animate them to the attack. "Despise," he said, "the savage uproar, the yells and shouts of undisciplined barbarians. In that mixed multitude, the women outnumber the men. Void of spirit, unprovided with arms, they are not soldiers who come to offer battle; they are bastards, runaways, the refuse of your swords, who often have fled before you, and will again betake themselves to flight when they see the conqueror flaming in the ranks of war. In all engagements it is the valor of a few that turns the fortune of the day. It will be your immortal glory that with a scanty number you can equal the exploits of a great and powerful army. Keep your ranks, discharge your javelins, rush forward to a close attack, bear down all with your shields, and hew a passage with your swords. Pursue the vanquished and never think of spoil and plunder. Conquer, and victory gives you everything." This speech was received with warlike acclamations. The soldiers burned with impatience for the onset, the veterans brandished their javelins and the ranks displayed such an intrepid countenance that Suetonius, anticipating the victory, gave the signal for the charge.

The engagement began. The Roman legion presented a close embodied line. The narrow defile gave them the shelter of a rampart. The Britons advanced with ferocity and discharged their darts at random. In that instant, the Romans rushed forward in the form of a wedge. The auxiliaries followed with equal ardor. The cavalry, at the same time, bore down upon the enemy, and, with their

---

[78] The standard formation of an ancient army.

[79] The Ninth Legion of Cerialis. Another, the Second Legion under Poenius Postumius, also refused to fight.

[80] It was a literary tradition that accounts of battles would be prefaced by speeches of generals to their troops, much like coaches will give a pregame speech to their teams in the modern day.

pikes, overpowered all who dared to make a stand. The Britons betook themselves to flight, but their wagons in the rear obstructed their passage. A dreadful slaughter followed. Neither sex nor age was spared. The cattle, falling in one promiscuous carnage, added to the heaps of slain. The glory of the day was equal to the most splendid victory of ancient times. According to some writers, not less than eighty thousand Britons were put to the sword. The Romans lost about four hundred men, and the wounded did not exceed that number. Boudicca, by a dose of poison, ended her life. Poenius Postumius, the Prefect on the Camp of the Second Legion,[81] as soon as he heard of the brave exploits of the Fourteenth and Twentieth legions, felt the disgrace of having, in disobedience to the orders of his general, robbed the soldiers under his command of their share in so complete a victory.[82] Stung with remorse, he fell upon his sword and expired on the spot.

---

[81] It is unclear why the Prefect of the Camp, who ranked beneath the Legate of the Legion and the Military Tribune, was in command of the legion.

[82] Thus, of the four British legions, only two, the Second and the Fourteenth, actually participated in Boudicca's defeat.

"THE LAW ON THE *IMPERIUM* OF VESPASIAN"

The *Lex de imperio Vespasiani* is inscribed on a bronze tablet now in the Church of St. John Lateran in Rome.

It is our good fortune to have preserved the concluding section of a recommendation of the Senate, the so-called Lex de imperio Vespasiani ("Law on the Imperium of Vespasian"), which granted imperial powers to Vespasian in the year 69 CE. The beginning of the law does not survive, so it is unclear exactly what all of the powers conferred were, but it appears that they were part of a unified, and expanding, package of powers that had been granted to earlier emperors. The grants of the proconsular imperium and tribunician power are missing, so they must have been part of the missing first section—no surprise given that they were the most important powers that an emperor received. The use of the word lex ("law") suggests that the resolution subsequently received the pro forma approval of a vestigial popular assembly, perhaps the Centuriate Assembly. For the Senate, the issuance of such a document, which would have been issued for all later emperors of the Principate as well, not only would have satisfied its requirement that an emperor rule according to the law but also would have asserted its own continued role in the government.

Source: Allan Johnson, Paul Coleman-Norton, and Frank Bourne, Ancient Roman Statutes
(Austin: Univ. of Texas Press, 1961), 149–150, n.183.

. . . or it shall be lawful for him to make a treaty with whom he wishes, just as it was lawful for the deified Augustus, for Tiberius Julius Caesar Augustus, and for Tiberius Claudius Caesar Augustus Germanicus;[83]

And that it shall be lawful for him to hold a session of the Senate, to make a motion in it, to refer a matter to it, to propose Recommendations of the Senate by a motion and by calling for a vote by division, just as it was lawful for the deified Augustus, for Tiberius Julius Caesar Augustus, for Tiberius Claudius Caesar Augustus Germanicus;[84]

And that, when a session of the Senate is held in accordance with his pleasure or authority or order or mandate or in his presence, the authority of all proceedings therein shall be maintained and shall be observed, just as if that session of the Senate had been announced and was held in accordance with a statute;

And that whatsoever persons seeking a magistracy, power, *imperium*, or charge of anything he commends to the Roman Senate and people and to whomsoever he gives or promises his electoral support special consideration of them shall be taken in every election;[85]

And that it shall be lawful for him to advance and to extend the boundaries of the pomerium whenever he considers it to be in accordance with the public interest, just as it was lawful for Tiberius Claudius Caesar Augustus Germanicus;[86]

And that whatever he considers to be in accordance with the public advantage and the dignity of divine and human and public and private interests he shall have the right and the power to do and to execute, just as had the deified Augustus and Tiberius Julius Caesar Augustus and Tiberius Claudius Caesar Augustus Germanicus;

And that by whatever laws or plebiscites it has been recorded that the deified Augustus or Tiberius Julius Caesar Augustus and Tiberius Claudius Caesar Augustus Germanicus were not bound, from these laws and plebiscites Emperor Caesar Vespasian shall be exempt; and whatsoever things it was proper for the deified Augustus or Tiberius Julius Caesar Augustus or Tiberius Claudius Caesar Augustus Germanicus to do in accordance with any law or proposed law, it shall be lawful for Emperor Caesar Vespasian Augustus to do all these things;

And that whatever before the passage of this law has been done, executed, decreed, ordered by Emperor Caesar Vespasian Augustus or by anyone at his order or mandate, these things shall be legal and valid, just as if they had been done by the order of the people or of the plebs.[87]

Sanction[88]

If anyone has done or does anything in consequence of this law[89] contrary to statutes or bills or plebiscites or decrees of the Senate, or if he does not do in consequence of this law what it is proper for him to do in accordance with statute or bill or plebiscite or Recommendation of the Senate, this shall not be to his prejudice nor shall he be liable to pay the people anything on this account, nor shall anyone have the right to an action or a judgment concerning this matter, nor shall anyone allow an action concerning this matter to be pleaded before him.

---

[83] This repeated list of previous emperors not only shows the importance of past precedent, but also underlines the Senate's power to designate, by deification, which emperors had the most favored status. Thus, Augustus, Tiberius, and Claudius are cited, but not Caligula, Nero, Galba, Otho, and Vitellius.

[84] This clause emphasizes the Senate's continued role in the legislative process.

[85] An acknowledgment of the emperor's rights of *nominatio* and *commendatio*, the rights to nominate and commend persons for election to the old Republican offices.

[86] A statement of the expectation that an emperor would be a *propagator imperii*—that is, one who expands the frontiers of the empire.

---

[87] A clause that grandfathered in Vespasian's actions and policies prior to the issuance of the law; it also underlines the continued theoretical sovereign power of the Council of the Plebs and the other Republican popular assemblies.

[88] The legal consequences if the law is disobeyed.

[89] *Lex*, suggesting approval by a popular assembly, as opposed to the Senate, which only proposed advice and did not pass *leges* ("laws").

8.5 THE FALL OF MASADA (74 CE)

JOSEPHUS, *THE WARS OF THE JEWS*, BOOK 7, CHAPTER 9

An aerial view of the site of Masada, showing the Herodian fortress atop the bluff, the Roman ramp up the side, and the remains of Roman siege camps scattered around the base of the escarpment.

In spite of Roman efforts to accommodate the religious sensibilities of the Jews of Palestine, there always were religious incompatibilities between the Jews and the Roman government, and the Jews easily were the most restive of all the peoples included in the Roman Empire. Large-scale Jewish revolts against Roman authority occurred in 66, 115, and 131 CE, after which the Jews were expelled from Palestine, thus augmenting the already extensive Jewish diaspora. The first of these rebellions occurred under the emperor Nero and resulted in a massive Roman response. The general Vespasian was appointed to suppress the revolt. While in Judaea, Vespasian became the patron of the Jewish historian Josephus, who later wrote a history of the war. In 69 CE, after Vespasian had been declared emperor, he left the revolt in the hands of his son, Titus. In the next year, Jerusalem was captured and sacked, but Jewish *Sicarii*, or Dagger-Carriers, a fanatic group of the Jewish Zealots who had attempted to expel the Romans, had retreated to and occupied what was thought to be the impregnable fortress of Masada, built atop a precipitous bluff in the Judaean desert by King Herod the Great in the 30s BCE. In 73 CE the Roman army besieged Masada and began constructing a massive earthen ramp to the top. The work initially was done by Roman soldiers, but when the besieged Jews bombarded them with rocks from the top of the bluff, the Romans also put captured Jews to work, and the Jews stopped throwing stones. After three months, the ramp was complete. The Romans broke into the fortress to find that 960 Jews had committed suicide; only 7 survived to report what had happened. The Jewish historian Josephus provides a detailed account of the siege.

Source: William Whiston, trans., *The Works of Josephus* (Peabody, MA: Hendrickson, 1987).

Now as Eleazar[90] was proceeding on in his exhortations, they all cut him off short[91] and made haste to do the work, full of an unconquerable ardor of mind and moved with a demoniacal fury. So they went their ways, with each one still endeavoring to be before the others, and as if they were thinking that this eagerness would be a demonstration of their courage and good conduct. So great was the zeal they were in to slay their wives and children, and themselves also! Nor, indeed, when they came to the work itself, did their courage fail them, as one might imagine it would have done. Then they held fast to the same resolution, without wavering, that they had upon hearing of Eleazar's speech, while every one of them still retained the natural passion of love for their families, because the reasoning they depended upon appeared to them to be very just, even with regard to those that were dearest to them. The husbands tenderly embraced their wives and took their children into their arms, and gave the longest parting kisses to them, with tears in their eyes. Yet at the same time did they complete what they had resolved on, as if they had been executed by the hands of strangers, and they had nothing else for their comfort but the necessity they were in of doing this execution to avoid that prospect they had of the miseries they were to suffer from their enemies. Nor was there at length any one of these men found that scrupled to act their part in this terrible execution, but every one of them dispatched his dearest relations.

Miserable men indeed were they, whose distress forced them to slay their own wives and children with their own hands, as the lightest of the evils that were before them. So, being not able to bear the grief they were under for what they had done any longer, and esteeming it an injury to those they had slain to live even the shortest space of time after them, they presently laid all their possessions in a heap and set fire to it. They

then chose ten men by lot out of them to slay all the rest, every one of whom laid himself down by his wife and children on the ground, and threw his arms about them, and they offered their necks to the stroke of those who by lot executed that melancholy office. And when these ten had, without fear, slain them all, they made the same rule for casting lots for themselves, that he whose lot it was should first kill the other nine, and after all, should kill himself. Accordingly, all these had courage sufficient to be no way behind one another in doing or suffering. So, for a conclusion, the nine offered their necks to the executioner, and he who was the last of all took a view of all the other bodies, lest perchance some or other among so many that were slain should want his assistance to be quite dispatched, and when he perceived that they were all slain, he set fire to the palace, and with the great force of his hands ran his sword entirely through himself and fell down dead near to his own relations.

So these people died with this intention, that they would leave not so much as one soul among them all alive to be subject to the Romans. Yet there was an ancient woman, and another who was of kin to Eleazar, and superior to most women in prudence and learning, with five children, who had concealed themselves in caverns underground, and had carried water thither for their drink, and were hidden there when the rest were intent upon the slaughter of one another. Those others were nine hundred and sixty in number, the women and children being withal included in that computation. This calamitous slaughter was made on the fifteenth day of the month Xanthicus.[92]

Now for the Romans, they expected that they would be fought in the morning, when accordingly they put on their armor and laid bridges of planks upon their ladders from their ramp, to make an assault upon the fortress, which they did. But they saw nobody as an enemy, only a terrible solitude on every side, with a fire within the place as well as a perfect silence. So they were at a loss to guess at

---

[90] Eleazar ben Ya'ir, the leader of the Jewish *Sicarii* ("Knife-Bearers") who had occupied Masada.

[91] When it became clear that the Romans had completed their ramp and were about to storm the fortress, Eleazar spoke in favor of committing suicide. His supporters needed no speeches to be convinced to do this.

[92] The first month in the Macedonian calendar, equivalent to the Jewish month of Nisan, or April.

what had happened. At length they made a shout, as if it had been at a blow given by the battering-ram, to try whether they could bring anyone out that was within. The women heard this noise and came out of their underground cavern and informed the Romans what had been done, and the second of them clearly described all that was said and what was done, and the manner of it. Yet the Romans did not easily give their attention to such a desperate undertaking, and did not believe it could be as the women said. They also attempted to put the fire out, and quickly cutting themselves a way through it, they came within the palace, and so met with the multitude of the slain, but could take no pleasure in the fact, although it was done to their enemies. Nor could they do other than wonder at the courage of their resolution and the immovable contempt of death that so great a number of them had shown, when they went through with such an action as that was.

TACITUS, *AGRICOLA*, 29–32

In 83 CE, the Roman general Agricola's advance into the highlands of Caledonia (modern Scotland) was resisted by Calgacus, the leader of a coalition of Caledonians, the only people of Britain not yet conquered by the Romans. The Caledonians occupied the high ground at an unknown place called Mount Graupius. According to Agricola's biographer Tacitus, his son-in-law, before the battle the two generals made the customary speeches to their troops. Agricola expressed the traditional sentiments about how the Romans were the bringers of civilization and prosperity. Tacitus also candidly put into Calgacus' mouth words very critical of the Romans, including the famous statement, "they make a desert and call it peace," indicating that not everyone in the Roman world was happy to be incorporated under the Roman umbrella. The battle then began with a charge by the Roman auxiliary foot soldiers and cavalry. The Caledonians were routed, and the legionaries did not even have to engage.

Source: Alfred John Church and William Jackson Brodribb, trans., *The Agricola and Germany of Tacitus* (London: MacMillan, 1868), pp. 24–34.

Early in the summer Agricola sustained a domestic affliction in the loss of a son born a year before, a calamity that he endured, neither with the ostentatious fortitude displayed by many brave men, nor, on the other hand, with womanish tears and grief. In his sorrow he found one source of relief in war. Having sent on a fleet, which by its ravages at various points might cause a vague and widespread alarm, he advanced with a lightly equipped force, including in its ranks some Britons of remarkable bravery, whose fidelity had been tried through years of peace, as far as Mount Graupius,[93] which the enemy already had occupied. For the Britons, indeed, in no way cowed by the result of the late engagement, had made up their minds to be either avenged or enslaved, and convinced at length that a common danger must be averted by union, had, by embassies and treaties, summoned forth the whole strength of all their states. More than 30,000 armed men were now to be seen, and still there were pressing in all the youth of the country, with all whose old age was yet hale and vigorous, men renowned in war and each bearing decorations of his own. Meanwhile, among the many leaders, one superior to the rest in valor and in birth, Calgacus by name, is said to have thus harangued the multitude gathered around him and clamoring for battle:

"Whenever I consider the origin of this war and the necessities of our position, I have a sure confidence that this day, and this union of yours, will be the beginning of freedom to the whole of Britain. To all of us slavery is a thing unknown; there are no lands beyond us, and even the sea is not safe, menaced as we are by a Roman fleet. And thus in war and battle, in which the brave find glory, even the coward will find safety. Former contests, in which, with varying fortune, the Romans were resisted, still left in us a last hope of succor, inasmuch as being the most renowned nation of Britain, dwelling in the very heart of the country, and out of sight of the shores of the conquered, we could keep even our eyes unpolluted by the contagion of slavery. To us who dwell on the uttermost confines of the earth and of freedom, this remote sanctuary of Britain's glory has up to this time been a defense. Now, however, the furthest limits of Britain are thrown open, and the unknown always passes for the marvelous. But there are no peoples beyond us, nothing indeed but waves and rocks, and the yet more terrible Romans,

---

[93] The actual site of the battle is unknown.

from whose oppression escape is vainly sought by obedience and submission. Robbers of the world, having by their universal plunder exhausted the land, they rifle the deep. If the enemy be rich, they are rapacious; if he be poor, they lust for dominion; neither the east nor the west has been able to satisfy them. Alone among men they covet with equal eagerness poverty and riches. To robbery, slaughter, plunder, they give the lying name of empire. They make a desert and call it peace.

"Nature has willed that every man's children and kindred should be his dearest objects. Yet these are torn from us by conscriptions to be slaves elsewhere. Our wives and our sisters, even though they may escape violation from the enemy, are dishonored under the names of friendship and hospitality. Our goods and fortunes they collect for their tribute, our harvests for their granaries. Our very hands and bodies, under the lash and in the midst of insult, are worn down by the toil of clearing forests and morasses. Creatures born to slavery are sold once for all, and are, moreover, fed by their masters; but Britain is daily purchasing, is daily feeding, her own enslaved people. And as in a household the last comer among the slaves is always the butt of his companions, so we in a world long used to slavery, as the newest and the most contemptible, are marked out for destruction. We have neither fruitful plains, nor mines, nor harbors, for the working of which we may be spared. Valor, too, and high spirit in subjects, are offensive to rulers; besides, remoteness and seclusion, while they give safety, provoke suspicion. Since then you cannot hope for quarter, take courage, I beseech you, whether it be safety or renown that you hold most precious. Under a woman's leadership the Brigantes were able to burn a colony, to storm a camp, and had not success ended in supineness, might have thrown off the yoke.[94] Let us, then, a fresh and unconquered people, never likely to abuse our freedom, show forthwith at the very first onset what heroes Caledonia has in reserve.

"Do you suppose that the Romans will be as brave in war as they are licentious in peace? To our strifes and discords they owe their fame, and they turn the errors of an enemy to the renown of their own army, an army that, composed as it is of every variety of nations, is held together by success and will be broken up by disaster. These Gauls and Germans, and, I blush to say, these numerous Britons, who, though they lend their lives to support a stranger's rule, have been its enemies longer than its subjects, you cannot imagine to be bound by fidelity and affection. Fear and terror there certainly are, feeble bonds of attachment; remove them, and those who have ceased to fear will begin to hate. All the incentives to victory are on our side. The Romans have no wives to kindle their courage; no parents to taunt them with flight; many have either no country or one far away. Few in number, dismayed by their ignorance, looking around upon a sky, a sea, and forests that are all unfamiliar to them; hemmed in, as it were, and enmeshed, the gods have delivered them into our hands. Be not frightened by idle display, by the glitter of gold and of silver, which can neither protect nor wound. In the very ranks of the enemy we shall find our own forces. Britons will acknowledge their own cause; Gauls will remember past freedom; the other Germans will abandon them, as but lately did the Usipii.[95] Behind them there is nothing to dread. The forts are ungarrisoned; the colonies in the hands of aged men; what with disloyal subjects and oppressive rulers, the towns are ill-affected and rife with discord. On the one side you have a general and an army; on the other, tribute, the mines, and all the other penalties of an enslaved people. Whether you endure these forever, or instantly avenge them, this field is to decide. Think, therefore, as you advance to battle, at once of your ancestors and of your posterity."

They received his speech with enthusiasm, and as is usual among barbarians, with songs, shouts and discordant cries. And now was seen the

---

[94] A reference to the earlier revolt of Boudiccca.

[95] An auxiliary cohort of Usipians, a Germanic people, recently had mutinied and sailed off in three ships. Reduced to cannibalism, they finally landed in Germania, where they were enslaved.

assembling of troops and the gleam of arms, as the boldest warriors stepped to the front. As the line was forming, Agricola, who, though his troops were in high spirits and could scarcely be kept within the entrenchments, still thought it right to encourage them, spoke as follows—

"Comrades, this is the eighth year since, thanks to the greatness and good fortune of Rome and to your own loyalty and energy, you conquered Britain. In our many campaigns and battles, whether courage in meeting the foe, or toil and endurance in struggling, I may say, against nature herself, have been needed, I have ever been well satisfied with my soldiers, and you with your commander. And so you and I have passed beyond the limits reached by former armies or by former governors, and we now occupy the last confines of Britain, not merely in rumor and report, but with an actual encampment and armed force. Britain has been both discovered and subdued. Often on the march, when morasses, mountains, and rivers were wearing out your strength, did I hear our bravest men exclaim, 'When shall we have the enemy before us?—when shall we fight?' He is now here, driven from his lair, and your wishes and your valor have free scope, and everything favors the conqueror, everything is adverse to the vanquished. For as it is a great and glorious achievement, if we press on, to have accomplished so great a march, to have traversed forests and to have crossed estuaries, so, if we retire, our present most complete success will prove our greatest danger. We have not the same knowledge of the country or the same abundance of supplies, but we have arms in our hands, and in them we have everything. For myself I have long been convinced that neither for an army nor for a general is retreat safe. Better, too, is an honorable death than a life of shame, and safety and renown are for us to be found together. And it would be no inglorious end to perish on the extreme confines of earth and of nature.

"If unknown nations and an untried enemy confronted you, I should urge you on by the example of other armies. As it is, look back upon your former honors, question your own eyes. These are the men who last year under cover of darkness attacked a single legion, whom you routed by a shout. Of all the Britons, these are the most confirmed runaways, and this is why they have survived so long. Just as when the huntsman penetrates the forest and the thicket, all the most courageous animals rush out upon him, while the timid and feeble are scared away by the very sound of his approach, so the bravest of the Britons have long since fallen; and the rest are a mere crowd of spiritless cowards. You have at last found them, not because they have stood their ground, but because they have been overtaken. Their desperate plight, and the extreme terror that paralyses them, have riveted their line to this spot, that you might achieve in it a splendid and memorable victory. Put an end to campaigns; crown your fifty years' service with a glorious day;[96] prove to your country that her armies could never have been fairly charged with protracting a war or with causing a rebellion."

While Agricola was yet speaking, the ardor of the soldiers was rising to its height, and the close of his speech was followed by a great outburst of enthusiasm. In a moment they flew to arms. He arrayed his eager and impetuous troops in such a manner that the auxiliary infantry, 8,000 in number, strengthened his center, while 3,000 cavalry were posted on his wings. The legions were drawn up in front of the entrenched camp; his victory would be vastly more glorious if won without the loss of Roman blood, and he would have a reserve in case of repulse. The enemy, to make a formidable display, had posted himself on high ground; his van was on the plain, while the rest of his army rose in an arch-like form up the slope of a hill. The plain between resounded with the noise and with the rapid movements of chariots and cavalry. Agricola, fearing that from the enemy's superiority of force he would be simultaneously attacked in front and on the flanks, widened his ranks, and though his line was likely to be too extended, and several officers advised him to bring up the legions, yet, so sanguine was he, so resolute in meeting danger,

---

[96] A bit of an exaggeration, given that the invasion of Britain had commenced in 43 CE, forty years earlier.

he sent away his horse and took his stand on foot before the colors.

The action began with distant fighting. The Britons with equal steadiness and skill used their huge swords and small shields to avoid or to parry the missiles of our soldiers, while they themselves poured on us a dense shower of darts, until Agricola encouraged three Batavian and two Tungrian cohorts to bring matters to the decision of close fighting with swords. Such tactics were familiar to these veteran soldiers, but were embarrassing to an enemy armed with small bucklers and unwieldy weapons. The swords of the Britons are not pointed, and do not allow them to close with the foe, or to fight in the open field. No sooner did the Batavians begin to close with the enemy, to strike them with their shields, to disfigure their faces, and overthrowing the force on the plain to advance their line up the hill, than the other auxiliary cohorts joined with eager rivalry in cutting down all the nearest of the foe. Many were left behind half dead, some even unwounded, in the hurry of victory. Meantime the enemy's cavalry had fled, and the charioteers had mingled in the engagement of the infantry. But although these at first spread panic, they were soon impeded by the close array of our ranks and by the inequalities of the ground. The battle had anything but the appearance of a cavalry action, for men and horses were carried along in confusion together, while chariots, destitute of guidance, and terrified horses without drivers, dashed as panic urged them, sideways, or in direct collision against the ranks.

Those of the Britons who, having as yet taken no part in the engagement, occupied the hill-tops, and who without fear for themselves sat idly disdaining the smallness of our numbers, had begun gradually to descend and to hem in the rear of the victorious army, when Agricola, who feared this very movement, opposed their advance with four squadrons of cavalry held in reserve by him for any sudden emergencies of battle. Their repulse and rout was as severe as their onset had been furious. Thus the enemy's design recoiled on himself, and the cavalry that by the general's order had wheeled round from the van of the contending armies, attacked his rear. Then, indeed, the open plain presented an awful and hideous spectacle. Our men pursued, wounded, made prisoners of the fugitives only to slaughter them when others fell in their way. And now the enemy, as prompted by their various dispositions, fled in whole battalions with arms in their hands before a few pursuers, while some, who were unarmed, actually rushed to the front and gave themselves up to death. Everywhere there lay scattered arms, corpses, and mangled limbs, and the earth reeked with blood. Even the conquered now and then felt a touch of fury and of courage. On approaching the woods, they rallied, and as they knew the ground, they were able to pounce on the foremost and least cautious of the pursuers. Had not Agricola, who was present everywhere, ordered a force of strong and lightly-equipped cohorts, with some dismounted troopers for the denser parts of the forest, and a detachment of cavalry where it was not so thick, to scour the woods like a party of huntsmen, serious loss would have been sustained through the excessive confidence of our troops. When, however, the enemy saw that we again pursued them in firm and compact array, they fled no longer in masses as before, each looking for his comrade; but dispersing and avoiding one another, they sought the shelter of distant and pathless wilds. Night and weariness of bloodshed put an end to the pursuit. About 10,000 of the enemy were slain; on our side there fell 360 men, and among them Aulus Atticus, the commander of the cohort, whose youthful impetuosity and mettlesome steed had borne him into the midst of the enemy.

Elated by their victory and their booty, the conquerors passed a night of merriment. Meanwhile the Britons, wandering amidst the mingled wailings of men and women, were dragging off their wounded, calling to the unhurt, deserting their homes, and in their rage actually firing them, choosing places of concealment only instantly to abandon them. One moment they would take counsel together, the next, part company, while the sight of those who were dearest to them sometimes melted their hearts, but oftener roused their fury. It was an undoubted fact that some of them vented their rage on their wives and children, as if in pity for their lot. The following day showed more fully the extent of the calamity, for the silence of desolation reigned everywhere: the hills were forsaken, houses were smoking in the distance, and no one was seen by the scouts. These were dispatched in all directions; and it having been ascertained that the track of the flying enemy was uncertain, and that there was no attempt at rallying, it being also impossible, as summer was now over, to extend the war, Agricola led back his army into the territory of the Boresti. He received hostages from them, and then ordered the commander of the fleet to sail round Britain. A force for this purpose was given him, which great panic everywhere preceded. Agricola himself, leading his infantry and cavalry by slow marches, so as to overawe the newly-conquered peoples by the very tardiness of his progress, brought them into winter-quarters, while the fleet with propitious breezes and great renown entered the harbor of Trutulium,[97] to which it had returned after having coasted along the entire southern shore of the island.

---

[97] Location unknown.

THE TRIAL OF JESUS BEFORE PONTIUS PILATE
(ca. 28/36 CE)

THE NEW TESTAMENT, MATTHEW 27:11–16; MARK 5:1–30; JOHN 18:28–40 AND 19:1–24;
AND LUKE 23:1–25

The Rossano Gospels, an illustrated manuscript produced in Italy in the sixth century CE, depicts the trial of Jesus before Pontius Pilate. Pilate is shown as a late Roman governor sitting on a raised dais and flanked by attendants holding standards bearing the portraits of two emperors. To his left lawyers make their case and to his right the crowd shouts its opinions. A stenographer records the proceedings as two imperial officials in military robes present Jesus and two underlings present the robber Barabbas.

During the early years of the Principate, Judaea was racked by dissension. Various Jewish popular leaders were thought to be the "Messiah," the person that many Jews believed would unify the Jewish people, give the Jews back their independence, and bring a new era of world peace. The Jewish teacher Yeshua bar Yosef of Nazareth, known as Jesus in English and Christos ("the anointed one") in Greek, was one of these. He caused so much anxiety for the established Jewish hierarchy that he was put on trial before the Sanhedrin, the Jewish high court, and was condemned when he declined to deny that he was the son of God. Because the Jewish court was located in the Roman province of Judaea, it had no authority to pass the death sentence. Only the Roman governor, in this case the Prefect of Judaea, Pontius Pilate, had the authority to do that. So Caïaphas, the Jewish High Priest, turned Jesus over to the Romans for an additional trial. During the proceedings, Pilate made several attempts to distance himself from what he saw as purely local bickering. The date of Jesus' trial is uncertain, but the book of Luke states that Jesus' baptism occurred at some time after the beginning of the ministry of John the Baptist, "In the fifteenth year of the reign of

Tiberius Caesar"—that is, in 28 CE. Pontius Pilate was replaced as governor circa 36 BCE; this would place Jesus' trial sometime between 28 and 36 BCE. The story of Jesus' trial before Pilate presented here is a conflation of the accounts given in all four of the New Testament gospels. The three synoptic gospels, Matthew (27:11–16), Mark (5:1–30), and Luke (23:1–25), repeat similar versions of the same account; the book of John gives a longer report.

Source: *The Bible, American Standard Version* (New York, 1901).

They led Jesus therefore from Caïaphas[98] into the *praetorium*[99]; and it was early, and they themselves entered not into the *praetorium*, that they might not be defiled, but might eat the Passover.[100] Pilate[101] therefore went out to them, and said, "What accusation bring you against this man?" They answered him, "If this man were not an evildoer, we should not have delivered him up to you." And they began to accuse him, saying, "We found this man perverting our nation and forbidding to give tribute to Caesar, and saying that he himself is Christ, a king." And Pilate asked him, saying, "Are you the King of the Jews?" And he answered him, "You say it."[102] And Pilate said to the chief priests and the multitudes, "I find no fault in this man." But they were the more urgent, saying, "He stirs up the people, teaching throughout all Judaea, and beginning from Galilee[103] even to this place." But when Pilate heard it he asked whether the man were a Galilaean. And when he knew that he was of Herod's jurisdiction, he sent him to Herod,[104] who himself also was at Jerusalem in these days. Now when Herod saw Jesus he was exceeding glad, for he was of a long time desirous to see him because he had heard about him,

and he hoped to see some miracle done by him. And he questioned Jesus in many words, but he answered him nothing. And the chief priests and the scribes stood by, vehemently accusing him. And Herod with his soldiers set him at nought, and mocked him, and arraying him in gorgeous apparel sent him back to Pilate. And Herod and Pilate became friends with each other that very day: for before they were at enmity between themselves.

And Pilate called together the chief priests and the rulers and the people, and said to them, "You brought to me this man as one that perverts the people, and behold, I, having examined him before you, found no fault in this man regarding those things of which you accuse him, no, nor yet Herod, for he sent him back to us, and behold, nothing worthy of death has been done by him. I will therefore chastise him, and release him." And when the chief priests and elders accused Jesus of many things, he answered nothing. And Pilate again asked Jesus, saying, "Do you answer nothing? Behold how many things they accuse you of." But Jesus no more answered anything, insomuch that Pilate marveled. Pilate therefore said to them, "Take him yourselves and judge him according to your law." The Jews said to him, "It is not lawful for us to put any man to death."

Pilate therefore entered again into the *praetorium*, and called Jesus, and said to him, "Are you the King of the Jews?" Jesus answered, "Do you say this yourself, or did others tell it to you concerning me?" Pilate answered, "Am I a Jew? Your own nation and the chief priests delivered you to me. What have you done?" Jesus answered, "My kingdom is not of this world. If my kingdom were of this world, then would my servants fight so that I should not be delivered to the Jews, but my

---

[98] The High Priest of the Jews in Jerusalem.

[99] The headquarters building of a Roman army camp.

[100] The Jews had many regulations relating to ritual purity, especially at the time of the celebration of festivals.

[101] Pontius Pilate, the Equestrian Prefect (Governor) of the Roman province of Judaea ca. 26–36 CE.

[102] Throughout the proceedings, Jesus refuses to speak to the Jewish officials and in so doing acknowledge their authority; he speaks only to Pilate.

[103] A region of Judaea neighboring the Sea of Galilee, north of Jerusalem.

[104] Herod Antipas, a Roman client, son of Herod the Great and Tetrarch of Galilee and Perea ca. 6–39 CE.

kingdom is not from here." Pilate therefore said to him, "Are you a king then?" Jesus answered, "You say that I am a king. To this end have I been born and to this end have I come into the world, that I should bear witness to the truth. Every one that is of the truth hears my voice." Pilate said to him, "What is truth?"

And when he had said this, he went out again to the Jews, and said to them, "I find no crime in him. But you have a custom, that I should release to you one prisoner at the Passover." And there was one called Barabbas, who for a certain insurrection made in the city, and for murder, was cast into prison.[105] Pilate said to them, "Whom do you wish that I release to you? Barabbas, or Jesus who is called Christ and the King of the Jews?" For he knew that it was for envy that they had delivered Jesus up. And while he was sitting on the judgment seat, his wife sent to him, saying, "Have nothing to do with that righteous man, for I have suffered many things this day in a dream because of him." Now the chief priests and the elders persuaded the multitudes that they should ask for Barabbas, and destroy Jesus. The governor said to them, "Which of the two do you wish that I release to you?" They cried out therefore again, saying, "Not this man, but Barabbas." Pilate said to them, "What then shall I do to Jesus, who is called Christ?" They all sad, "Let him be crucified."

And he said to them a third time, "Why, what evil has this man done? I have found no cause of death in him. I will therefore chastise him and release him." But they were urgent with loud voices, asking that he might be crucified. And their voices prevailed. So when Pilate saw that he achieved nothing, but rather that a tumult was arising, he took water and washed his hands before the multitude, saying, "I am innocent of the blood of this righteous man. See to it." And all the people answered and said, "His blood be on us, and on our children." And Pilate gave sentence that what they asked for should be done. And he released the one who for insurrection and

murder had been cast into prison, whom they asked for. Then Pilate therefore took Jesus and whipped him.

And the soldiers plaited a crown of thorns and put it on his head, and arrayed him in a purple garment, and they came to him, and said, "Hail, King of the Jews!," and they struck him with their hands. And Pilate went out again, and said to them, "Behold, I bring him out to you, so that you may know that I find no crime in him." Jesus therefore came out, wearing the crown of thorns and the purple garment. And Pilate said to them, "Behold, the man!" When therefore the chief priests and the officers saw him, they cried out, saying, "Crucify him, crucify him!" Pilate said to them, "Take him yourselves, and crucify him, for I find no crime in him." The Jews answered him, "We have a law, and by that law he ought to die, because he made himself the Son of God." When Pilate heard this saying, he was the more afraid, and he entered into the *praetorium* again and said to Jesus, "From where do you come ?" But Jesus gave him no answer. Pilate therefore said to him, "Do you not speak to me? Do you now know that I have power to release you, and have power to crucify you?" Jesus answered him, "You would have no power against me except if it were given to you from above. Therefore he that delivered me to you has greater sin." Upon this Pilate sought to release him, but the Jews cried out, saying, "If you release this man, you are not Caesar's friend. Every one that makes himself a king speaks against Caesar." When Pilate heard these words, he brought Jesus out and sat down on the judgment seat at a place called "The Pavement," but in Hebrew, Gabbatha. Now it was the Preparation of the Passover; it was about the sixth hour. And he said to the Jews, "Behold, your king!" They therefore cried out, "Away with him, away with him, crucify him!" Pilate said to them, "Shall I crucify your king?" The chief priests answered, "We have no king but Caesar."

Then therefore he delivered him to them to be crucified. Therefore they took Jesus, and he

---

[105] This from the books of Mark and Luke; according to the book of John, Barabbas was a robber.

went out, bearing the cross for himself, to the place called the place of a skull, which is called in Hebrew, Golgotha. There they crucified him, and with him two others, on either side one, and Jesus in the middle. And Pilate wrote a title also, and put it on the cross. And there was written, "Jesus of Nazareth, the King of the Jews." This title therefore many of the Jews read, for the place where Jesus was crucified was near to the city; and it was written in Hebrew, in Latin, and in Greek. The chief priests of the Jews therefore said to Pilate, "Write not, 'The King of the Jews,' but that he said, 'I am King of the Jews'." Pilate answered, "What I have written I have written." The soldiers therefore, when they had crucified Jesus, took his garments and made four parts, to every soldier a part, and also the coat. Now the coat was without seam, woven from the top throughout. They said therefore one to another, let us not rend it, but cast lots for it, whose it shall be, that the scripture might be fulfilled, which says, "They parted my garments among them, And upon my vesture did they cast lots."

CHAPTER 9

THE ROMAN PEACE (96–192)

The second century CE marked the height of the *Pax Romana*, or "Roman Peace," the period when the Roman Empire was most well administered, most peaceful, most inclusive, and most economically sound. As the Roman Empire became more socially, culturally, and economically integrated, it embraced all of the manifold peoples living within its diffuse frontiers and provided opportunities for advancement to all of its residents. The evolution of a Mediterranean Culture created the most cohesive and successful empire that the world had yet known.

THE ANTONINE DYNASTY (96–192)

The **Antonine Dynasty**, also known as the period of the Adoptive Emperors or the **Five Good Emperors**, represented the period of the *Pax Romana* during which the Roman Empire was absolutely at its height. Peace prevailed from Scotland to the Nile cataracts, from Gibraltar to the Caucasus Mountains; the empire was well governed and economically prosperous, and it offered opportunities to residents of all sections of the empire. Indeed, Edward Gibbon, who in 1776 published *The Decline and Fall of the Roman Empire*, opined that this was the best time to have lived in the whole history of the world. One of the reasons that the empire was well administered under the Antonines was that the first four had no blood sons, meaning that they could groom their successors and then adopt them to placate the army. The first five Antonine emperors thus went down in history as the Five Good Emperors.

Nerva (96–98)

After the assassination of Domitian, the Senate was prepared. It immediately granted imperial powers to the elderly senator Nerva (96–98), an experienced administrator under the Flavians, and affixed a sentence of Damnation of Memory upon Domitian. Nerva, as a nominee of the Senate and not of the

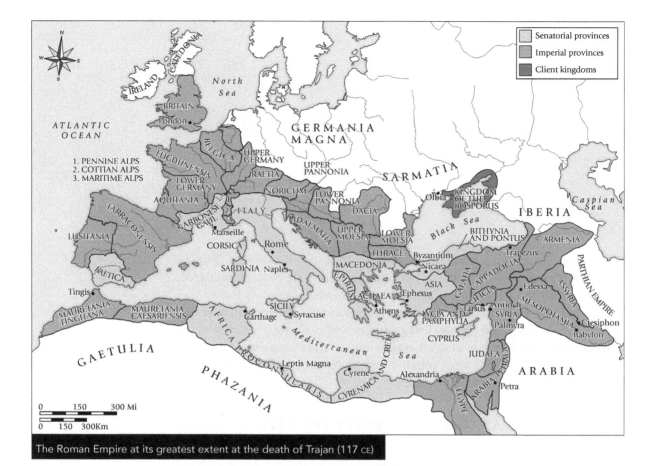

Senatorial provinces
Imperial provinces
Client kingdoms

1. PENNINE ALPS
2. COTTIAN ALPS
3. MARITIME ALPS

The Roman Empire at its greatest extent at the death of Trajan (117 CE)

TABLE 9.1   THE ANTONINE DYNASTY

Nerva (96–98)

Trajan (98–117)

Hadrian (117–138)

Antoninus (138–161)

Lucius Verus (161–169)

Marcus Aurelius (161–180)

Commodus (180–192)

army, attempted to gain army support by granting an even more enormous do-native of 5,000 *denarii* to each of the Praetorian Guards. In addition, he promised that no Senator would be put to death and recalled those who had been exiled by Domitian. But his hesitant manner of ruling—for example, he declined to execute senators who had been involved in a conspiracy—and his initial reluctance to name a successor led to a growing lack of confidence in his abilities. Only after being kidnaped by the Praetorian Guard did he finally adopt as his successor the popular army general Trajan (98–117), thus beginning the second-century tradition of selecting suitable successors by adoption. Otherwise, Nerva, who ruled barely more than a year, did not have the time to institute any significant policies. In January, 98, Nerva died of a fever and was smoothly succeeded by Trajan. Nerva and Trajan mark the beginning of a period in which emperors were chosen on the basis of their ability and were adopted by their predecessors in order to give the army the sons it loved.

Trajan (98–117)

As a native of Spain, Trajan was the first emperor of non-Italian origin, and power continued to diffuse out of Italy and into the provinces. Trajan was a popular emperor. He often consulted the Senate and received from it the title "the Best Prince." His building program in Rome included the construction of a huge bath complex and the vast Trajan's Forum, which included a marketplace for the distribution of free food, a basilica, column commemorating the Dacian Wars, libraries, and a temple in his name, anticipating his own deification. His reign was looked back on as the second Golden Age of the Roman Empire, the reign of Augustus having been the first. Trajan was the only emperor to undertake large-scale violations of Augustus' policy of non-expansion. Between 101 and 107 he conducted two wars in Dacia (101–102 and 105–107 CE), on the north side of the lower Danube River, and annexed it as a new province.

Subsequently, Trajan's attentions turned to the east. In 106, the Nabataean kingdom was annexed and became the new province of Arabia Petraea, named after the Nabataean capital of Petra. The province extended into the Sinai and northwestern Arabia. In 115, after the Parthians had laid claim to Armenia in violation of the treaty with Nero, Trajan invaded the Parthian Empire. He captured the capital city of Ctesiphon on the Tigris River and became the only Roman emperor to go wading in the Persian Gulf. He created new provinces in Armenia, Assyria, and Mesopotamia. But problems caused by Jewish insurrections in Trajan's rear made the situation difficult. In the Kitos War, the second Jewish rebellion against Rome, revolts for unknown reasons by Jews of the diaspora in Cyrenaica, Egypt, and Cyprus in 115 spread to Palestine, and then to the newly conquered territories, where the Jews of Mesopotamia massacred the small Roman garrisons. It was reported that over 200,000 Romans were killed in Egypt alone. Trajan entrusted the command in the war to Lusius Quietus, a Berber prince who had risen to high command. Quietus crushed the rebellion and gave his name to the war.

Meanwhile, still in 117, Trajan, who had been afflicted by sunstroke, proposed to return to Rome, but died unexpectedly in Anatolia. His wife, the Augusta Plotina, declared that just before his death Trajan had named another Spaniard, Hadrian, an experienced soldier and administrator, as his successor. This was a popular choice, and the claim went unchallenged.

Hadrian (117–138)

Hadrian (117–138) immediately returned to Augustus' policy of establishing strongly defended borders and avoiding adventures of foreign conquest. He made a treaty with Parthia that abandoned the new provinces of Armenia, Assyria, and Mesopotamia but gained very favorable trading privileges for Roman merchants. The frontier provinces of Arabia and Dacia, however, were retained, Arabia for its control of trade routes and Dacia for its gold mines, which were needed to replace the output of the depleted gold and silver mines of Spain, Egypt, and Anatolia. Hadrian spent much of his reign on the road, visiting nearly every province. He built one stone fortification known as Hadrian's Wall across northern Britain and another between the upper Rhine and Danube.

Hadrian was confronted with a serious military campaign when the Jews rebelled in the **Bar Kochba Revolt** (132–135), the third major Jewish revolt against Rome. The revolt was instigated when Hadrian unwisely proposed to build a new city on the ruins of Jerusalem, much like Gaius Gracchus had proposed building a Roman colony on the cursed site of Carthage in the 120s BCE, and to erect a temple to Jupiter on the site of the Jewish temple. This was something the Jews of Palestine could not tolerate, and they went so far as to establish their own country. Many Jews saw Simon Bar Kochba, the leader of the revolt, as the Jewish Messiah. Roman military losses were very heavy, with two legions eventually being disbanded, before the revolt finally was suppressed. Jewish losses were even greater, with reportedly 580,000 killed. Roman retribution was severe. Anti-Jewish legislation prohibited the use of Torah law and the Jewish calendar and many Jews departed, expanding the Jewish diaspora. The remaining rabbis, Jewish teachers, continued to preserve the Jewish way of life, now centered on places of worship known as synagogues.

Like other emperors, Hadrian adorned Rome with additional public buildings, including the Temple of Venus and Rome and the circular temple called the Pantheon, Greek for "All the Gods," not to mention a new mausoleum for himself,

A silver shekel of the Bar Kochba revolt, the third Jewish revolt against the Roman Empire, struck in 133–134 CE, depicts a temple facade that might be the Jewish temple destroyed by the Romans in 70 CE at the end of the first Jewish revolt. The reverse depictions of a *lulav* (palm branch, myrtle, and willow) and *ethrog* (citron fruit) refer to the Jewish feast of Sukkot (the Feast of the Tabernacles) and the legend reads "Year Two of the Freedom of Israel."

all of the previous emperors having been interred in the tomb of Augustus. In the countryside, about thirty miles (forty-eight kilometers) from Rome, he also constructed an elaborate villa at Tivoli.

The imperial bureaucracy continued to expand. Hadrian formalized the policy of using equestrians rather than ex-slaves in midlevel government posts in the central government and preferred to consult with *amici* ("friends") and a private *consilium* ("council") made up of high officials and jurists rather than with the Senate. When it came to the succession, Hadrian was a micromanager. After his first choice, Lucius Aelius, died, Hadrian not only adopted the middle-aged senator Antoninus but he also required Antoninus to adopt both Aelius' eight-year-old son Lucius Verus and seventeen-year-

Hadrian constructed the Pantheon, or Temple of "All the Gods," a round temple added to a porch built over a century earlier by Agrippa, the friend of Augustus.

old Marcus Aurelius Antoninus, a talented member of a distinguished senatorial family. Hadrian also required Antoninus to marry his daughter Faustina, when the time was right, to Verus.

Antoninus Pius (138–161)

On Hadrian's death in 138, **Antoninus** smoothly succeeded as emperor. He ruled over the Roman Empire during its most flourishing period and gave his name to the Antonine Dynasty. Another curious consequence of Antoninus' success is that little of interest to sensation-seeking historians occurred, and the historical record of Antoninus' reign thus is rather scanty. He demonstrated fiscal responsibility by cutting back on the extravagant building programs that had characterized the reigns of his predecessors. He was popular with the Senate, which granted him the epithet *Pius* ("The Dutiful"), a title that, like Augustus, was so popular that it also was used by many subsequent emperors. After his death, a temple honoring him and his wife, the Augusta Faustina, was constructed in the Roman forum.

Marcus Aurelius (161–180)

Antoninus Pius was succeeded in 161 by his own adopted sons, **Marcus Aurelius** (161–180) and Lucius Verus (161–169), marking the first time the empire had been ruled by more than one emperor at the same time. Even though Marcus was the senior, and much more able, member of the partnership, he accorded Verus full equality in the rule. Marcus was devoted to Stoic philosophy, which inculcated the necessity of doing one's duty. He even composed a book called the *Meditations* that preserves some of his personal thoughts on what it meant to be emperor. He had little chance, however, for

THE DARK SIDE OF ROMANIZATION

The Romans were not loath to use violence to terrorize peoples who resisted them, as seen in this scene from the Column of Marcus Aurelius, in which defeated Germans are forced to decapitate each other.

In the past, historians customarily saw the creation of a common Greco-Roman culture in the Roman Empire as a process of "Romanization" whereby the benefits of Roman culture were happily assimilated by provincial populations. But the Romans themselves realized that the situation on the ground was not so simple, and that many foreign peoples were very chary about being brought under Roman authority. Those who resisted Rome understood that any war would be fought with no quarter; thus, stringent measures were called for. During the Gallic revolt against Rome in 52 BCE, the Gallic leader Vercingetorix proposed to the Gauls (Caesar, *Gallic Wars* 7.14):

> That the towns ought to be burned . . . so that they would not be places of retreat for their own countrymen for declining military service, nor be exposed to the Romans as inducements to carry off abundance of provisions and plunder. If these sacrifices should appear heavy or galling, they ought to consider it much more distressing that their wives and children would be dragged off to

slavery, and themselves slain, the evils that necessarily must befall the conquered.

And this is what indeed came to pass shortly thereafter during the Roman sack of Avaricum (Bourges). Caesar continues (*Gallic Wars* 7.24):

> The Gauls threw their weapons away and, rushing in a mass, made for the farthest parts of the hill fort. There some of them were killed by our troops as they were crammed together in the narrow gateways; others got out through the gates but were then killed by our cavalry. None of our men stopped to think about booty. They were so infuriated by the massacre of Romans at Orléans, and by the efforts they had had to make over the siege, that they spared neither the old nor the women nor the children. Of the whole population, which had numbered some 40,000, barely 800 got through safely to Vercingetorix; these people had rushed out of the place at the very first sound of the attack.

On several occasions, the historian Tacitus presented the perspective of other side. For example, in explaining why the Britons revolted under Boudicca in 60 CE after the death of King Prasutagus, he noted that:

> His kingdom was plundered by Centurions, his house by slaves, as if they were the spoils of war. First, his wife Boudicca was scourged, and his daughters outraged. All the chief men of the Iceni, as if Rome had received the whole country as a gift, were stripped of their ancestral possessions, and the king's relatives were made slaves. Roused by these insults and the dread of worse, they flew to arms. It was against the veterans that their hatred was most intense. For these new settlers drove people out of their houses, ejected them from their farms, called them captives and slaves, and the lawlessness of the veterans was encouraged by the soldiers, who lived a similar life and hoped for similar license.

And in his account of the Battle of Mount Graupius in Scotland in 83 CE, Tacitus put words into the mouth of Caledonian leader Calgacus that again showed that peoples about to be incorporated into the empire might have a different perspective on the benefits of Roman rule: "They make a desert and they call it peace."

In addition, the Jewish revolts suggest that even after they had been incorporated into the empire, and offered benefits such as Roman citizenship, not all the provincials were happy with Roman occupation, which sometimes was portrayed as being rife with corruption. Josephus, for example, reports regarding the Roman Procurator of Judaea Albinus (62–64 CE):

> But then Albinus, who succeeded Festus, did not execute his office as ably; nor was there any sort of wickedness that could be named but he had a hand in it. Accordingly, he did not only, in his political capacity, steal and plunder every one's substance, nor did he only burden the whole nation with taxes, but he permitted the relations of such as were in prison for robbery, and had been laid there either by the senate of every city or by the former procurators, to redeem them for money. And nobody remained in the prisons as a malefactor but he who gave him nothing . . . Upon the whole, nobody dared speak their minds, but tyranny was generally tolerated; and at this time were those seeds sown which brought the city to destruction.

Even though other administrators, such as Albinus' predecessor Festus, behaved more responsibly, corruption in the provinces was a common phenomenon.

As a consequence, one always must balance the widespread accounts, ancient and modern, of the benefits of being part of the Roman Empire against the occasional, but nonetheless significant, evidence for dissatisfaction with what was seen as Roman oppression, self-interest, and self-righteousness.

private reflection, because several problems arose that required his full attention. For one thing, the empire was afflicted by a devastating plague brought back from a Parthian War in the mid-160s. In 169, Verus died, leaving Marcus as sole emperor.

In addition, for the first time, there were significant threats on the northern frontier. Germanic peoples such as the Marcomanni and Quadi were seeking to move south of the Danube. Marcus was compelled to spend most of his reign on campaign. By 180, the Germans had been pushed back, and the frontier was again secure. Individual defeated barbarians were settled on depopulated Roman land in exchange for their military service. At the time of his death, Marcus was on the verge of creating two new provinces on the northern banks of the Danube and the Rhine, but his desire to fulfill Augustus' plan to shorten the northern frontier died with him.

The Evolution of Roman Law

The *Pax Romana* saw significant developments in Roman law as emperors assumed a personal role in issuing legislation, absorbing the Republican roles of the Senate, the popular assemblies, and the magistrates. At the beginning of the Principate, emperors introduced legislation by presenting an *oratio* (speech) to the Senate, which dutifully issued a Recommendation of the Senate that was rubber-stamped at a pro forma meeting of the Council of the People. But the popular assemblies soon lost any role in government. The rights of the Centuriate Assembly to declare war, elect magistrates with imperium, and try cases were transferred to the emperor, Senate, and jury courts, respectively. The Council of the Plebs lost all power to the emperor by virtue of his tribunician power. The last vestigial meeting of Council of the People was held under Nerva for the passage of an agrarian law. By the second century, approval of imperial legislation by the Senate was assumed, and the imperial *oratio* itself gained the force of law. But no matter how much the emperor controlled the creation and issuance of new laws, there never was a sense that the emperor was above the law. As always in the Roman world, everyone, including the emperor, was subordinated to the rule of law.

Private legal cases were streamlined by combining the action and judgment phases of a case into a single hearing before a judge appointed by a Roman magistrate such as a provincial governor. The administration of private law also became more complicated because of the need to maneuver through a welter of provincial legal customs according to which non-citizen provincials still functioned. In the provinces, criminal law was overseen by the provincial governor, whereas in Italy, the Praetorian Prefect began to assume criminal jurisdiction.

The Principate also saw the rise of legal scholars known as **jurists** who either authored commentaries on Roman law or served as legal advisers to emperors. If a jurist was approved by the emperor, his legal opinions or commentaries could be cited as precedents in courts of law. Hadrian, in an attempt to consolidate legal authority in the emperor's hands even further, removed from the Praetor the right to issue new legal *formulae* and appointed the jurist Salvius Julianus to codify the Praetor's Edict into a standard, permanent form. In addition, every citizen had the right to appeal directly to the emperor, who responded to thousands of petitions a year. Thus, even more authority coalesced in the hands of the emperor. By the end of the Antonine Dynasty it was possible to say, as did the jurist Ulpian, that "whatever the emperor authorizes has the force of law." Imperial legal enactments, which had the generic name **constitutions**, included not only **edicts**—laws binding on the entire empire—but also mandates, instructions to imperial officials; decrees, decisions in court cases rendered by the emperor; and rescripts, replies to petitions.

The modern term "constitution," the general guiding legal principles of a country or organization, has a meaning quite different from the ancient term.

The End of the Antonines

There were five good emperors, but there were six members of the Antonine Dynasty, the last of whom was problematic. Unlike his predecessors, Marcus Aurelius had a son, Commodus (180–192), whose claims to the throne could not be ignored. Like Domitian, Commodus was popular with the army and in the provinces. He made a favorable peace with the Germans and supported the rights of oppressed tenant farmers in North Africa.

But, like Nero before him, Commodus also had a yen for luxurious living, including sponsoring extravagant circus and gladiatorial games, and his expenses could not be met by an empire still recovering from plague and invasion. He also went so far as to portray himself as the Greek hero Hercules. His excesses led to plots against him. He responded by giving a ready ear to delators and by using *frumentarii*, imperial foragers, as a sort of secret police. In 192 his mistress, Marcia, and several high officials, afraid for their lives, induced a professional athlete to strangle Commodus in his bath. Once again the empire was left adrift.

THE WORLD OF THE *PAX ROMANA*

The *Pax Romana* fully manifested Augustus' promise to bring peace and prosperity to the Roman world. New opportunities became available to greater numbers of people for social advancement, economic prosperity, and even religious worship. A common culture created a sense of connection among those with the means and opportunity to participate in the

This statue portrays the emperor Commodus wearing Hercules' lion skin and carrying Hercules' club. This kind of identification of living emperors with divinities was unusual at this time but common a hundred years later.

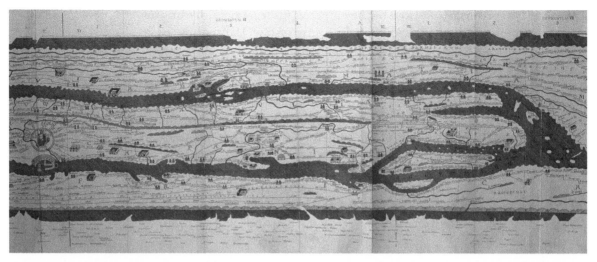

The "Peutinger Table" dates to the early fifth century but was compiled during the previous four centuries. The only surviving Roman roadmap, it depicts hundreds of roads along with the distances between rest stops from Britain to India. The Italian section, shown here, portrays the goddess Roma, representing the city of Rome, in a large circle at left, with Ostia, the port city of Rome, immediately below. The Apennine Mountains run the length of the peninsula. In this squeezed and flattened format, Greece is at the top and North Africa at the bottom.

opportunities Rome had to offer. Those living during this period would have had every reason to hope and believe that the good fortune of the Roman Empire would last forever.

Society and Culture

By the end of the second century CE, Roman citizenship had been extended to as many as half of the free inhabitants of the empire. The Senate represented more of a cross-section of the population and now included many North Africans and Greeks along with Italians and other western Europeans. Non-Romans, such as Greeks and Syrians, benefited from the economic opportunities available in the free market provided by the *Pax Romana*. Segments of the population that had been lacking in privilege in the past gained new rights. Under Hadrian, for example, the old authority of the "father of the family" was weakened, and the status of women and slaves was improved.

Indeed, women came to have greater rights than in any ancient civilization. By the first century CE, marriages *sine manu* ("without authority"), in which women did not come under the legal jurisdiction of their husbands or fathers, had become standard. Women retained control over their own property (usually their dowry) after the deaths of their fathers, and as a result a marriage consisted of not one but two economic units. Women also could manage their own property; they still needed a male to do the paperwork, but if one was not available, the court would appoint one. A divorce could be effected simply by saying "I divorce you" three times in front of witnesses. This is not to say, of course, that wives and husbands did not live amicably. Generally, women managed the household while their husbands oversaw business outside the home. Men often did not marry until after the age of thirty, but wealthy women, who would have slaves to assist them, married as young as twelve or thirteen and shared the rank and status of their husbands. They were well educated and participated in social and cultural activities as much as any man.

Slaves now were valued much more than they had been in the late Republic, for the wars of conquest and the days of cheap slaves were long gone. Regulations on one imperial estate worked by slaves stated that hospitals and baths were to be provided and that slave women were to be freed after bearing several slave children. Indeed, by this time many imperial and senatorial estates were managed by slaves, for senators, too, found it to their advantage to leave their estates in the hands of a few trusted slaves.

The Roman Peace also saw the continued evolution of a common culture that extended the length and breadth of the empire. An amalgam of old Roman traditions, Greek civilization, and provincial culture was created in which all those who partook in the world of Rome could participate. This hybrid Mediterranean Culture was most spectacularly manifested in urban areas, where the Roman presence was most deeply embedded. Rural regions, however, generally remained repositories of whatever native way of life always had been there.

With imperial support, urban life expanded immensely. Rome boasted a population of about one million, and Alexandria, Antioch, and Carthage each checked in at over a quarter of a million. On the frontiers, Roman garrison posts became cities such as Mainz, Strasbourg, Bonn, Vienna, Budapest, and Belgrade. Members of city councils, the decurions, manifested their civic responsibilities by vying with one another to endow their cities with amenities such as theaters, amphitheaters, temples, town halls, libraries, and aqueducts. The emperors often contributed imperial assistance for public works projects, and army troops sometimes provided the labor. On occasion, however, cities overspent on grandiose construction projects and fell into debt. If they were lucky, the emperor would bail them out.

Entertainment

Easily the most popular form of munificence, whether provided by emperors, cities, or private benefactors, was public entertainment, which took several forms and could be vastly expensive. The most visible, most grandiose, and best-liked entertainments were blood sports that took place in an amphitheater, which consisted of a central sand-covered arena surrounded by thousands or tens of thousands of spectator seats. There, one could observe wild beasts and gladiators (both male and female) fighting against one another in different combinations, often accompanied by music. Executions of condemned criminals who were not Roman citizens also could be carried out: they could be hunted down by starved wild animals, gored to death by maddened bulls, or forced to fight one another.

The most famous games were held in the Flavian amphitheater, or Colosseum, in Rome, which adjoined the Republican forum. It was completed in 80 CE and enlarged several times afterward. It could accommodate an audience of over fifty thousand, and the floor could be flooded to present mock naval combats. It even had an awning, operated by sailors detached from the Roman fleet at Misenum on the Bay of Naples, so spectators could watch the bloodletting in the shade. A series of tunnels provided access for both gladiators and wild animals, which could enter the arena through trapdoors.

Contrary to popular belief, not all gladiators were slaves. They also included defeated soldiers, criminals condemned *ad ludos* ("to the games"), and free persons, as many as half, looking for an adventurous life or an opportunity to gain riches. Not only did gladiators keep their prize money, but star gladiators commanded up to a hundred thousand *sestertii* (equivalent to about a quarter of a million dollars) in appearance money. Conceptually, gladiators were meant to inspire in viewers an appreciation of Rome's martial virtues. Gladiators were costumed and armed to represent certain standard kinds of figures: the *murmillo* carried an oblong shield and a *gladius*; the Thracian wore a broad-rimmed helmet and carried a small round shield and a curved sword; and the ever-popular *retiarius* ("net man") bore a trident and arm-guard, a net, and a dagger. Contrary to Hollywood portrayals, gladiators rarely fought to the death: if they had, the Romans soon would have run short of trained gladiators. Audiences were happy to see a good contest, and nearly always preferred to see even losing competitors get another chance in a future match. Fights to the death were special occasions and got special billing. In addition, star gladiators, like modern sumo wrestlers, fought only a few times a year. The rest of the time they lived a life of luxury, enlivened by trysts with their male or female admirers.

On the other side of the Palatine Hill from the Colosseum was the Circus Maximus ("great circus"), the site of chariot races, a very popular form of entertainment that often featured spectacular crashes. In Rome, there were four chariot racing teams, named after their team colors, the "blues," "greens," "reds," and "whites." Each of them had fan clubs, one of the few forms of permitted public organizations. The fan clubs, known as "factions," sometimes had political overtones; the members of a circus faction could shout out slogans intended for the ears of the emperor.

Many cities around the empire also had their own amphitheaters and circuses where similar entertainments were presented on a smaller scale. Cities

FEMALE GLADIATORS

During the Principate, gladiators were hugely popular and were the media darlings of the Roman world. They regularly appeared in frescoes, relief sculptures, and mosaics in the villas of the well-to-do. For the less wealthy, there was a multitude of gladiator memorabilia ranging from impressions on stamped tableware to gladiator-themed oil lamps. Nor were gladiatorial combats limited to men: anticipating the female competitors of modern Mixed Martial Arts matches, Roman women also fought in the arena. The biographer Suetonius, for example, reports that the emperor Domitian (81–96) "gave hunts of wild beasts, gladiatorial shows at night by the light of torches, and not only combats between men but between women as well." The poet Statius likewise spoke of spectacles at the same time, where "The unskilled sex, unused to swords, take positions in warlike combat; they seem like troops of Amazons." And female gladiators were in fact cast in the role of Amazons, as seen in this relief from Halicarnassus in Anatolia, now in the British Museum in London, which celebrates a successful combat of two female gladiators, the one on the left stage-named "Amazon" and the one on the right called "Achillia" (a reference to the Greek hero Achilles). The legend at the top, "having been discharged," could be taken to mean either that they had been set free from slavery, or that both had received a *missio*—that is, a release from a combat that was not fought to the death. Each is depicted as a *secutor*, a type of well-protected gladiator, with a large shield, greaves (shin guards), a belted loincloth, and a guard for the sword arm. Unlike men, female gladiators did not wear helmets or tunics in order to make it clear to the audience that they were women, as attested by the Roman poet Juvenal, who satirized a woman who participated in wild beast hunts, citing a time "when Mevia, with a naked breast, holds a hunting spear and pierces a Tuscan boar."

competed against one another, and things could get out of control. Athletes of all kinds could become immensely popular, much as in the modern day. Portrayals of athletes and athletic contests was a very common motif in Roman art—for example, in mosaics and as designs on clay lamps. Gladiatorial groupies could develop libidinous passions for their favorites. Regarding a senator's wife who ran off with a gladiator, for example, the satirist Juvenal commented, "There were sundry deformities in his face, a huge boil upon his nose. But then he was a gladiator! She preferred this to children and to country, to sister, and to husband. What these women love is the sword!" For people with more genteel tastes, theaters in both the Greek and Roman style also peppered the

THE *FORMA URBIS ROMAE*

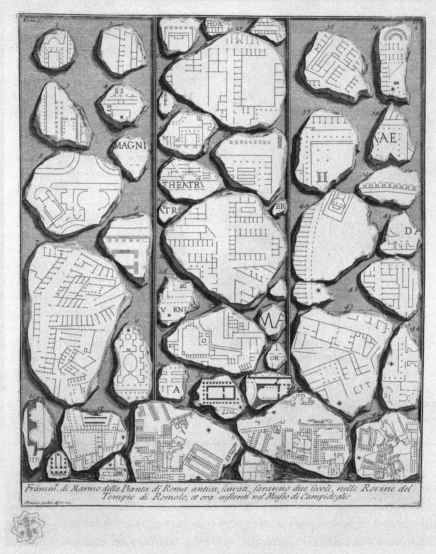

A drawing of a group of fragments from the *Forma Urbis Romae* published by the Renaissance artist Giovanni Batista Piranesi in 1756 suggests how complex the job of fitting them back together would be.

The site of the city of Rome has been continuously occupied since the middle of the eighth century BCE. As the city has grown and evolved over many centuries, remodeling, renovation, rebuilding, and urban renewal has meant that older parts of the city were constantly being destroyed to make way for new construction. In most cases, the only way that the plans of earlier phases of the city can be regained is through painstaking archaeological investigations, which are difficult to undertake because the site is occupied by the modern city. Thus, most modern excavation takes place in an "emergency" context during the construction of a new subway or high-rise building.

But another way to reconstruct what the city looked like at the height of the Roman Empire exists: a gigantic marble plan of the city created at the beginning of the third century CE and known as the *Forma Urbis Romae* ("Shape of the City of Rome"). The plan was sixty feet (eighteen meters) wide and forty-five feet (thirteen meters) high, and was cut onto 151 marble slabs mounted on the wall (which still survives because it later became part of a Christian church) of a room inside Vespasian's Temple of Peace. It was detailed enough to show every street and large building—including the floor plans of public buildings and *insulae* (residential tenements)—in the city. During the Middle Ages, the slabs either fell off the wall and accumulated at its base or were cannibalized as building material. Antiquarian interest in recovering and reconstructing the plan arose in the sixteenth century. When fragments were put on display in the eighteenth century, the edges of some were actually sawed off so they would fit their frames.

New fragments continue to turn up, as in 1999, when thirty more were excavated. Some 1,186 fragments—about 10 percent—of the plan survive and are preserved in the Conservatory and Capitoline Museums in Rome. There have been many efforts to try to determine where the surviving fragments fit on the original plan, and a project at Stanford University (http://formaurbis.stanford.edu/) currently is engaged in creating a digital reconstruction of the surviving fragments.

cities of the empire. Greek-style theaters featured just a bare stage, whereas the stage of Roman theaters had a multistoried backdrop that permitted characters to appear in all three dimensions. As in the Republic, comedies tended to be much more popular than tragedies. By the beginning of the Principate, mime had become the favorite form of Roman drama. Unlike traditional drama, mime was performed without masks and used both male and female actors. Mime encompassed a wide range of performances, including the dramatization of scenes from works of literature, satire, dance routines, and material of a sexually explicit nature. Another form of drama, pantomime, which included no spoken parts, also increased in popularity.

The Economy

The *Pax Romana* also saw an expansion in manufacturing and commerce. Ease of travel by water, either by sea or by river, made it possible to ship small-value items great distances, and the Roman road system made land transport much less expensive. After long use in the Near East, camels began to be used around 200 CE by the Garamantes to replace horses for transport in the Sahara Desert. The unified currency system eliminated complicated monetary transactions. Tolls and port dues were low, banditry had been suppressed, and piracy had been virtually eliminated. Much of the trade was in the hands of easterners, resulting in a shift of the economic center of gravity of the empire toward the east.

Different regions came to be known for different kinds of manufactured products and trade goods. Italy and Gaul were celebrated for their ceramics; Sidon in Phoenicia and northern Gaul were famous for glassblowing; Spain and Britain were centers of mining; and Britain also was a source of wool. Amber was imported from the Baltic Sea area, and exotic animals from Sub-Saharan Africa. But the most extensive foreign trade was with the east, to India and even China. Roman gold, silver, glassware, fabrics, and wine were exchanged for gems, silks, spices, and perfumes. Trajan reopened a canal between the Nile River and the Red Sea, and every year over one hundred trading ships set out from Egypt for India, Sri Lanka (Ceylon), and the east. The journey from Italy, through the canal, and on to India took about sixteen weeks. A second-century Indian poet wrote, "Drink the cool and fragrant wine brought by the Yavanas (Ionians) in their vessels." In 166, envoys claiming to be the representatives of the emperor "An-Tun," apparently a reference to Marcus Aurelius Antoninus, visited the Chinese court. One consequence of the eastern trade was a huge balance-of-payments deficit, which Pliny the Elder estimated at 550 million *sestertii* per year (enough to pay the annual expenses of the entire Roman army). The result was a growing scarcity of gold and silver in the empire that gradually made it more difficulty for the government to issue sufficient numbers of coins to meet its expenses.

The ancient canal from the Nile to the Red Sea silted up in the Middle Ages and was not reopened, as the Suez Canal, until 1869.

Even though the cities had great visibility, and in spite of the expansion in manufacturing and trade, the Roman economy remained essentially agricultural, and the great bulk of the population lived in rural areas. The cities always were parasites on the countryside. The second-century physician Galen, for example, reported that as a consequence of the great urban demand for foodstuffs, country dwellers sometimes were reduced to eating grass and acorns just to survive. The primary grain-growing areas were Egypt; North Africa, which was heavily irrigated; and Sicily. Each year a huge grain fleet departed from Alexandria and headed across the Mediterranean for Rome to help to meet Italy's insatiable need for grain. In addition, certain areas became known for particular kinds of agricultural products. Olive oil came from North Africa, Italy, and Spain; wine from Italy and southern Gaul; and a popular fish sauce known as *garum* from Spain.

Some farmland was held by small subsistence farmers, but huge *latifundia* were owned by senators. Initially, the *latifundia* were farmed mainly by a combination of slave and day labor, but by the second-century tenant farmers known as **coloni** were increasingly used. They remitted a portion of their crops to the landowner and kept the rest for themselves. The biggest landowner was the emperor himself, whose estates grew ever larger as a result of purchases, bequests, and confiscations.

The Silver Age of Roman Literature

Latin literature continued to thrive. Whereas the literature of the late Republic and Augustan period is called Golden Age Latin, that of the remainder of the first and the second century is called the Silver Age. Many Silver Age writers came from outside Italy, reflecting the much more representative nature of the post-Augustan empire. The expansion of literary culture resulted partly from a growing state-sponsored education system, for the expanding imperial bureaucracy had a constant and growing need for educated civil servants. Grammarians and rhetoricians were funded by cities and the imperial government, and many of the beneficiaries of these educational practices went on to serve in the imperial administration, giving administrators a kind of common culture. The education was purely literary, with little exposure to science and mathematics. Law was the most popular field for advanced study: even if orators had much less opportunity to engage in politics than in the Republic, they still could argue cases in court or enforce the law as imperial administrators, and many Silver Age writers practiced law at some point in their careers.

The Thracian slave Phaedrus wrote poetic fables under the first four Julio-Claudian emperors. Under Nero, Persius, a native of Etruria, wrote verse satire in the manner of Horace in which, among other things, he espoused Stoic philosophy and complained about a general decline in morality. Petronius, a member of Nero's court, was called Nero's "judge of elegance" and usually is identified as the author of a partly surviving novel, *The Satyricon*, which relates the attempts of

CULTURAL ENCOUNTERS

ROME AND THE FAR EAST

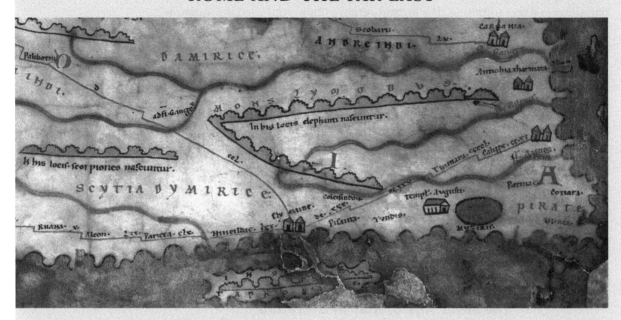

The easternmost section of the Peutinger Table depicts roads and sea routes leading to Ceylon (the island of Taprobane at the bottom here) and India. On the far right is the eastern ocean that was believed to mark the end of the world. The Ganges River flows into the Indian Ocean on the eastern coast of India, and China is omitted. The all-encompassing extent of Roman influence is marked by a "Temple of Augustus" just to the west of the "Pirates" who manifest the dangers that threatened merchants who dared to travel this far. The compiler comments, "In these places serpents appear" and "In these places elephants appear."

Roman cultural interactions extended far to the east. Every year, Roman trading fleets set out from Egypt and made their way to India, Sri Lanka, and even China. A detailed description of the peoples that were encountered on voyages from the Red Sea to India is given in "The Periplus ['sailing Around'] of the Red Sea," written in the first century CE by a merchant who listed market towns and goods that could be traded. Every summer, trading ships would make use of the annual etesian winds out of the southwest to strike out across the open sea from southern Arabia and western Africa for India, as seen in this passage.

Now to the left of Berenice is the adjoining country of Arabia, in its length bordering a great distance on the Erythrean [Red] Sea. Different peoples inhabit the country, differing in their speech. The country inland is peopled by rascally men speaking two languages, who live in villages and nomadic camps, by whom those sailing off the middle course are plundered, and those surviving shipwrecks are taken for slaves. And so they too are continually taken prisoners by the chiefs and kings of Arabia. Navigation is dangerous along this whole coast of Arabia, which is without harbors, with bad anchorages, foul, inaccessible because of breakers and rocks, and terrible in every way. Therefore, we hold our course down the middle of the gulf and pass on as fast as possible by the country of Arabia. [One also encounters] Charibael, lawful king of two peoples, the

Himyarites and the Sabaites; through continual embassies, he is a friend of the emperors.

After Eudaemon Arabia [Aden] there is a continuous length of coast, and a bay extending two thousand *stadia* [230 miles, or 370 kilometers] or more; just beyond the cape projecting from this bay there is another market-town, Cana, of the Kingdom of Eleazar, the Frankincense Country [Yemen]. The frankincense is gathered by the king's slaves and those who are sent to this service for punishment. For these places are very unhealthy, and pestilential even to those sailing along the coast; but almost always fatal to those working there. The inhabitants are foreigners, a mixture of Arabs and Indians and Greeks, who have emigrated to carry on trade there. Sailing along the coast, which trends northward toward the entrance of the Persian Sea, there are many islands known as the Calxi. The inhabitants are a treacherous lot, very little civilized. There follows not far beyond the mouth of the Persian Gulf. Sailing through the mouth of the Gulf, after a six-days' course there is a market-town of Parthia called Ommana [Oman].

Beyond this region, the continent making a wide curve from the east, there follows the coast district of Indo-Scythia, the whole marshy, from which flows down the river Sinthus [Indus River in India], the greatest of all the rivers that flow into the Erythrean Sea. This river has seven mouths, very shallow and marshy, except one by whose shore is the market town, Barbaricum [Karachi, Pakistan]. Inland is Minnagara, the metropolis of Indo-Scythia; it is subject to Parthian princes who are constantly driving each other out. There are imported into this market figured linens, topaz, coral, sweetgum, frankincense, vessels of glass, silver and gold plate, and a little wine, and there are exported ginger, myrrh, wolfberry, incense, turquoise, lapis lazuli, Chinese skins, cotton cloth, silk yarn, and indigo. Sailors set out thither with the Indian etesian winds,

about the month of July: it is more dangerous then, but through these winds the voyage is more direct, and sooner completed. The whole country of India has very many rivers, and very great ebb and flow of the tides; increasing at the new moon, and at the full moon for three days, and falling off during the intervening days of the moon.

This whole voyage, from Cana and Eudaemon Arabia, they used to make in small vessels sailing close around the shores of the gulfs; and Hippalus the pilot first discovered how to lay his course straight across the ocean. For at the same time when with us the etesian winds are blowing, on the shores of India the wind blows in from the ocean. From that time to the present day ships start, some direct from Cana and some from the Cape of Spices [Cape Guardafui in Somalia]; and those bound for Damirica [Malabar coast of southern India] throw the ship's head considerably off the wind; whereas those bound for Indo-Scythia hold the same course straight out to sea, quite away from the land.

Beyond this, the course turns toward the east again, and sailing with the ocean to the right and the shore to the left, the territory of Ganges comes into view, and near it the very last land toward the east, Chryse [Malaysia]. There is a river near it called the Ganges, and it rises and falls in the same way as the Nile. After this region under the very north, the sea outside ending in a land called This [China]. There is a very great inland city called Thinae there, from which raw silk and silk yarn and silk cloth are brought on foot through Bactria to Barygaza [Bharuch on the northwestern Indian coast], and are also exported to Damirica by way of the river Ganges. But the land of This is not easy of access; few men come from there, and seldom. The regions beyond these places are either difficult of access because of their excessive winters and great cold, or else cannot be sought out because of some divine influence of the gods.

Source: Wilfred E. Schoff, trans., *The Periplus of the Erythraean Sea: Travel and Trade in the Indian Ocean by a Merchant of the First Century* (London: Longman, Green and Co., 1919), 22–49.

Encolpius, an ex-gladiator, to keep his sixteen-year-old boyfriend Giton faithful to him. The *Satyricon* includes the famous "Trimalchio's Dinner," an account of the extravagant, but ultimately tedious, attempts of a social-climbing newly rich freedman to fit into Roman society. The rhetorician and philosopher Seneca, a Spaniard, wrote nine surviving tragedies, such as "The Madness of Hercules," and 124 letters on moral topics, such as "On Anger." In the late 40s he became the tutor of the young Nero, and early in Nero's reign was one of his chief advisers. And Lucan, a Spanish nephew of Seneca, initially was a good friend of Nero and wrote an epic poem, the *Pharsalia*, about the war between Pompey and Caesar. In 66, Petronius, Lucan, and Seneca all were implicated in the conspiracy of Piso and allowed to commit suicide. Clearly, writers who interacted too closely with emperors were risking their lives.

In the Flavian period, Latin authors continued to play with fire. The Spanish orator Quintilian wrote a rhetorical handbook, the *Institutes of Oratory*, and was made Consul by the emperor Vespasian in acknowledgment of his efforts to educate the Roman governing class. Statius, the author of a book of occasional verse known as the *Silvae* ("Groves"), flourished during the reign of Domitian, who presented Statius with a golden crown. And Pliny the Elder, who rose from a cavalry commander in Germany to command of the Roman fleet stationed on the Bay of Naples, wrote a *History of the German Wars* and a *History of His Times*, both now lost, and a surviving massive thirty-seven-book *Natural History* that summarized much of ancient knowledge, including geology, geography, zoology, botany, agriculture, architecture, and medicine. Along the way, Pliny added his own pithy observations, such as, "By a marvelous disease of the human intellect, it pleases us to record bloodshed and slaughter in histories, so that the wickedness of men might become known to those who are ignorant of the real world."

During the eruption of Mt. Vesuvius in August of 79, Pliny accompanied ships from the Roman fleet on a rescue mission, and in the course of his scientific observations he was asphyxiated by the volcanic gases. Other practical writers included Columella on agriculture and Frontinus on aqueducts, not to mention Vitruvius, who wrote on architecture a century earlier.

Pliny the Younger, the nephew and adopted son of Pliny the Elder, advanced through the Republican magistracies and became Consul in 100 CE. He subsequently served on the *consilium* of Trajan and died while serving as governor of Bithynia and Pontus. He is known primarily for a panegyric, or speech of praise, in honor of Trajan and for a collection of nine books of personal and official letters, which provide priceless insights into both private lives and administrative procedures during this period. His most famous two letters describe the eruption of Vesuvius and his own soul-searching about whether or not to prosecute Christians in 112.

Under the early Antonine emperors, writers who had felt inhibited under emperors such as Nero and Domitian felt that they could express themselves more freely. Tacitus, arguably the greatest of Roman historians, held several traditional Republican senatorial offices and married Julia, the daughter of the famous general Agricola. After being implicated in some of Domitian's purges, Tacitus, drawing on the histories of Pliny, turned to writing history under the Antonines. Surviving works include the *Germania*, a sympathetic account of the peoples and customs of Germany; the *Agricola*, a biography of his father-in-law; and longer historical narratives—the *Annals*, going from the death of Augustus to the death of Nero, and the *Histories*, covering the Flavian period. Tacitus carefully researched his source material, but although he claimed to be writing *sine ira et studio* ("without rancor or favoritism"), he pitched his presentation is such a way so as to make clear his general unhappiness with how the empire was governed. Like the Greek historian Thucydides, Tacitus provides insights into the nature of the acquiring and wielding of power and has little confidence that powerful persons, such as emperors, will do the right thing. Tacitus also believed that the Senate was largely complicit in the whittling away of Roman liberties.

Outspoken in another way was Suetonius, who served as director of the imperial archives under Trajan and as personal secretary to Hadrian. He therefore had access to a full range of imperial documents, which he put to good use in his *On the Life of the Caesars*, biographies of rulers from Julius Caesar through Domitian that overlap with much of Tacitus' account. Although Suetonius cites a wealth of detail, he also retails a great deal of salacious court gossip. Yet another outspoken writer was the satirist Juvenal, who may have lived into the reign of Hadrian. Juvenal criticized Roman customs and morals, sometimes in such an extravagant way that it is difficult to assess how much he should be believed. For example, he described the influx of easterners into Rome as "the waters of the Orontes [a river in Syria] flowing into the Tiber."

In the modern day, the most explosive volcanic eruptions are termed Plinian eruptions.

From later in the second century comes a writer of possible African origin, Aulus Gellius, whose work *Attic Nights*, written circa 170 CE, is a collection of literary extracts, many from authors whose works do not survive, made for his children. It provides precious insight into literary life and literary education at this time. At about the same time, the North African lawyer Apuleius composed the only Latin novel to survive in full, a bawdy farce known variously as the *Metamorphoses* or the *Golden Ass*, in which a certain Lucius experiments with magic, is turned into an ass, and has a series of adventures. The grammarian Fronto, yet another North African, was the most famous orator of his age, traveling from city to city making speeches. He was the teacher and later the friend of Marcus Aurelius and Lucius Verus, and was rewarded with a consulate in 142. Fronto is best known for his surviving private correspondence with Antoninus Pius, Lucius Verus, and Marcus Aurelius, which paints a sympathetic picture of the relations between a teacher and his imperial pupils and patrons.

In the Greek east, the writers of this period represent the period called the **"Second Sophistic"** (as opposed to the first Greek sophists of the fifth century BCE), a revival of Greek rhetoric and oratory lasting from about 60 to 230 CE that strove to attain a higher standard of education and rhetorical exposition. During this period, Roman emperors such as Hadrian (117–138) and Marcus Aurelius (161–180) served as patrons for and participated in literary activities. Around 100 CE, for example, **Plutarch**, a native of Greece, wrote *Moralia* ("Customs"), a collection of seventy-eight works dealing with matters such as "Brotherly Affection" and "On Peace of Mind," but he is best known as the most famous biographer of antiquity: his *Parallel Lives* contains comparative biographies of famous Greeks and Romans, such as Alexander the Great compared with Julius Caesar. In the mid-second century, Arrian of Nicomedia, a Roman governor and general, wrote the most thorough surviving account of the life of Alexander the Great. Appian of Alexandria, a lawyer who argued cases before emperors, wrote a *Roman History* covering Rome's wars from the founding of Rome until Trajan's Dacian wars. And Lucian of Samosata in Anatolia wrote wildly popular satires, such as "Praise of a Fly," "The Rooster's Dream," and "The Sky-Man," about a man who made a pair of wings, flew up to the gods, and discovered that Zeus intended to destroy all philosophers.

In the same way that Roman administrators shared the same literary culture, in the British Empire of the nineteenth and early twentieth centuries, British overseas administrators were taught a common classical culture in the British "public" (actually private) school system.

RELIGIOUS DIVERSITY

Religions always had a place of prime importance in the lives of ancient peoples. This remained the case during the Roman Empire, which incorporated a great multitude of populations and diverse religious practices. This multicultural environment saw the expansion of one of the most significant religious movements in the history of the world, Christianity. During the first few centuries of its existence, Christianity had some difficult times with the Roman government, but, even so, there were Christians who argued that without the existence of the Roman Empire, Christianity never could have grown to become the most influential religion that the Mediterranean world had ever seen.

Traditional Religious Practices

As was the case throughout antiquity, there were two fundamental kinds of religion in the Roman world: state religion and personal religion. During the Roman Empire, state religion focused on the imperial cult, participation in which was one's way of pledging allegiance to the empire and the emperor. As *Pontifex Maximus*, the emperor was responsible for maintaining the *pax deorum* (peace with the gods), which entailed carrying out appropriate sacrifices, such as the *suovetauralia*, the sacrifice of a pig, a ram, and a bull, before the army set out on campaign. In addition, an increasing catalogue of deified emperors could be depended on to continue to watch over the well-being of the empire.

Personal religion was much more varied. Of the philosophical schools, Stoicism, with its focus on duty and responsibility, maintained its great attraction for the Roman ruling elite. The Hellenistic mystery cults, such as those of Isis and Cybele, likewise retained their popularity, although in the case of Cybele, the staid Romans preferred to substitute bulls' testicles for their own as an offering.

These were joined by the cult of the Persian god sun god **Mithras**, the origins of which have aroused much modern controversy. Some would argue that the cult of Mithras was directly descended from the sun god Mithras, who was part of the Zoroastrian pantheon of the old Persian Empire and whose continued worship in the Hellenistic period was reflected in the royal name Mithridates ("Given by Mithras"). But given that the first solid evidence for Mithraism in the Roman world does not first appear until the first century CE and comes almost exclusively from the western Mediterranean, it also has been suggested that Mithraism as a mystery cult was essentially a Roman invention based on Roman understandings of eastern religions.

Initiates into Mithraism met in an underground shrine known as a Mithraeum, and much of what little can be deduced about Mithraic theology is inferred from the Tauroctony ("bull killing"), a standard depiction of Mithras slaying a sacred bull in a cave. Other scenes show the sun god Helius kneeling before Mithras, Mithras and Helius sharing a meal of bull parts, and Mithras riding to heaven in a chariot. Mithraism demanded lifetime participation and thus was different from other mystery cults that required no more than a few days of ini-

In this relief from Rome, the emperor Marcus Aurelius, veiled and acting as Pontifex Maximus, sacrifices a bull in front of the Temple of Capitoline Jupiter in Rome.

tiation rituals. Seven degrees of initiation, ranging from *Corax* ("raven") to *Miles* ("soldier") to *Pater* ("father"), gave worshippers the opportunity for greater ranks and privileges in the cult. The initial stage included a simulated murder of the initiate, which reinforced the salvific aspects of the cult, followed by baptism and a communal meal. Before moving up in rank, the initiate was required to meet tests of endurance, including not only ritual flogging but also ordeals involving water, fire, cold, hunger, and thirst. Initiates believed they were guaranteed immortality, for after death they would be judged by Mithras himself, whose tests they already had passed. For several reasons, the cult was especially popular in the Roman army: it admitted only men; the slaying of the bull was a brave, manly activity; and soldiers related to a religion that offered an afterlife based on the continued exercise of virtue, as opposed to a one-time initiation. Small Mithraic shrines holding no more than a hundred worshippers became a common attribute of military bases, especially in Europe.

Other kinds of personal religious practices included astrology and magic. Babylonian astrology, which taught that a future ordained by the gods could be read in the stars, had many followers. In the early third century, the Babylonian priest Berossus wrote a *Babyloniaca*, a history of Babylonia, and opened a school of astrology on the Greek island of Cos. In addition, the use of magical spells gave average people a sense of empowerment. It was believed, for example, that speaking a god's secret name gave a person control over the god. An Egyptian charm read, "Hear me, I am going to say the great name, Aoth, before whom every god prostrates himself and every demon shudders. Your divine name is Aeeioyo Iayoe Eaooyeeoia. I have spoken the glorious name, the name for all needs." In addition, there survive large numbers of curse tablets that were buried near a place in contact with the gods, such as a sacred well, an execution site, or a grave, and that invoked a god to bring misfortune on a wrongdoer, such as a thief, an opponent in a lawsuit, or a rival lover.

Not surprisingly, people also looked for help from the gods in curing their maladies. Incubation, or sleeping in the temple of a god known for healing, such as Asclepius, was done to treat maladies ranging from psoriasis to cancer, and temple walls were hung with plaques recording cures. A soldier left one that read, "As he was sleeping in the Temple the god extracted the spearhead and gave it to him into his hands. When day came he departed cured." Dreams also could convey signs of cures. According to another report, "Arata, a woman of Sparta, suffered from dropsy [an accumulation of fluid]. While she remained at home, her mother slept in the temple and saw a dream. It seemed that the god cut off her daughter's head and out came a huge quantity of fluid matter. Then he fitted the head back on the neck. Afterward she went home where she found her daughter in good health." People also attempted self-medication. And an ancient pregnancy test advised, "You should make the woman urinate on the Great-Nile plant. When morning comes, if you find the plant scorched, she will not conceive. If you find it green, she will conceive."

In addition, by the third century there was a growing sense that all of the traditional gods were representatives of a single overarching deity. In this form of henotheism (the belief in one primary god among multiple gods), often referred to as "**pagan monotheism**," it was especially common to see the sun as the manifestation of this single transcendent god, a belief known as "solar monotheism,".

Judaism in the Roman World

The most structured personal religion continued to be Judaism, and in the Jews' organization lay potential problems for the imperial government. By the mid-second century, there already had been no less than three Jewish rebellions against the Roman government. In general, the Roman government was tolerant of Jewish religious sensibilities and, based on their traditional and well-known monotheistic beliefs, exempted the Jews from making sacrifices to the emperors and to Rome. Nonetheless, the Jews were the only annexed people who ever engaged in large-scale organized resistance to Rome, in 66, in 115, and again in the Bar Kochba Revolt in 132. But the Jews could not hope to resist the might of the imperial armies, and after the suppression of the revolts, thousands of Jews were expelled from Judaea, resulting in an expansion of the Jewish diaspora throughout the Mediterranean world.

In order to try to maintain the Jewish way of life in the face of omnipresent Roman culture and political supremacy, Jewish scholars began to create texts that could be used in addition to the Hebrew Bible as a means of interpreting Jewish law. Jewish oral traditions dating from Pharisaic times were collected in the **Mishnah**, a work edited in the early third century by the Rabbi Judah the Prince. It contained accounts of debates held among rabbinic sages known as *Tannaim* who met during the first two centuries CE. The cases discussed in the Mishnah were intended to cover all aspects of human life as defined in the context of biblical teaching. Major topics covered include prayer, farming, the Sabbath and festivals, marriage and divorce, civil and criminal law, religious rituals, and dietary laws.

The Christians and Rome

Once the Roman government realized that Christians were not Jews, problems sometimes arose. Many Christians, as a consequence of their belief in only a single god, refused to participate in the state loyalty exercise, which involved sacrificing to the state gods. This was viewed by the government as high treason, for the Christians did not have the same exemption from sacrificing that the Jews did. Christians also were accused of "superstition"—that is, of not believing in the gods. In addition, the tendency of Christians, unlike participants in polytheistic religions, to meet in private, out of the public view, something totally contrary to Roman custom and Roman law, led to their being seen as a secret society engaged in subversive activities.

The term pagan, *commonly used in the modern day to refer to participants in polytheistic religions that recognized the existence of many gods, originated as a Christian insult from the word for "rustics."*

In spite of these perceptions, the Roman government generally was tolerant of the Christians, and only rarely was action taken against them. Circa 112, for example, after already having executed several Christians, Pliny the Younger, the rather officious Roman governor of Bithynia and Pontus, had second thoughts and consulted the emperor Trajan regarding how to deal with accused Christians. Trajan responded that they were not to be sought out and that anonymous accusations were to be ignored. Christian **apologists** such as Justin Martyr and Athenagoras of Athens, many of them converts from polytheistic religions, rebutted misconceptions about the Christians in tracts addressed to the emperors. In an "Apology" of 197 CE addressed to Roman magistrates, for example, the African Tertullian complained, "If the Tiber rises too high or the Nile too low, the cry is 'The Christians to the lions.'"

The occasional spates of prosecutions of Christians came to be known as **persecutions**. Some Christians suffered torture or were sentenced to the mines and became known as confessors. Others were executed and became **martyrs**, "witnesses" to the faith. Many died in the arena, because Christians often were of low social status, although those who held Roman citizenship,

This mosaic of ca. 200 CE from Zliten in North Africa shows the kind of punishment reserved for non-citizens—such as most Christians—sentenced to death.

like the apostle Paul, were sent to Rome for trial and suffered an honorable beheading on conviction. Both martyrs and confessors often were recognized as Christian **saints** in recognition of their steadfastness in their faith. The court records of their trials sometimes were preserved and served as the basis for popular biographies known as saints' lives, which provided models for how to lead a Christian life. As of the late second century, however, there still was no indication that Christianity would ever be much more than just one more eastern religion.

⇦ LOOKING BACK

During the Antonine Dynasty, from 96 until 192 CE, the Roman Empire was at its height, the most successful empire that the world had ever seen. Although nominally based on power being shared between the emperor and the Senate, it clearly was the emperor who had the real authority. The emperor oversaw a primarily peaceful and prosperous Roman world where the Roman army not only was successfully kept out of politics but also maintained a secure frontier defense system that prevented foreign invasions at the same time that it permitted travel across the borders. Commerce and social and cultural interchange freely flourished. The peoples living in the provinces were incorporated into Roman life and encouraged to feel that Rome's interests were their own interests. As the Roman Empire became more socially, culturally, and economically integrated, it embraced all of the manifold peoples living within its diffuse frontiers and provided opportunities for advancement to all of its residents. Provincial men could become senators or even emperors. Previously disadvantaged groups, such as women, foreigners, and slaves, gained greater rights under the law than persons in any other ancient society. The evolution of a Mediterranean Culture extending to the most distant frontiers created the most cohesive and successful empire that the world had yet known. In this context of empire-wide peace and security a new religion arose, Christianity. It met the spiritual needs of large numbers of converts who effectively were able to spread its message. But Christians also came into conflict with the Roman government when they refused to sacrifice to the imperial cult. Many were martyred, and it was unclear whether Christianity would be able to survive.

LOOKING AHEAD ⇨

Until the late second century, the history of Rome and the Roman Empire had been one of increasing consolidation of authority over an expanded Mediterranean world that extended to Scotland in the northwest and Arabia in the southeast. This consolidation brought with it a concomitant extension of social status and economic opportunity to all persons living under Roman authority, creating a degree of social, cultural, and political unity never before seen in the ancient world. As of the year 192, the Roman Empire looked deceptively stable. A few civil wars and barbarian invasions had been weathered. The economy was sound, the administration as efficient as one could expect. But forces had been at work that were undermining the Principate as it had been established by Augustus, and few living at the end of the second century would have guessed that there were some very tough times ahead.

FURTHER READING

Anderson, G. *The Second Sophistic: A Cultural Phenomenon in the Roman Empire*. London and New York: Routledge, 1993.

Ando, Clifford. *Imperial Ideology and Provincial Loyalty in the Roman Empire*. Berkeley: Univ. of California Press, 2000.

Ball, Warwick. *Rome in the East: Transformation of an Empire*. 2nd ed. London & New York: Routledge, 2016.

Bovill, Edward W. "The Camel and the Garamantes." *Antiquity* 30 (1956): 19–21.

Champlin, Edward. *Fronto and Antonine Rome*. Cambridge, MA: Harvard Univ. Press, 1980.

Duthoy, Robert. *The Taurobolium: Its Evolution and Terminology*. Leiden, Netherlands: Brill, 1969.

Fishwick, D. *The Imperial Cult in the Latin West: Studies in the Ruler Cult of the Western Provinces of the Roman Empire*. 4 vols. New York: Brill, 1987.

Gradel, Ittai. *Emperor Worship and Roman Religion*. Oxford: Oxford Univ. Press, 2002.

Keay, S., and N. Terrenato, eds. *Italy and the West: Comparative Issues in Romanization*. Oxford: Oxbow, 2001.

Lambert, R. *Beloved and God: The Story of Hadrian and Antinous*. New York: Viking, 1984.

MacMullen, Ramsay. *Enemies of the Roman Order: Treason, Unrest and Alienation in the Empire*. New York: Routledge, 1993.

Millar, Fergus. *The Emperor in the Roman World*. London: Duckworth, 2003.

Sheldon, Rose Mary. *Rome's Wars in Parthia: Blood in the Sand*. London & Portland: Valentine Mitchell, 2010.

Smallwood, E. Mary. *The Jews under Roman Rule: From Pompey to Diocletian*. Leiden, Netherlands: Brill, 2001.

Webster, Graham. *The Roman Imperial Army of the First and Second Centuries* A.D. Norman: Univ. of Oklahoma Press, 1998.

Webster, J., and N. Cooper, eds. *Roman Imperialism: Post-Colonial Perspectives*. Leicester, UK: Univ. of Leicester Press, 1996.

Whitmarsh, Timothy. *The Second Sophistic*. Cambridge, UK: Cambridge Univ. Press, 2006.

Ziolkowski, Adam. "Urbs direpta, or how the Romans Sacked Cities." In John Rich & Graham Shipley, eds. *War and Society in the Roman World*. London: Routledge, 1993, pp. 69–91.

SOURCES

THE LAMBAESIS INSCRIPTION

On the detailed reverse of this *sestertius*, the emperor Hadrian (117–138), in the course of his travels around the empire, delivers an *adlocutio*, or formal speech of greeting, to the British army, represented by an *aquilifer* (eagle bearer), *signifer* (standard bearer), and common soldier.

In the summer of 128 CE, during a tour of North Africa, the emperor Hadrian visited the legionary fortress at Lambaesis in Numidia (modern Algeria), the headquarters of the Third Augustan Legion. As was his practice, during the two-week visit he observed army units doing prepared maneuvers and then after each exercise he made an *adlocutio* (a formal address), in which he commented on what he had seen. The *adlocutio* made on this occasion is the only one to survive from antiquity, preserved on the base of a column erected to commemorate Hadrian's visit. The inscription began with a dedication by the legion and was followed by the text of the emperor's speech. Hadrian began by praising Quintus Fabius Catullinus, the "Legate of the Legion." Then, after a few words about the value of military exercise that he no doubt repeated in all such speeches, the inscription continued with Hadrian's comments on each unit in turn, in which the emperor mixed praise with occasional criticism, just enough to validate the praise. The text is fragmentary, so only the best-preserved sections are quoted here.

Source: Michael Speidel, *Emperor Hadrian's Speeches to the African Army. A New Text*
(Mainz: Römisch-Germanischen Zentralmuseums, 2006).

[Dedication]

The Third Augustan Legion to the Imperator Caesar Trajan Hadrian Augustus, bravest and most generous emperor, after the encampment and the army had passed inspection.

[Hadrian's adlocutio]

After the exercises had been observed, the Imperator Caesar Trajan Hadrian Augustus spoke these words that are written below, on the Kalends of July while Torquatus for the second time and Libo were Consuls.[1]

To the *pili*.[2]

Catullinus, my Legate,[3] is keen in your support. Indeed, everything that you might have had to put to me he has himself told me on your behalf; that a cohort[4] is away because, taking turns, one is sent every year to the staff of the Proconsul[5]; that two years ago you gave a cohort and five men from each century to the fellow Third Legion; that many far-flung outposts keep you scattered, that twice within our memory you have not only changed fortresses but built new ones. For this I would have forgiven you if something had come to a halt in your training. But nothing seems to have halted, nor is there any reason why you should need my forgiving.

To the cavalry of the legion.

Military exercises somehow have their own laws by which, if anything is added or taken away, the exercise gets either easier or harder. And the harder one makes it, the less graceful it becomes. You have made the hardest out of a hard task by throwing spears while wearing the *lorica*,[6] and thereby you lost in elegance. But I do approve the spirit in which you did this.

To the *principes*.[7]

Work that others would have spread out over several days you took only one day to finish. You have built a lengthy wall, made as if for permanent winter-quarters, in nearly as short a time as if it were built from turf that is cut in even pieces, easily carried and handled, and laid without difficulty, being naturally smooth and flat. You built with big, heavy, uneven stones that no one can carry, lift, or lay without their unevenness becoming evident. You dug a straight ditch through hard and rough gravel and scraped it smooth. Your work approved, you quickly entered camp, took your food and weapons, and followed the horse who had been sent out, hailing them with a great shout as they came back.

To the second cohort of the *Hamii*.[8]

Because you do not shoot at a signal, the foe being already upon you, your Prefect makes you try and shoot oftener and sharper, so that among the many missiles the foe dare not lift his head above the shield. You were slow to close ranks . . .

To the *ala*[9] . . .

I praise him[10] for having brought you over to this maneuver that has taken on the looks of true fighting, and for training you so well that I can praise you. Your Prefect Comelianus has done his duty undauntedly. I do not like counter-wheelings,[11] nor did the deified Trajan,[12] my model. A horseman should ride out from cover. If he does not see where he is going, or cannot rein in his horse when he wishes, he may come to grief from hidden traps and trenches he does not see. If you want to attack, you must charge across the middle of the field, as when facing the foe. Nothing ever must be done recklessly.

---

[1] 1 July 128 CE.

[2] The "spear carriers"—that is, the legionaries stationed in the first rank.

[3] The *Legatus legionis*—that is, the "Legate of the Legion," the commander of the legion.

[4] A subdivision of a legion, which had ten cohorts of rather less than six hundred men each.

[5] Because Africa was a senatorial province, its governor was a Proconsul, not a "Legate of Augustus."

[6] Roman body armor, made of metal scales or plates.

[7] The "leaders," the legionaries of the second rank.

[8] Hadrian now has moved on to the units of the auxilia, commanded by Prefects and composed of specialized troops such as cavalry and archers.

[9] A squadron of cavalry.

[10] Presumably Catullinus.

[11] Circling movements that do not allow a rider to see clearly what is ahead.

[12] The emperor Trajan (98–117 CE), Hadrian's predecessor.

The third day before the Ides of July.[13]

To the first squadron of the Pannonians.

You did everything according to the book. You filled the training ground with your wheelings, you threw spears not ungracefully, although with short and stiff spears.

Several of you hurled *lancea* spears with skill. Your jumping onto the horses here was lively and yesterday was swift. Had anything been lacking, I would note it; had anything stood out, I would mention it. You pleased equally throughout the whole maneuver. Noble Catullinus, my deputy, gives the same care to all.

To the cavalry of the sixth cohort of the Commagenians.[14]

It is hard for horsemen of a cohort to please, even as they are, and harder still not to displease after a show by horsemen of an *ala*: the training field differs in size, spear throwers are fewer, the right-wheel is tight, the Cantabrian formation[15] is cramped, the condition of the horses and the maintenance of the equipment in keeping with the pay level. But you have banished weariness by your eagerness, by doing briskly what had to be done. Moreover, you shot stones from slings and fought with javelins; everywhere you jumped nimbly onto your horses. The outstanding manhood of noble Catullinus, my Legate, shows itself in that under this man you are such men.

---

[14] Named after Commagene, a region in the southeastern corner of Anatolia.

[15] A tactic in which cavalry rode in a continuously rotating circle and thus kept up a steady stream of arrow, spear, or sling-stone fire.

---

[13] July 13.

JUVENAL, *SATIRE 6*

A fresco from the "House of the Chaste Lovers" in Pompeii shows men and women enjoying each other's company at a banquet. The kinds of pleasures being enjoyed here would have seemed tame compared to the kinds of activities in which, according to the Roman satirist Juvenal, upper-class Roman women indulged around 100 CE.

The Roman satirist Juvenal's Sixth Satire, which nominally attempts to dissuade Juvenal's friend Postumus from getting married, usually is taken as evidence for Roman attitudes toward gender in general and misogyny in particular, as Juvenal expounds on women's fundamental lack of morality. But the Satire also includes the famous line, "Who will guard the guards?"—not only making the point that it is impossible to impose standards of morality if those doing the imposing are themselves immoral, but also disclosing Roman men's anxieties about the paternity of their children. For example, men who divorce older wives in order to marry younger ones also are condemned. The Satire thus can be taken as being equally against the men who themselves have encouraged, participated in, and enabled immoral behavior. At the same time, the Satire also is full of jokes and mythological allusions—only some of which can be commented on here—that an educated audience would have appreciated.

Source: G. G. Ramsay, trans., *Juvenal and Persius*, Loeb Classical Library (London: Heinemann, New York, Putnam, 1918).

In the days of Saturn,[16] I believe, Chastity still lingered on the earth, and was to be seen for a time. These were the days when men were poorly housed in chilly caves; when one common shelter enclosed hearth and household gods, herds and their owners; when the hill-bred wife spread her sylvan bed with leaves and straw and the skins of her neighbors the wild beasts, a wife not like to you, O Cynthia,[17] nor to you, Lesbia,[18] whose bright eyes were clouded by a sparrow's death, but one whose breasts gave suck to lusty babes, often more unkempt herself than her acorn-belching spouse. For in those days, when the world was young, and the skies were new, men born of the riven oak, or

---

[16] The "Golden Age" of the early Greek poet Hesiod.

[17] The paramour of the Augustan poet Propertius.

[18] The paramour of the late Roman Republican poet Catullus.

formed of dust, lived differently from now, and had no parents of their own. Under Jove,[19] perchance, some few traces of ancient modesty may have survived, but that was before he had grown his beard, before the Greeks had learned to swear by someone else's head, when men feared not thieves for their cabbages or apples, and lived with unwalled gardens. After that Astraea[20] withdrew by degrees to heaven, with Chastity[21] as her comrade, the two sisters taking flight together.

To set your neighbor's bed a-shaking, Postumus,[22] and to flout the Genius[23] of the sacred couch, is now an ancient and long-established practice. All other sins came later, the products of the Age of Iron; but it was the Silver Age that saw the first adulterers. Nevertheless, in these days of ours, you are preparing for a covenant, a marriage-contract, and a betrothal; you are by now getting your hair cut by a master barber; you have also perhaps given a pledge to her finger. What! Postumus, are you, you who once had your wits, taking to yourself a wife? Tell me what Tisiphone, what snakes are driving you mad?[24] Can you submit to a she-tyrant when there is so much rope to be had, so many dizzy heights of windows standing open, and when the Aemilian Bridge[25] offers itself to hand? Or if none of all these modes of exit hits your fancy, how much better to take some boy bedfellow, who would never wrangle with you over nights, never ask presents of you when in bed, and never complain that you took your ease and were indifferent to his solicitations!

But Ursidius[26] approves of the Julian Law.[27] He purposes to bring up a dear little heir, although he will thereby have to do without the fine turtles, the bearded mullets, and all the legacy-hunting[28] delicacies of the meat-market. What can you think impossible if Ursidius takes to himself a wife? If he, who has long been the most notorious of gallants, who has so often found safety in the grain-bin of the luckless Latinus,[29] puts his head into the connubial noose? And what think you of his searching for a wife of the good old virtuous sort? O doctors, lance his over-blooded veins. A pretty fellow you! Why, if you have the good luck to find a modest spouse, you should prostrate yourself before the Tarpeian threshold and sacrifice a heifer with gilded horns to Juno,[30] so few are the wives worthy to handle the fillets of Ceres,[31] or from whose kisses their own father would not shrink! Weave a garland for your door-posts, and set up wreaths of ivy over your lintel![32]

But will Hiberina[33] be satisfied with one man? Sooner compel her to be satisfied with one eye! You tell me of the high repute of some maiden, who lives on her paternal farm. Well, let her live at Gabii, at Fidenae,[34] as she lived in her own country, and I will believe in your paternal farm. But will anyone tell me that nothing ever took place on a mountain side or in a cave?[35] Have Jupiter and Mars become so senile? Can our arcades[36] show you one woman worthy of your vows? Do all the tiers in all our theaters hold one whom you may love without misgiving, and

---

[19] Another name for Jupiter; the "Bronze Age" of Hesiod.
[20] The virgin goddess of innocence; she fled from the earth and became the constellation Virgo ("the virgin").
[21] Pudicitia, the goddess of chastity.
[22] A friend of Juvenal; the Satire purportedly is intended to dissuade him from getting married.
[23] Guardian spirit.
[24] One of the Furies, the avengers of crimes; she had snakes for hair.
[25] The oldest stone bridge across the Tiber in Rome, dating to the first half of the second century BCE.
[26] A notorious adulterer who finally decided to get married and raise a family.
[27] A law of Augustus against adultery.

[28] Marriages often were contracted with inheritances in mind; once he was married, Ursidius would have to give this up.
[29] In Roman comedies "Latinus," a stock character, often had to hide anyplace that was on hand to avoid being caught in the act of adultery.
[30] A shrine to Juno, part of the Capitoline temple, was near the Tarpeian Rock, from which unfaithful Vestal Virgins sometimes were flung, on the Capitoline Hill.
[31] Only chaste women were supposed to participate in the rites of the grain goddess Ceres.
[32] Decorations put on the homes of newlyweds.
[33] The putative fiancée of Postumus. This section turns to a discussion of unfaithfulness.
[34] Towns outside Rome.
[35] Juvenal refers to mythological sexual escapades that took place in the countryside.
[36] Fashionable Roman women promenading in sheltered arcades could see and be seen.

pick out thence? When the soft Bathyllus[37] dances the part of the gesticulating Leda,[38] Tuccia[39] cannot contain herself; your Apulian maiden heaves a sudden and longing cry of ecstasy, as though she were in a man's arms. Other women pay great prices for the favors of a comedian. Hispulla[40] has a fancy for tragedians; but do you suppose that any one will be found to love Quintilian?[41] If you marry a wife, it will be so that the flute player Ambrosius may become a father. Adorn your doors and doorposts with wreaths of laurel, so that your highborn son may exhibit, in his tortoiseshell cradle, the lineaments of a murmillo![42]

When Eppia, the senator's wife, ran off with a gladiator to Pharos[43] and the Nile, Canopus[44] itself cried shame upon the monstrous morals of our town. Forgetful of home, of husband, and of sister, without thought of her country, she shamelessly abandoned her weeping children. Although born in wealth, although as a babe she had slept in an ornamented cradle on the paternal down, she made light of the sea, just as she had long made light of her good name. And so with stout heart she endured the tossing and the roaring of the Tyrrhenian and Ionian Seas,[45] and all the many seas she had to cross. Now, when danger comes in an honorable way, a woman's heart grows chill with fear, and she cannot stand upon her trembling feet: but if she be doing a bold, bad thing, her courage fails not. For a husband to order his wife on board ship is cruelty; the bilge-water sickens her. But if she is running away with a lover, she feels no qualms. In the first case, she vomits over her husband, but in the second she flirts with

the sailors, roams about the deck, and delights in hauling at the hard ropes.

And what were the youthful charms that captivated Eppia? What did she see in him to allow herself to be called "a she-Gladiator"? Her dear Sergius[46] already had begun to shave[47]; a wounded arm gave promise of a discharge,[48] and there were sundry deformities in his face: a scar caused by the helmet, a huge boil upon his nose, a nasty humor always trickling from his eye. But then he was a gladiator! It is this that transforms these fellows into Hyacinths![49] It was this that she preferred to children and to country, to sister, and to husband. What these women love is the sword!

Do the concerns of a private household and the doings of Eppia affect you? Just look at those who rival the gods, and hear what Claudius [50]endured. As soon as his wife[51] perceived that her husband was asleep, this august harlot was shameless enough to prefer a common mat to the imperial couch. Assuming a night-cowl and attended by a single maid, she went out. Then she took her place in a brothel reeking with long-used coverlets. Entering an empty cell reserved for herself, she there took her stand, under the feigned name of Lycisca,[52] her nipples bare and gilded, and exposed to view the womb that bore you, O nobly-born Britannicus![53] Here she graciously received all comers, asking from each his fee, and when at length the keeper dismissed the rest, she remained to the very last before closing her cell, and with passion still raging hot within her went sorrowfully away. Then exhausted but unsatisfied, with soiled cheeks and begrimed with the smoke of lamps, she took back to the imperial pillow all the odors of the bordello.

---

[37] A male slave who introduced pantomime, where stories were told accompanied only by movements.

[38] The mortal woman whom Jupiter visited disguised as a swan.

[39] A Vestal Virgin who cleared herself of a charge of fornication by drawing water in a sieve.

[40] A Roman noblewoman.

[41] A famous rhetorician.

[42] A type of gladiator.

[43] The famous lighthouse at Alexandria in Egypt.

[44] An Egyptian city on the eastern edge of Alexandria.

[45] The Tyrrhenian Sea was just west of the boot of Italy and the Ionian Sea just east of it.

[46] The gladiator she had run off with.

[47] At this time, Roman men often did not begin to shave until forty years of age.

[48] A discharge from service as a gladiator.

[49] A beautiful boy loved by Apollo, who changed him into a flower after he was accidentally killed.

[50] Roman emperor, 41–54 CE.

[51] Claudius' third wife Valeria Messalina, who had a reputation for promiscuity.

[52] A word meaning "wasp."

[53] The son of Claudius and Messalina; murdered by the emperor Nero (54–68) when he was fourteen.

But tell me why is Censennia,[54] on her husband's testimony, the best of wives? She brought him a million *sestertii*; that is the price at which he calls her chaste. He has not pined under the darts of Venus; he was never burnt by her torch. It was the dowry that lit his fires, the dowry that shot those arrows! That dowry bought liberty for her: she may make any signals, and write any love letters she pleases, before her husband's face. The rich woman who marries a money-loving husband is as good as unmarried.

If you are not to love the woman betrothed and united to you in due form, what reason have you for marrying? Why waste the supper and the wedding cakes to be given to the well-filled guests when the company is slipping away? If you are honestly devoted to one woman, then bow your head and submit your neck to the yoke. Never will you find a woman who spares the man who loves her; for although she be herself aflame, she delights to torment and plunder him. So the better the man, the more desirable he is as a husband, the less good will he get out of his wife. No present will you ever make if your wife forbids; nothing will you ever sell if she objects; nothing will you buy without her consent. She will arrange your friendships for you; she will turn your now-aged friend from the door that saw the beginnings of his beard. Panders and trainers can make their wills as they please, as also can the gentlemen of the arena,[55] but you will have to write down among your heirs more than one rival of your own.

"Crucify that slave!" says the wife. Thus does she lord it over her husband. But before long she vacates her kingdom; she flits from one home to another, wearing out her bridal veil. Then back she flies again and returns to her own imprints in the bed that she has abandoned, leaving behind her the newly decorated door, the festal hangings on the walls, and the garlands still green over the threshold. Thus does the tale of her husbands grow; there will be eight of them in the course of five autumns, a fact worthy of commemoration on her tomb! There never was a case in court in which the quarrel was not started by a

woman. If Manilia[56] is not a defendant, she will be the plaintiff. She will herself frame and adjust the pleadings; she will be ready to instruct Celsus[57] himself how to open his case, and how to urge his points.

Why need I tell of the wrestling-oils used by women? Who has not seen one of them smiting a tree stump, piercing it through and through with a sword, lunging at it with a shield, and going through all the proper motions? A matron truly qualified to blow a trumpet at the Floralia![58] Unless, indeed, she is nursing some further ambition in her bosom, and is practicing for the real arena. What modesty can you expect in a woman who wears a helmet, abjures her own sex, and delights in feats of strength? Yet she would not choose to be a man, knowing the superior joys of womanhood. What a fine thing for a husband, at an auction of his wife's effects, to see her belt and armlets and plumes put up for sale, with a gaiter that covers half the left leg; or if she fight another sort of battle, how charmed you will be to see your young wife disposing of her greaves! Yet these are the women who find the thinnest of thin robes too hot for them; whose delicate flesh is chafed by the finest of silk tissue. See how she pants as she goes through her prescribed exercises; how she bends under the weight of her helmet; how big and coarse are the bandages that enclose her thighs; and then laugh when she lays down her arms and shows herself to be a woman!

I hear all this time the advice of my old friends: keep your women at home and put them under lock and key. Yes, but who will watch the watchers?[59] Wives are crafty. High or low their passions are all the same. She who wears out the black cobble-stones with her bare feet is no better than she who rides[60] upon the necks of eight stalwart Syrians. Ogulnia hires clothes to see the games; she hires attendants, a litter, cushions, female friends, a nurse, and a

---

[54] Not a clearly Roman name; Juvenal's point may be that as long as a woman has money, she can find a respectable, but perhaps impoverished, high-ranking Roman husband.
[55] That is, gladiators.

[56] A plebeian woman of this name was prosecuted for hitting a magistrate with a stone.
[57] Probably a Roman lawyer.
[58] A six-day festival, held in late April, in honor of the fertility goddess Flora. It was marked by theater performances and the participation of prostitutes, and was known for its licentiousness.
[59] "Quis custodiet ipsos custodes," one of the most famous ancient quotations.
[60] In a litter.

fair-haired girl to run her messages; yet she will give all that remains of the family plate, down to the last flagon, to some smooth-faced athlete. Many of these women are poor, but none of them pay any regard to their poverty, or measure themselves by the standard that that prescribes and lays down for them. Men, on the other hand, do sometimes have an eye to utility, but your extravagant woman is never sensible of her dwindling means; she never gives a thought to what her pleasures cost her.

Yes, I know well the advice and warnings of my old friends: Put on a lock and keep your wife indoors. And yes, just who will guard the guards? They get paid in kind for holding their tongues as to their young lady's escapades. The wily wife arranges accordingly, and begins with them. If your wife is musical, none of those who sell their voices to the Praetor can compete with her charms. Better, however, that your wife should be musical than that she should be rushing boldly about the entire city, attending men's meetings, talking with unflinching face and firm breasts to generals in their military cloaks, with her husband looking on! This same woman knows what is going on all over the world: what the Thracians[61] and Chinese are after; she knows who loves whom, what gallant is the rage; she will tell you who got the widow with child, and in what month; how every woman behaves to her lovers, and what she says to them.

She frequents the baths by night; she loves all the bustle of the hot bath, when her arms drop exhausted by the heavy weights,[62] the anointer passes his hand skillfully over her body, bringing it down at last with a resounding smack upon her thigh. Meanwhile her unfortunate guests are overcome with sleep and hunger, until at last she comes in with a flushed face and tosses off a couple of pints before her dinner to create a raging appetite; then she brings it all up; the stream runs over the marble pavement and the gilt basin reeks of Falernian,[63] for she drinks and vomits like a big snake that has tumbled into a vat. The sickened husband closes his eyes and so keeps down his bile.

If the woman is of humble rank, she will promenade between the turning-posts of the Circus.[64] Wealthy women will pay for answers from a Phrygian or Indian augur[65] well skilled in the stars and the heavens. These poor women, moreover, endure the perils of child-birth and all the troubles of nursing to which their lot condemns them; but how often does a gilded bed contain a woman that is lying in?[66] So great is the skill, so powerful the drugs, of the abortionist, paid to murder mankind within the womb. Rejoice, poor wretch, give her the stuff to drink whatever it be, with your own hand, for were she willing to get big and trouble her womb with bouncing babes, you might perhaps find yourself the father of an Ethiopian, and someday a tinted heir would fill all the places in your will.

A wife hates the children of a concubine, let none demur or forbid, seeing that it has long been deemed right and proper to slay a stepson. But I warn you wards, you who have a good estate, keep watch over your lives; trust not a single dish, for those hot cakes are black with the poison of a mother's baking. Whatever is offered you by the mother, let someone taste it first; let your trembling tutor[67] take the first taste of every cup. Now think you that all this is a fancy tale, and that our satire is taking to itself the high heels of tragedy?[68] Think you that I have out-stepped the limits and the laws of those before me? Would indeed that my words were idle! But here is Pontia[69] proclaiming "I did the deed; I gave aconite,[70] I confess it, to my own children; the crime was detected, and is known to all." "What, you most savage of vipers? You killed two, did you, two, at a single meal?" "Aye, and seven too, had there chanced to be seven to kill!"

---

[61] Thrace was a mountainous Balkan region northeast of Greece; modern Bulgaria.

[62] After a workout in the weight room.

[63] The most famous Roman wine, produced from grapes of Mt. Falernus in Latium.

[64] The Circus Maximus ("Great Circus"), the chariot-racing track, with turning posts at each end.

[65] In this case, a fortune teller.

[66] Waiting to give birth.

[67] In this case, a child-care worker.

[68] Actors wore shoes with several-inch soles in order to stand out more effectively.

[69] Otherwise unknown, but in a famous case from forty years earlier, the Tribune Octavius Sagitta had murdered Pontia, a woman who had swindled him out of his fortune.

[70] An extremely poisonous plant, also known as wolf's bane; the poison also was associated with rabid dogs.

PUBLIUS AELIUS ARISTIDES THEODORUS, *TO ROME*

During the Roman Empire, it was common for orators to present speeches to emperors on special occasions, such as birthdays or anniversaries of accession to power. These speeches not only conveyed lavish praise and often said what the emperor wanted to hear, but also expressed popular views of how influential individuals thought the empire was being or should be governed. One such orator was Publius Aelius Aristides Theodorus, a Greek orator who represented the "Second Sophistic." Aristides flourished during the reigns of Hadrian and Antoninus Pius (138–161). After a visit to Rome in 143 CE, Aristides returned to his native Smyrna in Anatolia. Around 150 CE, Aristides delivered an oration called "Praise of Rome" to the emperor Antoninus Pius, with Marcus Aurelius probably also in attendance, in which he fulsomely praised the advantages and opportunities offered by Roman rule. In the course of his speech Aristides also expressed the growing commonplace that Rome in fact ruled, or ought to rule, the entire world. The speech glorified the emperors as having created an ideal world where opportunities were open to all, which no doubt is exactly what the emperors wanted to hear. These sentiments might be compared with those expressed in the feature "The Dark Side of Romanization" earlier in the chapter.

Source: James H. Oliver, *The Ruling Power. A Study of the Roman Empire in the Second Century after Christ through the Roman Oration of Aelius Aristides* (Philadelphia: American Philosophical Society, 1953), 895–907.

It is an age-old tradition that travelers who journey forth on land or water offer a prayer whereby they pledge to fulfill some vow—something they have on their mind—on reaching their destination safely. The vow I took as I journeyed here was not the usual silly and irrelevant sort, nor was it one unrelated to the art I profess. I simply vowed that, if I arrived safely, I would salute your city with a public address.

Some writer referring to Asia asserted that one man ruled as much territory as the sun passed over, but his statement was false, because he placed all of Africa and Europe outside of the area where the sun rises in the east and sets in the west. Now, however, it has become fact. The land you possess equals what the sun can pass over, and the sun does encompass your land. You do not reign within fixed boundaries and another state does not dictate the limits of the land you control[71]; rather, the sea[72] extends like a belt, situated in the middle of the civilized world and in the middle of the land over which you rule. Around that sea lie the great continents[73] massively sloping down to it, forever offering you in full measure what they possess. Whatever each culture grows and manufactures cannot fail to be here[74] at all times and in great profusion. Here merchant vessels arrive carrying these many commodities from every region in every season and even at every equinox,[75] so that the city takes on the appearance of a sort of common market for the world. One can see cargoes from India and even, if you will, from southern Arabia in such numbers that one must conclude that the trees in those lands have been stripped bare and if the inhabitants of those lands need anything, they must come here to beg for a share of what they have produced. Your farmlands are Egypt, Sicily, and all of cultivated Africa. Seaborne arrivals and departures are ceaseless, to the point that the wonder is, not so much that the harbor[76] has insufficient space for all

---

[71] Reflecting the official view that the Roman Empire ruled, in reality or potentiality, the whole world.

[72] The Mediterranean.

[73] That is, Asia, Africa, and Europe.

[74] In Rome.

[75] The two moments during the solar year, roughly March 21 and September 21, when night and day are of equal length.

[76] Ostia, the port of Rome at the mouth of the Tiber River.

these merchant vessels, but that the sea has enough space, if it really does. Just as there is a common channel where all waters of the Ocean[77] have a single source and destination, so there is a common channel to Rome and all meet here: trade, shipping, agriculture, metallurgy, all the arts and crafts that are or ever were and all things that are produced or spring from the earth. What one does not see here does not exist. So it is not easy to decide which is the greater: the superiority of this city relative to cities that presently exist, or the superiority of this empire relative to all empires that ever existed.

As vast and comprehensive as its size is, your empire is much greater for its perfection than for the area its borders encircle. The entire civilized world prays with one voice that this empire will endure forever. For of all who ever have gained an empire, you alone rule over free men. You conduct public business throughout the whole civilized world exactly as if it were one city-state, you appoint governors, as if it were by election, to protect and care for the governed, not to act as slave masters over them. One could say that the people of today are ruled by governors sent out to them only to the degree that they wish to be ruled.

You have divided into two parts all men throughout your empire, everywhere giving citizenship to all those who are more accomplished, noble, and powerful, even as they retain their native-born identities, whereas the rest you have made subjects and the governed. Neither the sea nor the great expanse of intervening land keeps one from being a citizen, and there is no distinction between Europe and Asia. No one is a foreigner who deserves to hold an office or is worthy of trust. Rather, there is here a common "world democracy" under the rule of one man, the best ruler and director.

You have divided humanity into Romans and non-Romans, and because you have divided people in this manner, in every city throughout the empire there are many who share citizenship with you, no less than they share citizenship with their fellow natives. And some of these Roman citizens have not even seen this city! There is no need for troops to garrison the strategic high points of these cities because the most important and powerful people in each region guard their native lands for you.[78] Yet there is not a residue of resentment among those excluded. Because your government is both universal and like that of a single city-state, its governors rightly rule not as foreigners but, as it were, their own people. Additionally, all of the masses of subjects under this government have protection against the more powerful of their native countrymen, by virtue of your anger and vengeance, which would fall upon the more powerful without delay should they dare to break the law. Thus, the present government serves rich and poor alike, and your constitution has developed a single, harmonious, all-embracing union. What in former days seemed impossible has in your time come to pass. You control a vast empire with a rule that is firm but not unkind.

As on a holiday, the entire civilized world lays down the weapons that were its ancient burden and has turned to adornment and all glad thoughts, with the power to realize them. Cities glisten with radiance and charm, and the entire earth has been made beautiful like a garden. Like a perpetual sacred flame, the celebration is unending. You, better than anyone else, have proved the truth of the proverb: "The earth is everyone's mother and our common fatherland." It now is possible for Hellene[79] and non-Hellene, with or without property, to travel with ease wherever he wishes, as though passing from homeland to homeland. As far as security is concerned, it suffices to be a Roman citizen, or rather one of those people united under your rule.

Let us pray that all the gods and their children grant that this empire and this city flourish forever and never cease until stones float on water and trees cease to put forth shoots in spring, and that the Great Governor and his sons[80] be preserved and obtain blessings for all.

---

[77] The great ocean that it was believed encircled all of the continents.

[78] As of this period, nearly all Roman military forces except the Praetorian Guard were stationed on the frontier.

[79] Technically, a Greek, but here probably referring to Roman citizens.

[80] The emperor; Antoninus Pius had two adopted sons, Lucius Verus and Marcus Aurelius, both of whom became emperor when he died in 161 CE.

BABYLONIAN TALMUD, SANHEDRIN 39A, SABBATH 33B, ME'ILAH 17B

Under Roman rule, the Jews maintained their identity by the creation and circulation of the Talmud, a massive and comprehensive guidebook for Jewish life compiled beginning in the third century CE. It comprised oral tradition, interpretations of Mosaic Law, observations on faith and morality, Bible commentaries, and historical narratives. One version of the Talmud was completed in the late fourth century in Palestine and a Babylonian version was completed by circa 500. The Talmud illustrated the complex and conflicted relationship that the Jews had with the Romans. For example, stories circulated about how Jewish rabbis undertooktheological debates with the emperor or the emperor's daughter. One individual who was caught in the middle was Rabbi Simeon ben Yoḥai. Simeon's teacher, Rabbi Akiba ben Yoseph, had supported the Bar Kochba Revolt (132–135 CE), and after the defeat of the revolt, Akiba's followers, including Simeon, were discredited. Circa 140 CE, Simeon lost the election to be head of the Sanhedrin, the Jewish governing body, which only existed by sufferance of the Romans and could not offend them. At a subsequent Sanhedrin meeting, ben Yoḥai criticized Rabbi Yehudah ben Ilai, who praised Roman achievements. When this exchange was reported to the Romans, Yehudah was rewarded and Simeon was sentenced to death. After many years hiding in a cave, Simeon emerged and became a great Jewish teacher. He gained a reputation as a wonder worker and stories were told about his spiritual authority. In one story, he was said to have been sent to the emperor, perhaps Marcus Aurelius (180–192), to have the anti-Jewish legislation of the emperor Hadrian (117–138) rescinded. He accomplished the mission by having the emperor's daughter become possessed by a demon and then releasing her from it, a motif similar to later Christian traditions of holy men and women who released people from demonic possession.

Source: I. Epstein, trans., *Contents of the Soncino Babylonian Talmud*, 26 volumes (London: Soncino, 1935–1948).

The emperor once said to Rabbi Gamaliel,[81] "Your God is a thief, for it is written, 'And the Lord God caused a deep sleep to fall upon Adam and he slept, and he took one of his ribs'." Thereupon the emperor's daughter replied, "Leave him to me and I will answer him,"[82] and said, "Give me a military guard commander." "Why do you need him?," he asked. "Thieves visited us last night and robbed us of a silver pitcher, leaving a golden one in its place." "Would that such thieves visited us every day!," the emperor exclaimed. "Ah!," she retorted, "was it not to Adam's gain that he was deprived of a rib and a handmaid presented to him in its stead

to serve him?" The emperor replied: "This is what I mean: he should have taken it from him openly, when he was awake." Said she to him, "Let me have a piece of raw meat." It was given to her. She placed it under her armpit, then took it out and offered it to him to eat. "I find it loathsome," he exclaimed. "Even so would Eve have been to Adam had she been taken from him openly,"[83] she retorted.

The emperor proposed to Rabbi Tanhum,[84] "Come, let us all be one people." "Very well," he answered, "but we who are circumcised cannot possibly become like you unless you become circumcised like us." The emperor replied, "You have spoken well; nevertheless, anyone who gets the better of the king in debate must be thrown into the

---

[81] A rabbi known to have visited Rome at least twice, during the reigns of Domitian (81–96) and Nerva (96–98). Neither of these had a known daughter.

[82] That is, she would deal with the emperor's question in place of the rabbi.

[83] And he thus had known where she had come from.

[84] Tanhum ben Ḥanilai, a rabbi of the third century CE.

vivarium.[85] So they threw him in, but he was not eaten. Thereupon a heretic remarked, "The reason they did not eat him is that they are not hungry." They then threw the heretic in, and he was eaten . . .

Rabbi Judah, Rabbi Yose, and Rabbi Simeon were sitting, and Judah, a son of proselytes,[86] was sitting near them. Rabbi Judah commenced by observing, "How fine are the works of the Romans. They have made streets, they have built bridges, they have erected baths." Rabbi Yose was silent. Rabbi Simeon ben Yoḥai answered and said, "All that they made they made for themselves; they built market-places, to set harlots in them; baths, to rejuvenate themselves; bridges, to levy tolls for them."[87] Now, Judah the son of proselytes went and repeated this conversation, which was heard by the Roman government. The Romans decreed: "Judah, who exalted us, shall be rewarded by having the privilege to speak first on all occasions. Yose, who was silent, shall be exiled to Sepphoris.[88] Simeon, who censured, let him be executed." Simeon and his son went and hid themselves in the Beth Hamidrash[89] and his wife brought him bread and a mug of water and they dined. But when the decree became more severe he said to his son, "Women are of unstable temperament; she may be put to the torture[90] and expose us." So they went and hid in a cave. The whole day they studied. When it was time for prayers they robed, covered themselves, prayed, and then put off their garments again, so that they should not wear out. Thus they dwelt twelve years in the cave. Then Elijah[91] came and stood at the entrance to the cave and exclaimed, "Who will inform the son of Yoḥai that the emperor is dead and his decree annulled?"[92] So they emerged. Seeing a man ploughing and sowing, they exclaimed, "They forsake life eternal and engage in life temporal!" Whatever they cast their eyes upon was immediately burnt up. Thereupon a Heavenly Echo came forth and cried out, "Have you emerged to destroy my world? Return to your cave!'"[93] So they returned and dwelt there twelve months, saying, "The punishment of the wicked in Gehenna is limited to twelve months."[94] A Heavenly Echo then came forth and said, "Go forth from your cave!" Thus, they issued forth: wherever Rabbi Eleazar[95] wounded, Rabbi Simeon healed. Said he to him, "My son! You and I are sufficient for the world." Rabbi Phinehas ben Ya'ir his son-in-law went out to meet him. He took him into the baths and massaged his flesh. Seeing the clefts in his body he wept and the tears streamed from his eyes. "Woe to me that I see you in such a state!," he cried out. "Happy are you that you see me thus," he retorted, "for if you did not see me in such a state you would not find me so learned."[96] For originally, when Rabbi Simeon ben Yoḥai raised a difficulty, Rabbi Phinehas ben Ya'ir would give him thirteen answers, but subsequently when Rabbi Phinehas ben Ya'ir raised a difficulty, Rabbi Simeon ben Yoḥai would give him twenty-four answers . . .

---

[85] Enclosures where the Romans kept wild animals to be used in the games.

[86] Converts to Judaism.

[87] For similar negative views of "Romanization," see the feature "The Dark Side of Romanization" earlier in the chapter.

[88] A desert city west of the Sea of Galilee and a center of rabbinical activity at this time.

[89] A place for Jewish religious study.

[90] Jews who were not Roman citizens, such as Yeshua bar Yosef (Jesus of Nazareth) in the previous century, would be liable to torture should they be brought in for questioning by the Roman government.

[91] A prophet who lived in the northern Hebrew kingdom of Israel during the reign of King Ahab (ca. 885–850 BCE).

[92] Presumably the emperor Antoninus Pius (138–161); this would date Simeon's original condemnation to around 148 CE.

[93] This story is a rebuke of excessively pious Jews who believed they should only study religion and not do practical work.

[94] In general, Judaism had no concept of eternal punishment in Hell, but rather of limited, regenerative punishment in Gehenna.

[95] Eleazar ben Simeon, the son of Simeon; another disciple of Akiba. He later held office under the Romans.

[96] Making the point that he spent all his time studying.

The government[97] once issued a decree that Jews might not keep the sabbath, circumcise their children, and that they should have intercourse with menstruant women. The Jews then conferred as to who should go to Rome to work for the annulment of the decrees. "Let Rabbi Simeon ben Yoḥai go for he is experienced in miracles," said Rabbi Eleazar son of Rabbi Yose. "And who should accompany him?," they asked. Said Rabbi Yose to them, "I shall accompany him." Then ben Temalion[98] came to meet them and said, "Is it your wish that I accompany you?" Thereupon Rabbi Simeon wept and said, "Let the miracle be performed, no matter how." Thereupon ben Temalion went ahead and entered into the emperor's daughter. When Rabbi Simeon arrived in Rome he called out,[99] "Ben Temalion leave her, ben Temalion leave her," and as he proclaimed this the demon left her. The emperor said to them, "Request whatever you desire." They were led into the treasure house to take whatever they chose. They found that edict,[100] took it, and tore it to pieces. It was with reference to this visit that Rabbi Eleazar, son of Rabbi Yose, related: "I saw it[101] in the city of Rome and there were on it several drops of blood."

---

[97] Rulings of the emperor Hadrian (117–138 CE).
[98] A demon, also known as Asmodeus.

[99] After having been invited to cure the emperor's daughter based on his reputation as a wonder worker.
[100] That is, the anti-Jewish legislation.
[101] The curtain from the Jewish Temple in Jerusalem that had been carried off in the sack by the Romans in 70 CE.

DEALING WITH CHRISTIANS (ca. 112 CE)

PLINY, *LETTERS* 10.96–97

The Jews were not the only followers of a monotheistic religion who caused problems for the Romans. Around 112 CE, Gaius Plinius Secundus, or Pliny, the governor of the Roman province of Bithynia-Pontus on the southern coast of the Black Sea, wrote to the emperor Trajan (98–117) asking his advice about how to deal with a curious religious sect known as "Christians," who seemed to reject Roman religious practices and often refused to participate in the Roman loyalty oath. Trajan's brief reply spelled out the Roman government's "don't ask, don't tell" principle regarding the Christians, a rather more sympathetic policy than had been that of the Senate with respect to the Bacchanalians nearly three hundred years earlier.

Source: William Melmoth, trans., *Pliny: Letters*, revised by W. M. L. Hutchinson. 2 vols., Loeb Classical Library (London: Heinemann; New York: Macmillan, 1915).

Pliny to the Emperor Trajan.

It is my practice, my lord, to refer to you all matters concerning which I am in doubt. For who can better give guidance to my hesitation or inform my ignorance? I have never participated in trials of Christians. I therefore do not know what offenses it is the practice to punish or investigate, and to what extent. And I have been not a little hesitant as to whether there should be any distinction on account of age or no difference between the very young and the more mature; whether pardon is to be granted for repentance, or, if a man has once been a Christian, it does him no good to have ceased to be one; whether the name itself, even without offenses, or only the offenses associated with the name are to be punished.

Meanwhile, in the case of those who were denounced to me as Christians, I have observed the following procedure: I interrogated these as to whether they were Christians; those who confessed I interrogated a second and a third time, threatening them with punishment; those who persisted I ordered executed. For I had no doubt that, whatever the nature of their creed, stubbornness and inflexible obstinacy surely deserve to be punished. There were others possessed of the same folly, but because they were Roman citizens, I signed an order for them to be transferred to Rome.[102]

Soon accusations spread, as usually happens, because of the proceedings going on, and several incidents occurred. An anonymous document was published containing the names of many persons. Those who denied that they were or had been Christians, when they invoked the gods in words dictated by me, offered prayer with incense and wine to your image, which I had ordered to be brought for this purpose together with statues of the gods, and moreover cursed Christ, something that none of which those who are really Christians, it is said, can be forced to do, these I thought should be discharged. Others named by the informer declared that they were Christians, but then denied it, asserting that they had been but had ceased to be, some three years before, others many years, some as much as twenty-five years. They all worshipped your image and the statues of the gods, and cursed Christ.

They asserted, however, that the sum and substance of their fault or error had been that they were accustomed to meet on a fixed day before dawn and sing responsively a hymn to Christ as to a god, and to bind themselves by oath, not to some crime but rather not to commit fraud, theft, or adultery,

_____

[102] Roman citizens automatically had the right of appeal regarding accusations that could carry the death penalty,

_____

as occurred with the Christian leader Paul, who was sent from Judaea to Rome for trial during the reign of Nero (54–68) after it was discovered that he was a Roman citizen.

not falsify their trust, nor to refuse to return a trust when called upon to do so.[103] When this was over, it was their custom to depart and to assemble again to partake of food, but ordinary and innocent food.[104] Even this, they affirmed, they had ceased to do after my edict by which, in accordance with your instructions, I had forbidden political associations. Accordingly, I judged it all the more necessary to find out what the truth was by torturing two female slaves who were called deaconesses.[105] But I discovered nothing else but depraved, excessive superstition.[106]

I therefore postponed the investigation and hastened to consult you. For the matter seemed to me to warrant consulting you, especially because of the number involved. For many persons of every age, every rank, and also of both sexes are and will be endangered. For the contagion of this superstition has spread not only to the cities but also to the villages and farms. But it seems possible to check and cure it. It is certainly quite clear that the temples, which had been almost deserted, have begun to be frequented, that the established religious rites, long neglected, are being resumed, and that from everywhere sacrificial animals are coming, for which until now very few purchasers could be found. Hence it is easy to imagine what a multitude of people can be reformed if an opportunity for repentance is afforded.

Trajan to Pliny.

You observed proper procedure, my dear Pliny, in sifting the cases of those who had been denounced to you as Christians. For it is not possible to lay down any general rule to serve as a kind of fixed standard. They are not to be sought out. If they are denounced and proved guilty, they are to be punished, with this reservation, that whoever denies that he is a Christian and really proves it, that is, by worshiping our gods, even though he was under suspicion in the past, shall obtain pardon through repentance. But anonymously posted accusations ought to have no place in any prosecution. For this is both a dangerous kind of precedent and out of keeping with the spirit of our age.

---

[103] The same crimes of which the Bacchanalians had been accused in 186 BCE.

[104] Contradicting the popular belief that Christians were cannibals because they ate flesh and drank blood during their religious rites.

[105] Demonstrating that in early Christianity women were admitted to the clergy and that even slaves could be clerics.

[106] For the Romans, "superstition" was not believing in the gods—that is, atheism.

CHAPTER 10

THE SEVERANS AND THE THIRD-CENTURY CRISIS (192–284)

During the third century, it became clear that the carefully constructed Principate was no longer working. The empire began to disintegrate as a result of economic, political, and military problems that the Roman government found increasingly difficult to deal with. The Severan Dynasty saw an increasing focus on the army and a precipitous decline in the influence of the Senate. This was followed by a fifty-year Imperial Crisis that threatened the empire's very existence, and it looked very much like the empire was going to crumble.

THE SEVERAN DYNASTY (193–235)

The emperor Commodus failed to name a successor, and after his assassination in 192 there were no obvious candidates for the throne. So once again, as after the death of Nero in 68, the empire was up for grabs. The lack of a constitutional method for choosing new emperors meant that a series of claimants arose all around the empire. The eventual victor, the Libyan Septimius Severus, instituted policies that made it clear that the empire as it had been established by Augustus had become less and less relevant to the social and political realities of the time.

Jockeying for Power

The choice of Commodus' assassins fell on Pertinax, an old lieutenant of Marcus Aurelius. Pertinax (192–193), however, attempted to restore discipline among the Praetorian Guards and was murdered early in 193. The Guards then sank to a new low and auctioned off the emperorship. The high bidder was Didius Julianus (193), whose only qualification lay in being filthy rich. He reportedly paid each guardsman 25,000 *sestertii* (the modern equivalent of about $250,000) for the dubious privilege of becoming emperor during these troubled times.

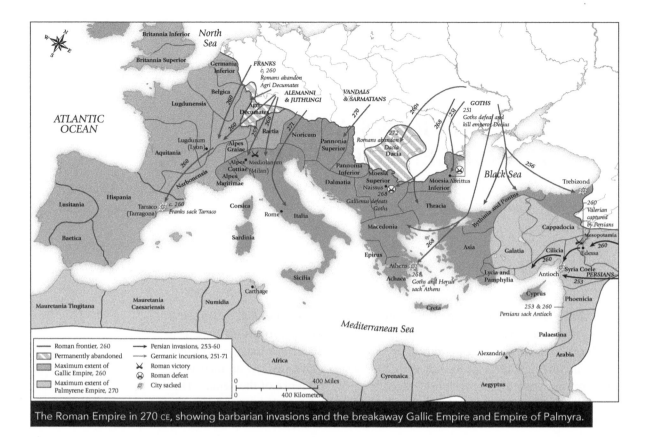

The Roman Empire in 270 CE, showing barbarian invasions and the breakaway Gallic Empire and Empire of Palmyra.

At this, the hard-bitten frontier legions became disgusted and named their own candidates: Clodius Albinus in Britain, Septimius Severus on the Danube, and Pescennius Niger in Syria. Severus dashed upon Rome and demanded recognition from the Senate. The senator and historian Cassius Dio, who was present, later reported, "Silius Messala, who was then Consul, assembled us. We thereupon sentenced Julianus to death, named Severus emperor, and bestowed divine honors upon Pertinax." Thus proper procedures were followed in this case and other similar ones, and the praetorians then murdered the hapless Julianus. After disingenuously designating Albinus as his successor by giving him the rank of **Caesar**, or junior emperor, Severus headed off to

A gold *aureus* of Didius Julianus, who purchased the right to be emperor in an auction held by the Praetorian Guard. The reverse legend reads, "Concord of the soldiers," a forlorn hope that died when he was beheaded after only nine weeks of rule.

the east where he defeated Niger. He then returned west and in 197, in a hardfought battle outside Lyon, polished off his erstwhile ally Albinus. By then, he had created the **Severan Dynasty** (193–235).

The Reign and Policies of Septimius Severus

Severus faced several problems in attempting to consolidate his authority. For one thing, he had no connection to the previous dynasties, although he attempted to remedy that issue by having himself posthumously adopted by Marcus Aurelius, giving himself and his sons the name Antoninus. He also was definitely not what the Italian senators had in mind for an emperor: he was a native of Libya, he had been a mere equestrian before gaining senatorial rank, and his wife, **Julia Domna**, came from Syria. The snobbish Romans made fun of his Libyan-accented Latin. In addition, during the civil wars many senators had preferred the more cultured Albinus. Severus' career had been solely in the army, and he understood very well where his real support lay.

Severus, therefore, had little reason to cooperate with the Senate, and the carefully maintained united front presented by the emperor and the Senate began to crumble. Severus created several new provinces (by subdividing existing ones) and army units, placing equestrians rather than senators in charge of them. Senators accused of crimes lost the right to be tried before the Senate; they now were heard before the Praetorian Prefect, who assumed legal jurisdiction over all of Italy. Severus also packed more provincials into the Senate; by the end of his reign, it was only about one-third Italian and even less cohesive than before. As the status of the Senate declined, the empire increasingly assumed the appearance of an open military dictatorship. One of the consequences of the emperor's distancing himself from the partnership with the Senate was that many senators no longer saw the empire as acting in their best interests. As a consequence, there was an increasing tendency for senators implicitly to withdraw their support from the state, to settle somewhere in the provinces, to pursue purely local interests, and to consolidate their local authority.

In 208, Severus traveled to Britain to deal with local unrest. After advancing into Scotland and repairing Hadrian's Wall, he withdrew to York, where he died in 211. His last words were, "Anything else to do? Give it here!" He was succeeded by his

TABLE 10.1 DYNASTIES AND RULERS OF THE THIRD CENTURY (193–275)

Successors of Commodus
Pertinax (192–193)
Didius Julianus (193)
Pescennius Niger (193–194)
Clodius Albinus (193–197)
Severan Dynasty
Septimius Severus (193–211)
Geta (211)
Caracalla (211–217)
Macrinus (217–218) (usurper)
Elagabalus (218–222)
Severus Alexander (222–235)
Imperial Crisis (selected)
Maximinus the Thracian (235–238)
Gordian III (238–244)
Philip the Arab (244–249)
Trajan Decius (249–251)
Trebonianus Gallus (251–253)
Valerian (253–260)
Gallienus (253–268)
Illyrian Emperors (selected)
Claudius II Gothicus (268–270)
Aurelian (270–275)
Severina (275) (interregnum, wife of Aurelian)
Tacitus (275–276) (not an Illyrian)
Probus (276–282)
Carus (282–283) (not an Illyrian)
Carinus (283–285) (not an Illyrian)
Breakaway Emperors and Rulers (selected)
Postumus (259–268) (Gallic Empire)
Tetricus I (271–274) (Gallic Empire)
Zenobia (267–272) (Queen of Palmyra, as Augusta)
Vaballathus (267–272) (son of Zenobia, as king)

The Severan tondo, one of the few panel paintings to survive from antiquity, shows the Severan family ca. 200: the empress Julia Domna and emperor Septimius Severus stand behind their sons, the Caesars Geta and Caracalla. Geta's face has been obliterated because he suffered "Damnation of Memory" after being murdered by his brother.

sons Marcus Aurelius Antoninus, better known by his nickname Caracalla (the word for a long Gallic cloak) (211–217) and Geta (211), both of whom he already had named first Caesar and then Augustus. This marked the first time that an emperor had been succeeded by multiple natural sons at the same time. Later in the year, however, Caracalla, the elder son, murdered his younger brother.

A Restive Army

The empire that Severus bequeathed to his sons once again had well-protected borders and was financially solvent. But he also left the seeds of some serious problems, one of which involved the army. By the Severan period, the army had assumed a different character from the army of Augustus. Few Italians enlisted anymore except in the privileged and pampered Praetorian Gaurd. The army became heavily provincialized, with large numbers of recruits coming from North Africa and the hinterlands of the Rhine and Danube Rivers. To meet chronic manpower shortages, emperors increasingly recruited barbarian units from across the frontiers. The soldiers had little in common with their educated and cultured senatorial commanders and often went out of control. Emperors who wished to remain in power would have to know how to maintain control over their increasingly unruly troops.

Severus reportedly advised his two sons to "treat the soldiers well and despise everybody else." He followed his own advice by extending several privileges to soldiers. He allowed them to marry while still in service. This made them happier, but it also made them less mobile, for they became reluctant to leave home and travel to some far-flung sector of the empire. He also dismissed the largely Italian Praetorian Guards and replaced them with soldiers from his own provincial legions.

Financial Collapse

To keep the army content, Severus raised army salaries from 300 to 500 *denarii* a year. Caracalla (211–217) continued this trend by raising the salaries to 750 *denarii* per year. These increases were far more than the imperial treasury could bear. The Roman Empire operated on a mandated balanced budget. There was no national debt and no paper money. Expenditures, primarily in silver, simply could not exceed income. And income, based mainly on the land tax, was essentially constant: the best that it could do was to remain the same. Until the reign of Severus, emperors, perhaps only by sheer good fortune, had been able to live within their financial limits. But the exorbitant pay increases granted by Severus and Caracalla broke the bank. The soldiers' salaries, the major imperial expenditure, had more than doubled, but there were no large new sources of income in sight.

In 212, Caracalla did his best to make up the difference by issuing the **Antonine Constitution**, a law that made all the inhabitants of the empire, except for slaves and certain freedmen, into Roman citizens. He did so not from a far-seeing desire to make everyone equal under the law but for more mundane reasons. For one thing, he was accused by the historian Cassius Dio of using the law as a moneymaking initiative, for only citizens were required to pay certain kinds of taxes, such as an inheritance tax. In addition, by now so many Romans were already citizens anyway that making nearly everyone a citizen streamlined civil legal processes that otherwise would have had to take into account differences in legal status between citizens and provincials. Furthermore, from the perspective of criminal law, Roman citizenship no longer determined how a person was treated. Another, easier to administer, form of legal distinction had taken its place. A person now was automatically classified either as one of the *honestiores*, "more distinguished people" (senators, equestrians, decurions, and soldiers), or as one of the *humiliores*, "more humble people" (everyone else). If arrested, *honestiores* retained the right of appeal to the emperor and could not be tortured. If convicted of a capital crime, they suffered a simple execution rather than being thrown to the wild beasts in the arena. This newer system was much more in line with traditional Roman ideas that one's social status should inform one's treatment under the law.

To deal with the monetary crisis, the emperors had no choice but to *debase* the currency—that is, to mix copper in with the silver. Doing so had the natural consequence of reducing the value of the coins. Caracalla, after his 50 percent pay increase to the soldiers, realized he could not add more copper, as this would make the debasement even more obvious. He came up with an ingenious solution that permitted him to pay out the increase without further debasing the coinage: he issued a new coin called the *antoninianus* (after his name, Antoninus) that was officially valued at 2 *denarii* but only weighed as much as 1½ *denarii*. These measures fooled no one, and as the weight and silver content of the coins decreased, so did their value. Perhaps the emperors anticipated and were willing to accept this on the assumption that the drop in value would be balanced by the increase in salary. But what they would not have foreseen was the effect of pouring into circulation more than double the accustomed number of coins every year. This brought the law of supply

An *antoninianus* of Julia Domna issued ca. 215 gives to her the same titles, "Pia," "Felix, "Augusta," given to male emperors, attesting to the status of Severan women. The reverse legend, "Venus the Ancestress," asserts Julia's almost divine origins. The *antoninianus'* value as a double *denarius* was indicated by a radiate solar crown for men and by a crescent moon under the bust for women.

In the modern day, money has no intrinsic value at all, and its value is determined by popular faith that the money is worth something and by government manipulation of the money supply.

and demand into play: as money became more and more plentiful than goods and services, the value of the goods and services increased and the value of the money decreased, resulting in spiraling inflation. Nor would the emperors have anticipated that Gresham's Law, a modern economic proposition that "bad money drives good money out of circulation," would go into effect: people hoarded the older, good silver coins and paid their taxes with the new, debased ones. The result was that when incoming coins were melted down to make new coins, there was less and less actual silver to use, and newly issued coins thus had an even smaller percentage of silver. In addition, another unforeseen factor was that as the value of the silver coinage plummeted, it no longer served to shore up the value of the fiduciary bronze coinage, which soon lost all of its good faith value and eventually stopped being issued altogether.

All of these factors eventually resulted in financial disaster for the Roman government. Accelerating cycles of debasement and inflation irretrievably ruined the old Roman coinage system based on the silver *denarius*. By mid-century, the silver coinage had fallen to 5 percent silver. This meant that the soldiers' salaries, rather than being increased, became nearly worthless: soldiers complained that they spent their entire salary on a single purchase. The only remaining money of any value was the gold coinage, which was distributed only in the form of donatives on the accession of a new emperor. It would not be long before the soldiers put this consideration to use.

Local administrative and economic problems also were exacerbated by the expanding financial catastrophe. Cities had been overspending and misspending as a consequence of poor management and the lack of an effective accounting system. Many had undertaken massive building projects, such as amphitheaters, aqueducts, and baths, that they could not complete. The emperors were called on to step in. They often made up the shortfall, resulting in another expense to the treasury, and appointed curators to oversee the city's finances. This fed the increasing bureaucratization of the government.

Yet another problem involved tax collection, which was a responsibility of the ecurions. In the case of shortfalls, the decurions had to make up the difference. In addition, what once had been voluntary municipal philanthropy by the mid-second century had become mandatory, a burden on the members of city councils. As a result, being a decurion sometimes was no longer the great honor it once had been, and decurions increasingly looked for ways to evade their responsibilities. The injudicious Severan military salary increases therefore had far-reaching effects that contributed to the ruin of the Roman economy in many different manners.

THE DEBASEMENT OF THE SILVER COINAGE

In the past, emperors had debased the coinage on a small scale without doing any harm to the value of the money, but Severus drastically reduced the silver content, creating gray-colored *denarii* as opposed to shiny silver ones. Later emperors were forced to debase the coinage even further. Chemical analysis of Roman silver coins of the third century graphically depicts the effect of debasement on the silver content of the coins. From the beginning of the empire until about the year 180, the beginning of the reign of Commodus, the *denarius* underwent a gradual decline from nearly 100 percent silver to about 80 percent silver. Subsequently, however, the silver percentage began a more precipitous decline that was exacerbated by Septimius Severus' massive military pay increase. By 230 CE, near the end of the Severan period, the *denarius* was down to 45 percent silver. For the next thirty years the silver percentage in the *antoninianus*, or double *denarius*, which had replaced the *denarius*, declined only minimally, but as of the mid 250s CE the bottom dropped out and by 260 the silver content had collapsed to only about 5 percent silver. As a consequence, the once mighty *denarius* lost nearly all of its purchasing power.

The decline in value of the silver money brought with it rampant inflation. As debasement increased, the value of the money declined, and prices consequently increased. In the modern day, U.S. currency went off the silver standard in 1964, when paper money was no longer exchangeable for silver. It was at about the same time that inflation in the United States took off and was brought back under control only when the government learned to balance the amount of money in circulation against the availability of goods and services that the money could purchase.

TABLE 10.2 WEIGHT AND SILVER CONTENT OF ROMAN SILVER COINS, 27 BCE–270 CE

Emperor	Denomination	Date	Total Weight (grams)	Silver Purity (%)	Weight of Silver (grams)
Augustus	*Denarius*	27 BCE–14 CE	3.50	98.0	3.43
Nero	*Denarius*	54–68	3.45	91.8	3.17
Vespasian	*Denarius*	69–79	3.40	78.0	2.65
Domitian	*Denarius*	81–96	3.45	93.5	3.11
Antoninus Pius	*Denarius*	138–161	3.33	86.5	2.88
Marcus Aurelius	*Denarius*	161–180	3.31	78.0	2.58
Commodus	*Denarius*	180–192	2.86	73.0	2.09
Septimius Severus	*Denarius*	193–211	3.21	55.5	1.78
Caracalla	*Denarius*	212–217	3.23	48.6	1.57
Elagabalus	*Denarius*	218–222	3.17	46.3	1.47
Severus Alexander	*Denarius*	222–235	3.13	42.2	1.32
Philip the Arab	*Antoninianus*	244–249	4.31	42.0	1.81
Gallienus	*Antoninianus*	253–268	3.30	5.0	0.17
Claudius II	*Antoninianus*	268–270	3.65	2.0	0.07

Imperial Women and Boy Emperors

In 217, Caracalla was assassinated by a conspiracy of ambitious army officers. The Praetorian Prefect Macrinus (217–218) became emperor, marking the first time that an equestrian had done so. To indicate his disdain for the Senate, Macrinus did not even bother to request recognition from the Senate, which technically left him as an illegal emperor.

But the dynastic principle soon reasserted itself. Julia Maesa, the sister of Septimius Severus' wife Julia Domna, passed off her fourteen-year-old grandson Elagabalus (218–222) as a son of Caracalla. The army went over, and Macrinus was murdered. The Romans then got more than they had bargained for. Elagabalus had been a pleasure-loving priest of the eastern sun god Elagabal, whose name he had taken. His agenda was to make Elagabal, whom he renamed "the Unconquered Sun," the primary god of the Roman Empire, supplanting the worship of Jupiter and the other Roman gods. This alienated his Roman subjects. Elagabalus' sexual practices likewise aroused disdain; he had five wives, including a Vestal Virgin, and a catalogue of male lovers. In an attempt to regain favor, Elagabalus adopted his nine-year-old cousin, Severus Alexander (222–235), as his successor. But when the Praetorian Guard favored Alexander over himself, Elagabalus ordered the arrest of anyone who did so. The soldiers responded by lynching Elagabalus and pitching him into the Tiber River. The young Alexander then assumed the emperorship.

A gold aureus of the emperor Elagabalus (218–222 CE) depicts the transfer of the sacred black stone of the sun god Elagabal from Emesa in Syria to Rome. The legend reads, "To the Blessed Sun God Elagabal." This scene reflects the increasing trend in the Roman Empire toward monotheism based on various forms of sun worship.

The reigns of these two young men were the closest that Rome ever came to having real empresses. The government was largely taken over by Julia Maesa, who received the title "Mother of the Camp and of the Senate," and Alexander's mother, Julia Mamaea, who was named not only Augusta but also "Imperial Consort." Mamaea attended meetings of the Senate and tried to restore its authority in order to counter the growing power of the army. She included senators in the emperor's *consilium* and opened up the office of Praetorian Prefect to senators. In the end, however, the army had its way. The senatorial Prefect Ulpian was murdered. In 234, army discipline became so bad that German raiders had to be bought off. In the next year, Alexander and his mother were killed during an army mutiny.

THE IMPERIAL CRISIS (235–284)

The murder of Severus Alexander marked not only the end of the Severan Dynasty but also the beginning of a very difficult period for the Roman Empire, the **Imperial Crisis**, also known as the **Military Anarchy**. In addition to economic collapse, many armies throughout the empire named their commanders emperor, marched on Rome to force the Senate to recognize them, and received their donatives. No single emperor was able to end the disorder or to reestablish normal dynastic succession. At the same time, the frontiers were menaced by foreign enemies. Germanic people coalesced into large and formidable coalitions: on the lower Rhine, there were the **Franks** (named after the *francisca*, their favored throwing axe), and the upper Rhine and upper Danube were threatened by the **Alamanni** ("All Men"). Moreover, on the north shore of the Black Sea the **Goths** appeared. And in the east, in 227 the Parthians were overthrown by a Persian dynasty, the **Sasanids**, who created the **New Persian Empire** and laid claim to all the territories of the Old Persian Empire of the fifth century BCE at its fullest extent, including Egypt, Palestine, and Anatolia, resulting in a state of war with the Roman Empire. All of these peoples were eager to take advantage of Roman weakness, especially when armies abandoned frontier posts in the course of civil wars. The empire thus was beset simultaneous attacks from all sides. Indeed, it was a wonder that the empire survived at all. Nor is it easy to reconstruct the political history of this chaotic period, for it is discussed at length in only one connected ancient source, the "Augustan History," a work of historical fiction written in the 390s.

A Multitude of Emperors

Between 235 and 284 there were about fifty emperors, some very short-lived. One was said to have "been proclaimed one day, reigned the next, and been assassinated the next." Few left much mark on history; indeed, some are known only from a few stray coins. But several are worthy of mention. Maximinus the Thracian (235–238), the second non-senatorial emperor after Macrinus, was denigrated by effete senators as a seven-foot barbarian, a description no doubt resulting from his provincial origin and army career. In an attempt to restore normalcy, he appointed his young son Maximus to the rank of Caesar. To no avail. After a revolt instigated by the Senate in Rome, Maximinus and his son were murdered and he was succeeded by the thirteen-year-old Gordian III (238–244), the youngest sole emperor so far.

In 243, the New Persians under Shapur I invaded the eastern provinces. After a Roman victory, young Gordian personally led an attack in 244, and Persian sources claim that he was killed in a battle not even mentioned in the Roman sources, which would make him the first Roman emperor to die in battle. Gordian was succeeded by his Praetorian Prefect Philip the Arab (244–249), who was rumored to have conspired against him and who quickly made his young son, also named Philip, into his co-emperor. Philip treated Christians fairly and even was considered to be a crypto-Christian; he also demonstrated that the emperorship was indeed open even to those from a distant frontier. In 247, he presided over secular games in honor of the one thousandth anniversary of the founding of Rome, but his attempt to equate the eternity of Rome with that of his own dynasty failed dismally.

In 249, Decius, whom Philip had appointed to suppress a revolt on the lower Danube, was proclaimed emperor by his soldiers after inflicting a defeat on the Goths. After Philip the Arab was defeated and killed, along with his son, Decius was acknowledged as emperor by the Senate. In order to gain legitimacy and inspire confidence, Decius assumed the name Trajan Decius (249–251), harking back to the glorious Roman past. To create a dynasty, he named his sons Herennius and Hostilian as co-emperors. He proposed to reunify the empire using religion as a common denominator by requiring all citizens to attest to their loyalty by sacrificing to the state gods. In return, they received a certificate: one reads, "I have always sacrificed to the gods, and now, according to the order, I have made sacrifice and libation, and tasted the victim's flesh." This was the first empire-wide ruling that, potentially, could affect all Christians. Many Christians apostatized by sacrificing, but others, such as Bishop Fabian of Rome, were martyred when they refused to do so. In 251, Decius and Herennius were killed in the frantic Battle of Abritus against the Goths and Carpi on the lower Danube. Rejoicing Christians saw this as the judgment of God and gleefully described Decius' body being devoured by wild animals on the battlefield.

After the death of Decius, his soldiers proclaimed as emperor Trebonianus Gallus (251–253), a provincial governor, even though Decius' surviving son Hostilian still was ruling in Rome. Gallus negotiated a shameful peace with the Goths, allowing them to depart with all their booty and captives, and a civil war was averted when Hostilian died of the plague. After a series of military disasters, including invasions by the New Persians and Goths, Trebonianus and his son Volusianus soon were murdered by their own troops.

Emperors such as Maximinus, Philip the Arab, Trajan Decius, and Trebonianus Gallus desperately tried to reestablish constitutional normality by creating new dynasties. Each of them appointed their young sons as either Caesars or Augustuses—indeed, Trajan Decius made two of his sons co-emperors. But these young men were obvious figureheads, and all but one (who died of the plague) were killed along with their fathers.

In 253, the senator Valerian (253–260) was made emperor. Realizing that the empire was confronted by too many problems and threats to be handled by a single emperor, he immediately named his thirty-five-year-old son, Gallienus (253–268), as his colleague. Gallienus was the first son to be named co-emperor who was not a child figurehead but was actually able to share the rule. The empire was faced with perils on all sides. The frontier defense system of Augustus crumbled, and foreign invaders broke through.

Valerian took charge of the east, which was threatened by Goths and Persians, but to no avail. In 260

This Persian sardonyx cameo shows the Persian King of Kings Shapur capturing the Roman emperor Valerian, all without even having to draw his sword, a tremendous propaganda coup for the New Persians.

he was defeated and captured by the New Persian king Shapur. He spent the rest of his life as Shapur's slave, and the Persians invaded the eastern provinces. In the aftermath of this disaster, bands of Goths and Heruls devastated Greece and the Black and Aegean seacoasts, and the rich and powerful Roman caravan city of Palmyra, in the Syrian desert, which in the previous century had succeeded the Nabataean city of Petra as the primary commercial center of the eastern frontier, declared its

A debased silver *antoninianus* of Queen Zenobia of Palmyra depicts her as Augusta, or empress, with the legend "Zenobia Aug(usta)" on the obverse and a standing figure of the goddess Juno Regina, "Juno the Queen (of the Gods)," on the reverse, emphasizing Zenobia's royal status. Zenobia was the only woman actually to have ruled as Augusta during the Roman Empire.

independence. The city's queen, **Zenobia** (267–272), created a Palmyrene Empire that included the Levant, part of Anatolia, and Egypt. She eventually took title of Augusta and became an empress of the Roman Empire not just in name but in fact.

In the west, Gallienus defeated the Alamanni in northern Italy in 259, but in the following year the fortification system between the upper Rhine and Danube Rivers collapsed, and the Alamanni permanently occupied the Roman territories on the far side of the rivers. Farther west, the Franks broke through into central Gaul and northern Spain. As a result, the army in Gaul, trusting that it could defend itself better than the emperors of Rome could, acclaimed its general, Postumus (259–268), as emperor. A breakaway Gallic Empire, consisting of Gaul, Spain, and Britain, was created. Postumus restored the frontier, but the unity of the empire had been shattered. On top of all this, the empire was decimated by another onslaught of the plague. By 260, Gallienus was left with only the core of the empire: Italy, North Africa, and the Balkans. The empire was disintegrating around him.

Faced with apparently insurmountable difficulties, Gallienus did the best he could with what he had. He transferred the command of armies from senators to equestrians, who came from social and cultural backgrounds more similar to those of the men in the ranks. He made greater use of cavalry, part of a trend to prefer quality over quantity as recruitment problems continued. And he experimented with a **defense in depth** policy with a mobile field army stationed well behind the frontiers that could respond more quickly to hotspots on and inside the frontiers. Eventually, however, he fell victim to a conspiracy among his own officers and was murdered in 268.

The Illyrian Emperors

Gallienus was succeeded by a series of emperors who came from the backwoods of Illyria, also known as the "Soldier Emperors." They had risen in the ranks of the army by dint of their own ability, and they were better able to relate to and control the troops. The first of them, Claudius II (268–270), was faced by a huge invasion of Goths intending not merely to raid but to settle in Roman territory. Assembling the last remnants of the Roman armies, Claudius dealt the Goths a devastating defeat in 269. The survivors were settled as tenant farmers near the Danube, and Claudius gained the epithet Gothicus, or "Slayer of the Goths." He then succumbed to the plague in 270 and became the only emperor of this period to die in his bed.

An *antoninianus* of Severina, probably issued after Aurelian's assassination, displays a male rather than a female reverse, depicting not Venus, Juno, or other feminine design but the goddess Concord holding two military standards, and the typical male legend "Concord of the soldiers."

Claudius was succeeded by another Illyrian, Aurelian (270–275), whose nickname "Hand on Sword" attested to his military prowess. Aurelian completed the task of reconstituting the empire. He drove the **Vandals**, a Germanic people from the area of modern Poland who had been spreading southward, back across the Danube, but, realizing that the province of Dacia could no longer be held (and that the gold mines had played out), he withdrew those Roman inhabitants who wanted to leave and abandoned it. He then marched east. In 272, Palmyra was captured, sacked, and destroyed and its proud queen Zenobia taken captive along with her teenage son and nominal co-ruler Vaballathus (267–272). Then, in 274, Aurelian likewise defeated the Gallic emperor Tetricus (271–274) at the Battle of Châlons. The empire had been recovered, and Aurelian gained a new nickname, "the Restorer of the World." In a show of magnanimity, Aurelian allowed his defeated rivals to live: Zenobia was given an estate outside Rome and became a Roman socialite, whereas Tetricus was appointed a provincial governor.

Like Gallienus, Aurelian attempted to deal with the problems that bedeviled the empire. He tried to restore the value of the currency by giving the essentially copper **antoninianus** a thin silver wash. It looked impressive, but the coating soon rubbed off, and few were fooled for long. Recognizing the popular trend toward monotheism, Aurelian attempted to give some religious unity to the empire by favoring the worship of the god **Sol Invictus** ("The Unconquered Sun"). Moreover, tacitly acknowledging the army's inability to defend even the inner reaches of the empire, he built Aurelian's Wall, the first new wall around Rome in 550 years. But he then suffered the same fate as Gallienus and was assassinated in 275 by a group of disgruntled army officers. Confusion then reigned. No successor was chosen, perhaps because the army was ashamed of its actions, and Aurelian's wife Severina (275) took charge of the government during the brief interregnum. Finally, the Senate, showing uncharacteristic initiative, named the elderly senator Tacitus (275–276) as emperor, although, typically for Senate choices, he died the next year.

The next emperor, Probus (276–282), another able Illyrian emperor, strengthened the northern frontier, defeating the Alamanni, Franks, Goths, and Vandals. He also expanded the practice of settling defeated barbarians as farmers and soldiers on vacant Roman lands. Like Aurelian, Probus also favored the god Sol Invictus. But the Imperial Crisis was not yet over: during a revolt led by Carus (282–283), a general from Gaul, Probus was assassinated, supposedly because he had ordered some of his soldiers to work on road repairs. Carus campaigned successfully against the New Persians, even sacking their capital at Ctesiphon, thus avenging the Persian defeat and capture of Valerian. Carus then was said to have been struck and killed during a violent storm by a lightning bolt; one must wonder whether this particular "lightning bolt" was in the hands of an assassin.

Hopeful Signs

In spite of problems restoring continuity in the emperorship, the empire was surviving the Imperial Crisis. One reason for this was that, even though there were many changes at the top, the Roman bureaucracy continued to operate

A PICTURE IS WORTH A THOUSAND WORDS

CHRIST AS THE SUN GOD

During the course of the Principate, there was an increasing belief among both intellectuals and the general public that all of the many pagan gods were different representations of a single overarching deity.

This belief, known as "pagan monotheism," often was manifested in "solar monotheism," wherein it was believed that the sun represented this unifying deity. At the same time, Christianity, which had begun as a largely misunderstood and even reviled religion, was gaining more and more converts and becoming increasingly intellectually and popularly accepted, if not even mainstream. After all, Christians could claim that they had been monotheists much longer than the pagan population had been. Points of contact between paganism and Christianity often were connected to the sun. Biblical scholars could point to description of the coming Messiah in the Old Testament book of Malachi as the "sun of righteousness." And because Christians met for worship on the "dies Solis," the "day of the Sun," it was thought that they must be sun worshippers. Thus, in this mosaic of the third century from a cemetery beneath St. Peter's Basilica in Rome, Christ is depicted as the sun god driving a four-horse chariot across the sky, suggesting that even Christians bought into the solar connection. Christ's radiate solar crown, representing the rays of the sun, evolved into the Christian halo, with the result that solar iconography perseveres as one of the most common Christian symbols.

at both the empire-wide and local levels. Imperial bureaucrats continued to be appointed and to carry out their duties, taxes were collected and distributed, and the government continued to function. Western European cities still were prosperous enough to be able to construct expensive walls, some with elaborate decorations, that served not only for defense but also as a means of expressing local chauvinism. In addition, not all areas of the empire were equally distressed. Indeed, some regions, such as Britain and North Africa, positively prospered during the third century.

Nor were the frontier regions as dangerous as might be thought. Yes, there were spates of raids and invasions on both the Rhine and Danube frontiers in the north and the Saharan frontier in the south, but by and large, frontier life remained not only relatively peaceful but also remarkably integrated. The frontier, rather than being a line in the sand, was a very fluid place, with constant coming and going and incessant interaction. It often would have been difficult to know just what side of the border one was on, for at the same time that barbarians were adopting Roman customs, the reverse also was true. Barbarian hairstyles and dress, such as trousers and footgear, became the height of Roman fashion, and the barbarian custom of raising a newly named ruler on a shield was adopted by the Roman army. Barbarians on the other side of the frontier likewise picked up Roman culture: the historian Cassius Dio remarked, "The barbarians were adapting themselves to the Roman world. They did not find it difficult to change their life, and they were becoming different without realizing it."

In addition, there was a long tradition of barbarian settlement within the empire, usually organized by a Roman government that always was struggling to find enough farmers to till the soil (and thus ensure the payment of the land tax) and enough soldiers to man the army. It was especially common to settle defeated barbarians, as individuals rather than groups, on Roman land that had been deserted and gone out of production for any number of reasons, such as falling into tax arrears, being abandoned by decurions who could no longer afford the costs of office, being overfarmed or ruined by drought, or even being devastated by barbarian raids. Augustus, for example, settled fifty thousand Getae, Tiberius found land for forty thousand Germans, Nero brought in more than a hundred thousand Transdanubian immigrants, and Trajan imported thousands of defeated Dacians. Most barbarians, it seems, were happy to have this opportunity, for, after all, throughout the history of Rome, a peaceful and prosperous life within the imperial frontiers had been the dream of many barbarians. As a consequence, these barbarian settlers soon were indistinguishable from their Roman neighbors, and after the issuance of the Antonine Constitution, they, too, became Roman citizens.

Now, as then, it is customary to use the term barbarian *in a generic, nonpejorative way to refer to peoples who lived beyond the Roman frontiers.*

Initially, literary activities continued to be pursued as before, although very often in Greek, a sign that the intellectual balance in the empire was shifting toward the east. The Asian senator **Cassius Dio** prospered under emperors from Commodus through Severus Alexander, but he ran into problems in 229 when he was given command of two legions and received death threats from the unruly soldiers. He then went into retirement and authored, in Greek, a massive *Roman History* in eighty books covering the period from the arrival of Aeneas in Italy until his own consulate in 229. In the 240s, a *History of the Roman Empire since Marcus Aurelius* was written, also in Greek, by Herodian, who may have been a minor government official. Subsequently, however, literary productions tailed off; perhaps the political uncertainties reduced the number of patrons willing to underwrite literary efforts. The Platonic philosopher Plotinus, a friend of the emperor Gallienus, did much to establish a new philosophical system known as **Neoplatonism**. His essays and lecture notes were compiled and published under the title *Enneads* by his pupil Porphyry. And the Greek historian Callinicus lived at the court of Queen Zenobia of Palmyra and was executed by Aurelian. In addition, the patriotic Athenian Dexippus, who as archon in the late 260s had raised an army to help drive off attacking Heruls, wrote a *Chronica*, a complete history up until the time of Claudius Gothicus, and a *Scythica*, on Rome's wars with the Scythians, as the Goths were poetically called. Unfortunately, only fragments of these two works survive.

All that said, the empire still was confronting serious political, military, and economic problems that would have to be dealt with. The emperors may have been getting the situation back under control, but much work clearly remained to be done. It was clear that the Principate as established by Augustus was no longer working and that radical changes would have to be made if the empire were going to return to normalcy.

⇦ LOOKING BACK

In the third century CE, the Roman Empire was confronted by crisis. The empire established by Augustus no longer functioned. Emperors were more dependent on the army, and the Senate was shut out of the rule. Overspending and the debasement of the coinage brought financial disaster to empire and cities alike. The government lost control of the armies, which often revolted and made their own commanders emperors. Civil wars gave foreign enemies the chance to raid and invade the empire. By the 260, the empire was breaking apart and looked like it might not survive. Soon thereafter, however, soldier emperors from Illyria began the task of getting the army back under control and putting the empire back together.

LOOKING AHEAD ⇨

The Imperial Crisis had many able emperors who recognized what the problems were and tried to deal with them, but simply lacked the authority and resources to do so. Even though the soldier emperors had made a start in dealing with the problems confronting the empire, much work remained to be done if the empire was going to survive. In the years after 284 CE, two exceptional emperors, Diocletian and Constantine, implemented a series of modifications and reforms that were intended to respond to over two centuries of accumulated problems.

FURTHER READING

Birley, Anthony R. *Septimius Severus: The African Emperor.* 2nd ed. New Haven, CT: Yale Univ. Press, 1988.

Brauer, George C. *The Age of the Soldier Emperors.* Park Ridge, NJ: Noyes, 1982.

Brauer, George C. *The Young Emperors: Prelude to the Fall of Rome, A.D. 193–244.* Springfield, OH: Crowell, 1967.

de Blois, L. *The Policy of the Emperor Gallienus.* Leiden, Netherlands: Brill, 1976.

Elliott, Colin P. "The Acceptance and Value of Roman Silver Coinage in the Second and Third Centuries AD." *Numismatic Chronicle* 174 (2014), 129–152.

Garnsey, Peter, and Caroline Humfress, eds. *The Evolution of the Late Antique World.* Cambridge, UK: Orchard Academic Press, 2001.

Haines, G. C. "The Decline and Fall of the Monetary System of Augustus." *Numismatic Chronicle* 6, no. 1 (1941), 17–47.

Potter, David S. *The Roman Empire at Bay: AD 180–395.* New York: Routledge, 2005.

Turton, G. E. *The Syrian Princesses: The Women Who Ruled Rome, A.D. 193–235.* London: Cassell, 1974.

Watson, Alaric. *Aurelian and the Third Century.* Oxford: Taylor & Francis, 2004.

SOURCES

PAPYRUS GISSENSIS 40; AND CASSIUS DIO, *ROMAN HISTORY*, BOOK 78, CHAPTER 9

The only surviving original version of the Antonine Constitution issued by the emperor Caracalla (211–217), also known as Antoninus, is preserved on a fragmentary papyrus copy now in Giessen in Germany. Although enough of the text survives to provide a general idea of what was in Caracalla's edict, there also remain areas of uncertainly as to the exact contents.

In 212 CE the emperor Caracalla (211–217), whose full legal name was Marcus Aurelius Severus Antoninus, issued an edict that made all of the inhabitants of the Roman Empire except slaves and *dediticii* (legally disadvantaged freedmen) into Roman citizens. Far from creating legal equality for all Romans, this edict merely acknowledged two realities: (1) by this time, well over half of all Romans already were citizens, which created complications in navigating among Roman, provincial, and local laws, and (2) by now, other legal distinctions, those between *honestiores* ("more distinguished people") and *humiliores* ("more humble people"), had replaced the distinctions between citizens and non-citizens. Caracalla's edict, therefore, had the benefits of simplifying legal procedures and raising a bit of extra tax income because some taxes, such as taxes on inheritances and slave manumissions, applied only to Roman citizens. Those persons enfranchised by Caracalla's law then took the name "Aurelius," the extended family name of Caracalla. It is unclear what "danger" Caracalla is referring to in the edict; it could be a purported conspiracy that led to the murder of his younger brother Geta at the end of 211 CE. The law attracted surprisingly little attention in antiquity: it survives only in a single ragged piece of papyrus and is mentioned in only four other ancient sources. The only contemporary historian to discuss it any length was Cassius Dio, a senator from Bithynia who served under emperors from Commodus (180–192) to Severus Alexander (222–235). After antagonizing the Praetorian Guard in 227 CE, Dio escaped into an honorable retirement. He is known primarily for his massive eighty-book *Roman History*, which covered the period from Aeneas until 229 CE. Dio's history is especially important for the invaluable information that it provides based on his personal experiences and knowledge.

Source: Allan Johnson, Paul Coleman-Norton, and Frank Bourne, *Ancient Roman Statutes* (Austin: University of Texas Press, 1961), no. 277, 225–226.

(a) *Papyrus Gissensis* 40

Emperor Caesar Marcus Aurelius Severus Antoninus Augustus proclaims: It is most fitting that, as I ascribe the causes and the reasons of events to divine origin, I should attempt to render thanks to the immortal gods for their preservation of me in so great a danger. I believe, therefore, that most magnificently and reverently I can perform a service not unworthy of their majesty, if I make my offerings to the gods in company with the foreigners[1] who at any time have entered the number of my subjects, as well as with my own people. I grant, therefore, the Roman citizenship to all foreigners throughout the Empire [. . .] except for the *dediticii*.[2] For it is proper that the populace not only should [. . .] everything, but also should share in the victory. This edict will enhance the majesty of the Roman people.

(b) Cassius Dio, *Roman History*, Book 78, Chapter 9

Earnest Gary, trans., *Dio's Roman History*, 9 vols. (Cambridge, MA: Harvard Univ. Press, 1927).

Now this great admirer of Alexander,[2] Antoninus,[3] was fond of spending money upon the soldiers, great numbers of whom he kept in attendance upon him, alleging one excuse after another and one war after another; but he made it his business to strip, despoil, and grind down all the rest of mankind, and the senators by no means least. In the first place, there were the gold crowns[4] that he was repeatedly demanding, on the constant pretext that he had conquered some enemy or other. And I am not referring, either, to the actual manufacture of the crowns—for what does that amount to?—but to the vast amount of money constantly being given under that name by the cities for the customary "crowning," as it is called, of the emperors. Then there were the provisions that we were required to furnish in great quantities on all occasions, and this without receiving any remuneration and sometimes actually at additional cost to ourselves, all of which supplies he either bestowed upon the soldiers or else peddled out. There also were the gifts that he demanded from the wealthy citizens and from the various communities; and the taxes, especially the new ones that he promulgated, and the ten percent tax that he instituted in place of the five percent tax applying to the emancipation of slaves, to bequests, and to all inheritances, for he abolished the right of succession and exemption from taxes that had been granted in such cases to those who were closely related to the deceased. This was the reason why he made all the people in his empire Roman citizens. Nominally he was honoring them, but his real purpose was to increase his revenues by this means, inasmuch as aliens did not have to pay most of these taxes. But apart from all these burdens, we also were compelled to build at our own expense all sorts of houses for him whenever he set out from Rome, and costly lodgings in the middle of even very shortest journeys; yet he not only never lived in them, but in some cases was not destined even to see them. Moreover, we constructed amphitheaters and racecourses wherever he spent the winter or expected to spend it, all without receiving any contribution from him; and they were all promptly demolished, the sole reason for their being built in the first place being, apparently, that we might become impoverished.

---

[1] Latin *peregrini*, referring to any "foreigner," including Roman provincials and barbarian immigrants.

[2] Not a reference to barbarians who had surrendered, as often is thought, but to stigmatized freedman who had been branded or tortured or had fought in the arena.

[3] The son of Septimius Severus (193–211), more usually known by his nickname "Caracalla," the word for a Gallic cloak that he liked to wear.

[4] What was known as "crown gold"; emperors expected the cities of the empire to provide gold crowns after victories over a foreign enemy, which led emperors to declare victories of dubious value.

PERVIGILIUM VENERIS

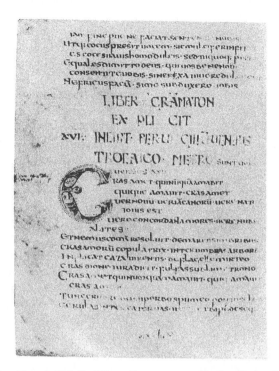

The first page of the *Pervigilium Veneris* ("Vigil of Venus") as preserved in the *Codex Salmasianus* ("Salmasian Manuscript"), now in Paris, a famous collection of late antique poetry copied around the year 700 CE.

The *Pervigilium Veneris*, or "Vigil of Venus," was written by an unknown author and is variously dated to between the second and fifth centuries CE; a third-century date certainly would fit its themes and presentation. It is preserved in only two manuscripts, both in Paris. It was written for a festival in honor of the goddess Venus that lasted for three nights, April 1-3, and reflects the deep and lasting hold that traditional religious practices could have on the popular mentality. The focus on the reawakening of plant and animal life in the spring makes it different from the typical poetry of antiquity and more of a harbinger of the Middle Ages. The repetitive refrain "Cras amet qui nunquam amavit; quique amavit cras amet" ("May one love tomorrow, who never has loved; may whoever has loved, love tomorrow") conveys the sense of longing that underlies the poem. This anonymous versified translation from 1843 uses archaic word forms and verbal elisions, such as "'tis" for "it is," "'twill" for "it will," and so on.

Source: "The Vigil of Venus. Translated from the Latin," *Blackwood's Edinburgh Magazine* 53.332 (June, 1843)

May one love tomorrow, who never has loved;
may whoever has loved, love tomorrow.
Spring, new spring, with song and mirth,
Spring is on the newborn earth.
Spring is here, the time of love—
The merry birds pair in the grove,
And the green trees hang their tresses,
Loosen'd by the rain's caresses.
Tomorrow she joins lovers all,
Where the woodland shadows fall,
On bowers of myrtle intertwined,[5]
Many a band of love she'll bind.
Tomorrow Dione[6] speaks her laws,
Seated in her justice hall.
May one love tomorrow, who never has loved;
may whoever has loved, love tomorrow.
Tomorrow is the day when first
From the foam of Ocean burst,[7]
Like one of his waves, the bright
Dione, queen of love and light,
'Mid the sea-gods' azure train,
'Mid the horses of the main.[8]
May one love tomorrow, who never has loved;
may whoever has loved, love tomorrow.
She[9] it is that lends the Hours[10]
Their crimson glow, their jewel-flowers:
At her command the buds are seen,
Where the west-wind's breath has been,
To swell within their dwellings green.
She abroad those dewdrops flings,
Dew that night's cool softness brings;
How the bright tears hang declining,
Glis'ning with tremulous shining,
Almost of weight to drop away,
And yet too light to leave the spray.
Hence the tender plants are bold

Their blushing petals to unfold:
'Tis that dew, which through the air
Falls from heav'n when night is fair,
That unbinds the moist green vest
From the floweret's[11] maiden breast.
'Tis Venus' will, when morning glows,
'Twill be the bridal of each rose.
Then the bride-flower[12] shall reveal,
What her veil cloth now conceal,
The blush divinest, which of old
She caught from Venus' trickling blood,
With Love's kisses mix'd, I think,
With blaze of fire, and rubies' pink,
And with many a crimson ray
Stolen from the birth of day.
May one love tomorrow, who never has loved;
may whoever has loved, love tomorrow.
All the nymphs[13] the queen of Love[14]
Summons to the myrtle-grove;
And see ye, her wanton boy,[15]
Comes with them to share our joy?
Yet, if Love[16] be arm'd, they say,
Love can't take a holiday,
Not without his bow laid down!
Come, ye nymphs, for Love says now,
His torch, his shafts, are now deferred,
From them no harm shall you incur,
Yet, I advise ye, nymphs, beware,
For your foe is passing fair;
Love is mighty, ye'll confess,
Mighty e'en in nakedness;
And most panoplied[17] for fight
When his charms are bared to sight.
May one love tomorrow, who never has loved;
may whoever has loved, love tomorrow.
Diana[18] a petition we,

---

[5] During the festivals of Venus her statues were crowned with myrtle leaves.

[6] A Titaness, daughter of Oceanus, personification of the sea, and mother of Venus (Greek Aphrodite), often, as here, identified with Venus herself.

[7] Venus was born from the sea foam that arose around the god Uranus' castrated testicles.

[8] Seahorses.

[9] Venus.

[10] The goddesses that control the sequence and attributes of the seasons.

[11] A small flower that is part of a larger flower.

[12] The rose, the flower of Venus.

[13] Young nubile female nature deities who live in woods, mountains, streams, and oceans.

[14] That is, Venus.

[15] Cupid, son of Venus.

[16] Cupid, who was armed with a bow and arrow. Before lovemaking can take place, Cupid must put down his bow.

[17] A panoply was a full complement of arms and armor, but in this case a panoply is lacking both.

[18] The virgin goddess of hunting.

By Venus sent, proffer to thee:
Virgin envoys, it is meet,
Should the Virgin huntress greet:
Quit the grove, nor it profane
With the blood of quarry slain.
She would ask thee, might she dare
Hope a maiden's thought to share—
She would bid thee join us now,
Should the maids our sport allow.
For three nights[19] thou may'st have seen,
Wandering through thine alleys green,
Troops of joyous friends, with flowers
Crown'd, amid their myrtle bowers.
Ceres and Bacchus[20] us attend,
And great Apollo[21] is our friend;
All night we must our vigil keep—
Night by song redeem'd from sleep.
Let Venus in the woods bear sway,
Dian, quit the grove, we pray.
May one love tomorrow, who never has loved;
may whoever has loved, love tomorrow.
Of Hybla's[22] flowers, so Venus will'd,
Venus' judgment-seat we build.
She is judge supreme; the Graces,[23]
As assessors, take their places.
Hybla, render all thy store
All the season sheds thee o'er,
Till a hill of bloom be found
Wide as Enna's[24] flowery ground.
Attendant nymphs shall here be seen,
Those who delight in forest green,
Those who on mountain-top abide,
And those whom sparkling fountains hide.
All these the queen of joy and sport
Summons to attend her court,
And bids them all of Love beware,

Although the guise of peace he wear.
May one love tomorrow, who never has loved;
may whoever has loved, love tomorrow.
Fresh your coronals of flowers,
Green your overarching bowers,
Tomorrow brings us the return
Of Aether's[25] primal marriage-morn.
In amorous showers of rain he came
T' embrace his bride's mysterious frame,
To generate the blooming year,
And all the produce Earth does bear.
Venus still through vein and soul
Bids the genial current roll;
Still she guides its secret course
With interpenetrating force,
And breathes through heaven, and earth, and sea,
A reproductive energy.
May one love tomorrow, who never has loved;
may whoever has loved, love tomorrow.
She old Troy's[26] extinguish'd glory
Revived in Latium's later story,
When, by her auspices, her son
Laurentum's[27] royal damsel won.
She vestal Rhea's spotless charms
Surrender'd to the War-god's arms;[28]
She for Romulus that day
The Sabine daughters bore away;[29]
Thence sprung the Ramnes'[30] lofty name,
Thence the old Quirites[31] came;

[19] April was the month of Venus; her festival lasted three nights, April 1–3.
[20] Ceres, goddess of the harvest, and Bacchus (Dionysus), god of wine.
[21] The sun god, brother of Diana.
[22] The name of several cities in Sicily, which has led to suggestions that the poem may have originated there.
[23] Known in Greek as the Charites, the Graces were minor female goddesses connected to nature and fertility; in some myths they are the companions of Venus.
[24] A city in central Sicily.

[25] In Greek mythology, the god of the upper atmosphere, the son of Darkness and Night and the brother of Day, thought to give the spark of life to all creatures.
[26] Venus favored Troy in the Trojan War because the Trojan prince Paris had declared her most beautiful in the competition with the goddesses Hera and Athena.
[27] Aeneas, the son of Venus, married Lavinia, daughter of the Latin king Latinus, whose capital city was Laurentum.
[28] The Vestal Virgin Rhea Silvia claimed that Mars was the father of the twins Romulus and Remus.
[29] In legend, the Sabines were an Italic people living near the original foundation of Rome; Romulus organized the kidnaping of Sabine women in order to provide wives for Roman men.
[30] One of the original three tribes (thirds) of Rome, their name supposedly derived from "Romulus."
[31] A name for Roman citizens, from the ancient Roman god Quirinus.

And thence the stock of high renown,
The blood of Romulus, handed down
Through many an age of glory pass'd,
To blaze in Caesar's age at last.[32]
May one love tomorrow, who never has loved;
may whoever has loved, love tomorrow.
All rural nature feels the glow
Of quickening passion through it flow.
Love, in rural scenes of yore,
They say, his goddess-mother bore;
Received on Earth's sustaining breast,
Th' ambrosial infant[33] sunk to rest;
And him the wild-flowers, o'er his head
Bending, with sweetest kisses fed.
May one love tomorrow, who never has loved;
may whoever has loved, love tomorrow.
On yellow field out yonder, see,
The mighty bulls lie peacefully.
Each animal of field or grove
Owns faithfully the bond of love.
The flocks of ewes, beneath the shade,

Around their gallant rams are laid;
And Venus bids the birds awake
To pour their song o'er plain and lake.
Hark! the noisy pools reply
To the swan's hoarse harmony;
And Philomel[34] is vocal now,
Perch'd upon a poplar-bough.
Thou scarce would'st think that dying fall
Could ought but love's sweet griefs recall;
Thou scarce would'st gather from her song
The tale of brother's barbarous wrong.
She sings, but I must silent be:—
When will the spring-tide come for me?
When, like the swallow, spring's own bird,
Shall my faint twittering notes be heard?
Alas! the muse, while silent I
Remain'd, hath gone and pass'd me by,
Nor Phoebus[35] listens to my cry.
And thus forgotten, I await,
By silence lost, Amyclae's[36] fate.

---

[32] Venus and her son Aeneas were the ancestors of the Julian family, which included Julius Caesar and Augustus.
[33] Cupid, son of Venus, who ate ambrosia, the food of the gods.

[34] Philomela, Greek mythology, a daughter of Pandion, king of Athens, who after being violated and having her tongue cut out by her brother-in-law was turned by the gods into a nightingale.
[35] An epithet of the god Apollo.
[36] A village conquered by the Spartans early in their history.

THE MARTYRDOM OF PERPETUA AND FELICITAS (7 MARCH 203 CE)

THE PASSION OF SAINT PERPETUA, SAINT FELICITAS, AND THEIR COMPANIONS

During the course of the Principate, traditional religious beliefs and practices were increasingly challenged by the expansion of Christianity, a new religion that better met the needs and desires of larger and larger numbers of people. Christianity offered a multitude of benefits, including a moral code for guiding one's life, easy access (compared to the Jewish requirement that male converts be circumcised), a community experience and social support system, the forgiveness of sins, and, in particular, an afterlife. Initially, Christianity often had been greeted by the Romans with hostility and skepticism that even could result in execution by the Roman government, but during the second and third centuries, Christianity developed the look and feel of a more mainstream religion. In the Severan period (193–235 CE), for example, a form of pagan monotheism focused on sun worship became increasingly popular and even was promoted by Roman emperors. In spite of increasing popular sympathy toward Christianity, Christians still could run afoul of the Roman government if they refused to take the loyalty oath to Rome and the emperor by participating in the imperial cult, which they believed was contrary to their monotheistic religious beliefs. As a consequence, many Christians suffered execution and became martyrs (from the Greek word for "witnesses") to their Christian beliefs. They were believed to receive the "crown of martyrdom" and to go directly to heaven, where they could intercede with God on behalf of persons who still were alive. Christian communities preserved many authentic accounts of martyrdoms that were intended to provide examples of commendable behavior to other members of the community. These "martyrs' acts" often included the verbatim minutes of the trial before a Roman magistrate. These accounts demonstrate that many Roman judges were sympathetic to the accused Christians, attempting to reason with them and offering them extra time to reconsider. One of the most famous Christian martyrs was Vibia Perpetua, an aristocratic woman of Carthage, who was married and nursing a child. Felicitas, a pregnant slave, was martyred with her. The account of the martyrdom, written in Latin, purportedly was a form of prison diary by Perpetua herself, making it one of the earliest surviving pieces of writing by a Christian woman. Additional material was added after her death. The account is viewed as being completely authentic.

Source: Walter H. Shewring, trans., *The Passion of SS. Perpetua and Felicity* (London: Sheed and Ward, 1931).

If ancient examples of faith kept, both testifying to the grace of God and working for the edification of man, have to this end been set in writing, that by their reading God may be glorified and man strengthened, why should not new witnesses also be so set forth which likewise serve either end? There were apprehended the young catechumens,[37] Revocatus, Felicitas his fellow servant, Saturninus, and Secundulus. With them also was Vibia Perpetua, nobly born, reared in a liberal manner, wedded honorably, and having a father and mother and two brothers, one of them a catechumen likewise, and a son, a child at the breast; and she herself was about twenty-two years of age. What follows here she shall tell herself; the whole order of her martyrdom as she left it written with her own hand and in her own words.

At that time when, she said, we were still with our companions and my father was liked to vex me with his words and continually strove to hurt my faith because of his love,[38] "Father," said I, "Do you see, for example, this vessel lying, a pitcher or

---

[37] Individuals receiving Christian instruction before being baptized.

[38] Because he knew that being a Christian could be dangerous.

whatsoever it may be?" And he said, "I see it." And I said to him, "Can it be called by any other name than that which it is?" And he answered, "No." "So can I call myself nought other than that which I am, a Christian." Then my father, angry with this word, came upon me to tear out my eyes, but he only vexed me, and he departed, vanquished, he and the arguments of the devil. Then, because I was without my father for a few days I gave thanks to the Lord and I was comforted because of his absence. In this same space of a few days we were baptized, and the spirit[39] declared to me that I must pray for nothing else after that water[40] save only endurance of the flesh. After a few days we were taken into prison, and I was much afraid because I never had known such darkness. O bitter day! There was a great heat because of the press, there was cruel handling by the soldiers. Lastly I was tormented there by care for the child.

Then Tertius and Pomponius, the blessed deacons[41] who ministered to us, obtained with money that for a few hours we should be taken forth to a better part of the prison and be refreshed. Then, when all of them went out from the dungeon and took their pleasure, I suckled my child who now was faint with hunger. And being careful for him, I spoke to my mother and strengthened my brother and commended my son to them. I pined because I saw they pined for my sake. Such cares I suffered for many days, and I obtained that the child should abide with me in prison,[42] and straightway I became well and was lightened of my labor and care for the child, and suddenly the prison was made a palace for me, so that I would sooner be there than anywhere else.

Then said my brother to me, "Lady, my sister, you are now in high honor, even such that you might ask for a vision, and it should be shown you whether this be a passion[43] or else a deliverance."

And I, as knowing that I conversed with the Lord, for whose sake I had suffered such things, promised him nothing, doubting, and I said, "Tomorrow I will tell you." And I asked,[44] and this was shown me. I beheld a ladder of bronze, marvelously great, reaching up to heaven; and it was narrow, so that not more than one might go up at one time. And in the sides of the ladder were planted all manner of things of iron. There were swords there, spears, hooks, and knives, so that if any that went up took not good heed or looked not upward, he would be torn and his flesh cling to the iron. And there was right at the ladder's foot a serpent lying, marvelously great, which lay in wait for those that would go up, and frightened them that they might not go up. Now Saturus went up first. And he came to the ladder's head, and he turned and said, "Perpetua, I await you, but take care that serpent bites you not." And I said, "It shall not hurt me, in the name of Jesus Christ." And from beneath the ladder, as though it feared me, it softly put forth its head, and as though I trod on the first step I trod on its head. And I went up, and I saw a very great space of garden, and in the midst a man sitting, white-headed, in shepherd's clothing, tall milking his sheep, and standing around in white were many thousands. And he raised his head and beheld me and said to me, "Welcome, child." And all that stood around said, "Amen." And at the sound of that word I awoke, yet eating I know not what of sweet. And at once I told my brother, and we knew it should be a passion, and we began to have no hope any longer in this world.

A few days after, the report went abroad that we were to be tried. In addition, my father returned from the city spent with weariness, and he beseeched me to cast down my faith, saying, "Have pity, daughter, on my grey hairs, have pity on your father, if I am worthy to be called father by you. If with these hands I have brought you to this flower of youth and have preferred you before all your brothers, give me not over to the reproach of men. Look upon your brothers, look upon your mother and mother's sister; look upon your son, who will not endure to live after you. Give up your resolution. Do

---

[39] The Holy Spirit.

[40] Of baptism.

[41] Christian clerics who managed the resources of the church. They were not arrested because no one had made an accusation against them.

[42] Roman prisons were used as holding areas for persons awaiting trial, not as places to which one was sentenced for punishment.

[43] That is, a martyrdom.

[44] For a vision.

not destroy us all together, for none of us will speak openly against men again if you suffer anything."

This he said, fatherly in his love, kissing my hands and grovelling at my feet, and with tears he named me, not daughter, but lady. And I was grieved for my father's case because, out of all my kin, he would not rejoice at my passion, and I comforted him, saying, "That shall be done at this tribunal,[45] whatsoever God shall please, for know that we are not established in our own power, but in God's." And he went from me very sorrowful.

Another day as we were at meal we were suddenly snatched away to be tried, and we came to the forum. Therewith a report spread abroad through the parts near to the forum, and a very great multitude gathered together.[46] We went up to the tribunal. The others being asked, confessed. So they came to me. And my father appeared there also, with my son, and would draw me from the step, saying, "Perform the sacrifice,[47] have mercy on the child." And Hilarian the Procurator,[48] who at that time, in the place of the deceased Proconsul[49] Minucius Timinianus, had received the right of the sword,[50] said, "Spare your father's grey hairs; spare the infancy of the boy. Make sacrifice for the emperor's[51] prosperity." And I answered, "I am a Christian." And when my father stood by me yet to cast down my faith, he was bidden by Hilarian to be cast down and was smitten with a rod. And I sorrowed for my father's harm as though I had been smitten myself; so sorrowed I for his unhappy old age. Then Hilarian passed sentence upon us all and condemned us to the beasts, and cheerfully we went down to the dungeon. Then, because my child had been used to being breastfed and to staying with me in the prison, straightway I sent Pomponius the deacon to my father, asking for the child. But my father would not give him. And as God willed, neither did he wish to be suckled any more, nor did I take fever, so that I might not be tormented by care for the child and by the pain of my breasts.

A few days after, while we were all praying, suddenly in the midst of the prayer I uttered a word and named Dinocrates, and I was amazed because he had never come to my mind save then, and I sorrowed, remembering his fate. And straightway I knew that I was worthy, and that I ought to ask for him. And I began to pray for him long, and to groan to the Lord. Forthwith the same night, this was shown me.[52] I beheld Dinocrates coming forth from a dark place, where there were many others also, both hot and thirsty, his raiment foul, his color pale, and the wound on his face which he had when he died. This Dinocrates had been my brother in the flesh, seven years old, who being diseased with ulcers of the face had come to a horrible death, so that his death was abominated of all men. For him therefore I had made my prayer, and between him and me was a great gulf, so that either might not go to the other. There was, moreover, in the same place where Dinocrates was, a font full of water, having its edge higher than was the boy's stature, and Dinocrates stretched up as though to drink. I was sorry that the font had water in it, and yet for the height of the edge he might not drink. And I awoke, and I knew that my brother was in travail. Yet I was confident I should ease his travail, and I prayed for him every day until we passed over into the camp prison, for it was in the camp games that we were to fight, and the time was the anniversary of Geta Caesar.[53] And I made supplication for him day and night with groans and tears, that he might be given me.

On the day when we were in chains, this was shown me.[54] I saw that place that I had seen before, and Dinocrates clean of body, finely clothed, in comfort; and where the wound was before, I saw a scar; and the font I had seen before, the edge of it

---

[45] The court of the magistrate.

[46] Criminal trials were a popular form of public entertainment.

[47] On behalf of the imperial cult; it involved dropping a pinch of incense on a fire.

[48] An official who usually had financial duties.

[49] The governors of the province of Africa still had the Republican office of Proconsul.

[50] The power to inflict the death sentence.

[51] In 203 CE there were three emperors, the Augustus Septimius Severus, and his sons, Caracalla, also Augustus, and the Caesar Geta.

[52] Perpetua has another vision.

[53] Either his birthday, March 7, or the day when he was proclaimed Caesar in 197 CE. The celebration would have been marked by entertainments ranging from gladiatorial contests to the execution of condemned criminals.

[54] Perpetua has a third vision.

being drawn down to the boy's navel, and he drew water thence which flowed without ceasing. And on the edge was a golden cup full of water; and Dinocrates came up and began to drink therefrom, and the cup failed not. And being satisfied he departed away from the water and began to play as children will, joyfully. And I awoke. Then I understood that he was translated from his pains.

Then a few days after, Pudens the adjutant, in whose charge the prison was, who also began to magnify us because he understood that there was much grace in us, let in many to us that both we and they in turn might be comforted.[55] Now, when the day of the games drew near, there came in my father to me, spent with weariness, and began to pluck out his beard and throw it on the ground and to fall on his face cursing his years and saying such words as might move all creation. I was grieved for his unhappy old age.

The day before we fought, I saw in a vision[56] that Pomponius the deacon had come hither to the door of the prison, and knocked hard upon it. And I went out to him and opened to him. He was clothed in a white robe ungirdled, having shoes curiously wrought. And he said to me, "Perpetua, we await you. Come." And he took my hand, and we began to go through rugged and winding places. At last with much breathing hard we came to the amphitheater, and he led me into the midst of the arena. And he said to me, "Be not afraid. I am here with you and labor together with you." And he went away. And I saw many people watching closely. And because I knew that I was condemned to the beasts I marvelled that beasts were not sent out against me. And there came out against me a certain ill-favored Egyptian with his helpers, to fight with me. Also there came to me comely young men, my helpers and aiders. And I was stripped naked, and I became a man. And my helpers began to rub me with oil as their custom is for a contest, and over against me I saw that Egyptian wallowing in the dust. And there came forth a man of very great stature, so that

he overpassed the very top of the amphitheater, wearing a robe ungirdled, and beneath it between the two stripes over the breast a robe of purple, having also shoes curiously wrought in gold and silver, bearing a rod like a master of gladiators, and a green branch whereon were golden apples. And he besought silence and said, "The Egyptian, if he shall conquer this woman, shall slay her with the sword, and if she shall conquer him, she shall receive this branch." And he went away. And we came nigh to each other, and began to buffet one another. He tried to trip up my feet, but I with my heels smote upon his face. And I rose up into the air and began so to smite him as though I trod not the earth. But when I saw that there was yet delay, I joined my hands, setting finger against finger of them. And I caught his head, and he fell upon his face, and I trod upon his head. And the people began to shout, and my helpers began to sing. And I went up to the master of gladiators and received the branch. And he kissed me and said to me, "Daughter, peace be with you. And I began to go with glory to the gate called the Gate of Life."[57] And I awoke, and I understood that I should fight, not with beasts but against the devil. But I knew that mine was the victory.

Thus far I have written this, until the day before the games, but as to the carrying out of the games themselves, if anyone wishes, let him write.

And blessed Saturus[58] too delivered this vision that he himself wrote down. We had suffered, he said, and we passed out of the flesh, and we began to be carried toward the east by four angels whose hand touched us not. And we went not as though turned upward upon our backs, but as though we went up an easy hill. And passing over the world's edge we saw a very great light, and I said to Perpetua, for she was at my side, "That which the Lord promised us, we have received his promise." And while we were being carried by these same four angels a great space opened before us, having rose trees and all kinds of flowers. The height of the trees was after the manner of the cypress, and their leaves sang without ceasing. And there in the garden

---

[55] Many of these persons also were Christians, but because they, like the deacons, had not been accused or denounced they could freely go in and out of the prisons and care for the condemned persons.

[56] A fourth vision.

[57] Victorious gladiators exited the arena through the Gate of Life on the eastern side, whereas dead gladiators were carried out the Gate of Death on the western side.

[58] Who also had been condemned.

were four other angels, more glorious than the rest, who when they saw us gave us honor and said to the other angels, "Lo, here are they, here are they," and marvelled. And the four angels who bore us set us down trembling, and we passed on foot by a broad way over a plain. There we found Jocundus and Saturninus and Artaxius, who in the same persecution had been burned alive, and Quintus, a martyr also, who in prison had departed this life, and we asked of them where were the rest. The other angels said to us, "Come first, go in, and salute the Lord."

And we came near to a place, of which the walls were such that they seemed built of light, and before the door of that place stood four angels who clothed us when we went in with white raiment. And we went in, and we heard as it were one voice crying "Holy, holy, holy" without any end. And we saw sitting in that same place as it were a man, white-headed, having hair like snow; youthful of countenance; whose feet we saw not. And on his right hand and on his left, four elders, and behind them stood many other elders. And we went in with wonder and stood before the throne, and the four angels raised us up and we kissed him, and with his hand he passed over our faces. And the other elders said to us, "Stand you." And we stood, and gave the kiss of peace. And the elders said to us, "Go you and play." And I said to Perpetua, "You have that which you desire." And she said to me, "Yes, God be thanked," so that I that was glad in the flesh am now more glad.

And we went out, and we saw before the doors, on the right Optatus the bishop,[59] and on the left Aspasius the priest and teacher, being apart and sorrowful. And they cast themselves at our feet and said, "Make peace between us,[60] because you departed and left us thus." And we said to them, "Are not you our father, and you our priest, that you should throw yourselves at our feet?" And we were moved, and embraced them. And Perpetua began to talk with them in Greek,[61] and we set them apart in the arboretum beneath a rose tree. And while we yet spoke with them, the angels said to them, "Let

them cool down, and whatsoever dissensions you have between you, put them away from you each for each." And they made them to be confounded. And they said to Optatus, "Correct your people, for they come to you as those that return from the games and arguing about the racing clubs."[62] And it seemed to us as though they would shut the gates. And we began to know many brothers there, martyrs also. And we were all sustained there with an inexpressible savor that satisfied us. Then in joy I awoke. These were the glorious visions of those martyrs themselves, the most blessed Saturus and Perpetua, that they themselves wrote down. But Secundulus by an earlier end God called from this world while he was yet in prison, not without grace, so that he should escape the beasts. Yet if not his soul, his flesh at least knew the sword.

As for Felicitas, she too received this grace of the lord. For because she was already eight months with child, for she was pregnant when she was arrested, she was very sorrowful as the day of the games drew near, fearing lest because of the child she would be kept back, for it is not permitted that pregnant women be presented for torment, and lest she should shed her holy and innocent blood after the rest, among strangers and malefactors.[63] Also her fellow martyrs were much afflicted lest they should leave behind them so good a friend and as it were their fellow-traveler on the road of the same hope. Therefore with joint and united groaning they poured out their prayer to the Lord three days before the games. Immediately after their prayer her pains came upon her. And when by reason of the natural difficulty of the eighth month she was oppressed with her travail and made complaint, there said to her one of the servants of the keepers of the door, "You that thus make complaint now, what wilt you do when you are thrown to the beasts, for whom you showed contempt when you would not sacrifice?" And she answered, "I myself now suffer that which I suffer, but there another shall be in me who shall suffer for me, because I am to suffer for

---

[59] Bishop of an unknown North African city.

[60] It was not uncommon for bishops to be defied by their clergy.

[61] The "Passion of Perpetua" circulated in both Latin and Greek.

[62] Generally, there were four chariot-racing factions, or clubs, identified by their colors, blue, green, red, and white.

[63] Christians were executed along with any other criminals who had been sentenced to death.

him." So she was delivered of a daughter, whom a sister reared up to be her own daughter.

Because therefore the Holy Spirit permitted this, and by permitting it has willed that the account of the games also should be written, even if though we are unworthy of describing such great glory as a supplement, nevertheless we follow the, so to speak, mandate[64] of the most holy Perpetua, or rather her trust, adding one testimony more of her own steadfastness and height of spirit.[65] When they were being more cruelly handled by the Tribune[66] because through the advice of certain most despicable men he feared lest by magic charms they might be withdrawn secretly from the prison house, Perpetua answered him to his face, "Why do you not allow us, the most noble guilty ones, the property, certainly, of Caesar, and about to fight on his anniversary, to take some comfort? Or is it not your glory that we should be taken out thither, fatter of flesh?" The Tribune trembled and blushed, and gave order that they should be more gently handled, granting that her brothers and the rest should come in and rest with them. Also the adjutant of the prison now believed.

Likewise on the day before the games, when at the last feast that they call "free" they made, as far as they might, not a Free Feast[67] but a Love Feast,[68] with like hardihood they cast these words at the people, threatening the judgment of the Lord, witnessing to the felicity of their passion, setting at nought the curiosity of those that ran together. And Saturus said, "Is not tomorrow sufficient for you? You are friends today, foes tomorrow. Yet mark our faces diligently, that you may know us again on that day." So they began all to go away thence astonished, of whom many believed.

Now dawned the day of their victory, and they went forth from the prison into the amphitheater as it were into heaven, cheerful and bright of countenance. If they trembled at all, it was for joy, not for fear. Perpetua followed behind, glorious of presence, as a true spouse of Christ and darling of God, at whose piercing look all cast down their eyes. Felicitas likewise, rejoicing that she had borne a child in safety so that she might fight with the beasts, came now from blood to blood, from the midwife to the gladiator, to wash after her travail in a second baptism. And when they had been brought to the gate and were being compelled to put on, the men the dress of the priests of Saturn, the women the dress of the priestesses of Ceres,[69] the noble Perpetua remained of like firmness to the end, and would not. She said, "For this cause came we willingly to this, that our liberty might not be obscured. For this cause have we devoted our lives, that we might do no such thing as this. This we agreed with you." Injustice acknowledged justice; the Tribune suffered that they should be brought forth as they were, without more ado. Perpetua began to sing, as if already treading on the Egyptian's head. Revocatus and Saturninus and Saturus threatened the people as they gazed. Then when they came into Hilarian's sight, they began to say to Hilarian, stretching forth their hands and nodding their heads, "You judge us, they said, and God judges you." At this the people, being enraged, sought that they should be vexed with scourges before the line of the beast-fighters. Then truly they gave thanks because they had received somewhat of the sufferings of the Lord.

But he who had said, "Ask and you shall receive,"[70] granted them that end that each had desired. For whenever they spoke together of their desire in their martyrdom, Saturninus for his part would declare that he wished to be thrown to every kind of beast, that so indeed he might wear the more glorious crown. At the beginning of the spectacle therefore, Revocatus himself and Saturninus first had suffered a leopard and then were torn by a bear on a scaffold. Now, Saturus detested nothing more than a bear, but was confident already that he should die by one

---

[64] A mandate was an imperial command issued to an imperial official.

[65] The rest of the account was composed by other authors.

[66] A junior officer, not a Military Tribune or Tribune of the Plebs.

[67] The *cena libera*, or "free meal," of gladiators. All of those who would be taking part, including condemned criminals and gladiators, were together, many of whom would be fighting against each other on the next day.

[68] The *agape*, a Christian communal meal that included taking communion.

---

[69] Saturn and Ceres were harvest deities.

[70] John 16:24.

bite of a leopard. Therefore when he was being given to a boar, the gladiator instead who had bound him to the boar was torn asunder by the same beast and died after the days of the games; nor was Saturus more than dragged. Moreover, when he had been tied on a bridge to be assaulted by a bear, the bear would not come forth from his den. So Saturus was called back unharmed a second time.

But for the women the devil had made ready a most savage cow, prepared for this purpose against all custom, for even in the beast he mocked their sex. They were stripped therefore and made to put on nets, and so they were brought forth. The people shuddered, seeing one a tender girl, the other her breasts yet dropping from her late childbearing. So they were called back and clothed in loose robes.[71] Perpetua was first thrown and fell upon her loins. And when she had sat upright, her robe being rent at the side, she drew it over to cover her thigh, mindful rather of modesty than of pain. Next, looking for a pin, she likewise pinned up her disheveled hair, for it was not meet that a martyr should suffer with hair disheveled, lest she should seem to grieve in her glory.[72] So she stood up; and when she saw Felicitas smitten down, she went up and gave her her hand and raised her up. And both of them stood up together and, the hardness of the people being now subdued, were called back to the Gate of Life. There Perpetua being received by one named Rusticus, then a catechumen,[73] who stood close at her side, and as now awakening from sleep, so much was she in the spirit and in ecstasy, she began first to look about her; and then, which amazed all there, she asked, "When, indeed, are we to be thrown to the cow?" And when she heard that this had been done already, she would not believe until she perceived some marks of mauling on her body and on her dress. Thereupon she called her brother to her, and that catechumen, and spoke to them, saying, "Stand fast in the faith, and love you all one another; and be not offended because of our passion."

Saturus also at another gate exhorted Pudens the soldier, saying, "So then indeed, as I trusted and foretold, I have felt no assault of beasts until

now. And now believe with all your heart. Behold, I go out thither and shall perish by one bite of the leopard." And immediately at the end of the spectacle, the leopard being released, with one bite of his Saturus was covered with so much blood that the people, in witness to his second baptism, cried out to him returning, "Well washed, well washed." Truly it was well with him who had washed in this wise. Then said he to Pudens the soldier, "Farewell. Remember the faith and me, and let not these things trouble you, but strengthen you." And therewith he took from Pudens' finger a little ring, and dipping it in his wound gave it back again for an heirloom, leaving him a pledge and memorial of his blood. Then as the breath left him he was cast down with the rest in the accustomed place for his throat to be cut.[74] And when the people besought that they should be brought forward, that when the sword pierced through their bodies their eyes might be joined thereto as witnesses to the slaughter, they rose of themselves and moved, whither the people willed them, first kissing one another, that they might accomplish their martyrdom with the rites of peace. The rest not moving and in silence received the sword. Saturus much earlier gave up the ghost, for he had gone up earlier also, and now he waited for Perpetua likewise. But Perpetua, that she might have some taste of pain, was pierced between the bones and shrieked out, and when the swordsman's hand wandered still, for he was a novice, herself set it upon her own neck. Perchance so great a woman could not else have been slain, being feared by the unclean spirit,[75] had she not herself so willed it.

O most valiant and blessed martyrs! O truly called and elected to the glory of Our Lord Jesus Christ! Which glory he that magnifies, honors and adores, ought to read these witnesses likewise, as being no less than the old, to the Church's edification; that these new wonders also may testify that one and the same Holy Spirit works ever until now, and with Him God the Father Almighty, and His Son Jesus Christ Our Lord, to Whom is glory and power unending forever and ever. Amen.

---

[71] Because they had gained the sympathy of the crowd.

[72] Having unkempt hair was a sign of being grief-stricken.

[73] An unbaptized Christian.

[74] To end his suffering and ensure that he actually was dead.

[75] The Devil.

THE SHAPUR I INSCRIPTION

In this cliff carving, Shapur I, with the Roman emperor Philip kneeling in front of him and holding the emperor Valerian by the hand, tramples the emperor Gordian III. Bishapur. The high priest Kartir and a Sasanian general stand on the right.

Like the kings of the Old Persian Empire (550–331 BCE), the kings of the New Persian, or Sasanid, Empire advertised their achievements with monumental reliefs and inscriptions carved on the sides of cliffs. A trilingual rock carving, in Parthian, Middle Persian, and Greek, at Naqsh-I Rustam in Iran gives a detailed account of the reign of the Sasanid king Shapur I (241–272 CE). Shapur described himself as "The Mazda-worshipping lord Shapur, King of Kings of Iran and non-Iran, whose lineage is from the gods, son of the Mazda-worshipping divinity Ardashir, King of Kings of Iran, whose lineage is from the gods, grandson of king Papak." Like the Roman emperors, Shapur I claimed to rule the entire world. Among other projects, he built the city of Bishapur using enslaved Roman soldiers, many of whom were captured after the defeat of Valerian in 260.

Source: R. N. Frye, *The History of Ancient Iran*, Vol. 7 (Beck: Munich, 1983), 370–373.

I, the Mazda-worshipping lord Shapur, King of Kings of Iran and non-Iran, whose lineage is from the gods, son of the Mazda-worshipping divinity Ardashir,[76] King of Kings of Iran, whose lineage is from the gods, grandson of King Papak,[77] am ruler of Iranshahr and these lands[78]: Persis, Parthia, Khuzistan, Characene, Assyria, Adiabene, Arabia, Azerbaijan, Armenia, Georgia, Segan, Arran, Balasakan, up to the Caucasus mountains and the Gates of Albania, and all of the mountain chain of Pareshwar, Media, Gurgan, Merv, Herat and all of Aparshahr, Kerman, Seistan, Turan, Makuran, Paradene, Sind, the Kushanshahr up to Peshawar, and up to Kashgar, Sogdiana and to the mountains of Tashkent, and on the other side of the sea, Oman. And we have given to a village district the name Peroz-Shapur and we made Hormizd-Ardashsir by name Shapur. And these many lands, and rulers and governors, all have become tributary and subject to us.

When at first we had become established in the empire, Gordian Caesar[79] raised in all of the Roman Empire a force from the Gothic and German realms[80] and marched on Asuristan[81] against the Empire of Iran and against us. On the border of Babylonia at Misikhe, a great "frontal" battle occurred. Gordian Caesar was killed and the Roman force was destroyed.[82] And the Romans made Philip Caesar.[83] Then Philip Caesar came to us for terms, and to ransom their lives gave us 500,000 *denarii* and became tributary to us. For this reason we have renamed Misikhe Peroz-Shapur.[84]

And Caesar lied again and did wrong to Armenia.[85] Then we attacked the Roman Empire and annihilated at Barbalissos a Roman force of 60,000 and Syria and the environs of Syria we burned, ruined, and pillaged.[86] In this one campaign we conquered of the Roman Empire the following fortresses and towns: the town of Anatha with surroundings, Birtha of Arūpān with surroundings, Birtha of Asporakan, the town of Sura, Barbalissos, Manbuk, Aleppo, Qennisrin, Rhephania, Zeugma, Urima, Gindaros, Armenaza, Seleucia, Antioch[87], Cyrrhe, another town of Seleucia, Alexandretta, Nicopolis, Sinzara, Hama, Rastan, Dikhor, Dolikhe, Dura,[88] Circusium, Germanicia, Batna, and Khanar, and in Cappadocia[89] the towns of Satala, Domana, Artangil, Suisa, Sinda, and Phreata, a total of thirty-seven towns with surroundings.

In the third campaign, when we were besieging Carrhae and Edessa, Valerian Caesar[90] marched against us. He had with him a force of 70,000 from Germany, Raetia, Noricum, Dacia, Pannonia, Moesia, Istria, Spain, Africa, Thrace, Bithynia, Asia, Pamphylia, Isauria, Lycaonia, Galatia, Lycia, Cilicia, Cappadocia, Phrygia, Syria, Phoenicia, Judaea,

---

[76] Ardashir I (224–241 CE) overthrew the Parthians and established the New Persian Empire in 224 CE.

[77] A Persian prince, the son of Sāsān, who gave his name to the Sasanian Dynasty.

[78] Regions extending from Arabia to western India.

[79] Roman emperor from 238 until 244.

[80] Auxiliary troops serving in the Roman army.

[81] Babylonia.

[82] In reality, after Shapur had invaded Roman territory he was defeated by Gordian at the Battle of Resaena in 243. Gordian was not killed there.

[83] Gordian III was assassinated in 244 and succeeded by Philip the Arab (244–249).

[84] Philip's offensive against the New Persians later in 244 was initially successful but he was ultimately defeated at the Battle of Misikhe.

[85] Armenia lay on the frontier between the Roman and New Persian Empires and was a constant bone of contention between them, just as it had been between the Romans and Parthians.

[86] This Roman incursion in 253 is known only from this inscription; Shapur probably took advantage of the troubled times relating to the fall of the emperor Trebonianus Gallus (251–253) and the proclamation of Valerian (253–260). The victory opened the way to the Persian capture of Dura Europa and Antioch in 256 CE.

[87] The most important Roman city of Syria and the Levant.

[88] Dura Europa, the site of major modern archaeological excavations.

[89] A Roman province of western Anatolia.

[90] Emperor from 253 until 260; he made his son Gallienus (253–268) his co-emperor.

Arabia, Mauritania, Germania, Rhodes, Osrhoëne, and Mesopotamia.[91] And beyond Carrhae and Edessa we had a great battle with Valerian Caesar.[92] We made prisoner ourselves with our own hands Valerian Caesar and the others, chiefs of that army, the Praetorian Prefect, and senators; we made all prisoners and deported them to Persis.[93] Syria, Cilicia, and Cappadocia we burned, ruined and pillaged. In that campaign we conquered from the Roman Empire[94] the town of Samosata, Alexandria on the Issus, Katabolos, Aegaea, Mopsuestia, Mallos, Adana, Tarsus, Augustinia, Zephyrion, Sebaste, Korykos, Anazarba, Kastabala, Neronias, Flavias, Nicopolis, Epiphaneia, Celenderis, Anemurion, Selinus, Mzd, Antioch, Seleucia, Dometiopolis, Tyana, Caesarea, Komana, Kybistra, Sebasteia, Birtha, Rakundia, Laranda, and Iconium, altogether all these cities with their surroundings.

Men of the Roman Empire, non-Iranians, we deported. We settled them in the Empire of Iran in Persis, Parthia, Khuzistan, Babylonia, and other lands where there were domains of our father, grandfathers, and of our ancestors. We searched out for our conquest many other lands, and we acquired fame for heroism that we have not engraved here, except for the preceding. We ordered it written so that whoever comes after us may know of our fame, heroism, and power. Thus, for this reason, that the gods have made us their ward, and with the aid of the gods we have searched out and taken so many lands, so that in every land we have founded many Bahram fires[95] and have conferred benefices upon many magians,[96] and we have magnified the cult of the gods. And here by this inscription, we founded a fire Khosro-Shapur by name for our soul and to perpetuate our name, a fire called Khosro-Aduranahid by name for the soul

of our daughter Aduranahid, Queen of Queens, to perpetuate her name, a fire called Khosro-Hormizd-Ardashir by name for the soul of our son, Hormizd-Ardashir, Great King of Armenia, to perpetuate his name, another fire called Khosro-Shapur by name, for the soul of our son Shapur, King of Characene, to perpetuate his name, and a fire called Khosro-Narseh by name, for the soul of our son, the noble, Mazda worshipping Narseh, King of Sind, Seistan, and Turan to the edge of the sea, to perpetuate his name.

And that which we have donated to these fires, and which we have established as a custom, all of that we have written upon the document of guaranty. Of those 1,000 lambs, of which custom gives us the excess, and which we have donated so these fires, we have ordered as follows[97]: for our soul each day a lamb, one and a half measures of bread and four quantities of wine; for that of Sāsān the Lord[98]; King Papak[99]; King Shapur, son of Papak; the King of Kings Ardashir[100]; the Empire's Queen Khoranzim; the Queen of Queens Aduranahid; Queen Dinak; the King of Gilan Bahram; the King of Characene Shapur; the Great King of Armenia Hormizd-Ardashir; the King of the Saka[101] Narseh; the Queen of the Saka Shapurdukhtak; the Lady of the Saka Narsehdukht; Lady Ćašmak; Prinz Peroz; Lady Mirdut, mother of the King of Kings Shapur; Prince Narseh; Princess Rud-dukhtak, daughter of Anošak; Varazdukht, daughter of Khoranzim; Queen Stahyrad; Hormizdak, son of the King of Armenia Hormizd;

---

[91] A catalogue of many of the Roman provinces; this information probably came from Roman prisoners of war.

[92] In 268 CE.

[93] In southwestern Iran.

[94] Some of these places were announced as having been captured previously, but in the interim had been retaken by the Romans.

[95] New Persian fire temples.

[96] Priests of the god Ahura Mazda.

[97] To stress his own legitimacy, Shapur lists the royal genealogy, from Sāsān, who gave his name to the Sasanid Dynasty, up to his own family, many of whom have royal titles in their own right attesting to the desire of the New Persian rulers to keep the real power within their own family circle.

[98] A priest of a fire temple of the water goddess Anahita and the first member of the Sasanid Dynasty.

[99] A Persian prince, son of Sāsān and grandfather of Ardashir.

[100] Ardashir I (224–241 CE), who revolted against the Parthians and founded the Sasanid, or New Persian, Empire.

[101] A generic term for the peoples of the Asian steppe east of the Caspian Sea.

Hormizdak; Odabakht; Bahram; Shapur; Peroz, son of the King of Characene; Shapurdukhtak, daughter of the King of Characene; and Hormizddukhtak, daughter of the King of the Saka, for their souls a lamb, a measure and a half of bread and four quantities of wine.

Now as we serve and worship the gods with zeal, because we are the wards of the gods and with the aid of the gods we have searched out these peoples, have dominated them, and have acquired fame for bravery, also whoever comes after us and rules, may he also serve and worship the gods with zeal, so the gods may aid him and make him their ward.

This is the writing by my hand, Hormizd, the scribe, son of Shirak, the scribe.[102]

---

[102] The subscription appears only in the Parthian version of the inscription.

THE *AUGUSTAN HISTORY*, "ODENATHUS" AND "ZENOBIA"

Zenobia, queen of the powerful trading city of Palmyra in Syria on the eastern frontier of the Roman Empire, was the wife of Odenathus, a Palmyrene prince who drove off the New Persians after their defeat and capture of the emperor Valerian in 260 CE. As a reward, Odenathus was placed in charge of the east by Valerian's son Gallienus. After further defeats of the Persians, Odenathus took the title "King of Kings" in 264. But when he appeared to be on the verge of declaring himself emperor in 267, Zenobia organized a conspiracy against him and he was assassinated. Zenobia then assumed his position as ruler of Palmyra. She took advantage of Roman weakness—Gaul, Spain, and Britain already had created an "Empire of Gaul" in 260 CE—to take the title of Augusta (Empress) and create an Empire of Palmyra, which included the Levant, part of Anatolia, and Egypt. Zenobia's story is told most fully in the sections "Odenathus" and "Zenobia" in the *Augustan History*, a compilation of the 390s CE that is part fact and part historical fiction.

Source: David Magie, trans., *Historia Augusta*, Vol. I (Cambridge, MA: Harvard Univ. Press, 1921).

[Augustan History, "Odenathus"]

Had not Odenathus, Prince of the Palmyrenes, seized the imperial power after the capture of Valerian,[103] when the strength of the Roman state was exhausted, all would have been lost in the east. He assumed, therefore, as the first of his line, the title of King, and after gathering together an army he set out against the Persians, having with him his wife Zenobia, his elder son, whose name was Herodes, and his younger sons, Herennianus and Timolaus. First of all, he brought under his power Nisibis[104] and most of the east together with the whole of Mesopotamia; next, he defeated the king himself and compelled him to flee. Finally, he pursued Shapur[105] and his children even as far as Ctesiphon,[106] and captured his concubines and also a great amount of booty;

When Gallienus[107] learned that Odenathus had ravaged the Persians, brought Nisibis and Carrhae[108] under the sway of Rome, made all of Mesopotamia ours, and finally arrived at Ctesiphon, put the king to flight, captured the satraps and killed large numbers of Persians, he gave him a share in the imperial power, conferred on him the name Augustus, and ordered coins to be struck in his honor that showed him haling the Persians into captivity.[109] This measure the Senate, the city, and men of every age received with approval.

Then, after he had for the most part put in order the affairs of the east, Odenathus was killed by his cousin Maeonius, who also had seized the imperial power together with his son Herodes, who, also, after returning from Persia along with his father, had received the title of emperor.[110] Some god, I believe, was angry with the Republic, who, after

---

[103] In 268 CE.

[104] A powerful fortress on the border between the Roman and Sasanid empires.

[105] Shapur I (241–272 CE), King of Kings of the New Persian Empire.

[106] The western capital of the New Persian Empire, on the Tigris River in Mesopotamia.

[107] Roman emperor from 253 until 268 CE, the son of the emperor Valerian.

[108] A city on the frontier of the Roman and Sasanid Empire that had been captured by Shapur.

[109] No such coins are known to exist.

[110] There is no other evidence that Maeonius or Herodes ever did so.

Valerian's death, was unwilling to preserve Odenathus alive. For of a surety he, with his wife Zenobia, would have restored not only the east, which he already had brought back to its ancient condition, but also all parts of the whole world. Hardened by these feats, he was able to bear the sun and the dust in the wars with the Persians, and his wife, too, was inured to hardship and in the opinion of many was held to be more brave than her husband, being, indeed, the noblest of all the women of the east, and, as Cornelius Capitolinus[111] declares, the most beautiful.

Then Zenobia, his wife, because the sons who remained, Herennianus and Timolaus, were still very young, assumed the power herself and ruled for a long time, not in feminine fashion or with the ways of a woman, but surpassing in courage and skill not merely Gallienus, than whom any girl could have ruled more successfully, but also many an emperor. As for Gallienus, indeed, when he learned that Odenathus was murdered, he made ready for war with the Persians, an over-tardy vengeance for his father,[112] and, gathering an army with the help of the general Heraclianus, he played the part of a skilful prince. This Heraclianus, however, on setting out against the Persians, was defeated by the Palmyrenes and lost all the troops he had gathered, for Zenobia was ruling Palmyra and most of the east with the vigor of a man.

[Augustan History, "Zenobia"]

Now all shame is exhausted, for in the weakened state of the Republic things came to such a pass that, while Gallienus conducted himself in the most evil fashion, even women ruled most excellently. For, in fact, even a foreigner, Zenobia by name, about whom much already has been said, boasting herself to be of the family of the Cleopatras and the Ptolemies, proceeded upon the death of her husband Odenathus to cast about her shoulders the imperial mantle; and arrayed in the robes of Dido[113] and even assuming the diadem, she held the imperial power in the name of her sons Herennianus and Timolaus,

[111] An otherwise unknown Roman author.
[112] Valerian, who had been defeated and captured in 268.
[113] The Queen of Carthage who was spurned by Aeneas and committed suicide.

ruling longer than could be endured from one of the female sex. For this proud woman performed the functions of a monarch both while Gallienus was ruling and afterward when Claudius[114] was busied with the war against the Goths, and in the end could scarcely by conquered by Aurelian[115] himself, under whom she was led in triumph and submitted to the sway of Rome.

There is still in existence a letter of Aurelian that bears testimony concerning this woman, then in captivity. For when some found fault with him, because he, the bravest of men, had led a woman in triumph, as though she were a general, he sent a letter to the senate and the Roman people, defending himself by the following justification:

> I have heard, Conscript Fathers, that men are reproaching me for having performed an unmanly deed in leading Zenobia in triumph. But in truth those very persons who find fault with me now would accord me praise in abundance, did they but know what manner of woman she is, how wise in counsels, how steadfast in plans, how firm toward the soldiers, how generous when necessity calls, and how stern when discipline demands. I might even say that it was her doing that Odenathus defeated the Persians and, after putting Shapur to flight, advanced all the way to Ctesiphon. I might add thereto that such was the fear that this woman inspired in the peoples of the east and also the Egyptians that neither Arabs nor Saracens nor Armenians ever moved against her. Nor would I have spared her life had I not known that she did a great service to the Roman state when she preserved the imperial power in the east for herself or for her children. Therefore let those whom nothing pleases keep the venom of their own tongues to themselves. For if it is not meet to vanquish a woman and lead her in triumph, what are

[114] Emperor Claudius II Gothicus (268–270).
[115] Emperor from 270 to 275.

they saying of Gallienus, in contempt of whom she ruled the empire well? What of the Deified Claudius, that revered and honored leader? For he, because he was busied with his campaigns against the Goths, suffered her, or so it is said, to hold the imperial power, doing it of purpose and wisely, in order that he himself, while she kept guard over the eastern frontier of the empire, might the more safely complete what he had taken in hand.

This speech shows what opinion Aurelian held concerning Zenobia.

Such was her continence, it is said, that she would not know even her own husband save for the purpose of conception. For when once she had lain with him, she would refrain until the time of menstruation to see if she were pregnant; if not, she would again grant him an opportunity of begetting children. She lived in regal pomp. It was rather in the manner of the Persians that she received worship and in the manner of the Persian kings that she banqueted; but it was in the manner of a Roman emperor that she came forth to public assemblies, wearing a helmet and girt with a purple headband, which had gems hanging from the lower edge whereas its center was fastened with the jewel called cochlis,[116] used instead of the brooch worn by women, and her arms were frequently bare. Her face was dark and of a swarthy hue, her eyes were black and powerful beyond the usual wont, her spirit divinely great, and her beauty incredible. So white were her teeth that many thought that she had pearls in place of teeth. Her voice was clear and like that of a man.

Her sternness, when necessity demanded, was that of a tyrant, her clemency, when her sense of right called for it, that of a good emperor. Generous with prudence, she conserved her treasures beyond the wont of women. She made use of a carriage, and rarely of a woman's coach, but more often she rode a horse; it is said, moreover, that frequently she walked with her foot-soldiers for three or four miles. She hunted with the eagerness of a Spaniard. She often drank with her generals, although at other times she refrained, and she drank, too, with the Persians and the Armenians, but only for the purpose of getting the better of them. At her banquets she used vessels of gold and jewels, and she even used those that had been Cleopatra's.[117] As servants she had eunuchs of advanced age and but very few maidens. She ordered her sons to speak Latin, so that, in fact, they spoke Greek but rarely and with difficulty. She herself was not wholly conversant with the Latin tongue, but nevertheless, mastering her timidity she would speak it; Egyptian, on the other hand, she spoke very well. In the history of Alexandria and the Orient she was so well versed that she even composed an epitome, so it is said. Roman history, however, she read in Greek.

After Aurelian took her prisoner he caused her to be led into his presence and then asked her, "Why is it, Zenobia, that you dared to show insolence to the emperors of Rome?" To this she replied, it is said: "You, I know, are an emperor indeed, for you win victories, but Gallienus and Aureolus[118] and the others I never regarded as emperors. Believing Victoria[119] to be a woman like me, I desired to become a partner in the royal power, should the supply of lands permit." And so she was led in triumph with such magnificence that the Roman people had never seen a more splendid parade. For, in the first place, she was adorned with gems so huge that she labored under the weight of her ornaments; for it is said that this woman, courageous although she was, halted very frequently, saying that she could not endure the load of her gems. Furthermore, her feet were bound with shackles of gold and her hands with golden fetters, and even on her neck she wore a chain of gold, the weight of which was borne by a Persian guardsman. Her life was granted her by Aurelian, and they say that thereafter she lived with her children in the manner of a Roman matron on an estate that had been presented to her at Tibur, which even to this day is still called Zenobia, not far from the palace of Hadrian.[120]

---

[116] An agate-like gem from Arabia.

[117] Presumably after her conquest of Egypt.

[118] A general who revolted against Gallienus in 268 and later was murdered by the Praetorian Guard.

[119] The goddess Victory.

[120] At Tivoli, nineteen miles east of Rome.

LATE ANTIQUITY

PART

LATE ANTIQUITY

CHAPTER 11

DIOCLETIAN, CONSTANTINE, AND THE CREATION OF THE LATE ROMAN EMPIRE (284–337)

The situation for Rome in 284 CE was eerily similar to what it had been in 31 BCE. Serious problems had arisen that the existing government was unable to deal with, and the Roman world had been beset by some fifty years or more of civil war. Roman governmental policies were in serious need of reformation. Thus, just as Augustus had to dealt with accumulated problems by establishing the Principate beginning in 27 BCE, the emperor Diocletian was confronted with the need virtually to reestablish the Roman Empire in a new form in order to respond to problems that had accumulated over the past 300 years. Diocletian's attempts, however, which built upon some of the efforts of his predecessors, were not uniformly successful, and the restructuring of his successor **Constantine I** bore greater fruit. Some of their reforms had an effect different from those of Augustus: instead of creating unity, they resulted in increasing fragmentation. The Roman Empire as it was reorganized by Diocletian and Constantine goes under several names, such as the Dominate, the Late Roman Empire, and, ultimately, the Byzantine Empire. The second half of the third century also marked the onset of **Late Antiquity**, the final phase of the ancient world. The world of Late Antiquity would be characterized by the breakdown of the unity of the Mediterranean world that had evolved during the Roman Empire. At the same time, many of the defining characteristics of the modern world, such as the genesis of the western European nations and the appearance and expansion of new religious movements, such as Christianity and Islam, also are to be sought here.

DIOCLETIAN AND THE LATE ROMAN EMPIRE

In 284, **Diocletian**, another Illyrian soldier, rebelled against the emperor Carinus (283–285), the son of Carus. After emerging victorious, Diocletian was in much the same position as the first emperor Augustus, having come to power after a

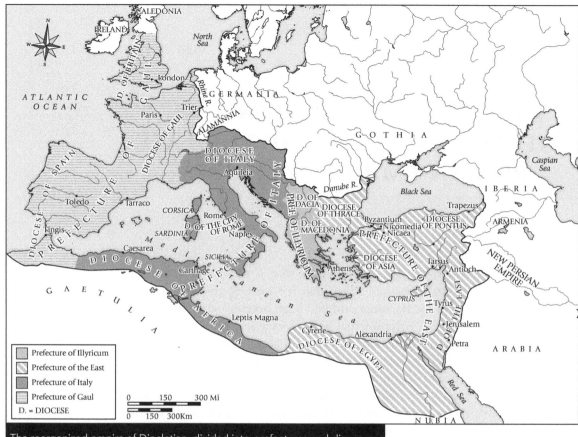

The reorganized empire of Diocletian, divided into prefectures and dioceses

lengthy period of civil war. Like Augustus, he was confronted, first of all, by the necessity of getting the empire back under control, and secondly, by the need to introduce reforms to deal with problems that had accumulated over the previous centuries. Also like Augustus, he was a better administrator than general, but the empire had an abundance of generals; a good administrator was just what it needed.

Diocletian and the Dominate

When Diocletian (284–305), a career soldier and another of the Illyrian Emperors, assumed the throne, the Roman Empire faced a multitude of problems that had accumulated during the Principate, had worsened during fifty years of civil war, and had threatened to undermine the unity that Augustus and his successors had worked so hard to create. These included an army that was difficult to control, a lack of an effective method for choosing emperors, threats of foreign attacks, a society in which certain classes felt disadvantaged or alienated, an economy in ruins, an expanding and expensive bureaucracy, and a state religion that engendered less and less devotion. To restore normality, Diocletian wanted to accomplish two things. On the one hand, in order to deal with the Imperial Crisis and ensure his own longevity, Diocletian desired to take complete control of the empire and end the civil wars. And on the other, he wished to implement reforms that would result in the long-term success and security of the empire.

Diocletian's first priority was to consolidate his own authority. He tried to do so in several ways. The last vestiges of the fictional partnership with the Senate were abandoned. At the same time that he ostentatiously refurbished the Senate house in Rome, Diocletian removed all authority from the Senate, which lost all of its former role in conferring power on emperors and became merely the city council of the city of Rome. Diocletian also altered the way that the emperor was perceived. Rather than being just another senator, he became the *Dominus*, or "Lord and Master," a godlike person elevated far above other men. He replaced the general's cloak with a floor-length purple robe and the laurel wreath with a pearl diadem. Everything associated with his person became "sacred." Those who met with him performed *proskynesis*, prostrating themselves face down on the floor. These practices made it more difficult for potential rivals to envisage themselves bridging the gap between subject and emperor. As a result, the empire was transformed from the Principate of Augustus to the **Dominate**, and we now move into what is called the Late Roman Empire.

Diocletian attempted to gain more direct control of the administration by greatly expanding the imperial bureaucracy. He regularized the custom of having multiple ruling emperors that had been introduced by Valerian in the third century by creating the **Tetrarchy**, or "Rule by Four," in which he appointed three other army officers as emperors to rule various sections of the empire. Two had the rank of Augustus, or Senior Emperor: Diocletian ruled the eastern provinces, and Maximianus administered Italy, Africa, and Spain. Two Caesars, or Junior Emperors, Galerius and Constantius, administered the Balkans in the east and Gaul and Britain in the west, respectively. Each emperor had his own *comitatus* (the imperial court, from the word *comites*, or comrades), consisting of his chief officials, bodyguard, and household personnel, and each established his own imperial capital—for example, Diocletian at Nicomedia in Anatolia and Constantius at Trier in northern Gaul. Rome, on the other hand, now far removed from the action, lost its status as an imperial capital, with Maximianus preferring Milan and Aquileia further north. If an emperor went on campaign, he was accompanied by his entire *comitatus*, and the government set up shop wherever the emperor happened to camp. Diocletian proposed to solve the problem of the imperial succession by designating each Caesar as the successor of his respective Augustus. In this way he hoped to eliminate rival claimants to the throne after emperors died.

This sculpture made from porphyry, a purple igneous stone that came from a single Egyptian quarry, depicts the emperors embracing each other, thus emphasizing the idealized cooperation among the four emperors of the Tetrarchy. Their other hands on their swords demonstrate the source of their authority. The sculpture was looted from Constantinople and taken to Venice when the city was sacked by Crusaders in 1204. Its original site is unknown, and it now is erected in a corner of St. Mark's Basilica in Venice.

In order to reduce the possibility of anyone gaining enough power to lead a revolt, Diocletian subdivided the sources of authority. Gallienus' experimental "defense in depth" policy was formalized. The army was split up into the *limetanei*, or border army, stationed on the frontier and commanded by Dukes, and the *comitatenses*, or field army, mobile units stationed at court and in internal areas and commanded by Counts. One consequence of this was that the border troops became even more tied to the regions in which they were stationed. They took up farming and lost their mobility, becoming little more than a citizen militia. Civil and military functions and offices were separated, so that generals did not govern provinces and provincial governors did not command troops. By a process of subdivision, the number of provinces was increased from fifty to one hundred and two, lessening the authority of each governor. In addition, Italy was demoted to the same status as the rest of the provinces, and Diocletian expanded the third-century policy of restricting the entry of senators into high-ranking governmental posts, especially military ones.

New levels of bureaucracy were introduced. The provinces, whose governors had the positions of Proconsul, Consularis, Praeses, and Corrector, were grouped into twelve **dioceses**, administered by **Vicars**, of about eight provinces each. And the dioceses were organized into four **Prefectures**, each administered by a Praetorian Prefect, who thus gained even greater authority. The Praetorian Prefect became the most powerful imperial official after the emperor: he was the only provincial administrator to report directly to the emperor and was permitted to wear a purple cloak extending to his knees. Measures such these not only brought an end to the repetitious cycles of revolts but also gave the imperial government an increased local presence—and greatly increased costs.

Strategies for Survival

Once Diocletian had put an end to the Military Anarchy, he could attempt to solve more long-term problems. The economy was in a very sorry state. The debased silver coinage was nearly worthless. Tax revenues could hardly meet expenses, and, in border areas, some land had gone out of cultivation as a consequence of fifty years of warfare. In an attempt to restore value to the currency, Diocletian reissued a good gold coin weighing one-sixtieth of a pound and known as the *aureus* or *solidus*, a good silver coin known as the *siliqua*, and a large, silver-coated copper coin called the *follis* ("bag of money"). But the *follis* fooled no one, and the attempt to reissue good gold and silver coins failed because there was not enough available metal. A Maximum Price Edict issued in 301 attempted to curb inflation by purely legal means by setting maximum prices that could be charged for goods and services. But this served only to drive goods onto the black market, and rampant inflation continued.

Ultimately, Diocletian accepted the ruin of the money economy and revised the tax system so that it was based on payments in kind, known as the *annona*, rather than on payments in the worthless coinage: farmers, for example, now paid taxes in produce rather than silver currency. In order to take into account changes in productivity levels over time and changes in the imperial budget, the *annona* was recalculated in periodic reassessments, called indictions, every fifteen years. Produce was gathered into imperial storehouses, and imperial factories manufactured uniforms and weapons. Soldiers were paid in kind, in ration units that also were called the *annona*. The soldiers' only monetary salary became the gold and silver donative, which now was issued at five-year intervals rather than just at the beginning of a reign, a policy that now gave the soldiers an incentive to keep a good emperor in office.

In another effort to ensure the long-term survival of the empire, Diocletian issued laws that identified certain jobs, known as **compulsory services**, that had to be performed. These included the occupations of soldier, baker, Decurion, and tenant farmer, to name a few. These positions were made hereditary, and those engaging in them were prohibited from changing their careers. The repeated reissuance of these laws, however, leads one to wonder just how widely they were obeyed.

Finally, like Augustus and Trajan Decius, Diocletian attempted to use the traditional state polytheistic religion as a unifying element. But Christianity, which rejected participation in polytheistic sacrifices made for the safety of the empire, had become attractive not just to the less privileged but also to senators, officials, soldiers, and intellectuals, and now was perceived by some as a direct threat to the empire's well-being. In a last-ditch effort to reverse the rise of Christianity and restore the polytheistic imperial cult, Diocletian, urged on by his Caesar Galerius, commenced the so-called **Great Persecution** in 303. A series of edicts began with a command to surrender Christian books, then seized Christian churches, then ordered the arrest of Christian clergy, and culminated in an order to "sacrifice or die." But by now there was increased popular acceptance

TABLE 11.1 THE TETRARCHIES

First Tetrarchy
Diocletian (Augustus) (284–305)
Maximianus (Augustus) (285–305)
Galerius (Caesar) (293–305)
Constantius I (Caesar) (293–305)
Second Tetrarchy
Galerius (Augustus) (305–311)
Constantius I (Augustus) (305–306)
Maximinus II (Caesar, Augustus) (305–313)
Severus II (Caesar, Augustus) (305–307)
Later Additions
Constantine (Caesar, Augustus) (306–337)
Maxentius (Augustus) (307–312)
Licinius (Augustus) (308–324)

Wage and price controls often have been used to try to control inflation; they were last used in the United States by President Richard Nixon in 1971–1973 after inflation had remained above 4 percent for several years.

DIGGING ANTIQUITY

PIAZZA ARMERINA

The fourth-century CE Roman villa preserved in the uplands of Sicily at Piazza Armerina is one of the most spectacular to survive from all of antiquity. The villa and its contents had the good fortune—from an archaeologist's perspective—to have been covered by a mudslide in 1141 and only brought back to light in the course of archaeological excavations beginning in 1950. The villa covers 43,000 square feet (four thousand square meters) and is accommodated to the terrain by being spread over three terraces. It contains no fewer than sixty-two rooms, including courtyards, living quarters, a large basilica (audience hall), a dining room, a gymnasium, and a thermal bath complex, which, given the Roman obsession with baths, probably accounts for the choice of this particular site. The villa even had its own private aqueducts.

The villa is best known for its well-preserved mosaics, which include the largest one preserved from antiquity. Probably constructed by North African artists, the mosaics display scenes of hunting, chariot races, cherubs and sea nymphs, everyday life, and athletic competitions, including one famously displaying bikini-clad women engaged in athletic activities. Most notably, a forty-meter-long corridor portrays scenes of African animals being captured alive and then being packed onto ships for use in wild beast hunts in the Colosseum in Rome.

The speculative identification of the villa's owner as the retired emperor Maximianus is based on the villa's level of grandeur; the view of the Circus Maximus in Rome from the perspective of the imperial box seats; and the great mosaic of the labors of Hercules, with whom Maximianus was identified. In addition, the depiction of an individual wearing an elaborate embroidered chlamys—the uniform of those in imperial service—and accompanied by soldiers would be consistent with a retired emperor. But the villa equally well could have been constructed by an enormously rich senatorial ex-magistrate of Rome. Whereas the early excavations focused on uncovering the mosaics, more recent digs, beginning in

This mosaic from the villa at Piazza Armerina is thought to depict the retired emperor Maximianus.

2004, are looking at the villa's sculptures, frescoes, and adjoining residential sections. The unearthing of large storerooms, for example, demonstrates that the villa was occupied year round and was not just a summer vacation spot.

See Patrizio Pensabene and Enrico Gallocchio, "The Villa del Casale of Piazza Armerina": https://www.penn.museum/documents/publications/expedition/PDFs/53-2/pensabene.pdf

of and even sympathy with Christian teachings. Christians, for example, were popularly seen as sun worshippers because they met on Sunday, and Christ was seen as a manifestation of the unifying sun god. Christian scripture, adopted from the Jews as the Old Testament, even referred to Christ the Messiah as the "sun of righteousness." There thus was little public support for the persecution. In most of the empire the edicts were ignored, and Christians were permitted to worship in peace.

In 305, saying that he had ruled long enough, Diocletian took a voluntary step unprecedented for a Roman emperor. He retired, taking his colleague Maximianus along with him. Another of his motives would have been to ensure that his method for dealing with the imperial succession went into effect. A Second Tetrarchy was created: Galerius and Constantius became the Augustuses in the east and the west, and two new Caesars, Maximinus II and Severus II, were appointed.

CONSTANTINE AND THE LATE ROMAN EMPIRE

Even though Diocletian often gets most of the credit for establishing the Late Roman Empire, many of his reforms turned out to be ineffective, and it was his successor Constantine, yet another Illyrian, who finished the job of creating programs and policies that would definitively deal with the accumulated problems and finish laying the groundwork for the Late Roman Empire.

The Rise of Constantine

Constantius died the very next year, and the Tetrarchy then collapsed. Its fatal error was that it could not supplant the army's preference for sons. The Second Tetrarchy had ignored Constantine and Maxentius, the sons of Constantius and Maximianus. Both were declared emperors by their fathers' soldiers, Constantine in Britain and Maxentius in Italy. Severus II was killed in 307 when he attacked Maxentius, and a new round of civil wars ensued. In 312, Constantine overcame Maxentius at the **Battle of the Milvian Bridge** underneath the walls of Rome and gained control of the entire western half of the empire. After a shaky period of peace with the eastern emperor Licinius (308–324), who had killed Maximinus II in 313 and taken control of the east, civil war again broke out. In 324, Constantine first defeated Licinius at the Battle of the Hellespont, the last major naval battle of antiquity, and then routed him at the Battle of Chrysopolis. Once again the empire was controlled by a single emperor.

Strategies for Survival

Constantine took a rather different approach to some of the problems confronted by Diocletian. Regarding the senators, Constantine, like Augustus, believed that the empire could not succeed without the support of its richest, most experienced, and most influential social class. Constantine thus reversed the third-century practice of alienating the senatorial aristocracy. He implemented a new accommodation with the senators: they were welcomed into imperial offices—mostly civil offices, although the occasional senator did become an army general—but the Senate, as a body, never regained its authority to name emperors; in the future its only role in the naming of emperors was to deliver congratulations.

With regard to the economy, Constantine decided that it was necessary to have credible hard currency to deal with imperial income and expenditures more efficiently. Instead of trying to revive the discredited silver coinage (a pound of gold now was valued at 120,000 debased denarii), he put the imperial economy on the gold standard in 312 by introducing a new form of the gold **solidus**, larger but thinner and weighing less, only one-seventy-second of a pound. In order for the solidus to succeed, the empire needed a constantly replenishable supply of gold. Because there were no new gold mines to exploit, the only way to do this was by getting hoarded gold back into circulation and keeping it there. The government thus implemented a multitude of measures intended to do so. Moneylenders and gold miners were compelled to sell their gold to the state. Merchants paid an income tax in gold. And taxpayers who preferred the convenience of cash to the cumbersome *annona* could pay in gold. These procedures resulted in a constant recycling of the gold coinage: it was paid out in expenses and received back in taxes and forced purchases. Constantine's solidus was so successful that it served as the main means of exchange in the Mediterranean world for nearly seven hundred years.

Constantine observed most of Diocletian's administrative reforms, retaining all of the tactics used to split up the sources of authority. Indeed, Constantine furthered the process by removing all military authority from the Praetorian Prefects and entrusting it to "Masters of Soldiers," who became the highest-ranking Roman generals. The transformation of the Praetorian Prefect from a military to a civil official now was complete. Praetorian Prefects still were the highest-ranking officials after the emperor, but the potentially dangerous consequences of combined civil and military authority were avoided.

A solidus issued ca. 313 in the name of Crispus, son of Constantine, in commemoration of a defeat of the Franks depicts on the reverse a trophy of captured weapons and a grieving woman representing "Francia" (the land of the Franks). The legend reads, "The joy of the Romans," emphasizing the popular expectation that Roman emperors would win victories over threatening barbarians.

Constantine also concurred with Diocletian's recognition of the growing importance of the east as the population, economic, and even cultural center of the empire. In 330 CE he therefore created a second, eastern, capital of the empire on the site of the old Greek city of Byzantium, located on the Bosporus, the strategic strait between Anatolia and Europe. Always the self-promoter, he named the new city **Constantinople**, after himself. In many ways, Constantinople was a copy of Rome. It supposedly was built on seven hills, and it soon had its own imperial court, its own new Senate, and its own circus (where the "blues" and "greens" became the favorite chariot-racing teams). In order to emphasize the city's role as the New Rome, Constantine placed beneath the Column of Constantine the *palladium*, an ancient wooden statue of Athena said to have been brought from Troy to Rome by Aeneas, the legendary ancestor of the Romans. The city was decorated with monuments removed from other famous sites. In the hippodrome stood the famous serpent column that had been dedicated at Delphi after the Greek victory over the Persians at Plataea in 479 BCE. Many statues of polytheistic gods, including the Pythian Apollo from Delphi, the Hera from Samos, and the Zeus from Olympia, were removed from their temples and brought to the city. And a milestone known as the *milliarium aureum* ("Golden Milestone") was the point from which the distances of all roads in the east were measured.

CONSTANTINE AND CHRISTIANITY

Among the many reforms instituted by Constantine easily the most important, and the one with the greatest impact, had to do with his religious policies. He believed that Diocletian was right to try to use religion to unify the empire, but he determined that Diocletian had supported the wrong religion. Rather than attempting to revive classical paganism, which had lost much of its past prestige, Constantine turned his support to the religion that now was creating real enthusiasm: Christianity.

Using Religion to Support the Empire

In 311, the persecuting emperor Galerius, afflicted with a terrible gangrenous wasting disease, acknowledged that the Great Persecution had failed. In an "Edict of Toleration" he declared, "Because most Christians persevered in their determination, we thought that we ought to grant our most prompt indulgence so that they may again be Christians and hold their meetings. Wherefore, for this our indulgence, they ought to pray to their God for our safety, so that they may be able to live securely in their homes." But any Christian prayers for Galerius' good health were to no avail, and he died shortly thereafter, it was said, "eaten by worms." Galerius' edict had merely ended the persecution and returned to the previous status quo, it had not made Christianity a legally recognized religion, and Christians would have had good cause to fear further persecutions in the future.

THE ARCH OF CONSTANTINE

The single monument most associated with the emperor Constantine is no doubt the arch that was built in Rome after his defeat of Maxentius in 312. In this case, one has not only an iconographical program establishing Constantine's legitimacy—for he was, after all, a usurper—but also a verbal inscription communicating the message that the Senate, which sponsored the building of the arch, wanted to promulgate. The arch was full of levels of meaning. For one thing, the inscription ambiguously attributed Constantine's victory to "the movement of the divinity," without specifying just what that divinity was. A Christian, of course, could see it as the Christian god, but a polytheist could see it as any of the other monotheistic divinities, such as the sun god. And the artwork was a curious mixture of original art, depicting Constantine's victories and then his generosity, and of art taken from earlier monuments of the Antonine emperors. In the past, it was thought that the use of earlier artwork was a sign of cultural decline and degeneracy, as if the best that late Roman emperors could do was cannibalize the monuments of earlier emperors. But historians now realize that the situation was much more nuanced. By connecting himself to the Antonine emperors, Constantine was not only stressing his legitimacy but also assuring the people that his reign would bring back the happy and secure times of the past. Thus, this relief from a monument of Trajan would have recalled to a viewer the Golden Age of the reign of Trajan.

Reliefs from a monument of the emperor Trajan reused on the Arch of Constantine.

The emperor Constantine had different ideas. Indeed, his most significant legacy lay in his policies toward the Christian church, and he is best known as the emperor who began to make Christianity into the most dominant force in the Mediterranean world and beyond. In early 313, not long after his victory over Maxentius, Constantine and the eastern emperor Licinius issued the **Edict of Milan**, which granted "to the Christians and others full authority to observe that religion that each preferred." It also ordered the restitution of Christian property that had been confiscated by the imperial treasury or acquired by private persons, with the latter being provided compensation by the state. This marked the first time that the imperial government recognized the Christian church as a lawful institution. Christianity thus was converted from a potentially persecuted to a legally recognized religion.

But Constantine went even further than that. He agreed with Diocletian that religion could be used as a unifying factor, but, realizing that popular enthusiasm for traditional Roman polytheism was on the decline, he saw in Christianity a religion that met the needs of his times much better than the traditional beliefs, for the organizational structure and standardized doctrine of the church, he believed, could be mobilized in support of imperial unity. In various ways, Constantine therefore threw his support to Christianity. He granted senior clergy the status of *honestiores*, exempted Christian priests from taxation, and made Sunday, the Christian day of worship, the official market day so that Christians would have liberty to attend church services. Constantine and his mother Helena also demonstrated their personal piety by building churches in Rome, Constantinople, and the Holy Land.

Constantine also believed that his support for Christianity should bring material benefits to the empire. For example, it allowed him to confiscate polytheist temple treasures and use the proceeds to issue large numbers of his new gold coins. It also permitted growing government reliance on Christian churches to provide social services, such as poor relief and the care of the incarcerated. In order to take some of the load off the Roman judicial system, Christian bishops even were granted legal jurisdiction in some cases, such as the manumissions of slaves.

LEGACY OF ROME
Constantine believed that Christianity was the religion that most suited the needs of his times. Do you believe that Christianity is still a religion suited to the needs of the times?

The Emperor's Role in the Christian Church

Constantine also soon discovered that he had been wrong about just how unified the Christian church was. The years of seclusion and persecution had isolated the many Christian communities from one another and had prevented the development of the kind of homogeneity that Constantine hoped for. The church was plagued by disagreements over questions of theology, organization, and authority. Dissension raged over just what Christians were supposed to believe and who was to have the right to decide this. Constantine solved the second of these questions in one stroke: the emperor now took the responsibility for compelling fractious churchmen to reach agreement on any number of divisive issues. Just as, during the Principate, the emperor had siphoned authority off from the Senate, he now did so from the church, and even greater power coalesced into his hands. The first step toward **Caesaropapism**, in which the head of state also was the head of the church, had been taken.

Constantine mobilized state authority in an attempt to create Christian unity, sometimes by issuing imperial regulations, but the preferred method for settling major quarrels was to convene **ecumenical** (Greek for "the whole world") **church councils** comprising bishops from all over the empire. The bishops were the heads of the church in each city; theoretically each was responsible only to God and had no earthly supervisor. An ecumenical council therefore represented the collective authority of the entire Christian church.

Some of the problems confronting the church involved church authority, especially the authority of priests and bishops. In North Africa, conflict arose when Christians known as **Donatists** (after their leader, Bishop Donatus of Carthage) taught that *traditores* ("betrayers"), Christian bishops and priests who had turned over Christian books during Diocletian's Great Persecution, had lost their spiritual authority and could no longer hold church office. Others, however, believed that spiritual authority lay in the office, not the man, and that after doing penance, the *traditores* could continue in office. The dispute was referred to Constantine, who in 314 convened a church council at Arles in southern Gaul. Donatism was condemned and became the first official **schism**, a branch of the church that did not recognize the authority of the rest of the orthodox, or official, church.

A much more serious controversy, involving belief rather than authority, arose in Alexandria in Egypt, where the priest Arius taught that Christ the Son was different in substance from and subordinate to God the Father. This teaching, known as **Arianism**, struck a chord with those who viewed the Christian Trinity (the father, son, and holy spirit) as analogous to a human family but was rejected by Christians who believed that all three persons of the Trinity were of the same substance and thus equal in status. In 325, at the first ecumenical **Council of Nicaea**, in Anatolia just south of Constantinople, Constantine persuaded 318 bishops, assembled with government support from throughout the empire, to condemn Arianism. The council formulated the **Nicene Creed**, an official statement of belief that all Christians were expected to accept. As a result, Arianism became the first official **heresy**, or illegal belief, within the Christian church. But many Arians refused to concede, and the Arian controversy continued to simmer. In spite of Constantine and future emperors' best efforts, schisms and heresies would continue to threaten Christian unity.

The Council of Nicaea also dealt with administrative issues, establishing the official date of Easter and formalizing an administrative model for the church based on the Roman provincial model. Within each province, the church in each *civitas* was under the authority of a bishop, and the bishop of the capital city of each province became an archbishop, who had a higher status than and a loose supervisory authority over the provincial bishops. The bishops of Alexandria, Antioch, and Rome were assigned the even higher status of **patriarch**, which conveyed great honor but not any additional authority; soon thereafter the bishops of Constantinople and Jerusalem received the same status. In addition, the bishops of Rome claimed to have the highest status of all the bishops based on the argument that they were the successors of the apostle Peter. But other bishops also claimed to be the successors of apostles, and they, along with most other bishops, refused to acknowledge the primacy of the bishop of Rome.

The Nicene Creed is still used in many modern Christian churches.

HISTORICAL CONTROVERSY

CONSTANTINE'S CHRISTIANITY

One of the great controversies of ancient history is the extent to which Constantine was a true Christian and the extent to which his motives for supporting Christianity were personal as opposed to political. The official Roman version of Constantine's conversion, according to the Christian historian Eusebius, was that in 312, in the midst of his war with Maxentius, he saw in the sky a cross of light above the sun, accompanied by the words "In hoc signo victor eris" ("In this sign you shall conquer"). ,Then, on the night before the crucial battle, the story continued, Christ came to Constantine in a dream and commanded him to create a sign bearing the overlapping letters X (chi) and P (rho), the first two letters in the Greek spelling of the name of Christ. After Constantine's victory at the Battle of the Milvian Bridge in October 312, the chi–rho sign became known as the **Christogram,** or sign of Christ, and Constantine's victory was attributed to the Christian God. Constantine not only did not contradict this opinion but also began to support Christianity openly and actively.

But Constantine might have been less a devout believer and more a political opportunist. It would have been clear from the failure of Diocletian's Great Persecution that the old imperial cult was no longer feasible as a unifying factor; to a political pragmatist, Christianity might have seemed a more viable possibility. And there are, in fact, many ambiguities about Constantine's religiosity. For one thing, even though he issued laws favorable to Christians, he never issued any anti-pagan legislation; even very late in his reign he approved the construction of a temple in central Italy in honor of his own family, where stage plays and gladiatorial games were overseen by a pagan priest. And Constantine never seems to have abandoned his devotion to Sol Invictus, the Unconquered Sun, whom many Romans, and especially Roman emperors, had looked on not only as the most important traditional god but even as the only god. At the same time that he issued coins bearing the Christogram, he continued to issue coins in honor of Sol Invictus, who also was portrayed rising to heaven on the Arch of Constantine. Even the chi–rho sign his soldiers placed on their shields had an alternate meaning as a sign of the sun god. But Constantine's devotion to the sun god need not mean that he was not a devoted Christian, for the common identification of Christ with the sun god would have made Constantine's solar monotheism very close to Christian monotheism.

THINKING OF THE FUTURE

Constantine handled the problem of the imperial succession by abandoning Diocletian's Tetrarchy and returning to **dynastic succession**: whenever possible, fathers were to be succeeded by sons. Sovereignty now rested in the hands of the emperor and the army. If an emperor existed, only the reigning emperor or emperors could make new emperors. A usurper, such as Constantine himself had been, could become legitimate only if he was recognized by, or defeated, the existing legitimate emperors. If there were no reigning emperors, then only the army attached to the imperial court had the authority to name a new one. Male emperors bore the title Augustus and female members of the imperial family the title Augusta. Although women were not constitutionally barred from ruling, no woman ruled alone until Irene in 799. This method of succession was remarkably stable—between 364 and 802, there were only five imperial dynasties and only two brief periods of anarchy.

Constantine's Successors

Constantine's plans for his own succession ran into several glitches. He initially named his eldest son Crispus as his successor, but in 326 he had Crispus executed based on a false charge of sexual assault made by Constantine's wife Fausta, who supposedly wanted to clear the way to the throne for her own three sons. When Constantine learned the truth, he then had Fausta executed as well. Subsequently, a story was told that when Constantine asked how he could relieve himself of the weight of guilt that he suffered, he was told that no god could possibly forgive such heinous crimes, except for the god of the Christians, who would forgive anything. However that may be, Constantine ultimately named his three other sons, Constantine II, Constantius II, and Constans, as his successors, along with his nephews Delmatius and Hanniballianus.

Constantine died in 337. Only on his deathbed was he finally baptized as a Christian, with the ceremony being performed by an Arian bishop who had retained his belief and had risen in the emperor's favor. Constantine was buried in the Church of the Apostles in Constantinople and later became a Christian saint. Constantine's plan for dynastic succession then went into effect, and this created another glitch. The empire was indeed divided among his three sons, but his two nephews were murdered as part of a purge of other family members who might have a claim on the throne.

The Legacy of Diocletian and Constantine

Curiously, even though Diocletian and Constantine get the credit for establishing the Late Roman Empire, the ideas for many of their policies go back to reform efforts of their predecessors during the Imperial Crisis. In addition, although Diocletian usually gets the credit for saving the empire after the Imperial Crisis, most of his reforms were dead ends. It was Constantine's initiatives, such as his establishment of a second capital, his introduction of the solidus, his rapprochement with the senators, his establishment of a principle of dynastic succession, and, in particular, his support of Christianity that were to be crucial in charting the future course of the Roman Empire. Once Constantine took sole control of the empire, the civil wars came to an end and stability returned.

⇦ LOOKING BACK

At the end of the third century and the beginning of the fourth, the Roman Empire recovered from the third-century crisis. Able emperors such as Diocletian and Constantine restored stability, but in the course of doing so they abandoned the Principate as established by Augustus, including the partnership with the Senate, and established the Late Roman Empire. The Late Roman Empire, which also marked the beginning of Late Antiquity, saw the implementation of a number of policies and institutions that continue to reverberate in the modern day, including the use of legislation as a means of trying to solve problems and, in particular, Constantine's favoring of the Christian church.

LOOKING AHEAD ⇨

The Late Roman Empire brought many administrative, social, and cultural changes to the Roman world. Christianity became an imperial religion and came to pervade all aspects of late Roman life. But Constantine's plan to use the church as a unifying factor in the service of the empire did not work out exactly as he had intended and brought with it new problems of its own that would continue to threaten Roman unity. Then, during the fifth century CE, one of the most momentous events of all of western civilization occurred: the fall of the Western Roman Empire.

FURTHER READING

Barnes, Timothy D. *The New Empire of Diocletian and Constantine.* Cambridge, MA: Harvard Univ. Press, 1982.

Brown, Peter. *The World of Late Antiquity: From Marcus Aurelius to Mohammed.* New York: Harcourt, Brace, Jovanovich, 1971.

Corcoran, Simon. *The Empire of the Tetrarchs, Imperial Pronouncements and Government AD 284–324.* Oxford: Clarendon Press, 1996.

Drake, Harold A. *Constantine and the Bishops: The Politics of Intolerance.* Baltimore: Johns Hopkins Univ. Press, 2000.

Garnsey, Peter, and Caroline Humfress, eds. *The Evolution of the Late Antique World.* Cambridge, UK: Orchard Academic Press, 2001.

Potter, David S. *The Roman Empire at Bay: AD 180–395.* New York: Routledge, 2005.

Rees, Roger. *Diocletian and the Tetrarchy.* Edinburgh: Edinburgh Univ. Press, 2004.

Wassink, A. "Inflation and Financial Policy under the Roman Empire to the Price Edict of 301 A.D." *Historia* 40 (1991), 465–493.

Williams, Stephen. *Diocletian and the Roman Recovery.* New York: Routledge, 1997.

SOURCES

11.1 THE "EDICT ON MAXIMUM PRICES" (301 CE)

EDICTUM DE PRETIIS RERUM VENALIUM

The "Edict on Maximum Prices," issued by Diocletian and his three colleagues in 301 CE, was posted in Latin and Greek on stone inscriptions throughout the Roman Empire. The largest surviving portions have been found in Turkey, Egypt, and Greece, and pieces have been found in no less than thirty different places, nearly all in the eastern part of the empire. This section, now in the Pergamon Museum in Berlin, lists the prices for slaves, ranging from 15,000 denarii for boys and girls to 35,000 for a male or eunuch aged sixteen through forty, with the proviso that "for a slave instructed in a skill, with regard to the type and experience and quality of the skills, it is fitting regarding the price to reach an agreement between the buyer and seller to the extent that a double price, at least, might exceed that established for the slave."

When the emperor Diocletian came to power in 284 CE, the Roman economy was in a shambles, primarily because of enormous pay raises given to soldiers by Septimius Severus (193–211) and his son Caracalla (211–217) that had resulted in the debasement of the silver coinage. When millions of these coins flooded the marketplace, the empire was struck by massive inflation, not only because of the lowered value of the coins, but also because the economy could not absorb the great increase in the money supply and because people hoarded good silver coins and paid their taxes in the debased silver coins. Diocletian initially attempted to solve the problem by reissuing good silver and gold coins, but there was not enough silver available for this to work. So in 301 he adopted the usual late Roman method for addressing problems: he issued a law to deal with it, a "Maximum Price Edict" that established not only the maximum prices that could be charged for a large list of items but also the maximum wages that could be paid for a long list of jobs. Prices and wages were given in "denarii." Although the *denarius* was no longer issued, it remained a standard unit of account and had to be converted into whatever currency one was using. Thus, the silver-coated copper coin called the *follis* was valued at twenty-five *denarii*, and a gold *aureus* was technically worth one thousand denarii (although it is doubtful that anyone would exchange a gold aureus for forty copper *folles*). The law was a total failure. It simplistically attributed inflation to greedy merchants and took no account of either a merchant's need to make a profit or differential prices that had to be charged for items manufactured in one place and sold hundreds or thousands of miles away. In any event, moreover, the emperors had no means of enforcing laws; all they could do was hope that people obeyed the laws of their own volition. Goods that could not be sold openly were simply sold on the black market. Acknowledging the failure of the law, Diocletian then introduced the *annona* system, the payment of taxes and expenditures in kind. It was cumbersome, but it worked.

Source: Elsa R. Graser, trans., "The Edict of Diocletian on Maximum Prices," in T. Frank, *An Economic Survey of Ancient Rome Volume V: Rome and Italy of the Empire* (Baltimore: Johns Hopkins Univ. Press, 1940), 307–421.

Diocletian, Maximianus, Constantius, and Galerius[1] declare:

As we recall the wars that we successfully have fought, we must be grateful for a world that is tranquil and reclining in the embrace of the most profound calm, and for the blessings of peace that was won with great effort. That the fortune of our Republic[2] be faithfully disposed and suitably adorned is the demand of public opinion and the dignity and majesty of Rome. Therefore, we, who by the gracious favor the gods have repressed the former tide of ravages of barbarian nations by destroying them, must guard by due defenses of justice a peace that was established for eternity.

If, indeed, any self-restraint might check the excesses with which limitless and furious avarice rages, avarice that, with no thought for mankind, hastens to its own gain and increase, not by years or months or days but by hours and even by minutes, or, if the general welfare could endure undisturbed the riotous license by which it, in its misfortune, is from day to day most grievously injured, there would perhaps be left some room for dissimulation and silence, since human forbearance might alleviate the detestable cruelty of a pitiable situation. Because those whose extremes of need have brought us to an appreciation of their most unfortunate situation, so that we no longer can close our eyes to it, we, the protectors of the human race, viewing have

agreed that justice should intervene[3] as arbiter, so that the long-hoped-for solution that mankind itself could not supply might, by the remedies of our foresight, be applied to the general betterment of all.

We, therefore, hasten to apply the remedies long demanded by this situation, satisfied that there can be no complaints that the intervention of our remedy may be considered untimely or unnecessary, trivial, or unimportant by the unscrupulous who, in spite of perceiving in our silence of so many years a lesson in restraint, have been unwilling to copy it. For who are so insensitive and so devoid of human feeling that cannot know, or rather, have not perceived, that in the commerce carried on in the markets or involved in the daily life of cities immoderate prices are so widespread that the uncurbed passion for gain is lessened neither by abundant supplies nor by fruitful years.

It is our pleasure, therefore, that the prices listed in the subjoined summary be observed in the whole of our empire in such fashion that everyone may know that whereas permission to exceed them has been forbidden, the blessing of low prices has in no case been restricted in those places where supplies are seen to abound, because special provision is made for these when avarice is definitely quieted. It is our pleasure that anyone who shall have resisted the form of this statute shall for this daring be subject to a capital penalty. And let no one consider the penalty harsh because there is at hand a means of avoiding the danger by observance of moderation. We, therefore, urge upon the loyalty of all our

---

[1] The four emperors who were members of the Tetrarchy, or "Rule by Four."

[2] Even though what we call the "Roman Empire" had begun over three hundred years in the past, it still was officially designated as the "Republic."

---

[3] The standard method used by late Roman emperors to try to solve problems was to issue laws.

people that a law constituted for the public good may be observed with willing obedience[4] and due care, especially because in such a statute provision has been made, not for single states and peoples and provinces, but for the whole world.[5]

The prices for the sale of individual items that no one may exceed are listed below.

Wheat	1 army *modius*[6] den.[7]	100
Barley	1 army *modius den.*	60
Rye	1 army *modius den.*	60
Millet, ground	1 army *modius den.*	100
Millet, whole	1 army *modius den.*	50
Panic grass[8]	1 army *modius den.*	50
Spelt, hulled	1 army *modius den.*	100
. . . .		
Beans, crushed	1 army *modius den.*	100
Beans, not ground	1 army *modius den.*	60
Lentils	1 army *modius den.*	100
Pulse	1 army *modius den.*	80
Peas, split	1 army *modius den.*	100
Peas, not split	1 army *modius den.*	60
. . . .		
Rice, cleaned	1 army *modius den.*	200
Barley grits,	1 *modius* cleaned *den.*	100
Spelt grits,	1 *modius* cleaned *den.*	200
Sesame	1 army *modius den.*	200
. . . .		

Likewise, for wines:

Picene	1 Italian *sextarius*[9] *den.*	30
Tiburtine	1 Italian *sextarius den.*	30
Sabine	1 Italian *sextarius den.*	30
. . . .		
Falernian[10]	1 Italian *sextarius den.*	30
Aged wine, first quality	1 Italian *sextarius den.*	24
Aged wine, second quality	1 Italian *sextarius den.*	16
Ordinary	1 Italian *sextarius den.*	8
Beer, Gallic or Pannonian[11]	1 Italian *sextarius den.*	4
Beer, Egyptian	1 Italian *sextarius den.*	2
. . . .		
Likewise, for oil:		
From unripe olives	1 Italian *sextarius den.*	40
Second quality	1 Italian *sextarius den.*	24
Salt	1 army *modius den.*	100
Spiced salt	1 Italian *sextarius den.*	8
Honey, best quality	1 Italian *sextarius den.*	40
Honey, second quality	1 Italian *sextarius* den	24
Likewise, for meat:		
Pork	1 Italian pound *den.*	12
Beef	1 Italian pound *den.*	8
Leg of pork, Menapic[12] or Cerritane,[13] best,	1 Italian pound *den.*	20
Pork mincemeat	1 ounce *den.*	2
Beef mincemeat	1 Italian pound *den.*	10
Pheasant,	fattened *den.*	250
Pheasant,	wild *den.*	125

---

[4] This because the government had no institutionalized means of enforcing the laws.

[5] In legal theory, the Romans claimed to rule the entire world.

[6] A civilian *modius* was a dry measure unit equivalent to about eight liters, two gallons, or one peck. An "army *modius*" was about one and a half times a civilian "Italian *modius.*"

[7] That is, "denarii." Even though the *denarius* no longer was issued, it remained as the standard accounting unit, much as the American "mil," one-thousandth of a dollar (or one-tenth of a cent), is not an actual coin, but still shows up at the gasoline pump, where prices are expressed in tenths of a cent, and in the "millage rate," a means of computing property taxes.

[8] Panicum, a type of grain.

---

[9] A *sextarius* was a liquid measure equivalent to about a half liter or a half quart.

[10] A famous Roman wine, with grapes from Mt. Falernus in Latium.

[11] That is, French or Hungarian.

[12] The Menapii were a Celtic people of Belgium.

[13] The Cerritani were a Pyrenaean people of northeastern Spain

Chickens	1 brace *den.*	60
Venison	1 Italian pound *den.*	12
Butter	1 Italian pound *den.*	16
Likewise, for fish:		
Sea fish with rough scales	1 Italian pound *den.*	24
Fish second quality	1 Italian pound *den.*	16
River fish, best quality	1 Italian pound *den.*	12
River fish, second quality	1 Italian pound *den.*	8
Salt fish	1 Italian pound *den.*	6
Oysters	100 *den.*	100

Regarding the prices of slaves:

For a masculine slave, either a eunuch or a male, from the age of seventeen years to forty years,	35,000 *denarii.*
For a female slave of the aforementioned age,	25,000 *denarii.*
Likewise, for a man from the age of forty to sixty,	25,000 *denarii.*
For a woman of the aforementioned age,	20,000 *denarii.*
For a boy from the age of eight to sixteen and a girl of the aforementioned age,	15,000 *denarii.*
For a man over sixty years and less than nine years,	15,000 *denarii.*
For a woman of the aforementioned age,	10,000 *denarii.*

For a slave skilled in an occupation, with regard to the type and the age and the quality of the skills it is suitable that there be an agreement between the buyer and the seller about the price to the extent that it is not at all permitted to exceed double the statutory price.

For wages:

Farm laborer, with maintenance (daily)	*den.* 25
Carpenter, as above (daily)	*den.* 50
Wall painter, as above (daily)	*den.* 75
Picture painter, as above (daily)	*den.* 150
Baker, as above (daily)	*den.* 50
Shipwright working on a seagoing ship, as above (daily)	*den.* 60
Shipwright working on a river boat, as above (daily)	*den.* 50
Muleteer, with maintenance (daily)	*den.* 25
Veterinary, for clipping and preparing hoofs (per animal)	*den.* 6
Veterinary, for bleeding and cleaning the head (per animal)	*den.* 20
Barber (per man)	*den.* 2
Sewer cleaner, working a full day, with maintenance (daily)	*den.* 25
Scribe, for the best writing (100 lines)	*den.* 25
Scribe, for second-quality writing (100 lines)	*den.* 20
Notary, for writing a petition or legal document (100 lines)	*den.* 10
Elementary teacher per boy (monthly)	*den.* 50
Teacher of arithmetic, per boy (monthly)	*den.* 75
Teacher of shorthand, per boy (monthly)	*den.* 75
Teacher of Greek or Latin language and literature, and teacher of geometry, per pupil (monthly)	*den.* 200
Teacher of rhetoric or public speaking, per pupil (monthly)	*den.* 250
Advocate or jurist, fee for a complaint	*den.* 250
Advocate or jurist, fee for pleading	*den.* 1000
Teacher of architecture, per boy (monthly)	*den.* 100
Check room attendant, per bather	*den.* 2

LACTANTIUS, *ON THE DEATHS OF THE PERSECUTORS*, 1–35

Although the four emperors of the Tetrarchy emphasized that they worked together in harmony and that there was only one empire, in practice, they did not always agree on policy. This is seen most clearly in the efforts of Diocletian (284–305) to use religion to unify the empire. Throughout the history of the Roman Empire, beginning with Augustus and the "Cult of Rome and Augustus," emperors used religion as a means of uniting the empire's otherwise disparate peoples. Participation in the imperial cult was meant to be a purely political act, a means of declaring one's loyalty to Rome and the emperor. Jews and Christians, however, saw things differently and often refused to participate, an act that would have been seen as treasonous and subject to a capital penalty. Jews, because of their long history of monotheism, received an exemption, but not Christians. As Christianity became more widespread, greater numbers of Christians were punished for refusing to sacrifice in the imperial cult. As Diocletian attempted to reorganize the empire to meet the needs of the times, his colleague Galerius, an ardent anti-Christian, prevailed on him to see the Christians as disloyal and thus worthy of extreme punishment. In 303, Diocletian thus undertook what was called the "Great Persecution," the only concerted effort during the entire history of the Roman Empire to suppress Christianity. The persecution was a complete failure. By then, Christianity was too firmly entrenched. In the realms of Diocletian and, especially, Galerius (293–311) there were some efforts to enforce the legislation, but by and large it was ignored. The western emperors Maximianus (286–305) and, in particular, Constantius (293–306) participated either in a lukewarm manner or not at all. In 311 Galerius, racked by a wasting disease, rescinded the anti-Christian legislation, but this did not keep him from an agonizing death, gleefully described in the work "On the Deaths of the Persecutors" by the Christian rhetorician Lactantius. Lactantius also commented on what he saw as the problems with Diocletian's reform attempts.

Source: William Fletcher, trans., *Lactantius. Of the Manner in That the Persecutors Died* (Buffalo, NY: Christian Literature Publishing, 1886).

The Lord has heard those supplications that you, my best beloved Donatus,[14] pour forth in his presence all the day long, and the supplications of the rest of our brethren, who by a glorious confession have obtained an everlasting crown, the reward of their faith.[15] Behold, all the adversaries are destroyed, and tranquility having been re-established throughout the Roman Empire, the late oppressed church arises again, and the temple of God, overthrown by the hands of the wicked, is built with more glory than before. For God has raised up princes[16] to rescind the impious and sanguinary edicts[17] of the tyrants and provide for the welfare of mankind, so that now the cloud of past times is dispelled, and peace and serenity gladden all hearts. And after the furious whirlwind and black tempest, the heavens now have become calm, and the wished-for light has shone forth. God, the hearer of prayer, by his divine aid now has lifted his prostrate and afflicted servants from the ground, has brought to an end the united devices of the wicked, and wiped off the tears from the faces of

---

[14] The dedicatee of Lactantius' work; he had been tortured three times for his Christian beliefs.

[15] A reference to the "crown of martyrdom."

---

[16] Including the emperors Constantine I and Licinius, who in early 313 issued the Edict of Milan, which legalized Christianity.

[17] Edicts were imperial laws addressed to the entire population that had empire-wide validity.

those who mourned. They who insulted the divinity lie low; they who cast down the holy temple are fallen with more tremendous ruin; and the tormentors of just men have poured out their guilty souls amid plagues inflicted by heaven and amid deserved tortures. For God delayed to punish them so that, by great and marvelous examples, he might teach posterity that he alone is God, and that with fit vengeance he executes judgment on the proud, the impious, and the persecutors.

Of the end of those men I have thought good to publish a narrative, so that all who are far off and all who shall arise hereafter may learn how the Almighty manifested his power and sovereign greatness in rooting out and utterly destroying the enemies of his name. And this will become evident, when I relate who were the persecutors of the church from the time of its first constitution, and what were the punishments by which the divine judge, in his severity, took vengeance on them.

While Diocletian,[18] that author of ill and deviser of misery, was ruining all things, he could not withhold his insults, not even against God. This man, by avarice partly, and partly by timid counsels, overturned the Roman Empire. For he chose three persons to share the government with him, and thus, the empire having been quartered, armies were multiplied and each of the four princes strove to maintain a much more considerable military force than any sole emperor had done in times past.[19] There began to be fewer men who paid taxes than there were who received wages, so that, with the means of the farmer exhausted by enormous impositions, the farms were abandoned, cultivated grounds became woodland, and universal dismay prevailed. The provinces, moreover, were divided into minute portions, and many governors and a multitude of inferior officers lay heavy on each

territory, and almost on each city.[20] There also were many stewards of different degrees, and deputies of Prefects.[21] Very few civil causes came before them, but there were criminal condemnations daily, and confiscations frequently inflicted, taxes on numberless commodities, and those not only often repeated, but perpetual, and, in exacting them, intolerable wrongs.

Whatever was laid on for the maintenance of the soldiery might have been endured, but Diocletian, through his insatiable avarice, would never allow the sums of money in his treasury to be diminished. He constantly was heaping together extraordinary aids and free gifts[22] so that his original hoards might remain untouched and inviolable. He also, when by various extortions he had made all things exceedingly dear, attempted by an ordinance to limit their prices. Then men were afraid to expose anything for sale, and the scarcity became more excessive and grievous than ever, until, in the end, the ordinance, after having proved destructive to multitudes, was from mere necessity abrogated.

I omit mentioning how many perished on account of their possessions or wealth, for such evils were exceedingly frequent, and through their frequency appeared almost lawful. But this was peculiar to him, that whenever he saw a field remarkably well cultivated, or a house of uncommon elegance, a false accusation and a capital punishment were straightway prepared against the proprietor; so that it seemed as if Diocletian could not be guilty of rapine without also shedding blood. I pass over Constantius,[23] a prince unlike the others, and worthy to have had the sole government of the empire.

Diocletian, as being of a timorous disposition, was a searcher into futurity and during his abode in the east he began to slay victims, so that from their

---

[18] Roman emperor from 284 to 305, he commenced the Great Persecution in 303 CE.

[19] In 293, Diocletian created the Tetrarchy, or "Rule by Four," in which the eastern and western halves of the empire each had an Augustus (senior emperor) and a Caesar (junior emperor).

[20] Diocletian subdivided the 50 provinces into 102, and the imperial bureaucracy was greatly expanded.

[21] The "Vicars," who stood intermediate between Praetorian Prefects and provincial governors.

[22] Such as the "crown gold."

[23] The father of Constantine I, Constantius (293–306) was the only member of the Tetrarchy to be praised by Lactantius.

livers he might obtain a prognostic of events,[24] and while he sacrificed, some attendants of his, who were Christians, stood by, and they put the immortal sign on their foreheads.[25] At this the demons were chased away and the holy rites interrupted. The soothsayers trembled, unable to investigate the wonted marks on the entrails of the victims. They frequently repeated the sacrifices, but the victims afforded no tokens for divination. At length Tages, the chief of the soothsayers, said, "There are profane persons here, who obstruct the rites." Then Diocletian, in furious passion, ordered all who resided within the palace to sacrifice, and, in case of their refusal, to be whipped. And further, he enjoined that all soldiers should be forced to perform the same impiety, under pain of being dismissed the service. Thus far his rage proceeded, but at that season he did nothing more against the law and religion of God.

After an interval of some time he went to winter in Bithynia,[26] and presently Galerius Caesar[27] came thither, inflamed with furious resentment and planning to excite the empty-headed old man to carry on that persecution that he had begun against the Christians. I have learned that the cause of his fury was as follows. The mother of Galerius, a woman exceedingly superstitious, was a votary of the gods of the mountains. She made sacrifices almost every day and she feasted her servants on the meat offered to idols, but the Christians of her family would not partake of those entertainments. On this account she conceived ill-will against the Christians and by woman-like complaints instigated her son, no less superstitious than herself, to destroy them. So, during the whole winter, Diocletian and Galerius held councils together, at which no one else assisted. The old man long opposed the fury of Galerius, arguing how pernicious it would be to raise

disturbances throughout the world and to shed so much blood, and suggesting that the Christians were wont with eagerness to meet death, and that it would be enough for him to exclude persons of that religion from the court and the army. Yet he could not restrain the madness of that obstinate man.[28] Diocletian determined above all to consult his gods; and he dispatched a soothsayer to inquire of Apollo at Miletus,[29] whose answer was such as might be expected from an enemy of the divine religion.

An edict was published, depriving the Christians of all honors and dignities, ordaining also that, without any distinction of rank or degree, they should be subjected to tortures and that every suit at law should be received against them, while, on the other hand, they were debarred from being plaintiffs in questions of wrong, adultery, or theft; and, finally, that they should neither be capable of freedom, nor have right of suffrage. A certain person tore down this edict and cut it in pieces, improperly indeed, but with high spirit, saying in scorn, "These are the triumphs of Goths and Sarmatians."[30] Having been instantly seized and brought to judgment he not only was tortured but also burnt alive, in accordance with the laws, and having displayed admirable patience under sufferings, he was consumed to ashes.

And now Diocletian raged, not only against his own domestics, but indiscriminately against all, and he began by forcing his daughter Valeria and his wife Prisca[31] to be polluted by sacrificing. Eunuchs, once the most powerful, and who had chief authority at court and with the emperor, were slain. Priests and other officers of the church were seized, without evidence by witnesses or confession, condemned, and together with their families led to execution. In burning alive, no distinction of sex or age was regarded, and because of their great multitude they were not burnt one after another but

---

[24] The Roman rite of taking the *haruspices*, the inspection of the livers of sacrificial animals, to ascertain the will of the gods.

[25] A sign of the cross made with chrism, or consecrated oil.

[26] A province on the southern coast of the Black Sea.

[27] Galerius (293–311) was the Caesar, or designated successor, of the Augustus Diocletian in the eastern half of the empire.

---

[28] Galerius.

[29] The location of another famous oracle.

[30] That is, of barbarians.

[31] Both of whom were Christians, attesting the degree to which Christianity now had infiltrated the highest levels of society.

a herd of them were encircled with the same fire. Servants, having millstones tied about their necks, were cast into the sea. Nor was the persecution less grievous on the rest of the people of God; for the judges, dispersed through all the temples, sought to compel everyone to sacrifice. The prisons were crowded; tortures, hitherto unheard of, were invented; and lest justice should be inadvertently administered to a Christian, altars were placed in the courts of justice, hard by the tribunal, that every litigant might offer incense before his cause could be heard.

Mandates[32] also had gone to Maximianus Herculius[33] and Constantius, requiring their concurrence in the execution of the edicts even though, in matters even of such mighty importance, their opinion never once was asked. Herculius, a person of no merciful temper, yielded ready obedience, and enforced the edicts throughout his dominions of Italy.[34] Constantius, on the other hand, lest he should have seemed to dissent from the injunctions of his superiors, permitted the demolition of churches—mere walls, and capable of being built up again—but he preserved entire that true temple of God, which is the human body.[35]

Having thus attained the highest power,[36] Galerius bent his mind to afflict the empire. Crucifixion was the punishment ready prepared in capital cases, and for lesser crimes, fetters. Matrons of honorable station were dragged into workhouses, and when any man was to be whipped, there were four posts fixed in the ground and to them he was tied, after a manner unknown even in the chastisement of slaves. He kept bears, most resembling himself in fierceness and bulk, that he had collected together during the course of his reign. As often as he chose

to indulge his humor, he ordered some particular bear to be brought in and men were thrown to that savage animal rather to be swallowed up than devoured, and when their limbs were torn asunder, he laughed with excessive complacency. Men of private station were condemned to be burnt alive, and he began this mode of execution by edicts against the Christians, commanding that, after torture and condemnation, they should be burnt at a slow fire. They were fixed to a stake, and first a moderate flame was applied to the soles of their feet, until the muscles, contracted by burning, were torn from the bones. Then torches, lighted and put out again, were directed to all the members of their bodies, so that no part had any exemption. Meanwhile cold water was continually poured on their faces and their mouths moistened, lest, by reason of their jaws being parched, they should expire. At length they did expire, when, after many hours, the violent heat had consumed their skin and penetrated into their intestines.

Already the judgment of God approached him and that season ensued in which his fortunes began to droop and to waste away. While occupied in the manner that I have described above, he did not set himself to subvert or expel Constantius, but waited for his death, not imagining, however, that it was so nigh.[37] And now, when Galerius was in the eighteenth year of his reign,[38] God struck him with an incurable plague. A malignant ulcer formed itself in the lower part of his genitals and spread by degrees. The physicians attempted to eradicate it and healed up the place affected. But the sore, after having been skinned over, broke out again. A vein burst, and the blood flowed in such quantity as to endanger his life. The blood, however, was stopped, although with difficulty. He grew emaciated, pallid, and feeble, and the bleeding then stanched. The ulcer began to be insensible to the remedies applied and a gangrene seized all the neighboring parts. It diffused itself the wider the more the corrupted flesh was cut away, and everything employed as the means of cure served but

---

[32] Mandates were administrative instructions sent to imperial officials; they, too, had the force of law.

[33] Maximianus (286–305) was the Augustus of the western part of the empire; Constantius was his Caesar.

[34] Other sources suggest that Maximianus only half-heartedly enforced the persecution.

[35] Other sources state that Constantius did not participate in the persecution at all.

[36] Diocletian retired in 305 and Galerius was promoted to Augustus, senior emperor, in the eastern half of the empire.

[37] Constantius died in 306 CE, the year after he had been promoted to the rank of Augustus.

[38] 310 CE.

to aggravate the disease. Already approaching to its deadly crisis, it had occupied the lower regions of his body. His bowels came out and his entire buttocks putrefied. The distemper attacked his intestines and worms were generated in his body. The stench was so foul as to pervade not only the palace but even the whole city. And no wonder, for by that time the passages from his bladder and bowels, having been devoured by the worms, became indiscriminate, and his body, with intolerable anguish, was dissolved into one mass of corruption.

They applied warm flesh of animals to the chief seat of the disease, so that the warmth might draw out those minute worms, and accordingly, when the dressings were removed, there issued forth an innumerable swarm. Nevertheless, the prolific disease had hatched swarms much more abundant to prey upon and consume his intestines. Already, through a complication of distempers, the different parts of his body had lost their natural form. The upper part was dry, meager, and haggard, and his ghastly-looking skin had settled itself deep among his bones while the inferior, distended like bladders, retained no appearance of joints. At length, overcome by calamities, he was obliged to acknowledge God, and he cried aloud, in the intervals of raging pain, that he would rebuild the church that he had demolished, and make atonement for his misdeeds; and when he was near his end, he published an edict of the tenor following:[39]

> Among our other regulations for the permanent advantage of the Republic, we have hitherto studied to reduce all things to a conformity with the ancient laws and public discipline of the Romans. It has been our aim in a special manner, that the Christians also, who had abandoned the religion of their forefathers, should return to right opinions. For such willfulness and folly had, we know not how, taken possession of them, that instead of observing those ancient institutions, which possibly their own forefathers had established, they, through caprice, made laws to themselves and drew together into different societies many men of widely different persuasions. After the publication of our edict, ordaining the Christians to betake themselves to the observance of the ancient institutions, many of them were subdued through the fear of danger and moreover many of them were exposed to jeopardy. Nevertheless, because great numbers still persist in their opinions, and because we have perceived that at present they neither pay reverence and due adoration to the gods, nor yet worship their own God, therefore we, from our wonted clemency in bestowing pardon on all, have judged it fit to extend our indulgence to those persons and to permit them again to be Christians, and to establish the places of their religious assemblies, yet so as that they offend not against good order. By another mandate we purpose to signify to magistrates how they ought herein to conduct themselves. Wherefore it will be the duty of the Christians, in consequence of this our toleration, to pray to their God for our welfare, and for that of the public, and for their own, so that the Republic may continue safe in every quarter, and that they themselves may live securely in their habitations. This edict was promulgated at Nicomedia[40] on the day preceding the Kalends of May, in the eighth consulship of Galerius and the second of Maximinus Daia.[41]

Then the prison-gates having been thrown open, you, my best beloved Donatus, together with the other confessors for the faith, were set at liberty from the prison that had been your

---

[39] The "Edict of Toleration," issued in 311 CE.

[40] The capital city of Diocletian, in Anatolia just east of the future site of Constantinople.

[41] 311 CE. Maximinus Daia was Caesar of Galerius, appointed in 305 on the retirement of Diocletian. After the death of Galerius in 311 he became the Augustus of the eastern half of the empire.

residence for six years. Galerius, however, did not, by publication of this edict, obtain the divine forgiveness. In a few days after he was consumed by the horrible disease that had brought on a universal putrefaction.

I relate all those things on the authority of well-informed persons; and I thought it proper to commit them to writing exactly as they happened, lest the memory of events so important should perish, and lest any future historian of the persecutors should corrupt the truth, either by suppressing their offenses against God, or the judgment of God against them. To his everlasting mercy ought we to render thanks, that, having at length looked on the earth, he deigned to collect again and to restore his flock, partly laid waste by ravenous wolves, and partly scattered abroad, and to extirpate those noxious wild beasts who had trod down its pastures, and destroyed its resting-places. Where now are the surnames of the Jovii and the Herculii, once so glorious and renowned among the nations; surnames insolently assumed at first by Diocles[42] and Maximianus, and afterward transferred to their successors? The Lord has blotted them out and erased them from the earth. Let us therefore with exultation celebrate the triumphs of God, and oftentimes with praises make mention of his victory; let us in our prayers, by night and by day, beseech him to confirm forever that peace that, after a warfare of ten years, he has bestowed on his own: and do you, above all others, my best beloved Donatus, who so well deserve to be heard, implore the Lord that it would please him propitiously and mercifully to continue his pity toward his servants, to protect his people from the machinations and assaults of the devil, and to guard the now flourishing churches in perpetual felicity.

---

[42] The original, Greek, name of Diocletian; Lactantius uses it as an insult.

LACTANTIUS, *ON THE DEATHS OF THE PERSECUTORS*, 45–48

Although Licinius shared in the promulgation of the Edict of Milan, there is no evidence that he had any Christian convictions himself. His coinage, for example, reveals only an allegiance to the traditional gods, as shown on this gold *aureus*, with the reverse legend, "To Jupiter, the Preserver of the Augustus Licinius."

After Constantine's victory over Maxentius at the Battle of the Milvian Bridge on 28 October 312 he traveled to Milan, where he met Licinius, Caesar of the eastern half of the empire. At the time, Licinius was engaged in a war with the eastern Augustus Maximinus Daia, who, like Galerius, was a devoted pagan. There, the two emperors sealed an alliance by the marriage of Constantine's half-sister Constantia to Licinius. At the same time, the two emperors issued an edict that made Christianity not into a merely tolerated religion, as Galerius' Edict of Toleration had done in 311, but into a fully legal and even favored religion. The Edict of Milan provided not only freedom of worship for Christians, but also the restitution of Christian property that had been confiscated by the imperial treasury or acquired by private persons, with the latter being provided compensation by the state. This marked the first time that the imperial government recognized the Christian church as a lawful institution. As reported by Lactantius, the only text of the Edict survives in a letter sent by Licinius to provincial governors ordering its publication. Embedded in Lactantius' account is a story about one of the many wars between the successors of Diocletian, a battle of Licinius against Maximinus Daia that is similar to the story of Constantine's victory over Maxentius.

Source: William Fletcher, trans., *Lactantius. Of the Manner in Which the Persecutors Died* (Buffalo, NY: Christian Literature Publishing, 1886).

Constantine, having settled all things at Rome, went to Milan about the beginning of winter. Thither also Licinius came to receive his wife Constantia.[43] When Daia[44] understood that they were busied in solemnizing the nuptials, he moved out of Syria in the depth of a severe winter, and by forced marches he came into Bithynia. Daia did not halt in his own territories; but immediately crossed the Bosporus,[45] and in a hostile manner approached the gates of Byzantium.[46] Licinius by expeditious marches had reached Adrianople,[47] but with forces not numerous. The armies, thus approaching each other, seemed on the eve of a battle. Then Daia made this vow to Jupiter, that if he obtained victory he would extinguish and utterly efface the name of the Christians. And on the following night an angel of the Lord seemed to stand before Licinius while he was asleep, admonishing him to arise immediately, and with his whole army to put up a prayer to the Supreme God, and assuring him that by so doing he should obtain victory.[48] At this all men took fresh courage, in the confidence that victory had been announced to them from heaven. Accounts came that Daia was in motion; the soldiers of Licinius armed themselves; and advanced. A barren and open plain called Campus Serenus lay between the two armies. The troops of Licinius charged.[49] The enemies, panic stricken, could neither draw their swords nor throw their javelins. After great numbers had fallen, Daia perceived that everything went contrary to his hopes. He threw aside the purple and, having put on the habit of a slave, hasted across the Bosporus. One half of his army perished in battle and the rest either surrendered to the victor or fled. Not many days after his victory, Licinius, having received part of the soldiers of Daia into his service and properly distributed them, transported his army into Bithynia, and having made his entry into Nicomedia,[50] he returned thanks to God, through whose aid he had overcome. On the Ides of June, while he and Constantine were Consuls for the third time,[51] he commanded the following letter[52] for the restoration of the church, directed to the governor of the province,[53] to be promulgated:

> When we, Constantine and Licinius, emperors, met at Milan and conferred together with respect to the good and security of the Republic, it seemed to us that, among those things that are profitable to mankind in general, the reverence paid to the divinity merited our first and chief attention, and that it was proper that the Christians and all others should have liberty to follow that mode of religion that to each of them appeared best, so that that God, who is seated in heaven, might be benign and propitious to us and to every one under our government. And therefore we judged it a salutary measure, and one highly consonant to right reason, that no man should be denied leave of attaching himself to the rites of the Christians, or to whatever other religion his mind directed him, that thus the supreme divinity, to whose worship we freely devote ourselves, might continue to grant his favor and beneficence to us. And accordingly we give you to know that, without regard to any provisos in our former orders to you concerning the Christians all who choose that religion are to

---

[43] The sister of Constantine; her tomb in Rome survives as the church of Santa Costanza.

[44] Maximinus Daia (305–313), the other Augustus in the eastern part of the empire.

[45] The eastern strait linking the Aegean Sea to the Black Sea.

[46] An ancient Greek city on the south end of the Bosporus; soon to become Constantinople.

[47] A city just northwest of Byzantium; in 378 the location of a disastrous Roman defeat by the Visigoths.

[48] Likewise, just before the Battle of the Milvian Bridge against Maxentius (306–312) the previous year Constantine also was said to have had a similar visit from an angel (that is, a "messenger") in a dream.

[49] The Battle of Tzirallum on 30 April 313.

[50] Capital city of the province of Bithynia.

[51] 13 June 313.

[52] Not an "edict," as in many translations, but a "letter," or "mandate," directed to a provincial governor that authorized the publication of the actual edict that had been promulgated by Licinius and Constantine previously at Milan.

[53] The same letter would have been forwarded to the governors of other eastern provinces.

be permitted, freely and absolutely, to remain in it, and not to be disturbed any ways or molested. And we thought fit to be thus special in the things committed to your charge, that you might understand that the indulgence that we have granted in matters of religion to the Christians is ample and unconditional; and perceive at the same time that the open and free exercise of their respective religions is granted to all others, as well as to the Christians.

For it befits the well-ordered state and the tranquility of our times that each individual be allowed, according to his own choice, to worship the divinity, and we mean not to remove anything from the honor due to any religion or its votaries. Moreover, with respect to the Christians, we formerly gave certain orders concerning the places appropriated for their religious assemblies, but now we desire that all persons who have purchased such places, either from our treasury or from anyone else, shall restore them to the Christians, without money demanded or price claimed, and that this be performed peremptorily and unambiguously. And we desire also that those who have obtained any right to such places by form of gift do forthwith restore them to the Christians, reserving always to such persons, who either have purchased them for a price or gratuitously have acquired them, to make application to the judge of the district if they look on themselves as entitled to any compensation from our beneficence.

All those places are, by your[54] intervention, to be restored immediately to the Christians. And because it appears that, besides the places appropriated to religious worship, the Christians possessed other places that belonged not to individuals but to their society in general, that is, to their churches, we include all such within the aforesaid regulation. We command that you cause them all to be restored to the society or churches without hesitation or controversy, always provided that the persons making restitution without a price paid shall be at liberty to seek indemnification from our bounty. In furthering all these things for the benefit of the Christians you are to use your utmost diligence, so that our orders are speedily obeyed and our gracious purpose in securing the public tranquility be promoted. So shall that divine favor that, in affairs of the mightiest importance, we have already experienced, continue to give success to us and in our successes make the Republic happy. And that the tenor of this our gracious ordinance may be made known to all, we desire that you cause it by your authority to be published everywhere.

Having published this letter, Licinius made a harangue in which he exhorted the Christians to rebuild their religious edifices. And thus, from the overthrow of the church until its restoration, there was a space of ten years and about four months.[55]

---

[54] The governor.

[55] That is, from 303, the beginning of the Great Persecution, until 313.

EUSEBIUS OF CAESAREA, *LIFE OF CONSTANTINE*, 2.61–71, 3.6–14

Although Constantine continued to issue coins in honor of Sol Invictus, the "Unconquered Sun," he also struck coins with clearly Christian motifs. This copper coin, one of the first to be issued at Constantinople, in 327, portrays an army standard bearing three dots, representing the equality of the Christian Trinity, and topped by a Christogram, the monogram of Christ. The base of the standard pierces a serpent, which represents heresy. The legend reads "Public Hope."

In 324 Constantine defeated Licinius and gained control of the entire Roman Empire. At the same time, he became responsible for refereeing the many quarrels regarding church authority, church practices, and church teachings that had arisen among competing Christian factions. The most serious theological issue related to the teachings of the priest Arius of Alexandria, who taught that Christ the son was of a different substance from and not co-eternal with God the Father. Other Christians taught that Christ and God were made of the same substance and were co-eternal (that is, had existed together since the beginning of time). In an attempt to force unity on the Christians, Constantine first naïvely suggested that the dispute was of little significance and that the disputants should simply make up. Finally realizing how serious the matter was, in 325 Constantine summoned an ecumenical (that is, world-wide) council of Christian bishops from both within and outside the Roman Empire to meet at the city of Nicaea in northwestern Anatolia. Around 318 of approximately 1,800 bishops, mostly from the eastern provinces, attended and were required to remain until they had reached an agreement. The resulting "Nicene Creed" condemned Arianism and became a Christian statement of belief that is still used in most Christian churches. The council also issued other regulations that mark the beginning of Christian "canon law," such as establishing a standard date for Easter and a model for Christian administration based on the administration of Roman provinces. Constantine's initiative began the process of placing the Roman emperor, in effect, at the head of the Christian church, and thus, paradoxically, in the process of gaining imperial favor, the Christian church lost control of its own destiny. In his *Life of Constantine*, the historian Eusebius, bishop of Caesarea, provided his version of the events surrounding the Council of Nicaea. A confidant of Constantine, Eusebius had access to many official documents that are not preserved by any other author.

Source: Arthur Cushman McGiffert, trans., *Eusebius Pamphilius: Church History, Life of Constantine, Oration in Praise of Constantine* (New York: Christian Literature Publishing, 1890).

The emperor, like a powerful herald of God, addressed himself by his own letter to all the provinces, at the same time warning his subjects against superstitious error and encouraging them in the pursuit of true godliness. But in the midst of his joyful anticipations of the success of this measure, he received tidings of a most serious disturbance that had invaded the peace of the church. This intelligence he heard with deep concern, and at once he endeavored to devise a remedy for the evil. The origin of this disturbance may be thus described. The people of God were in a truly flourishing state. No terror from without assailed them, but a bright and most profound peace, through the favor of God, encompassed his church on every side. Meantime, however, the spirit of envy at first crept in unperceived but soon reveled in the midst of the assemblies of the saints. At length it reached the bishops themselves, and arrayed them in angry hostility against each other, on pretense of a jealous regard for the doctrines of divine truth. Hence it was that a mighty fire was kindled, originating in the first instance in the Alexandrian church, and overspread the whole of Egypt and Libya. Eventually it extended its ravages to the other provinces and cities of the empire, so that not only the prelates of the churches might be seen encountering each other in the strife of words, but the people themselves were completely divided, some adhering to one faction and others to another. So notorious did the scandal of these proceedings become, that the sacred matters of inspired teaching were exposed to the most shameful ridicule in the very theaters of the unbelievers.

As soon as the emperor was informed, he forthwith selected from the Christians in his train one whom he well knew to be approved for the sobriety and genuineness of his faith and sent him to negotiate peace between the dissentient parties at Alexandria. He also made him the bearer of a most needful and appropriate letter to the original movers of the strife, and this letter, as exhibiting a specimen of his watchful care over God's people, it may be well to introduce into this our narrative of his life. Its purport was as follows:

> Victor Constantinus, Maximus Augustus, to Alexander and Arius.[56] I call God to witness that I had a twofold reason for undertaking the duty that I now have performed. My design was, first, to bring the diverse judgments formed by all nations respecting the deity to a condition of settled uniformity, and, secondly, to restore to health the system of the world, then suffering under the malignant power of a grievous distemper. I sought to accomplish the one by the secret eye of thought and the other by the power of military authority. For I was aware that if I should succeed in establishing, according to my hopes, a common harmony of sentiment among all the servants of God, the general course of affairs also would experience a change correspondent to the pious desires of them all.
>
> Finding, then, that the whole of Africa[57] was pervaded by an intolerable spirit of mad folly through the influence of those who with heedless frivolity had presumed to rend the religion of the people into diverse sects, I was anxious to check this disorder, and could discover no other remedy equal to the occasion, except in sending some of yourselves to aid in restoring mutual harmony among the disputants, after I had removed that common enemy of mankind who had interposed

---

[56] Alexander was bishop of Alexandria; Arius was one of his priests.

[57] That is, Egypt and Libya.

his lawless sentence for the prohibition of your holy synods.[58] As soon, therefore, as I had secured my decisive victory and unquestionable triumph over my enemies, my first enquiry was concerning that object that I felt to be of paramount interest and importance.

But, O glorious Providence of God! How deep a wound did not my ears only but my very heart receive in the report that divisions existed among yourselves more grievous still than those that continued in your country. And yet, having made a careful enquiry into the origin and foundation of these differences, I find the cause to be of a truly insignificant character, and quite unworthy of such fierce contention. Feeling myself, therefore, compelled to address you in this letter and to appeal at the same time to your unanimity and sagacity, I interrupt your dissension in the character of a minister of peace. For if I might expect to be able by a judicious appeal to the pious feelings of those who heard me to recall them to a better spirit, even though the occasion of the disagreement were a greater one, how can I refrain from promising myself a far easier and more speedy adjustment of this difference, when the cause that hinders general harmony of sentiment is intrinsically trifling and of little moment?

I understand, then, that the origin of the present controversy is this. When you, Alexander, demanded of the priests what opinion they maintained respecting a certain passage in the divine law, then you, Arius, inconsiderately insisted on what ought never to have been conceived at all. Hence it was that a dissension arose between you, fellowship was withdrawn,[59] and the holy people, rent into diverse parties, no longer preserved the unity of the one body. Now, therefore, you both must exhibit an equal degree of forbearance, and receive the advice that your fellow-servant[60] righteously gives. What then is this advice? It was wrong in the first instance to propose such questions as these. For those points of discussion that are enjoined by the authority of no law, but rather suggested by the contentious spirit that is fostered by misused leisure, even though they may be intended merely as an intellectual exercise, ought certainly to be confined to the region of our own thoughts, and not hastily produced in the popular assemblies or unadvisedly entrusted to the general ear. For how very few are there able either accurately to comprehend, or adequately to explain subjects so sublime and abstruse in their nature? Or, granting that one were fully competent for this, how many people will he convince? Or, who, again, in dealing with questions of such subtle nicety as these can secure himself against a dangerous declension from the truth? It is incumbent therefore on us in these cases to be sparing of our words, lest, in case we ourselves are unable, through the feebleness of our natural faculties, to give a clear explanation of the subject before us, or, on the other hand, in case the slowness of our hearers' understandings disables them from arriving at an accurate apprehension of what we say, from one or other of these causes the people to be reduced to the alternative either of blasphemy or schism.

Let therefore both the unguarded question and the inconsiderate answer receive your mutual forgiveness. For the cause of your difference has not been any of the leading doctrines or precepts of the divine law, nor has any new heresy respecting the worship of God arisen among you. You are in truth of one and the same judgment: you may therefore well join in communion and fellowship.

We are not all of us like-minded on every subject, nor is there such a thing as one disposition and judgment common to all alike. As far, then, as regards the divine providence, let there be one faith, and one understanding among you, one united judgment in reference to God. But as to your subtle disputations on questions of little or no significance, although you may be unable to harmonize in sentiment, such differences should be consigned to the secret custody of your own minds and thoughts. And now, let the preciousness of common affection, let faith in the truth, let the honor due to God and to the observance of his law continue immovably among you. Resume, then, your mutual feelings of friendship, love,

---

[58] A reference to Licinius (308–324), who had prohibited the holding of church councils.

[59] That is, the dissenting parties excommunicated each other.

[60] Constantine himself.

and regard: restore to the people their wonted embracing; and, having purified your souls, as it were, you once more must acknowledge one another. For it often happens that when a reconciliation is effected by the removal of the causes of enmity, friendship becomes even sweeter than it was before.

Then as if to bring a divine array against this enemy, he convoked a general council,[61] and invited the speedy attendance of bishops from all quarters, in letters expressive of the honorable estimation in which he held them. Nor was this merely the issuing of a bare command but the emperor's good will contributed much to its being carried into effect, for he allowed some the use of the public means of conveyance whereas he afforded to others an ample supply of horses for their transport.[62] The place, too, selected for the synod, the city Nicaea, named from "Victory," in Bithynia[63] was appropriate to the occasion. As soon as the imperial injunction was generally made known, all[64] with the utmost willingness hastened thither, for they were impelled by the anticipation of a happy result to the conference and the desire of beholding something new and strange in the person of so admirable an emperor. When they were all assembled, it appeared evident that the proceeding was the work of God, inasmuch as men who had been most widely separated, not merely in sentiment but also personally, and by difference of country, place, and nation, were here brought together and comprised within the walls of a single city.

In effect, the most distinguished of God's ministers from all the churches that abounded in Europe, Libya,[65] and Asia were here assembled. And a single house of prayer, as though divinely enlarged,

sufficed to contain at once Syrians and Cilicians, Phoenicians and Arabians, delegates from Palestine, and others from Egypt, Thebans and Libyans, with those who came from Mesopotamia. A Persian bishop too was present at this conference, nor was even a Scythian[66] found wanting to the number. Pontus, Galatia, and Pamphylia, Cappadocia, Asia, and Phrygia, furnished their most distinguished prelates, whereas those who dwelt in the remotest districts of Thrace and Macedonia, of Achaea and Epirus, were notwithstanding in attendance. Even from Spain itself, one whose fame was widely spread took his seat as an individual in the great assembly.[67] The prelate of the imperial city[68] was prevented from attending by extreme old age, but his priests were present and took his place. Constantine is the first prince of any age who bound together such a garland as this with the bond of peace and presented it to his savior as a thank-offering for the victories he had obtained over every foe. For the maintenance of all ample provision was daily furnished by the emperor's command.

When the appointed day arrived on which the council met each member was present in the central building of the palace.[69] On each side of the interior of this were many seats disposed in order, which were occupied by those who had been invited to attend according to their rank. As soon as the whole assembly had seated themselves a general silence prevailed, in expectation of the emperor's arrival. First of all, three of his immediate family entered in succession, then others also preceded his approach, not the soldiers or guards who usually accompanied him but only friends in the faith. And then, all rising at the signal that indicated the emperor's entrance, at last he himself proceeded through the midst of the assembly, clothed in raiment that glittered as it were with rays of light, reflecting the glowing radiance of a purple robe, and adorned with the brilliant splendor of

---

[61] Clearly after his personal efforts at reconciliation had failed.

[62] The government provided warrants so the bishops could use the public post system, which was used only for official business.

[63] A province on the southwestern coast of the Black Sea. Nicaea was not far from the imperial capital city at Nicomedia.

[64] Actually, only 318 of the approximately 1,800 Christian bishops attended.

[65] That is, Africa.

---

[66] A Gothic bishop from the Crimea.

[67] Hosius, bishop of Cordova. Few westerners attended; Hosius just happened to be there by chance.

[68] The bishop of Rome Silvester (314–335), who declined to attend.

[69] The so-called "Senatus Palace," actually a church.

gold and precious stones. Such was the external appearance of his person. With regard to his mind, he was distinguished by piety and godly fear as was indicated by his downcast eyes, the blush on his countenance, and his gait. He surpassed all present in height of stature and beauty of form as well as in majestic dignity of mien and invincible strength and vigor. As soon as he had advanced to the upper end of the seats, at first he remained standing, and when a low chair of wrought gold had been set for him, he waited until the bishops had beckoned to him, and then sat down, and after him the whole assembly did the same.

The bishop[70] who occupied the chief place in the right division of the assembly then rose, and, addressing the emperor, delivered a concise speech in a strain of thanksgiving to Almighty God on his behalf. When he had resumed his seat, silence ensued and all regarded the emperor with fixed attention, on which he looked serenely round on the assembly with a cheerful aspect, and, having collected his thoughts, in a calm and gentle tone gave utterance to the following words:

> It once was my chief desire, dearest friends, to enjoy the spectacle of your united presence, and now that this desire is fulfilled, I feel myself bound to render thanks to God because he has permitted me to see you all assembled together, united in a common harmony of sentiment. I pray therefore that no malignant adversary may henceforth interfere to mar our happy state. I pray that, now the impious hostility of the tyrants[71] has been forever removed, that spirit who delights in evil may devise no other means for exposing the divine law to blasphemous calumny, for, in my judgment, intestine strife within the church of God, is far more evil and dangerous than any kind of war or conflict, and these our differences appear to me more grievous than any outward trouble.[72]

Accordingly, when, by the will of God, I had been victorious over my enemies, I thought that nothing more remained but to sympathize in the joy of those whom he had restored to freedom through my instrumentality. As soon as I received the news of your dissension, I judged it to be of no secondary importance. With the earnest desire that a remedy for this evil also might be found through my means, I immediately sent to require your presence. And now I rejoice in beholding your assembly, and I feel that my desires will be most completely fulfilled when I can see you all united in one judgment, and that common spirit of peace and concord prevailing among you all. Delay not, then, you ministers of God. Begin from this moment to discard the causes of that disunion that has existed among you and remove the perplexities of controversy by embracing the principles of peace. For by such conduct you will at the same time be acting in a manner most pleasing to the supreme God, and you will confer an exceeding favor on me, your fellow-servant.

As soon as the emperor had spoken these words in the Latin tongue, which another translated,[73] he gave permission to those who presided in the council to deliver their opinions.

On this, some began to accuse their neighbors, who defended themselves and recriminated in their turn. In this manner numberless assertions were put forth by each party, and a violent controversy arose at the very commencement. Notwithstanding this, the emperor gave patient audience to all alike and received every proposition with steadfast attention. By occasionally assisting the argument of each party in turn,[74] he gradually disposed even the most vehement disputants to a reconciliation. At the same time, by the affability of his address to all and his use of the Greek language, with which he was not altogether unacquainted, he appeared in a truly attractive and amiable light, persuading some, convincing others by his reasoning, praising those who spoke well, and urging all to unity

---

[70] Eusebius of Caesarea, the author of this account.

[71] Maxentius, Licinius, Maximinus Daia, and Constantine's other rivals for power. Defeated emperors traditionally were stigmatized as "tyrants."

[72] Emperors always were much more concerned about internal trouble, from usurpers or other kinds of unrest, than about foreign attacks.

---

[73] Into Greek, the language of most of the participants.

[74] That is, by showing that he was paying attention and participating directly in the theological discussions.

of sentiment, until at last he succeeded in bringing them to one mind and judgment respecting every disputed question.

The result was that they not only were united as concerning the faith,[75] but also that the time for the celebration of the salutary feast of Easter[76] was agreed on by all. Those points also which were sanctioned by the resolution of the whole body were committed to writing, and received the signature of each several member.[77] Then the emperor, believing that he had thus obtained a second victory over the adversary of the church, proceeded to solemnize a triumphal festival in honor of God.

[75] That is, the condemnation of Arianism.

[76] A major point of contention was the means by which the date of Easter, which did not occur on the same day each year, was calculated.

[77] In fact, two Libyan bishops refused to subscribe.

CHAPTER 12

THE CHRISTIAN EMPIRE AND THE LATE ROMAN WORLD (337–395)

The late Roman world looked very different from the Principate. The most significant change was the evolution of Christianity into the primary religion of the Roman world. Even though emperors continued to be confronted by religious controversy, by the end of the fourth century, Christianity had prevailed and had become the only fully legal religion. Christianity muscled its way into every nook and cranny of the Roman world, and Christian culture became inextricably intertwined with virtually every aspect of Roman society, culture, and politics. At the same time, late Roman emperors oversaw a relatively peaceful and prosperous world that, if anything, offered even greater opportunities to the empire's inhabitants. It looked like the Roman Empire would last forever.

THE SUCCESSORS OF CONSTANTINE (337–395)

The successors of Constantine, including first his sons and then the families of the generals Valentinian I and Theodosius I, continued the policies that had been laid out by Diocletian and Constantine. At first, all appeared to be well, but any sense of security was illusory. As had occurred in the Principate, accumulating problems threatened the future of the empire.

The Dynasty of Constantine

In 337, the empire was divided among Constantine's three sons: the eldest, Constantine II (337–340), obtained Gaul, Spain, and Britain; Constantius II (337–361), received all of the east; and Constans (337–350), the youngest, inherited Italy and North Africa. But Constantine II was killed in 340 when he unadvisedly invaded

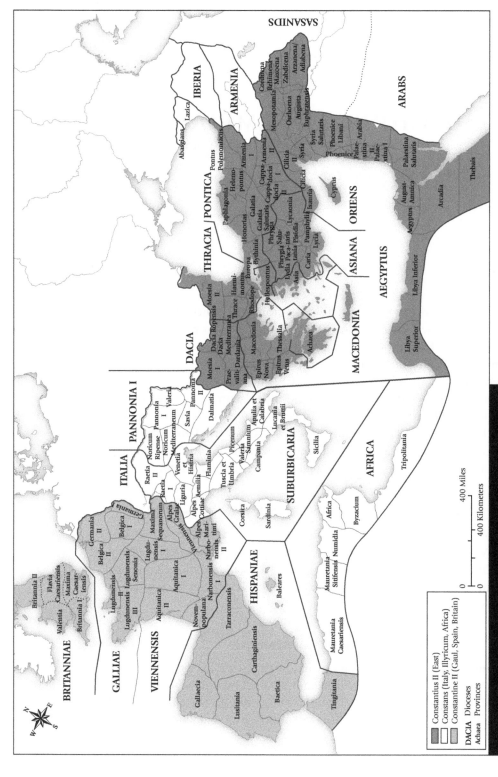

The Roman Empire as partitioned among the sons of Constantine in 337 CE

- Constantius II (East)
- Constans (Italy, Illyricum, Africa)
- Constantine II (Gaul, Spain, Britain)

DACIA Dioceses
Achaea Provinces

400 Miles
400 Kilometers

Constans' territory, and Constans in turn was killed by the Gallic usurper Magnentius (350–353). In 351, the armies of Constantius and Magnentius met at the Battle of Mursa in modern Croatia. After a bloody engagement in 351 at the Battle of Mursa, Magnentius finally retreated; a total of fifty thousand soldiers had been lost, severely weakening the military forces of both sides. Magnentius finally was defeated in 353, leaving the entire empire in Constantius' hands. In the east, meanwhile, the drawn-out wars with the New Persians continued, now often focusing on sieges of fortified sites as both sides dug in and attempted to preserve what they had.

During Constantius' reign, eastern bishops who denied they were Arians but refused to accept the Nicene Creed and supported the Arian teaching that the father and son were not of the same substance gained the support of Constantius II. They attempted to reach a compromise with Nicene Christians by proposing a **Homoian** theology, that is, that the father and son were "alike according to the scriptures." This interpretation, which was approved at a church council at Rimini in Italy in 359, left it up to the individual to decide just what the degree of likeness was. Meanwhile, circa 340, an Arian Gothic bishop, **Ulfilas**, was dispatched to convert the Goths north of the Danube, some of whom already were Nicene Christians, to Arian Christianity. Not only they but other barbarian peoples as well, such as the Vandals, Suevi, and Burgundians, soon adopted the Arian-appearing Homoian form of Christianity. For a time it looked as if some version of Arianism might yet prevail.

In 360, Constantius was faced by a revolt in Gaul by his nephew, **Julian**, whom he had raised to the rank of Caesar in 355 when barbarian problems arose in Gaul. The next year, however, Constantius died before the final confrontation, leaving Julian as sole emperor. Like all members of the imperial family, Julian had been raised as a Christian, but he harbored a secret devotion to Neoplatonic philosophy and traditional religious practices. He now showed his true colors. Preaching "tolerance for all," he announced his desire to revive polytheism, thus gaining the epithet "the Apostate." In several ways, Julian attempted to weaken the hold Christianity had on the empire. He disparagingly referred to Christians as "Galileans" and prohibited Christian professors from teaching the ancient Greek and Latin classic authors, arguing that it was hypocritical to teach material discussing gods in which one did not believe. In order to gain Jewish support, he promised to rebuild the temple in Jerusalem. And, using Christianity as a model, he even sought to create

TABLE 12.1 EMPERORS AND DYNASTIES OF THE FOURTH CENTURY (306–395)

The Dynasty of Constantine
Constantine I (306–337)
Constantine II (337–340)
Constans (337–350)
Constantius II (337–361)
Magnentius (350–353) (usurper)
Julian (360–363)

The Dynasty of Valentinian and Theodosius
West
Valentinian I (364–375)
Gratian (367–383)
Magnus Maximus (383–388) (usurper)
Valentinian II (375–392)
Eugenius (392–394) (usurper)
East
Valens (364–378)
Theodosius I (379–395)

A large copper coin portrays Julian on the obverse as a bearded philosopher and depicts on the reverse a bull, a characteristic symbol of traditional Roman religious practices. The legend, "Security of the Republic," indicates where Julian thought that the best interests of the empire lay.

an organized polytheistic church. But Julian's initiative fell on sterile ground. The days of large-scale state-sponsored polytheism were past.

In 363, engaged in preparations for an invasion of the Sasanid Empire, Julian consulted the Sibylline Books for the last attested time. He was strongly advised not to leave Roman territory that year. Julian invaded anyway. He should have listened. During a skirmish against the New Persians, he was killed, some said by one of his own Christian soldiers, thus ending the Constantinian Dynasty. Julian then became a pagan saint, but Christianity clearly was the way of the future for both individual persons and the empire as a whole.

The Dynasty of Valentinian and Theodosius

The following year, the army selected one of its own commanders, **Valentinian I** (364–375), as emperor. He immediately made his younger brother, **Valens** (364–378), co-emperor, assigning to him the eastern provinces while he took responsibility for the more demanding west. By doing so Valentinian continued the trend toward a de facto division of the empire into eastern and western halves. Whereas Valentinian generally kept out of Christian controversies, Valens was an open supporter of Arian-appearing Homoian Christianity. In the west, Valentinian was succeeded by his sons Gratian (367–383) and Valentinian II (375-392), and in the east, Valens was followed by **Theodosius I** (379–395), who married Valentinian's daughter Galla, thus preserving the dynastic connection. The Valentinianic–Theodosian Dynasty would provide an image of continuity for the empire until 457.

THE TRIUMPH OF CHRISTIANITY AND THE WORLD OF THE CHURCH

During the course of the fourth century, Christianity triumphed and became not only the only fully legal religion in the empire but also a part of virtually every aspect of life. The overwhelming impact of the spread of Christian beliefs and practices was felt not only in private but also in public life. Christian ideologies became imperial ideologies, and powerful Christian clerics came to be major players as makers of public policy and could exercise great influence even over Roman emperors. The success of Christianity thus was inextricably bound up with the favor that the church received from the imperial government, and Christian historians saw it as no accident that the rise of Christianity coincided with the rise of the Roman Empire, which, as attested by Christ's "render to

Caesar" and Paul's pride in his Roman citizenship, was an explicit part of the Christian world. According to **Augustine**, bishop of Hippo in North Africa, the creation of the Roman Empire was itself part of God's plan: "He, therefore, who is the one true God gave a kingdom to the Romans when he wished. He who gave power to Marius gave it also to Julius Caesar; He who gave it to Augustus gave it also to Nero."

Christian Competitors

During the fourth century, other religions continued to compete with variant forms of Christianity for the hearts, minds, and spirits of the people. Judaism, for example, continued to have a numerous and committed following in urban centers throughout the empire and beyond as a result of the diaspora. Despite previous expulsions, many Jews still lived in Palestine, where a Jewish patriarch served as a go-between with the imperial administration. To the east, by the fifth century over a million Jews, led by a "Prince of the Captivity," were living in Babylon under New Persian rule.

After the creation of the Mishnah in the early third century, Jewish scholars in Palestine and Judaea continued to debate the nature of Jewish life and created the Gemara, exhaustive commentaries on the Mishnah that often covered other topics as well. Joined together, the Gemara and the Mishnah made up the **Talmud**, a comprehensive guidebook for Jewish life that comprised oral tradition, interpretations of Mosaic Law, observations on faith and morality, Bible commentaries, and historical narratives. One version of the Talmud was completed in the late fourth century in Palestine, and a Babylonian version was completed by circa 500. Christian treatment of Jews ranged from tolerance to attempts to convert them to Christianity, by force if necessary. Jews also were subject to legal restrictions imposed by the imperial government, such as prohibitions on their holding government offices, testifying in court, making wills, and receiving inheritances. Although some Jews did convert under coercion, most remained steadfast in their faith.

Nor was traditional polytheism by any means dead. Indeed, some of the most committed pagans of all were the senators of Rome and Italy, who believed that Rome's past greatness had resulted from Roman faithfulness to the traditional Roman deities. But in other regards, large-scale classical urban paganism was on the decline. Most temples were unfrequented and unmaintained, and enthusiasm for Christianity had largely overwhelmed any remaining passion for paganism. Polytheistic practices continued to be the norm in the countryside, where polytheists continued to cling to their traditional beliefs. Some mystery cults also continued to flourish, especially that of Mithras, which had much in common with Christianity, such as baptism, group worship, communal meals that included communion with bread and wine, a moral code, and a belief in a life after death. By the fourth century, Mithras' birthday, December 25, even had come to be accepted as the birthday of the Christian God. The ability of Mithraism to become a mainstream religion was greatly hindered, however, by its exclusion of women.

Pagan philosophy also retained a strong following, especially Neoplatonism, a variant of the teachings of the Athenian philosopher Plato. Neoplatonism, which developed during the third century with the teachings of the philosopher Plotinus, taught that the source of all existence was a single, transcendent, impersonal, divine principle called **"The One."** Everything in the material world derived from The One in a series of hierarchical spheres, with the most distant sphere, earthly existence, reflecting the nature of The One only very imperfectly. From The One emanated the Divine Mind, known variously as the *logos, nous,* or demiurge, which contained the perfect forms of all existing things, and from the Divine Mind came the World Soul, which connected the intellectual world to the material world. A person's goal was to leave earthly existence behind, attain a higher consciousness through the World Soul, and thus gain a better sense of The One. Neoplatonism's stress on morality made it attractive to Christian intellectuals. Neoplatonism also had other several points of contact with Christianity, such as a disbelief in the independent existence of evil. In addition, Christians believed, based on the statement in the book of John, "In the beginning was the word (*logos*)," that the *logos* represented Christ.

One of the greatest competitors with Christianity at this time was another new religion, which likewise had arisen in the Near East, **Manichaeism.** The prophet Mani (ca. 215–275) was born in Babylon in the New Persian Empire. In his youth he received a divine revelation that led him to claim to be the successor of Zoroaster, Buddha, and Jesus. He incorporated aspects of all of these religions into Manichaeism, a new dualistic religion whose precepts, like those of Judaism and Christianity, were contained in books of sacred scripture. In essence, Manichaeism viewed the world as based on a constant struggle between God, representing the spiritual world of light and good on the one hand, and Satan, representing the material world of darkness and evil on the other. One's body was a battleground between good and evil, and a Manichaean's goal was to gain eternal life by setting the light part of the soul free from the matter-bound part. One purified oneself by living an ascetic life. There were two categories of Manichaeans: the Elect, who lived an ascetic life consisting of abstinence from meat, wine, sex, and property owning; and the Hearers, who accepted Manichaean beliefs but did not have the willpower to become members of the Elect. The emphasis on a constant conflict between good and evil, in which both had an independent existence, was easier to understand than the Christian concept of evil as a perversion of good and helps to explain the attraction that Manichaeism had for many people. Like Christianity, Manichaeism suffered persecution, in its case from both the Roman and New Persian governments: as early as 297, for example, Diocletian ordered that Manichaean leaders were to be burned alive together with their scriptures.

The Political Victory of Christianity

There was no stopping the rise of Christianity. After the death of Julian, Nicene Christianity consolidated itself in the face of both pagan survivals and competing Christian theologies. The eastern emperor Theodosius I was a devoted supporter of the Council of Nicaea and an avowed opponent of Arianism in any form. In 381 he summoned the second ecumenical **Council of Constantinople**; it reaffirmed the condemnation of Arianism, which then withered among the Roman population even as it continued to spread among barbarian peoples. In the western empire, the senators of Rome continued to support their ancient polytheistic traditions. During the 380s, the focus of senatorial devotion was the **Altar of Victory**, which stood in the Senate house in Rome. Powerful Christian bishops such as **Ambrose of Milan**, himself a senator and ex-provincial governor, successfully lobbied the emperor Gratian to have this decidedly non-Christian relic removed, creating hard feelings among senators who felt that their traditions were not being respected. Soon, however, even diehard traditionalists began to convert to Christianity, often for a combination of both spiritual and political reasons. The prominent pagan senator of Rome Praetextatus, for example, realizing the power that came from being bishop of an important city, was heard to exclaim, "Make me bishop of Rome, and I'll become a Christian, too!"

In 383, Magnus Maximus, commander of the British legions, crossed to Gaul and murdered Gratian. Theodosius, loath to engage in a civil war, recognized him as the colleague of the western emperor Valentinian II (375–392), the remaining son of Valentinian I. But after Maximus invaded Italy, Theodosius intervened, and in 388 Maximus was defeated and beheaded. Theodosius then became embroiled in a quarrel with Ambrose of Milan. Theodosius first angered Ambrose by ordering Christians who had destroyed a Jewish synagogue in Mesopotamia to rebuild it. Then, after a massacre of rioting citizens by the army in Greece, Ambrose excommunicated the emperor. Theodosius was not readmitted to Christian fellowship until after he had performed public penance. The emperor's humiliation served notice regarding the exalted status to which the Christian church now had risen. Suitably chastised, Theodosius also issued legislation further restricting pagan worship, culminating in a law of 392 that totally prohibited pagan practices and made Christianity the only legitimate religion within the empire. At the same time, Jews, who were grudgingly allowed to continue to worship, suffered legal disabilities, and followers of Christian variants that the government deemed heresies, such as Manichaeism, were treated even more harshly, often receiving the death penalty. As a consequence of his support for Nicene Christianity, Theodosius gained the epithet "the Great."

By the turn of the fifth century, Christianity had emerged completely triumphant. In the course of less than a century it had gone from being a persecuted religion to the only legal religion, and its devotees enjoyed a number of religious and legal privileges. Once it had become a favored religion, Christianity adopted many of the trappings of the Roman Empire. Christ himself, for example, was portrayed as manifesting many of the attributes, such as the role of lawgiver, of the Roman emperor.

Now that the tables were turned, some fanatical Christians assaulted pagans with a vengeance. Many pagan temples were demolished, sometimes against the violent opposition of rural pagans who continued to be devoted to their gods. Others, like the Parthenon in Athens, were converted into Christian churches and thus escaped destruction. Pagan statues were either smashed or Christianized by having crosses etched on their foreheads. And, in an extreme case, in 415, **Hypatia**, the leading Neoplatonist philosopher at Alexandria, was gruesomely lynched by a band of rampaging monks. It was said that she was torn limb from limb and the flesh was scraped from her bones with shells.

As time went on, the bishops of Rome, the old capital of the empire, laid increasing claims to preeminent authority in the church. Although the pretensions of the popes, as the bishops of Rome came to be called in the sixth century, to supreme authority were generally ignored in the east, the bishops of Rome gained increasing power in the west based on their claims to be the successors of the apostle Peter and on their willingness to hear appeals from disgruntled bishops who had already been condemned for various infractions in their own provinces. Thus powerful Roman bishops such as **Leo the Great** (440–461), who was able to enlist the authority of the Roman emperor on his behalf, gradually built up precedents for Rome as the greatest source of ecclesiastical authority in the west.

The Christian Life

The adoption of Christianity by greater and greater numbers of people brought changes in both public and private lifestyles. Social life—which never had been an important element of most polytheistic religions—came to center on the church. As in the modern day, some Christians expressed their

The sarcophagus of the Roman senator Junius Bassus, who converted to Christianity just before his death in 359, depicts Christ, portrayed like a Roman emperor, dispensing the law, demonstrating how Christian iconography often was modeled on Roman imperial iconography.

devotion and spirituality more publicly than others. There were nominal Christians, who made only occasional appearances in church, and people who converted for political reasons. But most Christians enthusiastically expressed their faith. Going to church on Sunday not only served spiritual needs but also provided entertainment. Church services incorporated choirs, singing, chanting, and sermons by trained orators. Basilicas in large cities held up to a thousand persons—it was standing room only then, for laypersons stood to worship—and sported marble columns and frescoes or mosaics on the walls. Even smaller churches and chapels boasted as much decoration as their sponsors could afford. The church calendar contained many festivals honoring Christian saints and martyrs. Some

The Liberian basilica in Rome, constructed by the bishop of Rome Liberius (352–366), was built on the Esquiline Hill atop a temple of the goddess Cybele. It was rebuilt by the bishop of Rome Sixtus III (432–440). It now is the basilica of Santa Maria Maggiore.

saints, such as the apostles, had empire-wide prominence, but others were of purely local significance, perhaps someone martyred during an imperial persecution.

Nor should one think that the adoption of a Christian lifestyle kept people from enjoying the good things in life. Worshippers would mingle before and after a service. The Gallo-Roman aristocrat Sidonius Apollinaris, for example, told of a gathering of people outside the church of Lyon while waiting for mass to begin. After a period of playful bantering, one group took to ball playing and another to playing dice. One of Sidonius' friends even made a risqué comment about Sidonius luring the Muses off to a private interview, and Sidonius then addressed an impromptu poem to a towel. At that point, the bishop appeared and the happy throng retreated into the church.

In their private lives, devoted Christians at least to some degree were expected to engage in prayer, fasting, and good works, such as helping the poor or at least making offerings to their local church. An increasingly popular activity was making **pilgrimages** to sacred sites, such as the site of a martyr's death or even the **Holy Land** itself, for reasons of personal piety, in search of a cure for an ailment, or in fulfillment of a vow.

Steadfast Christians constantly expected the second coming of Christ, also known as the Apocalypse and the **Last Judgment,** which they thought would mark the end of the world as they knew it. The biblical book of Revelation and other apocalyptic writings attempted to predict when the Judgment Day would occur. One approach was to combine the seven days it took to create the world

This mosaic from the villa at Piazza Armerina depicts bikini-clad women engaged in an athletic contest, in this case a ball game perhaps similar to beach volleyball. The woman on the lower left already has been awarded the palm and crown of victory.

with the biblical passage that "every day is like a thousand years" to predict that the Last Judgment would take place six or seven thousand years after the creation. Others believed that the Last Judgment would be foreshadowed by evil signs. For example, Bishop Cyprian of Carthage wrote, "It was foretold that evils would be multiplied in the last times. As the Day of Judgment is now drawing near, the censure of an indignant God will be more and more aroused for the punishment of humanity." To prepare themselves for the Apocalypse, many Christians experienced a second conversion, usually late in life, and adopted a life of penitence based on constant, and public, repentance for the many sins they believed they had committed.

Asceticism and Monasticism

The most enthusiastic Christians practiced extreme **asceticism**, or physical self-denial, a practice that also had been used by pagans and Jews who desired to become closer to God and reach a higher level of spirituality. An ascetic life provided a substitute for martyrdom, which generally was no longer available in a Christian empire. Christian ascetics rejected worldly pleasures, such as comfortable quarters, expensive clothing and food, and, in particular, sexual relations, which carried a reminder of the **original sin** of Adam and Eve. Bishops were expected to conform to the ascetic ideal by embracing **celibacy** even if they were married. The greater the degree of self-deprivation that one suffered, the greater degree of holiness and spiritual authority that one was thought to have gained.

Some Christian ascetics remained at home, but during the fourth century increasing numbers, especially in Egypt, Palestine, Syria, and Anatolia, abandoned the secular world and adopted the isolated lives of hermits, living in huts and caves. At the same time, groups of ascetic-minded men and women became **monks** and lived together in single-sex monasteries directed by an abbot or abbess. In the late fourth century, ascetic and monastic practices also were embraced in the west not only by persons such as Martin of Tours, who abandoned a military career and became a hermit, but also by Roman aristocrats, who created pseudo-monasteries in their town and country mansions. Some monastic communities, with monks called anchorites, attempted to recreate the seclusion of the desert, whereas others, with monks known as cenobites, focused on performing charitable services. In the fifth century and later, written monastic rules were created that defined a nontraditional family-style life based on obedience to the abbot and fixed routines of prayer, worship, and labor. Monks also distanced themselves from the authority of bishops, who lived in cities, and in so doing contributed to a decentralization of church authority. In general, monasticism created a world that was separated from urban life and was consistent with the withdrawal to the countryside and focus on local interests that characterized Late Antiquity.

The most zealous ascetics gave up all their earthly possessions, if they had any, and attachments. Because these **holy men and women** were thought to be isolated from earthly concerns and close to God, they were seen as impartial counselors and arbitrators and were consulted by all segments of the population. Thus women, who were excluded from church offices, and unprivileged men could acquire great authority outside the normal channels of social privilege or government jurisdiction. The holy man Simeon, for example, the son of a shepherd, sat atop a column in all weather in northern Syria for thirty years and, like an ancient Greek oracle, was consulted by privileged and unprivileged alike on account of his reputation for holiness.

Women found the ascetic life attractive for a variety of reasons. Matrona of Constantinople, for example, escaped her abusive husband by disguising herself as a man, adopting the ascetic life, and entering a male monastery. After later becoming abbess of her own convent, she possessed great spiritual authority and even instructed the emperor on matters of church teaching.

Many ascetics were considered to be Christian saints either during their lifetimes or after their deaths. For example, the Roman aristocrat Melania became an ascetic after her husband and two of her three children had died. During a pilgrimage to the Holy Land, she dressed in a slave's clothing so she could circulate freely among the poor and established two monasteries, one for men and one for women. She also convinced her daughter, also named Melania, and her husband to adopt the ascetic life. The two then renounced sex and built monasteries in North Africa and the Holy Land for virgins and ex-prostitutes. Women may have been prohibited from holding ecclesiastical office, but by becoming ascetics they still could gain spiritual authority, and wealthy women could do so very visibly by expending their wealth on religious endeavors.

THE LATE ROMAN WORLD

The rise of the Christian church and the creation of a Christian empire were just two of the things that made the Late Roman Empire very different from the Principate. Many of the more secular aspects of the late Roman world also had their own idiosyncrasies. Indeed, many of the institutions and attributes that we in the modern day consider to be aspects of the Middle Ages can be seen to have had their origins in the world of Late Antiquity.

The Role of the State

Late Roman emperors adopted the attitude that they had the authority to do whatever was necessary to get the empire back on its feet and keep it going. This policy has resulted in a modern assumption that the late empire was an authoritarian, military despotism, in which the emperors, in a big-brotherly kind of manner, assumed cradle-to-grave responsibility for supervising the lives of all of their subjects. More recent study, however, demonstrates that the late Roman world was a dynamically changing place, full of opportunity. Far from being unflaggingly oppressive, imperial humanity, as it was called, recognized certain personal rights regardless of an individual's gender or social status.

In the Late Roman Empire, the emperor was the "decider" who had the final word on everything.

The characteristic late Roman method of attacking problems was to issue laws, thousands of which still survive, which attests to the continued Roman belief in the rule of law. Every document issued by the emperor, even replies to memos, had the force of law. But this is not to say that emperors were out-and-out dictators. For one thing, it was understood that even emperors were subject to the increasingly extensive precedents of Roman law. Emperors also were careful to consult with an imperial advisory council known as the Consistory, which comprised the highest-ranking officials of state, including, along with the Praetorian Prefects and the Masters of Soldiers, the Quaestor of the Sacred Palace, the chief legal official, who oversaw the drafting of laws; the Master of Offices, a factotum who oversaw the office staffs, received foreign ambassadors, and even commanded a unit of the bodyguard; and the two chief treasury officials, who oversaw the tax income and the administration of imperial property.

The voluminous legislation has the appearance of being terribly prescriptive and inflexible, for it proposed to regulate some of the most intimate and personal aspects of Romans' lives. If it all had been enforced, as once was supposed, the Late Roman Empire would in fact have been a totalitarian establishment. But it was not. What the legislation in fact represents is the emperors' perceptions of what the problems were and methods that could be used to solve them. Very often, the legislation represents what was not happening rather than what was happening: for example, reiterated directives that sons of soldiers must be soldiers suggest only that the laws were not being obeyed.

Late Roman Economy and Infrastructure

The late Roman imperial economy revolved around the gold coinage, based on Constantine's gold *solidus*. Gold coins were paid out in salaries, expenditures on public works, and subsidies to barbarian peoples, and were returned to the treasury in taxes, fines, and other forms of income. To ensure that taxes did not fall into arrears—for if that happened for too long a period, taxpayers simply stopped paying—the land tax was paid in three installments per year, and to facilitate the accounting, a one-third *solidus* piece, the *tremissis*, was extensively minted. The use of gold allowed the government to hoard large amounts of currency in good times that could later be used to meet unexpected large expenditures.

A LATE ROMAN GOVERNOR HEARS A CASE

A sixth-century illustrated gospel written in Greek in silver ink on purple-dyed parchment and preserved in Rossano, Italy, recreates the trial of Christ before Pontius Pilate as if it were a late Roman courtroom scene. In late Roman law, the presiding magistrate, who would be a provincial governor in important cases, had complete authority to adjudicate all phases of the case, ranging from determining what the charges were to making the final judgment. Here, the governor, wearing a military robe pinned at his right shoulder—even civilian officials were technically in *militia*, or military service—sits on a dais that raises him above the level of others in the courtroom. The governor holds in his left hand a scroll that may contain his official letter of appointment or be intended to record his official disposition of the case; other scrolls of either upcoming or resolved cases lie on the floor beneath him. The governor's rank is attested by the large colored patch on his uniform (in real life, the uniform probably would have been white and the patch purple, as in the San Vitale mosaic illustrated in Chapter 14). Behind the governor stand two *apparitores* (bailiffs), also in military uniforms, who look warily at the postulants to their left and are flanked by standards bearing portraits of the two emperors; the emperors' portraits also appear on the cloth covering the desk in front of the governor. The imperial portraits serve as stand-ins for the emperors, just as portraits of the U.S. president often are found in modern U.S. courthouses. An inkpot and pens lie on the table, but the *tabellarius* (court stenographer) standing to the governor's left makes his transcript of the proceedings using a stylus to write on folding wax tablets. His own rank is attested by the colored patch on his uniform. On the right, litigants make their case to the governor, and on the left, members of the general public also express their opinion about how the case should be decided.

A mosaic of ca. 400 CE from Carthage in North Africa depicts the fortified villa of the estate owner Julius and the kinds of activities associated with it, including farming, hunting, and herding.

This form of economy was fine for the wealthy and for the government, which worked with huge amounts of money, but did little to benefit the poor, for whom three solidi could represent a year's wages. The lack of a viable silver or copper coinage (that is, one that was tied directly to the gold coinage) meant that local economies, and trade in small-value, high-volume items, suffered badly. Silver coins never were issued in large numbers, and the value of the copper coinage was allowed to float based on market forces, with the result that its value continued to plummet. The book value of the old *denarius*, no longer minted but still used to value the copper coinage, was 4,350 *denarii* per *solidus* in 324; 275,000 per *solidus* in 337; 4,570,000 per *solidus* in 360; and 45,000,000 per *solidus* thereafter. To counteract this inflation, the government attempted to revalue copper coins at higher values; for example, the *centenionalis* issued in the mid-fourth century may have been valued at 100 *denarii*. To meet the needs of local economies, some regions resorted to issuing their own small change in copper, to which the government turned a blind eye. Nor did long-distance trade completely stop. North African pottery known as red slipware, for example, was extensively exported until well into the seventh century.

Economic restructuring of the empire also was caused by the reorientation of the Roman army. With the decline of large frontier legionary forts and the dispersal of the army around the countryside, the large grain-producing villas of the northern frontier areas lost their economic underpinning. Those owned by absentee landlords were just abandoned, and those run by local senators were reoriented toward a more localized economy. Many frontier villas were subdivided, occupied by local peasants, and given over to subsistence farming. This agricultural pattern looked very different from that of the Principate, but it was well suited to the needs of its times. On the other hand, however, the fourth century was the great age of senatorial villas in southern Gaul, Spain, and North Africa, which continued to prosper. Excavations at the villa of Chiragan near Toulouse in southwestern France, for example, brought to light hundreds of sculptures dating from the first through the fourth centuries, perhaps the private collection of the villa owner.

The nature of urban settlement also changed. The overall decrease in long-distance trade meant a reduced role for cities as major centers of manufacture and economic exchange, just as the reduced role of the Roman government meant a decline in Roman imperial administrative services. The increasing withdrawal of the Roman army from frontier areas brought a parallel drop in the prosperity and population of the cities that had arisen to support it. In addition, senators, decurions, and other large landowners concentrated more on expanding, consolidating, enhancing, and fortifying their country villas, which also could serve as refuges for local people in times of trouble. City populations shrank as both rich and poor sought security in the countryside. The areas enclosed within city walls were as little as a tenth of some city's areas in the second century.

But cities by no means vanished. What economic life remained continued to be centered on cities, many of which, for example, still had communities of Jewish merchants and moneylenders. Town councils continued to function in many cities, even if at a reduced level. The decline in secular administration was at least partly compensated for by an increase in the role of bishops not only as ecclesiastical leaders but also, in the western provinces, as secular administrators. Funding that in the past had been allocated to the construction of temples, baths, amphitheaters, and buildings typical of the Principate was reallocated to church construction; indeed, churches, often built in the city suburbs and underwritten by the same public-spirited citizens who used to sponsor circus games, now became the most significant urban monuments. Many cities reoriented themselves to be centered on the churches; the old city centers were abandoned and used as stone quarries for material to build more churches. Some cities, such as Rome and the cities of the Holy Land, prospered as pilgrimage centers; people came from far and wide, for example, to be healed at the shrine of St. Martin of Tours.

Late Roman Society

The prescriptive nature of Late Roman legislation suggests that Late Roman society was very structured and stratified. But in other regards, there were new opportunities. When it came to getting things done, much happened outside the normal administrative, legislative, and judicial channels. Late Roman society and politics functioned through a complex process of behind-the-scenes interaction in which whom one knew often was crucially important. Influential individuals relied on each other to pursue their ambitions. The less privileged often attached themselves for dear life to someone of greater status, trading their independence of action for a legal and economic safety net. The institution of *clientela* remained just as pervasive in Late Roman society as it had been during the Roman Republic.

As always, most social, economic, and even political power lay in the hands of the senatorial aristocracy. Unlike the Principate, during which there were only perhaps six hundred true "members" of the Senate, by the Late Roman period thousands upon thousands of persons could lay claim to the title of "senator." One could become a senator by several means: by holding one of a multitude of civilian or military offices, by being a Christian bishop, or, most commonly, by being the son of a senator, for senatorial status was inherited. The old order of equestrians also was absorbed into the senatorial order.

For senators, their most important attribute continued to be their status—that is, how they ranked with regard to other senators. Status was measured by rank (usually obtained through office-holding); by wealth (in the form of landed property); by the number of one's clients; and by *potentia* ("power"), the ability to "get one's way." One senator wrote, "The glory of my status flourished, furnished with submission and supported by a crowd of clients." The most obvious determinant of status was rank: all senators had the entry-level rank of *clarissimus* ("most distinguished"); the higher ranks of *spectabilis* ("respectable") and *inlustris* ("illustrious") were obtained by holding high offices. And the highest rank, that of Patrician, could be received only by a special grant from the emperor.

Senators cultivated their role as patrons by doing favors for their friends and their clients. Even emperors got into the act, for they realized that they could hope to maintain the support of senators only by granting them what they wanted: offices, ranks, and opportunities to accumulate even greater wealth. All in all, however, the senators were not nearly as dependent on the goodwill of the emperor as they had been during the Principate. They now knew that, if need be, they could do quite well without him.

The ideal life of a senator consisted of a balance between *militia*, or state service, and *otium*, or leisure. Senators still coveted the power and prestige that came from holding high office. A senator's fondest dream was to be appointed Consul; not only would he give his name to the year, but he also would outrank nearly every other senator. But holding state office no longer was as important as before. Yes, it was a way to gain status, accumulate wealth, and advance the interests of one's family and friends, but a senator's real interests lay at home, somewhere in the provinces. The end result was a continuation of the withdrawal of senatorial support for the central government and the pursuit of local interests and authority. By retiring to the security of fortified villas on their estates, aristocrats could hope to isolate themselves from the vagaries of politics. In the western empire, where the Senate had a long tradition, most senators preferred to be big men in their home provinces rather than small fish, dependent on the goodwill of the emperor, in Rome. Some senators strengthened their local authority by recruiting bands of private retainers made up of mercenaries known as *bucellarii*, or "hard-tack men." In the east, however, where the Senate had been created only in the mid-fourth century CE, senators continued to be less independent and more under the thumb of the emperors.

Now that the equestrians had been incorporated into the senatorial order, the lowest-ranking members of the *honestiores* ("more distinguished people") were the decurions. They had the least *potentia* of all the aristocrats. Socially, they were squeezed between the senatorial elite and the mass of the unprivileged population. In a sense, they suffered the worst of both worlds, disdained by their senatorial superiors and distrusted by their plebeian or servile inferiors. More and more responsibilities for local administration, such as expensive road repairs, were foisted on them. And taxes that senators could evade or ignore would devolve on the decurions, who then were compelled to squeeze more out of the plebeian population. Municipal offices, once an honor, now often were a burden.

Decurions constantly confronted the possibility of falling into debt, losing their rung on the ladder of privilege, and falling into the ranks of the *humiliores* ("more humble people"). Yet, for the most ambitious and able, opportunities presented themselves. This was a world in which local interests were foremost, and decurions were experts at life on the local level. Audacious decurions sometimes even appropriated, quite illegally, the title of "senator." This allowed them to evade their municipal responsibilities, although their doing so only increased the burdens on their erstwhile brethren.

Lower still on the social scale was the majority of the population, the great mass of the "more humble" population, most of whom still were referred to generically as "plebeians." For most of them, little changed. The free plebeians, if anything, became even more dependent on either aristocrats or the church for support and continued employment. It remained possible to make a career in the army, but the opportunity to reach high political office by this means, as many had done in the third century, had largely vanished. Small peasant farmers who owned their own land still existed, but there often was pressure to sell out to land-hungry aristocrats, become their clients, and serve as tenants on what had been one's own property. The numerous tenant farmers, the *coloni*, often sank virtually to the level of *servi*, or slaves (the "serfs" of the Middle Ages); the restrictions on their legal freedom were balanced by the security they gained from being under the protection of a powerful aristocrat.

As for the slaves, the days of large slave gangs were gone. During the Principate, the number of agricultural slaves had decreased as tenant farming became the preferred method of cultivating large estates. Many slaves were engaged in various kinds of personal services. Even persons of modest means, such as soldiers and schoolteachers, had a slave or two, whose de facto status was little different from that of free plebeians. An occupation that was legally restricted to slaves was that of eunuch. Castration was illegal within the empire, and eunuchs had to be imported, often from Persia. For some, this was a good career choice. The Keeper of the Sacred Bedchamber in the imperial palace, for example, was a eunuch; he was in constant attendance on the imperial family and had very great influence.

Although this social system provided an economic and legal safety net for the less privileged (assuming they had a responsible patron), it also was designed to maintain the status quo. Not everyone was happy with the way that privileged persons often operated outside the legal system. One writer commented, "Who indeed is the rich man or noble who keeps his hands free from crime of all sorts? The socially great wish to have the privilege of committing the lesser crimes as of their right."

New Opportunities

The social, political, and religious transformations of Late Antiquity opened windows of opportunity for advancement and fulfillment to able and ambitious persons, from all segments of the population, whose aspirations might have been stifled or restricted in the past. These included lesser aristocrats, women, the poor, and even barbarians. In the past, for example, the highest-ranking state offices had been monopolized by the most influential senatorial families. Late Antiquity, however, saw old-guard aristocrats being challenged. It always was possible for a New Man, who came from the local landed gentry, if not from an even less privileged element of society, to gain the favor of the emperor, be granted a high office, and enter the aristocracy.

The expansion of Christianity also brought new career opportunities, and, for privileged persons, church office became an attractive alternative to state office. Christianity now attracted the brightest minds and most able individuals in the Roman world; indeed, it was not uncommon for individuals being tracked into government service, such as Ambrose of Milan and Augustine of Hippo, to do a sudden about-face and become bishops. Senators came to see the office of bishop as a way to culminate their careers. It not only permitted them to manifest their Christian piety but it also allowed them to display their public spirit, and to acquire the local authority that they cherished so much. Bishops oversaw the care of the poor, ill, and elderly, for whom the church was now responsible. They intervened on behalf of persons accused or convicted of crimes. They ransomed those captured by barbarians. Using the right of *episcopalis audientia* ("episcopal hearing") granted by the government, they judged civil and criminal cases. All these activities gained them both status and supporters. The office of bishop became so desirable that conflicts sometimes arose over episcopal elections, as rival factions supported their candidates. Further down the social scale, the less privileged likewise had the opportunity to enter ecclesiastical careers, not only as doorkeepers, readers, and gravediggers but also as deacons, priests, and even, on occasion, bishops.

Women, whose status generally was coupled with that of their fathers or husbands, also stood to benefit from the changing times. As always, women's activities usually took place in a family context, although some high-ranking women, both Romans and barbarians, played important roles in political and religious developments during Late Antiquity. Legally, women gained greater rights in choosing marriage partners; a law of the early fifth century stated, "If the suitors are equal in birth and character, the person whom the woman herself approves, consulting her own interests, shall be adjudged preferable." In addition, wealthy women had the opportunity to gain greater control over their own affairs; by adopting the religious life and devoting themselves to charitable

The Patrician Anicia Juliana also was a patroness of the arts. Her portrait appears, garbed in wedding regalia and flanked by the personifications of Magnanimity and Prudence, on the dedicatory page of a copy of the *Herbal* of Dioscorides, one of the earliest surviving illustrated manuscripts.

works or to church building, women could not only achieve spiritual fulfillment but also dispose of their property as they saw fit. No matter how much the family might want a rich woman to marry or remarry, it was impolitic to criticize women who expended their wealth on the church.

Imperial women provided role models for female philanthropy. For example, **Helena**, the mother of Constantine, rose from very humble beginnings as a stable girl to become a patroness of the church. After Constantine's adoption of Christianity, she made a pilgrimage to the Holy Land, during which she later was believed to have discovered the "True Cross" on which Christ was crucified. She also built a church on the site of Christ's tomb in Jerusalem. And Anicia Juliana, granddaughter of the emperor Valentinian III, eventually settled in Constantinople, where she had the rank of Patrician and married the barbarian general Areobindus. She displayed her religious devotion by building at least three churches, one of which was the largest church in Constantinople until the construction of the church of Hagia Sophia in the mid-sixth century. Other rich and influential women also devoted their lives to the pursuit of Christian piety. Some also built churches; others expended their wealth in other charitable acts, such as the care of the poor.

Late Antique Literary Culture

Contrary to the old-fashioned commonplace that literary culture went into decline after the Principate, Late Antiquity in fact was a time of great literary productivity, with most of the literary works that survive being written by members of the senatorial aristocracy. In their pursuit of leisure, senators placed a great emphasis on their cultural activities. Their education was a literary one, focusing first on grammar and then on rhetoric. Their estates were decorated with sculptures, frescoes, and mosaics modeled on themes from the literature of the Greek and Roman past. They prided themselves on their ability to compose extemporaneous poetry, and made **manuscript** copies of the past literature with their own hands. It is due to their efforts that much of the literature of classical antiquity survived to the modern day.

In the world of secular literature, the last great Latin historian of antiquity, **Ammianus Marcellinus,** an ex-army officer who was part of many of the events he discussed, writing in the 390s concluded his exquisitely detailed *Res gestae* ("Histories"), the surviving section of which covers the period 353–378. The "Augustan History," written at about the same time, is more a work of historical fiction and contains many absurd tales of the faults and foibles of emperors from Hadrian to Carus (282–283). Subsequent historical works consist primarily of jejune chronicles.

Late Antiquity also was a period of secular literary consolidation, as writers excerpted, summarized, and accumulated the learning of the past, often for use in schools, rather than creating new learning themselves. Textbook abridgments of Roman history, as by Aurelius Victor and Eutropius, became popular. Grammatical, rhetorical, and literary compendia in which authors displayed their erudition and learning likewise were composed. Around 400 CE, the grammarian Servius compiled a full edition and massive set of commentaries on the works of Vergil, and shortly thereafter the Roman Macrobius authored the *Saturnalia*, a treasure trove of arcane antiquarian lore relating to Roman mythological, philosophical, and grammatical learning. The greatest Late Roman grammarian was Aelius Donatus, an early proponent of the use of punctuation, whose *Art of Grammar*, composed in the mid-third century, became a standard school text in the Middle Ages. Another standard grammatical textbook, *Grammatical Institutes*, was compiled circa 500 CE by the North African grammarian Priscian. An abundance of technical handbooks also were written. Around 400 CE, for example, Marcellus of Bordeaux composed his *On Medications*, a catalogue of home remedies, and Vegetius wrote *On Military Matters*, a detailed discussion of military practices. The late fourth century also saw a great expansion in the composition of letters and the creation of letter collections as aristocrats who lived far apart looked for ways of maintaining their friendships with each other and preserving their cultural heritage.

Writers in the traditional literary genres of the classical Greek and Roman past gradually were overwhelmed by those writing in Christian genres. In the fourth and fifth centuries, Christianity demonstrated its intellectual stature with the creation of literary masterpieces by some of the most skilled writers of all time. Christian writers now known as the **Church Fathers**, most of whom came from aristocratic or curial backgrounds, authored works in Greek and Latin that include sermons, commentaries on scripture, theological treatises, letters, and Christian versions of Roman history that had a significant effect on the future course of Christian belief and practice.

In the east, Bishop Eusebius of Caesarea wrote a *Life of Constantine*, a *Church History*, and a massive *Chronicle* collating all the events of the human past up to the year 325. The theologian **Athanasius**, bishop of Alexandria, almost single-handedly preserved Nicene theology in the east during the period of Arian resurgence in spite of being sent into exile several times. He wrote several works against the Arians, including an "Apology" addressed to Constantius II, and his *History of the Arians* even portrayed Constantius II as the Antichrist. The "Cappadocian fathers," named after a province in Anatolia, also were strong supporters of Nicaea from the 360s into the 380s. They included Basil the Great of Caesarea, whose works included letters, sermons, and "On the Holy Spirit," which demonstrated the place of the Holy Spirit in the Trinity; Gregory of Nyssa, Basil's younger brother, whose important writings include a *Life* of his sister Macrina and works on the Trinity such as "Why There Are Not Three Gods"; and Gregory of Nazianzus, who likewise nuanced the nature of the Holy Spirit and is especially known for the orations he delivered during a brief tenure as bishop of Constantinople. And John Chrysostom, bishop of Constantinople from 398 until he was exiled in 403, authored the largest surviving collection of Greek patristic writings, including sermons, biblical commentaries, letters, and treatises such as "Against Those Who Oppose the Monastic Life."

The west produced equally talented Christian authors. **Jerome**, a native of Illyricum who settled as a monk near Bethlehem, wrote letters, scriptural commentaries, saints' lives and a catalogue of saints, and a Latin translation of the *Chronicle* of Eusebius that he continued up to 379. In addition, by the end of the fourth century, a standard **canon** of books of the Christian Bible had been defined. Thus, after learning Hebrew, Jerome translated the Old and New Testaments from Hebrew and Greek into Latin in a form known as the "**Vulgate**," which gradually replaced the variant versions of the Latin Bible used by different churches. In Milan, Ambrose authored sermons, biblical commentaries, letters, some of the first Christian hymns, and tracts such as "On the Faith, to the Emperor Gratian" and "On Virginity."

To the south, Aurelius Augustine, a North African, was raised as a Christian but then became a Manichaean Hearer. As a young man, he pursued a secular career and served as the official orator of Milan, the imperial capital, in the 380s. After receiving instruction from Ambrose, he was baptized as a Nicene Christian and adopted the Christian life, eventually becoming bishop of Hippo in North Africa. He was a strong proponent of the need for divine grace to gain salvation and of the theory of "predestination," whereby God knows in advance who will be saved and who will be damned, which severely weakened the role of free will. His literary output was prodigious: it later was said that "not only could no one ever write as many works as Augustine did, no one could even read that many." He wrote letters, sermons, biblical commentaries, and tracts both in support of his beliefs, such as "On the Trinity," and against a multitude of heresies. His account of his conversion experience, the *Confessions*, is the most important autobiographical account to survive from antiquity.

All of these Christian intellectuals had received the standard classical, and largely polytheistic, education, and they later debated the question of what role pagan literature might have in the Christian world. Some argued that the Greek and Latin classics were relics of paganism and should be simply abandoned. Jerome, who feared being condemned for his classical education, told of seeing himself in a dream standing before God in the Last Judgment and being told, "You are not a Christian. You are a Ciceronian." Augustine and Ambrose, on the other hand, believed that a classical literary education, with its emphasis on grammar and public speaking, could be used in the service of the church. When used cautiously, pagan wisdom likewise had value. Of course, in many instances Christian thinkers disagreed with their pagan predecessors. For example, in *The City of God*, Augustine promoted the Christian linear concept of history, which progressed from the Creation at the beginning to the second coming of Christ at the end, as opposed to the classical view that history was cyclical and repeated itself over and over.

Thanks to Christians who felt the same as Augustine, Greek and Latin classical literature was preserved in the Middle Ages and passed on to the modern day. Christian clerics and monks reproduced manuscripts that previously had been copied by and for cultured senators. And, in general, the preservation of both the pagan and Christian writings of antiquity was furthered by the use of the **codex**,

THE CREATION OF THE CHRISTIAN BIBLICAL CANON

In the modern day, most Christians assume that the Christian Bible, with its standardized contents of books, or "canon," has been around pretty much ever since the beginning of Christianity, but, at least as regards the New Testament, nothing could be further from the truth. The Old Testament was borrowed directly from the Jewish Septuagint, a Greek translation of the twenty-four books of the Jewish biblical canon that had been drawn up in Alexandria in the Hellenistic period. But the New Testament evolved in a more hit-and-miss fashion and went through many variations before achieving its final form. In the early church, books of scripture, including not only the modern Gospels and the letters of Paul but also a "Gospel of Peter," a "Gospel of Thomas," and the "Acts of Pilate," to name but a few, circulated independently in different churches. Churches often did not have the same collections of scripture.

Attempts to define a standard New Testament canon go back at least to the late second century and a document called the Muratorian Fragment; it listed not only many of the modern books but also others, such as the "Revelation of Peter," and it rejected Paul's letters to the Laodiceans and Alexandrians. In the early third century CE, the Christian scholar Origen of Alexandria used a canon containing all but four of the books in the modern canon, plus a book called "The Shepherd of Hermas." In 367, Bishop Athanasius of Alexandria became the first known writer to cite the books of the New Testament in the modern Roman Catholic order, but his list was not yet fully accepted, as some eastern churches, for example, rejected the book of Revelation. In the west, after much debate, the modern canon was approved at African church councils in the 390s and in a letter of Bishop Innocent of Rome in 407. The book of Second Peter barely gained endorsement. By the fifth century, therefore, by which time most eastern churches had accepted Revelation, the orthodox churches of both the Greek east and the Latin west were in full agreement on which books to include in the Old and New Testaments, and this became the definitive ordering in Jerome's *Vulgate*. But that did not end disputes over the biblical canon, because splinter groups of Christians still preferred to use other noncanonical, or apocryphal (meaning "hidden"), books of scripture; the Egyptian Coptic church, for example, still includes two "Letters of Clement," and the Ethiopian Orthodox church continues to recognize "The Shepherd of Hermas" and the "Acts of Paul." In addition, during the Christian Reformation, the biblical canon underwent several significant changes by Protestant groups, which reordered some of the New Testament books, eliminated some Old Testament books, and placed others in a special section, the *Apocrypha*.

or book format, which usually was made from virtually indestructible parchment, a writing material made from sheep and calf skins, as opposed to the old-fashioned scroll, which usually was made from papyrus and soon became fragile and disintegrated.

⇦ LOOKING BACK

The most significant transformation that occurred during Late Antiquity was the changing role of Christianity. In a remarkably short time, Christianity evolved from a religion that was persecuted by the government to a universal state-sponsored religion that transformed the politics, society, and culture of the Roman world. Christianity impacted the individual in incalculable ways. Many people lived Christian lives that emphasized self-denial, personal spirituality, and community service. The church offered opportunities for personal fulfill-ment and security that the empire was no longer able to provide. Women in particular benefited from participation in the Christian life. At the same time, emperors took a more hands-on approach to government by issuing thousands of laws intended to ensure the continued survival of the empire. But their efforts were hindered by difficulties in military recruitment, declining support from senators, and a growing split of the empire into eastern and western halves.

LOOKING AHEAD ⇨

At the same time, other trends led to a continued breakdown of the carefully constructed unity of the Roman Empire. One of the greatest changes was the ar-rival and settlement of various barbarian peoples, which during the fifth century would contribute to the end of the Western Roman Empire.

FURTHER READING

Arnheim, M. T. W. *The Senatorial Aristocracy in the Later Roman Empire.* Oxford: Oxford Univ. Press, 1972.

Bowersock, G. W. *Julian the Apostate.* London: Duckworth, 1978.

Bowersock, G. W., P. Brown, and O. Grabar. *Late Antiquity: A Guide to the Postclassical World.* Cambridge, MA: Harvard Univ. Press, 1999.

Brown, Peter. *The Body and Society: Men, Women, and Sexual Renunciation in Early Christianity.* New York: Columbia Univ. Press, 1988.

Brown, Peter. *Power and Persuasion in Late Antiquity: Toward a Christian Empire.* Madison: Univ. of Wisconsin Press, 1992.

Clark, Gillian. *Women in Late Antiquity.* Oxford: Oxford Univ. Press, 1993.

Hoare, F. R., ed. *The Western Fathers: Being the Lives of Martin of Tours, Ambrose, Augustine of Hippo, Honoratus of Arles and Germanus of Auxerre.* New York: Sheed and Ward, 1954.

Jones, Arnold H. M. *The Later Roman Empire, 284–602: A Social, Economic and Administrative Survey.* 3 vols. Oxford: Blackwell, 1964.

Kelly, Christopher. *Ruling the Later Roman Empire.* Cambridge, MA: Harvard Univ. Press, 2004.

Levine, L. I., ed. *The Synagogue in Late Antiquity.* Philadelphia: American Schools of Oriental Research, 1987.

Liebeschuetz, J. H. W. G. *The Decline and Fall of the Roman City.* Oxford: Oxford Univ. Press, 2001.

Mathisen, R. W. *People, Personal Expression, and Social Relations in Late Antiquity.* 2 vols. Ann Arbor: Univ. of Michigan Press, 2003.

Matthews, John F. *The Roman Empire of Ammianus.* Baltimore: Johns Hopkins Univ. Press, 1989.

McCormick, Michael. *The Origins of the European Economy: Communications and Commerce, A.D. 300–900.* Cambridge, UK: Cambridge Univ. Press, 2001.

McLynn, Neil B. *Ambrose of Milan: Church and Court in a Christian Capital.* Berkeley: Univ. of California Press, 1994.

Potter, David S. *The Roman Empire at Bay, AD 180–395.* London: Routledge, 2004.

Southern, P., and K. Dixon. *The Late Roman Army.* London: Batsford, 1996.

Whittaker, C. R. *Frontiers of the Roman Empire: A Social and Economic Study.* Baltimore: Johns Hopkins Univ. Press, 1994.

SOURCES

THE IMPERIAL OPPRESSION OF PAGANS, JEWS, AND HERETICS

THE *THEODOSIAN CODE* (437 CE)

During the Late Roman Empire, emperors issued thousands of *constitutions* (a generic word for laws) of various types, including edicts (laws addressed to the entire empire, akin to legislation of the U.S. Congress); mandates (instructions to imperial officials, akin to the executive orders of the U.S. president); decrees (decisions in courts cases, akin to decisions of the U.S. Supreme Court); and rescripts (replies to petitions addressed to the emperor, which have no modern equivalent). There was no standard method for archiving and accessing all this legislation, and it quickly became unmanageable. In 429 CE the eastern emperor Theodosius II (402–450) undertook a massive project to codify all imperial legislation going back to the reign of Constantine I (306–337), the first Christian emperor. Imperial constitutions dating from 18 January 313 to 16 March 437 were collected from both central and provincial archives and edited by an imperial commission of officials and legal experts in Constantinople. The final compilation of more than 2,500 entries (some constitutions were subdivided into multiple entries), organized into sixteen books, was issued in the eastern empire in November 437, on the occasion of the marriage of the young emperor Valentinian III (425–455) to Theodosius' daughter Licinia Eudoxia. In this legislation, the full weight of government authority was brought to bear against persons who did not subscribe to what the government deemed to be orthodox (or catholic) Christian beliefs—that is, beliefs that at some point had been agreed on at an imperial-sponsored church council, such as that at Nicaea in 325 CE. Hundreds of laws preserved not only in the Theodosian Code but also in the Code of Justinian, issued a century later in ten books under the emperor Justinian (527–565) in 534, supported orthodox Christians and disadvantaged everyone else, including pagans, Jews, and, in particular, Christian heretics (Christians with non-orthodox beliefs) and schismatics (Christians who did not recognize the authority of government-supported Christian authorities). The penalties against heretics, schismatics, Jews, and pagans included the imposition of *infamia* ("infamy"), which brought loss of social rank, the inability to act or appear for someone else at law (for instance, serving as a guardian or a witness), the inability to make or receive testamentary bequests, and the inability to initiate a civil case. Other penalties were dependent on one's social status: persons of "more humble" status could suffer corporeal punishment, whereas "more distinguished" people had to pay a fine. In both law codes, the topic of religion was allocated an entire book, subdivided into sections with multiple entries on the same topic, attesting to the significant place that Christianity had assumed in the life of the empire. For each constitution cited below, its date and place of issue, where known, also are given.

Source: J. C. Ayer, ed., *A Source Book for Ancient Church History* (New York: Scribner, 1913); Oliver J. Thatcher, ed., *The Library of Original Sources, Vol. IV, The Early Medieval World* (Milwaukee: University Research Extension, 1907). Unattributed translations are by the author.

Theodosian Code, Book 2, Section 1 ("On Jurisdiction, and Where it is Fitting for Anyone to Assemble")

(1) Entry 10 (Constantinople: 11 February 398)

Even though imperial legislation generally penalized non-orthodox Christians, Jews were permitted to continue to practice their ancestral religion so long as doing so did not conflict with the administration of Roman law.

The Imperators[1] Arcadius and Honorius[2] Augustuses to Eutychianus, Praetorian Prefect.[3] Jews who are living under Roman common law shall attend the courts in the usual way in those cases that do not concern so much their superstition[4] as court, laws, and rights, and all of them shall bring actions and defend themselves under the Roman laws. In sum, they shall be under our laws. Certainly, if some shall deem it necessary to litigate before the Jews or the patriarchs[5] through mutual agreement, in the manner of arbitration with the consent of both parties, at least in civil matters, they shall not be prohibited by public law from accepting their verdict, the governors of the provinces shall even execute their sentences as if they were appointed arbiters through the award of a judge.

---

[1] The ancient Roman Republican title given to victorious army generals; it remained part of the titulature of Roman emperors.

[2] The sons of the emperor Theodosius I (379–395), with Arcadius holding office in the eastern part of the empire from 395 to 408 and Honorius in the west from 395 until 423.

[3] The Praetorian Prefect was the highest-ranking official in the empire after the emperor and was the emperor's chief executive officer. Thus, much imperial legislation was addressed to the Praetorian Prefects, who then were expected to put it into effect.

[4] Any form of religion that was not Orthodox Christianity was conventionally referred to by the government as a "superstition."

[5] Jewish leaders recognized by the Roman government.

Theodosian Code, Book 9, Section 16 ("On Evil Doers and Astrologers and Other Similar Persons")

(2) Entry 2 (15 May 319)

Source: Ayer, 386.

The prohibition of private pagan sacrifices; public sacrifices still were allowed.

The Imperator Constantine Augustus to the people. *Haruspices*[6] and priests and those accustomed to minister in their rite we forbid to enter any private house, or under the pretence of friendship to cross the threshold of another, under the penalty established against them if they disobey the law. But those of you who choose to participate may approach public altars and shrines and celebrate the solemnities of your custom, for we do not indeed prohibit the duties of the old usurpation to be performed in broad daylight.[7]

Theodosian Code, Book 11, Section 7 ("On Taxation")

(3) Entry 13 (Aquileia: 3 November 386)

Source: Thatcher, 69–71.

The conducting of business and legal cases is prohibited on Sunday.

The Imperators Gratian,[8] Valentinian,[9] and Theodosius Augustuses to Principius, Praetorian Prefect. Let the course of all law suits and all business cease on Sunday, which our fathers rightly have called the Lord's day, and let no one try to collect either a public or a private debt, and let there be no hearing of disputes by any judges, either those required to serve by law or those voluntarily chosen

---

[6] Priests who read signs in the entrails of sacrificial animals, usually sheep.

[7] Ironically, in the past Christian worship had been condemned because it was carried out in private.

[8] The son of Valentinian (364–375) and emperor in the western empire from 375 until 383.

[9] Valentinian II (375–392), younger brother of Gratian.

by disputants. And he is to be held not only infamous[10] but also sacrilegious who has turned away from the service and observance of holy religion on that day.

Book 16 of the Theodosian Code dealt with matters of religion, and it covered in great detail the relative statuses of orthodox Christians, heretical and schismatic Christians, Jews, and pagans. Late Roman emperors took responsibility for ensuring the predominance of orthodox Christianity, so the first section of the book contained four rulings relating to how orthodox belief was to be established. Methods for establishing a person's Orthodox status ranged from accepting a permitted statement of faith to being in communion with a senior prelate whose orthodoxy was recognized by the government.

Theodosian Code, Book 16, Section 1, "On the Catholic Faith"

(4) Entry 3 (Heraclea[11]: 30 July 381)

Source: Ayer, 351.

The churches of those declared to be heretics are to be confiscated. In addition, one of the means of establishing orthodoxy was to be in communion with persons of proven orthodoxy. In this case, orthodox Christians are declared to be those who are in communion with the bishops listed here. As in the secular world, the ecclesiastical world was very status-conscious. Thus, the bishops of Constantinople and Alexandria, who had the rank of "patriarch," were listed first.

The Imperators Gratian, Valentinian, and Theodosius, Augustuses, to Auxonius, Proconsul of Asia. We command that all churches be forthwith delivered up to the bishops who confess the Father, the Son, and the Holy Spirit to be of one majesty and power, of the same glory and of one splendor, making no distinction by any profane division, but rather harmony by the assertion of the Trinity of the persons and the unity of the godhead, that is,

to the bishops who are associated in communion with Nectarius, bishop of the church of Constantinople, and with Timotheus in Egypt, bishop of the city of Alexandria; in the parts of the Orient,[12] who are in communion with Pelagius, bishop of Laodicaea and Diodorus, bishop of Tarsus; in Proconsular Asia and in the diocese of Asiana,[13] who are in communion with Amphilochius, bishop of Iconium, and Optimus, bishop of Antioch; in the diocese of Pontus,[14] who are in communion with Helladius, bishop of Caesarea, and Otreius, bishop of Melitina, and Gregory, bishop of Nyssa, Terennius, bishop of Scythia, and Marmarius, bishop of Marcianopolis. Those who are of the communion and fellowship of approved priests ought to be permitted to possess the catholic churches, but all who dissent from the communion of the faith of those whom the special list has named ought to be expelled from the churches as manifest heretics, and no opportunity whatsoever ought to be allowed them henceforth of obtaining episcopal churches that the priestly orders of the true and Nicene faith[15] may remain pure and no place be given to evil cunning, according to the evident form of our precept.

(5) Entry 4 (Milan: 23 January 386)

Many barbarian soldiers in the Roman army were "Homoians," following the Creed of Rimini, issued in 359 CE, which declared that "the Son was like ('homoios') the Father according to scripture," as opposed to the Creed of Nicaea of 325, which stated that the Son and Father were of the same substance. In the modern day, this divergence from the orthodox Nicene belief has resulted in the followers of the Creed of Rimini wrongly being labeled "Arians." The Roman government may have legitimated this non-Nicene belief because of the need to conciliate its barbarian soldiers.

---

[10] The legal status of *infamia* ("infamy") encompassed legal restrictions, such as the inability to make contracts or bequeath property.

[11] On the Black Sea coast east of Constantinople.

[12] The imperial diocese that included the easternmost provinces of the empire plus a few provinces in southeastern Anatolia.

[13] A diocese that included the provinces of southwestern Anatolia.

[14] A diocese that included the provinces of northwestern Anatolia.

[15] That is, based on the Creed of Nicaea, issued in 325 CE.

The Imperators Valentinian, Theodosius, and Arcadius Augustuses to Eusignius, Praetorian Prefect. We grant a full right of gathering to those who believe according to those things that during the times of Constantius[16] of blessed memory were decreed, to remain valid for eternity, at the Council of Rimini and in fact were confirmed at Constantinople.[17] Indeed, we command that the opportunity of assembling shall be open to them. Whoever thinks that too much of an opportunity of gathering has been granted to these people, if they think that anything disruptive should be done against the precept of Our Tranquility,[18] they should know that that as the authors of sedition and the disturbed peace of the church and even of treason, they will suffer punishments of capital punishment and bloodshed, with no lesser punishment awaiting those who attempt anything secretly or surreptitiously against this our disposition.

Theodosian Code, Book 16, Section 2, "On Bishops, Churches, and Clerics"

The forty-seven entries contained in the second section of Book 16 dealt with church clergy and practices.

(6) Entry 3 (20 October 319)

Beginning with the emperor Constantine, Christian clergy gained many privileges, such as, in this ruling, exemption from the performance of public services.

The Imperator Constantine Augustus to Octavianus, Corrector[19] of Lucania and Bruttium.[20] Those who engage in divine worship through the ministry of religion, that is, those who are called clergy, are altogether excused from public obligations, so that they may not be called away from divine services by the sacrilegious malice of certain persons.

Theodosian Code, Book 16, Section 5, "On Heretics"

As the enforcers of Christian orthodoxy, the emperors saw it as their duty to repress non-orthodox beliefs by a series of increasingly detailed and restrictive measures, as illustrated by the sixty-six entries in this section.

(7) Entry 40 (Rome: 22 February 407)

As time went on, the penalties against heretics became more numerous and more specific. This ruling was particularly directed against the Manichaeans, along with two other heresies that were thought to share many of their practices. Those associated with unorthodox beliefs lost many of their citizenship rights.

The Imperators Arcadius, Honorius, and Theodosius[21] Augustuses to Senator, Prefect of the City.[22] What we have thought concerning the Donatists[23] we recently have set forth. Especially do we pursue, with well-merited severity, the Manichaeans, the Phrygians, and the Priscillianists. Therefore, there is nothing in custom, nothing in laws that is common for these kinds of people. And first we declare that their crime is against the state, because what is committed against the divine religion is held to be an injury of all. And we will take vengeance upon them by the confiscation of their goods, which, however, we command shall fall to whomsoever is nearest of their kindred, in ascending or descending lines or cognates of collateral branches to the second degree, as the order is in succession to goods.[24] Finally, it shall be so that we allow to them the right to receive the goods only if they themselves are not in the same way polluted by the same belief. And it is our will that they be deprived of every grant or succession from whatever title derived. In addition, we do not leave to anyone convicted of this crime the right of giving,

---

[16] A son and successor of Constantine I, Constantius II (337–361 CE) had preferred the Homoian interpretation of the relationship between the Father and Son.

[17] A confirmation of the Creed of Rimini in 360 CE.

[18] That is, Nicenes who might not agree with this ruling.

[19] A type of provincial governor found only in Italy.

[20] Provinces of southern Italy.

[21] Theodosius II (402–450 CE).

[22] Rome.

[23] A schismatic African sect that was heavily persecuted by the western government.

[24] That is, according to standard Roman legal procedures relating to inheritances.

buying, selling, or finally of making a contract. The investigation shall continue until death. For if in the case of the crime of treason it is lawful to attack the memory of the deceased, not without desert ought this one to endure judgment.

Therefore, let his last will and testament be invalid, whether he leave property by testament, codicil, epistle, or by any sort of will, if ever he has been convicted of being a Manichaean, Phrygian, or Priscillianist, and in this case the same order is to be followed as in the grades above stated, and we do not permit sons to succeed as heirs unless they forsake the paternal depravity, for we grant forgiveness of the offence to those repenting. We will that slaves be without harm if, rejecting their sacrilegious master, they pass over to the catholic church by a more faithful service. The property on which a congregation of men of this sort assembled, with the owner knowing but not prohibiting, even if not implicated in participation in the crime, is to be confiscated to our patrimony.[25] If the owner was ignorant, let the agent or steward of the property, having been scourged with a lead-weighted whip, be sent to labor in the mines. The tenant, if he is of sufficient status, will be deported.[26] If the governors of provinces by fraud or favor defer what has been reported or fail to carry out the sentences, let them know that they will be inflicted with a fine of twenty pounds of gold.[27] A penalty of ten pounds of gold also will constrain the Defenders[28] and principals[29] of individual cities, and also the provincial office staffs unless they provide the most sagacious care and the most skillful labor in pursuing those

matters that were commanded by the governors regarding this law.

(8) Entry 59 (Constantinople: 9 April 423)

Because the government lacked effective means of enforcement, Roman laws against heretics in particular, and all Roman laws in general, tended not to be obeyed. As a consequence, laws often were reissued and repeated many times over, as in this ruling that merely reiterates previous anti-heretic legislation.

The Imperators Honorius and Theodosius Augustuses to Asclepiodotus, Praetorian Prefect. After other matters.[30] Let the Manichaeans and Phrygians, who, by a more disguised word are called Pepyzites or Priscillianists, the Arians likewise, the Macedonians and Eunomians, the Novatians[31] and Sabbatians,[32] and other heretics know that by this constitution too all things are denied to them that the authority of general legislation prohibits to them. Those persons who attempt to go against the interdicts of general constitutions must be punished.

(9) Entry 65 (Constantinople: 30 May 428)

The longest and most exhaustive list of heresies, accompanied by lists of penalties, came in 428, when the last of the reiterated condemnations of heresy contained in the Theodosian Code was issued. It is primarily eastern; only three groups cited here, the Priscillianists, Donatists,

---

[25] The branch of the imperial treasury that oversaw the personal property of the emperor.

[26] That is, if the tenant is not tied to the land.

[27] Extreme fines such as this—twenty pounds of gold amounted to 1,440 gold solidi, about 480 years' wages for an ordinary worker—would seem to have been intended primarily as deterrents.

[28] The "Defender of the City" was an imperial official whose responsibility was to protect local inhabitants from oppression by city council members, but because the Defenders often were members of the city council, the practice was not always effective.

[29] The "principals" were the highest-ranking and most influential members of the city council.

---

[30] The entries in the Theodosian Code often were extracted piecemeal from more lengthy pieces of legislation.

[31] At the end of the Decian Persecution in 251 CE, a schism arose in the church of Rome when two rival candidates, Novatian, who opposed the readmission of lapsed Christians into the church, and Cornelius, who had a more moderate policy, both were consecrated as bishops of Rome. Although Cornelius soon prevailed, a separate Novatian church persisted into the fifth century. Because it had no non-Orthodox theological beliefs, the emperors generally tolerated its existence.

[32] A subdivision of the Novatians who believed that Easter and the Jewish Passover should be celebrated on the same date.

and Novatians, originated in the west. Other western groups that in the past had received imperial condemnation, such as the Pelagians, who privileged free will over predestination, are omitted.

The Imperators Theodosius and Valentinian[33] Augustuses to Florentius, Praetorian Prefect. The insanity of heretics must be repressed to such an extent that there is no doubt that, before everything, the churches they hold everywhere that have been taken from orthodox believers must be surrendered immediately to the catholic church, because it cannot be tolerated that those who do not deserve to have their own property should any longer maintain possession of properties that were possessed or established by orthodox believers and were occupied by their temerity. Next, if they recruit to themselves other clerics or, as they style themselves, bishops, let a fine of ten pounds of gold be wrested away to our treasury for each violation from the one who did this or who allowed it to be done, or, if they claim poverty, from the common body of the clerics of the same superstition or even from the sanctuaries themselves.

In addition, because not all of them should be afflicted with the same harshness, it is permitted to the Arians certainly, and the Macedonians and Apollinarians, whose crime is this, that, having been deceived by harmful contemplation they believe lies about the fountain of truth, to have a church within no city;[34] to the Novatians[35] and Sabbatians, however, all freedom of new construction is removed,[36] if perchance they might attempt this. The Eunomians, truly, the Valentinians, the Montanists or Priscillianists, the Phrygians, the Marcianists, the Borborians, the Messalians, the Euchitae or Enthusiastae, the Donatists, the Audians, the Hydroparastatae, the Tascodrogitae, the Photinians, the Paulians, the Marcellians, and those who

have come all the way to the lowest wickedness of crimes, the Manichaeans, nowhere on Roman soil are to have the opportunity for gathering and praying—indeed, the Manichaeans are to be expelled from cities—because no place must be left to all of these in which injury could occur to the fundamental principles[37] themselves.

No official office is permitted to them at all beyond that of a clerk in provincial offices or military service,[38] with the right granted to no one, in turn, of making a donation, to no one at all of a final testament or will, and with all the laws that were once issued and promulgated at diverse times against these and others who oppose our faith to remain valid with enthusiastic observance,[39] whether regarding donations made to the churches of heretics, or regarding property of any kind bequeathed in a last will, or regarding private buildings, in which they meet with the permission or connivance of the owner, being surrendered to the catholic church, revered by us. Regarding a procurator[40] who did this without the knowledge of the owner, let him suffer a fine of ten pounds of gold or exile, if he is freeborn, or the mines after a whipping if he was of servile status. Thus, they should dare to contemplate neither meeting in a public place nor building churches for themselves nor any overreaching of the laws. They must be prohibited from receiving civil and military assistance, from city councils and even from Defenders and governors, under threat of a fine of twenty pounds of gold.

Indeed, with all of these regulations remaining in their firmness, which have been promulgated about diverse heretics regarding official position and the right of donating property and the making of a will, which are completely denied or barely conceded only to certain persons, in this manner, no special exception received against the laws shall be valid.

---

[33] Theodosius II (402–450), emperor in the east, and Valentinian III (425–455), emperor in the west.

[34] But they were permitted to have churches outside the cities, like the "Arians" of Constantinople.

[35] The Novatians, joined as above by the Sabbatians, as schismatics rather than heretics receive the most lenient treatment.

[36] That is, they were permitted to keep existing churches.

---

[37] That is, Orthodox beliefs.

[38] The emperors were so desperate for soldiers that even heretics were permitted to enlist.

[39] Another indication that the laws were not being obeyed.

[40] The manager of the property; much property was held by absentee landlords.

To no heretic must be given the freedom of conducting to baptism either freeborn persons or his own slaves who have been initiated into the mysteries of orthodox believers, nor indeed those whom they, prohibited from following the religion of the catholic church, acquired or in some manner have not yet associated with their superstition. But if anyone does this,[41] or, because he is freeborn, allowed this to be done to himself or did not avoid it being done, he will be condemned to exile and a fine of ten pounds of gold, with the freedom of making a will and a donation denied to each one.

We command that all these rulings are to be enforced thus, so that it is permitted to no judge to order for an accusation placed before him a lesser or no punishment, unless he wishes to suffer that which he conceded to others by his dissimulation.

Theodosian Code, Book 16, Section 10: "On Pagans, Sacrifices, and Temples"

Another section of Book 16 was devoted to dealing with, and suppressing, pagan practices. During the course of the fourth century the opportunity to engage in pagan ceremonies was increasingly restricted.

(10) Entry 12 (Constantinople: 8 November 392)

This constitution often is seen as the definitive ruling prohibiting pagan practices and making Christianity into the only fully legal Roman religion. The prohibitions cited here may be compared with the prohibitions against the Bacchanalians in 186 BCE.

The Imperators Theodosius, Arcadius, and Honorius Augustuses to Rufinus, Praetorian Prefect. No one at all of whatever sort or rank of people or offices, either serving in office or retired with honor, whether empowered by circumstances of birth or humble in nature, condition, and fortune, shall in any place or in any city sacrifice an innocent victim, or, on behalf of images lacking sense, kindle lights, place incense, or suspend garlands in a more

hidden shrine, having venerated the Lar with fire, the Genius with wine, or the Penates[42] with smoke.

If anyone, about to sacrifice, dares to burn an offering, or to consult the smoking entrails, let him, as guilty of treason, receive the appropriate sentence, having been accused by a lawful indictment, even if he has not sought anything against the safety of the princes[43] or concerning their welfare. It constitutes a crime of this nature to wish to repeal the laws, to spy into unlawful things, to reveal secrets, or to attempt things forbidden, to seek the end of another's welfare, or to promise the hope of another's ruin.

If anyone venerates, with incense placed upon them and in a laughable display, images made by mortal labor and intended to be permanent, suddenly fearing what he himself has made, or, with a tree encircled with garlands or an altar erected from excavated pieces of turf, attempts to worship empty images, even if with a humble reward for the service nevertheless with a great injury to religion,[44] he, just like one guilty of a religious violation, will be fined by the loss of the house or property in which it is established that he was a servant to pagan superstition. For we command that all places that are proven to have smoked with the vapor of incense, if moreover they are proven to be the lawful possessions of those burning the incense, are to be confiscated to our treasury.

But if in temples or public sanctuaries or in buildings and fields belonging to another anyone should venture to carry out this sort of sacrifice, if it should be established that the unlawful acts were performed with the owner being ignorant, let him be compelled to pay twenty-five pounds of gold in the form of a fine, and let an equal penalty constrain anyone conniving at this crime and anyone sacrificing.

We also desire that this ruling be enforced by governors, Defenders, and decurions[45] of individual cities, so that things learned by them immediately

---

[41] That is, is baptized as a heretic.

[42] The Lar, Genius, and Penates were household gods who looked after a home's welfare.

[43] The emperors.

[44] That is, Christianity.

[45] Members of city councils, who oversaw local administration.

will be brought to judgment and the matters reported through them shall be punished. Furthermore, if they think that anything should be passed over on account of personal favor or carelessness, they shall be subjected to a judicial action. Truly, after they have been warned, if they defer punishment by dissimulation, they will be fined by an exaction of thirty pounds of gold, with their office staffs also being constrained by a like punishment.

(11) Entry 24 (Constantinople: 8 June 423)

The full weight of imperial authority is imposed on the Manichaeans and others who dissent regarding the date of Easter, but restraint is ordered with respect to law-abiding Jews and pagans.

The Imperators Arcadius and Honorius Augustuses to Asclepiodotus, Praetorian Prefect. The Manichaeans and those who are called Pepyzites[46] and also those who in this one persuasion are worse than all the heretics, because they dissent from everyone regarding the venerable day of Easter. If they persevere in this same madness, we impose the same punishment, confiscation of property and exile. But this we especially demand of Christians, those who truly are such and those who are called such, that, having abused the authority of religion, they dare not lay their hands on the Jews and pagans living in peace and attempting nothing seditious contrary to the laws. For if they act violently against those who are peaceful or seize their property, they are to be compelled to restore not only those things alone that they carried off but also the things that they seized, assessed at threefold or fourfold.[47] Indeed, the governors of the provinces and their office staffs and the provincials should understand that, if they permit this, they themselves must be punished just as those who do this.

---

[46] Another name for Montanists.

[47] Thus, the emperor Theodosius I ordered that Christians who destroyed a Jewish synagogue had to replace, and was severely rebuked for this by Bishop Ambrose of Milan.

SOCRATES SCHOLASTICUS, *ECCLESIASTICAL HISTORY*, BOOK 7, CHAPTER 15; AND JOHN OF NIKIÛ, *CHRONICLE*, CHAPTER 84

Caption: An illustration from the "Alexandrian World Chronicle," written on papyrus in the early fifth century, shows Bishop Theophilus of Alexandria standing on top of the Serapeum, the famous Temple of Serapis in Alexandria, at the time of its demolition in 391 CE. The temple housed part of the Library of Alexandria and was a symbol of the pagan resistance to Christianity. A large number of other pagan monuments also were destroyed.

Source: A. C. Zenos and Chester D. Hartranft, trans., *Socrates, Sozomenus. Church Histories* (New York: Christian Literature, 1890).

The final triumph of Christianity came under the emperor Theodosius I (379–395), who definitively outlawed the performance of public pagan rituals and made Christianity the only fully legal religion in the empire. Zealous Christians then struck back and began to persecute both pagans and Jews with acts ranging from the destruction of pagan temples and monuments to the murder of professed pagans. A marquee example of this occurred in Alexandria, where at the Museum, the university that had been established in the third century BCE under the Ptolemies, the female philosopher and mathematician Hypatia was the head of the school of Neoplatonism. She was the teacher of later Christian bishops such as Synesius of Cyrene. In 415 a quarrel broke out between Orestes, the imperial Prefect of Egypt, and Cyril, the ambitious bishop of Alexandria. Hypatia was accused of arousing Orestes against Cyril and, as a consequence, she was assaulted and gruesomely murdered by a band of fanatical Christian monks, who also were angered because she was teaching men. Two accounts of the murder, both by Christian authors, provide rather different views of Hypatia. Socrates Scholasticus, who had received a classical education and wrote an "Ecclesiastical History" in the 440s CE, portrayed Hypatia sympathetically, but the hardline Miaphysite (anti-Chalcedonian) bishop John of Nikiû, who wrote a chronicle shortly after the Muslim capture of Alexandria in 640, portrayed her as a devotee of Satanism.

(a) Socrates Scholasticus, *Ecclesiastical History*, Book 7, Chapter 15

There was a woman at Alexandria named Hypatia, daughter of the philosopher Theon,[48] who made such attainments in literature and science so as to surpass by far all the philosophers of her own time. Having succeeded to the school of Plato and Plotinus, she explained the principles of philosophy to her students, many of whom came from a distance to receive her instructions. On account of the self-possession and ease of manner that she had acquired in consequence of the cultivation of her mind she not infrequently appeared in public in presence of the magistrates. Nor did she feel abashed in coming to an assembly of men, for all men on account of her extraordinary dignity and virtue admired her all the more. Yet even she fell a victim to the political jealousy that at that time prevailed. For, as she had frequent interviews with Orestes,[49] it was calumniously reported among the Christian populace that it was she who prevented Orestes from being reconciled to the bishop.[50] Some of them therefore, whose ringleader was a reader[51] named Peter, hurried away with a fierce and bigoted zeal. They waylaid her returning home, and, dragging her from her carriage, took her to the church called Caesareum, where they completely stripped her and then murdered her with tiles. After tearing her body in pieces, they took her mangled limbs to a place called Cinaron and there burnt them. This affair brought not the least opprobrium upon Cyril or upon the whole Alexandrian church. But surely nothing can be farther from the spirit of Christianity than the allowance of massacres, fights, and transactions of that sort. This happened in the month of March during Lent, in the fourth year of Cyril's episcopate, under the tenth consulate of Honorius and the sixth of Theodosius.[52]

(b) John of Nikiu, *Chronicle*, Chapter 84

R. H. Charles, *The Chronicle of John, Bishop of Nikiu* (London: Williams & Norgate, 1916).

And in those days there appeared in Alexandria a female philosopher, a pagan named Hypatia, and she was devoted at all times to magic, astrolabes,[53] and instruments of music, and she beguiled many people with her Satanic wiles. The governor of the city[54] honored her exceedingly, for she had captivated him through her magic. He ceased attending church as had been his custom. He also went once under circumstances of danger, and he not only did this, but he also drew many believers to her and he himself received the unbelievers[55] at his house. And on a certain day when the unbelievers were making merry over a theatrical exhibition connected with dancers, the governor of the city published an edict regarding the public exhibitions in the city of Alexandria, and all the inhabitants of the city had assembled in the theater.

Now Cyril, who had been appointed Patriarch[56] after Theophilus,[57] was eager to gain exact intelligence regarding this edict. And there was a man named Hierax, a Christian possessing understanding and intelligence, who used to mock the pagans and was a devoted adherent of the illustrious father, the Patriarch, and was obedient to his monitions. He also was well versed in the Christian faith. Now, this man attended the theater to learn the nature of this edict. But when the Jews saw him

---

[48] A Greek scholar who edited the works of the mathematician Euclid.

[49] The Augustal Prefect, the highest civil official of Roman Egypt.

[50] Cyril, the powerful and ambitious bishop of Alexandria from 412 until 444.

[51] The position of lector (reader) was a minor clerical position in the church.

[52] 415 CE.

[53] A scientific device for measuring the angular distance above the horizon of stars and planets.

[54] Orestes, the Augustal Prefect of Egypt.

[55] The non-Christians.

[56] Only the bishops of Alexandria, Antioch, Jerusalem, Constantinople, and Rome ranked as "Patriarchs."

[57] In 391 CE, Theophilus, bishop of Alexandria, had overseen the destruction of the Serapaeum, the great temple of the god Serapis and a symbol of Egypt's past respect for the traditional gods.

in the theater they cried out and said: "This man has not come with any good purpose, but only to provoke an uproar." And Orestes the Prefect was displeased with the children of the holy church and had Hierax seized and subjected to punishment publicly in the theater, although he was wholly guiltless. And Cyril was angry with the governor of the city for doing so, and likewise for his putting to death an illustrious monk of the convent of Pernôdj named Ammonius, and other monks also.

And when the chief magistrate of the city[58] heard this, he sent word to the Jews as follows, "Cease your hostilities against the Christians." But they refused to hearken to what they heard, for they gloried in the support of the Prefect,[59] who was with them, and so they added outrage to outrage and plotted a massacre through a treacherous device. They posted beside them at night in all the streets of the city certain men, while others cried out and said: "The church of the apostolic Athanasius[60] is on fire: come to its succor, all you Christians." And the Christians on hearing their cry came forth quite ignorant of the treachery of the Jews. And when the Christians came forth, the Jews arose and wickedly massacred the Christians and shed the blood of many even though they were guiltless. And in the morning, when the surviving Christians heard of the wicked deed that the Jews had wrought, they betook themselves to the Patriarch. And the Christians mustered all together and went and marched in wrath to the synagogues of the Jews and took possession of them, and purified them and converted them into churches. And one of them they named after the name of Saint George. And as for the Jewish assassins, they expelled them from the city and pillaged all their possessions and drove them forth wholly despoiled, and Orestes the Prefect was unable to render them any help.

And thereafter a multitude of believers in God arose under the guidance of Peter the magistrate[61]—now this Peter was a perfect believer in all respects in Jesus Christ—and they proceeded to seek out the pagan woman who had beguiled the people of the city and the Prefect through her enchantments. And when they learned the place where she was, they proceeded to her and found her seated on a lofty chair, and having made her descend they dragged her along until they brought her to the great church, named Caesareum.[62] Now this was in the days of the fast.[63] And they tore off her clothing and dragged her through the streets of the city until she died. And they carried her to a place named Cinaron and they burned her body with fire. And all the people surrounded the Patriarch Cyril and named him "the new Theophilus," for he had destroyed the last remains of idolatry in the city.

---

[58] Perhaps the official who presided over the city council.

[59] That is, Orestes.

[60] A famous fourth-century bishop of Alexandria who was instrumental in combating Arianism.

[61] In the preceding account of Socrates, Peter is merely a minor Christian cleric.

[62] A large temple of the imperial cult that rather than being destroyed had been converted into a Christian church.

[63] Lent.

MONASTIC LIFE ON THE EASTERN FRONTIER (ca. 350/390 CE)

JEROME, *THE LIFE OF MALCHUS THE CAPTIVE MONK*

A low-relief carving on basalt shows the stylite (pillar sitter) Simeon, a shepherd's son, atop his fifty-foot (sixteen-meter)-high column near Aleppo, Syria, where he resided on a nine-foot (three-meter)-square platform in all kinds of weather, never coming down, between 422 and 459 CE. As a result of his ascetic lifestyle, he gained a reputation for great sanctity, and his advice and blessings were sought by rich and poor alike. By adopting lives of extreme deprivation, ordinary people were able to attain great authority. Most persons who took up the monastic life, however, did not go to such extremes to gain holiness.

During the late Roman Empire, many individuals abandoned the secular world and adopted the monastic life. Some did so purely for reasons of piety, others to evade secular responsibilities, to flee barbarian incursions, or, especially women, to escape problematic domestic situations. Some monasteries were located conveniently close to cities, whereas others were in more isolated regions, such as deserts, islands, or mountains. Around 390 CE, Jerome of Bethlehem, one of the greatest Christian intellectuals, told the story of Malchus, a young man who abandoned his family to become a monk. Eventually, Malchus decided to return home, but on the way he got rather more than he had bargained for.

Source: Philip Schaff and Henry Wace, trans., *Jerome: Letters and Selected Works* (New York: Christian Literature, 1893).

Maronia is a little hamlet some thirty miles (forty-eight kilometers) to the east of Antioch in Syria. After having many owners or landlords at the time when I was staying as a young man in Syria it came into the possession of my intimate friend, the bishop Evagrius,[64] whose name I now give in order to show the source of my information. Well,

there was at the place at that time an old man by name Malchus, a Syrian by nationality and speech, in fact a genuine son of the soil. His companion was an old woman, very decrepit, who seemed to be at death's door. Both of them were zealously pious and constant frequenters of the church. With some curiosity I asked the neighbors what was the link between them; was it marriage, or kindred, or the bond of the spirit? All with one accord replied that they

---

[64] Bishop of Antioch from 388 to 392.

were holy people, well pleasing to God, and gave me a strange account of them. Longing to know more I began to question the man with much eagerness about the truth of what I heard, and learnt as follows.

My son, said he, I used to farm a bit of ground at Nisibis[65] as an only son. My parents, regarding me as the heir and the only survivor of their family, wished to force me into marriage, but I said I would rather be a monk. How my father threatened and my mother coaxed me to betray my chastity requires no other proof than the fact that I fled from home and parents. I could not go to the east because Persia was close by and the frontiers were guarded by the soldiers of Rome; I therefore turned my steps to the west, taking with me some little provision for the journey, but barely sufficient to ward off destitution. To be brief, I came at last to the desert of Chalcis, which is situated between Immae and Beroea[66] farther south. There, finding some monks, I placed myself under their direction, earning my livelihood by the labor of my hands and curbing the wantonness of the flesh by fasting. After many years the desire came over me to return to my country, and stay with my mother and cheer her widowhood while she lived (my father, as I had already heard, was dead) and then to sell the little property and give part to the poor, settle part on the monasteries and, I blush to confess my faithlessness, keep some to spend in comforts for myself.

My abbot began to cry out that it was a temptation of the devil, and that under fair pretexts some snare of the old enemy[67] lay hid. It was, he declared, a case of the dog returning to his vomit. Many monks, he said, had been deceived by such suggestions, for the devil never showed himself openly. When he failed to convince me he fell upon his knees and besought me not to forsake him, nor ruin myself by looking back after putting my hand to the plough. Unhappily for myself I had the misfortune to conquer my adviser. I thought he was seeking not my salvation but his own comfort. So he followed me from the monastery as if he had been going to a funeral, and at last bade me farewell, saying, "I see that you bear the brand of a son of Satan. I do not ask your reasons

nor take your excuses. The sheep that forsakes its fellows is at once exposed to the jaws of the wolf."

On the road from Beroea to Edessa[68] adjoining the highway is a waste over which the Saracens[69] roam to and fro without having any fixed abode. Through fear of them travelers in those parts assemble in numbers, so that by mutual assistance they may escape impending danger. There were in my company men, women, old men, youths, children, altogether about seventy persons. All of a sudden the Ishmaelites[70] on horses and camels made an assault upon us, with their flowing hair bound with fillets, their bodies half-naked, with their broad military boots, their cloaks streaming behind them, and their quivers slung upon the shoulders. They carried their bows unstrung and brandished their long spears, for they had come not to fight but to plunder. We were seized, dispersed, and carried in different directions. I, meanwhile, repenting too late of the step I had taken, and far indeed from gaining possession of my inheritance, was assigned, along with another poor sufferer, a woman, to the service of one and the same owner. We were led, or rather carried, high upon the camel's back through a desert waste, every moment expecting destruction, and suspended, I may say, rather than seated. Flesh half raw was our food, camel's milk our drink.

At length, after crossing a great river[71] we came to the interior of the desert, where, being commanded after the custom of the people to pay reverence to the mistress and her children, we bowed our heads. Here, as if I were a prisoner, I changed my dress, that is, learnt to go naked, the heat being so excessive as to allow of no clothing beyond a covering for the loins. Some sheep were given to me to tend, and, comparatively speaking, I found this occupation a comfort, for I seldom saw my masters or fellow slaves. I fed on fresh cheese and milk, prayed continually, and sang psalms that I had learnt in the monastery. I was delighted with my captivity, and thanked God because I had found in the desert the monk's estate that I was on the point of losing in my country.

---

[65] A powerful fortress on the border between the Roman and Sasanid empires.

[66] Modern Aleppo in Syria.

[67] Satan.

[68] Modern Şanlıurfa in Turkey, northeast of Beroea.

[69] A Roman name for Arabs.

[70] That is, Arabs. Traditionally, Arabs were the descendents of Ishmael, Abraham's son by his handmaid Hagar.

[71] The Euphrates, which lay between Beroea and Edessa.

But no condition can ever shut out the Devil. How manifold past expression are his snares! Hid although I was, his malice found me out. My master, seeing his flock increasing and finding no dishonesty in me and wishing to reward me in order to secure my greater fidelity, gave me the woman who once was my fellow servant in captivity. On my refusing and saying I was a Christian, and that it was not lawful for me to take a woman to wife so long as her husband was alive (her husband had been captured with us, but carried off by another master), my owner was relentless in his rage, drew his sword and began to make at me. If I had not without delay stretched out my hand and taken possession of the woman, he would have slain me on the spot. Well, by this time a darker night than usual had set in and, for me, all too soon. I led my bride into an old cave. Sorrow was bride's-maid; we shrank from each other but did not confess it.

Then I really felt my captivity; I threw myself down on the ground and began to lament the monastic state that I had lost, and said, "Wretched man that I am! Have I been preserved for this? Has my wickedness brought me to this, that in my gray hairs I must lose my virgin state and become a married man? What is the good of having abandoned my parents, country, and property for the Lord's sake, if I do the thing I wished to avoid doing when I abandoned them? Turn your weapon against yourself. I must fear your death, my soul, more than the death of the body. Chastity preserved has its own martyrdom. Let the witness for Christ lie unburied in the desert."

Thus speaking I drew my sword that glittered even in the dark, and turning its point toward me said, "Farewell, unhappy woman, receive me as a martyr not as a husband." She threw herself at my feet and exclaimed, "I pray you by Jesus Christ, and adjure you by this hour of trial, do not shed your blood and bring its guilt upon me. If you choose to die, first turn your sword against me. Let us rather be united upon these terms. Supposing my husband should return to me. I would preserve the chastity that I have learnt in captivity. I would even die rather than lose it. Why should you die to prevent a union with me? I would die if you desired it. Take me then as the partner of your chastity and love me more in this union of the spirit than you could in that of the body only. Let our master

believe that you are my husband. Christ knows you are my brother. We shall easily convince them that we are married when they see us so loving." I confess, I was astonished and, much as I had before admired the virtue of the woman, I now loved her as a wife still more. Yet I never gazed upon her naked person, I never touched her flesh, for I was afraid of losing in peace what I had preserved in the conflict. In this strange wedlock many days passed away. Marriage had made us more pleasing to our masters, and there was no suspicion of our flight. Sometimes I was absent for even a whole month like a trusty shepherd traversing the wilderness.

After a long time as I sat one day by myself in the desert with nothing in sight save earth and sky, I began quickly to turn things over in my thoughts, and among others called to mind my friends the monks, and especially the look of the father who had instructed me, kept me, and lost me. I began to tire of captivity and to miss the monk's cell, where toil is for the community, and, because nothing belongs to anyone, all things belong to all.

When I returned to my chamber, my wife met me. My looks betrayed the sadness of my heart. She asked why I was so dispirited. I told her the reasons, and exhorted her to escape. She did not reject the idea. We constantly spoke to one another in whispers, and we floated in suspense between hope and fear. I had in the flock two very fine he-goats; these I killed, made their skins into bottles, and from their flesh prepared food for the way. Then in the early evening when our masters thought we had retired to rest we began our journey, taking with us the bottles and part of the flesh. When we reached the river that was about ten miles (sixteen kilometers) off, having inflated the skins and got astride upon them, we entrusted ourselves to the water, slowly propelling ourselves with our feet, that we might be carried down by the stream to a point on the opposite bank much below that at which we embarked and that thus the pursuers might lose the track. But meanwhile the flesh became sodden and partly lost, and we could not depend on it for more than three days' sustenance. We drank until we could drink no more by way of preparing for the thirst we expected to endure, then hastened away, constantly looking behind us, and advanced more by night than day, on account both of the ambushes of the roaming Saracens, and of the excessive heat of the sun. I grow terrified even as I relate what happened, and, although my mind is perfectly at rest, yet my frame shudders from head to foot.

Three days after we saw in the dim distance two men riding on camels approaching with all speed. At once, foreboding ill, I began to think my master purposed putting us to death, and our sun seemed to grow dark again. In the midst of our fear, and just as we realized that our footsteps on the sand had betrayed us, we found on our right hand a cave that extended far underground. Well, we entered the cave, but we were afraid of venomous beasts such as vipers, basilisks,[72] scorpions, and other creatures of the kind, which often resort to such shady places so as to avoid the heat of the sun. We therefore barely went inside and took shelter in a pit on the left, not venturing a step farther, lest in fleeing from death we should run into death. We thought thus within ourselves: If the Lord helps us in our misery, we have found safety; if he rejects us for our sins, we have found our grave. What was our terror, when in front of the cave, close by, there stood our master and fellow-servant, brought by the evidence of our footsteps to our hiding place. How much worse is death expected than death inflicted! Again, my tongue stammers with distress and fear; it seems as if I heard my master's voice, and I hardly dared to mutter a word. He sent his servant to drag us from the cavern while he himself held the camels and, sword in hand, waited for us to come. Meanwhile the servant entered about three or four cubits,[73] and we in our hiding place saw his back although he could not see us, for the nature of the eye is such that those who go into the shade out of the sunshine can see nothing. His voice echoed through the cave, "Come out, you felons; come out and die. Why do you stay? Why do you delay? Come out, your master is calling and patiently waiting for you." He still was speaking when lo! through the gloom we saw a lioness seize the man, strangle him, and drag him, covered with blood, farther in. Good Jesus! How great was our terror now, how intense our joy! We beheld, although our master knew not of it,

our enemy perish. He, when he saw that he was long in returning, supposed that the fugitives being two to one were offering resistance. Impatient in his rage, and sword still in hand, he came to the cavern, and shouted like a madman as he chided the slowness of his slave, but was seized upon by the wild beast before he reached our hiding place. Whoever would believe that before our eyes a brute would fight for us?

One cause of fear was removed, but there was the prospect of a similar death for ourselves, although the rage of the lion was not so bad to bear as the anger of the man. Our hearts failed for fear. Without venturing to stir a step we awaited the issue, having no wall of defense in the midst of so great dangers except the consciousness of our chastity. Then, early in the morning, the lioness, afraid of some snare and aware that she had been seen took up her cub in her teeth and carried it away, leaving us in possession of our retreat. Our confidence was not restored all at once. We did not rush out, but waited for a long time; for as often as we thought of coming out we pictured to ourselves the horror of falling in with her.

At last we got rid of our fright. When that day was spent we sallied forth toward evening and saw the camels, called "dromedaries"[74] on account of their great speed, quietly chewing the cud. We mounted, and, with the strength gained from the new supply of grain, after ten days traveling through the desert arrived at the Roman camp.[75] After being presented to the Tribune[76] we told all, and were sent to Sabinianus,[77] who commanded in Mesopotamia, where we sold our camels. My dear old abbot now was sleeping in the Lord. I betook myself therefore to this place, and returned to the monastic life, whereas I entrusted my companion here to the care of the virgins.[78]

---

[72] A very poisonous small snake.

[73] The cubit was the length of a forearm, about eighteen inches (forty-six centimeters).

[74] From the Greek word *dromas,* or "runner."

[75] On the frontier between Roman and Persian territory.

[76] The commander of the legion.

[77] A Roman general said to have sought the aid of the "Martyrs of Edessa" against the New Persians in 359 CE. The two escapees would have been debriefed regarding their knowledge of the Saracens.

[78] Male monasteries often had an associated female monastery.

THE LATE ROMAN CRIMINAL LEGAL PROCESS
(ca. 370 CE)

JEROME, *LETTER* 1

A late Roman Coptic tapestry from Egypt, now in the Bode Museum in Berlin, depicts an execution scene. Here, the biblical sacrifice of Isaac by his father Abraham is depicted, with Abraham portrayed as a *carnifex* (executioner), with his military cloak pinned at the shoulder, about to apply *jugulatio* (throat slitting) to a condemned criminal.

Jerome of Bethlehem also provides a detailed account of the public trial and attempted execution of a woman who was tried before a Consular governor ca. 375 CE at Vercelli in northern Italy. His tendentious account, written in the form of a letter, relates how "a certain little woman" was accused by her husband of adultery with a young man. The subsequent investigation and trial demonstrates that legal proceedings were public and provided a popular spectacle, with the audience sometimes getting directly involved in the proceedings. After a botched execution attempt, the woman received a pardon from the emperor through the intercession of Evagrius, a priest, and later bishop, of Antioch.

Source: W. H. Fremantle, G. Lewis, and W. G. Martley, trans., *St. Jerome: Letters and Select Works*, Nicene and Post-Nicene Fathers, second series, Vol. 6. (New York: Christian Literature Publishing, 1893).

To Innocent. You frequently have asked me, dearest Innocent, not to pass over in silence the marvelous event that has happened in our own day. To begin, then, Vercelli is a Ligurian town, situated not far from the base of the Alps, once important, but now sparsely peopled and fallen into decay. When the Consular[79] was holding his visitation there, a certain little woman[80] and her paramour were brought before him—the charge of adultery had been fastened upon them by the husband—and were both consigned to the penal horrors of a prison. Shortly after an attempt was made to elicit the truth by torture, and when the blood-stained hook smote the young man's livid

---

[79] A *consularis*, a governor who had the rank of a Consul.

[80] A diminutive term suggesting unprivileged legal status.

flesh and tore furrows in his side, the unhappy wretch sought to avoid prolonged pain by a speedy death. Falsely accusing his own passions, he involved another in the charge. It appeared that he was of all men the most miserable and that his execution was just inasmuch as he had left to an innocent woman no means of self-defense. But the woman, stronger in virtue if weaker in sex, although her frame was stretched upon the rack, and although her hands, stained with the filth of the prison, were tied behind her, looked up to heaven with her eyes, which alone the torturer had been unable to bind, and while the tears rolled down her face, said, "You are witness, Lord Jesus, that it is not to save my life that I deny this charge. I refuse to lie because to lie is sin. And as for you, unhappy man, if you are bent on hastening your death, why must you destroy not one innocent person, but two? I also, myself, desire to die. I desire to put off this hated body, but not as an adulteress. I offer my neck. I welcome the shining sword without fear, yet I will take my innocence with me."

The Consular, who had been feasting his eyes upon the bloody spectacle, now, like a wild beast ordered the torture to be doubled, and threatened the executioner with like punishment if he failed to extort from the weaker sex a confession that a man's strength had not been able to keep back. Every species of torture is devised. She is bound by the hair to a stake, her whole body is fixed more firmly than ever on the rack, fire is brought and applied to her feet, her sides quiver beneath the executioner's probe. Still the woman remains unshaken and, triumphing in spirit over the pain of the body, enjoys the happiness of a good conscience. The cruel judge rises, overcome with passion. Her limbs are wrenched from their sockets. Another confesses what is thought their common guilt.[81] She, for the confessor's sake, denies the confession, and, in peril of her own life, tries to clear one who is in peril of his.

She has but one thing to say, "Beat me, burn me, tear me, if you will. I have not done it. If you will not believe my words, a day will come when this charge shall be carefully sifted. I have one who will judge me."[82] Wearied out at last, the torturer sighed in response to her groans; nor could he find a spot on which to inflict a fresh wound. Immediately the Consular cried, in a fit of passion, "Why does it surprise you, bystanders, that a woman prefers torture to death? It takes two people, most assuredly, to commit adultery, and I think it more credible that a guilty woman should deny a sin than that an innocent young man should confess one."

The same sentence, accordingly, was passed on both, and the condemned pair were dragged to execution. The entire people poured out to see the sight. Indeed, so closely were the gates thronged by the out-rushing crowd that you might have fancied the city itself to be migrating. At the very first stroke of the sword the head of the hapless youth was cut off and the headless trunk rolled over in its blood. Then came the woman's turn. She knelt down upon the ground, and the shining sword was lifted over her quivering neck. But although the executioner summoned all his strength, the moment it touched her flesh the fatal blade stopped short, and, lightly glancing over the skin, merely grazed it sufficiently to draw blood. The striker saw, with terror, his hand unnerved, and, amazed at his defeated skill and at his drooping sword, he whirled it aloft for another stroke. Again the blade fell forceless on the woman, sinking harmlessly on her neck, as though the steel feared to touch her. The enraged and panting officer, who had thrown open his cloak at the neck to give his full strength to the blow, shook to the ground the brooch that clasped the edges of his mantle, and not noticing this, began to poise his sword for a fresh stroke. "See," cried the woman, "Your jewel has fallen from your shoulder. Pick up what you have earned by hard toil, that you may not lose it."[83]

---

[81] Roman trials, even the torture, were public, and here one of the onlookers attempted to intervene.

[82] That is, God.

[83] The chlamys, or military cloak, was pinned at the right shoulder with a brooch called a *fibula*, an official insignia of rank.

What, I ask, is the secret of such confidence as this? Death draws near, but it has no terrors for her. When smitten she exults, and the executioner turns pale. Her eyes see the brooch, they fail to see the sword. And, as if intrepidity in the presence of death were not enough, she confers a favor upon her cruel foe. And now the mysterious power of the Trinity rendered even a third blow vain. The terrified soldier, no longer trusting the blade, proceeded to apply the point to her throat,[84] in the idea that although it might not cut, the pressure of his hand might plunge it into her flesh. Marvel unheard of through all the ages! The sword bent back to the hilt, and in its defeat looked to its master, as if confessing its inability to slay.

Now at length the populace rise in arms to defend the woman. Men and women of every age join in driving away the executioner, shouting round him in a surging crowd. Hardly a man dares trust his own eyes. The disquieting news reaches the city close at hand, and the entire force Lictors[85] is mustered. The officer who is responsible for the execution of criminals bursts from among his men, and staining his grey hair with soiling dust, exclaims, "What? Citizens, do you mean to seek my life? Do you intend to make me a substitute for her? However much your minds are set on mercy, and however much you wish to save a condemned woman, yet assuredly I, I who am innocent, ought not to perish."[86] His tearful appeal tells upon the crowd, they are all benumbed by the influence of sorrow, and an extraordinary change of feeling is manifested. Before it had seemed a duty to plead for the woman's life, now it seemed a duty to allow her to be executed.

Accordingly a new sword is fetched, a new executioner appointed. The victim takes her place. The first blow makes her quiver, beneath the second she sways to and fro, by the third she falls wounded to the ground.[87] She who previously had received four

strokes without injury, now, a few moments later, seems to die that an innocent man may not perish in her stead.

Those of the clergy whose duty it is to wrap the blood-stained corpse in a winding-sheet dig out the earth and, heaping together stones, form the customary tomb. Sunset comes on quickly. Suddenly the woman's bosom heaves, her eyes seek the light, her body is quickened into new life. A moment after she sighs, she looks round, she gets up and speaks. At last she is able to cry: "The Lord is on my side; I will not fear. What can man do to me?" Meantime an aged woman, supported out of the funds of the church, gave back her spirit to heaven from which it came. It seemed as if this thus purposely had been ordered, for her body took the place of the other beneath the mound. In the gray dawn the devil appears in the form of a Lictor, asks for the corpse of her who had been slain, and desires to have her grave pointed out to him. The clergy show him the fresh turf and meet his demands by pointing to the earth lately heaped up, taunting him with such words as these, "Yes, of course, tear up the bones that have been buried! Pluck her limb from limb for birds and beasts to mangle! Mere dying is too good for one whom it took seven strokes to kill."

Before such opprobrious words the executioner retires in confusion, whereas the woman is secretly revived at home. Then, lest the frequency of the doctor's visits to the church might give occasion for suspicion, they cut her hair short and send her in the company of some virgins to a sequestered country house. There she changes her dress for that of a man and scars form over her wounds. Yet even after the great miracles worked on her behalf, the laws still rage against her. It is so true that where there is the most law, there, there is also the most injustice.

But now see where the progress of my story has brought me. We come upon the name of our friend Evagrius.[88] Who can fittingly praise the

---

[84] The executioner thus turns from beheading to throat slitting as a means of execution.

[85] The axe-bearing attendants of the consular governor.

[86] For failing to do his duty.

[87] The executioner still is pulling his punches.

[88] A priest of Antioch who took refuge in Italy in 363; Jerome accompanied him back to the east in 373. In 388 he was named a competing bishop of Antioch.

vigilance that enabled him to bury before his death Auxentius of Milan,[89] that curse brooding over the church? Or who can sufficiently extol the discretion with which he rescued the Roman bishop[90] from the toils of the net in which he was entangled? I now am satisfied to record the conclusion of my tale. Evagrius sought a special audience of the emperor,[91] importuned him with his entreaties, won his favor by his services, and finally gained his cause through his earnestness. The emperor restored to liberty the woman whom God had restored to life.

---

[89] Arian bishop of Milan until his death in 374 CE; a metaphorical burial.

[90] Bishop Damasus of Rome, whose election in 367 involved much violence and controversy.

---

[91] The western emperor Valentinian I (364–375).

THE INSCRIPTION OF CLAUDIUS POSTUMUS DARDANUS

The inscription of Claudius Postumus Dardanus commemorating the construction of a refuge known as the "City of God," perhaps around the year 415.

During Late Antiquity, there was an increasing focus on local interests. Many senators retreated to the isolated splendor of their estates and consolidated their local authority by constructing fortified villas that not only allowed them to isolate themselves from political and economic changes but also protected them and their clients from more direct threats to personal security. During the second decade of the fifth century, the powerful senator Claudius Postumus Dardanus corresponded with some of the most distinguished Christian authors of his day, including Jerome and Augustine. As Praetorian Prefect of Gaul circa 411–413, Dardanus remained loyal to the Italian regime during several Gallic usurpations. For security reasons, he withdrew with his family to a fortified estate at Sisteron in the French Alps. The construction of this refuge was recorded in a lengthy inscription that proudly listed all of the titles of Dardanus, his wife, and his brother, and acknowledged the role of patronage in local politics: Dardanus' refuge, which would have provided protection not only in times of civil war but also from marauding barbarians, was intended to shelter not only his own family, but also the local population. Dardanus' decision to name his refuge *Theopolis*, Greek for "City of God," is almost certainly an allusion to Augustine's famous work *De civitate dei* ("On the City of God"), published at just the time Dardanus was building his private fort.

Source: R. W. Mathisen, *Roman Aristocrats in Barbarian Gaul: Strategies for Survival in an Age of Transition* (Austin: Univ. of Texas Press, 2011), 55.

In the place that has the name Theopolis, Claudius Postumus Dardanus, an illustrious man and of Patrician rank, ex-Consularis (governor) of the province of Viennensis, ex-Master of the Office of Petitions, ex-Quaestor, ex-Praetorian Prefect of Gaul, and his *materfamilias* ("mother of the family") Naevia Galla, also an illustrious woman, provided the use of roads, with the sides of the mountains pierced on both sides, and furnished walls and gates, which, established on their own estate, they wished to serve as a common refuge for everyone; with the assistance, indeed, of Claudius Lepidus, an illustrious man, a Count, and the brother of the aforementioned man, ex-Consular of the province of Germania Prima, ex-Master of Messages, ex-Count of the Private Purse. They did this so that it would be possible that their enthusiasm for the safety of all and a record of their public devotion would be displayed.

CHAPTER 13

THE FALL OF THE WESTERN ROMAN EMPIRE (375–476)

During the fifth century CE, the Roman Empire, and in particular the western part of it, was increasingly confronted by new sets of changes and problems. The most pivotal political development of Late Antiquity was the dissolution of the Western Roman Empire. By the 480s, the western empire was no more. By a process that still is not completely understood, bands of barbarians managed to settle within the imperial frontiers and carve the Roman west up into a number of independent successor kingdoms.

A NEW SET OF PROBLEMS

In the year 375, it appeared that the Roman Empire had been restored to virtually its full former glory. But appearances can be deceiving, and within a very short time indeed the Roman house of cards came crashing down with the fall of the Western Roman Empire. Barbarian invaders usually get the blame, but a number of other serious problems also contributed to the decline and fall of the west.

Cracks in the Façade

The reign of Valentinian I later was looked on as the third and last Golden Age of the Roman Empire. The borders were secure, the economy relatively sound, and society reasonably harmonious. To outward appearances, the empire looked much like it had in the first century: its borders still extended from Scotland to the Euphrates. Rural life flourished on **villas** in Gaul, Spain, Italy, and North Africa, not to mention throughout the east. The imperial treasury, with the gold standard firmly in place, was solvent. Even quarreling among the Christians had died down. Disputes between pagans and Christians were carried out in a genteel, drawing-room atmosphere. There were no serious threats on the horizon to suggest that the empire would not continue to thrive for centuries to come.

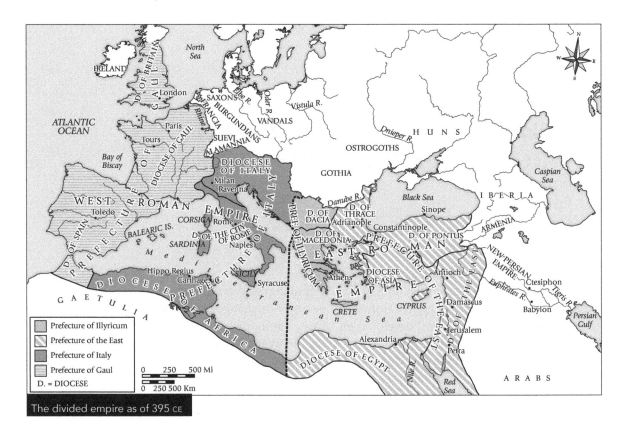

The divided empire as of 395 CE

On the other hand, however, this last bloom of normality did not mean a return to the heyday of the *Pax Romana*. There were signs that all was not well. The expansion of life in the countryside had been matched by a retrenchment of urban life, which, although still vital, functioned at a reduced level. The areas enclosed within city walls constructed in the late third and fourth centuries often enclosed as little as a tenth of what a city's area had been in the second century. And the gulf between the rich and poor was widening. Wealth was being concentrated in the hands of extremely wealthy senators who were intent on consolidating their rural estates. Their income could exceed a thousand pounds of gold a year. At the same time, more and more of the poor were reduced to a state of dependency on powerful potentates.

Furthermore, even though the army was back under control, it was now a very heterogeneous crowd. The old monolithic legions had been discarded in favor of smaller units of about a thousand men each, scattered about the countryside and often billeted with the local population. This was made necessary by the implementation not only of the new "defense in depth policy" but also of the *annona* income and payment system and the concomitant need to spread the burden of supplying the army more evenly. The military, therefore, was much more of an everyday presence than it had been two hundred years before.

Army recruitment continued to be a problem, especially after the loss of large numbers of troops in civil wars. Landowners responsible for furnishing conscripts as part of their tax assessment either provided men unsuited for military service or chose to pay an exemption fee in gold. Men eligible for the draft sometimes cut off various body parts in an attempt to avoid it. As a result, the emperors had to dip even further down into the recruitment pool and engage greater numbers of barbarian soldiers, either in ethnic units under Roman command or incorporated directly into the legions. It even became common for barbarians to be named as Masters of Soldiers. Thus many barbarians, such as the Franks Richomer, Arbogast, Merobaudes, and Bauto, the father-in-law of the future emperor Arcadius (383–408), entered Roman service and reached high office.

This **barbarization** of the Roman army was expanded by the increased hiring of *auxiliares* (auxiliaries) barbarian contingents serving under their own warlord chieftains. Initially, it was assumed that the *auxiliares* would return home after the end of the campaign for which they had been hired. At first they did, and they brought back with them not only elements of Roman culture but also tales of the wealth and opportunity that lay within the empire. But by the end of the fourth century, barbarian auxiliares and their warlord leaders were increasingly remaining within the imperial frontiers, preferably in imperial service, but if that failed, then they found other means to support themselves and their retinues.

In addition, a shift in the geographical balance of the empire came with Diocletian's and Constantine's choice to reside in the east, which reflected the increasing importance of this part of the empire. It was seen as more economically sound, more populous, more defensible, and even more civilized. Throughout antiquity, the center of gravity of civilization had been moving west, but during the Principate this process reached its high-water mark. A movement back toward the east accelerated, with Italy and the west losing their leading role as cultural incubators. Moreover, the two duplicate administrations contained the seeds of a future breach. Conflicts of interest became possible when the best interests of one half of the empire were not those of the other.

The Late Roman Empire and Its Neighbors

Ever since the beginning of the Roman Empire and even before, the Romans had been able to deal more or less effectively with the peoples living beyond the frontiers. But by the beginning of the fifth century, the emperors were confronted by growing problems on all sides, some of which appeared to be getting out of hand. On the Saharan frontier in North Africa, for example, Roman army units had been withdrawn from forward

TABLE 13.1 EMPERORS AND DYNASTIES OF THE FIFTH CENTURY (395–518)

The Dynasty of Valentinian and Theodosius
West
Honorius (393–423)
Valentinian III (425–455)
East
Arcadius (383–408)
Theodosius II (402–450)
Marcian (450–457)
Shadow Emperors (West, selected)
Petronius Maximus (455)
Avitus (455-456)
Majorian (457–461)
Anthemius (467–472)
Julius Nepos (474–480)
Romulus "Augustulus" (475–476)
The Dynasty of Leo (East)
Leo (457–474)
Zeno (474–491)
Anastasius (491–518)

A small copper coin issued by King Ezana of Aksum between 330 and 350 CE documents the spread of Christianity outside the Roman Empire. It bears a Christian cross and the legend, in Greek, "May this [cross] please the people."

posts and Roman farmers dug themselves into fortified farmhouses known as *centenaria* and grimly defended themselves against raids by the Garamantes, whose livelihood had been disrupted by increasing exhaustion of the fossil water supply.

Farther east in Africa, two nomadic desert peoples, the Blemmyes and Noubades (who gave their name to Nubia), had occupied Lower Nubia and even Egypt all the way to the first cataract on the Nile. In the fifth century, these two peoples alternately raided Roman Egypt or served as Roman allies. Farther south, on the Red Sea coast, the Kingdom of Aksum, with its capital at the city of the same name, had arisen by the first century CE, when it was mentioned in the "Periplus of the Red Sea." It grew to become an empire incorporating modern Eritrea, Ethiopia, Sudan, and even Yemen in Arabia. From the port city of Adulis its commerce extended to India and the Far East. In the mid-320s, King Ezana was converted to Christianity by the Roman missionary Frumentius, and the Kingdom of Aksum became the first major nation officially to become Christian.

The Arrival of the Visigoths

In 375 a group of defeated barbarians whom the emperor Valentinian I was interviewing became so insolent that Valentinian had an apoplectic fit and died. The able Valentinian, who was succeeded by his sixteen-year-old son Gratian (367–383), could not have perished at a less opportune time. A year later, Valentinian's brother Valens was confronted by a difficult decision. Thousands of **Visigoths**—the Goths had become subdivided into two groups that later came to be known as Visigoths, or Western Goths, and **Ostrogoths**, or Eastern Goths—had appeared on the Danube. They were fleeing from the **Huns**, steppe nomads of Mongolian origin with a reputation for terrible ferocity who had created a barbarian empire north of the Black Sea that incorporated many defeated barbarian peoples living on the central Eurasian steppes, including Alans, Gepids, Rugians, Scirians, Heruls, and the Visigoths' eastern relatives, the Ostrogoths. In exchange for being allowed to settle on deserted lands located safely within the Roman frontier, the Visigoths offered to provide military service. In the past, the Romans had permitted, and even compelled, defeated barbarians to do this on a regular basis, but never before had they allowed a large, unified group into the empire. Yet doing so would help to solve two needs at the same time: finding enough army recruits and bringing more land onto the tax rolls.

Valens accepted the Visigothic offer on condition that they turn over their weapons and that the Romans provide them with food until they could harvest

THE HUNS

During the Roman Empire, no peoples that the Romans encountered were more fascinating and feared than "barbarians," the generic name for all the peoples who lived beyond the Roman frontier. The more feared that barbarians were, the more that they were stereotypically portrayed as uncouth savages who represented the antithesis of everything that a civilized Roman or Greek stood for. The late Roman historian Ammianus Marcellinus described Roman perceptions of the Huns, the most terrifying of all the barbarians who threatened the Roman Empire, as they appeared to the Romans in the 390s.

The people of the Huns exceed every degree of savagery. Because the cheeks of the children are deeply furrowed with the steel from their very birth, in order that the growth of hair may be checked by the wrinkled scars, they grow old without beards and without any beauty, like eunuchs. Then all have compact, strong limbs and thick necks, and are so monstrously ugly and misshapen that one might take them for two-legged beasts. But although they have the form of men, however ugly, they are so hardy in their mode of life that they have no need of fire nor of savory food, but eat the roots of wild plants and the half-raw flesh of any kind of animal whatever, which they put between their thighs and the backs of their horses, and thus warm it a little.

They are never protected by any buildings, but they avoid these like tombs. Roaming at large amid the mountains and woods, they learn from the cradle to endure cold, hunger, and thirst. They dress in linen cloth or in the skins of field mice sewn together, and they wear the same clothing indoors and out. But when they have once put their necks into a faded tunic, it is not taken off or changed until by long wear and tear it has been reduced to rags and fallen from them bit by bit. They cover their heads with round caps and protect their hairy legs with goatskins; their shoes are shapeless, and prevent their walking with a free step. For this reason they are not at all adapted to battles on foot, but they are almost glued to their horses, which are hardy, it is true, but ugly, and sometimes they sit upon them woman-fashion and thus perform ordinary tasks. From their horses by night or day every one of that nation buys and sells, eats and drinks, and bowed over the narrow neck of the animal relaxes into a sleep so deep as to be accompanied by many dreams. And when deliberation is called for about weighty matters, they all consult as a common body on horseback.

You would not hesitate to call them the most terrible of all warriors, because they fight from a distance with missiles having sharp bone, instead of the usual metal points. Then they gallop over the intervening spaces and fight hand-to-hand with swords, regardless of their own lives; and while the enemy are guarding against wounds from the saber-thrusts, they throw strips of cloth plaited into nooses over their opponents and so entangle them that they fetter their limbs and take from them the power of riding or walking.

No one in their country ever plows a field or touches a plow-handle. They are all without fixed abode, without hearth, or law, or settled mode of life, and keep roaming from place to place, like fugitives, accompanied by the wagons in which they live. In wagons their wives weave for them their hideous garments, in wagons they cohabit with their husbands, bear children, and rear them to the age of puberty.

In truces they are faithless and unreliable. Like unreasoning beasts, they are utterly ignorant of the difference between right and wrong; they are deceitful and ambiguous in speech, never bound by any reverence for religion or for superstition. They burn with an infinite thirst for gold, and they are so fickle and prone to anger that they often quarrel with their allies without provocation, more than once on the same day, and make friends with them again without a mediator. This race of untamed men, without encumbrances, aflame with an inhuman desire for plundering others' property, made their violent way amid the neighboring peoples.

See Ammianus Marcellinus, *Histories* 31.2, translation from John C. Rolfe, *Ammianus Marcellinus*, vol 3, Loeb Classical Library (London: Heinemann, 1972), pp. 380–381.

their own crops. The Roman officials in charge of the transfer, however, pocketed much of the food money and accepted bribes to allow the Goths to keep their weapons. It was said that the Visigoths were faced with such famine that they were forced to trade their children for dogs they could eat. Soon after, starving, armed Visigoths began rampaging about the Balkans. Valens was forced to assemble the eastern Roman army in an attempt to bring the Visigoths to heel. In 378, rashly declining to await the arrival of Gratian and the western Roman army, Valens attacked the Goths in the **Battle of Adrianople**, northwest of Constantinople. The Roman army was virtually annihilated, and Valens was killed. The new eastern emperor Theodosius I (379–395), an experienced general, was unable to expel, or even defeat, the Visigoths. The most he could accomplish was to agree to a treaty that recognized the Visigoths as Roman *foederati* (allies). This subterfuge left the Visigoths free to wander about the empire, under their own chieftains, as they pleased.

Other peoples likewise posed threats. On the eastern frontier, the New Persians always were willing to probe for weaknesses in the Roman defenses and take advantage of Roman weaknesses. But the most serious barbarian problems usually were in the north, on the Rhine and Danube frontiers. Along with the Visigoths, any number of other barbarian peoples, pressured by the newly arrived Huns, had the means, motive, and opportunity to seek their fortunes within the empire.

In this illustration from the "Alexandrian World Chronicle" drawn in the early fifth century, the defeated emperor Eugenius begs for mercy after his defeat. His request was denied, and his head was paraded around the Roman camp.

The Final Separation

In 392, the western Master of Soldiers Arbogast murdered Valentinian II and proclaimed as emperor a teacher of rhetoric, Eugenius (392–394). In an effort to gain support, Eugenius became the last emperor to fund pagan ceremonies, something that created hostilities with both Theodosius and Christian bishops. Theodosius again invaded the west, and after his victory at the Battle of the Frigidus River Eugenius was beheaded and Arbogast committed suicide. Like the Battle of Mursa in 351, this battle resulted in tremendous military manpower losses that the government found very difficult to replace. Theodosius then became emperor of a united empire. No one could have known that this would be the last time that the Roman Empire would be united under a single ruler.

Theodosius died the following year and was succeeded by his two young sons. Arcadius (383–408), the elder, received the eastern part of the empire,

A PICTURE IS WORTH A THOUSAND WORDS

A GOLD MEDALLION OF VALENS

Roman emperors maintained their status as patrons by distributing gifts to their clients, who included powerful senators, high-ranking officials, military officers, and barbarian warlords and chieftains. The gifts they bestowed not only provided a very visible means of establishing their superior position but also gave them the opportunity to portray themselves in the best possible light. For ceremonial occasions, ranging from the observance of an imperial birthday to the commemoration of a military victory, emperors issued large gold medallions that were granted to favored subordinates, associates, and allies. This nine-solidus gold medallion of Valens (364–378), encased in an elaborate circular frame, would have been a special presentation piece, probably to a high-ranking subordinate or a barbarian chieftain. The obverse depicts Valens in a general's cloak holding a globe topped by the goddess Victory, who crowns him with a wreath. The reverse shows Valens driving a six-horse chariot and bears the legend "Our Lord Valens, Always Victorious." Barbarian chiefs who used these medallions as a means of enhancing their authority back home also implicitly acknowledged the preeminent status of the Roman emperor. Valens' grandiose claim to be ever-victorious did not keep him, however, from being defeated and killed at the Battle of Adrianople.

whereas Honorius (393–423) received the west. Neither showed much aptitude for rule, and both came under the influence of ambitious courtiers, female relatives, and Masters of Soldiers.

On the base of the Theodosian obelisk, erected in the hippodrome in Constantinople in 390 CE, Theodosius sits at court with the western emperor Valentinian II (375–392) at his left, and his two sons and successors, Arcadius and Honorius, at his right. The imperial family is flanked by military generals (with cloaks pinned at the right shoulder) and ex-consuls wearing decorated togas. Below, barbarian peoples offer tribute, signifying their submission to the empire.

The forces of fragmentation now reached their logical outcome, and the split between the Greek-speaking east and Latin-speaking west became more than merely linguistic. The creation of two separate courts resulted in two virtually separate empires. Henceforward there would be an emperor in the east, at Constantinople, and an emperor in the west, usually headquartered at Rome, Milan, or **Ravenna**. Constitutionally, there continued to be only one empire, and the eastern and western emperors continued to issue coins and laws in each other's names. But each emperor had sovereign jurisdiction in his own territories, and in reality the two halves of the empire now went their own ways, with each court pursuing interests that were not always compatible.

The loss of the traditional unity of empire would have disastrous consequences for the west. One particularly problematic issue had to do with finances. Even in the best of times, the west had barely been able to pay its own way. By the late fourth century, faced with mounting civil and military costs and reduced income, it was a financial liability. As long as there had been a unified rule, resources from the more prosperous east could be redistributed to prop up the unprofitable west. But the separate administrations changed this. The eastern government, faced with its own barbarian crisis, was reluctant to subsidize the costly west. In addition, disagreement over who controlled the territories in the western Balkans and their rich military recruiting grounds resulted in open hostilities. In the fifth century, the west was largely left to deal with its problems as best as it could by itself. Except for a few uncharacteristic bursts of activity, the eastern government passively sat by as the west collapsed.

THE FALL OF THE WEST

During the fifth century, the western empire was increasingly unable to deal with the problems confronting it. Traditionally, a western inability to cope with hordes of barbarian newcomers has been cited as the primary cause of the eventual fall of the Western Roman Empire.

The "Barbarian Invasions"

The eastern government found several ways to deal with its barbarian problem. For one thing, it was able to use its economic resources either to hire barbarians to serve in the Roman army or simply to pay them off. It also was not uncommon for it to play one barbarian off against another. In the year 400, for example, when Gaïnas, a Goth who had risen to the office of Master of Soldiers, the highest-ranking imperial general, attempted to seize control of Constantinople, the population rioted and killed thousands of his soldiers. Another barbarian Master of Soldiers, the Visigoth Fravitta, was called upon to defeat Gaïnas' navy. Gaïnas then fled to the Hun chieftain Uldin, who cut off his head and sent it to the emperor Arcadius as a present. Subsequently, the eastern government also was able to find sources of native Roman army recruits in Balkan uplands and, eventually, in the mountains of Isauria in southern Anatolia.

The increasing ability of the east to deal with its barbarian problem encouraged many barbarians to go west, where the barbarian invasions that first had afflicted the east soon had an even greater impact. Thus, in 401, the Visigoths invaded Italy. For a time, the half-Vandal, half-Roman Master of Soldiers Stilicho was able to keep the Visigoths at bay. But the situation worsened in 405, when the barbarian adventurer Radagaisus assembled a huge army in the Danubian region and invaded Italy. In order to defeat him the following year, Stilicho was compelled to withdraw troops from the northern frontier. He could not have done so at a worse time. On the last day of 406, several barbarian peoples, including the Vandals, Alans, and Burgundians, crossed the undefended and frozen Rhine River.

The situation went downhill from there. In 408, the emperor Honorius ordered the murder of his powerful Master of Soldiers. The lack of a competent Roman general opened up additional opportunities for barbarian invaders. In 409 the Vandals and Alans crossed from Gaul into the fertile and largely ungarrisoned provinces of Spain. Meanwhile, on the frontier, the Franks edged south of the Rhine. As a result of the withdrawal of Roman military forces, in 410 Honorius even told the isolated Britons to look to their own defense and to expect no help from the empire. Britain soon was invaded by Angles, Saxons, and Jutes from the area of modern Denmark.

But the greatest disaster occurred on 24 August 410, when the Visigoths, under the warlord **Alaric,** occupied and **sacked Rome** after the emperor Honorius had refused to make him Master of Soldiers. It was a rather polite sack, lasting only three days and leaving the churches untouched. But the point had been made: for the first time in eight hundred years Rome had fallen to a foreign enemy. "Unconquered Rome," as it had been called, now had been conquered. The psychological damage was even greater than the material destruction. The emperor Honorius, safely ensconced in **Ravenna,** in the swamps of northeastern Italy, eventually rid himself of the Visigoths by ceding to them Aquitania in southwestern France. Technically still Roman allies, they soon established their own independent kingdom. The dismemberment of the west was under way.

An ivory diptych (a bifolded plaque) portrays in the right panel the Master of Soldiers Stilicho, in military attire, and on the left his wife Serena and son Eucherius. In 405 CE, Stilicho, a Christian, burned the Sibylline Books, an act of piety that did not keep him from being murdered in 408 on the orders of the emperor Honorius (395–423). This opened the way for the sack of Rome by Alaric and the Visigoths in 410.

Year	Event
376	Visigoths cross the Danube
378	Battle of Adrianople
401	Visigoths invade Italy
406	Barbarians cross the Rhine
409	Barbarians enter Spain
410	Visigoths sack Rome
418	Visigoths settled in Aquitania
429	Vandals invade Africa
451	Battle of the Mauriac Plain
455	Vandals sack Rome
468	Expedition against Vandals
476	Odovacar deposes Romulus

ALTERNATIVE HISTORY

Do you think it would have made any difference in the long run if Attila and the Huns had been able to conquer the Western Roman Empire?

After the murder of Aëtius, a Roman joked that Valentinian had used his left hand to cut off his right hand.

In 425, Honorius was succeeded by his four-year-old nephew Valentinian III (425–455), whose mother, the Augusta Galla Placidia, served as regent and de facto ruler of the western empire. The political situation continued to worsen. The Vandals crossed to North Africa in 429 and ten years later occupied the great city of Carthage. The loss of North Africa was a disaster for the western empire. Not only did it put much of the grain supply of Italy into enemy hands, but it also gave the Vandals the opportunity to take to piracy. Vandal raiders fell upon the coasts of Sicily, Italy, Spain, and even Greece. By the 440s, the treasury was empty, and the army had disintegrated. What remained of the western empire was held together largely by the efforts of the Master of Soldiers **Aëtius**, often called the "Last of the Romans." He did his best at the dangerous game of playing one barbarian group off against another, often making use of *auxiliares* hired from the Huns, among whom he had been an honored hostage in his youth. When **Attila**, king of the Huns, invaded Gaul in 451, Aëtius cobbled together an unlikely alliance of Romans, Franks, Visigoths, and Burgundians. At the Battle of the Mauriac Plain, also known as the Battle of the Catalaunian Fields and the Battle of Châlons, in northern Gaul, the hitherto undefeated Huns were put to flight. The Roman coalition then collapsed, and the barbarians went back to expanding their holdings at Roman expense. In 452, Italy itself was invaded by the Huns, who, it was said, were turned back by the appeals of Leo, bishop of Rome. Plague and lack of supplies also played a role.

In 454 Aëtius was murdered by Valentinian, who in turn was murdered by two of Aëtius' comrades the following year. Although Valentinian was ineffectual as a ruler, his legitimate status and connection to the old ruling dynasty had provided a last vestige of unity for the increasingly fragmented Roman Empire. After his death, the collapse of the west accelerated. In 455, Rome again was sacked, this time by the Vandals, who conducted a thorough and lengthy fourteen-day looting, although Leo was said to have prevailed on King Gaiseric not to burn the city. The Vandals returned to Carthage not only with the spoils taken by Titus from Jerusalem in the year 70—the ship carrying them was said to have sunk—but also with the empress Licinia Eudoxia and Valentinian's two daughters Placidia and Eudocia; Eudoxia then was married to a the Vandal prince Huneric.

The different regions of the west then went their own way, and the remaining nine western emperors are known variously as the **Shadow Emperors** (because of their obscurity) or the **Puppet Emperors** (because they were often manipulated by their Masters of Soldiers). Few merit mention. In 455, the Gallic senator Avitus, supported by the Visigoths, seized power in Rome, but a year later he was deposed and killed by his Masters of Soldiers, the Roman

DIGGING ANTIQUITY

THE SACK OF ROME BY THE VISIGOTHS

An 1890 painting titled *The Sack of Rome by the Barbarians in 410* by the French painter Joseph-Noël Sylvestre reflects the popular modern belief in a destructive sack.

The Visigothic sack of Rome in 410 CE often is viewed as a horrifying event that was one of the most significant turning points in the history of the world, the point at which the Western Roman Empire began an inexorable decline and fall that culminated in 476 when the usurper Romulus was deposed by the barbarian warlord Odovacar. In people's minds at the time and later, the sack of 410 created a tidal wave of anguish, horror, and

disbelief. Some writers described extensive destruction. For example, in a comment reminiscent of the American capture of Baghdad in 2003, the church historian Socrates spoke of the Visigoths "burning the greatest number of the magnificent structures and other admirable works of art that [the city] contained." But in other regards this was the most genteel of sacks. The chronicler Prosper reported that the Visigoths "used their victory with clemency." Indeed, in some ways it hardly merits being called a sack at all, and has more the appearance of a troop of soldiers getting a bit out of hand.

Specific acts of destruction are rarely mentioned in the ancient sources. The best example came a century and a half later, when Procopius reported, "They set fire to the houses that were next to the gate, among which was the house of Sallust, who in ancient times wrote the history of the Romans, and the greater part of this house has stood half-burned up to my time." In addition, the *Book of the Popes* mentions damage in the Roman Forum to the Basilica Julia at about that time, but with no connection to the sack.

Modern archaeology also offers little support for a destructive sack. Despite diligent efforts by generations of Italian and other archaeologists, no certain evidence has been found for any material damage to the city. The most famous, and often cited, possible example of damage is supposed images of Roman coins that were etched into the marble floor of the Basilica Aemilia during a fire that burned the merchant stalls then occupying the basilica. But recent observations suggest that the supposed coin images are nothing more than stains left by drops of water falling from an overhanging tin roof.

Thus, the primary result of the sack of Rome of 410 was not the material damage to the city, but the psychological toll it took on the Roman mentality and the political use to which the sack was put in the future.

See R. W. Mathisen, "'Roma a Gothis Alarico duce capta est': The Sack of Rome in 410 CE," in L. Lipps, P. von Rummell, and C. Machado, eds., *410: The Sack of Rome* (Wiesbaden, 2013), 83–98.

Majorian and the barbarian **Ricimer**. Majorian (457–461) then became emperor, forced the Gallic barbarians to terms, reoccupied Spain, and was on the verge of attacking the Vandals when his fleet was treacherously burned in harbor. He was compelled to return to Italy, where he was beheaded by Ricimer. And in 468, a huge joint eastern–western expedition against the Vandals failed dismally, and the emperor Anthemius (467–472), who had been appointed by the eastern government, subsequently died during a civil war with Ricimer.

The term vandalism *comes from the thoroughness of the Vandal sack of Rome.*

The last legitimate western Roman emperor was **Julius Nepos** (474–480), another appointee of the eastern government. He was expelled in 475 by his Master of Soldiers Orestes, who once had been the secretary of Attila the Hun. Orestes named his son Romulus, nicknamed "Augustulus" ("the little emperor"), as emperor, but the child was deposed in 476 by **Odovacar**, a barbarian warlord. Odovacar informed the eastern emperor Zeno (474–491) that he would rule Italy in Zeno's name. Odovacar provides an excellent example of the barbarian adventurers who successfully pursued their careers in the midst of the decline of the Western Roman Empire. Four years later the exiled Nepos died and, with him, any hope of reviving the western emperorship. But, even though the Western Roman Empire legally lapsed in 480, Romulus' name—the same as the name of the founder of Rome—was too symbolic, and history generally views young **Romulus Augustulus** as the last western Roman emperor.

A nineteenth-century engraving depicts young Romulus Augustulus surrendering his diadem to Odovacar, marking the end of the Western Roman Empire and the beginning of barbarian Europe.

Perceptions of the Fall of the Western Roman Empire

Among the inventions proposed to the emperors was a paddlewheel ship powered by oxen. This contraption, which would have saved the hundred-plus sailors needed to man the oars, is not known to have been constructed, but vessels of a similar design operated on the lakes of upstate New York in the nineteenth century.

Ideas about why the western empire fell have exercised the popular imagination ever since the fall itself. Some contemporaries blamed Roman military inferiority. In an illustrated treatise titled "On Warlike Matters," a writer recommended to the emperors—perhaps Arcadius and Honorius—a number of inventions that he thought could be used to great effect against barbarian invaders, including various kinds of spear chuckers and even an oxen-driven paddlewheel ship. Although none of these inventions is known to have been implemented, they demonstrate that Romans were aware of the problems facing the empire and were suggesting imaginative ways of dealing with them.

Religious explanations for the Roman decline were particularly common, even standard. Pagans blamed it on the abandonment of the old gods. Augustine of Hippo responded to this charge in his *City of God* by arguing that what happened on Earth needed to be tolerated because it was God's will and much less important than what took place in the "heavenly city." Other Christians suggested that the disasters were God's punishment of Christians for their immoral lives. For example, around 439 the moralizing preacher Salvian of Marseille wrote, "Why does God suffer us to be conquered by the barbarians? To answer very briefly, he suffers us to endure these trials because we deserve to endure them. Let us consider the disgraceful habits, the vices and crimes of the Roman people, and we shall then understand."

In 1776, in his famous book *The Decline and Fall of the Roman Empire*, Edward Gibbon revisited the controversy and saw the fall of the western empire as the "triumph of Christianity and barbarism." He suggested that Christianity had attracted the best minds and that its message of love and peace had weakened the will of the Romans to resist, opening up the way for the more martial barbarians. This explanation, however, now is seen as too simplistic. After all, most of the barbarians were Christians themselves. And as for the barbarian invasions, for centuries the emperors had dealt with barbarian threats quite handily. In addition, aside from the Battle of Adrianople, it is difficult to identify many significant barbarian victories during their supposed military conquest. The barbarians occupied the west by means of infiltration, peaceful settlement, and persistence rather than by military superiority or right of conquest. The real question, it seems, is what factors made it possible for the barbarians to succeed at this point when they had been notable only for their failures in the past.

More recent thought identifies a multitude of interrelated causative factors. Some suggestions, ranging from volcanic eruptions to ethnic mixing to lead poisoning, can be easily dismissed. Others include the withdrawal of senatorial support, increasing administrative decentralization, barbarization of the army, the lack of organized resistance, economic collapse, overtaxation, corruption, manpower shortages, excessive bureaucracy, bad leadership, and just plain bad luck.

Furthermore, any satisfactory explanation for the fall of the west also must explain the survival of the east. It is clear, for example, that the east had more secure geographical frontiers, a stronger economy, a less well-entrenched senatorial order, a larger population, and a more dependable Roman military recruitment base, all of which increased the east's chances of survival. From this perspective, it may be that once the empire split into two halves, the decline of the west was virtually foreordained.

LEGACY OF ROME

The inventions suggested by the anonymous Roman reformer seem not to have been implemented in their own time. Can you think of other occasions on which imaginative ideas for weapons of war also have been ignored? Were any of them implemented at a later date?

And finally, it sometimes has been questioned whether the Western Roman Empire actually did fall: politically, it did, as barbarians—often Romanized barbarians—assumed the responsibility for governing different areas of the west. But most aspects of Roman culture, including language, literature, administration, law, and, in particular, the Christian religion, survived and were transmitted to later ages. In addition, the Western Roman Empire was revived under the Frankish king Charlemagne, who once again took the title of Augustus in the year 800, and the German-based Holy Roman Empire lasted from the eleventh century until its final dissolution in 1806. Meanwhile, however, the title of Caesar had been revived as *czar* in Russia, which claimed to be the successor of the Roman Empire until the end of the Russian monarchy in 1917. The whole question of the causes of and even the date of the fall of the Western Roman Empire is therefore full of complexity and nuance, and one can safely conclude that this controversy will never be definitively settled.

⇦ LOOKING BACK

During the fifth century, more and more of the Western Roman Empire fell under the control of barbarian leaders and peoples. By the end of the fifth century, the Western Roman Empire had ended; barbarians had established independent kingdoms throughout its former territory.

LOOKING AHEAD ⇨

Most surveys of Roman history stop at this point, if they get this far at all, leaving the reader believing that the barbarians had won and that the Roman Empire was effectively at an end. But by continuing the narrative of ancient history until the end of Late Antiquity, circa 650, a very different picture is presented.

THE BARBARIAN SETTLEMENT, CATASTROPHE VERSUS TRANSFORMATION

In a model prevalent since antiquity, which might be called the "Catastrophe Model," savage barbarian hordes have been blamed for waves of invasion during the fifth century CE that were the primary cause of the fall of the Western Roman Empire. This model was argued most persuasively in 1788 by Edward Gibbon in his *Decline and Fall of the Roman Empire*, one of the most influential historical studies of all time. These uncouth barbarians have been held responsible for the destruction of the western Roman government, for a decline in levels of economic productivity, and for the material destruction of Roman art and architecture. They also have been blamed for attempting, consciously or unconsciously, to destroy classical civilization and for creating a period of cultural decline and barrenness known ominously as the Dark Ages, when only faint glimmers of classical civilization were preserved by a few dedicated monks. The Catastrophe Model sees a barbarian settlement characterized by violent conquest, material destruction, severe economic decline, social and religious animosities between Romans and barbarians, and, in general, many changes from the Roman world. This view sees the fall of the western empire as being primarily due to external factors—the barbarian invaders—and continues to have eloquent supporters in the historical community.

Recent decades, however, informed by the work of Peter Brown in particular, as in his seminal study *The World of Late Antiquity* (1974), have brought the development of a different model regarding the causes and impact of the barbarian settlement on the Roman world. The "Transformation Model" posits largely peaceful integration and assimilation, punctuated only occasionally by spates of violence, in which, in most places, there was little actual conquest; minimal material destruction; economic decline caused not by the barbarians but by the general economic changes of the period; social and religious integration; and, in general, cultural, social, and administrative continuity from the Roman period. Proponents of the Transformation Model point out that it is difficult to find many battles that the barbarians won; indeed, most of the set battles were won by the Romans. It also is difficult to find signs of violent destruction in the archaeological record. The level of cultural decline, it is argued, was neither so precipitous nor so complete as once had been thought; indeed, there was an explosion of ecclesiastical writing. And religious animosities have been greatly exaggerated; except in Vandal Africa, Nicene Romans and Homoian barbarians in fact got along very well, even attending each other's services. The real issue, in this view, is what kind of internal changes allowed the barbarians to succeed when in the past the Roman government had been quite able to deal with barbarian threat.

Even more recently, however, proponents of the Catastrophe Model have pushed back. Bryan Ward-Perkins, in a slim book provocatively entitled *The Fall of Rome and the End of Civilization* (2005), argued that a catastrophic decline in the quality of life caused by the barbarian settlement could be quantitatively measured, and Peter Heather, in a massive study called *The Fall of the Roman Empire: A New History of Rome and the Barbarians* (2005), recapitulated decades of work arguing that the Roman Empire was indeed brought down by invading barbarians.

The proponents of both these models tend to be rather prescriptive in arguing their views. But what is more likely is that any ultimate answer to the question of the nature of the barbarian settlement, to the degree that one exists, will be a combination of elements drawn from both schools of thought.

FURTHER READING

Boak, Alfred E. R. *Manpower Shortage and the Fall of the Roman Empire in the West.* Ann Arbor: Univ. of Michigan Press, 1955.

Bowersock, G. W., P. Brown, and O. Grabar. *Late Antiquity: A Guide to the Postclassical World.* Cambridge, MA: Harvard Univ. Press, 1999.

Brown, Peter. *The World of Late Antiquity.* New York: Harcourt, Brace, Jovanovich, 1974.

Ferrill, Alfred. *The Fall of Rome: The Military Explanation.* London: Thames and Hudson, 1986.

Goffart, W., *Barbarians and Romans.* A.D. *418–584. The Techniques of Accommodation.* Princeton: Princeton Univ. Press, 1987.

Gordon, C.D., trans., *The Age of Attila. Fifth-Century Byzantium and the Barbarians.* Ann Arbor: Univ. of Michigan Press, 2013.

Harper, Kyle. *The Fate of Rome: Climate, Disease, and the End of an Empire.* Princeton: Princeton Univ. Press, 2017

Heather, Peter. *The Fall of the Roman Empire: A New History of Rome and the Barbarians.* Oxford: Oxford Univ. Press, 2005.

Kelly, Christopher. *Ruling the Later Roman Empire.* Cambridge, MA: Harvard Univ. Press, 2004.

Lenski, Noel E. *Failure of Empire: Valens and the Roman State in the Fourth Century A.D.* Berkeley: University of California Press, 2002.

MacGeorge, Penny. *Late Roman Warlords.* New York: Oxford Univ. Press, 2002.

Nathan, Geoffrey. "The Last Emperor: The Fate of Romulus Augustulus." *Classica et Mediaevalia* 43 (1992), 261–271.

O'Flynn, J. M. *Generalissimos of the Western Roman Empire.* Edmonton, Alberta, Canada: Univ. of Alberta Press, 1983.

Southern, P., and K. Dixon. *The Late Roman Army.* London: Batsford, 1996.

Ward-Perkins, Bryan. *The Fall of Rome and the End of Civilization.* Oxford: Oxford Univ. Press, 2005.

SOURCES

13.1 THE BATTLE OF ADRIANOPLE (378 CE)

AMMIANUS MARCELLINUS, *HISTORIES*, BOOK 31, CHAPTERS 12–14

In 376 CE, one year after the death of his elder and much abler brother, Valentinian I (364–375), the emperor Valens (364–378) allowed groups of Visigoths who were fleeing the Huns to settle in Roman territory south of the Danube River on the understanding that they would become taxpaying farmers and serve in the Roman army. Because of Roman mismanagement, the Visigoths revolted and in 378 Valens assembled the eastern Roman army to attack them. The subsequent Roman defeat at the Battle of Adrianople, chronicled by Ammianus Marcellinus, an army officer who became, with Livy and Tacitus, one of Rome's three greatest historians, was as disastrous as the previous Roman defeats at Cannae (216 BCE) and the Teutoburg Forest (9 CE). It also has been seen as marking the beginning of the "barbarian invasions" of the Roman Empire.

Source: C. D. Yonge, trans., *The Roman History of Ammianus Marcellinus during the Reigns of the Emperors Constantius, Julian, Jovianus, Valentinian, and Valens* (London: Bell, 1911), 609–618.

At this time Valens[1] was disturbed by a twofold anxiety,[2] having learned that the Lentienses[3] had been defeated and also because Sebastianus,[4] in the letters that he sent from time to time, exaggerated what had taken place by his pompous language. Therefore he advanced from Melanthias,[5] being eager by some glorious exploit to equal his youthful nephew,[6] by whose virtue he was greatly excited. He was at the head of a numerous force, neither unwarlike nor contemptible, and had united with them many veteran bands, among whom were several officers of high rank, especially Trajan,[7] who a little while before had been commander of the forces. And as by means of spies and observation it was ascertained that the enemy were intending to blockade the different roads by which the necessary supplies must come, with strong divisions he sent a sufficient force to prevent this, dispatching a body of the archers of the infantry and a squadron of cavalry, with all speed, to occupy the narrow passes in the neighborhood.

Three days later, when the barbarians, who were advancing slowly because they feared an attack in the unfavorable ground that they were traversing, arrived within fifteen miles (twenty-four kilometers) from the station of Nicaea,[8] which was the aim of their march, the emperor, with wanton impetuosity, resolved on attacking them instantly, because those who had been sent forward to reconnoiter (what led to such a mistake is unknown) affirmed that their entire body did not exceed ten thousand men. Marching on with his army in battle array, he came near the suburb of Adrianople,[9] where he

---

[1] Named co-emperor by Valentinian I (364–375) in 364, he became senior emperor when Valentinian died in 375.

[2] Resulting from his envy of the military successes of others.

[3] An Alamannic people of southern Germany, mentioned only by Ammianus, defeated by the western Roman army.

[4] A Roman general whose task it was to organize the Roman armies in Thrace and who won a few minor skirmishes with the Visigoths.

[5] An imperial villa in Thrace.

[6] Valens was jealous of the successes of the young western emperor Gratian (367–383), who had succeeded his father Valentinian I as western Augustus in 375.

[7] A Roman general who previously had defeated the New Persians.

[8] A city in Thrace, not the Nicaea in Anatolia.

[9] A city in Thrace west of Constantinople.

pitched his camp, strengthening it with a rampart of palisades, and then impatiently waited for Gratian. While here, Richomer, Count of the Domestics,[10] arrived, who had been sent on by that emperor with letters announcing his immediate approach and imploring Valens to wait a little while for him that he might share his danger, and not rashly face the danger before him single handed.

Valens took counsel with his officers as to what was best to be done. Some, following the advice of Sebastianus, recommended with urgency that he should at once go forth to battle, whereas Victor, Master of the Cavalry, a Sarmatian[11] by birth and a man of slow and cautious temper, recommended that he wait for his imperial colleague, and this advice was supported by several other officers, who suggested that the reinforcement of the Gallic army would be likely to awe the fiery arrogance of the barbarians. The fatal obstinacy of the emperor, however, prevailed, fortified by the flattery of certain barbarian chieftains, who advised him to hasten with all speed so that Gratian might have no share in a victory that, as they fancied, already almost was gained.

And while all necessary preparations were being made for the battle, a priest of the Christian religion, as he called himself, having been sent by Fritigern[12] as his ambassador, came, with some colleagues of low rank, to the emperor's camp. Having been received with courtesy, he presented a letter from that chieftain, openly requesting that the emperor would grant to him and to his followers, who now were exiles from their native homes, from which they had been driven by the rapid invasions of savage nations,[13] Thrace,[14] with all its flocks and all its crops, for a habitation. And if Valens would consent to this, Fritigern would agree to a perpetual peace. In addition to this message, the same Christian, as one acquainted with his commander's

secrets, and well trusted, produced other secret letters from his chieftain who, being full of craft and every resource of deceit, informed Valens, as one who was hereafter to be his friend and ally, that he had no other means to appease the ferocity of his countrymen, or to induce them to accept conditions advantageous to the Roman state, unless from time to time he showed them an army under arms close at hand, and by frightening them with the name of the emperor, recalled them from their mischievous eagerness for fighting. The ambassadors retired unsuccessful, having been looked on as suspicious characters by the emperor.

When the day broke that the annals mark as the fifth before the Ides of August,[15] the Roman standards were advanced with haste, the baggage having been placed close to the walls of Adrianople under a sufficient guard of soldiers of the legions. The treasures and the chief insignia of the emperor's rank were within the walls, with the Prefect and the principal members of the council.[16] Then, having traversed the broken ground that divided the two armies, as the burning day was progressing toward noon, at last, after marching eight miles (thirteen kilometers), our men came in sight of the wagons of the enemy, which had been stated by the scouts to be all arranged in a circle. According to their custom, the barbarian host raised a fierce and hideous yell while the Roman generals marshaled their line of battle. The right wing of the cavalry was placed in front; the chief portion of the infantry was kept in reserve. But the left wing of the cavalry, of which a considerable number were still straggling on the road, were advancing with speed, although with great difficulty. While this wing was deploying, not as yet meeting with any obstacle, the barbarians being alarmed at the terrible clang of their arms and the threatening crash of their shields, because a large portion of their own army was still at a distance, under Alatheus and

---

[10] A western general; the "Protectors and Domestics" were elite palace guards attendant on the emperor.

[11] A barbarian people of the southern Russian steppes.

[12] One of the leaders of the Visigoths who had crossed the Danube.

[13] The Huns.

[14] A Balkan region south of the lower Danube River.

---

[15] August 9.

[16] The most important officials of the imperial court traveled with the emperor.

Saphrax,[17] and, although sent for, had not yet arrived, again sent ambassadors to ask for peace.

The emperor was offended at the lowness of their rank, and replied that if they wished to make a lasting treaty they must send him nobles of sufficient dignity. They designedly delayed, in order by the fallacious truce that subsisted during the negotiation to give time for their cavalry to return, whom they looked upon as close at hand, and for our soldiers, already suffering from the summer heat, to become parched and exhausted by the conflagration of the vast plain, for the enemy had, with this object, set fire to the crops by means of burning faggots and fuel. To this evil another was added, that both men and cattle were suffering from extreme hunger.

In the meantime Fritigern, being skilful in divining the future and fearing a doubtful struggle, on his own authority sent one of his men as a herald, requesting that some nobles and picked men should at once be sent to him as hostages for his safety, whereas he himself would fearlessly bring us both military aid and supplies. The proposition of this formidable chief was received with praise and approbation, and the Tribune Equitius, a relation of Valens who was at that time Caretaker of the Palace, was appointed, with general consent, to go with all speed to the barbarians as a hostage. But he refused, because he had once been taken prisoner by the enemy, and had escaped from Dibaltum,[18] so that he feared their vengeful anger. Upon this Richomer voluntarily offered himself, and willingly undertook to go, thinking it a bold action, and one becoming a brave man; and so he set out, bearing vouchers of his rank and high birth. As he was on his way toward the enemy's camp, the accompanying archers and the Scutarii,[19] who on that occasion were under the command of Bacurius, a native

of Iberia,[20] and of Cassio, yielded, while on their march, to an indiscreet impetuosity, and on approaching the enemy first attacked them rashly and then by a cowardly flight disgraced the beginning of the campaign. This ill-timed attack frustrated the willing services of Richomer, as he was not permitted to proceed. In the meantime the cavalry of the Goths had returned with Alatheus and Saphrax, and with them a battalion of Alans.[21] These, descending from the mountains like a thunderbolt, spread confusion and slaughter among all whom in their rapid charge they encountered.

And while arms and missiles of all kinds were meeting in fierce conflict and Bellona,[22] blowing her mournful trumpet, was raging more fiercely than usual to inflict disaster on the Romans, our men began to retreat. But presently, roused by the reproaches of their officers, they made a fresh stand, and the battle increased like a conflagration, terrifying our soldiers, numbers of whom were pierced by strokes from the javelins hurled at them and from arrows. Then the two lines of battle dashed against each other, like the beaks or rams of ships, and thrusting with all their might were tossed to and fro, like the waves of the sea. Our left wing had advanced actually up to the wagons, with the intent to push on still further if they were properly supported, but they were deserted by the rest of the cavalry and so pressed upon by the superior numbers of the enemy that they were overwhelmed and beaten down, like the ruin of a vast rampart. Presently, our infantry also was left unsupported and the different companies became so huddled together that a soldier could hardly draw his sword or withdraw his hand after he had once stretched it out. And by this time such clouds of dust arose that it was scarcely possible to see the sky, which resounded with horrible cries; and in consequence, the darts, which were bearing

---

[17] Regents for the boy Viderichus, chieftain of another band of Goths.

[18] An ancient Roman military colony in modern Bulgaria on the Black Sea, site of a Roman defeat by the Visigoths in 376.

[19] Shield-bearing cavalry.

[20] Not Spanish Iberia but the Iberia north of Armenia between the Black and Caspian seas. The Christian Kingdom of Iberia was sometimes independent, sometimes a client state of Rome, and sometimes a vassal of the New Persians.

[21] Iranian steppe nomads living north of the Black Sea who often served in the Roman army.

[22] An ancient Italian war goddess.

death on every side, reached their mark, and fell with deadly effect, because no one could see them beforehand so as to guard against them.

But when the barbarians, rushing on with their enormous host, beat down our horses and men and left no spot to which our ranks could fall back to deploy, while they were so closely packed that it was impossible to escape by forcing a way through them, our men at last began to despise death, and again took to their swords and slew all they encountered, while with mutual blows of battle-axes, helmets and breastplates were dashed in pieces. Then, you might see the barbarian towering in his fierceness, hissing or shouting, fall with his legs pierced through, or his right hand cut off, sword and all, or his side transfixed, and still, in the last gasp of life, casting round him defiant glances. The plain was covered with carcasses, strewing the mutual ruin of the combatants and the groans of the dying or of men fearfully wounded were intense, and caused great dismay all around.

Amid all this great tumult and confusion our infantry were exhausted by toil and danger, until at last they had neither strength left to fight nor spirits to plan anything. Their spears were broken by the frequent collisions, so that they were forced to content themselves with their drawn swords, which they thrust into the dense battalions of the enemy, disregarding their own safety and seeing that every possibility of escape was cut off from them. The ground, covered with streams of blood, made their feet slip, so that all that they endeavored to do was to sell their lives as dearly as possible, and with such vehemence did they resist their enemies who pressed on them, that some were even killed by their own weapons. At last one black pool of blood disfigured everything and wherever the eye turned, it could see nothing but piled-up heaps of dead and lifeless corpses trampled on without mercy.

The sun being now high in the heavens scorched the Romans, who were emaciated by hunger, worn out with toil, and scarcely able to support even the weight of their armor. At last our columns were entirely beaten back by the overpowering weight of the barbarians, and so they took to disorderly flight, which is the only resource in extremity, each man trying to save himself as well as he could. While they were all flying and scattering themselves over roads with which they were unacquainted, the emperor, bewildered with terrible fear, made his way over heaps of dead and fled to the battalions of the Lancearii and the Mattiarii,[23] who, until the superior numbers of the enemy became wholly irresistible, stood firm and immovable. As soon as he saw him, Trajan exclaimed that all hope was lost, unless the emperor, thus deserted by his guards, could be protected by the aid of his foreign allies.

When this exclamation was heard, a Count named Victor hastened to bring up with all speed the Batavians,[24] who were placed in the reserve and who ought to have been near at hand, to the emperor's assistance; but as none of them could be found, he too retreated, and in a similar manner Richomer and Saturninus[25] saved themselves from danger. So now, with rage flashing in their eyes, the barbarians pursued our men, who were in a state of torpor. Many were slain without knowing who smote them, some were overwhelmed by the mere weight of the crowd that pressed upon them, and some were slain by wounds inflicted by their own comrades. The barbarians spared neither those who yielded nor those who resisted. Besides these, many half slain lay blocking up the roads, unable to endure the torture of their wounds, and heaps of dead horses were piled up and filled the plain with their carcasses. At last a dark moonless night put an end to the irremediable disaster that cost the Roman state so dear.

Just when it first became dark, the emperor being among a crowd of common soldiers, as it was believed, for no one said either that he had seen him, or been near him, was mortally wounded with an arrow, and, very shortly after, died, although his body was never found. For as some of the enemy loitered for a long time about the field in order to plunder the dead, none of the defeated army or of the inhabitants ventured to go to them.

---

[23] Elite units of the Roman army.

[24] A Roman military unit named after peoples from the mouth of the Rhine River.

[25] Roman Master of Soldiers who eventually negotiated a treaty with the Visigoths in 382 and was named Consul for 383.

A similar fate befell the Caesar Decius,[26] when fighting vigorously against the barbarians, for he was thrown by his horse falling, which he had been unable to hold, and was plunged into a swamp, out of which he could never emerge, nor could his body be found.

Others report that Valens did not die immediately, but that he was borne by a small body of picked soldiers and eunuchs to a cabin in the neighborhood, which was strongly built, with two storeys; and that while these unskillful hands were tending his wounds, the cottage was surrounded by the enemy, although they did not know who was in it. Still, however, he was saved from the disgrace of being made a prisoner. For when his pursuers, while vainly attempting to force the barred doors, were assailed with arrows from the roof, they, not to lose by so inconvenient a delay the opportunity of collecting plunder, gathered some faggots and stubble and setting fire to them, burnt down the building along with those who were in it. But one of the soldiers dropped from the windows, and, being taken prisoner by the barbarians, revealed to them what had taken place, which caused them great concern, because they looked upon themselves as defrauded of great glory in not having taken the ruler of the Roman state alive. This same young man afterward secretly returned to our people and gave this account of the affair. When Spain had been recovered after a similar disaster, we are told that one of the Scipios was lost in a fire, the tower in which he had taken refuge having been burnt.[27] At all events it is certain that neither Scipio nor Valens enjoyed that last honor of the dead, a regular funeral.

Many illustrious men fell in this disastrous defeat, and among them one of the most remarkable was Trajan, and another was Sebastian. There perished also thirty-five unassigned Tribunes, many unit commanders, and Valerianus and Equitius, one of whom was Master of the Horse and the other Caretaker of the Palace. Potentius, too, Tribune of the Promoti,[28] fell in the flower of his age, a man respected by all persons of virtue, and recommended by the merits of his father, Ursicinus,[29] who had formerly been Master of Soldiers, as well as by his own. Scarcely one-third of the whole army escaped.

Nor, except the Battle of Cannae,[30] is so destructive a slaughter recorded in our annals, although even in the times of their prosperity, the Romans have more than once had to deplore the uncertainty of war and have for a time succumbed to evil fortune. Such was the death of Valens, when he was about fifty years old and had reigned rather less than fourteen years.

---

[26] Trajan Decius (249–251), killed by the Goths at the Battle of Abritus on the lower Danube, was the first Roman emperor to die in battle.

[27] Gnaeus Scipio, the uncle of Scipio Africanus, killed in Spain in 211 BCE when, pursued by the Carthaginians, he took refuge in a tower and was burned to death.

[28] A cavalry unit.

[29] A high-ranking Roman general during the 350s, highly praised by Ammianus.

[30] In 216 BCE, when the Romans were defeated by Hannibal.

OROSIUS, *HISTORY AGAINST THE PAGANS*, BOOK 7, CHAPTERS 38–40

In the early years of the fifth century, barbarian groups made their way into the western empire. In 401, the Visigoths invaded Italy, and on the last day of 406, a barbarian horde crossed the frozen Rhine. For a time, the crafty western general Stilicho was able to keep the barbarians at bay, but after the emperor Honorius had Stilicho executed for treason in 408, the fall of the west began in earnest, punctuated by the Visigothic sack of Rome in 410. Although the sack caused little or no actual architectural damage and was more akin to some rowdy soldiers getting out of hand, the psychological damage was immense. "Roma invicta," "Unconquered Rome," was no longer unconquered. Encouraged by Bishop Augustine of Hippo, the Christian historiographer Orosius painted a rather biased picture of Rome's past military history, arguing that throughout its history, when the pagan gods still were worshipped, Rome had suffered military defeats, a point already acknowledged, however, by Ammianus in his account of the Battle of Adrianople.

Source: Irving W. Raymond, trans., *Seven Books of History against the Pagans. The Apology of Paulus Orosius* (New York: Columbia Univ. Press, 1936).

Meanwhile Count Stilicho,[31] who was sprung from the Vandals, that unwarlike, greedy, treacherous, and crafty people, thought it a small matter that he held the rule under the emperor, and, as was reported by many, was attempting in some manner to place upon the throne his own son Eucherius, who had been planning the persecution of the Christians ever since he was a boy and a private citizen. Hence, when Alaric and the whole Gothic nation begged humbly and straightforwardly for peace on very favorable terms and also for some place to settle, Stilicho supported them by a secret alliance, but in the name of the state refused them the opportunity of either making war or peace, reserving them to wear down and to intimidate the state. Moreover, other nations irresistible in numbers and might who are now oppressing the provinces of Gaul and Spain, namely, the Alans, Suevi, and Vandals, as well as the Burgundians,[32] were induced by Stilicho to take arms on their own initiative and were aroused when once their fear of Rome was removed. Stilicho's plan was to batter the Rhine frontier and strike against the Two Gauls.[33] This wretched man hoped that in this dangerous situation he could thereby wrest the imperial dignity from his son-in-law[34] and give it to his son, and that it would be as easy to repress the barbarian nations as it was to arouse them.

When the character of these crimes was openly revealed to the emperor Honorius and to the Roman army, the soldiers very properly mutinied and killed Stilicho, who, in order to clothe one boy with the royal purple had imperiled the blood of the whole human race. Eucherius also was slain, who for the sake of gaining the favor of the pagans had threatened that he would celebrate the beginning of his reign by the restoration of the temples and by the overthrow of the churches. Several accomplices also were punished for their wicked plots. Thus the churches of Christ and the devout

---

[31] Stilicho was the son of a Roman mother and a Roman general of Vandal origin; although in the modern literature he often is portrayed as a barbarian, he was thoroughly Roman.

[32] All of whom crossed the frozen Rhine River into Gaul on the last day of the year 406; there is no other evidence that Stilicho was involved in this.

[33] The two imperial dioceses of Gaul, "Viennensis" and "Gallia."

[34] The emperor Honorius (395–423), who married, in succession, Stilicho's two daughters Maria and Thermantia. Stilicho himself was married to Honorius' cousin Serena.

emperor were freed as well as avenged with very little trouble and with the punishment of but a few persons.

After this great increase of blasphemies without any evidence of repentance, the final, long-impending doom overtook the City.[35] Alaric appeared before trembling Rome, laid siege, spread confusion, and broke into the City. He first, however, gave orders that all those who had taken refuge in sacred places, especially in the basilicas of the holy Apostles Peter and Paul, should be permitted to remain inviolate and unmolested. He allowed his men to devote themselves to plunder as much as they wished, but he gave orders that they should refrain from bloodshed. A further proof that the storming of the City was due to the wrath of God rather than to the bravery of the enemy is shown by the fact that the blessed Innocent, the bishop of Rome, who at that time was at Ravenna through the hidden providence of God,[36] even as Lot the Just[37] was withdrawn from the Sodomites, did not witness the destruction of the sinful populace.

While the barbarians were roaming through the City, one of the Goths, a powerful man and a Christian, chanced to find in a church building a virgin advanced in years who had dedicated herself to God. When he respectfully asked her for gold and silver, she declared with the firmness of her faith that she had a large amount in her possession and that she would bring it forth at once. She did so. Observing that the barbarian was astonished at the size, weight, and beauty of the riches displayed, even though he did not know the nature of the vessels, the virgin of Christ then said to him: "These are the sacred vessels of the Apostle Peter. Presume, if you dare! You will have to answer for the deed.

As for me, because I cannot protect them, I dare not keep them."

The barbarian, stirred to religious awe through the fear of God and by the virgin's faith, sent word of the incident to Alaric. He ordered that all the vessels, just as they were, should be brought back immediately to the basilica of the Apostle, and that the virgin also, together with all Christians who might join the procession, should be conducted thither under escort. The building, it is said, was at a considerable distance from the sacred places, with half the city lying between. Consequently the gold and silver vessels were distributed, each to a different person. They were carried high above the head in plain sight, to the wonder of all beholders. The pious procession was guarded by a double line of drawn swords; Romans and barbarians in concert raised a hymn to God in public. In the sacking of the City the trumpet of salvation sounded far and wide and smote the ears of all with its invitation, even those lying in hiding. From every quarter the vessels of Christ mingled with the vessels of Peter, and many pagans even joined the Christians in making profession, although not in true faith. In this way they escaped, but only for a time, that their confusion might afterward be the greater.

The more densely the Roman refugees flocked together, the more eagerly their barbarian protectors surrounded them. O sacred and inscrutable discernment of the divine judgment! O glorious trumpet of Christian warfare that, inviting by its sweet notes all without distinction to life, leaves those who, for want of obedience, cannot be roused to salvation, to meet their death for want of excuse!

The third day after they had entered the City, the barbarians departed of their own accord. They had, it is true, burned a certain number of buildings, but even this fire was not so great as that which had been caused by accident in the seven hundredth year of Rome.[38] Indeed, if I review the conflagration produced during the spectacles of Nero, her own emperor, this later fire, brought on

---

[35] Rome was referred to simply as "the City."

[36] The bishop of Rome Innocent (401–417) fled Rome and took refuge with the emperor Honorius in Ravenna before the sack, an act that, despite Orosius' spin, rather damaged his credibility.

[37] In the Bible, Lot was given by God the opportunity to flee with his family from the city of Sodom before it was destroyed.

---

[38] 52 BCE, when a funeral pyre in the forum for the murdered politician Clodius got out of control and burned the Senate house and a basilica built by Cato the Elder.

by the anger of the conqueror, will surely bear no comparison with the former, which was kindled by the wantonness of the prince. Nor do I need in a comparison of this sort to mention the Gauls, who, after burning and sacking the City, camped upon her ashes for almost an entire year.[39] Moreover, to remove all doubt that the enemy were permitted to act in this manner in order to chastise the proud, wanton, and blasphemous City, it may be pointed out that her most magnificent sites, which the Goths were unable to set on fire, were destroyed at this time by lightning.[40]

It was in the one thousand one hundred and sixty-fourth year of the City that Alaric stormed Rome. Although the memory of the event is still fresh, anyone who saw the numbers of the Romans themselves and listened to their talk would think that "nothing had happened," as they themselves admit, unless perhaps he were to notice some charred ruins still remaining. When the City was stormed, Placidia,[41] the daughter of the princely Theodosius[42] and sister of the emperors Arcadius and Honorius, was captured and taken to wife by Alaric's kinsman,[43] as if she had been a hostage given by Rome as a special pledge, according to divine decree. Thus, through her alliance with the powerful barbarian king, Placidia did much to benefit the state.

Meanwhile, as I have said, the Alans, Suevi, and Vandals, as well as many others with them, overwhelmed the Franks, crossed the Rhine, invaded Gaul, and advanced in their onward rush as far as the Pyrenees. Checked for the time being by this barrier, they poured back over the neighboring provinces.[44]

---

[39] The sack of Rome by the Gauls in 390 BCE, in this interpretation the last time that Rome had been captured by a foreign enemy

[40] This is the only evidence for lightning strikes during this sack.

[41] Galla Placidia, mother of the emperor Valentinian III (425–455) and virtual ruler of the western empire during much of his reign.

[42] The emperor Theodosius I (379–395), who was succeeded by his sons Arcadius (395–408) in the eastern empire and Honorius in the west.

[43] In 414, Galla Placidia married the Gothic king Athaulf (410–415); their son Theodosius died in infancy.

[44] The Vandals and Alans crossed into Spain in 409 CE, the year before the sack of Rome, when the Pyrenees passes were left undefended.

AUGUSTINE, *CITY OF GOD*, BOOK 1

The popular perception of the sack of Rome by the Visigoths in 410, as portrayed in this 1962 depiction in *National Geographic*, is one of hulking, savage barbarians looting property, burning buildings, and harassing respectable Roman matrons. The reality, as portrayed by Orosius above and Augustine below, was rather different.

After the sack of Rome in 410, dedicated pagans argued that Rome was suffering misfortunes because of the abandonment of the old Roman gods who had made Rome great. These arguments were very convincing, so in response, Bishop Augustine of Hippo in North Africa wrote his massive work, *On the City of God*, in which he made the counterargument that everything that happened on earth was part of God's plan and that people should be more concerned not with the earthly city but with the heavenly city. He proposed that the barbarian sack of Rome in fact had been quite genteel, as far as sacks went, as a result of God's influence because any show of mercy or clemency during wartime must have come from God. In the course of discussing the question of why the good and the wicked suffered equally, Augustine argued that the misfortunes that he acknowledged were besetting the Roman world were the fault of sinful Christians, not only those who were guilty of gross wickedness but also those who were guilty of petty sins. Thus, Augustine proposed that Christian virgins deserved blame for their own violation at the hands of barbarians because they supposedly indulged in secret pride about their chastity.

Source: Marcus Dods, trans., *The Works of Augustine, Bishop of Hippo. The City of God* (Edinburgh: Clark, 1871).

Preface

The glorious City of God is my theme in this work, which you, my dearest son Marcellinus,[45] suggested, and which is due to you by my promise. I have undertaken its defense against those who prefer their own gods to the founder of this city, a city surpassingly glorious, whether we view it as it still lives by

---

[45] An imperial Tribune and Notary (all-purpose functionary) who oversaw the Council of Carthage in 411, which condemned the Donatists, a schismatic Christian sect that had originated during the Great Persecution of Diocletian.

faith in this fleeting course of time, and sojourns as a stranger in the midst of the ungodly, or as it shall dwell in the fixed stability of its eternal seat, which it now with patience waits for. A great work this, and an arduous one, but God is my helper. For I am aware of what ability is requisite to persuade the proud how great is the virtue of humility, which raises us, not by a quite human arrogance but by a divine grace above all earthly dignities that totter on this shifting scene. For the king and founder of this city of which we speak has in scripture uttered to his people a dictum of the divine law in these words, "God resists the proud, but gives grace to the humble."[46] But this, which is God's prerogative, the inflated ambition of a proud spirit also affects, and dearly loves that this be numbered among its attributes, to "show pity to the humbled soul, and crush the sons of pride."[47] And therefore, as the plan of this work we have undertaken requires, and as occasion offers, we must speak also of the earthly city, which, although it be mistress of the nations, is itself ruled by its lust of rule.

Chapter 1: Of the Adversaries of the Name of Christ, whom the Barbarians for Christ's Sake Spared when they Stormed the City.

For to this earthly city belong the enemies against whom I have to defend the City of God. Many of them, indeed, being reclaimed from their ungodly error have become sufficiently creditable citizens of this city,[48] but many are so inflamed with hatred against it and are so ungrateful to its redeemer for his signal benefits as to forget that they would now be unable to utter a single word to its prejudice had they not found in its sacred places, as they fled from the enemy's steel, that life in which they now boast themselves.[49] Are not those very Romans, who were spared by the barbarians through their respect for Christ, become enemies to the name of Christ? The reliquaries of the martyrs and the churches of the apostles bear witness to this, for in the sack of the city they were open sanctuary for all who fled to them, whether Christian or pagan. To their very threshold the bloodthirsty enemy raged; there his murderous fury owned a limit. Thither did such of the enemy as had any pity convey those to whom they had given quarter, lest any less mercifully disposed might fall upon them. And, indeed, when even those murderers who everywhere else showed themselves pitiless came to those spots where that was forbidden which the license of war permitted in every other place, their furious rage for slaughter was bridled and their eagerness to take prisoners[50] was quenched.

Thus escaped multitudes who now reproach the Christian religion, and impute to Christ the ills that have befallen their city. But the preservation of their own life, a boon that they owe to the respect entertained for Christ by the barbarians, they attribute not to our Christ but to their own good luck. They ought rather, had they any right perceptions, to attribute the severities and hardships inflicted by their enemies to the divine providence that is accustomed to reform the depraved manners of men by chastisement and that exercises with similar afflictions the righteous and praiseworthy, either translating them, when they have passed through the trial, to a better world, or detaining them still on earth for other purposes. And they ought to attribute it to the spirit of these Christian times, that, contrary to the custom of war, these bloodthirsty barbarians spared them, and spared them for Christ's sake, whether this mercy actually was shown in random places or was manifested in those places specially dedicated to Christ's name, of which the very largest were selected as sanctuaries, so that full scope thus might be given to the expansive compassion that desired that a large multitude might find shelter there. Therefore they ought to give God thanks and with sincere confession flee for refuge to his name, so that they may escape the punishment of eternal fire, they who with lying lips took upon them this name so that they might escape the punishment of present

[46] From the book of James 4:6 in the New Testament.
[47] A quotation from Vergil's *Aeneid*, where, in the underworld, Aeneas' father Anchises advises the Romans to "spare the vanquished and beat down the proud."
[48] A reference to barbarian Christians, perhaps even to those who espoused the so-called Arian creed.
[49] Pagans who took refuge in Christian churches in order to be secure from barbarians.

[50] Captives, who could be held for ransom or sold as slaves, were another form of loot.

destruction. For of those whom you see insolently and shamelessly insulting the servants of Christ, there are numbers who would not have escaped that destruction and slaughter had they not pretended that they themselves were Christ's servants. Yet now, in ungrateful pride and most impious madness, and at the risk of being punished in everlasting darkness, they perversely oppose that name under which they fraudulently protected themselves for the sake of enjoying the light of this brief life.

Chapter 4: Of the Churches of the Apostles that Protected from the Barbarians all who Fled to Them.

Troy itself, the mother of the Roman people, was not able to protect its own citizens in the sacred places of their gods from the fire and sword of the Greeks, although the Greeks worshipped the same gods. The place consecrated to a great goddess was chosen not so that no one might be led out from it as a captive but so that all the captives might be detained in it.[51] Compare now this "asylum," the asylum not of an ordinary god, not of one of the rank and file of gods, but of Jupiter's own sister and wife, the queen of all the gods, with the churches built in memory of the apostles. Into it were collected the spoils rescued from the blazing temples and snatched from the gods, not that they might be restored to the vanquished but to be divided among the victors, whereas into the churches was carried back, with the most religious observance and respect, everything that belonged to them, even though found elsewhere. There liberty was lost; here preserved. There bondage was strict; here it was strictly excluded. Into that temple men were driven to become the chattels of their enemies; into these churches people were led by their relenting foes so that they might be at liberty. In sum, the "gentle" Greeks appropriated that temple of Juno to the purposes of their own avarice and pride, whereas these churches of Christ were chosen even by the savage barbarians as the fit scenes for humility and mercy.

---

[51] In Vergil's *Aeneid,* when Aeneas was looking for his wife Creusa, he saw Trojan captives being kept in the Temple of Juno (Greek Hera).

Chapter 7: That the Cruelties that Occurred in the Sack of Rome were in Accordance with the Custom of War, whereas the Acts of Clemency Resulted from the Influence of Christ's Name

All the despoiling that Rome was exposed to in the recent calamity, all the slaughter, plundering, burning, and misery, was the result of the custom of war. But what was novel was that savage barbarians showed themselves in so gentle a guise, that the largest churches were chosen and set apart for the purpose of being filled with the people to whom quarter was given, and that in them none were slain, from them none forcibly dragged. That into them many were led by their relenting enemies to be set at liberty, and that from them none were led into slavery by merciless foes. Whoever does not see that this is to be attributed to the name of Christ, and to the Christian temper, is blind. Whoever sees this, and gives no praise, is ungrateful. Whoever hinders anyone from praising it is mad. Far be it from any prudent man to impute this clemency to the barbarians. Their fierce and bloody minds were awed and bridled and marvelously tempered by him who so long before said by his prophet, "I will visit their transgression with the rod, and their iniquities with stripes; nevertheless my loving-kindness will I not utterly take from them."[52]

Chapter 8: Of the Advantages and Disadvantages that often Indiscriminately Accrue to the Good and the Wicked

As for the good things of this life, and its ills, God has willed that these should be common to both, that we might not too eagerly covet the things that wicked people are seen equally to enjoy, nor shrink with an unseemly fear from the ills that even good people often suffer. If every sin were now visited with manifest punishment, nothing would seem to be reserved for the final judgment; on the other hand, if no sin received a plainly divine punishment, it would be concluded that there is no divine

---

[52] Psalms 89:32–33.

providence at all. And so of the good things of this life. If God did not by a very visible liberality confer these on some of those persons who ask for them, we should say that these good things were not at his disposal. And if he gave them to all who sought them, we should suppose that such were the only rewards of his service, and such a service would make us not godly, but greedy rather, and covetous. Wherefore, although good and bad people suffer alike, we must not suppose that there is no difference among the people themselves because there is no difference in what they both suffer. And thus it is that in the same affliction the wicked detest God and blaspheme, whereas the good pray and praise. So material a difference does it make, not what ills are suffered, but what kind of person suffers them.

Chapter 9: Of the Reasons for Administering Correction to Bad and Good Together

What, then, have the Christians suffered in that calamitous period that would not profit everyone who duly and faithfully considered the following circumstances? First of all, they must humbly consider those very sins that have provoked God to fill the world with such terrible disasters, for although they be far from the excesses of wicked, immoral, and ungodly persons, yet they do not judge themselves so clean removed from all faults as to be too good to suffer for these even temporal ills. For all persons, however laudably they live, yet yield in some points to the lust of the flesh. Even if they do not fall into gross enormity of wickedness, and abandoned viciousness, and abominable profanity, yet they slip into some sins, either rarely or so much the more frequently as the sins seem of less account. But not to mention this, where can we readily find anyone who holds in fit and just estimation those persons on account of whose revolting pride, luxury, and avarice, and cursed iniquities and impiety, God now smites the earth as his predictions threatened? Where is the person who deals with them in the manner in which it becomes us to deal with them? For often we wickedly blind ourselves to opportunities for teaching and admonishing them, sometimes even for reprimanding and chiding them, either because we shrink from the labor or are ashamed to offend them, or because we

fear to lose good friendships, lest this should stand in the way of our advancement, or injure us in some worldly matter, which either our covetous disposition desires to obtain, or our weakness shrinks from losing. So that, although the conduct of the wicked is distasteful to the good, and therefore they do not fall with them into that damnation which in the next life awaits such persons, yet, because they spare their damnable sins through fear, therefore, even though their own sins be slight and venial, they are justly whipped with the wicked in this world, although in eternity they quite escape punishment. Justly, when God afflicts them in common with the wicked, do they find this life bitter, through love of whose sweetness they declined to be bitter toward these sinners.

Chapter 28: By what Judgment of God the Enemy was Permitted to Indulge his Lust on the Bodies of Continent Christians

Even faithful women, I say, must not complain that permission was given to the barbarians so grossly to outrage them, nor must they allow themselves to believe that God overlooked their character when he permitted acts that no one with impunity commits. For some most flagrant and wicked desires are allowed free play at present by the secret judgment of God, and are reserved to the public and final judgment. Moreover, it is possible that those Christian women, who are unconscious of any undue pride on account of their virtuous chastity, whereby they sinlessly suffered the violence of their captors, had yet some lurking infirmity that might have betrayed them into a proud and contemptuous bearing, had they not been subjected to the humiliation that befell them in the taking of the city. As, therefore, some men were removed by death, so that no wickedness might change their disposition, so these women were outraged lest prosperity should corrupt their modesty. Neither those women then, who were already puffed up by the circumstance that they were still virgins, nor those who might have been so puffed up had they not been exposed to the violence of the enemy, lost their chastity, but rather gained humility; the former were saved from pride already cherished, the latter from pride that would shortly have grown upon them.

PROCOPIUS, *HISTORY OF THE WARS*, BOOK 3, CHAPTER 5

A gold solidus of the short-lived emperor Petronius Maximus (455), who had the misfortune to be emperor during the Vandal sack of Rome in 455. The obverse legend reads "Our Lord Petronius Maximus Dutiful and Fortunate Augustus," whereas the reverse reads "Victory of the Emperors" and shows Maximus holding a long cross in one hand and the goddess Victory in the other and trampling the serpent of heresy. The letters "RM" denote the Rome mint, and "COMOB" is an abbreviation for the "Count of Pure Gold," who was responsible for the gold content in the coin.

As the fifth century progressed, barbarian kingdoms coalesced in the Western Roman Empire: the Visigoths in Aquitania in Gaul, the Vandals in North Africa, and the Burgundians in central Gaul. It appeared that barbarians were taking over. Paradoxically, however, this barbarian expansion was not accomplished by military means. There were only a few marquee battles, and most of those, such as the Battle of the Mauriac Plain in 451 against the Huns, were won by the Romans. But the western empire was clearly weakened, as seen in the much less well-attested sack of Rome by the Vandals in 455 CE, which demonstrated that the Roman government no longer could protect even the city of Rome. This sack lasted some eighteen days and was much more lengthy and more thorough than the genteel sack by the Visigoths in 410, which went on for only three days. By 455 it was clear that the Western Roman Empire was failing fast, not because of barbarian invasion but because of its own weaknesses. One more sack of the venerable city simply did not have the same shock-and-awe factor that it had forty-five years earlier. The account of the sack, given nearly a century later by the Byzantine historian Procopius, begins with a typical attempt to blame it on personal animus, the result of the lust of Valentinian III for the virtuous wife of the senator Petronius Maximus, in much the same way that the creation of the Roman Republic resulted from the lust of Sextus Tarquin for the virtuous Lucretia.

Source: H. B. Dewing, trans., *Procopius. History of the Wars, Books III and IV* (Cambridge, MA: Harvard Univ. Press, 1916), 57–49..

And I shall now relate in what manner Valentinian died. There was a certain Maximus,[53] a Roman senator, of the house of that Maximus,[54] who, while usurping the imperial power, was overthrown by the elder Theodosius and put to death, and on whose account also the Romans celebrate the annual festival named from the defeat of Maximus.[55] This younger Maximus was married to a woman discreet in her ways and exceedingly famous for her beauty. For this reason a desire came over Valentinian to have her to wife. And because it was impossible, much as he wished it, to meet her, he plotted an unholy deed and carried it to fulfillment. For he summoned Maximus to the palace and sat down with him to a game of dice, and a certain sum was set as a penalty for the loser. The emperor won in this game, and receiving Maximus' ring as a pledge for the agreed amount. He sent it to Maximus' house, instructing the messenger to tell the wife of Maximus that her husband bade her come as quickly as possible to the palace to salute the queen Eudoxia.[56] And she, judging by the ring that the message was from Maximus, entered her litter and was conveyed to the emperor's court. She was received by those who had been assigned this service by the emperor and led into a certain room far removed from the women's apartments, where Valentinian met her and violated her.[57] She, after this outrage, went to her husband's house weeping and feeling the deepest possible grief because of her misfortune, and she cast many curses upon Maximus as having provided the cause for what had been done. Maximus, accordingly, became exceedingly aggrieved at what had come to pass and straightway entered into a conspiracy against the emperor.

Maximus slew the emperor[58] with no trouble and secured the tyranny, and he married Eudoxia against her will. For the wife to whom he had been wedded had died not long before. And on one occasion in private he made the statement to Eudoxia that it was all for the sake of her love that he had carried out all that he had done. And because she felt a repulsion for Maximus even before that time, and had been desirous of exacting vengeance from him for the wrong done Valentinian, his words made her swell with rage still more against him, and led her on to carry out her plot, because she had heard Maximus say that on account of her the misfortune had befallen her husband. And as soon as day came, she sent to Carthage entreating Gaiseric to avenge Valentinian,[59] who had been destroyed by an unholy man, in a manner unworthy both of himself and of his imperial station, and to deliver her, because she was suffering unholy treatment at the hand of the tyrant. And she impressed it upon Gaiseric that, because he was a friend and ally and so great a calamity had befallen the imperial house, it was not a holy thing to fail to become an avenger. For from Constantinople she thought no vengeance would come, because Theodosius[60] already had departed from the world and Marcian[61] had taken over the empire.

And Gaiseric, for no other reason than that he suspected that much money would come to him, set sail for Italy with a great fleet. And going up to Rome, because no one stood in his way, he took possession of the palace. Now while Maximus was trying to flee, the Romans threw stones at him

---

[53] Petronius Maximus, a powerful Roman senator who was twice Consul and became emperor for a few months in 455 after the murder of Valentinian III.

[54] Magnus Maximus, commander in Britain who seized the throne in 383 and was defeated and executed by Theodosius I (379–395) in 388.

[55] Probably in August, the month of Theodosius' victory.

[56] Licinia Eudoxia, the daughter of the eastern emperor Theodosius II (402–450), who had married the young Valentinian III in 437.

[57] This entire tale has striking parallels with the story of the violation of Lucretia in 509 CE, which led to a conspiracy against the Etruscan kings of Rome and the creation of the Roman Republic.

[58] Valentinian III actually was murdered in 455 by two comrades of the Patrician and Master of Soldiers Flavius Aëtius, whom Valentinian had murdered the year before.

[59] In the same manner that Justa Grata Honoria, the sister of the emperor Valentinian III, was said to have sent for Attila the Hun in 451.

[60] Eudoxia's father, the eastern emperor Theodosius II (402–450).

[61] The eastern emperor Marcian (450–457), the successor of Theodosius II.

and killed him, and they cut off his head and each of his other members and divided them among themselves. But Gaiseric took Eudoxia captive, together with Eudocia and Placidia, the children of herself and Valentinian, and placing an exceedingly great amount of gold and other imperial treasure in his ships sailed to Carthage, having spared neither bronze nor anything else whatsoever in the palace. He plundered also the Temple of Jupiter Capitolinus and tore off half of the roof.[62] Now this roof was of bronze of the finest quality, and because gold was laid over it exceedingly thick, it shone as a magnificent and wonderful spectacle. But of the ships with Gaiseric, one, which was bearing the statues, was lost,[63] they say, but with all the others the Vandals reached port in the harbor of Carthage. Gaiseric then married Eudocia to Huneric,[64] the elder of his sons, but the other of the two women, being the wife of Olybrius,[65] a most distinguished man in the Roman Senate, he sent to Constantinople[66] together with her mother, Eudoxia, at the request of the emperor.[67] Now the power of the east had by now fallen to Leo, because Marcian had already passed from the world.

---

[62] The Temple of Jupiter on the top of the Capitoline Hill.

[63] This ship also was said by some to have carried the temple treasures taken when the Jewish Temple in Jerusalem was sacked by Titus in 70 CE.

[64] King of the Vandals, 477–484.

[65] That is, Placidia, the other daughter of Valentinian and Eudoxia; Olybrius later became a short-lived emperor in the year 472.

[66] That is, Constantinople.

[67] The emperor Leo I (457–474).

A gold solidus of Romulus struck at Rome in 475 or 476. The obverse legend reads "Romulus Augustus, Dutiful and Happy Emperor." The reverse depicts an angel (or the goddess Victory) holding a long cross with the legend "Victory of the Emperors." The letters "R M" indicate that the coin was minted at Rome, and the abbreviation "COMOB" refers to the "Count of Pure Gold," who attested to the coin's purity.

In 475, the western emperor Julius Nepos (474–480) was forced into exile in Dalmatia on the Greek Adriatic coast by his Master of Soldiers Orestes, formerly secretary of Attila the Hun. Even though Nepos continued to be recognized as western Roman emperor by the eastern emperor Zeno (474–491), Orestes then had his son Romulus, perhaps fourteen years old, named as western emperor, albeit a usurper. In 476, just a year later, young Romulus was forced into retirement by the barbarian Master of Soldier Odovacar, who, rather than setting up another emperor or declaring allegiance to Nepos, had Romulus announce to the eastern emperor Zeno that the west no longer needed its own emperor and that Odovacar would rule as "King of Italy" in Zeno's name. Although Romulus has gone down in history as the last western Roman emperor—historians, beginning with Count Marcellinus in the mid-sixth century, just could not pass up the opportunity to have Rome begin and end with someone named Romulus—Nepos remained the last legal emperor of the western empire until his death in 480. Meanwhile, the story of the rise and fall of little Romulus and even of the final extinction of the Western Roman Empire passed with barely a mention in the ancient sources and must be pieced together from stray bits and snippets of information.

Source: Ralph W. Mathisen, "Romulus Augustulus (475–476)," *De imperatoribus Romanis. An Online Encyclopedia of Roman Emperors*: https://www.roman-emperors.org/auggiero.htm.

(1) "And another emperor, Nepos,[68] upon taking over the empire and living to enjoy it only a few days, died of disease, and Glycerius[69] after him entered into this office and suffered a similar fate.

---

[68] The legal western Roman emperor from 474 until 480 CE; he had been appointed western emperor by the eastern emperor Leo.

[69] Procopius has confused Nepos with Olybrius (472), who actually ruled a few days and died of disease; he was succeeded by Glycerius (473–474), who in turn was succeeded by Nepos.

And after him Augustulus[70] assumed the imperial power. There were, moreover, still other emperors in the west before this time, but although I know their names well, I shall make no mention of them whatsoever. For it so fell out that they lived only a short time after attaining the office and as a result of this accomplished nothing worthy of mention."[71] (Procopius, *Vandal War* 7.15–17: H. B. Dewing, trans., *Procopius. History of the Wars, Books III and IV* [Cambridge, MA: Harvard Univ. Press, 1916], 69)

(2) "Orestes,[72] having taken charge of the army and having departed from Rome against the enemies, arrived at Ravenna,[73] and remaining there he made his son Augustulus[74] emperor. When he learned this, Nepos fled to Dalmatia."[75] (Jordanes, *Gothic History* 241)

(3) "Soon Nepos arrived at Ravenna, pursued by the Patrician Orestes and his army. Fearing the arrival of Orestes, Nepos boarded a ship and fled to Salona."[76] (*Anonymous Valesianus* 7.36, year 474)

(4) "While Nepos was in the city,[77] the Patrician Orestes was sent against him with the main force of the army. But because Nepos dared not undertake the business of resisting in such desperate conditions, he fled to Dalmatia in his ships. When Nepos had fled Italy and departed from the city, Orestes assumed the primacy and all the authority for himself and made his son Augustulus emperor at Ravenna." (*Auctuarii Hauniensis ordo prior*, year 475)

(5) "After Augustulus had been established as emperor at Ravenna by his father Orestes, not long afterward Odovacar, King of the Turcilingi,[78] who had with him the Scirians, Heruls,[79] and auxiliaries from diverse peoples, occupied Italy and, after killing Orestes, deposed his son Augustulus from the rule and condemned him to exile in the Castle of Lucullus[80] in Campania." (Jordanes, *Gothic History* 242)

(6) "Odovacar, King of the Goths,[81] occupied Rome. Odovacar immediately killed Orestes. Odovacar condemned Augustulus, the son of Orestes, to exile in the Castle of Lucullus in Campania." (Count Marcellinus, *Chronicle*, year 476)

(7) "Entering Ravenna, Odovacar deposed Augustulus from the rule, and taking pity on his youth he granted him his life, and because he was comely he even granted to him an income of six thousand solidi and sent him to Campania to live freely with his relatives." (*Anonymous Valesianus* 8.38)

(8) "In this year, Orestes and his brother Paulus were killed by Odovacar, and Odovacar assumed the title of King, although he made use of neither the purple nor the imperial regalia." (Cassiodorus, *Chronicle*, year 476, no. 1303)

(9) "When Augustus,[82] the son of Orestes, heard that Zeno, having expelled Basiliscus,[83] had again gained the kingship of the east, he caused the Senate to send an embassy to tell Zeno that they had no need of a separate empire but that a single common emperor would be sufficient for both territories.[84] And also to say that Odovacar had been chosen by the Senate as a suitable man to safeguard their affairs because he had political understanding along with military skill. They asked Zeno to

---

[70] That is, Romulus (475–476), who followed Nepos.

[71] A sad epitaph for the last emperors of the Western Roman Empire.

[72] The Patrician and Master of Soldiers, the highest-ranking western Roman general; he previously had been the secretary of Attila the Hun.

[73] The imperial capital on the coast of the Adriatic Sea in northeastern Italy

[74] His actual name was Romulus; "Augustulus," or, "the Little Augustus," was a nickname based on his young age.

[75] Just across the Adriatic Sea on the western coast of Greece.

[76] A city in Dalmatia.

[77] That is, Ravenna.

[78] A poorly known barbarian people who might have been part of the horde of Attila the Hun.

[79] Peoples who had been part of the horde of Attila the Hun.

[80] Sometimes identified as the estate of the Roman Republican general Lucullus.

[81] Odovacar in fact was not king of the Goths.

[82] Young Romulus.

[83] The brother of Verina, the wife of Zeno's predecessor Leo; Basiliscus had rebelled against Zeno in 475.

[84] Paradoxically, after the end of the western Roman Empire the Senate regained some of its old status, sending embassies to the eastern emperor and even recovering the right to issue copper coinage.

award Odovacar the Patrician honor and grant him the government of the Italies. The men from the Senate in Rome reached Constantinople carrying these messages. On the same day messengers from Nepos also came to congratulate Zeno on the recent events concerning this restoration, and at the same time to ask him zealously to help Nepos, a man who had suffered equal misfortunes, in the recovery of his empire. They asked that he grant money and an army for this purpose and that he co-operate in his restoration in any other ways that might be necessary. Nepos had sent the men to say these things. Zeno gave the following answer to those arrivals and to the men from the Senate: the western Romans had received two men from the eastern empire and had driven one out, Nepos, and killed the other, Anthemius.[85] Now, he said, they knew what ought to be done. While their emperor was still alive they should hold no other thought than to receive him back on his return. To the barbarians he replied that it would be well if Odovacar were to receive the Patrician rank from the emperor Nepos and that he himself would grant it unless

Nepos granted it first. He commended him in that he had displayed this initial instance of guarding good order, suitable to the Romans, and trusted for this reason that, if he truly wished to act with justice, he would quickly receive back the emperor[86] who had given him his position of honor. He sent a royal letter about what he desired to Odovacar and in this letter named him a Patrician. Zeno gave this help to Nepos, pitying his sufferings because of his own, and holding to the principle that the common lot of fortune is to grieve with the unfortunate.[87] At the same time Verina[88] also joined in urging this, giving a helping hand to the wife of Nepos, her relative." (Malchus, *Chronicle*, fragment 10: Gordon, trans., *Age of Attila*, 127–128)

(10) "The western empire of the Roman people, which first began in the seven hundred and ninth year after the founding of the City with Octavian Augustus, the first of the emperors, perished with this Augustulus, in the five-hundred and twenty-second year of the reign of Augustus' successor emperors. From this point on Gothic kings held power in Rome."[89] (Count Marcellinus, *Chronicle*, year 476)

---

[85] Named western Roman emperor in 467 by the eastern emperor Leo; he was killed in 472 during a civil war with the barbarian Patrician and Master of Soldiers Ricimer.

[86] Nepos.

[87] Zeno had been expelled by Basiliscus in the same year as Julius Nepos, although he regained his throne the next year.

[88] The wife of Zeno's predecessor as eastern emperor Leo (457–474) and mother of Zeno's wife Ariadne.

[89] In was not until 489, in fact, that the Ostrogoths under Theoderic the Great invaded Italy; in 493 he defeated and killed Odovacar.

CHAPTER 14

THE BARBARIAN SUCCESSOR KINGDOMS: THE END OF ANTIQUITY IN THE WEST (476–751)

By the end of the fifth century, the Roman world looked very different from the way it had appeared at the time of Augustus. The hard-won political unity of the Mediterranean world had been fractured. Whereas the Roman Empire continued to thrive in the eastern Mediterranean, the western part of the empire had been partitioned among several barbarian peoples, who had created barbarian "successor kingdoms." This designation makes good sense, given that in many ways the barbarian kingdoms made use of many Roman traditions and administrative methods and barbarian kings saw themselves as successors of Roman emperors.

THE POST-ROMAN WEST

Even though the year 476 often is considered to mark the end of the Roman Empire in the west, some elements of the western Roman population continued to hold out. But by 500, all of the western empire had been incorporated into barbarian kingdoms, with the Visigoths in southwestern Gaul and Spain, the Vandals in North Africa, the Angles and Saxons in Britain, Burgundians in central Gaul, Alamanni on the upper Rhine, the Franks on the lower Rhine, and the Ostrogoths in Italy. One of the curiosities of historical writing is that most modern accounts of ancient history stop here, leaving the reader thinking that the barbarians had won and the Romans had lost. But by continuing forward in time for another few hundred years, one discovers that this was not the case. After not very long, the Romans had reconquered most of the western Mediterranean world, and smaller barbarian kingdoms had been gobbled up by larger ones. By the early eighth century, Spain had fallen to the Muslims, and the only barbarian kingdoms left were those of the Franks in France and the Angles and Saxons in England.

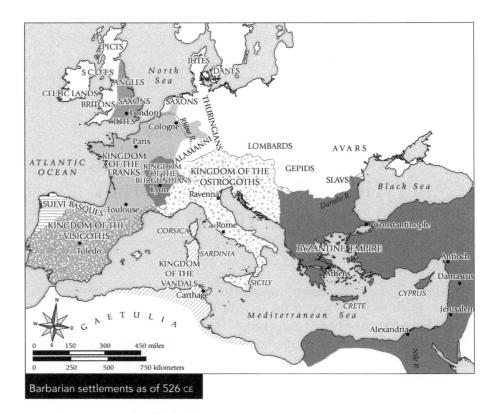

Barbarian settlements as of 526 CE

The Nature of Barbarian Rule

Eventually, all the inhabitants of western Europe felt the effects of the barbarian presence. Some fled, others faced life as captives, but most had to make whatever kind of private peace they could. In some cases, powerful Roman magnates may have preferred a local barbarian ruler who acknowledged their property rights and did not ask too many questions to a distant yet intrusive emperor. In many regards, the barbarian settlement caused little disruption, and, on a local level, life went on much as before, with barbarians becoming not only political rulers but also neighbors and social acquaintances. Indeed, in some ways all that made the sixth century different from the fourth was that the supreme political authority was a barbarian king rather than a Roman emperor.

The barbarians could not escape the power and prestige of either the Roman Empire or classical culture—not that they would have wanted to. After all, most of the barbarian peoples who occupied the western empire had been living in close contact with the Roman world and had even been working inside the empire for centuries and had enthusiastically absorbed much of its culture even before they crossed the Roman frontier. Except in Britain, Roman culture continued as before. The Latin language was adopted by all of the barbarian settlers except for the Anglo-Saxons, and it gradually evolved into the modern-day **Romance** (from "Roman")

languages, including Spanish, Portuguese, French, Italian, and Romanian. Classical literature was appreciated, pursued, and preserved by the educated elite. Over the course of time, barbarians, too, were assimilated into the classical cultural tradition.

In most regards, barbarian kingdoms looked like small-scale models of the Roman Empire. The barbarian governments adopted, to a greater or lesser degree, Roman procedures, making use of Roman law and administrative practices and continuing to use Roman officials. Barbarian kings were kings of peoples, not of territories; but, like Roman emperors, they continued to issue laws that were binding on all of the people living in territories under their control and compiled law codes just as Roman emperors did. None of the barbarian kingdoms, however, had an economy or bureaucracy that was nearly as complex as the Roman ones.

Older scholarly suggestions that there was one law for Romans and one for barbarians generally are no longer considered credible.

One concern that barbarian rulers had was how to maintain their individuality and authority in the midst of so many Romans, for the barbarians were but a drop in a Roman sea. In an attempt to preserve their identity and justify their authority, barbarians often created an origin myth that gave their ruling families, which often were of very recent derivation, the luster of great antiquity. The rulers of the Franks, for example, tried to work their way into the classical tradition by claiming to be descended from the Trojans, just like the Romans were. Barbarian rulers realized that if they could not conciliate their Roman subjects, they risked provoking uprisings in which they could be overwhelmed. The only way to survive was by respecting Roman traditions and values and making common cause with the powerful Roman landowners, much as Augustus had preserved ancient traditions and ruled with the cooperation of the senators at the beginning of the Principate.

In particular, the Christian church thrived under barbarian rule. If barbarian peoples were not already Christian when they entered they empire, they soon became Christian. And Christian culture at this time involved not only spiritual life but also secular life. In much of the western Mediterranean world, and especially in Gaul, Christian bishops had taken over many of the duties of city councils and Roman local officials. This often left bishops as de facto secular administrators on the local level. Many Roman cities shrank to little more than episcopal centers, overseen by a bishop. Bishops administered justice, oversaw local public works, and were able to mobilize local populations. By the fifth century, Roman senators, who by then were focusing on pursuing local interests anyway, had come to monopolize episcopal office in many cities. Thus, when barbarian kings dealt with Christian bishops, they often were dealing with Roman senators. This made it even more important for barbarian rulers to be on good terms with powerful Roman senators and to respect their ancient rights.

Potential Problems

This is not to say, of course, that there were not any difficulties during the course of the barbarian settlement. A very obvious possible source of conflict concerned property. Barbarian settlers, first and foremost, were seeking land on which to settle.

ETHNICITY VERSUS HISTORY VERSUS CULTURE

The Greeks and Romans left extensive literary remains, but other ancient peoples, especially those living beyond the frontiers of the Roman Empire, left no written records. These barbarian peoples are known only by occasional references in Greek and Latin authors, which historians use to try to establish when and where they lived. Archaeologists, on the other hand, use the material remains left behind by different peoples to identify characteristic archaeological cultures, whose extent in space and time likewise can be established. A popular armchair sport of scholars lies in attempting to match up the archaeological cultures with historical peoples. The fit often is less than perfect.

Others attempt to identify the ethnicity of peoples who left no written records on the basis of the material attributes—including elements such as hairstyle, dress,

Different barbarian peoples favored particular styles of ornate fibulae, clasps used to hold garments together at the shoulder (note the jeweled fibula worn by Justinian in the mosaic pictured in the figure on p. 530). For example, the Visigoths liked ornate "eagle" fibulae made from bits of colored glass set in a metal frame.

jewelry, and weapons—that are associated with them in both literature and archaeological excavations. But doing so can be tricky. Ancient authors loved to categorize different peoples and cultures based on their appearance. Diodorus of Sicily, for example, regarding the Celts, described "shirts that have been dyed and embroidered in varied colors, and breeches that they call in their tongue 'bracae,' and striped coats, fastened by a buckle on the shoulder." One can still recognize here the tartans of the modern Scots. Germans were known for dyeing their hair red. More specifically, Visigoths were said to favor mustaches, Suevi the "Suevic knot" in their hair (attested in literature, art, and physical remains), and *Longobardi* (Lombards), or "long beards," sported long unshaven beards. Barbarians also could be categorized based on their weaponry. Franks favored the *francisca*, a throwing ax that gave them their name, and the Saxons were named after the *seax* (also known as the *scramasax*), a large single-edged knife.

On the other hand, some historians have challenged the identification of ethnicity based on cultural attributes by citing counterexamples, such as a Frank who did not use the *francisca* or a Visigoth who did. But it is well known that people of one culture (including Romans) often used words and material used by other groups, a process linguists refer to as "code switching," and the act of doing so does not lessen the identification of the word or item with a particular ethnic group.

Nor are these merely academic discussions, for modern governments have attempted to lay claim to modern territory that their putative ancestors of thousands of years ago supposedly occupied. Thus in the 1930s the Nazi government of Germany used the findings of scientific archaeology to claim ownership of Poland because their ancestors, the Goths and Vandals, supposedly had lived there. Others, however, argued that it was the ancestors of the Slavs, not the Germans, who had dwelt in ancient Poland. And the debate continues.

Where was it to come from? Several solutions were implemented. Sometimes, barbarians were granted either land that in the past had belonged to the Roman government or shares in Roman tax receipts that could be used to purchase land. On other occasions, large Roman landowners shared their land with barbarian settlers, turning over to barbarians meadows that had not been leased out to tenants and keeping for themselves the more valuable rented lands. Despite some squabbling over how the division was to be made, the system was generally effective; after all, there were a great many Roman landowners and just not that many barbarians, and large landowners often saw the advantage of having barbarian neighbors who now had an interest in protecting property rights.

Another potential incompatibility, at least in some places during the early years of the settlement, lay in the area of religion. Both Romans and barbarians were Christians, but the Romans followed the Nicene Creed, whereas most barbarians practiced what was disparagingly called Arianism by Nicene writers but actually was Homoianism, the belief that the Father and Son were "alike according to the scriptures." Recent study, however, suggests that this dissimilarity usually was of little consequence. Arians and Nicenes generally were tolerant of each other, even going so far as to attend each other's church services and dinner parties. And when barbarians did become Nicene, as all of them eventually did, by choice or by compulsion, they, including their clergy, were incorporated into the Nicene church with a minimum of fuss.

A third factor that characterized the European post-Roman world was a perceived general increase in the level of violence, for the reduced level of government oversight meant that powerful persons often ended up taking justice, and the pursuit of their own advantage, into their own hands. This meant that it was all the more important for unprivileged and powerless persons to become clients and put themselves under the protection of powerful persons—barbarian nobles, Roman senators, and bishops—whom they hoped would look out for their interests.

Based on long tradition, the term "Arianism" will still be used here for barbarian Christianity, although it must be remembered that barbarians were in fact "Homoians," not "Arians."

BARBARIAN KINGDOMS

Not all of the barbarian settlers on Roman territory formed independent kingdoms; indeed, only a few of them did, in particular those, such as the Visigoths, Franks, Burgundians, and Ostrogoths, that had regularly supplied contingents of *auxiliares* for the Roman army. By doing so, they gained access to Roman resources and had the Roman stamp of approval on their occupation of Roman territory. The exception to this rule was the Vandals, who had forcibly occupied North Africa, although the consequence of this was that the Vandals were constantly confronted by the possibility of a Roman counter-invasion. Other peoples existed on the margins, such as the Suevi, holding out in the mountains of northwestern Spain, and the Gepids, who formed a kingdom on the Danube in the area of Belgrade. A multitude of others peoples, including Rugians, Heruls, and Scirians, continued to serve as *auxiliares* but never formed a territorial nation.

TABLE 14.1 BARBARIAN RULERS

Visigoths (Kingdom of Toulouse)

Athaulf (410–415)

Theoderic II (453–466)

Euric (466–484)

Alaric II (484–507)

Vandals (North Africa)

Gaiseric (428–477)

Huneric (477–484)

Hilderic (523–530)

Gelimer (530–534)

Ostrogoths (Italy)

Theoderic "the Great" (493–526)

Athalaric (526–534)

Amalasuintha (534–535)

Theodahad (534–536)

Totila (541–552)

Anglo-Saxons (Britain/England)

Alfred "the Great" (871–899)

Aethelstan (924–939)

Burgundians (Sapaudia)

Gundioc (ca. 437–473)

Gundobad (473–516)

Sigismund (516–524)

Franks (Gaul/France and Germany)

Merovingian Dynasty

Merovech (ca. 446–457)

Childeric (464–481)

Clovis (481–511)

Chloderic, King of Ripuarian Franks

Ragnacharius, King of Cambrai

Theoderic I (511–533)

Chlodomer (511–524)

Childebert I (511–558)

Chlothar I (511–561)

Dagobert I (623–639)

Childeric III (743–751)

Mayors of the Palace

Charles Martel (718–741)

Pepin the Short (741–751)

The Visigoths

As the first barbarian invaders to settle and maintain their independence on Roman soil, the Visigoths adapted themselves readily to Roman practices. In 412, the Visigothic warlord Athaulf (410–415) even went so far as to marry the Roman princess Galla Placidia, who had been kidnapped during the sack of Rome in 410. The death of their infant son, Theodosius, ended the hopes of a joint Roman–Visigothic union.

After settling in Aquitania in 418, with their capital at Toulouse, the Homoian/Arian Visigoths established an independent Kingdom of Toulouse. Technically the Visigoths were Roman *foederati*, and they did cooperate with Aëtius in 451 at the Battle of the Catalaunian Fields against the Huns. But they also took advantage of Roman weakness to occupy more and more Roman territory. Under King Theoderic II (453–466), for example, the Visigoths defeated the Suevi, who had occupied northwestern Spain and began to occupy Roman Spain. The most able Visigothic king in Gaul was Euric (466–484), who conquered the remainder of southwestern Gaul, expanding from Provence to the Loire River and ruling the largest and most powerful barbarian kingdom in Europe. To demonstrate that he was just as good a ruler as a Roman emperor, Euric issued a law code, "The Code of Euric," that dealt with issues, such as land tenure, of interest to Romans and Visigoths alike. Doing so reassured his subjects that the Visigothic kingdom was administered according to the rule of law. But, unlike his Homoian predecessors, Euric was increasingly harsh in his treatment of the Nicene church hierarchy. Some bishops were exiled, and cities that had lost their bishops were forbidden to ordain successors.

Euric's son Alaric II (484–507), however, was threatened by the Franks. In 506, he attempted to conciliate the Roman population by sponsoring a compilation of Roman law known as the *Breviarium* ("Summary") intended to reassure nervous Romans that their legal rights were protected. Alaric even permitted Nicene bishops to hold a church council. But it was too little too late. The final confrontation came in 507 at the **Battle of Vouillé**, just outside Poitiers, where Alaric was defeated and killed by the Franks and the Visigoths lost nearly all their Gallic possessions. Subsequently, the Visigothic kingdom was limited to Spain and an adjoining narrow strip of southern Gaul.

The Visigothic kingdom in Spain, the Kingdom of Toledo, survived by making extensive use of Romans in both secular and ecclesiastical positions. Unlike Gaul, which returned to a largely agrarian society, Spain continued to have an active urban culture, and some of the Visigothic kings even founded new cities. The kingdom of the Suevi was completely absorbed, and in 589 the Visigoths officially converted from Arian to Nicene Christianity at the Third Council of Toledo. This created a uniform Nicene Christian world in western Europe, nominally all under the authority of the bishop of Rome. In the seventh century, Visigothic kings issued a massive legal compilation known as the Book of Judgments. The Visigothic kingdom survived until 711, when it fell to a Muslim invasion from North Africa.

The Vandals

After their occupation of Roman North Africa between 429 and 439 and their subsequent seizure of Sicily, Sardinia, and Corsica, the Vandals established a powerful kingdom centered at Carthage. Under the leadership of their very able and long-reigning ruler Gaiseric (428–477), several Roman attempts to retake Africa were repulsed, and the Vandals became the most oppressive of the barbarian rulers of the western empire, adopting a policy of weakening the Roman senatorial class. Large tracts of Roman land were confiscated, and Romans who held office in the Vandal administration were expected to convert to Arianism. Many Roman senators simply abandoned their property and fled, often to Constantinople. In addition, Christian writers accused the Arian Vandals of savage persecutions of Christians, although it was primarily the Nicene clergy that the Vandals targeted. In an attempt to break the powerful hold of Christian clergy on the people, many Christian bishops were exiled, often to Sardinia. Vandals were prohibited from converting to Nicene Christianity, and persons dressed in the Vandal style who were apprehended entering Nicene churches were severely punished by having their hair torn from their scalps. In other regards, however, ordinary Nicenes generally were permitted to worship in peace.

Soon after the sack of Rome in 455 and the kidnapping of the imperial women, Gaiseric's son Huneric was married to Eudocia, the daughter of Valentinian, and when Gaiseric died in 477, Huneric succeeded him. Under Huneric (477–484), the persecution of Nicenes intensified. Some Nicene Christians were executed for refusing to convert to Arianism, many bishops were banished to Corsica, and influential Romans were exiled to the Sahara Desert. During his reign, outlying areas of the Vandal kingdom came under attack from the native Moors of North Africa. After Huneric's

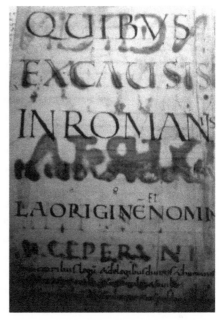

The opening section of the *Breviarium* of Alaric II, a compilation of earlier Roman laws and legal theory, preserved in a manuscript of the eighth century.

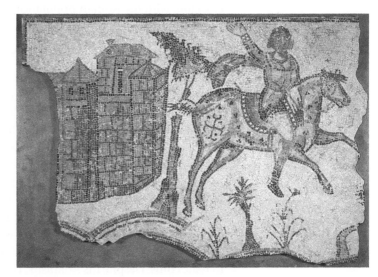

In this fifth- or sixth-century mosaic now in the British Museum, a pants-clad and mustachioed Vandal landowner waves farewell while riding away from his fortified villa, which likely had been confiscated from a departed Roman senator.

death, the Vandal kingdom was ruled by his descendents. Sporadic persecutions of Nicenes continued, and the Moors made further encroachments onto Vandal territory. The fall of the Roman Empire in the west, however, for the time being prevented any further Roman attempts to reconquer Africa.

Even though the Vandals usually are portrayed as the most anti-Roman of the barbarian settlers in the Mediterranean world, they absorbed Roman culture as much as anyone. Vandal kings issued coins and laws in the same way as Roman emperors. Latin literature also survived. The work of several poets survives in a work known as the *Latin Anthology*. Luxorius, for example, authored ninety-one surviving poems before and after 500 CE.

In 523, Hilderic (523–530), the son of Huneric and the imperial princess Eudocia, succeeded to the Vandal throne. Because Hilderic was sympathetic to the Nicene views of his mother, he was supported by the Byzantine emperor but disliked by many Vandals, especially the nobles. Hilderic lifted the restrictions on Nicene worship, and when ordinary Vandals began to convert to Nicene Christianity, Vandal nobles became alarmed and formed a conspiracy against him. In 530, Hilderic was imprisoned, and his cousin Gelimer (530–534), a staunch Arian, seized the throne. This gave the Byzantine emperor Justinian (526–565) just the pretext that he needed for launching an attack on the Vandals in 533.

Within a few months, and after two battles, the Vandal kingdom had been destroyed and North Africa reintegrated into the Roman-cum-Byzantine Empire. Many surviving Vandal soldiers were recruited into the Byzantine army and sent to the Persian frontier. The Vandals then virtually disappeared from history, and of all the Germans who occupied the Roman Empire, the Vandals probably had the least lasting impact, largely, perhaps, because of the difficulties they had engaging with the Roman population.

The Ostrogoths

In 488, the east Roman emperor Zeno rid himself of the troublesome **Ostrogoths** by sending them west to take control of Italy, which they and their warlord king, Theoderic, were happy to do. Theoderic invaded Italy in 489, and after being besieged in Ravenna for three years, Odovacar, the barbarian king of Italy, finally surrendered on condition that the two would rule Italy jointly. Soon thereafter, however, he and his family were murdered by Theoderic.

The Ostrogoths developed a kingdom that looked very much like the Roman Empire. King Theoderic, called "the Great" (493–526), had his capital at the Roman imperial city of Ravenna and issued legislation that looked like that of emperors. Many high-ranking officials were wealthy and powerful Roman senators, and the Senate in Rome even regained some of its old authority, such as the right to issue coins. Despite his Arianism, Theoderic also allowed Nicene Christians full freedom of religion and even became involved in Nicene church controversies, intervening in 502 in a disputed episcopal election at Rome. Even the bishop of

A PICTURE IS WORTH A THOUSAND WORDS

THE MEDALLION OF THEODERIC THE GREAT

Barbarian kings, in their attempts to demonstrate that they were the successors of Roman emperors, likewise issued medallions. This gold medallion of the Ostrogothic king Theoderic the Great (493–526), now in Palazzo Massimo in Rome, exemplifies the interaction between Roman and barbarian culture. It bears a Latin legend, *Theodoricus pius princis* ("King Theoderic, Dutiful Prince"), and depicts Theoderic wearing a Roman military uniform and holding a globe topped by the representation of Victory who is placing a crown on Theoderic's head. But it also ostentatiously shows Theoderic with a characteristic barbarian mustache, albeit a small one, and the long hair typical of Germanic royalty. The medallion could have been intended for distribution to a palace official, an Ostrogothic noble, or one of the several barbarian kings, such as the Visigoth Alaric II, the Burgundian Gundobad, and the Frank Clovis, with whom Theoderic had diplomatic relations.

Rome had little cause for complaint, for, freed from imperial oversight, he was able to expand his own authority. He began to monopolize the title of **Pope**, which in the past had been applicable to any distinguished bishop.

Theoderic also was well connected in the barbarian world, being related by marriage to the kings of the Vandals, Burgundians, Franks, and Visigoths. In 507, after the defeat of the Visigoths at Vouillé, he occupied Provence in southern Gaul and became the titular king of Visigothic Spain. It appeared that an Ostrogothic Empire was in the making. But toward the end of Theoderic's reign, problems arose. In 522 the influential senators Symmachus and Boethius were accused of treason and executed, resulting in a breakdown in the carefully nurtured partnership with the Roman senators. Theoderic died in 526, and the dream of an Ostrogothic empire died with him.

Roman culture continued unabated in the Ostrogothic kingdom. Boethius, for example, authored a number of works that enjoyed immense popularity in the Middle Ages, including school texts on music, arithmetic, astronomy, and geometry. These subjects became the "Quadrivium" of Medieval and Renaissance education and were studied after a student had mastered the "Trivium" of grammar, rhetoric, and logic. Boethius' most famous work, the *Consolation of*

Philosophy, was written while he was awaiting execution and has been called the last great work of classical antiquity. Here, Lady Philosophy consoles Boethius about the transitory nature of the things of this earth and suggests that true happiness comes from within. In addition, the senator Cassiodorus served in several high-level government offices and compiled a collection of official correspondence known as the "Variae" that shows the Ostrogothic kings stepping seamlessly into the role of Roman emperors. And the Gothic monk Dionysius Exiguus translated a number of ecclesiastical works from Greek into Latin and invented the "Anno Domini" dating system that begins with the birth of Christ.

The "Anno Domini" ("AD") dating system is still used, although it now often is called the "Common Era" ("CE") system. Because Dionysius' calculations were a bit off, the birth of Christ now is dated between 6 and 4 BC.

Theoderic was succeeded by his daughter Amalasuintha (534–535), who first served as regent for her young son Athlaric (526–534) and then ruled as queen in her own right. But making her cousin Theodahad (534–536) her co-ruler was a mistake, for in 535 he had her murdered in her bath. Because Amalasuintha had been an ally of the eastern Roman emperor Justinian, this gave Justinian a pretext to send the general Belisarius to invade Italy. After a desperate defense led mainly by King Totila (541–552), the Ostrogothic kingdom finally fell in 553.

The Anglo-Saxons and Irish

In Britain, the Roman population simply retreated in the face of barbarian invasions of **Angles**, **Saxons**, and Jutes that began not long after the Romans abandoned the island in 410. Contact with the mainland became restricted. Between 429 and 446, Germanus, bishop of Auxerre in Gaul, who formerly had been a Roman Duke, visited the island to combat Pelagianism, a Christian teaching of the Briton Pelagius that emphasized free will. Gradually, the eastern half of the island was occupied by the invaders, who, at least initially, retained their Germanic culture.

The closest thing to a contemporary account of the barbarian occupation, and nearly the only literary work to survive from Britain during the fifth and sixth centuries, is a late-sixth-century sermon titled "On the Destruction and Conquest of Britain" written by the monk Gildas the Wise. From what can be pieced together, it appears that some Britons fled to Armorica in western Gaul, which then became known as Brittany. But other western Britons continued to resist, led first by Aurelius Ambrosius, also sometimes called "the last of the Romans," and then by warlords such as Arthur, the "Duke of Battles," as he was called in an early-ninth-century source. As "King Arthur," he later became the subject of legends and medieval romances. Circa 500, the Britons inflicted a major defeat on the invaders at the Battle of Mount Badon, the last western Roman victory over the barbarians. Soon after, however, the Britons were overwhelmed, and Britain became partitioned into several independent Anglo-Saxon kingdoms, including Wessex (from West Saxons), Sussex (from South Saxons), Essex (from East Saxons), Mercia (Angles), East Anglia (from East Angles), Kent (Jutes), and Northumbria (Angles). By the ninth century, Britain came to be known as England (from "Angle-Land").

At the end of the sixth century, Britain began to be pulled back into the classical sphere. In 597, Augustine, a Roman monk sent by Pope Gregory I, arrived in England for the purpose of "converting" the Anglo-Saxons to Christianity, even though England already had communities of so-called Celtic Christians, the descendents of the previous Roman population. Augustine was appointed bishop of Canterbury, which became the archiepiscopal see of the English church. Within a few years, bishops had been appointed in several English cities, and Roman Catholic Christianity then quickly spread throughout England. At the Council of Whitby in 664, Roman Catholic traditions, such as the date of Easter, were imposed on the surviving Celtic bishops. Meanwhile, the Anglo-Saxon kingdoms continued to bicker among themselves. In the 880s King Alfred of Wessex (871–899), later Alfred "the Great," first took the title King of the Anglo-Saxons, but the Anglo-Saxons were not finally united into a single kingdom until 924 by Aethelstan (924–939), who also laid claim to Scotland and Wales and took the title King of All Britain.

One of the ironies of history is that even though Ireland never had been occupied by the Romans, after the end of the Western Roman Empire, Ireland was to become one of the most important bastions of classical culture. Although Roman culture certainly had penetrated into Ireland during the Roman period and there already were a few Christian communities, formal Roman influence in Ireland did not begin until the 430s, when Patrick, a Briton of curial stock who had been carried off to Ireland as a slave but then escaped, became the self-proclaimed bishop of the Irish. Patrick and other missionaries then converted much of Ireland to the Celtic form of Christianity, which retained its own way of calculating the date of Easter and in which church authority was centered in monasteries. After his death Patrick became the national saint of Ireland. After the fall of the western empire, Irish monks took a leading role in the preservation of classical culture.

The Burgundians

The short-lived Burgundian kingdom was the most Romanized barbarian kingdom of all. In 437, the Burgundians who had crossed the Rhine in 406 were nearly destroyed by Hun *auxiliares* in Roman service, a campaign that later was commemorated in the medieval poem the "Niebelungenlied." The surviving Burgundians were established under their king Gundioc (ca. 437–473) by the Roman general Aëtius as Roman allies in Sapaudia in the central Rhône River valley. The Burgundians then served as more or less loyal *foederati*, taking part, for example, in the Battle of the Catalaunian Fields against the Huns in 451. As Roman authority declined, the Burgundians expanded and established their own independent barbarian kingdom. Several Burgundian kings got their start as Masters of Soldiers in Roman service. Gundobad (473–516), for example, had been the successor to Ricimer in Italy.

The "Niebelungenlied" served as the basis for the "Ring Cycle" of operas by Richard Wagner.

Like the Visigoths, the Burgundians issued two forms of law codes. One, the "Roman Law of the Burgundians," was a compilation of past Roman law. The other, "The Law of Gundobad," was a collection of legislation issued by Burgundian kings to deal with more contemporary issues. In all cases, however, as in the Roman Empire, the laws were applicable to everyone in the kingdom; there was not one law for Romans and another for Burgundians, as once was thought. Although nominally Arian, the Burgundian kings enjoyed good relations with Nicene Gallo-Roman senators. In 516 the Burgundian king Sigismund (516–524) converted to Nicene Christianity, making the Burgundians the first group of Arian barbarians to do so. In 534 the Burgundian kingdom was absorbed into the expanding kingdom of the Franks.

The Franks

The Franks followed a rather different trajectory. They had originated in the third century CE as a confederation of different groups living on both sides of the lower Rhine. The most influential Frankish population was the Sicambrians, who already had been mentioned by Tacitus circa 100 CE. By the fifth century, the Salian Franks were settled in Toxandria (northern Belgium), with their center at Tongres. Subsequently, the Ripuarian Franks crossed the middle Rhine. Other Franks remained across the Rhine in Franconia. In the traditional model, most other barbarian peoples abandoned their original homelands when they occupied the Mediterranean regions of the empire. But the Franks stayed home and simply expanded their original territory into formerly Roman lands. Indeed, the Franks never really invaded the empire, but they were assigned the responsibility for guarding increasingly large areas of northern Gaul by the imperial government. Even during the barbarian invasion of 406, and although they later sacked Trier four times, the Franks remained remarkably loyal to Rome, serving, for example, with Aëtius in 451 at the Battle of the Catalaunian Fields against the Huns. Thus, with greater justification than any other barbarian people, the Franks could claim that they had simply succeeded to the Roman administration by default.

The different Frankish subgroups were united and the kingdom was greatly expanded under **Clovis** (481–511), a member of the **Merovingian dynasty** of Frankish kings, named after Clovis' grandfather Merovech (ca. 446–457), who in later legend was said to have been the son of the Quinotaur, a five-headed sea monster that mated with Clovis' great-grandmother. Clovis' father Childeric (464–481) founded a kingdom of Salian Franks centered on the city of Soissons; his elaborate tomb, containing the regalia of a Roman general, was discovered at Tournai in 1653. In 486, Clovis defeated the last Roman holdout in Gaul, Syagrius—another person who sometimes is called "the last of the Romans"—and occupied much of north-central Gaul. Ten years later, during a hard-fought battle with the Alamanni, it was said that Clovis promised to become a Christian.

After the Frankish victory, Clovis, encouraged by his Nicene Christian wife, the Burgundian princess Clotilda, was baptized as a Nicene Christian by Remigius, the Roman bishop of Reims.

His Nicene faith gained Clovis valuable Roman support during his subsequent war with the Visigoths. At the pivotal Battle of Vouillé in 507, Clovis defeated and killed Alaric II, and the Franks occupied most of the Visigothic territories in Gaul, thus becoming the primary barbarian power in Gaul. Immediately afterward, Clovis overthrew other Frankish kings, such as Chloderic, king of the Ripuarians, and Ragnacharius, king of Cambrai, and brought all the Franks under his own rule.

Clovis shrewdly conciliated the Gallo-Roman aristocracy, and especially the powerful Gallo-Roman bishops, by recognizing their social status and their

In a medieval manuscript illumination, the Frankish king Clovis, with Roman clerics on his right and Frankish nobles to his left, is baptized by Bishop Remigius at Reims.

property rights. Like other barbarian kings, Clovis demonstrated that he was a worthy successor of the Romans by issuing a law code known as the Salic Law. His successors likewise issued laws in the manner of Roman emperors.

After Clovis' death in 511, his kingdom, which was considered to be his personal property, was divided among his four sons: Theoderic I of Metz (511–533), Chlodomer of Orléans (511–524), Childebert I of Paris (511–558), and Chlothar I of Soissons (511–561). This policy of partition, which was followed by subsequent Merovingian kings, was to be the bane of the Merovingian dynasty. Not only did it prevent the unification of the kingdom, but it also encouraged the intrigues, quarrels, and conflicts for which the Merovingian kings became so well known. At the same time, the Frankish kings could not restrain themselves from interfering in ecclesiastical affairs, bestowing episcopal sees on their favorites, and often appropriating church property.

During the 530s, the Franks occupied Provence, which had been controlled by the Ostrogoths, and absorbed the Burgundian kingdom. This gave the Franks control of all of Roman Gaul excepting a coastal strip north of Spain known as Septimania, which continued to be held by the Visigoths. The Frankish kingdom also extended east into Swabia and Thuringia, and north and east of the Rhine all the way to the border of Saxony, thus spreading well beyond the old frontiers of the Roman Empire.

Frankish rule never was very tight or centralized, and kings had to be circumspect in their dealings not only with their own nobles but also with the powerful oGallo-Roman landed aristocracy. The central administration consisted primarily only of the king's household. There, a Referendary (also called a Chancellor) oversaw legal matters. Local administration was mostly in the hands of local potentates, including Frankish officials such as Dukes (military governors) and

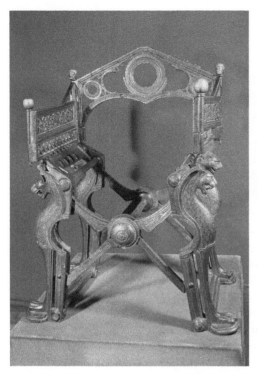

The throne believed to have belonged to Dagobert I was made in the shape of the curule chair of a Roman Consul (the sides and back were added centuries later), attesting to barbarian continuity with the Roman past. Subsequent French kings were enthroned using this chair.

Counts (city administrators), bishops, and landed magnates. Geographically, the Merovingian kingdom came to be divided into several sections that corresponded only approximately to the political divisions of the kingdom. In the northeast was Austrasia, the most heavily Germanic section, consisting of areas on both sides of the Rhine and with its chief city at Metz. To the south and west lay the more Romanized Neustria, consisting primarily of the Loire and Seine River valleys, with its main city at Paris. In the southwest was Aquitania, and in the Rhône valley Burgundy.

The remainder of the sixth century saw repetitious conflicts among the multiple kings and their various offspring, all of whom were contending to improve their own positions and holdings at the expense of the others. During the second half of the sixth century, an official called the **Mayor of the Palace**, the rough equivalent of a prime minister, achieved increasing importance in the Frankish administration. In the seventh century, the Mayors of the Palace began to compete for authority with the king, and the last effective Merovingian king was Dagobert I (623–639), who briefly reunited all of **Francia**, as Gaul now sometimes was called and which gave its name to modern France, under a single rule. Dagobert even entered into a treaty of "perpetual peace" with the Byzantine emperor Heraclius. Dagobert's reign later was looked back on as being the height of Merovingian Frankish civilization, and the image of "good king Dagobert" still survives in France. But, much like the reign of the Roman emperor Valentinian I, it also marked the calm before the storm, and this was the last time that the Merovingian kingdom could be called politically stable.

After the death of Dagobert in 639, the kingdom once again was partitioned. The remaining kings were known as the "do-nothing kings," and the real power lay in the hands of the Mayors of the Palace, such as Charles Martel (718–741), who in 732 defeated a massive Muslim invasion of France. The Merovingian decline culminated in 751, when the Mayor of the Palace, Pepin the Short (741–751), deposed Childeric III (743–751), the last Merovingian king, and established the Carolingian Dynasty.

CLASSICAL CULTURE IN POST-ROMAN EUROPE

It often is thought that the fall of the Western Roman Empire and the creation of the barbarian kingdoms brought a break with the classical Roman past. But, as has been seen, the barbarians largely absorbed Roman culture, so that the Roman world continued to persevere under their auspices. Even though there was a political change (and there had been many political changes throughout the course of antiquity), there was no obvious cultural break with the ancient world.

The Last Latin Classical Writers

One of the great misconceptions about the European post-Roman period is that it was a period when education and literary activity virtually ceased, giving rise to the "**Dark Ages**." This view was largely promulgated by classicists and historians who applied the standards of the classical period to Late Antiquity and who regretted the decline in the composition of secular histories, poetry, and so on in the classical style and disparaged the quality of the religious literature that was being written.

But western Late Antiquity in fact was a vibrant period of literary activity that was, however, different from that of the classical period. The literary works of Late Antiquity were very largely Christian in nature, consisting of sermons, biblical commentaries, and saints' lives. This does not mean, however, that the writing of secular works ceased. Far from it. In the mid-sixth century, Jordanes, an Arian Goth who converted to Nicene Christianity, wrote, probably in Constantinople, one work, *On the Origin and History of the Goths,* covering Gothic history up to his own times, and another, *On the Origin and History of the Roman People,* which did the same for the Romans. His works are interesting in that they discuss relations between Romans and barbarians from the barbarian perspective.

In Gaul, in the later sixth century, Bishop Gregory of Tours composed ten books of "Histories" from the Creation to his own time, but concentrating on Gaul in the sixth century. His stories of the antics of Frankish kings, and his personal involvement in many of them, make him one of the most readable historians of all time. Gregory's work was continued up to 641 by a chronicler known as Fredegar, and this work then was extended by others up to the coronation of Charlemagne in 768. Other historical writing, however, consisted of year-by-year chronicles with just a few or no entries per year. In addition, poetry, of both secular and religious nature, was composed for a joint Roman and barbarian audience by Venantius Fortunatus, an Italian who relocated to Gaul circa 580 and became bishop of Poitiers.

In Visigothic Spain, a spectacular outburst of literary work in the seventh century has been called the "**Visigothic Renaissance**" and gives the lie to popular perceptions of the "Dark Ages" in post-Roman Europe. This explosion of classical culture helped to preserve classical learning at the same time that it manifested many of the characteristics of the Middle Ages, in particular the compulsion to distill, summarize, and categorize ancient knowledge. Isidore, bishop of Seville from 600 to 636, for example, was a great writer of encyclopedias. Along with the religious works expected of any ecclesiastical writer, such as a compilation of 610 biblical homonyms and synonyms, he also compiled a massive year-by-year chronicle from the Creation to his own day. In addition, his great twenty-book collection of "Etymologies," a catalogue of word derivations drawn from a multitude of classical works, became standard reading in the Middle Ages. Elsewhere, the Goth John of Biclara, who had studied in Constantinople, wrote a chronicle, and even Visigothic kings participated: Sisebut (612–620) wrote biography and poetry; and poetry also survives written by Chintila (636–640), Reccesvinth (649–672), and Wamba (672–680). So, during the sixth and even the seventh century, the classical tradition was still going strong in western Europe.

Nor did educational institutions vanish. Yes, education often was carried out under the auspices of the church, with much reading of scripture and sacred texts. But this was not always the case. Secular education continued to be just as important for training secular officials as it had been in the Roman period, but there was less of it, so it is less visible in the sources. Grammar, literature, and law (with particular attention to the Theodosian Code) continued to be taught well into the seventh century. In the mid-seventh century, for example, Bonitus, a young man of Clermont in Gaul, "was imbued with the elements of grammar and trained in the Theodosian decrees, and excelling the others of his age, he was examined by the *sophistae* (sophists) and advanced." His legal education then led to his appointment as royal Referendary.

At the same time, King Dagobert I assembled at court, in a sort of "palace school," a group of young men who later served as royal advisers, government officials, and bishops. Some of them came from distinguished Roman families. Desiderius of Cahors, for example, belonged to the family of Ruricius, bishop of Limoges circa 485–510, who in turn was descended from the Anicii, the most aristocratic family of late imperial Rome. After holding the offices of royal treasurer, Count of Albi, and Patrician of Marseille, in 630 Desiderius was named bishop of Cahors. He and his companions created a literary circle that was the last direct link not only to the classical culture of antiquity but also, and in particular, to the people who had created this culture. Desiderius' surviving letter collection, which maintains the tradition of Roman aristocrats whose letters to each other were the glue that bound the aristocratic elite together, is the last Latin letter collection with a direct connection to classical antiquity. But Desiderius and his fellows had no successors, and in this regard they might truly be called, for western Europe, "the last of the Romans."

The Preservation of Classical Culture

Subsequent European writers saw the classical tradition only at a distance and classical literature as a relic of a bygone day rather than as a living tradition with which they had a traceable relationship. Thus, in Europe, the end of antiquity was marked in the mid-seventh century by the passing of the last generation with a direct link to the classical past. In the future, the preservation of the traditions of classical antiquity would be the responsibility of those who looked at it secondhand, as an artifact of great value that certainly deserved preservation and emulation but not one back to which they could trace a personal connection.

The work of preserving classical culture already had begun during the sixth century, when Christian monasteries in Ireland, such as Clonard Abbey, became the focal points of a completely new tradition of Latin literature, known as Hiberno-Latin, which was characterized by obscure classical vocabulary, including Hebrew and Greek, and abstruse, sometimes incomprehensible, allusions. During the sixth and seventh centuries, Irish monks, such as Columbanus (ca. 540–615), pursued missionary work in England, Scotland, and backwoods areas of Europe and established many monasteries, as at Iona, an island on the western coast of England, and Bobbio in northern Italy, where the copying of manuscripts and building of libraries played an important role in the transmission of classical culture.

The renewal of classical culture is attested by several "Renaissances," in which classical culture was "reborn." The Visigothic one was just the first. The next was the **Carolingian Renaissance**, which began in France under the auspices of Charlemagne (768–814) and his successors as rulers of the Carolingian Empire. By this time, barbarian and Roman intellectuals had long since formed a unified group, and in the Carolingian period scholars with barbarian names such as Notker, Theodulf, Einhard, and Alcuin oversaw a revival of education and literary composition and also the preservation of thousands of late antique Latin manuscripts, which by then had moldered to the point of disintegration.

Another Renaissance, in the twelfth century, brought a new burst of interest in classical philosophical and scientific ideas and resulted largely from renewed contact with the Byzantine and Islamic worlds as a result of the Crusades, which brought ancient Greek texts and medieval Arabic texts back to western Europe. And finally, of course, there was "the" Renaissance of the fourteenth century and later, which saw a great surgeof learning based on the study of classical sources. At the same time, the **fall of Constantinople** and the Byzantine Empire in 1453 brought to western Europe many refugee Greek scholars, bearing with them the cultural heritage of the ancient Greek world. All of these renaissances attest to the continuing significance that classical culture had for the development of western culture.

⇦ LOOKING BACK

The end of the Roman Empire in the western Mediterranean is more complex than many historical surveys would have one believe. For one thing, most barbarian successes were short-lived. Only the Franks in Gaul and Anglo-Saxons in Britain stood the test of time, with the Franks giving their name to France and the Angles to England. All the rest sooner or later were conquered, absorbed, or simply disappeared. In addition, barbarian kingdoms in the old western empire continued to look very "Roman," adopting Roman laws, administration, coinage, literature, and even language. The synthesis of Roman and barbarian culture not only preserved classical culture, but also evolved seamlessly into the Middle Ages. There was no break with the past, and the concept of the "Dark Ages" is largely a creation of classical historians and philologists who fail to appreciate and understand post-Roman Europe on its own terms.

LOOKING AHEAD ⇨

Given the great degree of continuity with the Roman world, the transition from the ancient to the medieval world in western Europe is much better characterized as resulting from transformation rather than from catastrophe. The seeds of modern France, Germany, Spain, and Italy already can be seen in the post-Roman barbarian kingdoms.

FURTHER READING

Bury, J. R. *History of the Later Roman Empire from the Death of Theodosius I to the Death of Justinian.* 2 vols. London: Macmillan, 1923.

Clover, F. M. *The Late Roman West and the Vandals.* Aldershot: Ashgate, 1993.

Drew, Katherine F. *The Burgundian Code. Book of Constitutions or Law of Gundobad. Additional Enactments.* Philadelphia: Univ. of Pennsylvania Press, 1972.

Ferreiro, Alberto, ed. *The Visigoths. Studies in Culture & Society.* Brill: Leiden, 1999.

Geary, Patrick. *Before France and Germany. The Creation and Transformation of the Merovingian World.* New York: Oxford Univ. Press, 1988.

Ghosh, Shami. *Writing the Barbarian Past: Studies in Early Medieval Historical Narrative.* Leiden: Brill, 2015.

Goffart, W. *Barbarians and Romans.* A.D. *418–584. The Techniques of Accommodation.* Princeton: Princeton Univ. Press, 1987.

Goffart, Walter. *The Narrators of Barbarian History, AD 550–880: Jordanes, Gregory of Tours, Bede and Paul the Deacon.* Princeton: Princeton Univ. Press, 1988.

Halsall, Guy. *Barbarian Migrations and the Roman West, 376–568.* Cambridge, UK: Cambridge Univ. Press, 2007.

James, Edward. *The Origins of France: From Clovis to the Capetians, 500–1000.* New York: St. Martin's Press, 1982.

Mathisen, R. W. *Ruricius of Limoges and Friends: A Collection of Letters from Visigothic Gaul.* Liverpool: Liverpool Univ. Press, 1999.

Mathisen, R. W., and D. R. Shanzer, eds. *Romans, Barbarians, and the Transformation of the Roman World: Cultural Interaction and the Creation of Identity in Late Antiquity.* Farnham: Ashgate, 2011.

Moorhead, John. *The Roman Empire Divided, 400–700.* London: Longman, 2001.

Pohl, Walter, ed. *Kingdoms of the Empire: The Integration of Barbarians in Late Antiquity.* Leiden: Brill, 1997.

Ward-Perkins, Bryan. *The Fall of Rome and the End of Civilization.* Oxford: Oxford Univ. Press, 2005.

Wood, I. N. *The Merovingian Kingdoms 450–751.* London: Routledge, 1994.

SOURCES

14.1 A VISIGOTHIC KING AND HIS COURT (ca. 455/465 CE)

SIDONIUS APOLLINARIS, *LETTERS 2.1*

The remains of the Visigothic palace in Toulouse, built during the fifth century and large enough to include all the amenities described by Sidonius in his letter about King Theoderic II, were discovered in 1988 during the demolition of an old military hospital.

In the early 450s, the blue-blooded Gallo-Roman aristocrat Sidonius Apollinaris, a native of Lyon, married Papianilla, the daughter of the emperor Eparchius Avitus (455–456). Sidonius later served first as Prefect of Rome in 468 and then bishop of Clermont from CA. 469 until his death CA. 485. He thus experienced the last years of the Roman Empire and the rise of the Visigothic kingdom of Toulouse. Like most Roman aristocrats, he made his peace with the barbarian settlers. In a letter to his brother-in-law Agricola, he provided a description of the court of the Visigothic king Theoderic II (453–484).

Source: O. M. Dalton, trans., *The Letters of Sidonius*, 2 vols. (Oxford: Clarendon, 1915).

Very soon after its discovery in 1988, in an act of archaeological vandalism, the remains of the Visigothic palace in Toulouse were bulldozed to make way for the construction of these apartment buildings.

Sidonius to Agricola. You often have begged a description of Theoderic the Gothic king, whose gentle breeding fame commends to every nation. You want him in his quantity and quality, in his person, and the manner of his existence. I gladly accede, as far as the limits of my page allow, and highly approve so fine and ingenuous a curiosity. Well, he is a man worth knowing, even by those who cannot enjoy his close acquaintance, so happily have providence and nature joined to endow him with the perfect gifts of fortune. His way of life is such that not even the envy that lies in wait for kings can rob him of his proper praise.

First as to his person. He is well set up, in height above the average man, but below the giant. His head is round, with curled hair retreating somewhat from brow to crown. His nervy neck is free from disfiguring knots. The eyebrows are bushy and arched; when the lids droop, the lashes reach almost half-way down the cheeks. The upper ears are buried under overlying locks, after the fashion of his people. The nose is finely aquiline; the lips are thin and not enlarged by undue distension of the mouth. Every day the hair springing from his nostrils is cut back; that on the face springs thick from the hollow of the temples, but the razor has not yet come upon his cheek, and his barber is assiduous in eradicating the rich growth on the lower part of the face. Chin, throat, and neck are full, but not fat, and all of fair complexion. Seen close, their color is fresh as that of youth, they often flush, but from modesty and not from anger.

His shoulders are smooth, the upper-and forearms strong and hard; hands broad, breast prominent; waist receding. The spine dividing the broad expanse of back does not project, and you can see the springing of the ribs; the sides swell with salient muscle, the well-girt flanks are full of vigor. His thighs are like hard horn; the knee-joints firm and masculine; the knees themselves the comeliest and least wrinkled in the world. A full ankle supports the leg, and the foot is small to bear such mighty limbs. Now for the routine of his public life. Before daybreak he goes with a very small retinue to attend the service of his priests.[1] He prays with assiduity, but, if I may speak in confidence, one may suspect more of habit than conviction in this piety. Administrative duties of the kingdom take up the rest of the morning. Armed nobles stand about the royal seat; the mass of guards in their garb of skins are admitted that they may be within call, but kept at the threshold for quiet's sake; only a murmur of them comes in from their post at the doors, between the curtain and the outer barrier.

And now the foreign envoys are introduced. The king hears them out, and says little. If a thing needs more discussion he puts it off, but he accelerates matters ripe for dispatch. The second hour[1] arrives; he rises from the throne to inspect his

---

[1] During antiquity and the Middle Ages, the day's activities started at sunrise and daylight was divided into twelve parts. Thus, the "second hour" began at approximately 5 AM in the summer and 8 AM in the winter.

treasure-chamber or stable. If the chase is the order of the day, he joins it, but never carries his bow at his side, considering this derogatory to royal state. When a bird or beast is marked for him, or happens to cross his path, he puts his hand behind his back and takes the bow from a page with the string all hanging loose; for as he deems it a boy's trick to carry it in a case, so he considers it effeminate to receive the weapon ready strung. When it is given to him, he sometimes holds it in both hands and bends the extremities toward each other; at others he sets it, knot-end downward, against his lifted heel and runs his finger up the slack and wavering string. After that, he takes his arrows, adjusts, and lets fly. He will ask you beforehand what you would like him to transfix; you choose, and he hits. If there is a miss through either's error, your vision will mostly be at fault and not the archer's skill.

On ordinary days, his table resembles that of a private person. The board does not groan beneath a mass of dull and unpolished silver set on by panting servitors; the weight lies rather in the conversation than in the plate; there is either sensible talk or none. The hangings and draperies used on these occasions are sometimes of purple silk, sometimes only of linen. Art, not costliness, commends the fare, as spotlessness rather than bulk does the silver. Toasts are few, and you will oftener see a thirsty guest impatient than a full one refusing cup or bowl. In short, you will find the elegance of Greece, the good cheer of Gaul, Italian nimbleness, the state of public banquets with the attentive service of a private table, and everywhere the discipline of a king's house. What need for me to describe the pomp of his feast days? No man is so unknown as not to know of them.

But to my theme again. The siesta after lunch is always slight and sometimes omitted. When inclined for the board game, he is quick to gather up the dice, examines them with care, shakes the box with expert hand, throws rapidly, humorously addresses them, and patiently waits the issue. Silent at a good throw, he makes merry over a bad, annoyed by neither fortune and always the philosopher. He is too proud to ask or to refuse a revenge;[2] he disdains

to avail himself of one if offered and if it is used by an opponent he will quietly go on playing. You effect recovery of your own gaming pieces without obstruction on his side; he recovers his without collusion upon yours. You see the strategist when he moves the pieces; his one thought is victory. Yet at play he puts off a little of his kingly rigor, inciting all to good fellowship and the freedom of the game: I think he is afraid of being feared. Vexation in the man whom he beats delights him; he will never believe that his opponents have not let him win unless their annoyance proves him really victor. You would be surprised at how often the pleasure born of these little happenings may favor the march of great affairs. Petitions that some wrecked influence had left derelict come unexpectedly to port. I myself am gladly beaten by him when I have a favor to ask, because the loss of my game may mean the gaining of my cause. About the ninth hour,[3] the burden of government begins again. Back come the appellants, back the ushers to remove them. On all sides buzz the voices of petitioners, a sound that lasts until evening and does not diminish until interrupted by the royal repast. Even then they only disperse to attend their various patrons among the courtiers, and are astir until bedtime. Sometimes, although this is rare, supper is enlivened by sallies of mimes,[4] but no guest is ever exposed to the wound of a satirical tongue. On the other hand, there is no noise of a hydraulic organ or a choir with its conductor intoning a set piece. You will hear no lyre or flute players, no director of the music, no girls with tambourine or lute. The king cares for no strains but those that no less charm the mind with virtue than the ear with melody. When he rises to withdraw, the treasury watch begins its vigil; armed sentries stand on guard during the first hours of slumber.

But I am wandering from my subject. I never promised a whole chapter on the kingdom, but a few words about the king. I must stay my pen; you asked for nothing more than one or two facts about the person and the tastes of Theoderic; and my own aim was to write a letter, not a history. Farewell.

---

[2] Apparently an opportunity to retake a throw.

[3] About 2 PM in summer and 1 PM in winter.

[4] A popular form of entertainment.

PROCOPIUS, *HISTORY OF THE WARS*, BOOK 3, CHAPTERS 10–20

A silver *siliqua* of Gelimer (530–534), the last king of the Vandals. The legend on the obverse reads, "Our Lord King Geilamir." The reverse shows a Christian cross in a wreath, along with the number "L" and the abbreviation "D N", signifying the coin's value as "50 *denarii.*" The *denarius* by this time was strictly a notional value and had no direct connection with the *denarius* of the Roman Principate.

Traditional accounts of the fall of the Western Roman Empire leave the reader supposing that as of 476 the barbarians had "won," having established kingdoms throughout the old western empire. But appearances, and popular perceptions, can be deceiving. A mere seventy-five years later much of the western empire had been reconquered by the Roman emperor Justinian (527–565), thus recreating an empire that extended from the cataracts of the Nile to the Strait of Gibraltar. The reconquest commenced in 533, when Justinian sent his general Belisarius to North Africa in an effort to defeatthe Vandals and their king Gelimer (530–534). At the Battle of Ad Decimum the Vandal army was destroyed and Gelimer put to flight. Belisarius then occupied Carthage, just as the Vandals themselves had done almost a century earlier. Later in the same year the remaining Vandal resistance was mopped up at the Battle of Tricamarum, which effectively brought the Vandal Kingdom to an end. After being displayed in Justinian's triumph in Constantinople, Gelimer spent the rest of his life in honorable retirement on estates granted to him in Galatia. A detailed account of the war was written by the historian Procopius, who, as an Assessor, or legal expert, accompanied Belisarius on his campaigns.

Source: H. B. Dewing, trans., *Procopius. History of the Wars, Books III and IV* (Cambridge, MA: Harvard Univ. Press, 1916).

And when the emperor Justinian[5] considered that the situation was as favorable as possible, both as to domestic affairs and as to his relations with Persia,[6] he took under consideration the situation in Libya.[7] But when he disclosed to the magistrates

---

[5] Byzantine emperor from 527 until 565; often looked upon as a model Byzantine emperor.

[6] The Sasanid, or New Persian, Empire to the east, which often was in a state of war with the Byzantine Empire.

[7] In this case, a reference to the Vandal Kingdom in modern Tunisia and Algeria in North Africa.

that he was gathering an army against the Vandals and Gelimer,[8] most of them began immediately to show hostility to the plan, and they lamented it as a misfortune, recalling the expedition of the emperor Leo and the disaster of Basiliscus,[9] and reciting how many soldiers had perished and how much money the state had lost. The emperor Justinian, hearkening, checked his eager desire for the war. But one of the bishops, who had come from the east, said that he wished to have a word with the emperor. And when he met Justinian, he said that God had visited him in a dream, and bidden him go to the emperor and rebuke him, because, after undertaking the task of protecting the Christians in Libya from tyrants, he had for no good reason become afraid. "And yet," God had said, "I will myself join with him in waging war and make him lord of Libya."

When the emperor heard this, he was no longer able to restrain his purpose, and he began to collect the army and the ships, and to make ready supplies of weapons and of food, and he announced to Belisarius[10] that he should be prepared, because he was very soon to act as general in Libya. He had in readiness for the expedition against Carthage ten thousand foot-soldiers and five thousand horsemen,[11] gathered from the regular troops and from the *foederati*. Now at an earlier time only barbarians were enlisted among the *foederati*, those, namely, who had come into the Roman political system, not in the condition of slaves, because they had not been conquered by the Romans, but on the basis of complete equality. For the Romans call treaties with their enemies "foedera." But at the present time there is nothing to prevent anyone from assuming this name.[12]

And after this the general Belisarius and Antonina,[13] his wife, set sail. And there was with

them also Procopius, who wrote this history. When they came near the shore, the general bade them furl the sails, throw out anchors from the ships, and make a halt. They made the disembarkation as quickly as possible, about three months later than their departure from Byzantium. And indicating a certain spot on the shore the general bade both soldiers and sailors dig the trench and place the stockade about it.[14]

And Belisarius, having arrayed his army as for battle, began the march to Carthage. And accomplishing eighty stades[15] each day, we completed the whole journey to Carthage, passing the night either in a city, should it so happen, or in a camp made as thoroughly secure as the circumstances permitted. Thus we passed through the cities of Leptis[16] and Hadrumetum[17] and reached the place called Grasse, three hundred and fifty stades distant from Carthage. But Gelimer, as soon as he heard in Hermione[18] that the enemy were at hand, wrote to his brother Ammatas in Carthage to kill Hilderic[19] and all the others, connected with him either by birth or otherwise, whom he was keeping under guard. He commanded him to make ready the Vandals and all others in the city serviceable for war, in order that, when the enemy got inside the narrow passage at the suburb of the city that they call Ad Decimum,[20] they might come together from both sides and surround

---

[8] The last king of the Vandals (530–534 CE).

[9] A failed attempt made in 468 CE to reconquer North Africa by the eastern emperor Leo (457–474) was led by Leo's incompetent brother-in-law Basiliscus.

[10] Justinian's best and most reliable general.

[11] A remarkably small number compared to the much larger armies of antiquity.

[12] The *foederati* were still random auxiliary units.

[13] The wife of Belisarius. She came from a family of entertainers; her father and grandfather were charioteers and her mother an actress, an occupation that often involved prostitution. Like Theodora, the wife of the emperor Justinian,

who also had been an entertainer (Source 15.2), Antonia, who also accompanied her husband on the campaign, manifests the opportunities for social advancement, especially for able women, that characterized Late Antiquity.

[14] As they had ever since the days of the Republic, Roman armies on the march fortified their camps.

[15] A *stade* was approximately six hundred feet, making eighty stades about nine and a half miles.

[16] Leptis Magna, a Roman city on the Libyan coast eighty miles east of modern Tripoli.

[17] A Phoenician trading colony of the ninth century BCE that predated Carthage.

[18] A small inland city.

[19] Grandson of the Vandal king Gaiseric and son of Gaiseric's son Huneric and Eudocia, daughter of the emperor Valentinian III. Hilderic served as king of the Vandals from 523 until 530, when he was deposed by his cousin Gelimer. Gelimer's rude responses to Justinian's protests gave Justinian the pretext for invading North Africa.

[20] A town located at the tenth mile post of one of the Roman roads leading out of Carthage.

them and, catching them as in a net, destroy them. Belisarius commanded Archelaus, the Prefect, and Calonymus, the Admiral, not to put in at Carthage, but to remain about two hundred stades away until he himself should summon them. And departing from Grasse we came on the fourth day to Ad Decimum, seventy stades distant from Carthage.

Belisarius, seeing a place well adapted for a camp, thirty-five stades distant from Ad Decimum, surrounded it with a stockade that was very well made, and placing all the infantry there and calling together the whole army, he spoke as follows:

> Fellow-soldiers, the decisive moment of the struggle is already at hand, for I perceive that the enemy are advancing upon us. The ships have been taken far away from us by the nature of the place, and it has come round to this that our hope of safety lies in the strength of our hands. For there is not a friendly city, no, nor any other stronghold, in which we may put our trust and have confidence concerning ourselves. But if we should show ourselves brave men, we shall overcome the enemy, but if we should weaken at all, we will fall under the hand of the Vandals and be destroyed disgracefully. And yet there are many advantages on our side to help us on toward victory; for we have with us both justice, with which we have come against our enemy, for we are here in order to recover what is our own, and the hatred of the Vandals toward their own tyrant. For the alliance of God follows naturally those who put justice forward, and a soldier who is ill-disposed toward his ruler knows not how to play the part of a brave man. And apart from this, we have been engaged with Persians and Scythians[21] all the time, but the Vandals, since the time they conquered Libya, have seen not a single enemy except naked Moors.[22] And who does not know that in every work practice leads to skill, whereas idleness leads to inefficiency? Now the stockade, from which we shall have to carry on the war, has been made by us in the best possible manner. And we are able to deposit here our weapons and everything else that we are not able to carry

> when we go forth; and when we return here again, no kind of provisions can fail us. And I pray that each one of you, calling to mind his own valor and those whom he has left at home, may so march with contempt against the enemy.

After speaking these words and uttering a prayer after them, Belisarius left his wife and the barricaded camp to the infantry, and himself set forth with all the horsemen. For it did not seem to him advantageous for the present to risk an engagement with the whole army, but it seemed wise to skirmish first with the horsemen and make trial of the enemy's strength, and later to fight a decisive battle with the whole army. Sending forward, therefore, the commanders of the *foederati*, he himself followed with the rest of the force, and his own spearmen and guards.[23] And when the *foederati* and their leaders reached Ad Decimum, they saw the corpses of the twelve comrades from the forces of John and near them Ammatas and some of the Vandals.[24] Hearing from the inhabitants of the place the whole story of the fight, they were vexed, being at a loss as to where they ought to go. But while they were still at a loss and from the hills were looking around over the whole country thereabouts, a dust appeared from the south and a little later a very large force of Vandal horsemen. They sent to Belisarius urging him to come as quickly as possible because the enemy were bearing down upon them. The opinions of the commanders were divided. Some thought that they ought to close with their assailants, but the others said that their force was not sufficient for this.

While they were debating thus among themselves, the barbarians drew near under the leadership of Gelimer, who was following a road between the one that Belisarius was traveling and the one by which the Massagetae who had encountered Gibamundus had come. But the land was hilly on

---

[21] Huns.

[22] The native inhabitants of North Africa.

[23] The Roman generals of Late Antiquity had attendant upon them large numbers of personal retainers.

[24] In one skirmish on the previous day, Roman Massagetae had defeated a Vandal force led by Gibamundus, and in another Roman forces led by John the Armenian had killed Gelimer's brother Ammatus.

both sides and did not allow him to see either the disaster of Gibamundus or Belisarius' stockade nor even the road along which Belisarius' men were advancing. But when they came near each other, a contest arose between the two armies as to which should capture the highest of all the hills there, for it seemed a suitable one to encamp upon, and both sides preferred to engage with the enemy from there. The Vandals, coming first, took possession of the hill by crowding off their assailants and routed the enemy, having already become an object of terror to them. And the Romans in flight came to a place seven stades distant from Ad Decimum, where, as it happened, Uliaris, the personal guard of Belisarius, was, with eight hundred guardsmen. All supposed that Uliaris would receive them and hold his position, and together with them would go against the Vandals, but when they came together, these troops all unexpectedly fled at top speed and went on the run to Belisarius.

From then on I am unable to say what happened to Gelimer because, having the victory in his hands, he willingly gave it up to the enemy. For if, on the one hand, he had made the pursuit immediately, I do not think that even Belisarius would have withstood him and our cause would have been utterly and completely lost, so numerous appeared the force of the Vandals and so great the fear they inspired in the Romans. Or if, on the other hand, he had even ridden straight for Carthage, he would easily have killed all John's men,[25] who, heedless of everything else, were wandering about the plain one by one or by twos and stripping the dead. He would have preserved the city with its treasures and captured our ships, which had come rather near, and he would have withdrawn from us all hope both of sailing away and of victory. But in fact he did neither of these things. Instead, he descended from the hill at a walk, and when he reached the level ground and saw the corpse of his brother, he turned to lamentations, and, in caring for his burial, he blunted the edge of his opportunity, an opportunity that he was not able to grasp again.

Meantime Belisarius, meeting the fugitives, bade them stop and arrayed them all in order

and rebuked them at length. Then, after hearing of the death of Ammatas and the pursuit of John and learning what he wished concerning the place and the enemy, he proceeded at full speed against Gelimer and the Vandals. The barbarians, having already fallen into disorder and being now unprepared, could not withstand the onset of the Romans, but fled with all their might, losing many there, and the battle ended at night. Now the Vandals were in flight, not to Carthage nor to Byzacium,[26] whence they had come, but to the plain of Boulla and the road leading into Numidia.[27] So the men with John and the Massagetae returned to us about dusk, and after learning all that had happened and reporting what they had done, they passed the night with us in Ad Decimum.

On the following day the infantry with the wife of Belisarius came up and we all proceeded together on the road toward Carthage, which we reached in the late evening. We passed the night in the open, although no one hindered us from marching into the city at once. For the Carthaginians opened the gates and burned lights everywhere and the city was brilliant with the illumination that whole night, and those of the Vandals who had been left behind were sitting as suppliants in the sanctuaries. But Belisarius prevented the entrance in order not only to guard against any ambush being set for his men by the enemy but also to prevent the soldiers from having freedom to turn to plundering, as they might under the concealment of night.

On the following day Belisarius commanded those on the ships to disembark, and after marshalling the whole army and drawing it up in battle formation, he marched into Carthage; for he feared lest he should encounter some snare set by the enemy. There he reminded the soldiers at length of how much good fortune had come to them because they had displayed moderation toward the Libyans, and he exhorted them earnestly to preserve good order with the greatest care in Carthage. Because no enemy was seen by them, he went up to the palace and seated himself on Gelimer's throne.

---

[25] From the battle the day before.

[26] A coastal region south of Carthage.

[27] A region of North Africa west of Carthage.

GREGORY OF TOURS, *HISTORIES*, BOOK 2, CHAPTERS 28–31

Constantine was not the only ruler who was confronted by a choice of religions. The king of the Franks Clovis (481–511), who also had been raised as a pagan, faced the same dilemma. And like Constantine, his decision was believed to have been made as a result of a military victory. Gregory of Tours, writing a century later, reported that circa 496 CE, during a hard-fought battle with the Alamanni, Clovis promised to become a Christian if he won. After the Frankish victory, Clovis, encouraged by his Nicene Christian wife, the Burgundian princess Clotilda, was baptized as a Nicene Christian by Remigius, the Roman bishop of Reims. As a result, barbarians and Romans in the Frankish kingdom shared the same religious beliefs and practices, greatly facilitating the integration of the two populations. His Nicene faith gained Clovis valuable Roman support during his subsequent war with the Visigoths, who espoused a non-Nicene form of Christianity. At the pivotal Battle of Vouillé in 507, Clovis defeated and killed the Visigothic king Alaric II (484–507), and the Franks occupied most of the Visigothic territories in Gaul, thus becoming the primary barbarian power in Gaul.

Source: Ernest Brehaut, *History of the Franks, by Gregory, Bishop of Tours* (Oxford: Oxford Univ. Press, 1916), 38–41.

Now the king of the Burgundians was Gundioc, of the family of king Athanaric[28] the persecutor. He had four sons: Gundobad,[29] Godegisel, Chilperic, and Godomar. Gundobad killed his brother Chilperic with the sword and sank his wife in water with a stone tied to her neck. His two daughters he condemned to exile; the older of these, who became a nun, was called Chrona, and the younger Clotilda. And as Clovis[30] often sent embassies to Burgundy,[31] the maiden Clotilda was encountered by his envoys. And when they saw that she was of good bearing and wise, and learned that she was of the family of the king, they reported this to King Clovis, and he sent an embassy to Gundobad without delay asking her in marriage. Gundobad was afraid to refuse and surrendered her to the men. They took the girl and brought her swiftly to the king. The king was very glad when he saw her, and married her, having already by a concubine a son named Theoderic.[32]

He had a first-born son by queen Clotilda, and as his wife wished to consecrate him in baptism, she tried unceasingly to persuade her husband, saying, "The gods you worship are nothing, and they will be unable to help themselves or anyone else. For they are graven out of stone or wood or some metal. And the names you have given them are names of men and not of gods, such as Saturn, who is declared to have fled in fear of being banished from his kingdom by his son; such as Jupiter[33] himself, the foul perpetrator of all shameful crimes, committing incest with men, mocking at his kinswomen, not able to refrain from intercourse with his own sister."[34]

But the spirit of the king was by no means moved to belief, and he said, "It was at the command of our gods that all things were created and came forth, and it is plain that your god has no power and, what is more, he is proven not to

[28] There is no other evidence that the Burgundian king Gundioc was related to the Visigothic chieftain Athanaric, who lived more than a century earlier and died as an exile in Constantinople in 381. Athanaric had persecuted Gothic Christians.

[29] King of the Burgundians from 473 until 516.

[30] King of the Franks from 481 until 511 CE

[31] The Burgundian kingdom, the region around Lyon in France.

[32] Later the Frankish king Theoderic I (511–534).

[33] Jupiter (Greek Zeus) overcame his father Saturn (Greek Cronus) and became king of the gods.

[34] Juno (Greek Hera) the sister and wife of Jupiter.

belong to the family of the gods." Meantime, the faithful queen made her son ready for baptism. She gave command to adorn the church with hangings and curtains, so that he who could not be moved by persuasion might be urged to belief by this mystery. The boy, whom they named Ingomer, died after being baptized, still wearing the white garments in which he became reborn. At this the king was violently angry and reproached the queen harshly, saying: "If the boy had been dedicated in the name of my gods he would certainly have lived; but as it is, because he was baptized in the name of your god, he could not live at all." After this she bore another son, whom she named Chlodomer[35] at baptism, and when he fell sick, the king said, "It is impossible that anything else should happen to him than what happened to his brother, namely, that being baptized in the name of your Christ, he should die at once." But through the prayers of his mother, and the Lord's command, he became well.

The queen did not cease to urge him to recognize the true God and cease worshipping idols. But he could not be influenced in any way to this belief, until at last a war arose with the Alamanni,[36] in which he was driven by necessity to confess what before he had of his free will denied. It came about that as the two armies were fighting fiercely, there was much slaughter, and Clovis' army began to be in danger of destruction.

He saw it and raised his eyes to heaven, and with remorse in his heart he burst into tears and cried, "Jesus Christ, whom Clotilda asserts to be the son of the living God, who are said to give aid to those in distress and to bestow victory on those who hope in you, I beseech the glory of your aid, with the vow that if you will grant me victory over these enemies and I shall know that power that she says that people dedicated in your name have had from you, I will believe in you and be baptized in you name. For I have invoked my own gods but, as I find, they have withdrawn from aiding me, and therefore I believe that they possess no power, because they do not help those who obey them. I now call upon

you, I desire to believe you, only let me be rescued from my adversaries." And when he said thus, the Alamanni turned their backs and began to disperse in flight. And when they saw that their king was killed, they submitted to the dominion of Clovis, saying, "Let not the people perish further, we pray. We are yours now." And he stopped the fighting, and after encouraging his men, he retired in peace and told the queen how he had had merited to win the victory by calling on the name of Christ. This happened in the fifteenth year of his reign.

Then the queen asked saint Remigius, bishop of Reims, to summon Clovis secretly, urging him to introduce the king to the word of salvation. And the bishop sent for him secretly and began to urge him to believe in the true God, maker of heaven and earth, and to cease worshipping idols, which could help neither themselves nor anyone else. But the king said, "I gladly hear you, most holy father; but there remains one thing: the people who follow me cannot endure to abandon their gods; but I shall go and speak to them according to your words." He met with his followers, but before he could speak the power of God anticipated him, and all the people cried out together, "O pious king, we reject our mortal gods and we are ready to follow the immortal God whom Remigius preaches." This was reported to the bishop, who greatly rejoiced and bade them get ready the baptismal font. The squares were shaded with tapestried canopies, the churches adorned with white curtains, the baptistery[37] set in order, the aroma of incense spread, candles of fragrant odor burned brightly, and the whole shrine of the baptistery was filled with a divine fragrance and the lord gave such grace to those who stood by that they thought they were placed amid the odors of paradise.

The king was the first to ask to be baptized by the bishop. Another Constantine[38] advanced to the baptismal font, to terminate the disease of ancient leprosy and wash away with fresh water the foul spots that long had been borne. And when he entered to be baptized, the saint of God

---

[35] Later king of the Franks from 511 to 524.

[36] A people living between the upper Rhine and upper Danube rivers.

[37] A chapel, inside or outside a church, used for baptisms.

[38] Constantine I (306–337), who likewise had adopted Christianity after being raised as a pagan.

began with ready speech, "Gently bend your neck, Sicamber,[39] worship what you burned; burn what you worshipped." The holy bishop Remigius was a man of excellent wisdom and especially trained in rhetorical studies, and of such surpassing holiness that he equaled the miracles of Silvester.[40] For there is extant a book of his life that tells that he raised a dead man. So the king confessed all-powerful God in the Trinity, and was baptized in the name of the Father, Son, and Holy Spirit, and was anointed with the holy ointment with the sign of the cross of Christ. And of his army more than 3000 were baptized. His sister also, Albofleda, was baptized, who not long after passed to the Lord. And when the king was in mourning for her, the holy Remigius sent a letter of consolation that began in this way, "The reason of your mourning pains me, and pains me greatly, that Albofleda your sister, of good memory, has passed away. But I can give you this comfort, that her departure from the world was such that she ought to be envied rather than be mourned." Another sister also converted, Lanthechildis by name, who had fallen into the heresy of the Arians,[41] and she confessed that the Son and the Holy Spirit were equal to the Father, and was anointed.[42]

---

[39] The Sicambrians were one of the peoples who made up the Franks.

[40] The bishop of Rome (314–335), who in the Middle Ages was said to have baptized Constantine and to have issued the "Donation of Constantine," a forged document that granted dominion of the Western Roman Empire to the bishop of Rome.

---

[41] The derogatory name used by Gregory for the Homoian Christians.

[42] That is, she accepted the Nicene Creed and abandoned Homoian theology.

THE PERSISTENCE OF THE CLASSICAL TRADITION IN BARBARIAN EUROPE (ca. 575 CE)

THE POEM OF EUCHERIA

Even barbarian kings assisted in the preservation of the classical poetic tradition, as when the Frankish king Chilperic (561–584) authored a poem in honor of Saint Medardus, the only surviving copy of which is found in a tenth-century manuscript preserved in Zurich, Switzerland: the subscription reads, "King Chilperic composed this hymn." Chiliperic was so engaged with literature and learning that he even ordered four letters to be added to the alphabet.

The only surviving poem of the author Eucheria was written in Gaul around the last quarter of the sixth century and is preserved in a collection of secular poems known as the "Latin Anthology." It is unclear what her connection is to the Rusticus, named in the last line, to whom the poem is addressed; he could be a paramour, or perhaps "Rusticus" is a nickname for her husband, the Patrician Dynamius of Marseille, who served in Provence in the middle to late sixth century. The poem exhibits many of the characteristic traits of late Roman poetry, such as overblown rhetoric; obscure allusions, especially to mythology and the heroic Roman past; and the use of such literary tricks as antithesis (opposites), alliteration, and rhyme. Eucheria survived Dynamius by eight years and died circa 605. Their epitaph, in the Church of St. Hippolytus at Marseille, was erected by a grandson, also named Dynamius. Eucheria's literary activities demonstrate the continued survival and vitality of the Roman secular literary tradition in barbarian Europe into the late sixth century CE and beyond.

Source: Ralph W. Mathisen, *People, Personal Expression, and Social Relations in Late Antiquity. Volume I. With Translated Texts from Gaul and Western Europe* (Ann Arbor: Univ. of Michigan Press, 2003), 38–40.

I wish to fuse golden threads, shining with harmonious metal, with masses of bristles.

Silken coverings, gem-studded Laconian[43] fabrics,

I say, must be matched with goat skins.

Let noble purple be joined with a frightful red jacket;

let the gleaming gemstone be joined to ponderous lead.

Let the pearl now be held captive by its own brightness,

and let it shine enclosed in dark steel.

Likewise, let the emerald be enclosed in Leuconian[44] bronze,

and let now hyacinth[45] be the equal of flint.

Let jasper be said to be like rubble and rocks;

let now the moon embrace the nether void.

Now, indeed, let us decree that lilies are to be joined with nettles,

and let the menacing hemlock oppress the scarlet rose.

Now, similarly, let us therefore, spurning the fish, choose

to disdain the delicacies of the great sea.

Let the rock-dwelling toad love the golden serpent,

and likewise let the female trout seek for herself the male snail.

And let the lofty lioness be joined with the foul fox;

let the ape embrace the sharp-eyed lynx.

Now let the doe be joined to the donkey, and the tigress to the wild ass;

now let the fleet deer be joined to the torpid bull.

Let now the foul silphium juice[46] taint the nectared rose-wine,

and let now honey be mixed with vile poisons.

Let us associate sparkling water with the muddy cesspool;

let the fountain flow saturated with a mixture of filth.

Let the swift swallow cavort with the funereal vulture;

let now the nightingale serenade with the doleful owl.

Let the unhappy coop-dweller[47] abide with the pellucid partridge,

and let the beautiful dove lie coupled with the crow.

Let the times manipulate these monstrosities with uncertain consequences,

and in this way let the slave Rusticus seek Eucheria.

---

[43] From Laconia, in Greece, the homeland of Sparta.

[44] A reference to Leuci (modern Toul) in Gaul.

[45] A gemstone, possibly a kind of sapphire or dark amethyst, the color of the hyacinth flower (perhaps a larkspur).

---

[46] A bad-smelling gum resin obtained from the silphium plant and used medicinally as an antispasmodic drug.

[47] The inhabitant of a bird coop.

CHAPTER 15

BYZANTIUM AND ISLAM: THE END OF ANTIQUITY IN THE EAST (402–650)

After the fall of the Western Roman Empire, in the east the Roman Empire, now known to modern historians as the Byzantine Empire, continued to survive and even flourish, adapting to changing times just as it had done in the past. During the seventh century, the ancient world was even more dramatically changed with the appearance of a new religion, Islam, in Arabia. The Persian Empire disappeared, and Muslims soon occupied much of the ancient world.

THE BYZANTINE EMPIRE

During the course of the fifth century, the Eastern Roman Empire (in the modern day also known as the Byzantine Empire, after the ancient Greek colony of Byzantium, where Constantinople had been established) confronted many of the same problems as the west but was able to deal with them more effectively and, as a result, continued to survive. In the sixth century, under the emperor Justinian, the empire again became a Mediterranean-wide empire, and the emperor became the head of both state and church.But afterward, the empire was faced by growing foreign threats. In the early seventh century, after barely winning a long and devastating war with the New Persian Empire, the emperor Heraclius was confronted by an even greater threat to the empire's survival.

The east Romans always called themselves Romans. The term "Byzantine" arose because of a modern western European reluctance to acknowledge the Roman identity of eastern Greeks.

The Age of Theodosius II

The emperor Theodosius II (402–450) ruled for nearly half a century. For much of this period he was very much under the influence of his elder sister Pulcheria, a consecrated virgin who in 414, at the age of sixteen, was made Augusta. He was much more of a scholar than a soldier and thus was nicknamed "the Calligrapher." His intellectual interests were manifested in several ways. He reorganized

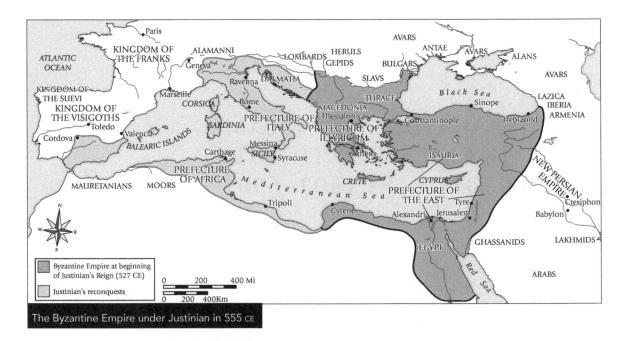

The Byzantine Empire under Justinian in 555 CE

the university of Constantinople, giving it thirty-one professors teaching grammar, rhetoric, philosophy, and law. And in 437, he issued the **Theodosian Code**, a compilation of all the significant Roman laws going back to the time of Constantine. It provides a wealth of information about Roman administration and society and the economy and gives us insight into what the emperors thought were some of the most important issues facing them.

During Theodosius' reign there was a continuing lack of Christian unity. After the demise of Arianism, other beliefs arose to challenge Nicene theology. The third ecumenical church **Council of Ephesus** in 431 condemned **Nestorianism**, which taught that Christ's divine and human natures were completely separate rather than intermingled. Many Nestorians then went into exile in the New Persian Empire, where they survived as the Church of the East; some even settled in China, where their descendents were encountered by Marco Polo.

But the most immediate problem faced by Theodosius was the continuing barbarian threat. Massive new walls were built on the landward side of Constantinople, and, because the government was reluctant to recruit too many barbarians, the empire continued to be plagued by military recruitment problems. The greatest pressure came from the Huns, who had settled in the former Roman province of Dacia (modern Romania) and were dealt with by the simple expedient of buying them off and calling them allies. Their demands became increasingly onerous. Circa 445, Attila, the king of the Huns, adopted a much more adversarial attitude toward the empire, eventually requiring annual subsidies of 2,100 pounds of gold. Numerous embassies,

A portrait bust, now in the Louvre Museum in Paris, depicts the emperor Theodosius II (402–450), who in 437 issued the Theodosian Code, a compilation of all the significant Roman laws going back to the time of Constantine.

discussed by the Byzantine ambassador Priscus, went back and forth between the Byzantine and Hunnic courts. In order to enforce his claims to Roman largess, Attila periodically invaded the Eastern Roman Empire. After a campaign of 447, the Romans were compelled to evacuate a strip south of the Danube five-days'-march wide. Paradoxically, however, the general freedom from attack resulted in some return of economic prosperity; even much of the subsidy paid to the Huns eventually made its way back to the Roman world in the form of commerce. The Huns also were something of a blessing in disguise: because they also threatened the New Persian Empire, the Romans and Persians found it advantageous to maintain generally peaceful relations.

Marcian and the Quarrel over the Nature of Christ

In 450 Theodosius II died and was succeeded by Marcian (450–457), an elderly senator whose nominal marriage to Pulcheria made him a part of the old dynasty. Marcian decided to call the Huns' bluff and terminated the payment of the subsidy. He was rewarded when, as already seen, the Huns were defeated by the western Roman general Aëtius in 451. Two years later, Attila died of a hemorrhage on his wedding night. He subsequently obtained a reputation as the stereotypical savage barbarian. Christian moralists referred to him as the "scourge of God" for his perceived role in punishing sinful Christians. Meanwhile, Attila's barbarian Empire of the Huns disintegrated when the subject peoples revolted and defeated the Huns in 454 at the Battle of the Nedao River in Hungary. In this case, however, the cure may have been worse than the disease. During the days of Attila, the Byzantine government had only him to deal with; after the defeat of the Huns, the subject peoples scattered and caused a multitude of problems for the Byzantines.

An even more serious religious problem now was caused by the **Miaphysites**, also known as Monophysites—Greek terms for "one nature"—who argued that the human and divine natures of Christ were united into a single nature, with the human portion being inconsequential in comparison to the divine part. In 448, at the "Robber Council" of Ephesus, the Miaphysites were cleared of heresy. But the accession of Marcian brought a reconsideration of the matter. With the vociferous encouragement of Leo, the powerful and able bishop of Rome, Miaphysite teachings were condemned at the fourth ecumenical **Council of Chalcedon** summoned by Marcian in 451. It validated the teaching that the human and divine natures of Christ were united while at the same time retaining their individual identities. The Chalcedonian definition, which accepted and more closely defined the Nicene Creed, then became the orthodox teaching of the imperial church.

TABLE 15.1 EMPERORS, RULERS, AND DYNASTIES OF THE BYZANTINE EMPIRE AND THE ISLAMIC CALIPHATE (402–668)

The Dynasty of Valentinian and Theodosius
Theodosius II (402–450)
Marcian (450–457)
The Dynasty of Leo
Leo (457–474)
Zeno (474–491)
Anastasius (491–518)
The Dynasty of Justinian
Justin (518–527)
Justinian (527–565)
Justin II (565–578)
Tiberius II (578–582)
Maurice (582–602)
Phocas (usurper) (602–610)
The Dynasty of Heraclius
Heraclius (610–641)
Heraclius Constantine (641)
Heracleonas (641)
Constans II (641–668)
Rashidun Caliphate
Abu Bakr (632–634)
Umar (634–644)
Uthman (644–656)
Ali (656–661)

But the Chalcedonian definition continued to be opposed by the Miaphysites of Syria and Egypt, where the Miaphysites—who simply called themselves Christians—eventually developed into the modern-day Jacobites and Copts. The controversy was never resolved, and it created a continuing sense of alienation in the eastern provinces. The Council of Chalcedon also sowed the seeds of future bickering between east and west by giving the bishop of Constantinople the same status as the bishop of Rome. Leo and his successors found this difficult to swallow, and the offensive clause was expunged from western editions of the council.

The Dynasty of Leo

Marcian's successor Leo (457–474), acclaimed by the army with the support of the barbarian Master of Soldiers Aspar, established a rather short-lived imperial dynasty. He largely solved the east's military manpower shortage by locating a new source of Roman recruits in Isauria, in the backwoods of Anatolia. In 474, an Isaurian chieftain named Tarasicodissa, who adopted the more acceptable Greek name **Zeno** (474–491), even became emperor, in much the same way that the Illyrian soldier-emperors had done so in the third century. Zeno attempted to deal with continued religious dissent by issuing in 492 the **Henotikon**, which proposed to satisfy both theological factions by condemning or approving only theologies that both sides already agreed on and by saying nothing at all about Christ's natures. Although this initiative attests to Zeno's good faith, it says little about his sense of political realities, for his compromise in fact satisfied no one, and religious dissent continued to rage.

Under the emperor Anastasius (491–518), who married Zeno's widow Ariadne, economic prosperity returned to the east. He gave tax abatements to devastated areas, allowing them get to back on their feet, and relieved the decurions of the responsibility for collecting taxes, which henceforth was done directly by imperial officials. Anastasius also reintroduced a copper coinage that could be exchanged for gold coinage. This restored confidence in the copper currency and meant that the government could issue large numbers of copper coins that circulated as if they were gold coins, resulting in a great expansion of the money supply. It also facilitated exchange at the local level, leading to economic expansion and increased tax revenues. By the end of Anastasius' reign, there were 320,000 pounds of gold in the treasury.

Other problems were not so easily solved. Religious dissent continued to simmer: Anastasius' own religious sympathies were so suspect that he was compelled to subscribe to the Henotikon by those who feared he would support the Miaphysites. The reign of Anastasius also saw an increase in urban violence. The **"Blue"** and **"Green"** chariot-racing fan clubs served as thinly veiled political activist groups that often used violence to support their views on matters such as theological beliefs and imperial appointments. In the course of one riot, Anastasius presented himself bareheaded and offered to resign. The fickle mob declined this magnanimous offer.

THE AGE OF JUSTINIAN

By the early sixth century, the Byzantine Empire was back on its feet. The barbarian threat had been subdued, economic prosperity had been restored, and religious dissent had been muffled. At the same time that the western Roman world was coping with the realities of the barbarian settlement, the Byzantine world was on the verge of momentous developments. In 518, after Anastasius died without an heir, a Thracian general, Justin (518–527), was named emperor without any fuss. His reign was generally peaceful and uneventful, and he soon associated his nephew, **Justinian**, in the rule with himself.

The Policies of Justinian

When Justinian assumed the throne in 527, he acted in many ways like Augustus and Diocletian before him as he attempted to restore past Roman glory. Like them, he was a better administrator than general. He also was greatly influenced by his able wife, Theodora. Early in his reign, Justinian faced political unrest in his own capital. In 532, "Blue" and "Green" rioters, disgusted with misadministration, rampaged throughout the city for six days shouting "Nika!" ("Conquer"). Justinian was on the point of fleeing when Theodora stiffened his backbone by quoting a saying that exile would be worse than death and that "the purple would make a fine burial shroud." The general **Belisarius** was ordered to suppress the **Nika Rebellion**, as it was called, and some thirty thousand rioters reportedly were massacred.

Justinian's vision for the future was ambitious indeed. In civil affairs, Justinian oversaw the codification all past Roman law, establishing a commission that by the mid-530s had published the *Corpus juris civilis* ("Body of Civil Law"). It consisted of three parts: the *Institutes* (a legal textbook), the *Code of Justinian* (a compilation of imperial statute law from Hadrian until his own day that rendered the Theodosian Code obsolete), and the *Digest* (a synthesis of all past jurists' opinions). At the same time, however, a millennium of tradition came to an end when the philosophical school of Athens was closed in 529.

Along with unifying the law, Justinian also proposed to unify the church, with himself at its head, a form of government known as Caesaropapism, in which the head of state also is the head of the church. At the fifth ecumenical Council of Constantinople in 553, Justinian made his own attempt to unify Chalcedonians and Miaphysites by condemning three Nestorian writers (known as the "Three Chapters"), something both sides could agree on. Once again, however, this conciliatory move had little success. Justinian also undertook a massive and expensive building program epitomized by the ostentatious and elaborate reconstruction of the Constantinian church of **Hagia Sophia**, or Holy Wisdom, in Constantinople.

DIGGING ANTIQUITY

HAGIA SOPHIA

The church of Hagia Sophia in Constantinople initially was built by either Constantine I or his son Constantius II. It was dedicated to Christ as the *Logos*—that is, the "Word" (or "Wisdom") of God. After this church burned during rioting in 404 it was rebuilt by Emperor Theodosius II. When the second church was itself burned during the Nika Rebellion in 532, the emperor Justinian used the opportunity to construct, between 532 and 537, the grandest church in the Christian world. Justinian collected building material from throughout the eastern empire, including columns taken from the ancient Temple of Artemis (Diana) in Ephesus and porphyry (purple stone) from Egypt. The eight largest columns, taken from the pagan temple complex in Baalbek, Syria, weigh some seventy tons each. Elaborate mosaics and frescoes covered the walls. After the dome collapsed during an earthquake in 558, it was strengthened and enlarged to 102 feet (thirty-one meters) in diameter, rising to a height of 182 feet (fifty-six meters). Finally completed in 562, Hagia Sophia became the largest church in Christendom. It has been described as the greatest architectural work

of Late Antiquity. When the church was finished, Justinian reportedly exclaimed, referring to the temple in Jerusalem, "Solomon, I have surpassed you!"

The church survived not only several subsequent earthquakes but also a sack by Crusader allies in 1204, when it was converted into a Roman Catholic cathedral. After the Byzantine recapture of Constantinople in 1261, Hagia Sophia remained the cathedral church of the Patriarch of Constantinople until the capture of Constantinople by the Ottoman Turks in 1453. It was looted and then converted into a mosque, and its mosaics were destroyed or plastered over. It remained the largest church in the world until the Seville cathedral was completed in 1520.

In 1951, Hagia Sophia was converted into a museum and many of the plastered mosaics have been restored. Additional restoration work between 1997 and 2006 helped to stabilize a cracked roof and deteriorating mosaics.

See Cyril Mango and Ahmed Ertuğ, *Hagia Sophia: A Vision for Empires* (Istanbul: Ertug & Kocabiyik, 1997).

In the realm of foreign policy, Justinian was determined to reconquer much of the Western Roman Empire. In 533–534, his able general Belisarius, yet another who has been called "the last of the Romans," destroyed the Vandal kingdom in a lightning campaign and began the recovery of North Africa. Then, in 536, Belisarius invaded the Ostrogothic kingdom of Italy and by the end of the year had captured Rome and Naples. In 540, he captured Milan and Ravenna—after the Ostrogoths had offered to make him emperor, an offer he declined—and it looked as though the war was over. But at this point Belisarius was recalled to the east to deal with an attack by the New Persians, and the war in Italy then bogged down. Italy now suffered much the same kind of ruinous warfare as it had during the war against Hannibal. During several sieges of Rome, the aqueducts were cut, the walls were broken, and the city often was virtually deserted. In 550, Justinian concocted a scheme to marry his cousin Germanus to Matasuintha, the daughter of the Ostrogothic queen Amalasuintha, and thus unite the Romans and Ostrogoths, but Germanus' death the next year foiled that plan. The elderly Armenian eunuch Narses then was placed in charge of Byzantine forces. At the Battle of Busta Gallorum in 552 the Ostrogoths were decisively defeated, and by 553 Italy was back in Byzantine hands.

Justinian's plans for reconquest even extended to Spain, and the southeastern part of the peninsula was reoccupied. But at that point the Byzantine offensive ran dry. The Byzantine Empire thus reached its greatest extent; by recovering much of the western empire, Justinian expanded the territory of the empire by over 40 percent. Justinian's western wars had drained the economy, and, except occasionally for Africa, the newly recovered western territories proved to be a financial and political burden. In addition, Justinian's preoccupation with the west gave the Persians a free hand in the east: in 540 Antioch, the queen city of the Orient, was captured and sacked. Justinian then paid dearly for peace treaties with the Persians. And in the north, the Byzantines faced incursions from across the Danube by a whole catalogue of barbarians, including Slavs, Bulgars, Avars, Gepids, Huns, and Catrigurs, who were defeated only with great difficulty.

Justinian's attempts to reform the administration were hindered, moreover, by his increasing need to squeeze out as much revenue as he could to support his extravagant military and building enterprises. Of great benefit was the development of an imperial silk monopoly. Ultimately, however, Justinian's extravagant spending could no longer be maintained. Military cutbacks led to the failure to maintain frontier defenses and army revolts. Other problems included a great plague in 542 that afflicted even Justinian himself, although he, unlike tens of thousands of others, survived.

The Successors of Justinian

After Justinian's death in 565, his successors had to deal with the consequences of his grandiose schemes. Justinian was followed by his nephew Justin II (565–578). Justin attempted to deal with religious incompatibilities by persecuting the Miaphysites and was confronted in 568 by an invasion of Italy by the **Lombards**, who had lived for centuries on the fringes of the Roman world and who became the last of the barbarian invaders of the old empire. The Lombards occupied much of inland Italy but were too weak to dislodge the Byzantines, who controlled the sea, from strongholds near the coast, such as Ravenna and Rome. The Lombards were disunited both politically, with a nominal king attempting to control more than thirty Dukes, and religiously, with the population adhering variously to paganism, Arianism, and Nicene Christianity. The last Lombard king surrendered to Charlemagne in 774, but the legacy of the Lombards survives in Lombardy, the name of the northern region of Italy around Milan.

In 573, overwhelmed by the news of defeats by the **Avars** and Persians, Justin apparently had some form of mental breakdown, and his wife, the Augusta Sophia, now the effective ruler of the empire, arranged the promotion of the influential general Tiberius (578–582) to the rank of Caesar, with the surname Constantine. Further attacks by the **Slavs** soon followed, which continued after Justin's death in 578, along with additional attacks on the Balkans by the Avars and by the Persians in the east. In 582, gravely ill, Tiberius crowned the general Maurice (582–602) as Augustus. Maurice did the best he could. In the west, the

THE COURT OF JUSTINIAN AND THEODORA

Justinian's role as head of both state and church is graphically illustrated in this famous mosaic of 547, depicting a communion scene, from the semicircular apse of the church of San Vitale in Ravenna. Justinian, sporting a halo signifying his near divinity even in the Christian era, processes toward the altar carrying the communion bread in a golden paten. His garb includes a full-length purple chlamys with a large embroidered golden bar, an elaborate jeweled fibula that pins the chlamys at his right shoulder, and the typical imperial red shoes. To the emperor's right are secular officials, each wearing a white chlamys with a purple bar pinned with a rather less elaborate fibula. The bearded person to the emperor's immediate right may be his general Belisarius, who earlier appeared to have defeated the Ostrogoths in Italy. Farther to Justinian's right are soldiers carrying spears, wearing torques, and holding shields that bear the Christogram. Three clerics stand to the emperor's left. To his immediate left is the bishop of Ravenna, Maximianus, the only person actually named: as the person who had underwritten the cost of the church and mosaic, he wanted to make sure that no one forgot him. His attire includes a white tunic, or "alb"; a golden planeta (or paenula, later a chasuble) worn very much like the emperor's chlamys; and a narrow pallium, a symbol of his archiepiscopal status, decorated with a cross. Next to Maximianus, another cleric, probably a deacon, holds the Gospels, and a third, perhaps a subdeacon, carries a censer for spreading incense smoke. The person between Justinian and Maximianus, who is rather out of place and lacks feet, seems to have been added at a later date. Directly opposite this mosaic is a parallel mosaic, shown in Source 15.2, of the court of the empress Theodora, also depicted with a halo and likewise carrying a communion bowl. She is accompanied by the women and palace eunuchs of her own retinue.

last Spanish possessions were lost, but Maurice also created the largely autonomous **exarchates** of Ravenna and Carthage, which were intended to maintain themselves independently without great assistance from the east. The Avars were kept from Constantinople, barely, and Maurice had a success in the east when his daughter Miriam married the Persian king Chosroes (or Xusru) II (590–628). But his plans to reestablish an emperor in Rome came to naught in 602 when he was killed in a revolt by his general Phocas (602–610). During the reign of Phocas, the last monument in the forum in Rome, a column in his honor, was erected by Pope Gregory I.

Heraclius and the Greek Empire

The reign of the usurper Phocas came to an end in 610, when a fleet commanded by **Heraclius** (610–641), the Exarch of Africa, arrived at Constantinople. The senators and army deserted to Heraclius, who executed Phocas with his own hand and then was crowned Byzantine emperor. The reign of Heraclius is looked on by some as the beginning of a truly Byzantine Empire, for it brought a number of great changes. Heraclius was immediately confronted by serious military problems. In 610, the New Persian king Chosroes II invaded Syria. In 613, Damascus fell, and in the following year Jerusalem was sacked; the True Cross and other Christian treasures were taken back to Persia. In 615, the Persians attacked Chalcedon, just opposite Constantinople, while in 617 the king of the Avars appeared before the land walls of the Byzantine capital. Heraclius almost abandoned the city for North Africa, especially after Egypt, the main source of grain for the empire, was occupied by the Persians in 619, by which time the Persians also had occupied nearly all of Anatolia. The relative ease of the Persian conquest is explained at least in part by religious differences within the Byzantine Empire: many eastern Nestorians and, in particular, Miaphysites, after years of persecution by the imperial government, preferred a Zoroastrian Persian ruler to what they saw as a Christian heretic.

Although Chosroes had succeeded in extending the frontiers of the Sasanian Empire almost to the limits of the old Achaemenid Empire, Heraclius still had a few tricks up his sleeve. Using a shrewd mixture of diplomatic and military moves, and supported by the populace as well as by contributions of the church, Heraclius took the offensive. Because the Byzantines controlled the seas, Heraclius resolved on a bold stroke. Leading the army

On this silver plate gilded with gold, the New Persian king Chosroes II engages in the traditionally aristocratic pastime of hunting, shooting a bow from horseback in much the same way that Iranians of over a thousand years earlier had done.

On this twelfth-century French plaque, the Byzantine emperor Heraclius overcomes the Persian king Chosroes, whose crown falls to the ground.

himself, the first time since Theodosius I that an eastern emperor had done so, in 622 he sailed into the Black Sea with an expeditionary force that penetrated into Armenia. Sasanian forces were defeated, and Heraclius advanced into Persian territory. An attempt of the Persians to induce Heraclius to return by making a joint attack on Constantinople with the Avars in 626 failed when the Avars were bought off and induced to withdraw. Chosroes recalled all the Persian forces, but after being unable to defeat Heraclius, he was deposed and killed. In 628, the new Persian king, Kavad, whose kingdom had been devastated, made peace with Heraclius, returning all the territory, treasures (including the True Cross), and prisoners that the Persians had captured.

By 628, therefore, Heraclius had been able to defeat, and virtually destroy, the New Persian Empire. The next year, as a consequence not only of this great victory but also of the changing times, Heraclius adopted the ancient Greek title of *Basileus*, or "King," and Roman emperors finally had an official title. Heraclius acknowledged the Greekness of the Byzantine Empire in other ways as well, by making Greek the official language. But, after nearly twenty years of warfare in which neither side had gained anything, both empires were totally exhausted. Even worse, in their attempts both to prosecute and to recover from the wars, both empires had imposed additional taxation on the population that resulted in popular discontent.

At the same time, Heraclius also made yet one more attempt to reconcile the eastern Miaphysites by supporting a new doctrine known as Monotheletism, according to which Christ had a single nature but two wills. Initially, this new doctrine made some headway in reconciling the eastern Christians; even the bishop of Rome concurred.

THE RISE OF THE ARABS AND ISLAM

Ever since the beginning of Near Eastern civilization circa 3000 BCE, the centers of cultural, political, and religious innovations had been located either in major river valleys or in the lands bordering on the Mediterranean Sea. Other regions, such as the steppes of central Asia, the Arabian Peninsula, and Sub-Saharan Africa, usually had been marginalized in the eyes of their Mediterranean neighbors. All this changed in the seventh century CE, when the peoples of the Arabian Peninsula burst dramatically into the Mediterranean world.

DESERT NOMADS, THE ARABS AND SARACENS

The desert fringes of the Levant and Egypt were inhabited by many nomadic peoples who either traded with or raided settled Roman territory. The contested region between the Roman and Parthian Empires—that is, western Mesopotamia and northern Arabia—was inhabited by Arab peoples. In a digression, the late-fourth-century historian Ammianus Marcellinus discussed the characteristics of the "Saracens," as the Arabs often were called.

The Saracens, however, whom we never found desirable either as friends or as enemies, ranging up and down the country, in a brief space of time laid waste whatever they could find, like rapacious kites which, whenever they have caught sight of any prey from on high, seize it with swift swoop, and directly they have seized it make off. Although I recall having told of their customs in my history of the emperor Marcus [Aurelius], and several times after that, yet I will now briefly relate a few more particulars about them. Among those peoples whose original abode extends from the Assyrians to the cataracts of the Nile and the frontiers of the Blemmyae all alike are warriors of equal rank, half-nude, clad in dyed cloaks as far as the loins, ranging widely with the help of swift horses and slender camels in times of peace or of disorder. No man ever grasps a plough-handle or cultivates a tree, none seeks a living by tilling the soil, but they rove continually over wide and extensive tracts without a home, without fixed abodes or laws; they cannot long endure the same sky, nor does the sun of a single district ever content them. Their life is always on the move, and they have mercenary wives, hired under a temporary contract. But in order that there may be some semblance of matrimony, the future wife, by way of dower, offers her husband a spear and a tent, with the right to leave him after a stipulated time, if she so elect: and it is unbelievable with what ardor both sexes give themselves up to passion. Moreover, they wander so widely as long as they live, that a woman marries in one place, gives birth in another, and rears her children far away, without being allowed an opportunity for rest. They all feed upon game and an abundance of milk, which is their main sustenance, on a variety of plants, as well as on such birds as they are able to take by fowling; and I have seen many of them who were wholly unacquainted with grain and wine. So much for this dangerous people.

Ammianus Marcellinus, *Histories* 14.4.1

Arabia in the Classical World

For centuries, Arabia had existed on the fringes of the classical world. Most of it was extremely arid, punctuated only by occasional oases and a few coastal areas, and at best permitted the Arab inhabitants to pursue a pastoral way of life based on herding camels, goats, and horses. The population was organized into mobile family groups, much as in the days of the early Hebrews. Agriculture was possible only in a more fertile strip along the Red Sea coast, the **Hejaz**, where a few small urban centers were located. The Arab population spoke the Arabic language, another of the branches of the Afroasiatic linguistic family. It was polytheistic, with a multitude of gods, although Arabs also generally believed in a remote supreme creator god known as **Allah**, a word that meant simply "God."

In the central Hejaz, the most important city was **Mecca**, which waslocated just inland from the Red Sea in a barren wilderness with little water. As of the fifth century CE, Mecca was controlled by an Arab group called the Quraysh, who became merchants and traders in the sixth century when, as a result of conflicts with the Persians, the Byzantines fostered an alternate trade route to the east going from Damascus to Mecca and thence east to obtain spices from India and silks from China. Other urban centers included Yathrib (later **Medina**), a center of agriculture two hundred miles (322 kilometers) north, but Mecca was the most significant, and eventually became more important than Palmyra as a caravan center. Along with being a trading center, Mecca also was a religious center, with a shrine called the **Ka'aba** that was frequented by the Arab population.

Once a year, the disunited and often warring peoples of Arabia declared a truce and congregated at Mecca, where disputes were resolved and trade was pursued. This made Mecca into a loose political center as well and gave the Arabs a common sense of identity. The merchants of Mecca entered into agreements with both the Bedouin peoples of the desert and the Byzantines to the north. As the city became more powerful, it became the center of a loose confederation of Arab peoples.

As of the second century CE, northwestern Arabia, populated by Saracens (a Roman name for Arabs), was incorporated into the Roman province of Arabia, but the Roman and Byzantine governments only rarely made any attempt to extend their influence any farther into the peninsula. Once Christianity became the state-sponsored religion in the Roman Empire, emperors began to use Christianity for political purposes and to encourage foreign allies to become Christians. Christianity began to penetrate the Arabian Peninsula. For example, a group of Saracens who had migrated from northern Arabia to southern Syria converted to Christianity circa 374 under their queen, Mavia, on condition that a certain Moses, another Saracen, be made their bishop. Likewise, after some experiments with Judaism, the Himyarite Kingdom of southern Arabia, which had controlled the trade in frankincense and myrrh since the first century CE, was provided with bishops by the emperors Anastasius and Justin I.

Meanwhile, in the semi-arid regions of northern Arabia and southern Syria, two Arab peoples, the Ghassanids and the Lakhmids, who had migrated all the way from Yemen, became involved in the frontier mix. The Ghassanids became Christians and clients of the Byzantine Empire and guarded the frontier against the attacks of other Arab peoples. But the Lakhmids became Nestorian Christians, were opposed to the Miaphysite Ghassanids, and allied themselves with the Persians after Nestorianism was condemned by the Romans. In addition, several Arab peoples, especially in southern Arabia, also adopted Judaism. By the sixth century, therefore, monotheism was gaining a strong presence among the Arab peoples.

Muhammad and the Rise of Islam

Around 570, the future prophet **Muhammad** was born into the Quraysh group in Mecca. His father Abdallah (a word meaning "the servant of Allah") died before he was born, and after being orphaned at the age of six he was raised by his uncle. After initially working as a merchant on caravans to Syria, around 610 Muhammad began to have visions in which he received divine revelations from the angel Gabriel. Three years later he began to preach a monotheistic religion with the messages that "God is one," that it was necessary to surrender to Allah, and that he was Allah's messenger. Whereas pagan Arabs had believed in blind irresistible fate over which people had no control, Muhammad taught that Allah was a merciful God who listened to prayers. Muhammad's religion became known as **Islam** (a word meaning "submission [to the will of Allah]") and the followers of Islam became known as **Muslims** (a word meaning "one who submits"). Muhammad was believed to be Allah's prophet, and the statement of faith of all Muslims became "There is no God but Allah, and Muhammad is His messenger."

The first converts to Islam were members of Muhammad's own family and unprivileged persons. Muhammad's efforts to spread his teachings more widely, and especially his condemnation of idol worship, met much resistance from the established pagan community, especially from wealthy merchants in Mecca. Civil war came to Arabia as Arabs attached to the old religion attempted to suppress Muhammad and his followers. Some Muslims fled to Ethiopia to escape persecution, and in 622 Muhammad himself took sanctuary in Yathrib, where he already had many supporters. This journey became known as the **Hegira** (or Hijra), and its date became the first year in a new Muslim calendar. Yathrib was renamed Medina-ul-Nabi, or "City of the Prophet," and became the center of operations for several battles with Mecca. Although neither side was able to achieve a decisive victory, Muhammad's skillful strategies and tactics (such as building an impregnable ditch to defend Yathrib) resulted in his gaining increasing prestige.

Eventually, after a series of mostly peaceful negotiations, Mecca surrendered to Muhammad in 630. Except for a sacred black stone, about seven inches (eighteen centimeters) in diameter, which the Muslims believed had fallen from heaven at the time of Adam and Eve, all of the stone idols in the Ka'aba were destroyed. Otherwise, however, Muhammad was very lenient toward his former enemies, pardoning most of them, and this spirit of tolerance toward defeated enemies later became one of the hallmarks of Muslim policy. Mecca, with the Ka'aba, became the holiest site in Islam, which all Muslims faced both during prayer and in death, and which was the destination of the pilgrimage now known as the Hajj that all devout Muslims were expected to make at least once in their lives. Medina, meanwhile, continued as the Muslim capital. Before his death in 632, Muhammad and his followers were able to convert nearly all Arabia to Islam and to bring the Arabs under a single political and religious authority.

Islam did not acquire many of its fundamental unifying and organizational characteristics until after the death of Muhammad. In particular, the revelations that Muhammad had received from Allah were collected and codified during and soon after his lifetime in a book of scripture called the **Qu'ran** (or "Recitation"), which became the supreme authority not only for Muslim beliefs but also for Muslim law and life. The Qu'ran, which contains 114 chapters known as "suras," placed great emphasis on morality, preferring moral rather than historical discussions of past events; this can make it difficult to use as a historical source.

The Qu'ran also referred to many events from Jewish and Christian scriptures, thus attesting to the close connections among these three religions. For example, the Muslims, like the Jews and Christians, believed that they were descended from the Hebrew prophet Abraham, thus creating a familial, albeit distant, bond among the adherents of all three religions. And according to Islamic tradition, in one of his miraculous journeys Muhammad was said to have met earlier prophets such as Abraham, Moses, and Jesus. Subsequently, Jews and Christians living under Muslim rule, who came from the same religious traditions as the Muslims, were termed **"People of the Book"** and were accorded special treatment, such as being allowed to practice their religion if they paid a special tax and did not resist. As in the case of Judaism and Christianity, it was the written scripture that gave Islam its continuity over centuries of time and large geographical spaces. The Qu'ran assumed its standard form almost immediately, and even in the modern day Muslims of different sects use the same Qu'ran.

After the death of Muhammad, controversy arose in the Muslim community over who would succeed him; no arrangements had been made, although it was understood that it should be someone from his family. Subsequent Muslim rulers formed **caliphates**, groups of related rulers who were seen as the religious successors of Muhammad. The choice to be the first **caliph**, establishing the Rashidun Caliphate (632–661 CE), fell on Muhammad's father-in-law Abu Bakr, although others had supported Ali, Muhammad's cousin and son-in-law, who later became the fourth caliph. This early dispute over leadership later was one of the factors in the Muslim split into two main denominations: the Sunnis (who recognized Abu Bakr) and the Shi'as (who recognized Ali). Abu Bakr and later caliphs succeeded to Muhammad's spiritual and temporal authority, but not to his position as prophet, and had no authority to rule in matters of religious doctrine, even though some early caliphs did believe that their authority extended to religious matters not discussed in the Qu'ran. In this regard, Islamic government could be considered to be a **theocracy**, in which the leaders of the church also govern the state, as opposed to the Caesaropapism of the Byzantine Empire.

Islamic conquests to 644 CE.
Between 636 and 644, in the space of just a few years, Muslims advanced out of Arabia, occupied Byzantine Syria, Palestine, and Egypt, and also defeated the New Persians.

The Confrontation between Byzantium and the Arabs

Under Abu Bakr, Islam began to expand out of Arabia proper, initially in an attempt to convert the Arabs living under Sasanid and Byzantine rule.

During 633, southwestern Mesopotamia (Iraq) was occupied by the Muslim general Khalid, and the Lakhmids were successfully incorporated, even though many of them preferred to remain Christians. Then, in 634, Abu Bakr sent Khalid with an army of nearly ten thousand to invade Byzantine Palestine. After defeating several Byzantine contingents, Khalid captured Damascus in 634, by which time Abu Bakr had been succeeded as caliph by Umar, who replaced Khalid as commander in chief with Abu Ubaida, although Khalid continued as the de facto Muslim commander. Muslim holdings in Palestine continued to expand.

Meanwhile, the Byzantine emperor Heraclius, residing in Antioch, not far from the battlefront, pulled together Byzantine contingents from throughout the empire, including Ghassanid Arabs and even Armenian allies, in an attempt to resist the Arab advances. In August of 636, the Muslim army of about forty thousand met a combination of five Byzantine armies under different commanders totaling about fifty thousand in the **Battle of the Yarmuk River** just east of the Sea of Galilee, on a plain that offered good room to maneuver for the Muslim cavalry. After five days of seesaw battle, the Muslim cavalry worked its way around to attack the Byzantine infantry from the rear. Lack of coordination among the Byzantine commanders forced the Byzantine army into a retreat that became a rout. Many Byzantines escaped, but others were killed in the panic, and those who surrendered were massacred. Heraclius, blaming the defeat on God's wrath, retreated to Constantinople and prepared for the defense of Egypt. Meanwhile, the Muslims consolidated their gains. Antioch fell in 637, and the Muslim conquest of Byzantine territory in western Asia was complete.

Egypt, meanwhile, as often in the past, was a hotbed of religious controversy. The population remained largely Miaphysite. After the Byzantine reoccupation from the Persians in the late 620s, the Miaphysites were persecuted by the Byzantine government, which was attempting to impose religious unity on the empire. In 639, Egypt was invaded by a Muslim army led by General 'Amr, a veteran of the Yarmuk campaign. In 641, after a Byzantine defeat at the Battle of Heliopolis in 640, Heraclius died, putting the Byzantine resistance into disarray when quarreling arose over the succession. Without reinforcements, Alexandria was surrendered shortly thereafter. The rest of Egypt was occupied relatively easily, and Byzantine efforts to retake the province were unsuccessful.

But at that point, the Muslim invasion of Africa ground to a halt. Two attempts to invade the Christian kingdom of Makuria south of Egypt, which included Nubia and the ancient Kingdom of Alodia farther south near the sixth cataract on the Nile, met dismal failure. The Nubian archers gained the sobriquet "pupil smiters" because of their ability to put out the eyes of Muslim attackers. As a result, the Muslims concluded a treaty with Makuria known as the Baqt, which guaranteed Nubia freedom from Muslim invasion and was in force for some six hundred years. Nubia thus became the only region in the world that was not included in either of the Muslim categories, the "House of the Faithful," inhabited

THE DESTRUCTION OF THE LIBRARY OF ALEXANDRIA

One of the most famous monuments of antiquity was the great library of Alexandria, initially established by the Ptolemaic kings in the third century BCE and said to contain, rather like the modern Library of Congress, copies of works written by virtually every ancient author. Estimates of its holdings ranged in antiquity from 400,000 to 700,000 scrolls. One of the great mysteries of history is what happened to the library. Many accounts circulated in antiquity and continue to be proposed about the library's fate.

In the first century CE, the Roman writer Seneca mentioned "forty thousand books burned at Alexandria" but said nothing about the date or circumstances. Several writers blamed Julius Caesar, including Plutarch, who said in the second century that a fire Caesar set to burn his own ships "spread and destroyed the great library." Other writers, such as Ammianus and the Christian historian Orosius, also blamed Caesar; Aulus Gellius, writing about 180, reports that 700,000 books were accidentally burned. But in the early third century Cassius Dio reported that on this occasion only some warehouses of books by the docks were accidentally burned. And this clearly was not the end of the library or libraries at Alexandria, for Plutarch also notes that in the mid-30s BCE, Mark Antony gave Cleopatra 200,000 books from the library of Pergamum, perhaps to replace the ones burned by Caesar. And there is evidence not only that during the second century CE the library established by the Ptolemies was moved to the Serapaeum, the most important temple of Alexandria, but also that works continued to be deposited there as late as the fourth century.

Meanwhile, several other dates for the destruction of the library have been suggested, including (1)

In this illustration from the fifth-century "Alexandrian World Chronicle," Bishop Theophilus of Alexandria, holding the Bible as the proper sort of book to read, stands atop the Serapaeum, which may still have contained the Library of Alexandria, just before its destruction ca. 391.

by Muslims, or the "House of the Enemy," inhabited by non-Muslims. And on the southern Red Sea coast of Africa, the Empire of Aksum fell to the Muslims in the early eighth century CE.

The Muslim invaders of the Byzantine Empire had succeeded beyond their wildest expectations. They encountered not only a greatly weakened Byzantine

273, when sections of the city were destroyed during Aurelian's suppression of Zenobia's revolt; (2) 365, when a tidal wave destroyed much of the city; and (3) circa 391, when the Serapaeum was torn down, although because a fourth-century writer attests that the books were stored in a colonnade adjoining the temple proper, the books perhaps escaped destruction.

Perhaps the most famous story about the destruction of the library, which first appears in the work of the thirteenth-century Arab historian Abd-al-Latif, places it in 642, at the time of the Muslim capture of Alexandria. The Muslim general 'Amr is said to have asked the caliph Umar what to do with the famous library, and the caliph supposedly replied, "The books will either contradict the Qu'ran, in which case they are heresy, or they will agree with it, so they are superfluous. Burn it!" The books then supposedly provided six months' worth of fuel for the furnaces heating water at Arab bathhouses.

The loss of the collected wisdom stored in the library at Alexandria continues to pique the modern imagination. For example, the thesis of the 1988 Clive Cussler novel *Treasure* is that at the end of the fourth century the library—full of lost knowledge about oil wells and gold mines—was spirited off to a hiding place in the Rio Grande valley, and in the 2004 movie *National Treasure*, a collection of scrolls from the library is discovered. In addition, the modern city of Alexandria now boasts a new "Library of Alexandria" established in 2002 that is intended "to recapture the spirit of openness and scholarship of the original Bibliotheca Alexandrina."

army but also a population rendered unhappy by the government's financial exactions and persecutions of the largely Miaphysite population. In Egypt, in particular, the relatively small Muslim invasion force was assisted by many Miaphysites, who were happy to pay taxes to them instead of to the Byzantine government in the hopes of getting better treatment under Muslim authority.

The Expansion of the Muslim World

After the conquest of Egypt, the Muslim advance continued. The Sasanids were defeated in 642 at the Battle of Nahavand, bringing the New Persian Empire to an end. In Constantinople, Heraclius' grandson, Heraclius Constantine, better known as Constans II (641–668), consolidated his hold on the throne, but the situation looked so dire that Constans, also confronted by urban unrest, withdrew to the west and settled in Syracuse. In 663, he was the last Roman emperor to visit Rome. Five years later, when rumors arose that Constans planned to move the capital to Syracuse, he was assassinated in his bath. Meanwhile, in 698 Carthage and Byzantine North Africa were taken by the Arabs, and in 711 the Visigothic kingdom of Spain also fell. The Muslim advance was halted only in 732, when the Frankish Mayor of the Palace, Charles Martel, defeated a Muslim invasion of western Europe at the Battle of Tours.

Back in the Levant, Muslim expansion stalled in the 670s when the Byzantines developed a secret weapon called "Greek Fire," a combustible compound that ignited on contact with water and incinerated enemy ships. The Byzantines did not experience another major setback until 1071, when at the Battle of Manzikert most of Anatolia was lost to the Seljuk Turks. A shrunken empire then held out until 1453, when the last desperate resistance of seven thousand Roman defenders against eighty thousand Ottoman Turks was led by Constantine XI Palaeologus (1449–1453). As the city was being overwhelmed, Constantine's final words were, "The city has fallen and I still live!" The last emperor of the Romans then threw himself into the thick of the fighting and perished. His body later was recognized only by the imperial red shoes. Constantine XI, like his namesake Constantine I, later was considered a saint in Eastern Orthodox churches. Constantinople subsequently was renamed Istanbul (from a Greek phrase "in the city").

A twelfth-century manuscript from Syracuse portrays the use of Greek Fire, which was propelled out of a siphon device to create a flame-thrower that destroyed enemy ships.

THE END OF ANTIQUITY

It is difficult to say exactly when the ancient world ended. Some scholars see the beginning of the Middle Ages as early as the reign of Marcus Aurelius and the Severan period of the Roman Empire, the same point at which many scholars would place the beginning of Late Antiquity. Others see the break occurring with Diocletian and Constantine just before and after the year 300, or with the beginning of a Christian Empire during the fourth century, or with the transformation of the Roman Empire into the so-called Byzantine Empire anywhere from the fourth to the sixth century. For our purposes, several developments suggest that the end of the ancient world came in the seventh century, which was a very different world even from the sixth. Europe saw the culmination of several trends, ranging from the diminishing of the Roman cultural tradition in Europe to the final merging of the Roman and barbarian populations. In the Byzantine Empire, Greek replaced Latin as the official language. The New Persian Empire, the successor of the Parthian and Old Persian Empires, vanished completely. And Arabia saw the rise of a third great monotheistic religion.

By the mid-seventh century, the changes that came during Late Antiquity had resulted in the culturally unified Roman world being fragmented into the three geographical and religious spheres of the Middle Ages, with Catholic Christians in western Europe, Orthodox Christians in the Balkans and Anatolia, and Muslims in the Levant, Egypt, and North Africa. One therefore can state with some confidence that the ancient world ended around 650. The Roman Empire itself continued to survive much longer, for nearly a thousand years after the fall of the western empire. But by the mid-seventh century CE the world had changed so much that one is justified in ending a history of ancient Rome at this point: the ancient world was over.

> **LEARNING FROM HISTORY**
>
> Every past empire in history, including the Roman Empire, eventually has fallen. Do you think that there is any way to prevent this cycle from recurring? Or do you think that all empires, even those of the modern day, are doomed eventually to fall?

⇦ LOOKING BACK

The Roman Empire certainly did not die in 476; it rather was largely reconstituted by Justinian in the sixth century and continued to develop and evolve under the modern misnomer "Byzantine Empire" until 1453 CE. And the rise of Islam in the early seventh century CE marks yet one more development of Late Antiquity that continues to reverberate in the modern world.

LOOKING AHEAD ⇨

As of the seventh century, much of the history of the Mediterranean world would be influenced or even determined by the religious differences among Catholic Christians, Orthodox Christians, and Muslims, which would prevent, and indeed continue to prevent, the kind of cultural unity of the Mediterranean and Near Eastern worlds that came to full fruition during the Roman Empire. The succeeding Middle Ages would last until the fourteenth-century Renaissance. But by the end of antiquity, the germs of modern Europe were already there. The divisions of the Frankish kingdom presaged the creation of modern France and Germany; indeed, the Franks gave their name to France, and the Alamanni to the French name for Germany ("Allemagne"). The Anglo-Saxon kingdoms in Britain eventually became **England**. Spain already was a separate entity, ruled first by Visigoths, then by Muslims. Even Italy, increasingly under the authority of the pope in Rome, had its own identity.

FURTHER READING

Bagnall, R. S. *Egypt in Late Antiquity.* Princeton: Princeton Univ. Press, 1993.

Beckwith, J. *Early Christian and Byzantine Art.* Harmondsworth, UK: Penguin Books, 1970.

Browning, Robert. *Justinian and Theodora.* 2nd ed. London: Thames and Hudson, 1987.

Bury, J. R. *History of the Later Roman Empire from the Death of Theodosius I to the Death of Justinian.* 2 vols. London: Macmillan, 1923.

Dagron, G. *Emperor and Priest: The Imperial Office in Byzantium.* Cambridge, UK: Cambridge Univ. Press, 2003.

Donner, F. M. *The Early Islamic Conquests.* Princeton: Princeton Univ. Press, 1981.

Frend, W. H. C. *The Rise of the Monophysite Movement.* Cambridge, UK: Cambridge Univ. Press, 1972.

Goffart, Walter. *The Narrators of Barbarian History, AD 550–880: Jordanes, Gregory of Tours, Bede and Paul the Deacon.* Princeton: Princeton Univ. Press, 1988.

Gordon, C. D. *The Age of Attila: Fifth-Century Byzantium and the Barbarians.* Ann Arbor: Univ. of Michigan Press, 1960.

Haldon, John F. *Byzantium in the Seventh Century: The Transformation of a Culture.* 2nd ed. Cambridge, UK: Cambridge Univ. Press, 1997.

Holum, K. G. *Theodosian Empresses: Women and Imperial Dominion in Late Antiquity.* Berkeley: Univ. of California Press, 1982.

Johnson, James-Howard. *East Rome, Sasanian Persia, and the End of Antiquity.* Aldershot, UK: Ashgate, 2006.

Kaegi, Walter E. *Heraclius: Emperor of Byzantium.* Cambridge, UK: Cambridge Univ. Press, 2003.

Moorhead, John. *The Roman Empire Divided, 400–700.* London: Longman, 2001.

Nicol, Donald M. *The Last Centuries of Byzantium.* Cambridge, UK: Cambridge Univ. Press, 1993.

Pharr, Clyde, trans. *The Theodosian Code and Novels, and the Sirmondian Constitutions.* Princeton: Princeton Univ. Press, 1952.

Shahid, Irfan. *Byzantium and the Arabs in the Fifth Century.* Washington, DC: Dumbarton Oaks Press, 1989.

Williams, S., and G. Friell. *The Rome That Did Not Fall: The Survival of the East in the Fifth Century AD.* London and New York: Routledge, 1999.

SOURCES

15.1 THE ACCLAMATIONS OF THE SENATE OF ROME (438)

THEODOSIAN CODE, "ACTS OF THE SENATE"

In December 438 the Theodosian Code (see Source 12.1) was officially introduced to the western empire at a meeting of the Senate in Rome. The verbatim minutes of the meeting were preserved and prefaced to the official copies of the code that were circulated throughout the west. This process shows the continuing role of the Senate, no longer in policymaking, but in distributing information received from the emperors. The only remaining means that the Senate had of communicating its desires to the emperors was by shouting acclamations after they had heard the emperors' wishes.

Source: Clyde Pharr, trans., *The Theodosian Code and Novels, and the Sirmondian Constitutions* (Princeton: Princeton Univ. Press, 1952), 5–7.

Acts of the Senate.

In the year of the sixteenth consulship of Our Lord Flavius Theodosius Augustus[1] and the consulship of the Most Noble Anicius Acilius Glabrio Faustus.[2] When the Most Noble and Illustrious Anicius Acilius Glabrio Faustus, thrice Ex-Prefect of the City, Praetorian Prefect, and Ordinary Consul,[3] in his home, which is at Palma,[4] and the Most Noble and Illustrious Flavius Paulus, Prefect of the City, the Respectable Junius Pompolius Publianus, Vicar of the Eternal City, men of noble rank, and the Most August Order of the Senate had assembled and conferred together for a considerable time, and the Constitutionaries[5] Anastasius and Martinus had entered pursuant to an order, the Most Noble and Illustrious Anicius Acilius Glabrio Faustus, thrice Ex-Prefect of the City, Praetorian Prefect, and Consul Ordinary, spoke as follows: "The felicity that emanates from our immortal emperors proceeds in its increase to the point that it arrays with the ornaments of peace those whom it defends in the fortunes of war.[6] Last year when I attended, as a mark of devotion, the most felicitous union of all the sacred ceremonies, after the nuptials had been felicitously solemnized,[7] the most sacred emperor, Our Lord Theodosius, desired to add the following high honor also to his world, namely, that he should order to be established the regulations that must be observed throughout the world,[8] in accordance with the precepts of the laws that had been gathered together in a compendium of sixteen books and these books he had desired to be consecrated by his most sacred name. The immortal emperor, Our Lord Valentinian, with the loyalty of a

---

[1] The emperor Theodosius II (402-450).

[2] The year 438 CE.

[3] The first Consul appointed during any given year, who gave his name to the year; subsequent appointees were called Suffect Consuls.

[4] An area near the center of Rome. The Senate often met not in the Curia (Senate house), which was rather spartan and small, but in the luxurious city house of a distinguished senator, which was a great honor and not, as suggested by Pharr (*Theodosian Code*, p. 3), "one of the many indications of the low status of the Senate."

[5] Officials responsible for making and preserving official copies of the Code.

[6] A rather optimistic statement, as in the east, the Huns were becoming a serious problem, and in the west the Vandals had invaded Africa and were on the verge of capturing Carthage.

[7] The marriage in 437 at Constantinople between Theodosius' cousin, the young western emperor Valentinian III (425–455), and Theodosius' daughter Licinia Eudoxia.

[8] In theory, the Romans claimed to rule the whole world.

colleague and the affection of a son, approved this undertaking.[9]

The Assembly shouted: "You are newly eloquent! Truly eloquent!"

The Most Noble and Illustrious Anicius Acilius Glabrio Faustus, thrice Ex-Prefect of the City, Praetorian Prefect, and Ordinary Consul, said, "Therefore, the most sacred emperor summoned me and the illustrious man who was Prefect of the East at that time and ordered copies of the Code to be delivered from his own divine hand, one to each of us, in order that they might be dispatched throughout the world with all due reverence. Thus, it was among the first of his provisions that his forethought should be brought to the knowledge of Your Sublimity.[10] The Code as directed by the order of both emperors was received into our hands. The Constitutionaries are present. If it please Your Magnificence, let Your Magnificence order that these very laws be read to you by which the emperors ordered that this undertaking should be performed, in order that we may obey with proper devotion the most carefully considered precepts of the immortal emperors."

The assembly shouted, "It is right! So be it! So be it!"

The Most Noble and Illustrious Anicius Acilius Glabrio Faustus, thrice Ex-Prefect of the City, Praetorian Prefect, and Ordinary Consul, read from the first book of the Theodosian Code, under the title, "Constitutions and Edicts of the Emperors":[11]

"The emperors Theodosius and Valentinian Augustuses to the Senate. We decree that, after the pattern of the Gregorian and Hermogenian Codes,[12] a collection shall be made of all the constitutions that were issued by the renowned Constantine, by the sainted emperors after him, and by us and that rest upon the force of edicts or sacred imperial law of general force. First, the titles, which are the definite designations of the matters therein, shall be so divided that when the various headings have been expressed, if one constitution should pertain to several titles, the materials shall be assembled wherever each is fitting.[13] Second, if any diversity should cause anything to be stated in two ways, it shall be tested by the order of the headings, and not only shall the year of the consulship be considered and the time of the reign be investigated, but also the arrangement of the work itself shall show that the laws that are later are more valid.[14] Furthermore, the very words themselves of the constitutions, in so far as they pertain to the essential matter, shall be preserved, but those words that were added, not from the very necessity of sanctioning the law, shall be omitted.[15]

Although it would be simpler and more in accordance with law to omit those constitutions that were invalidated by later constitutions and to set forth only those that must be valid, let us recognize that this Code and the previous ones were composed for more diligent men, to whose scholarly efforts it is granted to know those laws also that have

---

[9] The principle of "unanimity of Empire." Even though the Roman Empire now was effectively split into eastern and western halves, in legal practice there was still only a single empire and laws issued in one part of the empire were issued also in the name of the other emperor(s).

[10] High-ranking officials were endowed with elaborate titles of address, such as "Your Sublimity" and "Your Magnificence."

[11] Faustus then read out verbatim the legislation that had authorized the compilation of the Code. As can be seen, not all of it actually was put into effect.

[12] The existing Gregorian and Hermogenian Codes were not "compilations of imperial enactments or constitutions," per Pharr (*Theodosian Code*, p. 4), but were collections of rescripts (that is, replies to petitions); and they were compiled under Diocletian in the 290s, not "in the early fourth century."

[13] That is, the laws were dismembered so different sections pertaining to different topics could be added to the appropriate sections of the Code.

[14] A full record of laws on any given topic was included, even laws that had been overridden or superseded by subsequent laws. So these overridden laws, too, could be cited in court.

[15] The authors of late Roman laws could be very verbose, and the editors were instructed to omit material, sometimes a great amount, not directly relevant to the law being issued.

been consigned to silence and have passed into desuetude, because they were destined to be valid for cases of their own time only.

Moreover, from these three Codes and from the treatises and responses of the jurists what are attached to each of the titles, through the services of the same men who shall arrange the third code there shall be produced another Code of ours.[16] This Code shall permit no error, no ambiguities; it shall be called by our name, and shall show what must be followed and what must be avoided by all. For the consummation of so great a work and the composition of the Codes, the first of which shall collect all the diversity of general constitutions,[17] shall omit none outside itself that now are permitted to be cited in court,[18] and shall reject only an empty copiousness of words, and the other of which shall exclude every contradiction of the law and shall undertake the guidance of life—men must be chosen of singular trustworthiness, of the most brilliant genius. When they have presented the first Code[19] to our wisdom and to the public authority, they shall undertake the other, which must be worked over until it is worthy of publication.[20] Let Your Magnificence acknowledge the men who have been selected: the Illustrious Antiochus, Ex-Quaestor and Ex-Prefect; the Illustrious Antiochus, Quaestor of the Sacred Imperial Palace;[21] the Respectable Theodorus,

Count and Master of the Bureau of Memorials;[22] the Respectable Eudicius and Eusebius, Masters of the Bureaux; and the Respectable Johannes, Ex-Count of our Sacred Consistory; the Respectable Comazon and Eubulus, Ex-Masters of the Bureaux; and Apelles, most eloquent jurist.

We are confident that these men who have been selected by Our Eternity will employ every exceptionally learned man in order that by their common study a reasonable plan of action may be apprehended and fallacious laws may be excluded.

Furthermore, if in the future it should be our pleasure to promulgate any law in one part of this very closely united empire, it shall be valid in the other part on condition that it does not rest upon doubtful trustworthiness or upon a private assertion. From that part of the empire in which it will be established, it shall be transmitted with the most sacred imperial letters, it shall be received in the bureaux of the other part of the empire also, and it shall be published with the due formality of edicts. For a law that has been sent must be accepted and must undoubtedly be valid, and the power to emend and to revoke shall be reserved to Our Clemency. Moreover the laws must be mutually announced, and they must not be admitted otherwise.

Given on the seventh day before the Kalends of April at Constantinople in the year of the consulship of Florentius and Dionysius."[23]

The assembly shouted:

"Augustuses of Augustuses, the Greatest of Augustuses!"	Repeated 8 times
"God gave you to us! God save you for us!"	Repeated 27 times.
"As Roman Emperors, pious and felicitous, may you rule for many years!"	Repeated 22 times.

---

[16] A comprehensive Code consisting of the Gregorian, Hermogenian, and Theodosian Codes along with the writings of jurists (legal scholars) was not produced until the publication of the *Corpus iuris civilis* under the emperor Justinian in the early 530s.

[17] That is, the existing Theodosian Code, which only included statute law issued by emperors.

[18] Once the Code had been issued, any laws that had not been included in it, even by inadvertence, no longer were valid.

[19] That is, the Theodosian Code, also referred to above as the "third Code," to distinguish it from the earlier Gregorian and Hermogenian Codes.

[20] Only the first of these two codes was ever completed. The second was not assembled until a hundred years later as the *Digest* of the emperor Justinian, which compiled the opinions of Roman jurists.

[21] The chief legal official at the imperial court.

---

[22] The Bureaux were all of the high-ranking, specialized secretarial and office staffs in charge of correspondence, archives, and record keeping.

[23] 26 March 429.

[24] The acclamations would be repeated in unison until no one continued. The number of repetitions then were reported to the emperors.

"For the good of the human race, for the good of the Senate, for the good of the state, for the good of all!"   Repeated 24 times.

"Our hope is in you, you are our salvation!"   Repeated 22 times.

"May it please our Augustuses to live forever!"   Repeated 22 times.

"May you pacify the world and triumph here in person!"   Repeated 24 times.

"There are the prayers of the Senate, these are the prayers of the Roman people!"   Repeated 10 times.

"Dearer than our children, dearer than our parents!"   Repeated 16 times.

"Suppressors of informers, suppressors of trickery!"[25]   Repeated 28 times.

"Through you our honors, through you our patrimonies, through you our all!"   Repeated 28 times.

"Through you, our military strength; through you, our laws!"   Repeated 20 times.

"We give thanks for this regulation of yours!"   Repeated 23 times.

"You have removed the ambiguities of the imperial constitutions!"   Repeated 23 times.

"Dutiful emperors act wisely in this manner!"   Repeated 26 times.

"You wisely provide for lawsuits, you provide for the public peace!"   Repeated 25 times.

"Let many copies of the Code be made to be kept in the governmental office!"   Repeated 10 times.

"Let them be kept under seal in the public bureaux!"[26]   Repeated 20 times.

"In order that the established laws not be falsified, let many copies be made!"   Repeated 25 times.

"In order that the established laws may not be falsified, let all copies be written out in letters!"[27]   Repeated 12 times.

"To this copy that will be made by the Constitutionaries let no annotations be added to the law!"   Repeated 12 times.

"We request that the copies to be kept in the bureaux shall be made at public expense!"[28]   Repeated 16 times.

"Hail, Faustus!"[29]   Repeated 17 times.

"A second term for you in the consulship!"   Repeated 15 times.

"You regulate everything, you harm no man!"   Repeated 13 times.

"Let copies be made and dispatched to the provinces!"   Repeated 11 times.

"Worthy purveyor of such great benefits!"   Repeated 10 times.

"Hail Paulus!"[30]   Repeated 12 times.

"A Consulship for you!"   Repeated 11 times.

---

[25] This and the next acclamation, which received the greatest number of repetitions, reflect two of the Senate's greatest concerns: (1) a fear of informers, and (2) the acknowledgment that the ranks, titles, and honors that the senators valued so much came from the emperors.

[26] So unauthorized changes could not be made.

[27] Written out in full without abbreviations that could be misconstrued.

[28] Roman laws were full of unfunded mandates, so the senators did not want to be made responsible for paying for the copies.

[29] The senator who made the opening address. He never got a second consulship.

[30] A senator who, with Faustus, had convoked the meeting.

"We request that the Codes be kept in the public bureaux!"   Repeated 15 times.

"Let this duty be assigned to the office of the Prefects!"[31]   Repeated 12 times.

"Let each Prefect affix his own seal!"   Repeated 15 times

"Let each have a copy in his own office!"   Repeated 12 times.

"We ask that no laws be promulgated in reply to supplications."[32]   Repeated 21 times.

"Hail Aëtius!"[33]   Repeated 15 times.

"A third term for you in the consulship!"   Repeated 13 times.

"Through your vigilance we are safe and secure!"   Repeated 12 times.

"Through your vigilance, through your labors!"   Repeated 15 times.

"Hail, Faustus!"   Repeated 13 times.

"A second term for you in the consulship!"   Repeated 10 times.

"We ask that you report to the emperors the desires of the Senate!"[34]   Repeated 20 times.

"Preserver of the laws, preserver of the decrees!"   Repeated 16 times

"All the rights of landholders are thrown into confusion by such surreptitious actions."   Repeated 17 times.

The Most Noble and Illustrious Anicius Acilius Glabrio Faustus, thrice Ex-Prefect of the City,

Praetorian Prefect, and Ordinary Consul, said, "Pursuant to the orders of Our Lords[35] and the desires of Your Eminences, it now shall be an object of my care to provide for the transcription of this code in three copies, through the reliable services of the Respectable Veronicianus, who was selected by agreement between Your Magnificences and me, and with the reliable services of the Constitutionaries Anastasius and Martinus, whom we already have approved as having given long and faultless services to this office. Then, whereas the copy that I have presented shall remain in the exalted office of the praetorian[36] archives, the bureau of the magnificent Prefect of the City, a man of equal trustworthiness, shall hold the second, and the Constitutionaries shall be ordered to retain the third in their own custody faithfully and at their own risk, in order that they may publish it to the people, with this provision, that no copies may be published except such as have been transcribed from this copy by the Constitutionaries, in their own hand. Likewise it shall be an object of my care to arrange for this also, that another copy of the Code shall be transcribed by these men and shall be dispatched with like devotion to the Province of Africa,[37] in order that there, too, a model of equal reliability may be preserved."

The assembly shouted,

"Hail Faustus!"   Repeated 16 times.

"A second term for you in the consulship!"   Repeated 15 times.

"To a man of all virtues!"   Repeated 10 times.

And by another hand.[38] I, Flavius Laurentius, Secretary of the Most August Senate, have published this on the eighth day before the Kalends of January.[39]

---

[31] The Praetorian Prefects were the highest-ranking civil officials, ranking just below the emperor.

[32] Many Late Roman laws were issued in response to requests from special-interest groups: the emperors had a hard time saying "no" to these kinds of requests.

[33] The Patrician and Master of Soldiers and, along with Valentinian's mother Galla Placidia, the virtual ruler of the western empire. He did get a third consulship.

[34] This was important, for the reporting of such acclamations was the only remaining institutionalized way that the Senate of Rome had of communicating its desires to the emperors.

[35] The emperors.

[36] Of the Praetorian Prefects.

[37] The senators could not have known that less than a year later, on 19 October 439, Carthage and the Roman province of North Africa would fall to the Vandals. After less than a hundred years, however, North Africa would be reconquered by the Romans; see Source 14.2.

[38] A formula that indicates a scribal addendum.

[39] 25 December 438, Christmas Day.

THE CHARACTER OF JUSTINIAN AND THEODORA (527–548 CE)

PROCOPIUS, *SECRET HISTORY*, PROLOGUE, 1–12

The retinues of Justinian and Theodora are depicted in this composite view of a mosaic dating to 547 CE in the church of San Vitale in Ravenna. Theodora is just as resplendent if not even more so than Justinian, attesting to the important role she played in the imperial hierarchy. (Photo: R. W. Mathisen)

During the Roman Empire it always was potentially dangerous for writers to speak too candidly about current events. One had to wait until after the death of a problematic ruler, as Tacitus waited for the death of Domitian (81–96), before one could express oneself more freely. This also was the case for the historian Procopius, who glorified the emperor Justinian while the latter was alive but vilified him and his wife Theodora after their deaths. After beginning with a lengthy character assassination of Belisarius, punctuated by the liaisons and schemes of his wife Antonina (see Source 14.2 above), Procopius turns to extravagant tales of the character flaws and misdeeds of Justinian and Theodora, who predeceased her husband in 548 CE. As in the case of the salacious tales retailed in the second century CE by the biographer Suetonius (see Source 8.1 above), one must be cautious about accepting the literal truth of all of Procopius' stories.

Source: Richard Atwater, trans., *The Secret History of Procopius* (New York: Covici-Friede, 1927).

It was not possible, during the life of certain persons, to write the truth of what they did, as a historian should. If I had, their hordes of spies would have found out about it, and they would have put me to a most horrible death. I could not even trust my nearest relatives. These secrets it is now my duty to tell and reveal the remaining hidden matters and motives. Yet when I approach this different task, I find it hard indeed to have to stammer and retract what I have written before about the lives of Justinian and Theodora. Worse yet, it occurs to me that what I am now about to tell will seem neither probable nor plausible to future generations, especially as time flows on and my story becomes ancient history. I fear they may think me a writer of fiction, and even put me among the poets. But I was constrained to proceed with this history, for the reason that future tyrants may see also that those who thus err cannot avoid retribution in the end. For who now would know of the unchastened life of Semiramis[40] or the madness of Sardanapalus[41] or Nero,[42] if the record had not thus been written by men of their own times?

I now come to the tale of what sort of beings Justinian and Theodora were, and how they brought confusion on the Roman State. During the rule of the emperor Leo[43] in Constantinople, three young farmers of Illyrian birth, named Zimarchus, Ditybistus, and Justin of Bederiana, after a desperate struggle with poverty, left their homes to try their fortune in the army. They made their way to Constantinople on foot, carrying on their shoulders their blankets in which were wrapped no other equipment except the biscuits they had baked at home. When they arrived and were admitted into military service, the emperor chose them for the palace guard, for they were all three fine-looking men.

As time went on, this Justin came to great power. The emperor Anastasius[44] appointed him Count of the Palace Guard; and when the emperor departed from this world, by the force of his military power Justin seized the throne. By this time he was an old man on the verge of the grave, and so illiterate that he could neither read nor write, which never before could have been said of a Roman ruler. It was the custom for an emperor to sign his edicts with his own hand, but he neither made decrees nor was able to understand the business of state at all. The man on whom it befell to assist him as Quaestor[45] was named Proclus, and he managed everything to suit himself. But so that he might have some evidence of the emperor's hand, he invented the following device for his clerks to construct. Cutting out of a block of wood the shapes of the four letters required to make the Latin word, they dipped a pen into the ink used by emperors for their signatures,[46] and put it in the emperor's fingers. Laying the block of wood I have described on the paper to be signed, they guided the emperor's hand so that his pen outlined the four letters, following all the curves of the stencil, and thus they withdrew with the "FIAT"[47] of the emperor. This is how the Romans were ruled under Justin. His wife was named Lupicina, a slave and a barbarian who was bought to be his concubine. With Justin, as the sun of his life was about to set, she ascended the throne.

[The character of Justinian]

Now, Justin was able to do his subjects neither harm nor good. For he was simple, unable to carry on a conversation or make a speech, and utterly bucolic. His nephew Justinian, while still a youth, was the virtual ruler and the cause of more and worse calamities to the Romans than any one man in all their previous history. He had no scruples, against murder or the seizing of other persons property, and it was nothing to him to make away with myriads of men, even when they gave him no cause. He had no care for preserving established customs, but was always eager for new experiments, and, in short, was the greatest corrupter of all noble traditions.

When the plague attacked the whole world, no fewer men escaped than perished of it, for some never were taken by the disease, and others recovered after it had smitten them.[48] But this man not one of all the Romans could escape. As if he were a second pestilence sent from heaven, he fell on the nation and left no man untouched. For some he slew without reason, and some he released to struggle with penury, and their fate was worse than that of those who had perished, so that they prayed for death to free them from their misery. Others he

---

[40] A legendary Assyrian queen said to have been the daughter of the fertility goddess Astarte, to have fought many wars as far away as India, and to have constructed many Near Eastern monuments.

[41] The legendary last king of Assyria whose decadent pleasure-seeking lifestyle led to the fall of the Assyrian Empire.

[42] Roman emperor from 54 to 68 CE, known for his decadent lifestyle.

[43] Leo I (457–474 CE).

[44] East Roman emperor from 491 until 518.

[45] Quaestor of the Sacred Palace, the chief legal official.

[46] The emperors used purple ink. Only one original imperial signature, of Theodosius II, survives from antiquity.

[47] Latin for "let it be so." The same urban legend was told about the Ostrogothic king Theoderic the Great (493–525 CE).

[48] The Plague of Justinian (541–542 CE) afflicted much of Near Eastern and Mediterranean worlds, killing an estimated twenty-five million people.

robbed of their property and their lives together. When there was nothing left to ruin in the Roman state, he determined the conquest of Libya and Italy, for no other reason than to destroy the people there, as he had those who were already his subjects. Justinian was very complacent and resembled most the silly ass, which follows, only shaking its ears, when one drags it by the bridle. As such Justinian acted, and threw everything into confusion.

As soon as he took over the rule from his uncle, his measure was to spend the public money without restraint, now that he had control of it. He gave much of it to the Huns who, from time to time, entered the state, and in consequence the Roman provinces were subject to constant incursions, for these barbarians, having once tasted Roman wealth, never forgot the road that led to it. He gathered to himself the private estates of Roman citizens from all over the empire, some by accusing their possessors of crimes of which they were innocent, others by juggling their owners' words into the semblance of a gift to him of their property. And many, caught in the act of murder and other crimes, turned their possessions over to him and thus escaped the penalty for their sins.

This emperor, then, was deceitful, devious, false, hypocritical, two-faced, cruel, skilled in dissembling his thought, never moved to tears by either joy or pain, although he could summon them artfully at will when the occasion demanded, a liar always, not only offhand but also in writing and when he swore sacred oaths to his subjects in their very hearing. Then he would immediately break his agreements and pledges, like the vilest of slaves, whom indeed only the fear of torture drives to confess their perjury. A faithless friend, he was a treacherous enemy, insane for murder and plunder, quarrelsome and revolutionary, easily led to anything evil but never willing to listen to good counsel, quick to plan mischief and carry it out but finding even the hearing of anything good distasteful to his ears.

How could anyone put Justinian's ways into words? These and many even worse vices were disclosed in him as in no other mortal nature seemed to have taken the wickedness of all other men combined and planted it in this man's soul. And besides this, he was too prone to listen to accusations and

too quick to punish. For he decided such cases without full examination, naming the punishment when he had heard only the accuser's side of the matter. Without hesitation he wrote decrees for the plundering of countries, sacking of cities, and slavery of whole nations, for no cause whatever. So that if one wished to take all the calamities that had befallen the Romans before this time and weigh them against his crimes, I think it would be found that more men had been murdered by this single man than in all previous history.

He had no scruples about appropriating other people's property, and did not even think any excuse necessary, legal or illegal, for confiscating what did not belong to him. And when it was his, he was more than ready to squander it in insane display, or give it as an unnecessary bribe to the barbarians. In short, he neither held on to any money himself nor let anyone else keep any, as if his reason were not avarice but jealousy of those who had riches. Driving all wealth from the country of the Romans in this manner, he became the cause of universal poverty. Now this was the character of Justinian, so far as I can portray it.

[The character of Theodora]

Justinian took a wife, and in what manner she was born and bred, and, wedded to this man, tore up the Roman Empire by the very roots, I now shall relate. Acacius was the keeper of wild beasts used in the amphitheater in Constantinople. He belonged to the Green faction[49] and was nicknamed the Bearkeeper. This man, during the rule of Anastasius, fell sick and died, leaving three daughters named Comito, Theodora, and Anastasia, of whom the eldest was not yet seven years old. When these children reached the age of girlhood, their mother put them on the local stage, for they were fair to look upon. Forthwith, Theodora became a courtesan,

---

[49] The two most popular chariot-racing fan clubs were known as the "Blues" and the "Greens" from the colors the charioteers wore. These "circus factions" provided an outlet for popular political expression, often by shouting orchestrated acclamations (as in Source 15.1 above) and slogans during performances in the hippodrome (chariot racetrack).

for she was not a flute or harp player, nor was she even trained to dance, but only gave her youth to anyone she met, in utter abandonment. She took part in the low comedy scenes, for she was very funny and a good mimic, and immediately became popular in this art. Frequently, she conceived but as she employed every artifice immediately, a miscarriage was straightway effected.

Later, she followed Hecebolus, a Tyrian[50] who had been made governor of Pentapolis,[51] serving him in the basest of ways, but finally she quarreled with him and was sent summarily away. Consequently, she found herself destitute of the means of life, which she proceeded to earn by prostitution, as she had done before this adventure. She came thus to Alexandria, and then traversing all the east, worked her way to Constantinople, in every city plying a trade as if the devil were determined there be no land on earth that should not know the sins of Theodora.

Thus was this woman born and bred. But when she came back to Constantinople, Justinian fell violently in love with her. At first he kept her only as a mistress, although he raised her to Patrician[52] rank. Through him, Theodora was able immediately to acquire an unholy power and exceedingly great riches. She seemed to him the sweetest thing in the world, and like all lovers, he desired to please his charmer with every possible favor and requite her with all his wealth. The extravagance added fuel to the flames of passion. With her now to help spend his money he plundered the people more than ever, not only in the capital, but throughout the Roman Empire.

Justin, doting and utterly senile, now was the laughing stock of his subjects. He was disregarded by everyone because of his inability to oversee state affairs; but Justinian they all served with considerable awe. His hand was in everything, and his passion for turmoil created universal consternation. It was then that he undertook to complete his marriage with Theodora. Because it was impossible for a man of senatorial rank to make a courtesan his wife, this being forbidden by ancient law, Justinian made the emperor nullify this ordinance by creating a new one, permitting him to wed Theodora and consequently making it possible for anyone else to marry a courtesan.[53] Immediately after this he seized the power of the emperor, veiling his usurpation with a transparent pretext, for he was proclaimed colleague[54] of his uncle as emperor of the Romans by the questionable legality of an election inspired by terror.

So Justinian and Theodora ascended the imperial throne three days before Easter, a time, indeed, when even making visits or greeting one's friends is forbidden. And not many days later Justin died of an illness,[55] after a reign of nine years. Justinian now was sole monarch, together, of course, with Theodora. Thus it was that Theodora, although born and brought up as I have related, rose to royal dignity over all obstacles. What she and her husband did together must now be briefly described, for neither did anything without the consent of the other. For some time it was generally supposed they were totally different in mind and action, but later it was revealed that their apparent disagreement had been arranged so that their subjects might not unanimously revolt against them, but instead be divided in opinion.

As soon as Justinian came into power he turned everything upside down. As the Romans were now at peace with all the world and he had no other means of satisfying his lust for slaughter, he set the barbarians all to fighting each other. And for no reason at all he sent for the Hun chieftains and with idiotic magnanimity gave them large sums of money, alleging he did this to secure their friendship. This, as I have said, he also had done in Justin's time. These Huns, as soon as they had got this money, sent it together with their soldiers to others of their chieftains, with the word to make inroads into the land of the emperor, so that they might collect further tribute from him, to buy them off in a second peace. Thus the Huns

---

[50] From the Phoenician city of Tyre.

[51] A province in Libya, west of Egypt.

[52] Patricians outranked even Consuls.

[53] A law issued by Justin between 520 and 523.

[54] Justinian actually was appointed quite legally, on 1 April 527.

[55] On 1 August 527.

enslaved the Roman Empire, and were paid by the emperor to keep on doing it.

To me, and many others of us, these two seemed not to be human beings but veritable demons, and what the poets call vampires. They laid their heads together to see how they could most easily and quickly destroy the race and deeds of men, and assuming human bodies, became man-demons, and so convulsed the world. Some of those who have been with Justinian at the palace late at night, men who were pure of spirit, have thought they saw a strange demoniac form taking his place. One man said that the emperor suddenly rose from his throne and walked about, and indeed he was never wont to remain sitting for long, and immediately Justinian's head vanished, while the rest of his body seemed to ebb and flow, whereat the beholder stood aghast and fearful, wondering if his eyes were deceiving him. But presently he perceived the vanished head filling out and joining the body again as strangely as it had left it. Another said he stood beside the emperor as he sat, and suddenly the face changed into a shapeless mass of flesh, with neither eyebrows nor eyes in their proper places nor any other distinguishing feature, and after a time the natural appearance of his countenance returned. I write these instances not as one who saw them myself, but heard them from men who were positive they had seen these strange occurrences at the time.

AL-TABARI, *HISTORY OF THE PROPHETS AND KINGS*, 1619

This manuscript illustration comes from "The Universal History" of Rashid Al-Din Hamadani, created in Tabriz, Persia, for the Mongol Ilkhanate in the early fourteenth century CE. It depicts the encounter in Syria of the ten-year-old Muhammad with the Arab Nestorian Christian monk Bahira, otherwise known as Sergius the Monk. The historian al-Tabari reported that Bahira saw a vision above Muhammad's head and foretold to Muhammad's uncle his future role as the Prophet and warned him to protect Muhammad from the Byzantines (https://upload.wikimedia.org/wikipedia/commons/3/36/Muammad-as-youth-meeting-monk-bahira-compendium-persia-1315-edin-550.jpg).

The Persian scholar Abu Ja'far Muhammad ibn Jarir al-Tabari (839–923 CE), one of the earliest Islamic historians, was the author of the "Tarikh al-Rusul wa al-Muluk" ("History of the Prophets and Kings"), which covered the period from the creation to 915 CE. The "Tarikh al-Tabari," its short title, meticulously cites its sources and is considered one of the most accurate accounts of early Islamic history. The section on the rise of Islam discusses the processes by which Muhammad extended his authority over the peoples of Arabia. Ancient Arabia was a welter of many different clans who were identified by the word "Banu" ("the descendents of"), for each clan was believed to have had a single original progenitor. The clans all were interrelated to a closer or more distant degree and interacted with each other on many different levels, both friendly and hostile. In 627 CE, after Muhammad had fled from Mecca and established himself in Medina in 622 CE (the Hijra), the two sides made peace. But this did not last. It was only a matter of time before the quarrels among the different clans led to a further outbreak of hostilities. In 629 CE fighting broke out between the Khuza'ah clan, which supported Muhammad, and the Banu Bakr clan, which supported Mecca. As a result the peace collapsed, and in the next year Muhammad was able to gain control of Mecca. al-Tabari also wrote that Christians had deleted from the original Christian gospels references to the coming of Muhammad.

Source: Michael Fishbein, trans., *The History of Al-Tabari: The Victory of Islam*, vol. 8 (Albany: State Univ. of New York Press, 1997), 160–163.

After sending his expedition to Mut'ah,[56] the Messenger of God[57] stayed in Medina[58] during Jumada II and Rajab.[59] Then the Banu Bakr bin 'Abd Manat bin Kinanah[60] assaulted the Khuza'ah[61] while the latter were at a watering place called al-Watir belonging to the Khuza'ah in Lower Mecca. The cause of the strife between Banu Bakr and the Banu Khuza'ah was a man from the Banu al-Hadrami[62] named Malik bin 'Abbad. This man of the Banu al-Hadrami had a covenant of protection[63] at that time with al-Aswad bin Razn. Malik set out on a journey as a merchant. When he was in the middle of Khuza'ah territory, the Khuza'ah assaulted him, killed him, and took his property. The Banu Bakr therefore attacked and killed a man from Khuza'ah.[64] Just before Islam, the Khuza'ah in turn assaulted Salma, Kulthum, and Dhu'ayb, the sons of al-Aswad bin Razn al-Dili—they were the leading men and dignitaries of the Banu Bakr—and killed them at 'Arafah, by the border markers of the sacred territory.

According to Ibn Humayd, Salamah, and Muhammad bin Ishaq,[65] a man from the Banu al-Dil, said, "In pagan times two payments of blood money would be paid for each of the sons of al-Aswad, whereas a single payment of blood money would be paid for us, and that because of their excellence compared with us."[66]

Matters stood thus between the Banu Bakr and the Khuza'ah when Islam intervened to separate them and occupy people's minds. When the peace of al-Hudaybiyah[67] was concluded between the Messenger of God and the Quraysh[68] (this information is according to Ibn Humayd, Salamah, Muhammad bin Ishaq, Muhammad bin Muslim bin 'Abdallah bin Shihab al-Zuhri, 'Urwah bin al-Zubayr, al-Miswar bin Makhramah, Marwan bin al-Hakam, and other learned men of ours), among the terms they imposed on the Messenger of God and that he granted to them was that whoever wanted to enter into a treaty and pact with the Messenger of God might do so, and whoever wanted to enter into a treaty with the Quraysh might do so. The Banu Bakr entered into a pact with the Quraysh, and the Khuza'ah entered into a pact with the Messenger of God.

The truce having been concluded, the Banu al-Dil of the Banu Bakr took advantage of it against Khuza'ah. To retaliate for the sons of al-Aswad bin Razn they wanted to kill the persons from Khuza'ah who had killed their men. Nawfal bin Mu'awiyah al-Dili set out with the Banu al-Dil (at that time he was a leader of the Banu al-Dil, although not all the Banu Bakr followed him). He made a night raid on the Khuza'ah while the latter were at their watering place of al-Watir, and they killed a man. They tried to drive each other away and fought. The Quraysh aided the Banu Bakr with weapons, and some members of the Quraysh fought on their side under cover of darkness until they drove the Khuza'ah into the sacred territory.[69]

According to al-Waqidi: Among the members of the Quraysh who helped the Banu Bakr against Khuza'ah that night, concealing their identity, were Safwan bin Umayyah, 'Ikrimah bin Abi Jahl, Suhayl bin 'Amr, and others, along with their slaves.

Resumption of the account of Ibn Ishaq, who said: When they reached the sacred territory, the Banu Bakr said, "Nawfal, we have entered the sacred territory. Be mindful of your God! Be

---

[56] A town in eastern Jordan.

[57] Muhammad.

[58] The city to which Muhammad had fled after being expelled from Mecca in 622 CE.

[59] The sixth and seventh months of the Muslim calendar.

[60] A people of western Arabia south of Mecca. The word "bin" ("son of") indicates the family lineage of the person believed originally to have established the clan.

[61] The Banū Khuza'a, an Arab people of west central Arabia who once ruled Mecca.

[62] A people of the Hadramat area of Yemen in southern Arabia.

[63] A promise not to attack or kill each other.

[64] The standard "law of retaliation" in force at the time.

[65] Earlier sources cited by al-Tabari.

[66] Blood money was paid to bring the cycles of retaliation to an end.

[67] Following several battles, the Treaty of Hudaybiyyah in March 628 specified a ten-year peace between Muhammad and the city of Medina on the one hand and the Quraysh clan of Mecca on the other.

[68] The clan that controlled the city of Mecca at this time.

[69] The territory of Mecca, marked out by sacred stones.

mindful of your God!" To which Nawfal replied blasphemously, "Today he has no God! Banu Bakr, take your revenge! By my life you steal in the sacred territory; will you not take your revenge in it?"

The night that the Banu Bakr attacked the Khuza'ah at al-Watir, they killed a man of the Khuza'ah named Munabbih. Munabbih was a man with a weak heart. He had gone out with a clansman of his named Tamim bin Asad. Munabbih said to him, "Tamim, save yourself! As for me, by God, I am a dead man whether they kill me or spare me, for my heart has ceased beating." Tamim ran away and escaped; Munabbih they caught and killed. When the Khuza'ah entered Mecca, they took refuge in the house of Budayl bin Waqa' al-Khuza'i and the house of one of their *mawlas*[70] named Rafi'.

When the Quraysh leagued together with the Banu Bakr against the Khuza'ah and killed some of their men, breaking the treaty and covenant that existed between them and the Messenger of God by violating the Khuza'ah, who had a pact and treaty with him, 'Amr bin Salim al-Khuza'i, one of the Banu Ka'b, went to the Messenger of God in Medina. 'Amr stood before the Messenger of God while he was in the mosque sitting among the people, and he recited, "Oh God, I will remind Muhammad of the venerable alliance of our father and his father. Parent were we, and you were child."[71] This was one of the things that prompted the conquest of Mecca.

---

[70] Patrons, protectors, or supporters.

[71] Arab peoples were very aware of family relationships going back for generations and were expected to preserve ancient loyalties.

JOHN OF NIKIÛ, *CHRONICLE*, CHAPTERS 111–120

A gold *solidus* of the Byzantine emperor Heraclius (610–641) depicts on the obverse Heraclius with his son and short-lived successor Heraclius Constantine (641). The legend reads "Our Lords Heraclius and Heraclius Constantinus, Perpetual Augustuses." On the reverse is a cross on steps and the legend "Victory of the emperors," with the abbreviation for "Count of Gold" below. After repelling and disastrously defeating the New Persians in the 620s, the weakened Heraclius was unable to withstand the onslaught of the Muslim Arabs during the 630s.

In late 639 CE, Byzantine Egypt was invaded by the Muslim general 'Amr. After a series of small victories, 'Amr totally destroyed the Roman army at the Battle of Heliopolis on 6 July 640. Any hope of reinforcements and continued resistance ended with the death of the Byzantine emperor Heraclius in February 641. After additional defeats, what was left of the Roman forces congregated in Alexandria. After a further nine-month siege, with further resistance having become futile, Cyrus, the Melchite (eastern supporters of the Council of Chalcedon in 451) Patriarch of Alexandria, who also had been appointed Prefect of Egypt, made a humiliating treaty with 'Amr that surrendered Alexandria to the Muslims. With the loss of Alexandria, the Romans had no hope of holding Egypt, and thus the richest of all the Roman provinces was abandoned to the Muslims and with it any hope of being able to recover the eastern provinces. This account is given by John, the Miaphysite (anti-Chalcedonian) bishop of Nikiû in the Nile Delta, whose later seventh-century chronicle is often the only source for these events. The tale begins in the spring of 640.

Source: R. H. Charles, *The Chronicle of John, Bishop of Nikiu* (London: Williams & Norgate, 1916).

Now, Theodorus was Master of Soldiers in Egypt. And when the messengers of Theodosius the Prefect of Arcadia[72] informed him regarding the death of John, general of the local levies, he thereupon turned with all the Egyptian troops and his auxiliary forces and marched to Lôkjôn,[73] which

---

[72] A Roman province in the northernmost part of Upper Egypt.

[73] All of the locations in this account, some of which are otherwise unknown, are located in Lower Egypt.

is an island. Moreover he feared lest, owing to the dissensions prevailing among the inhabitants of that district, the Muslims should come and seize the coast of Lôkjôn and dislodge the communities of the servants of God who were subjects of the Roman emperor. His lamentations were more grievous than the lamentations of David over Saul when he said, "How are the mighty fallen, and the weapons of war perished!"[74] For not only had John the Master of Soldiers perished when the Arabs took Bahnasâ[75] and attacked Arsinoë,[76] but likewise John the general, who was of the city of Mârôs, had been slain in battle and fifty horsemen with him.[77]

I will acquaint you briefly with what befell the former inhabitants of Arsinoë.

John and his troops had been appointed by the Romans to guard the district. They posted other guards near the rock of the city of Lâhûn in order to keep guard continually and to give information to the chief of the forces of the movements of their enemies. And subsequently they got ready some horsemen and a body of soldiers and archers, and these marched out to fight the Muslims, purposing to prevent their advance. And these Ishmaelites[78] came and slew without mercy the commander of the troops and all his companions. And forthwith they compelled the city of Arsinoë to open its gates, and they put to the sword all that surrendered, and they spared none, whether old men, babes, or women. And they proceeded against the general John.

Tidings of these events were brought to the general Theodosius and to Anastasius,[79] who were then twelve miles (nineteen kilometers) distant from Nikiû.[80] And they betook themselves immediately to the citadel of Babylon,[81] and they remained there. And such Romans as were in Egypt sought refuge in the citadel of Babylon. And they also were awaiting the arrival of the general Theodorus in order to join with him in attacking the Ishmaelites before the rise of the river and the time of sowing.

[The Battle of Heliopolis]

Theodosius and Anastasius went forth to the city of Heliopolis,[82] on horseback, together with a large body of foot soldiers, in order to attack 'Amr the son of Al-As.[83] And 'Amr showed great vigilance and strenuous thought in his attempts to capture the city of Babylon. But he was troubled because of his separation from a part of the Muslim troops, who being divided into two corps on the east of the river were marching toward Heliopolis, which was situated on high ground. And 'Amr the son of Al-As sent a letter to Omar the son of Al-Khattab in the province of Palestine to this effect, "If you do not send Muslim reinforcements, I shall not be able to take Babylon." And Omar sent him 4,000 Muslim warriors whose general's name was Walwarja. He was of barbarian descent. And 'Amr divided his troops into three corps. One corps he placed near Tendunias,[84] the second to the north of Babylon in Egypt, and he made his preparations with the third corps near the city of Heliopolis. And he gave the following orders, "Be on the watch, so that when the Roman troops come out to attack us, you may rise up in their rear, while we shall be on their

---

[74] 2 Samuel 1:27.

[75] A Christian episcopal see.

[76] Arsinoë in Arcadia, the capital city of the Fayum district. Known to the Egyptians as Shedet and the Greeks as Crocodilopolis, it was renamed Arsinoë by the Ptolemaic king Ptolemy II (309–246 BCE) in honor of his sister and wife Arsinoë.

[77] John was an exceptionally common name during this period.

[78] In the Bible, the descendents of Ishmael, the son of Abraham and his maid Hagar. By the time of Muhammad, the Arabs were thought to be the descendents of Ishmael.

[79] The military governor of Alexandria.

[80] The episcopal see of the author of this account.

[81] The most important Roman fortress in Lower Egypt, on the Nile River south of modern Cairo.

[82] Lunu to the ancient Egyptians and On in the Bible, the worship center of the Egyptian gods Atum and Ra, located just north of modern Cairo near the border between Lower and Upper Egypt.

[83] 'Amr ibn al-'As, an early enemy of Islam who converted in 620 CE and became one of Muhammad's chief generals. After the Muslim conquest of Syria, he proposed an invasion of Roman Egypt, which he led in late 639 CE.

[84] Muslim Umm Dûnayn, a Roman fortress on the Nile River.

front, and so having got them between us, we shall put them to the sword."

And thus when the Roman troops, unaware, set out from the fortress to attack the Muslims, these Muslims thereupon fell upon their rear, as they had arranged, and a fierce engagement ensued. And when the Muslims came in great numbers against them, the Roman troops fled to their ships. And the Muslim army took possession of the city of Tendunias, for its garrison had been destroyed, and there survived only 300 soldiers. And these fled and withdrew into the fortress and closed the gates. But when they saw the great slaughter that had taken place, they were seized with panic and fled by ship to Nikiû in great grief and sorrow. And when Domentianus[85] heard of these events, he set out by night without informing the inhabitants of Abûît that he was fleeing to escape the Muslims, and they proceeded to Nikiû by ship. And when the Muslims learnt that Domentianus had fled, they marched joyously and seized the city of Abûît, and they shed much blood there.

Such of the governors as were in the city of Nikiû fled and betook themselves to the city of Alexandria, leaving Domentianus with a few troops to guard the city. Then a panic fell on all the cities of Egypt and all their inhabitants took to flight and made their way to Alexandria, abandoning all their possessions and wealth and cattle. And when those Muslims, accompanied by the Egyptians who had apostatized from the Christian faith and embraced the faith of the beast, had come up, the Muslims took as booty all the possessions of the Christians who had fled, and they designated the servants of Christ enemies of God.[86] And 'Amr the chief of the Muslims spent twelve months in warring against the Christians of northern Egypt, but failed nevertheless in reducing their cities.

And when the Muslims saw the weakness of the Romans and the hostility of the people to the emperor Heraclius[87] because of the persecution he had visited on all the land of Egypt in regard to the catholic faith, at the instigation of Cyrus the Chalcedonian Patriarch,[88] they became bolder and stronger in the war. And the inhabitants of the city of Antinoë[89] sought to concert measures with John their Prefect with a view to attacking the Muslims, but he refused, and arose with haste with his troops, and, having collected all the imposts of the city, betook himself to Alexandria, for he knew that he could not resist the Muslims and he feared lest he should meet with the same fate as the garrison of Arsinoë. Indeed, all the inhabitants of the province submitted to the Muslims and paid them tribute. And the Muslims put to the sword all the Roman soldiers whom they encountered.

Heraclius fell ill with fever and died in the thirty-first year of his reign in the month Yakâtî-tof the Egyptians, that is, February of the Roman months, in the 357th year of Diocletian.[90] Pyrrhus, the Patriarch of Constantinople, nominated Constantine the son of the empress Eudocia[91] and made him head of the empire in succession to his father.[92] Constantine mustered a large number of ships and

---

[85] A Roman patrician and general known for his cowardice and love of intrigue.

[86] Many Miaphysite Christians made common cause with the Muslims against what they viewed as persecuting emperors.

[87] Emperor from 610 to 641 CE.

[88] A supporter of the ecumenical Council of Chalcedon, which in 451 CE had condemned the Miaphysite view that Christ had a single divine nature as opposed to an equally divine and human nature, Cyrus had been made Patriarch of Alexandria by Heraclius in 631 in opposition to the exiled Miaphysite patriarch Benjamin. Most of Egypt was Miaphysite, and many Egyptians therefore welcomed the Muslim invasion, thinking they could thus gain greater religious tolerance.

[89] City in Upper Egypt built by the emperor Hadrian (117–138) in honor of his lover Antinoüs.

[90] 11 February 641, counting from the accession of Diocletian (284–305), who had reorganized the administration of Egypt.

[91] The first wife of Heraclius; after her death in 612 CE, Heraclius married his niece Martina.

[92] Heraclius Constantine died only four months later of tuberculosis and was succeeded by his younger half-brother and co-emperor Heracleonas (641). He, in turn, soon was deposed by his brother Constans II (641–668), the last Roman emperor to hold the office of Consul (642). This instability grievously affected the Byzantine ability to resist the Arabs.

entrusted them to Kîrjûs and Salâkriûs and sent them to bring the Patriarch Cyrus to him so that he might take counsel with him as to the Muslims regarding whether he should fight, if he were able, or, if not, should pay tribute.[93] Constantine sent orders to Theodorus to come to him and leave Anastasius to guard the city of Alexandria and the cities on the coast. And he held out hopes to Theodorus that he would send him a large force in the autumn in order to war with the Muslims.

And 'Amr the chief of the Muslim forces had encamped before the citadel of Babylon and besieged the troops that garrisoned it. Now, the latter received his promise that they should not be put to the sword and undertook to deliver up to him all the munitions of war, which were considerable. And thereupon he ordered them to evacuate the citadel. And they took a small quantity of gold and set out. And it was in this way that the citadel of Babylon in Egypt was taken.[94]

'Amr and the Muslim army, on horseback, then proceeded by land until they came to the city of Kebrias of Abâdjâ. And on this occasion he attacked the general Domentianus. When the latter learned of the approach of the Muslim troops he embarked on a ship and fled and abandoned the army and their fleet and entered the city of Alexandria. Now when the soldiers saw that their commander had taken flight, they cast away their arms and threw themselves into the river in the presence of their enemies. And the Muslim troops slaughtered them with the sword in the river. Thereupon the Muslims made their entry into Nikiû, and took possession, and finding no soldiers they proceeded to put to the sword all whom they found in the streets and in the churches, men, women, and infants, and they showed mercy to none. And after they had captured the city, they marched against other localities and sacked them and put all they found to the sword.

And Egypt became enslaved to Satan. A great strife had broken out between the inhabitants of Lower Egypt,

and these were divided into two parties. Of these, one sided with Theodorus, but the other wished to join the Muslims. And straightway the latter party rose against the other, and they plundered their possessions and burnt their city. But the Muslims distrusted them. And 'Amr sent a large force of Muslims against Alexandria, and they captured Kariun, which lies outside the city. And Theodorus and his troops who were in that locality fled and withdrew into Alexandria. And the Muslims began to attack them but were not able to approach the walls of the city, for stones were hurled against them from the top of the walls and they were driven far from the city.

Subsequently, Constantine gave Cyrus power and authority to make peace with the Muslims and check any further resistance against them, and to establish a system of administration suitable to the government of the land of Egypt. Now, not only Cyrus the Chalcedonian Patriarch desired peace with the Muslims but also all the people and the patricians and Domentianus, who had enjoyed the favor of the empress Martina.[95] So all these assembled and took counsel with Cyrus the Patriarch with a view to making peace with the Muslims. And all the inhabitants of Alexandria, men and women, old and young, gathered together to meet the Patriarch Cyrus, rejoicing and giving thanks for the arrival of the Patriarch of Alexandria.[96]

And the Patriarch Cyrus set out and went to Babylon to the Muslims, seeking by the offer of tribute to procure peace from them and put a stop to war in the land of Egypt.[97] And 'Amr welcomed his arrival, and said to him, "You have done well to come to us." And Cyrus answered and said to him, "God has delivered this land into your hands. Let there be no enmity from henceforth between you and Rome. Hitherto there has been no persistent strife with you." And they fixed the amount of tribute to be paid. And as for the Ishmaelites, they were not to intervene in any matter, but were to keep to themselves for eleven months. The Roman troops in Alexandria were to carry off their possessions and their treasures and proceed home by sea,

---

[93] By now, Cyrus also had been appointed Prefect of Egypt, an extraordinary union of religious and secular authority and an indication of how serious the situation in Egypt was.

[94] On 21 December 640.

---

[95] Widow of the deceased emperor Heraclius.

[96] After his return from consulting with the emperor.

[97] 8 November 641.

and no other Roman army was to return. And the Romans were to cease warring against the Muslims and the Muslims were to desist from seizing Christian churches and were not to meddle with any concerns of the Christians. And the Jews were to be permitted to remain in the city of Alexandria. The Egyptians, who, through fear of the Muslims, had fled and taken refuge in the city of Alexandria, made the following request to the Patriarch, "Get the Muslims to promise that we may return to our cities and become their subjects." And he negotiated for them according to their request. And the Muslims took possession of all the land of Egypt, southern and northern.

GLOSSARY

See page xxvii for a note on spelling and punctuation. The chapter references indicate the chapter in which the term first appears, not its only occurrence.

ADLECTION (*Adlec'tion*) The power of Censors to appoint members of the Senate, later used by the Roman emperors (Chapter 7)

AENEID (*Aene'id*) Vergil's account of the adventures of Aeneas and the most influential of all Roman literary works (Chapter 7)

AĒTIUS (*A ë'tius*) Western Roman Master of Soldiers who defeated the Huns in 451 CE (Chapter 13)

AGRICULTURAL-MILITARY CRISIS Roman inability in the second century BCE to recruit sufficient men for the army (Chapter 5)

ALAMANNI (*Alaman'ni*) A Romano-Germanic people living north of the upper Rhine and Danube Rivers during the third century CE and later (Chapter 10)

ALARIC (*Alar'ic*) Visigothic chieftain who captured Rome in 410 CE (Chapter 13)

ALLAH (*Al'lah*) The creator god of the Arabs (Chapter 15)

ALTAR OF VICTORY Altar in the Senate house in Rome that symbolized the senators' pagan beliefs in the Late Roman Empire (Chapter 12)

AMBROSE OF MILAN (*Am'brose of Milan'*) Christian bishop who enforced church authority over the emperor Theodosius I (Chapter 12)

AMMIANUS MARCELLINUS (*Ammia'nus Marcelli'nus*) Historian who wrote of the period 350–378 CE (Chapter 12)

ANACHARSIS (*Anachar'sis*) A Scythian philosopher (Chapter 1)

ANGLES (*An'gles*) A barbarian people from far northern Europe who eventually settled in Britain (Chapter 14)

ANNONA (*anno'na*) Income and payments in kind by the late Roman government (Chapter 11)

ANTIGONID DYNASTY (*Anti'gonid*) Macedonian dynasty that ruled Macedon 277–168 BCE (Chapter 1)

ANTIGONUS Macedonian general, nicknamed "One-Eyed," whose family gained control of Macedonia after the death of Alexander the Great (Chapter 1)

ANTIGONUS GONATAS (*Anti'gonus Gona'tas*) Macedonian ruler 277–239 BCE who solidified the control of the Antigonid dynasty (Chapter 1)

ANTONINE CONSTITUTION (*An'tonine*) Law issued by the Roman emperor Caracalla in 212 CE granting Roman citizenship to nearly everyone in the empire (Chapter 10)

ANTONINE DYNASTY (*An'tonine*) Dynasty of Roman emperors ruling from 96 to 192 CE (Chapter 9)

ANTONINIANUS A debased silver coin introduced by the emperor Caracalla (Chapter 10)

ANTONINUS PIUS Roman emperor from 138 until 161, when the Roman Empire was at its height (Chapter 9)

ANTONY (MARCUS ANTONIUS) (*An'tony [Mar'cus Anto'nius]*) Roman senator, a member of the

Second Triumvirate, defeated by Octavian at Actium in 31 BCE (Chapter 7)

APOLOGISTS (*Apol'ogists*) Christians who attempted to rebut accusations made against the Christians (Chapter 9)

ARIANISM (*Ar'ianism*) Christian teaching that Christ the son was subordinate to God the father (Chapter 11)

ARMINIUS (*Armi'nius*) A Romanized German who led the German revolt against Rome in 9 CE (Chapter 7)

ARSACID DYNASTY (*Arsa'cid*) Ruling family of the Parthians (Chapter 1)

ASCETICISM (*Asce'ticism*) Practicing a life of physical self-denial (Chapter 12)

ASIA Roman province in Anatolia in 133 BCE that incorporated the old kingdom of Pergamum (Chapter 4)

ATHANASIUS (*Athanas'ius*) Bishop of Alexandria who defended Nicene theology in the mid-fourth century CE (Chapter 12)

ATTILA (*Attil'a*) King of the Huns ca. 434–454 (Chapter 13)

AUGUSTA (*Augus'ta*) Title given to women of the Roman imperial family (Chapter 7)

AUGUSTINE (*Au'gustine*) Bishop of Hippo in North Africa and Christian writer in the late fourth and early fifth centuries (Chapter 12)

AUGUSTUS (*Augus'tus*) Honorary title given to Octavian in 27 BCE, later used as a title by all Roman emperors (Chapter 7)

AUSPICIUM (*auspi'cium*) The power that allowed Roman rulers to assess the will of the gods (Chapter 2)

AUXILIA (*auxil'ia*) The auxiliary forces of the army during the Roman Empire, recruited from provincials (Chapter 7)

AVARS (*A'vars*) Barbarian people who threatened the Byzantine Empire as of the late sixth century CE (Chapter 15)

BARBARIZATION (*barbariza'tion*) The process by which the Roman army included increasing numbers of barbarians (Chapter 13)

BAR KOCHBA REVOLT (*Koch'ba*) Revolt of the Jews against Rome, 132–135 CE (Chapter 9)

BASILEUS (*basile'us*) The Greek word for "King," the title taken by Heraclius and later Byzantine emperors (Chapter 15)

BATTLE OF ACTIUM (*Ac'tium*) Battle in 31 BCE in western Greece where Octavian defeated Mark Antony (Chapter 7)

BATTLE OF ADRIANOPLE (*Adriano'ple*) Victory of the Visigoths over the Romans northwest of Constantinople in 378 CE (Chapter 13)

BATTLE OF THE MILVIAN BRIDGE (*Mil'vian*) Victory of Constantine over Maxentius outside Rome in 312 CE (Chapter 11)

BATTLE OF THE TEUTOBURG FOREST (*Teu'toburg*) Battle in Germany in which three Roman legions were destroyed by the Germans in 9 CE (Chapter 7)

BATTLE OF VOUILLÉ (*Vouillé'*) Victory of the Franks over the Visigoths near Poitiers in 507 CE (Chapter 14)

BATTLE OF THE YARMUK RIVER (*Yar'muk*) Victory of the Arabs over the Romans east of the Sea of Galilee in 636 CE (Chapter 15)

BELISARIUS (*Belisar'ius*) General of Justinian who conquered the Vandals and began the conquest of the Ostrogoths (Chapter 15)

BERBERS (*Ber'bers*) North African peoples dwelling between Tunisia and the Atlantic Ocean (Chapter 1)

BISHOP (*bish'op*) The leader of a Christian community in a city (Chapter 8)

BLUES AND GREENS Chariot-racing factions (fan clubs) in Constantinople that served as political action groups (Chapter 15)

BOUDICCA (*Boudic'ca*) British queen who led a revolt against the Romans in 60 CE (Chapter 8)

BYRSA (*Byr'sa*) The acropolis of Carthage (Chapter 1)

CAESAR (*Cae'sar*) Imperial rank intended to show the designated successor of an emperor (Chapter 10)

CAESAR (GAIUS JULIUS CAESAR) (*Cae'sar [Gai'us Ju'lius Cae'sar]*) Roman senator and member of the First Triumvirate who used his army to seize Rome (Chapter 6)

CAESAROPAPISM (*Caesaropa'pism*) The principle whereby the head of state also is the head of the church (Chapter 11)

CALIPH (*caliph'*) Muslim rulers who were the successors of Muhammad (Chapter 15)

CALIPHATE (*caliph'ate*) Islamic rulers who saw themselves as religious successors of Muhammad (Chapter 15)

CANON (*ca'non*) The standard list of books of the Christian Bible (Chapter 12)

CAROLINGIAN RENAISSANCE (*Carolin'gian*) Period of literary activity in western Europe during the reign of Charlemagne, 768–814 CE (Chapter 14)

CARTHAGE (*Car'thage*) Phoenician colony founded in modern Tunisia in 814 BCE (Chapter 1)

CATILINE (LUCIUS SERGIUS CATILINA) (*Ca'tiline [Lu'cius Ser'gius Catili'na]*) Roman senator killed in 63 BCE attempting to overthrow the state (Chapter 6)

CELIBACY (*cel'ibacy*) Sexual abstinence practiced by those leading an ascetic life (Chapter 12)

CELTIBERIANS (*Celtiber'ians*) Celtic peoples of Spain (Chapter 1)

CELTS Indo-European peoples inhabiting inland Europe from Spain to the Balkans, the British Isles, and central Anatolia (Chapter 1)

CENSOR Roman official chosen every five years to assess property holding among the Roman citizen body; also had the right to admit new members to the Senate (Chapter 3)

CENTURIATE ASSEMBLY (*Centur'iate*) Roman popular assembly comprising 193 centuries (Chapter 3)

CENTURION A senior noncomissioned officer who commanded a unit of one hundred men (Chapter 7)

CHRIST "The anointed one," whom Jews believed was the Messiah; a title applied by Christians to Jesus of Nazareth (Chapter 8)

CHRISTOGRAM (*Chris'togram*) The sign of Christ, the Greek letters chi and rho superimposed (Chapter 11)

CHURCH COUNCIL An assembly of Christian bishops that ruled on issues relating to the church (Chapter 11)

CHURCH FATHERS Christian writers of Late Antiquity (Chapter 12)

CICERO (MARCUS TULLIUS CICERO) (*Ci'cero [Mar'cus Tul'lius Ci'cero]*) Roman Consul in 63 BCE, responsible for the execution of Catiline's supporters (Chapter 6)

CIMBRI (*Cim'bri*) A Celtic people who invaded Gaul in the late second century BCE (Chapter 6)

CLEOPATRA SELENE (*Cleopa'tra Seh-lee'nee*) Daughter of Cleopatra VII and wife of King Juba II (Chapter 7)

CLEOPATRA VII (*Cleopa'tra*) Queen and pharaoh of Egypt, 51–30 BCE (Chapter 6)

CLIENTELA (*cliente'la*) Roman social system based on patrons and clients rendering mutual services to each other (Chapter 2)

CLIENT KING Native king installed by the Romans in a frontier area (Chapter 7)

CLOVIS (*Clo'vis*) King of the Franks 481–511 CE (Chapter 14)

COHORT (*co'hort*) Six-hundred-man unit of a Roman legion (Chapter 6)

COLLEGIALITY (*collegial'ity*) A principle of Roman government in which no office was overseen by a single person (Chapter 3)

COLONI (*colo'ni*) Tenant farmers who worked on the estates of large landowners in the Late Roman Empire (Chapter 9)

COMITATENSES (*comitaten'ses*) The mobile troops of the late Roman army (Chapter 11)

COMITATUS (*comita'tus*) The court of a late Roman emperor (Chapter 11)

COMPULSORY SERVICES Jobs that late Roman emperors believed had to be performed for the empire to survive (Chapter 11)

CONFLICT OF THE ORDERS The struggle of the plebeians to obtain expanded rights and opportunities ca. 500–287 BCE (Chapter 3)

CONSTANTINE I (*Con'stantine*) Roman emperor 306–337 CE who supported Christianity (Chapter 11)

CONSTANTINOPLE (*Constantino'ple*) Second capital of the Roman Empire; established in the east by Constantine in 330 CE (Chapter 11)

CONSTITUTION Generic name for legal enactments in the Roman Empire (Chapter 9)

CONSULS (*con'suls*) The two chief magistrates of the Roman Republic (Chapter 3)

CORPUS JURIS CIVILIS (*Cor'pus yu'ris civi'lis*) "The Body of Civil Law"; a compilation of past Roman law made under Justinian (Chapter 15)

COUNCIL OF 104 Carthaginian council that oversaw the government and generals (Chapter 1)

COUNCIL OF CHALCEDON (*Chal'cedon*) Ecumenical council in 451 that condemned Miaphysite teachings (Chapter 15)

COUNCIL OF CONSTANTINOPLE (*Constantino'ple*) Christian ecumenical church council in 381 that definitively condemned Arianism (Chapter 12)

COUNCIL OF EPHESUS (*Eph'esus*) Ecumenical council in 431 that condemned Nestorianism (Chapter 15)

COUNCIL OF NICAEA (*Nicae'a*) Christian ecumenical church council in northeastern Anatolia that defined a statement of Christian belief in 325 CE (Chapter 11)

COUNCIL OF THE PEOPLE BY TRIBES Roman popular assembly consisting of all male citizens organized by geographical tribes (Chapter 3)

COUNCIL OF THE PLEBS Roman popular assembly consisting of plebeians organized by geographical tribes (Chapter 3)

CRASSUS (MARCUS LICINIUS CRASSUS DIVES) (*Cras'sus [Mar'cus Lici'nius Cras'sus Di'ves]*) Roman senator, a member of the First Triumvirate (Chapter 6)

CTESIPHON (*Ctes'iphon*) City on the Tigris River, capital of the Parthians and New Persians (Chapter 1)

CULT OF ROME AND AUGUSTUS The imperial cult in the Roman Empire, participation in which demonstrated one's loyalty to Rome and the emperor (Chapter 7)

CURIATE ASSEMBLY (*Cur'iate*) Roman popular assembly composed of the thirty *curiae* (Chapter 3)

CYBELE (*Cy'bele*) An Anatolian mother goddess (Chapter 5)

DAMNATION OF MEMORY The process by which the Senate condemned a memory of a deceased emperor it disliked (Chapter 7)

DARK AGES Former view of the period in western Europe after the end of the Western Roman Empire (Chapter 14)

DEBASEMENT (*debase'ment*) Mixing a base metal such as copper with silver or gold coinage to be able to create more coins (Chapter 10)

DECEMVIRS (*De'cemvirs*) Board of ten Roman patricians who created the Twelve Tables in 451 and 450 BCE (Chapter 3)

DECIMATION (*decima'tion*) Roman military punishment in which every tenth man in a disgraced army unit was executed (Chapter 6)

DECURION (*decur'ion*) A member of the *curia* of a Roman city (Chapter 7)

DEFENSE IN DEPTH The Roman military strategy of stationing soldiers at strong points behind the frontiers (Chapter 10)

DEFENSIVE AGGRESSION Roman policy of preemptively attacking neighbors who were thought to be too powerful (Chapter 4)

DEIFICATION (*deifica'tion*) The process by which a human is made into a god (Chapter 7)

DELATOR (*dela'tor*) A Roman informer who received part of the property of anyone convicted on the basis of his report (Chapter 8)

DENARIUS (*denar'ius*) Standard Roman silver coin, introduced in 212 BCE (Chapter 5)

DIADOCHI (*Diadoch'i*) The generals of Alexander the Great who divided up his empire (Chapter 1)

DICTATOR A limited-term single chief magistrate of the Roman Republic (Chapter 3)

DIDO (*Di'do*) Refugee Phoenician queen who founded Carthage (Chapter 1)

DIO CASSIUS Author of a *Roman History* covering the period from Aeneas until 229 CE (Chapter 10)

DIOCESE (*di'ocese*) Administrative unit of the Late Roman Empire consisting of several provinces (Chapter 11)

DIOCLETIAN (*Diocle'tian*) Roman emperor 284–305 CE who began the Late Roman Empire (Chapter 11)

DOMINATE (*Dom'inate*) One of the terms applied to the Late Roman Empire (Chapter 11)

DOMINUS (*Do'minus*) "Lord and Master"; the title of Late Roman emperors (Chapter 11)

DONATISTS (*Do'natists*) Christian splinter group that taught that clerics who surrendered scriptures lost their spiritual authority (Chapter 11)

DONATIVE (*don'ative*) A thanks offering given by newly proclaimed Roman emperors to the army (Chapter 7)

DRUIDS (*Dru'ids*) Celtic class of priests (Chapter 1)

DYNASTIC SUCCESSION (*dynas'tic*) The principle whereby rulers are succeeded by their children or other family members (Chapter 11)

ECUMENICAL COUNCIL (*ecumen'ical*) A church council sponsored by the Roman government that legislated for all Christian churches in the world (Chapter 11)

EDICT A law issued by an emperor that had empire-wide validity; also, rulings issued by Republican magistrates with *imperium*.

EDICT OF MILAN Law issued in 312 by Constantine and Licinius ordering freedom of religion and return of Christian property (Chapter 11)

EPICUREANISM (*Epicure'anism*) Hellenistic philosophy based on the teachings of Epicurus of Samos (Chapter 5)

EQUESTRIAN CLASS (*eques'trian*) Roman social class ranking below Senators, also known as the Knights (Chapter 3)

ETRUSCANS (*Etrus'cans*) A people of northwestern Italy (Chapter 2)

EXARCHATES (*ex'archates*) Largely autonomous units of the Byzantine Empire in Italy and North Africa (Chapter 15)

EXTORTION COURT (*Extor'tion*) Roman court established in 149 BCE to try cases of extortion in the provinces (Chapter 5)

FALL OF CONSTANTINOPLE Capture of Constantinople by the Turks in 1453 CE, the end of the Byzantine Empire (Chapter 14)

FIRST TRIUMVIRATE (*Trium'virate*) Alliance among Crassus, Pompey, and Caesar begun in 60 BCE to control the Roman government (Chapter 6)

FIVE GOOD EMPERORS The first five emperors of the Antonine Dynasty, 96–180 CE (Chapter 9)

FLAVIAN DYNASTY (*Fla'vian*) The family of Roman emperors begun by Vespasian, 69–96 CE (Chapter 8)

FOEDERATI (*foedera'ti*) Barbarian "allies" of the Roman Empire serving under their own chieftains (Chapter 13)

FOGGARA (*fog'gara*) Underground water channels used for irrigation (Chapter 1)

FORUM (*for'um*) The central meeting place of a Roman city (Chapter 2)

FOSSIL WATER Unreplenished water sources that exist deep underground (Chapter 1)

FRANCIA (*Fran'cia*) Name of the kingdom of the Franks (Chapter 14)

FRANKS A Germanic people living on the lower Rhine River during the third century CE and later (Chapter 10)

FREEDMAN/FREEDWOMAN During the Roman Empire, a freed slave who did not yet have all the rights of a Roman citizen (Chapter 7)

GAETULI (*Gae'tuli*) Berber people known for horses and purple dye (Chapter 1)

GAIUS GRACCHUS (*Gai'us Grac'chus*) Roman Tribune of the Plebs assassinated in 121 BCE (Chapter 5)

GARAMANTES (*Garaman'tes*) A Libyan people of North Africa (Chapter 1)

GAULS An alternate name for the Celts (Chapter 1)

GOLDEN AGE OF ROMAN LITERATURE Period of Roman literary activity from the Late Republic through the reign of Augustus (Chapter 7)

GOTHS A Germanic people initially living north of the Black Sea during the third century CE and later (Chapter 10)

GREATER PROCONSULAR IMPERIUM (*Procon'sular Imper'ium*) Power used by Roman emperors of the Principate to command the army (Chapter 7)

GREAT PERSECUTION The last persecution of Christians by the Roman government, 303–311 CE (Chapter 11)

HAGIA SOPHIA (*Ha'gia Sophi'a*) Church of Holy Wisdom built at Constantinople by Justinian (Chapter 15)

HALLSTATT CULTURE (*Hall'statt*) European culture of the early Iron Age (Chapter 1)

HANNO (*Han'no*) Carthaginian king who explored the western African coast (Chapter 1)

HEGIRA (*Hegir'a*) The journey undertaken by Muhammad from Mecca to Medina in 622 CE (Chapter 15)

HEJAZ (*Hejaz'*) A fertile strip of Arabia on the Red Sea coast (Chapter 15)

HELENA (*Hel'ena*) Mother of Constantine who built a church on the site of Christ's tomb (Chapter 12)

HELLENISTIC AGE (*Hellenis'tic*) Period of Greek history from 323 to 31 BCE (Chapter 1)

HENOTIKON (*Heno'tikon*) Ruling of the Byzantine emperor Zeno that attempted to end quarrels about religion (Chapter 15)

HERACLIUS (*Hera'clius*) Byzantine emperor 610–642 CE who led a crusade against the New Persians (Chapter 15)

HERESY (*her'esy*) An illegal Christian belief as determined by church councils and the Roman government (Chapter 11)

HEROD THE GREAT (*Her'od*) Roman client king of Judaea (Chapter 7)

HIMILCO (*Himil'co*) Carthaginian who explored the western European coast (Chapter 1)

HOLY LAND The area of Palestine discussed in the Bible, the destination of many pilgrimages in Late Antiquity (Chapter 12)

HOLY MEN/WOMEN Christian ascetics who gained spiritual authority by becoming close to God (Chapter 12)

HOMOIAN (*ho'moian*) Christian doctrine that held that the Father and Son were alike "according to the scriptures." (Chapter 12)

HONESTIORES (honestio'res) Romans with greater legal privilege in the third century CE and later (Chapter 10)

HORTENSIAN LAW (Horten'sian) Roman law of 287 BCE by which plebiscites automatically became laws of all the people (Chapter 3)

HUMILIORES (humilio'res) Romans with lesser legal privilege in the third century CE and later (Chapter 10)

HUNS Steppe nomads of Mongolian origin during the Late Roman Empire (Chapter 13)

HYPATIA (Hypa'tia) Female Neoplatonist philosopher of Alexandria murdered by a mob of Christian monks in 415 CE (Chapter 12)

HYPERBOREANS (Hyperbore'ans) A mythical people living in the far north (Chapter 1)

IDES OF MARCH March 15; on this day in 44 BCE Julius Caesar was assassinated (Chapter 6)

IMPERIAL CRISIS Period of Roman history from 235 to 284 CE (Chapter 10)

IMPERIAL SUCCESSION The process by which one Roman emperor was succeeded by the next (Chapter 7)

IMPERIUM (impe'rium) The power that allowed Roman rulers to command armies (Chapter 2)

INDEMNITY A payment for the costs of the war made by states defeated by Rome (Chapter 4)

INITIATION The rituals that allowed one to participate in a mystery cult (Chapter 5)

ISLAM (Is'lam) A word meaning "submission"; the religion established by Muhammad (Chapter 15)

ITALIA (Ital'ia) The new nation established by the Italian Allies when they revolted against Rome in 90 BCE (Chapter 6)

ITALIAN ALLIANCE The system of alliances established by the Romans in Italy during the Roman Republic (Chapter 4)

ITALIC PEOPLES Italian peoples who primarily occupied the uplands of central and southern Italy; also known as Sabellians (Chapter 2)

JEROME (Jerome') Christian author who made the definitive translation of the Bible into Latin in the late fourth century CE (Chapter 12)

JESUS OF NAZARETH (Je'sus of Na'zareth) The Jewish founder of Christianity during the reigns of Augustus and Tiberius (Chapter 8)

JUBA II (Ju'ba) Roman client king, 28 BCE to 23 CE, of Numidia and Mauretania (Chapter 7)

JULIA DOMNA (Dom'na) A Syrian, the wife of Septimius Severus (Chapter 10)

JULIAN Roman emperor 361–363 CE; the last major pagan Roman emperor, known to Christians as "the Apostate" (Chapter 12)

JULIAN CALENDAR (Ju'lian) A calendar with 365 days per year and a leap year every fourth year introduced by Julius Caesar (Chapter 6)

JULIO-CLAUDIAN DYNASTY (Ju'lio-Clau'dian) The family of Roman emperors related to Augustus, 27 BCE–68 CE (Chapter 8)

JULIUS NEPOS (Ju'lius Ne'pos) The last western Roman emperor, 474–480 CE (Chapter 13)

JURISTS (jur'ists) Legal scholars who advised Roman emperors on points of law (Chapter 9)

JUSTINIAN (Justin'ian) Byzantine emperor 527–565 CE who reconquered much of the western empire (Chapter 15)

KA'ABA (Ka'aba) A religious shrine in Mecca in Arabia (Chapter 15)

LAND LAW A Roman law for distributing public land to landless persons (Chapter 5)

LAST RECOMMENDATION OF THE SENATE A command given by the Roman Senate to the Consuls to save the state (Chapter 5)

LAST JUDGMENT The event that Christians believed would bring the second coming of Jesus Christ and the end of the world (Chapter 12)

LATE ANTIQUITY The final phase of the ancient world, from ca. 200 to ca. 750 CE (Chapter 11)

LA TÈNE CULTURE European Iron Age culture that evolved from the Hallstatt Culture (Chapter 1)

LATIFUNDIA (latifun'dia) "Wide fields"; the extensive estates of Roman senators (Chapter 6)

LATIUM (La'tium) Agricultural plain south of the lower Tiber River (Chapter 3)

LEGATES OF AUGUSTUS (Le'gates) Provincial governors who administered the provinces that the emperor was responsible for (Chapter 7)

LEGION The largest unit of the Roman army, nominally six thousand men but usually rather less (Chapter 3)

LEO THE GREAT Bishop of Rome 440–461 (Chapter 12)

LEPIDUS (MARCUS AEMILIUS LEPIDUS) (Le'pidus [Mar'cus Ae'milius Le'pidus]) Roman Consul, leader of an unsuccessful revolt in 78 BCE (Chapter 6)

LEPIDUS (MARCUS AEMILIUS LEPIDUS) (Le'pidus [Mar'cus Ae'milius Le'pidus]) Roman senator, son of the rebel of 78 BCE, a member of the Second Triumvirate (Chapter 7)

LICINIO-SEXTIAN LAW (*Lici'nio-Sex'tian*) Roman law of 367 BCE requiring that one Consul be a plebeian (Chapter 3)

LICTOR (lic'tor) Official who carried the fasces, a bundle of wooden rods with an ax embedded in it, and symbolized the authority of Roman magistrates with *imperium* (Chapter 3)

LIMETANEI (*limeta'nei*) The troops of the late Roman army stationed on the frontier (Chapter 11)

LOMBARDS (*Lom'bards*) Barbarian people who invaded Italy in 568 CE (Chapter 15)

MAGO (*Ma'go*) Carthaginian writer about agriculture (Chapter 1)

MANICHAEISM (*Ma'nichaeism*) Near Eastern religion developed in the third century CE that saw the world as a struggle between God and Satan (Chapter 12)

MANIPLES (*man'iples*) Units of 120 men making up a Roman legion during the Republic (Chapter 3)

MANUSCRIPT Handmade copies of literary works (Chapter 12)

MARCUS AURELIUS (*Mar'cus Aure'lius*) Roman emperor 161–180 CE (Chapter 9)

MARIUS (GAIUS MARIUS) (*Mar'ius [Gai'us Mar'ius]*) Roman general who created the volunteer army ca. 107 BCE (Chapter 6)

MARTYRS (*mar'tyrs*) Christians who were executed for their beliefs (Chapter 9)

MAURI (*Mau'ri*) The Moors, a Berber people of the Atlas Mountains in North Africa (Chapter 1)

MAYOR OF THE PALACE Frankish official who competed for authority with the Merovingian kings (Chapter 14)

MECCA (*Mec'ca*) A city of the central Hejaz in Arabia (Chapter 15)

MEDINA (*Medi'na*) An urban center of Arabia (Chapter 15)

MEDITERRANEAN CULTURE Composite culture shared by the Romans and all the peoples under their authority (Chapter 7)

MEROVINGIAN DYNASTY (*Merovin'gian*) The family of Frankish kings after the fall of the Western Roman Empire (Chapter 14)

MIAPHYSITES (*Mia'physites*) Also known as Monophysites, Christians who taught that Christ had only a single divine nature (Chapter 15)

MILITARY ANARCHY Period of Roman history from 235 to 284 CE (Chapter 10)

MISHNAH (*Mish'nah*) Jewish oral interpretations of Mosaic law (Chapter 9)

MITHRAS (*Mith'ras*) Persian sun god popular in the Roman army during the Roman Empire (Chapter 9)

MITHRIDATES VI (*Mithrida'tes*) King of Pontus 119–63 BCE who engaged in several wars with Rome (Chapter 6)

MOS MAIORUM (*mos maio'rum*) "The ways of our ancestors"; the sum total of Roman traditions (Chapter 2)

MUHAMMAD (*Muham'mad*) Islamic prophet active ca. 610–632 CE (Chapter 15)

MUSLIMS (*Mus'lims*) The followers of Islam (Chapter 15)

MYSTERY CULTS Religions that promised a happy afterlife to initiates (Chapter 5)

NABATAEANS (*Nabatae'ans*) Arab people living between Syria and Arabia (Chapter 1)

NASAMONIANS (*Nasamo'nians*) A Libyan people of North Africa (Chapter 1)

NEOPLATONISM (*Neopla'tonism*) Philosophical system of the Late Roman Empire loosely based on teachings of Plato (Chapter 10)

NESTORIANISM (*Nestor'ianism*) Christian teaching that the divine and human natures of Christ are completely separate (Chapter 15)

NEW MAN or **NOVUS HOMO** (*no'vus ho'mo*) A Roman Consul who had no ancestor who had been a Consul (Chapter 3)

NEW PERSIAN EMPIRE Successor to the Parthian Kingdom as of 227 CE (Chapter 10)

NEW TESTAMENT Christian scriptures based on the teachings of Jesus of Nazareth (Chapter 8)

NICENE CREED (*Ni'cene*) Statement of Christian belief defined at the Council of Nicaea in 325 CE (Chapter 11)

NIKA REBELLION (*nika'*) Popular rebellion in Constantinople in 532 CE put down with great slaughter (Chapter 15)

NOBLES Persons of high status who served as state officials and controlled large tracts of land (Chapter 3)

NUMEN (*Nu'men*) Inchoate force of nature that the early Romans believed controlled their environment (Chapter 2)

NUMIDIANS (*Numi'dians*) A Berber people of North Africa famous for their cavalry (Chapter 1)

OCTAVIAN (*Octa'vian*) Originally Gaius Octavius, then C. Julius Caesar Octavianus after his adoption in Caesar's will; defeated Antony in 31 BCE (Chapter 7)

ODOVACAR (*Odova'car*) Barbarian Master of Soldiers who seized Italy in 476 CE and made himself king (Chapter 13)

OPPIDUM (*Op'pidum*) A Celtic hill fort (Chapter 1)

ORIGINAL SIN The Christian doctrine that the sin of Adam and Eve was inherited by all humans who thus were guilty of sin (Chapter 12)

OSTROGOTHS (*Os'trogoths*) A barbarian people from north of the Black Sea who eventually settled in Italy (Chapter 13)

PAGAN MONOTHEISM (*mon'otheism*) The general trend toward monotheism during the Roman Empire (Chapter 9)

PATERFAMILIAS (*paterfami'lias*) "Father of the family"; the head of a Roman family (Chapter 2)

PATRIARCH (*pa'triarch*) During Late Antiquity, Christian bishops of Rome, Constantinople, Jerusalem, Antioch, and Alexandria (Chapter 11)

PATRICIANS (*patri'cians*) The aristocrats of early Rome (Chapter 2)

PEOPLE OF THE BOOK Jews, Christians, and Muslims, who base their beliefs on written scriptures (Chapter 15)

PERSECUTION (*persecu'tion*) An attempt by the Roman government to punish Christians for their beliefs (Chapter 9)

PETRA (*Pe'tra*) Capital city of the Nabataeans (Chapter 1)

PILGRIMAGE (*pil'grimage*) A journey to a sacred site for the purpose of gaining some blessing from a god (Chapter 12)

PLEBEIANS (*plebei'ans*) The less privileged citizens of Rome (Chapter 2)

PLEBISCITE (*pleb'iscite*) Law passed by the Council of the Plebs (Chapter 3)

PLUTARCH (*Plu'tarch*) Greek author of biographies and moral advice in the mid-second century CE (Chapter 9)

POMPEII (*Pompeii'*) City on the Bay of Naples destroyed by eruption of Mt. Vesuvius in 79 CE (Chapter 8)

POMPEY (GNAEUS POMPEIUS) (*Pom'pey [Gnae'us Pom'pei'us]*) Roman senator, a member of the First Triumvirate (Chapter 6)

PONTIFEX MAXIMUS (*Pon'tifex Max'imus*) Chief priest of Rome (Chapter 2)

PONTIUS PILATE (*Pon'tius Pi'late*) Roman Prefect of Judaea who ordered the execution of Jesus of Nazareth ca. 28 CE (Chapter 8)

POPE Title given to a distinguished bishop, during the sixth century CE reserved for the bishop of Rome (Chapter 14)

POTENTIA (*poten'tia*) The "power" of Roman senators and other powerful persons that allowed them to get their way (Chapter 12)

PRAETOR (*prae'tor*) Roman magistrate who oversaw law courts or, later, served as a provincial governor (Chapter 3)

PRAETORIAN PREFECT (*Praetor'ian Pre'fect*) In the Principate, the commander of the Praetorian Guard; later the administrator of a Prefecture (Chapter 7)

PREFECT (*Pre'fect*) A high-ranking equestrian office during the Roman Empire (Chapter 7)

PREFECTURE (*pre'fecture*) A large Late Roman administrative unit made up of dioceses (Chapter 11)

PRINCEPS SENATUS (*Prin'ceps sena'tus*) The highest-ranking member of the Roman Senate (Chapter 3)

PRINCIPATE (*Prin'cipate*) The Roman Empire in the form that was established by Augustus, 27 BCE–284 CE (Chapter 7)

PROCONSUL (*Pro'consul*) Roman provincial governor who in the past had held the office of Consul (Chapter 5)

PROCURATOR (*Pro'curator*) An equestrian official during the Roman Empire in charge of tax collection (Chapter 7)

PROLETARIATE (*proletar'iate*) The lowest-ranking class of the Centuriate Assembly (Chapter 3)

PROSCRIPTIONS (*proscrip'tions*) The lists of enemies published by Sulla (Chapter 6)

PROVINCE A foreign territory annexed by Rome (Chapter 4)

PTOLEMAIC DYNASTY (*Ptolema'ic*) Macedonian dynasty that ruled Egypt 323–31 BCE (Chapter 1)

PTOLEMY I (*Ptol'emy*) Macedonian general whose family gained control of Egypt after the death of Alexander the Great (Chapter 1)

PUPPET EMPERORS The western Roman emperors from 455 until 480 CE (Chapter 13)

QU'RAN (*Qu'ran'*) The book of Islamic scripture (Chapter 15)

RAVENNA (*Raven'na*) City in northeastern Italy that served as a refuge for western Roman emperors in the fifth century (Chapter 12)

REPUBLIC The "Public Thing"; the form of Roman government in which sovereign authority lay with the people, lasting from 509 to 27 BCE (Chapter 2)

REPUBLICAN EMPIRE Term referring to the Roman acquisition of many foreign provinces during the Roman Republic (Chapter 5)

RHODES Island city off the southwestern coast of Anatolia (Chapter 1)

RICIMER (*Ri'cimer*) Barbarian Master of Soldiers who virtually ruled the western Roman Empire during the time of the Shadow Emperors (Chapter 13)

ROMANCE LANGUAGES Modern languages, such as French and Italian, derived from Latin (Chapter 14)

ROMAN CITIZENSHIP The legal status that conveyed the private and public rights of a Roman citizen (Chapter 7)

ROMANIZATION The process by which provincials absorbed Roman culture and Romans absorbed provincial culture (Chapter 7)

ROME OF THE KINGS The first period of Roman history, 753–509 BCE (Chapter 2)

ROMULUS "AUGUSTULUS" (*Rom'ulus "Augus'tulus"*) Child western usurper deposed by Odovacar in 476 CE, often viewed as the last western emperor (Chapter 13)

RUBICON RIVER (*Ru'bicon*) Shallow river in northern Italy crossed by Caesar in 49 BCE to begin the civil war (Chapter 6)

RULE OF LAW The principle that everyone in a society is subject to the law (Chapter 3)

SACK OF ROME Capture and sack of Rome by the Visigoths in 410 CE, also sack of Rome by the Vandals in 455 (Chapter 13)

SAINTS Christians who were accorded special recognition for steadfastness in their faith (Chapter 9)

SAKA (*Sa'ka*) Name given by the Persians to the Scythians (Chapter 1)

SAMNITES (*Sam'nites*) The most powerful of the Italic peoples (Chapter 2)

SASANIDS (*Sa'sanids*) Persian dynasty that created the New Persian Empire in 227 CE (Chapter 10)

SAXONS A barbarian people from far northern Europe who eventually settled in Britain (Chapter 14)

SCHISM A division in the Christian church caused by a disagreement over authority (Chapter 11)

"SECOND SOPHISTIC" A revival of Greek rhetoric and oratory that strove to attain a higher standard of exposition (Chapter 9)

SECOND TRIUMVIRATE (*Trium'virate*) Alliance among Antony, Lepidus, and Octavian begun in 43 BCE to control the Roman government (Chapter 7)

SEJANUS (*Seja'nus*) Praetorian Prefect who tried to seize the throne during the reign of Tiberius (Chapter 8)

SELEUCID DYNASTY (*Seleu'cid*) Macedonian dynasty that ruled Syria and the east 312–63 BCE (Chapter 1)

SELEUCUS (*Seleu'cus*) Macedonian general whose family gained control of the eastern part of the empire of Alexander the Great (Chapter 1)

SENATE An advisory body that served as the true ruling body of the Roman Republic but lost authority to the emperors during the Principate and Dominate (Chapter 2)

SENATOR A member of the Senate at Rome; in the late empire, also a member of a wider senatorial aristocracy (Chapter 2)

SENATORIAL CLASS In the Roman Empire, men who owned enough property to be eligible for membership in the Senate (Chapter 7)

SERVIAN REFORMS (*Ser'vian*) Roman reforms CA. 500/450 that restructured the army and society (Chapter 3)

SESTERTIUS (PL. SESTERTII) (*sester'tius [pl. ses'ter-tee-ees]*) A large copper coin of the Roman Empire valued at one-fourth of a denarius (Chapter 7)

SEVERAN DYNASTY (*Se'veran*) Dynasty of Roman emperors 193–235 CE founded by Septimius Severus (Chapter 10)

SHADOW EMPERORS The western Roman emperors from 455 until 480 CE (Chapter 13)

SHELL DEFENSE SYSTEM The Roman military strategy of stationing nearly all the soldiers on the frontier to prevent invasions (Chapter 7)

SILK ROAD Trade route between China and the West opened in the second century BCE (Chapter 1)

SLAVS Barbarian people who threatened the Byzantine Empire as of the late sixth century CE (Chapter 15)

SOCIAL WAR The Revolt of the Italian Allies, 90–88 BCE (Chapter 6)

SOLIDUS (*so'lidus*) The gold coin used by Constantine to put the empire on the gold standard (Chapter 11)

SOL INVICTUS (*Sol Invic'tus*) "The Unconquered Sun," seen by many in the Late Roman Empire as being the only true god (Chapter 10)

SPARTACUS (*Spar'tacus*) Slave who led a revolt against Rome in 73 BCE (Chapter 6)

STOICISM (*Stoi'cism*) Hellenistic philosophy based on the teachings of Zeno of Citium (Chapter 5)

SUFFETS (*suf'fets*) Chief officials of the Carthaginian government (Chapter 1)

SULLA (LUCIUS CORNELIUS SULLA) (*Sul'la [Lu'cius Corne'lius Sul'la]*) Roman general who used his army to seize Rome in 88 BCE (Chapter 6)

TACITUS (*Ta'citus*) Roman historian writing ca. 100 CE who covered the Julio-Claudian and Flavian emperors (Chapter 8)

TALMUD (*Tal'mud*) Guide to Jewish life written in the fourth and fifth centuries CE (Chapter 12)

TANIT (*Ta'nit*) Carthaginian fertility goddess (Chapter 1)

TARIM BASIM (*Tarim'*) Area of northwestern China that linked China with the west (Chapter 1)

TARTESSUS (*Tartes'sus*) An early trading city of southern Spain (Chapter 1)

TEMPLE (JEWISH) Jewish temple in Jerusalem first built by Solomon ca. 950 BCE; destroyed by the Romans in 70 CE (Chapter 8)

TETRARCHY (*Te'trarchy*) The system of rule by four emperors introduced by Diocletian (Chapter 11)

TEUTONES (*Teuto'nes*) A Celtic people who invaded Gaul in the late second century BCE (Chapter 6)

THEOCRACY (*theo'cracy*) A society in which the leaders of the church also govern the state (Chapter 15)

THEODOSIAN CODE (*Theodo'sian*) Compilation of Roman laws going back to the time of Constantine issued in 437 CE (Chapter 15)

THEODOSIUS I (*Theodo'sius*) Roman emperor 379–395; called "the Great" because he outlawed pagan practices (Chapter 12)

THE ONE Neoplatonic transcendent, impersonal, divine principle (Chapter 12)

TIBERIUS GRACCHUS (*Tiber'ius Grac'chus*) Roman Tribune of the Plebs assassinated in 133 BCE (Chapter 5)

TITHE A land tax consisting of one-tenth of the crops raised during the year (Chapter 5)

TORAH (*Tor'ah*) The first five books of the Hebrew Bible (Chapter 1)

TRIBES Divisions of the Roman population based on family membership or residence (Chapter 3)

TRIBUNES OF THE PLEBS Ten officials elected by the plebeians to protect their interests (Chapter 3)

TRIBUNICIAN POWER (*Tribuni'cian*) Power used by Roman emperors of the Principate to control legislation (Chapter 7)

TRIUMPH Victory parade granted to a victorious Roman general (Chapter 4)

TRUE CROSS The cross on which Christ was crucified, believed to have been discovered by Constantine's mother Helena.

TURDETANI (*Turdeta'ni*) Iberian people who inherited the culture of Tartessus (Chapter 1)

TWELVE TABLES The first written Roman law, created by the Decemvirs 451–450 BCE (Chapter 3)

ULFILAS (*Ulfi'las*) Gothic bishop who brought Arian-appearing Christianity to the Visigoths in the 340s CE and later (Chapter 12)

VALENS (*Va'lens*) Eastern Roman emperor 364–378, brother of Valentinian I, killed at the Battle of Adrianople (Chapter 12)

VALENTINIAN I (*Valentin'ian*) Western Roman emperor 364–375 during the last Golden Age of the Roman Empire (Chapter 12)

VANDALS (*Van'dals*) Germanic people originally from the area of modern Poland (Chapter 10)

VARUS (*Var'us*) Roman general who lost three legions at the Battle of the Teutoburg Forest in 9 CE (Chapter 7)

VERCINGETORIX (*Vercinge'torix*) Leader of a Gallic revolt against Julius Caesar in 52 BCE (Chapter 6)

VESTAL VIRGINS Six Roman priestesses responsible for keeping the sacred fire of the goddess Vesta burning (Chapter 2)

VETO The power of the Roman Tribunes of the Plebs to halt any activity they disapproved of (Chapter 3)

VICAR (*vi'car*) The administrator of a late Roman diocese (Chapter 11)

VILLA (*vil'la*) A late Roman rural estate that produced most of its own needs (Chapter 13)

VISIGOTHIC RENAISSANCE (*Visigo'thic*) Period of literary activity in Visigothic Spain in the seventh century CE (Chapter 14)

VISIGOTHS (*Vi'sigoths*) Germanic people from north of the Danube River who entered the Roman Empire in 376 CE (Chapter 13)

VOLUNTEER ARMY Roman army that accepted men who owned no property (Chapter 6)

VULGATE (*Vul'gate*) Latin translation of the Bible made by Jerome in the late fourth century CE (Chapter 14)

YEAR OF THE FOUR EMPERORS The year 69 CE in the Roman Empire (Chapter 8)

ZENO (*Ze'no*) Eastern Roman emperor who ruled 474–491 CE (Chapter 15)

ZENOBIA (*Zeno'bia*) Queen of Palmyra 267–274 CE (Chapter 10)

CREDITS

Number preceding credit refers to page number

ART CREDITS

CHAPTER 1

7 Luis García
9 Ralph W. Mathisen
10 Ralph W. Mathisen
14 Jean Baradez, Fossatum
  Africae. Recherches Aériennes sur l'organisation des confins Sahariens a l'Epoque Romaine. Arts et Métiers Graphiques, Paris
15 Image Courtesy U. Leicester/Digitalglobe/Google
16 Classical Numismatic Group, Inc.
  http://www.cngcoins.com
19 BishkekRocks / Wikimedia Commons
20 damian entwistle / Wikimedia Commons
24 © Gilles Mermet / Art Resource, NY
24 Ralph W. Mathisen
28 Heritage Image Partnership Ltd / Alamy Stock Photo
30 Griffins attacking a horse (gold) (detail of 343656 and 343171), Greek School, (4th century BC) / Historical Museum, Kiev, Ukraine / Photo © Boltin Picture Library / Bridgeman Images
31 Ralph W. Mathisen
41 Classical Numismatic Group, Inc.
  http://www.cngcoins.com
45 Classical Numismatic Group, Inc.
  http://www.cngcoins.com

CHAPTER 2

58 Ralph W. Mathisen
59 Gold foils with Phoenician (left) and Etruscan (right) inscriptions, from Pyrgi, Italy / De Agostini Picture Library / G. Dagli Orti / Bridgeman Images
63 Ralph M. Mathisen
63 Scala / Art Resource, NY
64 The Metropolitan Museum of Art / Art Resource, NY
65 Ralph M. Mathisen
65 Ralph M. Mathisen
66 Ralph M. Mathisen
68 The Portable Antiquities Scheme

CHAPTER 3

90 © Araldo de Luca

CHAPTER 4

109 Scala / Art Resource, NY
113 © The Trustees of the British Museum

CHAPTER 5

142 Numismatica Ars Classica NAC AG
154 Palazzo Torlonia, Rome

CHAPTER 6

167 De Agostini / A. Dagli Orti / Getty Images
169 Classical Numismatic Group, Inc.
  http://www.cngcoins.com

CHAPTER 14

496 Ralph M. Mathisen

499 Ralph M. Mathisen

499 Ralph M. Mathisen

505 Art Resource, NY

506 Throne of King Dagobert, (gilded metal),
Merovingian, (7th century) / Bibliotheque Nationale,
Paris, France / Bridgeman Images

511 © Raphaël de Filippo, Inrap

512 Ralph M. Mathisen

514 Classical Numismatic Group, Inc.
http://www.cngcoins.com

521 Zürich, Zentralbibliothek,
Ms. C 10i, f. 69r – Passionarius maior, http://
www.e-codices.unifr.ch/de/zbz/C0010i/69r

CHAPTER 15

524 © Marie-Lan Nguyen / Wikimedia Commons

530 Cameraphoto Arte, Venice / Art Resource, NY

531 Erich Lessing / Art Resource, NY

532 RMN-Grand Palais / Art Resource, NY

538 Ralph M. Mathisen

540 Sonia Halliday Photo Library / Alamy Stock Photo

548 Ralph W. Mathisen

556 Classical Numismatic Group, Inc.
http://www.cngcoins.com

TEXT CREDITS

236 Erik Wistrand, The So-called Laudatio Turiae. Vol. 34
of Studia Graeca et Latina Gothoburgensia (Göteborg :
Acta Universitatis Gothoburgensis, 1976)

287 © 1961 University of Texas Press. All rights reserved.

328 Reprinted with permission of Michael P. Speidel.

336 Reprinted with permission of the American
Philosophical Society.

372 "Handbuch der Altertumswissenschaft, Vol. III,7: The
History of Ancient Iran by Richard N. Frye © Verlag
C.H.Beck oHG, München 1984, pp. 371–373.

396 "The Edict of Diocletian on Maximum Prices,"
Elsa R. Graser, trans., in T. Frank, An Economic
Survey of Ancient Rome Volume V: Rome and Italy
of the Empire (Baltimore: Johns Hopkins Univ.
Press, 1940).© The Johns Hopkins University Press.
Reprinted with permission of the Johns Hopkins
University Press.

480 Republished with permission of Columbia
University Press, from Irving W. Raymond, trans.,
Seven Books of History against the Pagans. The
Apology of Paulus Orosius (New York: Columbia
University Press, 1936); permission conveyed
through Copyright Clearance Center, Inc.

521 Republished with permission of University of
Michigan Press, from Ralph W. Mathisen, People,
Personal Expression, and Social Relations in Late
Antiquity. Volume I. With Translated Texts from Gaul
and Western Europe (Ann Arbor: Univ. of Michigan
Press, 2003); permission conveyed through Copyright
Clearance Center, Inc.

543 Republished with permission of Princeton University
Press, from Clyde Pharr, trans., The Theodosian
Code and Novels, and the Sirmondian Constitutions
(Princeton: Princeton Univ. Press, 1952); permission
conveyed through Copyright Clearance Center, Inc.

553 Reprinted by permission from The History of al-Tabari
Vol. 8: The Victory of Islam: Muhammad at Medina
A.D. 626-630/A.H. 5-8 translated by Michael Fishbein,
the State University of New York Press ©1997, State
University of New York. All rights reserved.

INDEX